MW01005813

משנה

ArtScroll Judaica Classics®

a treasury of chassidic

by

Rabbi Shlomo Yosef Zevin

Translated by Uri Kaploun

a treasury of chassidic tales on the torah

VOL. I

בראשית/Genesis

שמות/Exodus

ספורי חסידים על התורה

tales on the torah

A COLLECTION OF INSPIRATIONAL CHASSIDIC STORIES RELEVANT TO THE WEEKLY TORAH READINGS

Published by

Mesorah Publications, ltd / *New York*

in conjunction with

HILLEL PRESS / *Jerusalem*

FIRST EDITION VOL. I
First Impression . . . February 1980
Second Impression . . . August 1980
Third Impression . . . October 1980
Fourth Impression . . . November 1981
Fifth Impression . . . January 1984

FIRST EDITION VOL. II
First Impression . . . July 1980
Second Impression . . . November 1980
Third Impression . . . August 1981
Fourth Impression . . . January 1984

ONE VOLUME EDITION
First Impression . . . August 1992
Second Impression . . . December 1994
Third Impression . . . January 1997

Published and Distributed by
MESORAH PUBLICATIONS, Ltd.
4401 Second Avenue
Brooklyn, New York 11232

Distributed in Europe by
J. LEHMANN HEBREW BOOKSELLERS
20 Cambridge Terrace
Gateshead, Tyne and Wear
England NE8 1RP

Distributed in Israel by
SIFRIATI / A. GITLER—BOOKS
10 Hashomer Street
Bnei Brak 51361

Distributed in Australia & New Zealand by
GOLDS BOOK & GIFT CO.
36 William Street
Balaclava 3183, Vic., Australia

Distributed in South Africa by
KOLLEL BOOKSHOP
22 Muller Street
Yeoville 2198, Johannesburg, South Africa

THE ARTSCROLL JUDAICA CLASSICS®
A TREASURY OF CHASSIDIC TALES ON THE TORAH

ISBN:
0-89906-900-2 (hard cover)
0-89906-901-0 (paperback)

Typography by CompuScribe at ArtScroll Studios, Ltd.
4401 Second Avenue / Brooklyn, N.Y. 11232 / (718) 921-9000

Printed in the United States of America by Moriah Offset
Bound by Sefercraft Inc., Quality Bookbinders, Brooklyn, N.Y.

Table of Contents

Table of Contents

ספר ויקרא / Leviticus

ספר במדבר / Numbers

ספר דברים / Deuteronomy

◆ Preface

The publication of this *sefer* is a privilege for me and a milestone for the Torah community. Hagaon Rav Shlomo Yosef Zevin זצ״ל was one of the marvels of our age. To those who knew him well, it seemed almost incredible that one human being could combine within himself so much Torah knowledge, so much gentility, so much piety, and so much ability to articulate the most complex subjects in a manner that made them accessible to the masses of his people.

I am grateful to the Zevin family for their permission to reprint the many fruits of his prolific pen. The Hebrew editions have already been published to the delight and benefit of many thousands of avid readers. This volume marks the first in the projected series of English translations of Rav Zevin's works.

The Torah public is most fortunate that the translation has been done by Mr. Uri Kaploun, an artist of acknowledged excellence. Although his work is in demand by famous authors and renowned publishers, his first love is Torah literature and this translation is clearly a labor not only of impeccable skill, but of inspiring love.

I am grateful for my association in this endeavor with Rabbi Meir Zlotowitz and Rabbi Nosson Scherman of Mesorah Publications, creators of the justly famous ArtScroll Series. I am also deeply appreciative to Reb Shea Brander of Mesorah who skillfully provided the graphic enhancement that makes the book so visually appealing. No effort or expense has been spared to craft a book worthy of its illustrious author.

Finally, my wife תחי׳ and I offer humble thanks to Hashem Yisbarach for permitting us to begin this great service to the people of Israel.

Meir Holder
HILLEL PRESS

Jerusalem/Rosh Chodesh Adar, 5740

Translator's Foreword

Wherever half a dozen chassidim may find themselves thrown together, they cannot remain strangers for long. One of them is bound to have a story to tell — whether of a fearless tzaddik, or of a selfless chassid of years ago — and as his listeners share in his relived experience, they are all soon welded into one brotherhood. Whether they are in an underground *shul* in Moscow or at a *Melaveh Malkah* in Melbourne, the picture is always the same: A hushed knot of eager listeners straining to catch every nuance from the lips of an earnest, artless storyteller.

It was my good fortune to grow up in such a comradely brotherhood — in this case, a circle of Russian Lubavitcher chassidim who in their own life were not very different from the chassidim of long ago who people these pages. Into the wee hours of the night we would crowd around a softly-spoken elder chassid with a twinkle in his eye, who did not realize that the protagonist of his recollections — himself — was a hero. He told stories that had never yet been printed, side by side with well-loved classics — including, by the way, many of those appearing in this book. They were stories of men whose clear mission in life was to teach themselves how to love the undeserving, how to lend a kindly word to the faltering, how to reveal the divine spark hidden in the corporeal world, and how to transmute their own baser natures, being daunted by no tyrants from without or within. And it seemed a pity that treasures such as these should be cloistered away, and enjoyed by so few.

What a privilege, therefore, to be able now to throw the doors wide open, and to invite the English reader in his thousands to join me in listening to some five hundred chassidic stories told the way only chassidim tell stories — from the mouth of one of the luminaries of this century, Rav Shlomo Yosef Zevin, זצ"ל, a man who was in every way a scholar, and every inch a chassid.

For my part in this enterprise, I am grateful to the Providence which at a timely moment introduced me to the sage and cheerful company of Reb Meir Holder of Hillel Press, and thankful too for the cordial relationship which has ensued with Rabbis Meir Zlotowitz and Nosson Scherman of Mesorah Publications.

❦❦❦

אֵשֶׁת חַיִל מִי יִמְצָא: "A woman of valor who can find?" asked the author of *Proverbs*.

A Woman of Valor I have found, and to her this *Treasury* is dedicated.

U.K.

Jerusalem, 10 Shvat 5740 (1980)

בס"ד, ירושלים עיה"ק ת"ו
י' שבט
שנת דבקינ"ו במצותי"ך

◈ Biographical Sketch

Rav Shlomo Yosef Zevin זצ״ל
(1890-1978)

Jerusalem has seen prodigiously-attended funerals in its time — but rarely one with such a *diverse* multitude of followers as those who in 1978 crowded the streets of its Geulah section near the modest apartment of Rav Shlomo Yosef Zevin. When he died, still active and alert at 88, he was universally acknowledged as one of the great Talmudic and Halachic prodigies of his era.

The most eminent *poskim* were there in their black frock-coats, men who at critical moments had consulted him for a few measured sentences before taking weighty decisions on complex halachic questions; veteran fur-hatted Jerusalemites of all conceivable groups and shades of opinion, who from their youth to their old age had missed hardly one of the weekly *shiurim* which he gave in his home; Talmudic researchers in more Western garb, who had come to know and respect him through his editorship of the *Talmudic Encyclopedia;* Yiddish-speaking yeshivah students, who were fond of quietly making themselves at home in his booklined study, simply in order to watch a great man at work, and occasionally to be able to do him the favor of taking down a volume from the highest shelves, each inch of which he knew in precise order; thinkers and leading figures of the Mizrachi movement, and Mercaz HaRav students wearing crocheted white *kippot;* a busload of sun tanned farmers from Kfar Chabad, who recalled with what warmth and patience he had dealt with the halachic problems that their chassidic village had encountered when they had first migrated from Russia and begun tilling the Holy Land; his distinguished Ashkenazi and Sephardic colleagues of the Supreme Rabbinical Council of Israel, who revered him for his erudition, and felt ennobled by his unaffected dignity; and, mingling modestly with all these, עַמְּךָ יִשְׂרָאֵל in his thousands — the Jewish man in the street, who loved the compiler of *Sippurei Chassidim* for the spice which it added to his *Shabbos,* when week by week he could be sure to find in it a topical and inspiring Chassidic story to retell to his children and guests at the Friday night table.

Rav Zevin, then, was a man of such stature that each of these circles was able to regard him — and with justice — as *unzerer,* one of their own.

Born in Kazimirov, Belorussia, where his father was rabbi, he attracted attention early as a Talmudic prodigy. He studied at the Mir Yeshivah under R' Eliyahu Baruch Kamai and then at Bobruisk, near his home town, under R' Shemariah Noach Schneerson. When he was only 18, he began a lifelong correspondence with some of the greatest *geonim* of the century, such as R' Yosef Rosen of Ragatchov and R' Yechiel Michel Epstein of Slobodka.

He succeeded his father as rabbi of Kazimirov, and served several other Russian communities as well. He came to the fore as a Jewish spokesman, participating in conferences in Moscow, Vilna, and Kiev, and being elected as a Jewish representative to the Ukraine National Assembly. After the Bolshevik Revolution, he continued to serve as a rabbi despite increasing government pressure against Jewish religious life. In a surprising development, he and R' Yechezkel Abramsky received permission to co-edit a monthly Torah journal, *Yagdil Torah,* which appeared in 1928, but the permission was soon withdrawn. Rabbi Abramsky was later arrested as part of the intensification of official oppresion of Jewish religious leaders.

Arriving in *Eretz Yisrael* in 1934, Rav Zevin began to publish prolifically, his output including a weekly review of contemporary halachic literature; critical appraisals of the scholarly approaches of prominent religious personalities; essays which demonstrated by their own example that there is no area of modern life on which the halachah does not have a definable stance; and discourses on the principles underlying the laws regulating the observance of the festivals. In addition, in 1942 he founded and began to edit the monumental *Talmudic Encyclopedia,* in which the reader finds the entire massive complex of Talmudic literature organized for him in concise form.

These publications are all distinguished by his unique contribution to halachic literature — a style which is both decisive and appealing. He had a rare ability to simplify and clarify, and he was almost unique in his knack of presenting complex material in a form that could be grasped by knowledgeable laymen as well as accomplished scholars. Rav Zevin was thus simultaneously a scholar respected by scholars, and an authoritative popularizer of learned literature. This rare feat was publicly acclaimed in 1959 by the award of the Israel Prize for Religious Literature.

A Treasury of Chassidic Tales is a masterful translation by Uri Kaploun of Rav Zevin's classic Hebrew anthology *Sippurei Chassidim,* which has been reprinted many times since its original publication in 1955. The anthology on the Torah follows the order of the weekly readings of the Torah; its companion anthology is set out according to the yearly cycle of the festivals. Apart from the *Talmudic Encyclopedia,* the present work is the first of Rav Zevin's books to appear in English, but it is intended to be the forerunner of many others in a project that will enormously enrich the growing store of English-language Torah literature.

◆§ Author's Introduction

Chassidic stories lead to many destinations. There are those whose aim is to show how the Hand of God is revealed — often supernaturally — through the wondrous workings of tzaddikim. Their message: וְרָאוּ בָנָיו גְּבוּרָתוֹ, שִׁבְּחוּ וְהוֹדוּ לִשְׁמוֹ — "As His children beheld His might, they extolled and offered praise to His Name." Others seem rather to highlight the role of the tzaddik in these wonders, as if to echo the dictum of the Sages: צַדִּיק גּוֹזֵר וְהַקָּבָּ"ה מְקַיֵּים — "A tzaddik decrees; the Almighty fulfills." Yet others conceal a moral, pointing to the reward that is bestowed upon the righteous, and the retribution that awaits the godless. Some stories set their sights on a didactic target, in particular those which dwell on the uprightness and holiness of tzaddikim in their exemplary dealings with their fellows and in their enviable rapport with their Maker. There are stories in which a point deserving of contemplation is taught — whether directly or indirectly — through an original scholarly insight, such as a novel interpretation of a Biblical verse or Talmudic teaching. What captures our attention in some of the narratives is the spiritual and psychological motivation that steers the actions of tzaddikim and chassidim alike. In other stories these same protagonists fascinate us by their wit, intellectual prowess, or sage understanding of human nature. Then again, the very backdrop to a story is sometimes as attractive as its personages or its action, allowing us a peek into the ethos and lifestyle of a vanishing age in a faraway world. And indeed, in certain of the stories one can savor many of the above ingredients, if not all.

The chassidim of bygone generations disapproved of stories which merely recorded miraculous feats, for these are things which are rather to be tasted than consumed in quantity. Such stories used to be seen by the school of Pshischah as suiting the spiritual sophistication of pagans. They would take the innocent phrase from the Evening Prayer — אוֹתוֹת וּמוֹפְתִים בְּאַדְמַת בְּנֵי חָם, which, in the context of the plagues inflicted upon the

Egyptians, refers to "signs and miracles in the land of the Hamites" — and drily rephrase it to mean: "Signs and miracles belong best in the land of the Hamites ... " Reb Menachem Mendel of Kotsk likewise underplayed the role of miracle stories in the growth of the man of faith. There is a verse in Psalms: אֲבוֹתֵינוּ בְמִצְרַיִם לֹא הִשְׂכִּילוּ נִפְלְאוֹתֶיךָ, which in fact means that "Our forefathers in Egypt paid no heed to Your wonders." Reading this verse on a less literal level, Reb Menachem Mendel understood it to imply that it was not the miracles that refined the faith of our forefathers in Egypt.

This attitude can in fact be traced back to the Talmud, where the following is related: "There was a man whose wife died, leaving him an infant, and he had no money with which to hire a wetnurse. A miracle was worked for him, and he developed breasts like those of a woman so that he was able to nourish his baby. Hearing this, Rav Yosef exclaimed: 'How great is this man, that such a miracle should be wrought for him!' Said Abbaye: 'On the contrary — how blameworthy is this man, that the natural order of Creation should be disturbed for him!'" A similar view is evident in a comment by Rashi: "The further a man can keep his distance from miracles, the better." Indeed, even concerning a miracle that does not defy the natural order of things, the Talmud says that a person for whom a miracle is performed has this privilege subtracted from his account of merits.

In the teachings of Chabad Chassidism we find the following: "The miracle of Purim, it is true, was clothed in the ways of nature through the story of Achashverosh -- but for this very reason it is clear that the divine light then manifested was derived from a lofty source indeed." It is apparent, then, that it is more praiseworthy to listen to the voice of God as He walks about the garden of everyday life in the natural world than to witness miracles that burst the bounds of nature. So, too, writes Reb Shlomo Zalman of Kopust, relating his exposition to the two classic categories of divinity — the four-letter Name (compounded of the letters *yud-hei-vav-hei,* and here referred to as *Havayah),* which represents God as an infinite, transcendent essence, and the Name *Elokim,* which signifies His connection with the finite, created universe, through His seeming self-limitation in nature. Reb Shlomo Zalman, then, writes as follows: "Yisro had long known of these two divine Names. He knew well that when the Name *Havayah* rules supreme, the laws of nature are suspended altogether, and that when the Name *Elokim* holds sway, nature comes into its own. Accordingly, when he heard from afar of the miracle of the splitting of the Red Sea, he assumed that the divine Power had utterly withdrawn from the confines of nature — and did not see this as remarkable. When, however, he came to Moshe Rabbeinu who told him that the conduct of the laws of nature through the Name *Elokim* had not lapsed at all, he was overcome with wonderment, and exclaimed: עַתָּה יָדַעְתִּי כִּי גָדוֹל ה' מִכָּל הָאֱלֹהִים." [The plain meaning of this verse is: "Now I know that God is greater than all gods." For the purposes of his interpretation on the plane of *derush*, however, the rebbe of Kopust understood the last word of the verse — *ha-elohim* — to refer not to gods, but to *Elokim*, God. The verse thus reads as follows: "Now I know that even when the Name *Elokim* is the perceptible force in the natural universe, the Name *Havayah* — *through it* — yet reigns supreme."]

Typical of this outlook is the story told by Reb Yosef Yitzchak of Lubavitch (passed away in New York, 1950). During the imprisonment in St. Petersburg of Reb Shneur Zalman of Liadi, he was taken to the Senate one night via the River Neva for cross-examination. On the way there he asked the official who was taking him to stop the boat for a short while so that he could recite *Kiddush Levanah*, the prayer which is said during the waxing of the moon. Since the official refused, the Rav said: "If I wanted to, I could stop the boat myself." The official was adamant, and the boat stopped of its own accord. When the Rav later requested the favor again, the official obliged — in exchange for a blessing which the tzaddik gave him in writing.

"When I was a child," commented Reb Yosef Yitzchak, "I used to wonder: Since the rebbe had already stopped the boat by himself, why did he not go ahead and say the prayer instead of requiring the favors of that gentile? But as I grew older and studied Chassidism, I understood that the rebbe had no choice but to act as he did. For a mitzvah should be performed only when it is clothed in nature, and not in supernatural miracles."

Notwithstanding all the above, the fact remains that both the Jerusalem and the Babylonian Talmuds are replete with innumerable accounts of miraculous deeds wrought by the *tannaim* and *amoraim* of ancient times. Some of these have been anthologized in recent generations, as have been the many extant accounts of supernatural feats performed by the post-Talmudic Sages, from the period of the *geonim* until modern times. The careful reader will observe, however, that in the main, these stories were told not as miracles or wonders for their own sake, but as vehicles for conveying a certain moral or educational message.

Moreover, for all their reservations about mere miracle stories, tzaddikim and chassidim have always valued highly the telling of stories — particularly those proceeding from reliable sources — that illustrate the ways in which saintly men have lived their lives and served their Maker. This evaluation is expressed by Reb Menachem Mendel of Lubavitch (the author of *Tzemech Tzedek)* in a *derush*-level reading of the well-known passage in the Passover *Haggadah* which begins וַאֲפִילוּ כֻּלָּנוּ חֲכָמִים. The straightforward translation of that sentence is simply: "Even if we were all wise (חֲכָמִים) and understanding (נְבוֹנִים), and we all knew (יוֹדְעִים) the Torah, we are still obliged to recount the story of the Exodus from Egypt." Reb Menachem Mendel bases his interpretation of this verse on the three nouns which lie at the root of the above three Hebrew words: חָכְמָה, בִּינָה, דַּעַת. These latter three words, better known by their acronym חַבַּ"ד *(Chabad),* represent the demand of that school of Chassidism that the love and awe of God be generated by intellectual means. Reb Menachem Mendel's *derush*-level reading of the passage is thus as follows: "Even if we have fulfilled the demand that God be served through the intellectual effort required by the *Chabad* system, it is still a mitzvah for us to retell chassidic stories. Moreover, the very act of recounting them enables us to free ourselves from the worldly straits (מֵיצָרִים) which confine each of us in the psychological bondage of his own individual מִצְרַיִם, his own personal Egypt."

The same tzaddik wrote: "When one hears a story of a good deed from one's rebbe, one becomes bound to the rebbe's faculty of action; when one hears a Torah discourse from one's rebbe, one becomes united with his faculty of speech; when one listens to one's rebbe singing a *niggun,* one cleaves to his faculty of thought. The bond with one's rebbe is thus on the levels corresponding to each of the three names for the soul — *Nefesh, Ruach, Neshamah."* And his grandfather, Reb Shneur Zalman of Liadi, recalled: "When we used to hear a Torah discourse from the rebbe — Reb Dov Ber, the Maggid of Mezritch

— we saw this as the Oral Law, and when we heard a story from his mouth, this was our Written Law."

Reb Shlomo of Radomsk writes in a similar vein — "A story which retells the deeds of tzaddikim is Torah" — and borrows support for his statement by a novel reading of a familar Talmudic dictum. In explaining the seemingly excessive coverage alloted by the Torah to the lengthy account which Eliezer the servant of Avraham gives of his movements, the Talmud says: "The conversation of the Patriarchs' servants is loftier than the Torah as studied by their sons." Reb Shlomo explains: "This is so because the conversation — the storytelling — of the servants of the Patriarchs *becomes* the Torah of the sons." In a verse from Psalms, Reb Shlomo found a similar teaching: הַלְלוּ עַבְדֵי ה׳ הַלְלוּ אֶת שֵׁם ה׳. The straightforward construction of this sentence gives the following translation: "Offer praise, you servants of God; praise the name of God." However, instead of seeing the first half of the verse as a call to the servants to God to praise Him, Reb Shlomo treated "the servants of God" as the *object* of the first verb in Hebrew, so that the first clause reads: "Praise the servants of God." The verse as a whole could thus be taken to mean that the praise of God consists of the praise of his servants, the tzaddikim.

"Through telling stories of tzaddikim," concurs Reb Nachman of Breslov, "one draws down the light of the *Mashiach* into This World, and repels from it all manner of darkness and tribulations." And in another place he writes: "It is given to him who is in Eretz Yisrael to tell stories of true tzaddikim, and thereby to cleanse his thoughts." Reb Shalom of Belz found the merits of such storytelling hinted at in the verse from Malachi which opens with the words אָז נִדְבְּרוּ: "Then they who feared God spoke, one man to another; and God hearkened, and heard it, and a book of remembrance was written before Him for those who feared God, and took heed of His Name." Reb Shalom took the verb נִדְבְּרוּ literally, in a passive sense, so that the verse means: "Those who feared God *were spoken of* after their passing by one man to another; to this God hearkened, and heard it; and a book of remembrance was written before Him — both for those of the departed who feared God, in that 'their lips speak on in the grave' by virtue of the stories told of them, as well as for those who took heed of His Name, that is, those who tell these stories." And the final word on the subject comes from the Baal Shem Tov himself, the founder of Chassidism: "To speak of the praises of tzaddikim is as praiseworthy as meditating on the loftiest mysteries of the Divine Chariot."

It can fairly be said, then, that the doctrines of Chassidism are the *halachah* of Chassidism, and the stories of chassidim are its *aggadah*. Its *halachah* speaks to the intellect; its *aggadah* speaks to the heart. Its *halachah* delves earnestly into abstruse scholarly questions involving the knowledge of divinity, the mystery of creation, the descent of the divine light, the hidden truths of the Torah, the secrets of the mitzvos, and the profoundest enigmas and tortuous byways of the human soul. On the one hand this *halachah* of Chassidism bursts its way into the highest heavens, directing its words ever upward; on the other hand, it plunges to the depths, revealing the sanctity of creation in the innermost essence of the material existence that constitutes the universe. The *aggadah* of Chassidism, with its stories of the roadbuilders and trailblazers of the movement — the tzaddikim, their lives and deeds, attitudes and attributes, their customs and conduct, their words and their wonders — this *aggadah* of stories rouses the heart, revives the soul, and breathes the spirit of life into the driest of bones.

* * * * *

The narrative literature of Chassidism is rich indeed. In addition to the hundreds of books that have been compiled, and the tens of thousands of stories that have been handed down in writing, an oral tradition lives on, rebbe to rebbe, chassid to chassid. From these written and oral sources the present writer has chosen and arranged some five hundred stories. He has neither adapted them to suit his taste nor tampered with the facts as related, whether in content or in detail; he has simply aimed at rewriting them in an intelligible style. The stories chosen were those in which he found a moral or didactic point, regardless of whether they involved some supernatural wonder or not. Finally, he set them out according to the weekly Portion of the Torah, assigning each story to the verse that best suited it. That is not to say, obviously, that he exhausted all the resources which could have served his aim, for have our Sages not taught: "You are not obliged to complete the work"?

There may well be such as will raise objections to some of the stories included, but it seems to the author — rather: the compiler and editor — that in each of these stories there is something instructive to be found. Not that this "something" will be seen in the same light by all readers, for a single story can sometimes reflect a subtle variety of hues and shades. On the first story, for example, the rebbe of Gostynin commented: "We may be expert in assessing the value of gold and silver and gems — but to appreciate the true worth of a Jew is way, way beyond us." Another may be impressed chiefly by the esteem in which tzaddikim and chassidim hold the mitzvah of saving a life. A third may prefer to contemplate the spiritual cataclysm which overwhelmed that soldier when "the Jewish spark inside me flared up," and motivated him to act as he did. And yet a fourth may find the center of gravity in a different direction altogether: the privilege of healing children is one of heaven's ways of rewarding a man; one would have to be rich in merits to be allowed to attain a level such as that ...

This variety of reaction applies not only to a story with a whole plot of its own — in which case, too, some reader might perhaps enjoy it simply for its narrative value. It applies even to a brief story, boasting neither the suspense of a plot nor the mystique of the fanciful. Consider, for example, one of the last stories in the second volume, *Brevity is the Soul of Wit.* One reader will simply be interested to learn the interpretation it offers of the words in Deuteronomy עַד תֻּמָּם. Another will note the sharp-witted brevity characteristic of Reb Yaakov Yitzchak of Pshischah — a discourse of exactly two words, with no explanations offered. A third reader will perceive the continuity of style within the school of Pshischah, for the disciple and eventual successor, Reb Simchah Bunem, finds the two succinct words both ample and eloquent. And what may impress a fourth reader is the demand of that disciple that others too determine the essence of that novel teaching, unaided. In the words of Reb Simchah Bunem to Reb Heinich: "Here, you're a clever fellow. You work out the rebbe's meaning yourself!"

The affinity that links the stories to their respective Biblical verses is likewise bound by no one rule. Sometimes the connection is straightforward and obvious. It is natural, for example, that the stories on hospitality should be attached to *Vayera,* the passage in the Torah which describes the way the Patriarch Avraham received his angelic guests. Likewise, stories on prayer have been connected with *Eikev,* the passage which includes the Biblical source from which the Sages derived the mitzvah of prayer — "and to serve Him with all your heart."

Stories on prayer are nonetheless matched with other verses as well, each according to its own distinctive emphasis and flavor. Thus, for example, *The Light of Liberated Sparks* on page 92 finds itself linked with the verse that tells how "Yitzchak went out to speak in the field." Some stories interpret the verse to which they are joined, whether by design — as with *Intent*, on page 133 — or by their mere juxtaposition, by virtue of which the story causes the verse, or the commentary that accompanies it, to speak to us with greater immediacy. An example of this is *Head and Heart*, in the second volume. Conversely, there are cases in which the verse or its commentary lend seasoning or depth to the story, as in *The Rebbe and the Shtreimelmacher*, on page 273, or *The Land of the Living*, in the second volume. Then again, there are instances in which the verse and the story enhance each other's flavor, as in *Eyes that See Not*, on page 97.

In keeping with the narrative nature of this anthology, well-loved snippets of chassidic lore and teaching — no matter how quotable — were not included, unless they were connected with an incident of some sort.

S. Y. Z.

Jerusalem
Adar 5715 (1955)

ספר בראשית

GENESIS

סדר בראשית
Sidra Bereishis

◆§ *From Earth to Heaven*

בָּרָא אֱלֹקִים אֵת הַשָּׁמַיִם וְאֵת הָאָרֶץ *God created the heaven and the earth (1:1)*

A question of divine service was once being debated between the saintly brothers, Reb Elimelech of Lyzhansk and Reb Zusya of Hanipoli: since a person is obliged on the one hand to meditate on the exaltedness of the Creator, and on the other hand to contemplate his own worthlessness — where should he start? One argued that the worshiper should first cultivate such a degree of humility that he would then come to a true appreciation of the greatness of his Maker; the other maintained that he should first become overawed by the omnipotence of the Creator, and this would bring him to a due awareness of his own insignificance.

They brought the question to Reb Dov Ber, the Maggid of Mezritch, for adjudication, and received the following answer: "Both your approaches are the words of the living God, but the view that one should first consider one's own worthlessness is the loftier."

A chassid who heard of this interchange commented that in essence these two views reflect the classic dispute between the House of Shammai and the House of Hillel: the House of Shammai holds that the heaven was created before the earth, while the House of Hillel holds that the earth was created before the heaven.

◆§ *One Man's Life*

וַיִּבְרָא אֱלֹקִים אֶת־הָאָדָם *And God created Man (1:27)*

For this reason was Adam created solitary: to teach us that whoever saves the life of one Jew is given credit for having saved the whole world (Talmud, Tractate Sanhedrin).

A childless villager once journeyed with his wife to visit Reb Yisrael, the Maggid of Koznitz, to request that he pray for them, and give them his blessing that they be granted a child. The Maggid blessed them, and in due course the woman gave birth to a son. Some time later, however, the baby became grievously ill, so at the mother's request, her husband visited Koznitz again. The Maggid gave him his blessing for a speedy recovery, and sent him on his way. But instead of rallying, the infant became weaker from day to day, and the distraught mother barely left his cradleside.

One day, having dozed off exhausted at her usual place, she woke up to see a soldier leaning over the cradle, and spoonfeeding her baby from a vessel which he held. She screamed in alarm, and the soldier fled. From that moment, however, the child's condition began to improve, until he recuperated completely. The parents were overjoyed, to be sure, but at the same time they were haunted by fears. Who knows — perhaps this was a sorcerer, or a spirit perchance? So once again they made their way to Koznitz, and the Maggid reassured them that they had no cause to fear evil.

As soon as they had taken their leave, the Maggid handed his cane to his *shammes* and sent him off to the local cemetery. There he was to strike the grave of a certain soldier, and tell him that the Maggid wished to see him. The beadle did as he was told, and soon after the Maggid addressed his question to the soldier who stood before him: "Who made you a children's doctor?"

Whereupon the soldier unfolded his story. "It's as simple as this. When I was taken away for military service, I mixed with the gentiles and behaved like a gentile, until there was almost no difference between them and me, except that I appeared in their records as a Jew.

"It once happened that while I was strolling with some of my comrades, we came upon a poor Jew who was on his way home from a nearby village. The soldiers fell upon him from all sides, searched his pockets, and robbed him of 75 rubles. Then, to make sure that he would never get to tell the story to our commanding officer, they hanged him from the nearest tree, and off they went. This was too much. The Jewish spark inside me flared up, and I felt sorry for the poor devil. I quickly slipped away from my unit, found my way back, and with my little pocket-knife cut through the rope. He was still breathing. I gave him 75 rubles out of my pocket, and he went off home, as happy as you please.

"The soldiers got back to our base, but of course when my name was called on parade, I wasn't there. The officer sent them off to search for me, and soon enough they found me standing near that tree. Seeing that the poor old Jew wasn't hanging up there any more, they figured out what I'd done, and again they were afraid that word would get back to the officer. So they grabbed me, hanged me on the same tree, and reported back that they'd found me like that. Then they took me down and buried me in the cemetery of Koznitz.

"After I died, I found myself facing the Heavenly Court. They said they couldn't send me straight to the Garden of Eden, because I'd been sinning all my life. But they couldn't send me to the other place, either, because I had saved one man's life, and whoever saves the life of one Jew is given credit for having saved the whole world — especially since I'd actually given my life for that mitzvah. So they decided to send me down again as a children's doctor, and gave me permission to save the lives of little children whenever the situation is desperate."

❀ ❀ ❀

This story was told by Reb Yechiel Meir of Gostynin, who used to add: "We may be expert in assessing the value of gold and silver and gems — but to appreciate the true worth of a Jew is way, way beyond us."

◆§ *Whoever Saves a Life*

In the town of Reb Yisrael, the Maggid of Koznitz, there lived a butcher named Aizik, whose conduct in his younger years had given rise to considerable gossip. A few weeks after his premature death he appeared in a dream to the local *shochet*, and summoned him to a lawsuit to be heard before the Heavenly Court. The ritual slaughterer awoke agitated, but decided to make nothing of it, for is it not written that "dreams speak vanities"? But the next night the butcher summoned him once more, and again on the third night. He could not be ignored. The *shochet* sobbed out his story to Reb Yisrael, and asked the holy man for advice.

"It is written," said the Maggid, "that 'the Torah is not in the heavens.' The law of the Torah is to be dispensed in *this* world, and the law prescribes that the plaintiff must follow the defendant. When, therefore, the plaintiff appears to you again, tell him that if he has any claim against you he should come with you for a hearing before me, and that if he does not comply, he will regret it."

That night, when the butcher duly appeared and repeated his summons, the *shochet* replied as instructed, and the butcher agreed at once.

In the morning, as soon as the *shochet* arrived, the Maggid had a partition of boards set up in the corner of the room, and dispatched his *shammes* to the cemetery, where he was to approach the grave of the butcher, and summon him to the hearing by order of the Rabbi. A few moments later, the butcher's voice was heard behind the partition, weeping bitterly. He claimed that in the course of slaughtering, the *shochet* had made many of the animals *trefah,* and because they became unfit for kosher consumption, and had not belonged to him in the first place, he had fallen deeply into debt until, poverty-stricken and heartbroken, he had died, leaving a widow and children hungry and penniless, and plagued by creditors. Now, in the World of Truth, he had found out that the animals had in fact been healthy and kosher, until the *shochet,* out of sheer spite, had intentionally and unlawfully rendered them *trefah.* What with the debts he had left behind him, and the thought of the daily anguish of his widow and children, he could find no rest in the World Above, and therefore demanded that the *shochet* be brought to justice.

When the *shochet* heard these words he was overwhelmed with shame, confessed his guilt, and undertook to carry out whatever penance the Maggid would see fit to impose on him. Reb Yisrael ordered him to settle all of the butcher's debts, and to set aside a certain sum weekly for the support of the widow and children. This settlement was accepted by both parties.

As the butcher was leaving the house, the Maggid

beckoned him back: "Aizik'l, Aizik'l! Come here, please! It amazes me that so soon after your passing you have no other worries, and have time to concern yourself with financial claims. Tell me, have you finished all your accounts up there? What did you answer them concerning the sins of your youth?"

"Rabbi," answered the butcher, "your question is certainly in place, and I'll tell you how it all came about. In my youth I was a wagon-driver, and my work took me from town to town. One day I was driving with my passengers — fine, pious, upright folk — and far out on a highway we were surprised by a band of armed brigands, who wanted to kill my tzaddikim and take their money. I wasn't afraid. I jumped up, and pitched into those scoundrels tooth and nail like they deserved, until with God's help they ran for their lives.

"Years later, after I'd gone the way of all flesh, along came troops of avenging angels to take me down to the place of punishment. But in a flash there appeared all those tzaddikim whose lives I'd saved, every single one of them, and they objected loudly: 'Come, now, that's the man who saved us from the sword, and whoever saves the life of one Jew is given credit for having saved the whole world. You can't take him down there! It's only thanks to him that we remained alive, and were able to continue studying Torah and doing mitzvos and serving our Maker!'

"In brief, they wouldn't let them touch me, and they saved me from all evil, and spoke up for me during my trial, and the Court decided to send me to the Garden of Eden. But since God doesn't forgive sins that are left uncorrected between man and man, and I'd left a huge stack of debts behind me, they wouldn't let me into the Garden of Eden. So when I found out that the cause of all my troubles was the *shochet*, I decided to take him to court, and now that he's agreed to pay off all my outstanding debts, I can go back to my place in peace, to enjoy the light of life everlasting."

◆§ Where are You?

וַיִּקְרָא ה׳ אֱלֹקִים אֶל הָאָדָם וַיֹּאמֶר לוֹ אַיֶּכָּה
And God called to Adam and said to him, "Where are you?"

When Reb Shneur Zalman of Liadi was imprisoned in 1798 under capital sentence by the dreaded Secret Service of St. Petersburg, the Chief of the Gendarmes came to his cell to interrogate him. As soon as he opened the door he realized that the saintly visage before him, deep in thought, was the face of no ordinary prisoner. The officer, who was a thinking man, and familiar with Scripture, addressed the Alter Rebbe as follows: "I have a question on Scripture to ask you. Are you willing to answer it?"

"Ask your question," replied the Alter Rebbe.

"Please explain me the meaning of the verse, 'And God called to Adam, and said to him: Where are you?' Didn't the Almighty know where he was?"

"Do you believe," countered the Alter Rebbe, "that the Torah is eternal, and remains true for every generation and for every man?"

"Indeed, I so believe," replied the officer.

"This, then, is the meaning of the verse. At all times the voice of God calls out to every man, and asks him, 'Where are you? Where are you up to in your world? For every man has been apportioned a certain number of days and years, so that every day and every year he should live righteously with God and with man. Think, therefore: where are you up to in your world? How many years have gone by, and what have you done with those years?' You, for example, have lived so and so many years (and here he gave the officer's age exactly): what have you done with those years? Have you been of any good to anyone?"

The officer was overwhelmed. He clapped his prisoner on the shoulder, and cried, "Bravo!"

After several more such episodes, the Chief of the Gendarmes reported to the Czar on this wise man of God, and added his opinion that the charges brought against him by his slanderers were no doubt unfounded.

◆§ The Soul of a Brigand

ולְאָדָם אָמַר כִּי שָׁמַעְתָּ לְקוֹל אִשְׁתֶּךָ
And to Adam He said: Because you listened to the voice of your wife (3:17)

One of the many disciples who flocked from all over the Ukraine to the court of Reb Yisrael of Rhuzin was a chassid from a hamlet near Zhitomir, who became closely attached to the tzaddik, and visited him twice a year, for the festivals of Shavuos and Chanukah.

It once happened that during one of his midwinter visits, a fierce blizzard overtook all the carriages and wagons on the highway — in those days the railway had not yet reached that part of the world — and our chassid was forced to abandon his wagon, and find a haven for the night. He made his way to the inn of a Jewish leaseholder in the nearby village of Piliva where, being known from earlier visits as a respectable and upright man, he was given a cordial welcome. It had been his habit for years to spend a night there on his way, and this time, as always, he sat for hours with the innkeeper and his family, exchanging the conversation of chassidim, recounting wondrous stories of Reb Yisrael of Ruzhin, and treating them to choice morsels of Torah insights. Until the wee hours they listened, fascinated, until they could no longer keep their eyelids open. They murmured their thanks, tiptoed upstairs, and curled up in their eiderdowns to enjoy the sleep of the righteous.

They were rudely awakened by a violent knocking on the door: "Open up, there!" At first the innkeeper assumed that one of the local peasants had run out of vodka for a wild midnight party, and pretended not to hear. But the knocking continued — not of one man, but of a noisy rabble. Trembling, the innkeeper's family got up from their beds. Their guest, too, was roused by the uproar outside. He washed his hands, and recited the morning benedictions in a whisper.

Before any of them reached the door to open it, it was broken down, and a gang of robbers burst their way in. As they threw off their outer garments it became clear to the horrified family that they were armed with swords. First of all, the uninvited guests found the barrels of vodka and drank their fill. They then trussed up all the members of the family, laid them out in a row on the floor, and warned them not to utter the merest whisper.

The overnight guest, who had been listening to all this from his room, realized that he had now reached his last moments in this life — he, and all of the innkeeper's family. He wept the tears of a true penitent, and devoutly recited *Shema Yisrael.* Then he took out the volume of the *Zohar* which he always carried with him, and read out of it in a subdued voice, with pious concentration. And as he read, he became so carried away by the words of the holy *Zohar* that he quite forgot where he was, and was soon reading so loudly that his voice could be heard by the murderers downstairs.

A buzz of excitement went through the gang: Who was this man who was reading so happily at a time like this? Their chief silenced them: "You all stay right where you are and wait a moment, while I go and fix him up good and proper!"

But no sooner had he reached the chassid's room than he saw before him a countenance of rare nobility. He scrutinized the kingly features, and recognized the man: it was his schoolmate, Moshe Yehudah; they had learned together, years earlier, in the local *cheder*...

The chief stood dumbstruck. Then, pulling himself together, he went down to his cronies, and ordered them to free their captives and go on their way. Surprised as they were, they did as they were told.

He went back to the guest's room, offered his hand gently with the greeting of *Shalom Aleichem,* and asked the chassid to tell him all that had happened to him since they had last met. Even though it was clear that a sheer miracle had removed the threat of death from him, and through him from the whole household, the poor man's bones still trembled within him, and only with great difficulty did he manage to recount the bare outlines of his life story. It was now the other man's turn.

"Years after we parted ways, I married the daughter of the village innkeeper. In order to enable me to continue my studies, my father-in-law undertook to support us for the duration of his lifetime, and to bequeath me the lease on the liquor sales thereafter. I was well liked by my father-in-law as well as by my wife, and occupied myself only with my studies, while my parents-in-law and my wife ran the business.

"One day, while I was poring over my books, my wife came in, excused herself for disturbing me during my study, and said: 'My dear Binyamin. You have, thank God, a gift with figures, but you've never used it to earn even a single kopek. It's true we are supported by my father, and lack nothing, but it wouldn't hurt if we had a little something of our own, so that we wouldn't have to ask him for money every time we need anything. Fortunately,' she went on, 'now is an opportune moment to do something in that direction. Do you hear the loud argument going on between the gentiles in the drinking parlor? They earned a sum of money in partnership, and are utterly incapable of dividing it up correctly. If you go there now, and make their calculations for them, I'm sure they'll rely on you — they respect you as an honest man — and they'll pay you for your efforts, and go their way.' I in all innocence followed my wife's advice. I made calculations to their satisfaction, they paid me generously for my trouble; they went their way, and I returned to my books.

"A couple of months later I heard exactly the same din in the drinking parlor. I guessed my wife would repeat her earlier suggestion, and sure enough she did. She excused herself as before, proposed the same business, but added that since they had apparently earned more than last time, the devil wouldn't take them if they'd pay me more, too.

"So off I went again to the bar, heard out all their arguments, saw their accounts, arranged their earnings between them, and was paid well myself. But this time my conscience bothered me. I gathered from their arguments that their gains were not earned honestly, that there was some kind of shady business involved. When I mentioned this suspicion to my wife, she only said: 'What affair is that of yours? If the gentiles are doing something criminal, the sin is on their heads, and we're innocent.'

"From then on this same task came my way more and more frequently, until I was familiar with all the ins and outs of their affairs. In short, they were a bunch of murderers. I realized that I'd been trapped into becoming the accomplice of criminals, and it cost me a lot of heartache. I felt I wasn't the same old Binyamin, that my soul had become contaminated. I decided several times that I would never look at their evil faces again, nor at their dirty money — but each time my wife would calm my anguish with soft words, and reassure me that Jews never become murderers, only gentiles do; that I couldn't really be called an accomplice to their crimes; that I was only keeping their accounts; and other such empty words of consolation. With all of this I was unable to free myself from the trap in which I'd been ensnared, and habit became second nature, until it no longer bothered me; and for a long time I did my bit calmly, as if there were nothing wrong with it all.

"Then one night, when all my family were fast asleep, I see the face of one of these gentiles at the window of our room. He signals to me that I should open the door quickly. My wife opens it, and he stands in the doorway, all aghast. 'Terrible news!' he gasps. 'Right near here, only a mile away, our gang is in serious trouble. We waited in ambush for the local squire, who was coming home loaded with cash from his bank in Kiev. We attacked him, but he and his wagon-driver are fighting back furiously. If they get the upper hand, then we're all finished, and of course you'll have had it too!' I stood thunderstruck. I didn't know what to do. But my wife clung to me and sobbed: 'Binyamin, my dear. Do something to save us!'

"I grabbed a small hammer that happened to be handy, and ran off together with the gentile. He managed to get hold of the squire by the neck, and I bashed him in the temple with my hammer. He fell to the ground, and never got up.

"I went home, and things went from bad to worse. One sin drags along another, and I sank up to the neck in muck. I eventually became one of the gang. We killed a lot of people, and I've got sins over my head. One day they made me their chief. I've become a wild beast of the jungle.

"But now God has arranged for me to find you here ... I want to save my life! I'm not going back to that gang of murderers! I'll wander anywhere. If somebody kills me, that'll bring me consolation. Perhaps even atonement..."

The chassid, hearing this awful confession, advised his old-time friend to visit his rebbe, Reb Yisrael of Ruzhin, to ask him how to undertake repentance, and he agreed to do so. But what the tzaddik of Ruzhin told him, and what came of him, is not known.

☙ *A Question of Approach*

בְּזֵעַת אַפֶּיךָ תֹּאכַל לֶחֶם
By the sweat of your face shall you eat bread (3:19)

A poor man once brought his plaint to Reb Mordechai of Neshchiz: he barely managed to make a livelihood, and then only with hard toil.

Said the tzaddik: "But that is written in the Torah: 'By the sweat of your face shall you eat bread!' "

"At least," said the man, "if after all that toil I had plenty of bread, I wouldn't complain."

The tzaddik reassured him: "They say it's not healthy to eat a lot after perspiring..."

☙ *The Tempter Untempted*

לַפֶּתַח חַטָּאת רֹבֵץ
Sin crouches at the door (4:7)

In his childhood Reb Eliezer of Dzikov had got up to a mischievous prank, for which he was scolded by his father, Reb Naftali of Ropshitz.

"It's not my fault," the boy argued, "because I've got an Evil Inclination that seeks to tempt me, and I was enticed."

"All the more so," answered the father. "You should take an example from the Evil Inclination. Look how faithfully he carries out his duty of seducing people, exactly as he was commanded to do."

"True," countered the boy, "but the Evil Inclination hasn't got an evil inclination to tempt him not to do his duty, while with a person, 'sin crouches at the door' — that's the Evil Inclination — ready to mislead him."

☙ *My Brother's Keeper*

הֲשֹׁמֵר אָחִי אָנֹכִי
Am I my brother's keeper? (4:9)

Reb Avraham of Parisov recounted that when Reb Yaakov Aryeh of Radzymin once visited Reb Menachem Mendel of Kotsk, his host turned to him with a question: "Yaakov! For what reason was man created in This World?"

His guest answered: "Man was created in This World in order to set his soul aright."

The Kotsker Rebbe rebuked him loudly: "Yaakov! Is that what we learned from our rebbe, Reb Yaakov Yitzchak of Pshischah? Man was created in order to elevate the heavens!"

On this exchange Reb Avraham of Parisov commented as follows: "Both statements are true, and in both approaches we see that the ultimate purpose of man's creation is to reveal the Divine Presence in This World. Moreover, the common element in these two approaches is hinted at in the statement of the *Mechilta* that the first five of the Ten Commandments are parallel to the second five, respectively. 'Thou shalt not kill' (which is the Sixth Commandment) thus corresponds to אָנֹכִי ה׳ אֱלֹקֶיךָ — I am HASHEM your God' (the First Commandment). A person who commits murder thereby diminishes the cosmic influence of the divine statement 'I am.' Therefore, when God asked Cain: 'Where is Abel your brother?' — Cain answered: 'I do not know; הֲשׁוֹמֵר אָחִי אָנֹכִי? — Am I my brother's keeper?' That is to say, 'I did not know that *my brother* was the *keeper* of *I am;* I did not know that through killing *my brother* I was diminishing the divine *I am* in this world.' "

סדר נח

Sidra Noach

◆§ *A Time to Toil*

אֵלֶּה תּוֹלְדֹת נֹחַ
These are the offspring of Noach (6:9)

A certain scholarly rabbi, who used to exert himself teaching his yeshivah students all day long, once came to envy the more leisurely life-style of those pious folk who had the time to sit back for a few hours every day smoking their pipes, while meditating on the kabbalistic mysteries of the Supernal Unity. Why should he not do likewise? But it would not be proper for him to set out on such a different path in his service of his Maker without first consulting his rebbe, Reb Asher of Ropshitz (who was the son-in-law of Reb Naftali Ropshitzer). Without sharing his thoughts with a soul, he set out for Ropshitz.

The rabbi found the tzaddik in bed, surrounded by chassidim, for he was indisposed. As soon as the tzaddik saw him, he extended his hand to say *Shalom* to his guest and, without giving him a chance to say a word, proceeded: "Let me teach you the verse from the Torah that says *'These* are the *offspring of* Noach.' *These* brings to mind the verse, 'These are thy gods, O Israel' and the name *Noach* means *easy* or *convenient*. In brief: the various forms of idolatry are the *offspring* of an easy and idle life. Now you may argue that my teaching is contradicted by the continuation of that very same verse: *'Noach* [signifying ease and idleness] *was a righteous and perfect man'* — we see around us righteous folk who have the leisure to meditate on lofty kabbalistic mysteries while smoking their pipes. And the answer to your objection is to be found in the words that follow in the same verse: 'And Noach walked with God.' The very *Noach* of such tzaddikim — even their ease and leisure — walks with God. But as for you, my son, do not forsake your accustomed path in the service of your Maker — toiling day and night in the advancement of your studies and in the dissemination of Torah among your students."

☙ *Relative Righteousness*

נֹחַ אִישׁ צַדִּיק תָּמִים הָיָה בְּדֹרֹתָיו

Noach was a righteous and perfect man in his generations (6:9)

In his generations: Some cite this phrase to his credit; others — to his discredit *(Rashi).*

Reb Aryeh Leib of Shpola was once told that Reb Nachman of Breslov was in the habit of telling exceedingly miraculous stories. Reb Aryeh Leib (who was affectionately known as "the Shpoler Zeide" — the Grandfather, or Grand Old Man, from Shpola) reacted as follows: "It is true that in the last generations before the coming of the Messiah there will be such chassidim as will refresh their souls with stories — but it is stories of tzaddikim of earlier generations that they will delight in.

If, however, he tells miraculous stories like those exaggerations cited in the Talmud in the name of Rabbah bar Bar Chanah, how will this help those living in the last generations?"

His chassidim asked him: "Does this mean that there will then be no tzaddikim, so that chassidim will have to refresh their souls with stories of the tzaddikim of earlier generations?"

"Be assured," said the Shpoler Zeide, "that then too there will be tzaddikim and chassidim — but things will be different. For just as there are *esrogim* of various qualities, so, too, are there different levels of tzaddikim. You may have an *esrog* that is barely valid for use on Sukkos — but it is still called an *esrog:* you can pronounce a benediction over it, and meditate devoutly on all the appropriate kabbalistic connotations, and with it draw down to This World all the divine light that this mitzvah elicits. Yet for all that, it is not the ideal 'goodly fruit' that an *esrog* is meant to be — the kind with which one refreshes his soul far more than with an *esrog* that is barely valid."

❦ ❦ ❦

The above conversation took place at the Third Meal of a *Shabbos* during which the weekly Portion of *Noach* was read. "This subject," resumed the Shpoler Zeide, "is hinted at in today's reading from the Torah. We read: 'Noach was a righteous and perfect man in his generations.' Rashi quotes the comment of our Sages, that 'Some cite this phrase to Noach's discredit: in *his* generations he was accounted a tzaddik; had he been a contemporary of the Patriarch Avraham, he would have counted for nothing.' Now this is a remarkable comment. For if we find it possible to understand this phrase in a favorable sense, why should we cite it to his discredit? Do not our Sages teach us: 'Give every man the benefit of the doubt'?

"But in fact those who understood the phrase to Noach's discredit did a lasting favor to the Jewish people. Since the tzaddikim of the last generations before the coming of the Messiah would not be of the same stature as those of the earlier generations, the Torah mentions explicitly that even a person who is a tzaddik only when compared to his contemporaries — and in earlier times would have been overlooked — is also a tzaddik in the eyes of the Torah. Being so called, it is within his power to draw divine blessings down to This World, just as did the tzaddikim of yesteryear."

❦ ❦ ❦

It happened on another occasion that certain foolish chassidim heard of the opposition of Reb Aryeh Leib of Shpola to Reb Nachman of Breslov, and decided to travel to Zlatopol, where Reb Nachman lived at that time, in order to make life difficult for him. When word of this plan reached Reb Aryeh Leib, he summoned them, and warned them sternly that they were not to cause the slightest inconvenience to Reb Nachman, again by referring to the above quotation: "Those who cited this phrase to Noach's discredit did Jewry a lasting favor, for they saw through Divine Inspiration that almost all the tzaddikim who would arise throughout the generations until the coming of the Messiah would have to contend with opponents. Why, even Moses our teacher — and who greater than he? — had to face the envy and suspicion of certain individuals within that great generation of men of understanding. Now the first tzaddik mentioned in the Torah is Noach. If all our Sages had spoken only in his favor, we would measure every tzaddik thereafter in the same way, thinking that a man was a tzaddik only if all his contemporaries praised him, and rejecting him if he had any opponents. This would be a very bad thing for the world. For this reason some of our Sages intentionally pointed out an imperfection in the first tzaddik, so that in the case of later tzaddikim we should not take undue notice of the fact that they have opponents; so long as the man has as many admirers as critics, he may be called a tzaddik."

◆§ Make the Word a Window (i)

צֹהַר תַּעֲשֶׂה לַתֵּבָה
Make a window for the ark (6:16)

Make a window for the ark [the word תֵּבָה may be translated *ark* as it must be in the simple sense of *this* verse, or *word* as it is in this homiletical interpretation]: Make the words of your prayer luminous *(Baal Shem Tov).*

In the days of the Baal Shem Tov there lived a man who found an assurance written in some holy book that anyone who for forty consecutive days refrained from idle talk would be granted Divine Inspiration. After forty days had passed without the merest sign of such a visitation, the man decided to journey to the Baal Shem Tov. There must be *some* explanation...

When he had told the Baal Shem Tov his melancholy tale, the tzaddik asked him: "Did you pray during those forty days?"

"What a question! Three times a day!"

"And did you read any *Psalms?*"

"Of course!" answered the man.

"In that case," said the Baal Shem Tov, considering the questionable devoutness with which the sacred words had probably been babbled, "everything is clear. *This* must have been your idle talk..."

◆§ Make the Word a Window (ii)

A similar story took place a hundred years later, in the days of Reb Yisrael of Ruzhin: a well-meaning Jew, yearning desperately for the delights of Divine Inspiration, vigilantly shunned any syllable of idle talk for forty days and forty nights. The prescribed period passed — but neither word nor whisper of the holy spirit. What could be the matter? He would take his riddle to the tzaddik of Ruzhin.

The court of Reb Yisrael, as is well known, was conducted in regal style: gold and silver and the choicest of delicacies tantalized the senses of the bewitched beholder. Now when this visitor beheld all this luxury, he was dumbstruck. Was this the lifestyle that befitted a tzaddik? Was this the path laid out by the Torah? And the longer he tarried in Ruzhin, the more he was amazed, until he decided that this could be no tzaddik; one could hardly discuss matters of the holy spirit with a man like this.

On the very day that the guest was about to leave Ruzhin, without calling on the tzaddik, he saw Reb Yisrael preparing to go riding in his carriage. Four sturdy stallions were harnessed, and the tzaddik was about to take his seat. Before doing so, however, he approached one of the horses, and gently patted its back three times. The visitor was stupefied. Acting on impulse, he approached Reb Yisrael and asked: "Rabbi, what kind of divine service is this, for a tzaddik to pat his horse?"

"For your information," explained the tzaddik, "not a single word of idle talk has passed the lips of this horse for forty whole days."

◆§ *Make the Word a Window (iii)*

Reb Yitzchak Luria, known as the Ariz*al*, prayed with extraordinary devoutness during the Days of Awe. Then he was told from heaven that there was one man in a certain town who prayed better than he did. The celebrated kabbalist traveled there, called for the man, and asked him:

"Are you a Torah scholar?"

"No."

"Do you know how to pray?"

"No."

"Then what did you do during the Days of Awe?"

"Rabbi," answered the man, "I don't even know the whole alphabet — only from *aleph* to *yud*. So when I came to the synagogue, and I saw all the congregation praying so devotedly, all aloud, while I can't pray at all, my heart broke inside me, and this is what I said: '*Aleph, beis, gimmel, daled, hei, vav, zayin, ches, tes, yud*. Master of the Universe! Put together all these letters into words the way You understand, and I hope You'll find them acceptable.' That's what I said with a broken heart, but with all my strength, then I started all over again from the beginning."

And these were the words that made more impact on High than the prayers of the saintly Ariz*al*.

⌘ Make the Word a Window (iv)

Make a window of the word: Make a window out of the words of the Torah and of the prayers through which to gaze from one end of the world to the other *(Baal Shem Tov).*

The Baal Shem Tov was once asked a certain matter. He opened a volume of the *Zohar* which was on the table, looked inside, and then told his listeners all about the incident involved. It later transpired that things had been exactly as he had described them. So he was asked: "Is it by opening up the *Zohar* and looking inside it for a moment that you can tell what is going on at a distance?"

Replied the Baal Shem Tov: "Our Sages teach us that the light with which the Almighty created the world illumined from one end of the world to the other; Adam, too, was able to see with this light. But when the Almighty saw that the world was not worthy of using this light, he hid it away for the righteous in the World to Come. Now," asked the Baal Shem Tov, "where did He hide it? — In the Torah; and when a person studies the Torah for *its own sake*, a path is lit up for him, enabling him to understand and see from one end of the world to the other, just as things were before God hid the light."

⌘ A Simple Deduction

וַיִּזְכֹּר אֱלֹקִים אֶת-נֹחַ וְאֵת כָּל-הַחַיָּה וְאֶת-כָּל-הַבְּהֵמָה

And God remembered Noach, and every living thing, and all the cattle (8:1)

Reb Simchah Bunem of Pshischah once came to spend Rosh HaShanah at the court of Reb Yaakov Yitzchak, the Chozeh (or Seer) of Lublin. After the prayer service, he told the chassidim who surrounded him: "I can tell you what verse the rebbe is going to base his teaching on at today's festive meal; and the content of his lesson, too."

His hearers were amazed at this statement, and in order to be able to put his claim to the test, they asked him to tell them what he knew.

"Well," said Reb Simchah Bunem, "the rebbe is going to speak today on the verse: 'And God remembered Noach, and every living thing, and all the cattle which were with him in the ark.' This text he will expound as follows: 'God remembered Noach' — this refers to the tzaddik in a given generation; and through the tzaddik he will also remember 'every living thing and all the cattle' — an allusion to the common people, as is mentioned in the Book of *Jeremiah ('I will sow the House of Israel ... with the seed of man and the seed of cattle'),* and in the Talmud (where the words 'of the cattle' are taken to include such men as resemble cattle)."

Soon after, the Chozeh joined his chassidim at the table, and in the course of the meal expounded this verse, exactly as their guest had predicted. The chassidim were stupefied, and asked him how he knew all this in advance. Reb Simchah Bunem explained: "At today's *Musaf* service, I was praying near the rebbe. When, in the course of the passage on *Zichronos*, he came to the verse 'And God remembered Noach', I observed that he meditated on it deeply and at length, in the service of the heart which is called prayer. He repeated it many times, too; and I gathered that this was the verse which he would expound today, and that this was what he was going to say."

☙ *A Lesson in Self-Effacement*

וַיָּמָת הָרָן עַל־פְּנֵי תֶּרַח אָבִיו
And Haran died before his father Terach (11:28)

Before his father Terach: He died *because* of his father, for Terach complained to Nimrod that his son Avraham had shattered his idols *(Rashi).*

The townsfolk of Nikolsburg were not chassidim, and they disapproved of the seemingly odd behavior of their communal rabbi, Reb Shmelke, who was a chassidic rebbe. The most prominent burghers therefore called a meeting, decided to dismiss him, and instructed the *shammes* to inform the rabbi of their decision. This beadle, who was a simple fellow, but honest and upright, asked them why they had suddenly decided to do such a thing.

"It's no business of yours," they told him brusquely. "Your job is to do as you're told."

But since the *shammes* pleaded for an answer to his question, they told him simply that Reb Shmelke's odd behavior made him unfit for the post of rabbi.

 The *shammes* was insistent: "I know for a fact that our rabbi is a perfect tzaddik."

His employers knew their *shammes* to be a truthful man, so they asked him: "How do you know that he is a tzaddik?"

"Very well," he answered. "You know as well as I do that it is the custom in this city for someone to knock on the doors of all the Jewish townsfolk before dawn, to wake everyone up for the service of the Creator. Every night as I go a-knocking on my rounds, I come to the rabbi's house, and I drop in, and I always find him sitting up studying Torah; and next to him sits another man, whom I don't know. So one day I asked him who it was. So he told me. It was Eliyahu the Prophet, of blessed memory. It once happened that for some reason I came around later than usual, and saw the rabbi at the door of his house, holding two candlesticks. Two men were with him — one was the one I see there always, and the other wore a golden crown. The two men left and went their way, and the rabbi went back inside. I asked him who was the visitor with the crown of gold, and he told me that it was Menashe ben Chizkiyahu, king of Judah. When I asked the rabbi what business brought Menashe ben Chizkiyahu to his home, he explained that he was concerned regarding the outcome of a halachic query that a certain rabbi had sent our rabbi that very day.

"In the city of that other rabbi there lived a chassid, who had taken it upon himself to smash all of the images and crucifixes in the local church. He was handed over to the courts, sentenced to death, and hanged. Now that city has a welfare brotherhood, whose task it is to give financial support to poor widows whose husbands have left them penniless. But when the widow of this poor chassid came to them, and asked them for a little money, they refused, because they claim that their regulations only allow them to support the widows of men who have died a natural death, not the widows of men who have suicided — and they say her husband, by doing what he did, was such a man. Their dispute came up for adjudication by their local rabbi, and he referred the question to our Reb Shmelke, here in Nikolsburg. Our rabbi was in two minds over the whole business, when along came Menashe ben Chizkiyahu, and told him that he had been reincarnated in that very chassid, in order that he should be able to set right the evil that he had done in his earlier life, when he had set up an image in the Temple. And now he had come to ask our rabbi to see that the poor widow of that chassid should get her due."

❦ ❦ ❦

This story was told by Reb Simchah Bunem of Pshischah, who concluded in these words: "How beautiful is the modesty of that *shammes!* Night by night Eliyahu the Prophet stood revealed before his eyes, but it never occurred to him that he had any reason to be proud. All he did was to speak in praise of his rabbi: to *him* Eliyahu had appeared, and had revealed to him the secrets of the Torah."

סדר לך לך
Sidra Lech Lecha

◆§ *The Fall of a Giant*

לֶךְ־לְךָ מֵאַרְצְךָ *Go thee forth from your land (12:1)*

Among the disciples of Reb Dov Ber, the Maggid of Mezritch, there was a scholar of repute known as the Rav of Volpa. His first name is not recorded. Early in his career he was the greatest among the brotherhood, and his colleagues were wont to visit him in order to hear how he faithfully repeated the chassidic discourses which together they had heard from the lips of the Maggid, for his phrases were chosen with discernment. But after many years he was overtaken by a grave spiritual crisis, and the unfortunate man became a drunkard. "A worm was eating away at him from within," said the disciples of the Maggid. (So wrote Reb Menachem Mendel of Lubavitch, known as the Tzemach Tzedek, in a letter to one of his sons.) From that time on, like a vagabond, he wandered about with his knapsack and his staff, from town to town and from province to province. But even then, though errant and in exile, his tongue was yet able to conjure up perfectly fashioned pearls of wisdom. Indeed, the more wine he imbibed, the more freely flowed the mysteries he had savored in happier days.

In the course of his wanderings he lighted upon the town of Liozna, where Reb Shneur Zalman, the author of *Tanya*, lived before his imprisonment. The Rav of Volpa entered the local *beis midrash* in time to hear his former colleague, that illustrious disciple of the Maggid of Mezritch, delivering a chassidic discourse. For a quiet hour he stood and listened. Then he said to a bystander, "We all ate together out of the same bowl, but all the choicest morsels ended up with him."

With that, he turned and went on his way, and no one knew who he was. But when Reb Shneur Zalman was later told that there had been such a visitor, he understood that this must have been the Rav of Volpa and was grieved that he had not known of this earlier, so that he could have persuaded him to stay with him, and no longer live the life of a vagabond.

❀ ❀ ❀

Finding himself once in Vilna, the homeless wayfarer entered a tavern, drank deeply according to his habit, and lay down over the built-in fireplace to rest. Up there all alone, he repeated to himself aloud such secrets of the Torah that few ears ever hear. During this reverie, a learned stranger entered the tavern — a pious disciple of the Gaon of Vilna, Reb Yudel by name. As he went about, collecting donations for some worthy cause, he overheard from high up over the fireplace the most awesome words being uttered by an unseen speaker. He sought out the voice, and asked: "My good man, where did you acquire such wares?"

"From where I acquired, Sir, you can no longer acquire; but if you do want such wares I'd advise you to journey to Liozna. There you will find peace for your soul."

Reb Yudel took heed, and set out at once for Liozna.

There he grew close to Reb Shneur Zalman and became one of his foremost chassidim, and in time the rebbe sent him to be a rabbi in the town of Liepli.

❀ ❀ ❀

On another occasion the fallen wanderer was seen at an inn by Reb Baruch Mordechai of Bobruisk, a disciple of Reb Shneur Zalman, who gathered from his conduct that this was the Rav of Volpa. So eager was he to lay eyes on some rare manuscript of the mystical teachings of the Maggid, that when the stranger left the inn for a while, Reb Baruch Mordechai took the liberty of rummaging through his knapsack. At that moment, in walked the Rav of Volpa, who challenged him: "What are you looking for there? Have I stolen something from you?"

"I thought perhaps there might be a manuscript..."

"With you folk today," said the owner of the knapsack, "the chassidim are one thing, and the rebbe and his teachings are something apart; that's why you need manuscripts. But in our day, we and our rebbe and his teachings were all one, so we had no need for manuscripts."

And he took up his staff and his knapsack, and went his way.

◈§ *Just an Ordinary Jew*

וֶהְיֵה בְּרָכָה

And you shall be a blessing (12:2)

And you shall be a blessing: The blessings are entrusted to your hand *(Rashi)*.

Reb Elimelech of Lyzhansk was once walking along with another man on his way to a ritual immersion in a *mikveh*, when a heavenly voice was heard, promising a spiritual reward in the World to Come for whoever would help to free Reb Shmelke of Nikolsburg from the bitter opposition of his antagonists.

"Did you hear a voice just now?" Reb Elimelech asked his companion.

"Nothing," said the other.

"Since only I heard it," thought the tzaddik, "it is clear that I am the one who ought to go to Nikolsburg."

Arriving there, he asked Reb Shmelke for permission to preach in the synagogue in order to rebuke the congregation. Said Reb Shmelke: "What good can that do, when they never listen to any words of rebuke?"

But since his guest entreated him earnestly, he finally gave his permission.

Soon enough, the synagogue was filled with people who were eager to hear out the guest preacher. In the course of his sermon, Reb Elimelech proved to them by all manner of specious arguments that there were ways and means of voiding various prohibitions specified in the Torah — after the style of the ingenious hairsplitter mentioned in the Talmud, who succeeded in finding one hundred and fifty pseudo-logical justifications for pronouncing a reptile ritually clean. This kind of teaching was very much to their liking. The guest announced that on the morrow he would preach again, and almost all the townsfolk flocked to hear him. He ascended the pulpit, and proved to them — this time with genuine arguments — that the previous day he had not taught them the truth: that in fact it was forbidden to transgress not only those prohibitions explicitly set out in the Torah, but also the slightest prohibition ordained by the Sages. His words, proceeding from the heart, aroused a feeling of repentance in the hearts of all his listeners. They wept, contrite, and said to each other, "He's telling us exactly what our rabbi had been telling us all along, but we didn't want to take notice. We really ought to go to his house and ask for his forgiveness!"

So they went to Reb Shmelke, and fell on their faces, and asked him for pardon, and promised to heed his words from then on — for the visiting preacher had shown them that he had been in the right.

As for Reb Elimelech, he took his leave of Reb Shmelke, and took to the road. A little way out of Nikolsburg, he was addressed by a voice from heaven: "Because you helped Reb Shmelke, whomever you will bless during the next twenty-four hours will be blessed."

Reb Elimelech walked on, overjoyed at his gift — but deep was his disappointment when after many long hours on the road he had not encountered one solitary fellow Jew on whom to bestow his blessing. Heartbroken, he sobbed out his plaint to his Maker: "So You've given me a gift for twenty-four hours. But I cannot use it, because I have not met a single Jew. Tell me, whom can I bless?"

As he finished his prayer, he saw a woman walking in the fields, and immediately began to bless her. Seeing that the poor woman was taken aback, he put her at ease. "Be not afraid, my good woman," he said, "for I am no malevolent being. Tell me, please, where you come from, and what brings you here."

Reassured, the woman told her story; the tzaddik blessed her, and she went on her way.

Arriving home, she told her husband that an unknown man had met her on the way and had blessed her. And from that day on, all their affairs prospered so much that they became extremely wealthy, moved to another city, and there conducted their merchandising on a grand scale. They decided that without a doubt the unknown stranger who had blessed them was none other than the Prophet Eliyahu, of blessed memory. The merchant became a great philanthropist, and instructed his servants that they could disburse charity on his account to the extent of one gold coin without consulting him, while for larger amounts they were to ask him.

Many years passed. Then one day, Reb Elimelech and his brother Reb Zusya of Hanipoli decided to take to the road in order to collect money for the ransom of captives. Hearing that in a certain city there was a very generous magnate, they set out to visit him. His servants offered them a dinar of gold, and when this offer was declined, they explained that for greater sums they would have to ask their master's permission. The guests were admitted to the room of the merchant, but no sooner did his wife set eyes upon Reb Elimelech, then she fell into a swoon from sheer fright. The household was in turmoil. When she came to, she told her husband: "Do you know who that is? That is Eliyahu the Prophet, who blessed me many years ago. Now he has returned, no doubt to take back all the wealth that he gave us!"

"Do not fear," said Reb Elimelech. "I am not Eliyahu the Prophet, and I have not come to take away your wealth, God forbid. I'm just an ordinary Jew, except that (thank God) I blessed you, and my blessing was fulfilled."

The merchant then asked: "How much do you need to ransom your captives?"

When they told him that they needed five hundred gold coins in all, he went out for a moment and fetched them the whole sum.

"But we want to enable other Jews to have a share in this great mitzvah," they said, and refused to accept his offer. After he implored them to change their minds, they agreed to accept half the sum and, amid a warm exchange of farewells, they took their leave.

◆§ *A Pauper's Blessing*

And you shall be a blessing: The blessings are entrusted to your hand *(Rashi).*

In the days of the Baal Shem Tov there lived in Vilna two simple tailors. They were not particularly expert in their craft, but stitched together homespun clothes for the common folk, and for the peasants in the surrounding hamlets. In the course of time they became partners, and decided to make some money by leaving Vilna for a time, and making the rounds of the villages, plying their trade. On their way home with their earnings after some years, they came to a certain village where, according to their custom, they called on the Jew who lived there, and whose livelihood was the collection of taxes by contract with the local squire who owned the entire village. Seeing that he was downcast, they asked him what troubled him, and eventually persuaded him to unburden himself of his woes. It transpired that the local squire, about to marry off his daughter, had ordered this hapless Jew to find him an expert tailor to make up the bridal gown. The tax farmer had brought him the most fashionable tailors from all the towns in the vicinity, but none of them had satisfied him. He had now warned him that if he could not provide him with what he demanded, he would drive him penniless out of the village.

The two tailors listened intently and a wild idea

flickered in their minds: perchance Divine Providence had brought this job their way?

"Look here," they said; "you're talking to two tailors. Go along and tell your squire that you've come across two experts, and that he should give them a chance to try their hand at his daughter's bridal outfit."

The tax farmer laughed bitterly. "Do you think I want to go and make fun of the man? I just told you that the fanciest tailors weren't good enough for him; so how can I recommend two tailors like yourselves, who travel around the countryside sewing breeches for farmhands and yokels?"

The tailors were persistent. "But what do you lose by telling him about us? On the contrary. Perhaps just because he's behaving so crazily as to reject all the experts, he'll feel like giving us the job."

At length, the tax farmer succumbed to their barrage of arguments along these lines, and to the amazement of all concerned, the squire not only agreed to allow them to sew him a sample job, but was effusive in his praises of it when it was completed. What is more, he commissioned them to make up the entire bridal wardrobe of his daughter, which they did on the premises. Finally, he thanked them kindly, paid them generously, and before they left called in his Jewish tax farmer to thank him for having found him such fine workmen. In token of his appreciation, he told him that he had decided to allow him to retain his home and his livelihood.

Now the squire's wife, seeing how pleased the tailors were to hear this last piece of news, took her husband aside: "I am sure you noticed how overjoyed those Jews are that their coreligionist will not be thrown out of our village after all. Why don't you tell them about our other Jewish tax collector, the one we threw into the dungeon? They may feel like paying us a ransom in order to free him."

The squire thereupon told the tailors that one of his Jewish tax farmers had not paid his dues, for which reason he had imprisoned him and all his family in his underground lock-up. After a long time there, they were already begging to die.

"How much does he owe you?" they asked.

"Three hundred silver rubles," was the answer.

One of the tailors turned to his friend: "What do you say?"

"What *can* I say?" answered the other. "If it were a question of a smaller sum, I would agree that we should share the mitzvah of redeeming captives. But could we possibly lay out such an amount as this?"

After a few moments of thought, the first tailor said: "Listen, brother. I'd like to dissolve our partnership. Let's work out how much my share comes to, and I'll take it in cash."

They made their calculations, and each man's share came to three hundred silver rubles. Seeing that his friend was about to give away his entire earnings, the second tailor tried to dissuade him — but to no avail. They divided up the money, and the first tailor gave the squire his three hundred silver rubles. As soon as the wretched prisoners were freed, and told who was responsible for their sudden change of fortune, they embraced the tailor with tears of joy and gratitude — and he too rejoiced in their happiness.

Continuing their journey homeward, the two tailors arrived at length at Vilna. The one who brought his savings with him opened a business of readymade clothes and soon prospered, while his friend, who had come emptyhanded, fell on hard times. He walked with the stoop of a broken man, and people nicknamed him "the tailor with the funereal face." When he was overcome by the pangs of hunger, he would ask bypassers for alms, and what he had lived through was known to no one.

It so happened that one day, when he stopped one of the citizens of Vilna in the street and asked him for a little money to buy some bread, the stranger asked him: "And if I give you a donation, what happens then?"

"I can give you my blessings," he said.

The man smiled: the blessings of some fool.... He gave the tailor some small change, and forgot about the incident.

Now this man, who was a flax merchant, used to travel periodically to the homesteads of various landowners, buy up their flax, and bring it back to town. On the day that he had met the tailor, he had to go to the farm of a particularly tough customer, with whom he always had trouble in clinching a deal. This time, strangely enough, the transaction was completed quickly and profitably. The flax merchant thought for a moment. Perhaps, after all, it was the blessing of that pauper that was helping him? But he kept the thought to himself.

After some time, he had to go out on another such visit. This time he made a point of seeking out the tailor, giving him a donation, and asking him for his blessing. This he gave, and again things worked out well for the merchant. Seeing that it was clearly the poor man's blessing that made his affairs prosper, the merchant made it a rule to repeat the same procedure before every business venture, and within half a year he was a wealthy man. Still not a soul knew what transpired between them.

At a festive meal one day, the merchant sat surrounded by his relatives and friends and, happy with wine, he told them the secret of his success. But since (as the Talmud says) "your friend has a friend, and your friend's friend has a friend," the secret was no longer a secret, and in no time word got around that the blessings of this melancholy man actually came true. People thronged to him from all sides to request his blessing, and they found that they were in fact blessed.

At this time two disciples of the Baal Shem Tov happened to be passing through Vilna. They too heard about the tailor and his blessings, and on their return home told their rebbe about this phenomenon. The Baal Shem Tov asked them to try to bring this man with them next time they came home from Vilna, and indeed on their next visit there they succeeded in persuading him to come with them.

When they met, the Baal Shem Tov queried him as to the cause by virtue of which he had been granted this gift from heaven. The tailor had no answer. It did not occur to him that the incident of the ransom was involved. It could even be that he was not aware of the fact that his blessings were fulfilled. At any rate, the Baal Shem Tov asked him to recount his life story.

The tailor proceeded to tell of all the ups and downs of his life, until he came to the episode of the squire, and the bridal gown, and the prisoners, and the ransom ...

"That's it!" the Baal Shem Tov exclaimed.

He asked the tailor to stay with him, and took him into his hands, curing him of his melancholia, and teaching him both the revealed and the hidden sides of the Torah. So richly did he open up to him the fountains of wisdom, that as the tailor thirstily drank the mystical teachings of the Baal Shem Tov, he grew to become a great tzaddik himself, and wrote a book on the sacred mysteries of the Kabbalah.

A Misnaged's Curse

וּמְקַלֶּלְךָ אָאֹר
And him that curses you shall I curse (12:3)

In the town of Pinsk there lived a *misnaged,* an opponent of Chassidism, who while studying the *Zohar* came across a passage that he could not understand. He decided to visit the chassidic rebbe of the neighboring town, Reb Shlomo of Karlin, in order to have the difficulty clarified.

Said Reb Shlomo: "But you're a *misnaged,* so I shall not explain you the words of the *Zohar* until you curse the Gaon of Vilna in my name, exactly as I tell you."

The *misnaged* was alarmed at hearing such a reference to the leader of the opposition to Chassidism, and left disappointed. Back at home, he grappled again with the problematic passage, but without success. There was no alternative: he would go back to that chassidic rebbe and do as he was told. What harm could his curse do, especially when in his heart he didn't really mean what he would say?

Hearing of his consent, Reb Shlomo said: "Curse him in my name that some of his descendants will be chassidim!"

A curse as grim as this took the *misnaged* quite by surprise. Much relieved, he uttered the awesome words ...

And his words were duly fulfilled. Reb Eliyahu Zvi of Berisov and Reb Zalman of Dissna, both prominent chassidim of Reb Menachem Mendel of Lubavitch, were grandsons of the Gaon of Vilna.

A Curse with a Silver Lining

וְנִבְרְכוּ בְךָ כֹּל מִשְׁפְּחֹת הָאֲדָמָה
And in your name shall all the families of the earth be blessed (12:3)

It was the custom of Reb Yehudah Aryeh Leib of Ger, the author of *Sfas Emes,* to examine his young children in the weekly Portion of the Torah that they had studied. This was their time for asking questions, and one of them once asked as follows: "We read this week, 'And him that curses you shall I curse, and in your name shall all the families of the earth be blessed.' Now if all the families of the earth are to bless by wishing that others be like Avraham, who will curse?"

Replied his father: "It's rather like a person who curses chassidim — while deep down he would like his children to resemble them ... "

Living without a Rebbe

וְאֶת־הַנֶּפֶשׁ אֲשֶׁר־עָשׂוּ בְחָרָן
And the souls that they had acquired in Charan (12:5)

> *And the souls that they had acquired in Charan:* Avraham gathered them in under the wings of the Divine Presence — he would convert the menfolk, and Sarah the women *(Rashi).*

Reb Chanoch of Alexander once asked: "Where are all those who were converted by Avraham and Sarah? For in the Torah we find mentioned thereafter only the *children* of Avraham, Yitzchak and Yaakov. What happened to all those others?"

And he answered his own question: "During Avraham's lifetime, the converts cleaved to him and walked in his path. After his passing, they saw that his successor taught a different mode of divine service — while Avraham had epitomized the attribute of lovingkindness, Yitzchak represented the attribute of strict justice, and awe. This change was not to their liking, and they understood it to mean that the son was less worthy of being followed than the father. So they parted ways with Yitzchak, then gradually lost their previous degree of spirituality, and eventually returned to their former habits and became heathens again.

"From this we see," concluded Reb Chanoch, "that every man should cleave to the tzaddik of his generation, even if that tzaddik's path in the service of God is not to his liking. For if not, he will fall from his current spiritual level, and lose even whatever he acquired from his previous rebbe."

◆§ Feel Pity for the Prosperous

וַיְהִי רָעָב בָּאָרֶץ
And there was famine in the land (12:10)

In famine You have sustained us, and in plenty have You nourished us *(Sabbath Liturgy).*

A band of prosperous grain merchants once came to request the advice and blessing of Reb David of Tolna. Since the drought of the previous year had raised the grain prices considerably, they had assumed that their merchandise would fetch the same prices this year, and had therefore held it back in anticipation of greater profits. In fact, however, the prices were continually dropping — to their loss.

The tzaddik answered: "He Who sustains and nourishes the paupers in years of famine will doubtless sustain and nourish the magnates in years of prosperity..."

◆§ No Shadow of a Doubt

אִם־מִחוּט וְעַד שְׂרוֹךְ־נַעַל
I will take nothing, from a thread even to a shoelace (14:23)

Reb Meir of Premishlan was a great pauper all his days, subsisting on the merest pittance. Then whatever was left after the day's meager expenditure he would distribute to the poor on the very same day, in order that no money should spend the night in his house. Finding one night that he was utterly unable to fall asleep, he got up, and asked his family to search out the house lest some coins had been overlooked. Sure enough, they found a little money, and gave it to the poor, and the tzaddik went to sleep.

On another occasion a woman came to him from Rumania, with the request that he give her his blessing that she be granted a child, and Reb Meir gave his blessing that the Almighty answer her prayer. In due course

the sum of three hundred coins arrived in the mail, together with a letter from a stranger that explained that since his wife had borne him a child in the wake of the tzaddik's blessing, he was now sending him this gift. Reb Meir showed the letter to his sons, protesting that it was "full of mistakes. In the first place," he pointed out, "it addresses me as 'tzaddik' and 'saintly man' and so forth. Now since when am I a tzaddik and a saintly man? Secondly, the body of the letter is all wrong. Do I have the power to bless barren women that their prayers should be answered? It is clear, therefore, that the writer didn't mean me at all, and that is why I am going to return the gift to its sender."

His sons were incensed. If the Almighty arranged that some money should come the way of their poverty-stricken household so that they could at last buy the most basic necessities, why throw it away with their own hands? They remonstrated with their father, but he was determined. At length it was agreed that they should put their arguments before a rabbinical court of three judges, for adjudication.

After hearing out both sides, the court ruled that Reb Meir was indeed permitted to use the money: though he in his modesty did not regard himself as a tzaddik, it was certain that the writer thought otherwise and definitely had Reb Meir in mind when he sent the gift. Likewise, feeling sure that it was the tzaddik's blessing that had brought about his good fortune, it was beyond doubt that his gift had been given wholeheartedly and unconditionally.

"I would still like to ask my wife's opinion," said Reb Meir, "as to whether we should use this money."

So they called in the *rebbitzin*, and Reb Meir told her that since he had had such a *she'elah*, he had brought this legal query to the notice of a court, which had duly ruled that they could in fact use the money — but he nevertheless wanted to ask her opinion.

Replied the *rebbitzin:* "But your custom has always been that as soon as a *she'elah* arises in the kitchen as to whether a chicken or whatever is kosher, you never eat it anyway, even if a rabbi rules that it is permissible!"

And the tzaddik returned the gift to its sender.

◆§ Mutual Enrichment

וּמַלְכִּי־צֶדֶק ... הוֹצִיא לֶחֶם וָיָיִן וְהוּא כֹהֵן לְאֵל עֶלְיוֹן

And Malki-Tzedek ... brought out bread and wine, and he was a priest of God Most High (14:18)

Reb Meir of Premishlan once wrote to the renowned scholar, Rabbi Shlomo Kluger of Brody, asking that they should meet, which they arranged to do in a certain village near Zlotchov. Arriving there separately at the appointed time, they found lodgings in different houses. The chassidic rebbe then sent his beadle to ask the learned rabbi who of them, according to the Torah, should go to greet the other — since both were guests in this village. The famous rabbi returned his learned opinion that according to the Torah it was his prerogative to wait at his lodgings and be greeted there by Reb Meir.

Having done his duty, Reb Meir asked for the source of this ruling, and Rabbi Shlomo answered: "Its source is to be found in the passage in *Exodus:* 'And Moses went out to meet his father-in-law ... and they asked each other [literally: *a man asked his fellow*] of their welfare.' *Rashi,* following the interpretation of the *Mechilta,* explains that 'a man' refers to Moses. Now since he and Yisro were both journeying in the wilderness, why did Moshe go ahead and greet Yisro? In my opinion, the reason is that he had traveled only a short distance, while Yisro had come all the way from Midian. I, likewise, have come all the way from Brody, while you had only a few miles to travel. The prerogative of being greeted is therefore mine."

When they had spent some hours in scholarly discourse, and were about to part, Reb Meir — whose days and earnings were wholly devoted to charity — shared the following thought with the rabbi from Brody: "Regarding the meeting of Avraham and Malki-Tzedek, we read in the Torah — 'And Malki-Tzedek king of Shalem brought out bread and wine, and he was a priest of God, the Most High.' When two such tzaddikim meet, they each cleave to the sanctity of the other, and partake of each other's divine service. Avraham was chiefly occupied with the mitzvah of hospitality, with his house wide open to every wayfarer; Malki-Tzedek, who is traditionally identified with Shem, was cloistered in his House of Study, pondering the depths of the divine Law. When they met, each learned a lesson from the ways of the other, and this is hinted at by a homiletical reading of the very same text: 'And Malki-Tzedek brought out — from Avraham — bread and wine'; that is, he learned from him the attribute of giving succor to the needy. *And he* — that is to say, Avraham — learned from Shem how to be *a priest of God, the Most High,* how to serve Him through the study of the divine Law day and night."

◆§ A Mitzvah Untainted

וְאַתָּה אֶת־בְּרִיתִי תִשְׁמֹר
And you shall keep My covenant (17:9)

One of the young chassidim of Reb Mordechai of Lechovitch was always berated mercilessly by his father-in-law, who was an outstanding scholar — but an incorrigible *misnaged.* "You are just too lazy to study," he would taunt, "*that* is why you have chosen to be a chassid!"

Now one day a son was born to the young man so, being a loyal chassid, he hastened to honor his rebbe Reb Mordechai, an expert *mohel,* with the coveted mitzvah of circumcising the newborn infant. The eighth day arrived, and the father rose early, as was his custom, to pray the morning service in the synagogue of his rebbe. This was the very opportunity that his *misnagdisher* father-in-law had been waiting for. Once and for all he would put them in their place, both of them, this young chassidic son-in-law of his with his favorite chassidic rebbe. He lost no time, hired another *mohel,* mustered ten men for a *minyan,* and while his son-in-law and Reb Mordechai were still at their devotions, the circumcision was over and done with.

Radiant with innocent expectation the father and his rebbe returned from *shul,* accompanied by a retinue of joyful chassidim, all ready for the great mitzvah. But what a surprise awaited them! The young man was understandably distressed, firstly, because he had not been present at the circumcision of his own son, and secondly, because of the calculated insult to his revered rebbe. But there are things in this world which, once done, cannot be undone. There was nothing to do but to quietly go to the rebbe's home for the *seudas mitzvah,* the traditional festive meal that follows a joyful mitzvah. There, to the wonderment of all the crestfallen chassidim, the rebbe was clearly happier than on all the other occasions when he had *in fact* carried out the mitzvah of circumcision.

His explanation was simple: "The mitzvah of circumcising a baby is, of course, a singularly great one — but it is almost always tainted by the shadow of a hankering after honor, or pride. Now our Sages teach us that 'if an emergency prevented a person from doing a mitzvah, Scripture accords him credit for his good intention, as if he had actually performed the mitzvah.' Obviously, a mitzvah of this kind has no ulterior motive, and is reckoned by the Almighty as having been executed in the most perfect way possible. And that is why I have cause to rejoice more than usual: for how often do I get a chance to do a mitzvah that is absolutely untainted?"

◈ *The Alacrity of Abraham*

So eager was Reb Mordechai of Lechovitch to perform the mitzvah of circumcision that he never once declined an invitation to act as *mohel.* One short midwinter's day, on the Sabbath eve of Chanukah, he was honored with the performance of two circumcisions in villages far apart from each other, one to the north of his town, one to the south. When his chassidim heard that he had accepted both invitations, they asked him whether he thought he could manage so much in such a short day.

He answered: "Regarding a certain passage in the Torah, the Talmud tells us that 'it comes to teach us of Avraham's alacrity,' which I understand to mean that the Torah *teaches us* Avraham's alacrity; nay, the Torah *implants* it in us."

And, indeed, Reb Mordechai rose at the crack of dawn, hastened to set out and circumcise the infants in both villages, and sped home — weary, but in time to prepare for *Shabbos.*

❧ ❧ ❧

By his grave there sprang a myrtle *(hadas* in Hebrew), and people said that this was because all his life he had pursued this mitzvah of bringing children into the covenant of the Patriarch Avraham — for is it not written in the *Zohar* that the Angel of the Covenant is called Hadas?

◆§ *The Merits of an Informer*

וְהָיָה לְאוֹת בְּרִית
And it shall be a sign of the covenant (17:11)

In the Polish town of Chmielnik there lived an unscrupulous scoundrel whose career as an informer brought countless calamities upon his fellow Jews. Things came to such a pass that the local chassidim decided that when they would next go to visit Reb Yaakov Yitzchak, the clairvoyant Chozeh of Lublin, they would hand him a note asking that he save them by praying for the death of the traitor.

When he read the note, with the informer's name and the name of his mother, according to custom, the Chozeh expressed amazement: "What do you want of this man? His countenance shines forth like the face of a *kohen* offering sacrifices on the altar in the Temple!"

The chassidim were even more amazed, and explained the rebbe the pressing reasons for their drastic request. Again he read the note, and again — to their surprise — he spoke the same words. Some days later, before setting out for home, they decided that when taking their leave from the rebbe, they would try once more. This time, no sooner had the Chozeh read the name on the note, than he uttered a curse, and added that the law prescribes that one does not save the life of an informer. The chassidim could not understand.

When they arrived home, however, they discovered that on the very day on which they had first handed their note to the Chozeh, the informer had brought his son into the covenant of the circumcision — and this the Sages of the Talmud compare to one who offers a sacrifice on the altar in the Temple.

סדר וירא
Sidra Vayeira

Patient Hospitality

To extend hospitality is loftier than to greet the Divine Presence *(Talmud, Tractate Shabbos).*

And Avraham planted a tamarisk (אֵשֶׁל) *in Beer Sheva (Gen.* 21:33): This word hints at Avraham's hospitality, being an acrostic of the initial letters of the Hebrew words for eating, drinking, and accompanying *(Traditional).*

אַל־נָא תַעֲבֹר מֵעַל עַבְדֶּךָ
Please do not bypass your servant (18:3)

Reb Eliezer, the father of the Baal Shem Tov, was so hospitable that he used to send people out to bring in wayfarers who were passing by his village. When they had eaten, he would give them gifts, and provisions for their further travels. The Heavenly Court took due note of his exemplary conduct, and it was decided to put him to the test.

Satan spoke up first: "I am willing to go and test him."

But Eliyahu the Prophet said: "No, perhaps it would be better if I were to go."

His suggestion was accepted, and the prophet appeared at the door of Reb Eliezer on *Shabbos* afternoon in the guise of a destitute vagabond, with a staff in his hand and a knapsack on his back, as if in flagrant breach of the sanctity of the Sabbath. Then, when the door was opened, he said *Gut Shabbos,* and entered.

Reb Eliezer remained calm in the face of his guest's insolence in desecrating the Sabbath before his very eyes, and let no harsh word pass his lips that might put him to shame. On the contrary, he hastened to serve him the

Third Meal of *Shabbos*, and in the evening, when the Sabbath had passed, prepared for him the *Melaveh Malkah*, the meal which ushers out the Sabbath Queen. The next morning he gave him a liberal donation for his further upkeep, still without breathing a word about his guest's shameful conduct of the previous day.

At this moment, the prophet revealed himself, and said: "Know that I am the Prophet Eliyahu, come to test you. And because you withstood your test, and did not shame the one who came to your door, you have been found worthy of begetting a son who will illumine the eyes of all Israel."

And in due course the blessing was fulfilled, and to this patient host was born the Baal Shem Tov.

◆§ *Hospitality Incognito*

Reb Yaakov Yitzchak, the Chozeh (or Seer) of Lublin, was distressed that he was not given the opportunity of fulfilling the mitzvah of hospitality the way it should be fulfilled — that is, personally.

One night, in the midst of a bitter winter, in a town three miles from Lublin, a woman was in such straits during travail that her family hired someone to make haste to Lublin, there to ask the rebbe to intercede in heaven on her behalf. By the time he reached the town everyone was asleep, and all the windows were shuttered — except for one lighted window, in the house of the Chozeh. Never having laid eyes on the Chozeh or his house, the man knocked on the window, and the owner of the house brought him in, and made him a fire. When he had warmed up a little, the man told his host that he was hungry. The Chozeh brought him food and drink and then asked him: "From where do you come, and where are you headed?"

"I have come to your city," said the traveler, "in order to ask your rebbe to pray for an unfortunate woman who is having a difficult labor; but now in the middle of the night I won't be able to search all over town to find out where he lives. Besides, I'm exhausted from this difficult walk I have had, so now I would really like to sleep a bit."

"Who is this woman?" asked the rebbe, as if nonchalantly. "What is her name? And her mother's name?"

The man showed him the *kvitl*, the note which he had been given to present to the Chozeh and which, according to custom, bore both the woman's name and the name of her mother.

"I'd suggest you go to bed now," said the Chozeh, "and in the morning go along to see the rebbe."

With that, he showed him to the bed which was prepared for him, and the man slept through until close to midday. When he awoke, he recalled he had come on a mission of life and death. Wanting to make good his shameful delay, he made haste to set out to find the Chozeh. But his host stopped him: "What is your hurry? Go along and first say your morning prayers, then have some breakfast. Meanwhile, if you would like to give me the *kvitl* and the alms for the poor, the *pidyon*, that no doubt accompanies it, I'll send along one of my family to see the rebbe."

The man agreed. After a little while, his host conveyed to him "the rebbe's answer": *Mazel Tov*, the woman had given birth to a son during the night, and he could go home in peace. Much relieved, the messenger ate his breakfast, and arrived home to find that things were exactly as the rebbe had told his host.

And the Chozeh for his part said that Providence had so arranged circumstances in order to enable him to carry out the mitzvah of hospitality.

◆§ *Hospitality and the Divine Presence*

A troubled householder once complained to Reb Menachem Mendel of Rimanov that though he would dearly love to perform this choice *mitzvah* he was unable to do so, because his wife looked so unkindly on guests that bringing people into the house disrupted their domestic harmony.

"You will note," replied the rebbe, "that our Sages teach us that to extend hospitality is *loftier* than to greet the Divine Presence. Now would it not have sufficed for them to say that it is *as lofty as* the other ideal? But the Sages teach us elsewhere that 'when a man and a wife live together in harmony, the Divine Presence dwells in their midst.' It follows that if the Sages had merely *equated* hospitality with the greeting of the Divine Presence, no man would fulfill that mitzvah for fear that his wife might look unkindly upon his guests, and then, with the disruption of domestic harmony, the Divine Presence would leave their home — and this loss would cancel out his gain.

"For this reason the Sages teach us that to extend hospitality is *loftier* than to greet the Divine Presence, and it should therefore be practiced even at the risk of losing the company of the Divine Presence."

◆§ *The Inhospitable Leaseholder*

In a certain village there was a Jew who made a quiet livelihood from the profits of his *arenda*, the lease for his tavern or merchandising which he held by arrangement with the local squire. Late one night a party of chassidim on their way to visit Reb Chaim of Kosov knocked on his door, wanting to spend the night in his house. But since the leaseholder pretended not to hear them, they had no option but to continue on their way, despite the bitter cold and the drenching rain. They reached Kosov at daybreak, and when they went in to greet the rebbe, he asked them about their journey, and they mentioned the incident involving the leaseholder.

The rebbe said: "There will come a time when he will need *you*."

Not long thereafter, the lessee came to Reb Chaim in great distress: a few days earlier the local squire had summoned him, and had ordered him to leave the village within three months, ignoring all his pleas. What should he do?

"There is something that has always been puzzling me," began Reb Chaim. "Supposing a leaseholder lives in some village somewhere, where he has no *mikveh* at hand for his ritual immersion before prayers, and no quorum for communal prayer in which he can say *Amen* and all the other responses which are possible only with a *minyan*, and where he cannot hear the Reading of the Torah in synagogue: how can such a man fulfill his religious obligations? — What makes such a life permissible is the dictum of our Sages, that to extend hospitality is loftier than to greet the Divine Presence': the mitzvah of hospitality, which is commonest in faraway villages, compensates for all the rest.

"So long as you used to fulfill this mitzvah properly," concluded the rebbe, "the very merit of the mitzvah protected you, and no man could harm you. But now, as I hear, you don't even take in people who come by your way; so what justification is there for you to remain in the village? Surely it would be preferable for you to live in a big city of sages and scholars, where you could join in the prayer services with a *minyan* morning and evening, and immerse yourself in the *mikveh* every day before prayers, like all good and pious chassidim do..."

"Rebbe," sobbed the leaseholder, "from what will I make a living?"

"Very well," answered Reb Chaim. "Undertake that from this day on your house will be open wide. The Almighty will restore you to your accustomed position, and no harm will come your way."

The lessee went home a new man, and the Almighty softened the heart of the squire, so that the Jew was able to maintain his *arenda* for many quiet years.

☙ *Too Precious to Give Away*

When Reb Levi Yitzchak of Berditchev was a young man, before he was appointed rabbi of the city, he lived with his wife in the home of his father-in-law, in accordance with the custom of the times. His father-in-law was a wealthy and respectable citizen, and Reb Levi Yitzchak always made a point of personally waiting on the many guests who stayed in the house, bringing in bundles of straw for bedding and arranging the bed linen.

Seeing this, his father-in-law once asked him: "Why do you have to go to all that trouble yourself? Couldn't you pay some gentile to drag about the bundles of straw?"

"Now tell me," replied Reb Levi Yitzchak. "Is it right

to give a *goy* the privilege of doing the mitzvah, and on top of that to *pay* him for it?"

◆§ *The Uncompromising Host*

A Jew traveling about on business from town to town arrived in the middle of a winter's night in Gostynin, and made his way to the only house where lights were still shining. The householder — Reb Yechiel Meir of Gostynin, whom he did not know — gave him a warm welcome, and when he heard that his guest was hungry, served him strong drink and refreshments. But since the traveler was still hungry, the tzaddik searched about the house for food of some kind, and found a quantity of uncooked porridge and a saucepan full of fat. Unschooled in the finer points of cooking, he emptied one into the other, and put the result into the oven, which was still heaped with red-hot coals. The famished traveler ate with gusto, and was sated. The tzaddik then settled him in for the night in his own bed, where he slept soundly, galoshes and all (for he was weary from his travels), while his host, having nowhere to sleep, stayed awake through the night.

When his family awoke early, Reb Yechiel Meir did not allow them to enter the room lest they disturb their guest, and he too walked about on tiptoe. The time came for morning prayers, and he went to synagogue as usual. The guest, waking up soon after, also went to *shul*; and there, in the course of conversation after prayers, people told him who the illustrious personage was who had gone to so much trouble for him.

He was much abashed, and hastened to offer his apologies to the tzaddik, explaining that he did not know whose room he was in or whose house he was visiting.

The tzaddik's reply was disconcerting: "I refuse to accept any apology from you."

The traveler tried even harder to explain that he was the innocent victim of ignorance, and so on and so forth, until the tzaddik finally said: "If you promise to carry out an instruction which I will give you, then I will accept your apology."

The unfortunate fellow solemnly gave his promise,

after which the tzaddik spoke: "This is my condition — that every time you ever pass by Gostynin, you will be my guest. For when do I ever get a chance to fulfill this mitzvah as I was able to this time? — and they all spoil it for me!"

◆§ A Lecture in Practical Ethics

One winter's evening, when Reb Simchah Bunem of Pshischah was a child of five, a group of learned guests came to visit his father, who was the rabbi of Viedislav. While they were partaking of the meal which he had prepared for them, the rabbi called in his son, and said: "Run along, my boy, and prepare us some novel interpretation of the laws of hospitality."

When the child returned after a little while, his father asked: "Well, have you thought up something original?"

The boy replied that he had, and the guests, who had heard that he was a prodigy, eagerly anticipated hearing some halachic novellae. And indeed, as soon as the meal was over, his father said to them: "Let us come along together and see what he has to show us."

Sure enough, as they entered another room, his original interpretation of the laws of hospitality caught them pleasantly by surprise: for each of them the boy had made up a bed for the night, with pillows and quilts all neatly in place.

◆§ A Welcome for the Wretched

Reb Zusya of Hanipoli and Reb Elimelech of Lyzhansk were the sons of a village innkeeper who was unusually hospitable. One day a band of beggars lighted on the doorstep of his inn. The master of the house and his wife received them warmly, served them food and drink, and prepared them a place to sleep. Seeing that their guests wanted to bathe, they then went down to the bathhouse and heated water for them.

Among them was a pauper whose entire body was covered in repulsive sores, and none of the other vagrants was willing to help him wash himself. The innkeeper's wife felt sorry for the poor wretch, and helped him wash, whereupon he turned to her and said: "In return for your kindness, let me bestow upon you my blessing — that you bear sons like me."

Dismay overcame her: sons like that leper? ... But within seconds this man and all his companions and their wagon vanished before her very eyes. It then dawned on her and her husband that God had put them through a test, in order to allow them to earn the divine gift of saintly sons.

❦ ❦ ❦

When Reb Shneur Zalman of Liadi once recounted this story, one of his listeners asked him: "Who was that leper?"

But the rebbe gave not a word in reply.

☙ *Relying on Remedies*

וַתִּצְחַק שָׂרָה *And Sarah laughed (18:12)*

The daughter of Reb Shmuel of Kamenka was childless. Once, when her father was not at home, Reb Raphael of Bershad came to their town, so she decided to call on the visiting tzaddik in order to receive his blessing that she bear children.

Reb Raphael told her: "A spiritual remedy for children is — joy."

When she later repeated these words to her father, he said: "The visiting tzaddik derived his answer from the *Chumash*, from the *Nevi'im*, and from the *Ksuvim*. From the Pentateuch — as it is written: 'And Sarah laughed,' and thereafter she bore Yitzchak; from the Prophets — as it is written: 'Rejoice, you barren one'; and from the Writings — as it is written: 'The mother of children is joyful' ".

The daughter asked: "Since Sarah's laughter was intended as a spiritual remedy, as a *segulah*, why did God find fault with her conduct?"

Replied the father: "A *segulah* should be used only when a tzaddik gives a promise; but when the promise comes from the Almighty Himself, there is need for neither remedies nor talismans. This, then, was Sarah's transgression."

◆§ A Statute with a Precedent

הַכְּצַעֲקָתָהּ
Like her outcry (18:21)

Like her outcry: The outcry of a maiden whom the people of Sodom had tortured to death because she had given alms to a pauper *(Rashi).*

When Reb Levi Yitzchak accepted the appointment of *rav* of Berditchev, he stipulated that the local lay leaders were not to burden him with attendance at communal meetings, unless some new custom was to be ordained.

In due course they called a meeting which was to introduce a new regulation: that paupers would be forbidden henceforth to knock on the doors of householders; instead, they would be given a monthly grant from the community chest. In anticipation of the new statute, they invited Reb Levi Yitzchak and, at the meeting, proceeded to explain their proposition.

Reb Levi Yitzchak protested: "My brothers! Did we not agree that I was not to be bothered with discussions over old regulations?"

"Begging your pardon, rabbi, this is a new piece of legislation!'

Reb Levi Yitzchak was not convinced: "There is nothing novel in your proposal. In fact it has an ancient history, dating all the way back to Sodom and Amora. They too had a statute forbidding people to give alms to the needy..."

The proposal was removed from the agenda there and then.

◆§ For Everything there is a Season

וְאֶת־הָאֲנָשִׁים ... הִכּוּ בַּסַּנְוֵרִים
And they smote the men ... with blindness (19:11)

Reb Simchah Bunem of Pshischah maintained a haberdashery shop in his younger days, where all the imported merchandise was duly wrapped and stamped to indicate that the excise dues had been paid. It so happened that at one time a number of bundles found their way into his shop without having received their customs clearance — and just then a squad of customs officers appeared on his doorstep and began their search for contraband goods. The shopkeeper and his wife were filled with trepidation. The goods would be found within moments, and then in addition to the financial ruin involved, they would no doubt be thrown into prison.

The distraught woman appealed to her husband: '-'Listen, you've got a good head. Quick! Let's figure out what we should do. We're in terrible danger!''

''You're right,'' he said. ''Look, I'll go into the next room, and consider what should be done.''

His wife meanwhile waited, confident that he would return any minute with a practical suggestion — but in vain. Reb Simchah Bunem did not appear. The officers continued with their thoroughgoing search, but — as if stricken blind — they saw no trace of the contraband goods, and left emptyhanded.

The tzaddik's wife was curious: what was her husband doing there all that time? She opened the door, and found him sitting in front of an open volume of the Talmud, and saying to himself: ''Thank God! At long last the commentary of the Tosafos is perfectly clear.''

''Is this what you came here for?'' she asked.

''For weeks now,'' he explained, ''I have been baffled by this commentary. So when these villains arrived with their wicked designs, I realized that I had just been presented with an ideal opportunity to get to the bottom of this problematic passage, for in *Psalms* it is written clearly: 'The wicked have waited for me to destroy me — but I will meditate upon Your testimonies?' And that's exactly how it worked out. Thank God, at long last I've fathomed the depths of that commentary!''

◆§ *A Providential Pilgrimage*

וְיִתְפַּלֵּל בַּעַדְךָ וֶחְיֵה

And he shall pray for you, and you shall live (20:7)

In St. Petersburg there lived a wealthy merchant who was a chassid of Reb Menachem Mendel of Lubavitch, known as the Tzemach Tzedek. He was accustomed to travel to the big regional fair in Nizhni-Novogorod every year, but on his way he would always first make a detour to Lubavitch, to see his rebbe, and then to a neighboring townlet called Dobromishl to visit a certain pious sage who many years earlier had been his Torah teacher. After leaving a certain sum for the upkeep of the aging scholar, he would proceed to the annual fair.

It happened that one year he was forced by the pressure of business to defer his departure from home until after the fair had already begun in Nizhni-Novogorod. Nevertheless, he did not cancel the first of his two annual stations and, as always, visited the rebbe in Lubavitch. It did occur to him, though, to save time by dispensing for once with his visit to his childhood *melamed* in Dobromishl, so he asked for the rebbe's opinion on this subject when he came to take his leave.

The Tzemach Tzedek counseled as follows: "Since this is a custom of long standing, it is not advisable to diverge from it."

The chassid had his horses harnessed forthwith, and of course headed for Dobromishl. The *melamed* was overjoyed that he had at last arrived, and immediately heated a samovar in his honor. His guest pleaded with him that he not trouble himself on his account, for he was in a great hurry, and after saying his afternoon prayers would be on his way. However, as he was reciting the *Minchah* prayer, the sky became overcast, and the village was drenched with such a downpour that the *melamed* suggested that he stay the night, because the local roads would be impassable. At first he insisted that he would have to leave as scheduled, but since he developed a persistent headache, he was forced at length to submit to the redoubled arguments of his host, and to stay the night.

He awoke feeling very ill indeed, and it was clear that he had a dangerously high fever. But Dobromishl was only a modest little hamlet, and did not boast a doctor of its own, so a doctor was urgently summoned from the nearby town of Orsha. As soon as it became clear that the guest was stricken with typhus, his host telegraphed St. Petersburg, in order that some member of his family should come to help him through his illness, and notified the rebbe in Lubavitch, so that he should pray for his recovery. After eight difficult weeks he was strong enough to set out for Lubavitch.

The fact is that he went there out of a sense of grievance toward the rebbe, who had advised him to visit his *melamed* this year as always; no doubt he had caught cold on his way to Dobromishl, and that was what had brought on the typhus. Indeed, as soon as he entered the rebbe's study he broke into tears: "Why, rebbe, did you send me to Dobromishl?"

The Tzemach Tzedek answered by quoting a Talmudic dictum which,in its usual meaning, runs as follows: "A man's legs may be depended upon to take him to that place where he is summoned" — i.e., where Providence has ordained that his life is to end. In this case, however, the rebbe gave the quotation a topical flavor by punning on the Aramaic word דְּמִתְבְּעֵי which can connote either *to summon* or *to pray*. What he told the disgruntled chassid was therefore the following: " 'A man's legs may be depended upon to take him to that place where there is someone who is able to pray for him.' You owe your life to the prayers of your *melamed* in Dobromishl!"

◆§ *The Blessing that Went Astray*

כִּי־עָצֹר עָצַר ה׳
For God had utterly closed (20:18)

Chernobyl is surrounded by mighty forests, in which merchants used to buy the felling rights for a number of years at a time, and then float their lumber downstream in rafts to the cities in the south. A Vilna timber merchant once bought a forest near Chernobyl, set up an office in a nearby village, and manned it generously with clerks who were all from Vilna, and all — predictably — *misnagdim.* Their favorite pastime was making fun of a certain villager who was a devoted chassid of Reb Aharon of Chernobyl (the oldest son of Reb Mordechai of Chernobyl), especially when he told stories of his rebbe's wondrous exploits.

Seeing that the cashier of the timber company was childless, this villager tried repeatedly to persuade him to accompany him on his next visit to his rebbe, in order to receive the rebbe's blessing that he be granted children. The cashier laughed off the suggestion as nonsense, but the villager was so persistent that in the end even the cashier's *misnagdish* friends joined in the campaign — if only "to see what would become of his dreams."

Arriving in Chernobyl, the villager introduced his companion to the rebbe as a childless *misnaged* who had come to seek his blessing. The cashier, according to custom, gave Reb Aharon a *pidyon* of eighteen rubles for charity, and the rebbe gave him his blessing that he would father a child within a year.

This meeting took place in the winter, which was when the timber used to be felled and transported across the snow to the coast; in the summer, when the logs would be floated down the rivers, the offices in the forest were closed. The following winter, then, when the office staff reassembled in readiness for another season's felling, the villager asked the cashier whether the rebbe's blessing had been fulfilled. The answer was an uncouth mouthful of abuse of the rebbe, who had taken eighteen rubles for nothing: his wife was still as barren as ever. The villager tried to convince him to visit the rebbe once more, but the cashier would hear nothing of it. Once again, ironically, it was his own *misnagdish* friends who persuaded him to go: it would be interesting to see what explanation this chassidic rebbe could offer.

Off they went again to Chernobyl, and the villager spoke first: "Forgive me, rebbe, for asking — but I told you that this man was a *misnaged*, and childless, and had come to seek your blessing; why did you mislead him?"

Replied Reb Aharon: "Surely it is not my fault if someone takes my blessing and gives it to some gentile woman ... "

The cashier recalled at once that the blessing had indeed been fulfilled ... He fell at the feet of the rebbe, confessed, and asked how he should repent — and, in time, became a devoted chassid of Reb Aharon of Chernobyl.

◆§ *To Do Your Will*

קַח־נָא אֶת־בִּנְךָ
Take now your son (22:2)

Renowned scholars from far and wide used to converge on Mezritch, there to sit at the feet of the great Maggid, Reb Dov Ber. Only a select few were admitted to the inner circle of close disciples; many were told that this way of divine service was not suited to them, and many were told that they were not yet ripe for it. Very many nevertheless chose to remain in Mezritch: if they were not able to be disciples of the Maggid, they could at least still be of service to the Maggid and to his disciples. They thus became known (in Russian Yiddish) as *hrubnikess,* which means fireplace-kindlers.

Reb Shneur Zalman of Liadi, in order to show that these *hrubnikess* were men of stature, once reported a conversation which he had overheard in the days when he was studying under the Maggid. He had gone to bed, though had not yet fallen asleep, when three of these men stole into his room in order to light his fire. While they were so occupied, one of them said to his friends: "What's so remarkable about the Patriarch Avraham being prepared to slaughter his son Yitzchak, that everyone makes so much fuss about? Who would not have done that, if the Almighty Himself had told him to? Look how many people there have been over the ages who have sacrificed their lives in sanctification of the divine Name, even though God never spoke to them!"

"So what's your explanation?" asked his companion.

"This is the way I see it," he said. "It is no great achievement for other Jews to act this way, because they have inherited the power to do so from the Patriarchs. For Avraham, who was the son of Terach, to stand up to such a test was a major accomplishment."

This explanation did not satisfy his friends. After all one of them argued, it was the Almighty Himself Who had given the command: who in such circumstances would not have obeyed, whoever he might be? And if there was anything remarkable about Avraham, it lay in the fact that even though he was the son of Terach, he recognized his Maker at the age of three. Once he had come to this recognition, though, surely there was nothing particularly praiseworthy in the fact that he obeyed God when addressed directly by Him.

The second man therefore proposed an alternative explanation: "The wonder lies in Avraham's eagerness to act. He rose early in the morning, instead of dallying a day or two, or at least a few hours, in which to enjoy his son's company — even though God did not specify that he should leave forthwith."

The third man found this approach inadequate: had he received a command from the Mouth of God, he would not even have waited for daybreak, but would have made haste in the dead of night to fulfill it. He felt that the uniqueness of Avraham's obedience had to be explained otherwise, and said: "The Torah itself indicates what was remarkable here. We read: 'And you did not withhold your son ... *from Me.*' These last two words appear to be redundant, until we realize that the Torah is telling us therewith that after the episode of the binding on the altar, Avraham's joy stemmed not from the fact that his son had been spared, but from the fact that he had been able to fulfill another Divine command by not sacrificing him. That is, his joy came *from Me* — from the fulfillment of God's Will."

Having quoted this conversation of the three *hrubnikesss,* Reb Shneur Zalman averred that each of them had in fact attained the spiritual level of which he had spoken.

◆§ *Of Angels and Men*

וַיִּקְרָא אֵלָיו מַלְאַךְ ה׳
And an angel of Hashem called to him (22:11)

In the 1770's, when the *misnagdim* issued bans and excommunications in the course of their campaign against the chassidim, one such document was sent to the renowned sage, Rabbi Raphael of Hamburg, with the request that he append his signature. The covering letter noted that the enclosed ban had already been signed by "the rabbi who resembles an angel of the Lord of Hosts" — a reference to Rabbi Eliyahu, the Gaon of Vilna.

Rabbi Raphael declined to sign, replying as follows: "When the Almighty commanded Avraham to sacrifice his son, He did not convey the instruction through an angel, but gave the order Himself; when He later commanded him not to slaughter him, this He conveyed through an angel. This comes to teach us that when it is a matter of saving a person, it suffices that we should heed even an instruction that comes to us through the intermediacy of an angel; but when it comes to slaughtering someone, we should believe no angel — the order must come from the Almighty Himself."

☙ Selflessness

גֵיחֲזִי
Gechazi (Haftarah)

Reb Yitzchak Meir of Ger once recounted that in the days of Reb Elimelech of Lyzhansk there lived a hidden tzaddik, who was rabbi of a small town. The local *shammes* noticed that every day two venerable sages used to visit the *rav,* and after their departure a certain individual would call on him, asking whether the two had visited, and whither they had gone. Seeing this unusual sight repeating itself day after day, the beadle was overcome with curiosity, and finally mustered the courage to ask the *rav* for an explanation. The *rav* assumed in his innocence that just as these two guests came to him, they were likewise in the habit of calling on other folk as well, so he answered in surprise: "How is it you don't know? The two elders are the Prophets Eliyahu and Elisha, and the man who always comes asking after them is Gechazi, Elisha's servant. This is his punishment — that he must always chase after them, but not catch up with them nor see them; for though he desires to learn from them how to rectify himself through repentance, he has not yet been found worthy of this."

The *shammes* was seized with trembling in the face of such unassuming saintliness; such news he could not possibly keep to himself. In no time the whole town was bustling with excitement over his sensational discovery — until word of it reached the *rav,* and at the same time the *shammes* stopped seeing the wondrous sight.

He asked the rav: "What has changed? Why did the two elders not visit you today?"

And the rav answered: "As soon as I heard of the excitement in town, and discovered that these tzaddikim visit me alone, I told them, 'Since you come only to me and not to others, I would rather you didn't visit me any more.' "

סדר חיי שרה

Sidra Chayei Sarah

◆§ The Unconventional Litigant

וַיָּבֹא אַבְרָהָם לִסְפֹּד

And Avraham came to mourn (23:2)

One day, when Reb Levi Yitzchak was rabbi of Berditchev, there died a wealthy householder who was known as a skinflint. The burial society asked for a considerable sum for the cemetery plot, but his heirs refused to pay, though at length they agreed to abide by whatever Reb Levi Yitzchak would rule.

The tzaddik was most distressed to hear of this man's passing, and ruled that not a single kopek was to be demanded of the heirs; the burial society was to take only whatever they would freely offer. He further asked to be notified of the time of the funeral, so that he would be able to attend.

Surprised as they were to hear these words, the townsfolk faithfully carried out the instructions of their *rav*, and as soon as word got around that he was personally going to honor the deceased by following him to his resting place, the whole town turned out to honor him likewise.

Returning from the funeral, some of the townsfolk asked the tzaddik what reason had he to show such honor to a citizen who was so undistinguished, and a miser to boot.

"This man," said the tzaddik, "was a party to three lawsuits which were heard before me, and he won all three. He is therefore deserving of our honor. Let me tell you about the first lawsuit.

"There was once an agent who used to accept payment from the shopkeepers of his town on account for wine which he was to bring them from a big city nearby. It once happened that after he had bought his wine and was about to pay, he discovered that the huge sum of money which had been in his pocket had disappeared. He cried out loud in horror, and fainted. Since no one succeeded in bringing him to, people called doctors, but they only said that so long as his money was not restored to him, nothing would help, because every time he regained consciousness and realized afresh what had happened to him, he fell again into a swoon. Now the gentleman whose funeral we attended today happened to be passing at that moment. Seeing all the panic and commotion around the poor fellow, he drew near and announced loudly that he had found the money. The wine agent came to, received the whole sum from the hands of the stranger, thanked him warmly, and went his way.

"Now in fact the money had been found by someone else altogether, and the passing stranger had found nothing. He had simply decided to save the unfortunate fellow's life by saying what he said, and paying out of his own pocket. The man who had in fact found the money was one of those who were standing around watching the spectacle, except that he had succumbed to the counsel of his Evil Inclination, and did not return what he had found. However, from the moment that he had observed the noble deed of the passing stranger, who had not only given away such a vast sum from his own pocket, but had announced as well that he had found the money, his conscience pricked him sharply. As time went on, he came to regret his earlier action so earnestly, that he was able to find no rest until he was on his way to Berditchev, to seek out the stranger and to return him his due. He finally found our townsman, the same man whom we honored today, explained that he was the man who had found the money, and therefore knew that our townsman had given the wine merchant that sum out of his own pocket. He had now come to return it.

"Our townsman refused. 'Your arguments are no affair of mine,' he insisted. 'The mitzvah of saving a life was brought my way by a kind Providence, and I'm not giving it away.' At length they decided to go to court with their dispute, and each of them set forth his arguments before me. One claimed: 'I am the finder, so I have to pay.' The other argued: 'You should have paid at the time to the man who fainted. *I* can't be forced to accept anything from you.' And the deceased won the case: the court ruled that he could not be obliged to accept the money against his will.

"The second lawsuit involved a poor man here in Berditchev, who wanted to leave home and try his luck in distant pastures — but his wife would not hear of such a plan. One day he hit upon a stratagem. He told his wife that a certain magnate had employed him to attend to some of his businesss interests, which would require him to travel about in various cities. He had stipulated that every Thursday the cashier of the local office would pay her an agreed sum as his salary. The wife agreed, and the poor man took to the road. When Thursday came, the unsuspecting woman duly called on the cashier to collect the first of her weekly payments. He of course did not know what she was talking about, and in fact had never heard of her husband. She tried to convince him in her most powerful voice that her husband was no common liar. The cashier remained unconvinced, and pleaded with her to free him from her wild imaginings. Their shouts reached the inner chamber, where the proprietor had his office. He came out and asked what the hubbub was all about, and when he was told the story, said: 'The woman is right. I myself engaged her husband, and arranged with him that his wife would be paid an agreed sum every week.' And he instructed his cashier to pay out that sum punctually, every Thursday.

"In the meantime, the Almighty prospered the poor man's efforts, until at length — now a rich man — he came home. When the excitement of his homecoming had subsided, his wife told him that she had never suffered want during his long absence, because the wealthy merchant had always made his weekly payments on time. Her husband was amazed, but quickly guessed what must have transpired. He calculated the sum that the merchant had evidently paid out as his so-called salary, and set out immediately to repay it — to the very man whose funeral we attended today. He flatly refused, and here too he told the husband: 'Your arguments are no affair of mine. I don't know you from Adam, and whatever I gave was not given to you. I gave it to your wife as a gift, and am not obliged to receive anything from you.' Again the dispute was brought to me for settlement, and again the deceased won his case.

"The third lawsuit revolved around a Berditchever householder who had fallen on hard times. A certain lucrative business proposition once presented itself, but it would require a considerable capital outlay. Since he was down to his last kopek, he decided to approach our deceased townsman for an interest-free loan for the amount.

"The deceased told him: 'But you are not exactly a man of means. If I lend you money, on whose guarantee am I to lay my trust?'

"The borrower replied: 'On the guarantee of Him in Whom all lay their trust.'

"Hearing this, the deceased said: 'On His guarantee I am willing to rely without any hesitation' — and lent him the entire sum.

"The transaction was exceedingly profitable, and in due course the borrower came to return the loan. The deceased once again refused, saying: 'I have already received the amount in full.'

" 'When did you receive the amount?' shouted the borrower. 'I have not yet repaid you a single kopek!'

" 'True,' said the lender. 'But did I not agree, on your own suggestion, to lend you the money against the guarantee of Him in Whom all lay their trust? And already, I assure you, my Guarantor has repaid me the whole amount, with interest!'

"Again a lawsuit — and again the deceased won the case.

"Now do you not agree," concluded Reb Levi Yitzchak, "that following three lawsuits like these, our townsman is worthy of being honored by us after his passing?"

◆§ *Where You Lodge, I Will Lodge*

בְּמִבְחַר קְבָרֵינוּ *In the choicest of our sepulchres (23:6)*

Before his death, Reb Shmelke of Nikolsburg told the local burial society that when his time came he would like to be buried next to one of his predecessors in office a century earlier, Reb Menachem Mendel, author of *Tzemach Tzedek* (not to be confused with Reb

Menachem Mendel of Lubavitch, author of a later work of the same name).

While the grave was being dug next to the tomb of the earlier incumbent, an old man came and told the members of the burial society that his late father had been told by Reb Menachem Mendel before his death that he wanted no man to be buried next to his grave. The burial society was in a dilemma, for both the old man and his late father were known to be honest and reliable men. The whole town soon became involved in their quandary: should they obey the earlier sage, or the later? At length it was decided that they would search through the *pinkas* of the burial society. If in that register they would find the will of Reb Menachem Mendel, they would follow its instructions; if not, then they would ignore the words of the old man, for he was but a sole witness, and conveyed secondhand testimony — whereas they had all personally heard the will of Reb Shmelke from his very mouth.

They carefully searched through the records of the burial society and, sure enough, they found the explicit instruction of Reb Menachem Mendel that no man should be buried next to his grave until a certain day in a certain year — the exact date of their search. The whole community saw this as the Word of God, and proceeded to fulfill the will of both sages.

◆§ *A Place to Rest*

When Reb Yaakov Yitzchak, the Chozeh of Lublin, passed away, his disciple — Reb Naftali of Ropshitz — bundled together a pick and shovel over his shoulder like a common laborer, and set off to dig a grave for his rebbe.

The local rabbi, who had been an antagonist of the Chozeh, meanwhile instructed the heads of the burial society not to allocate a prestigious plot in the cemetery for his gravesite. Reb Naftali therefore made a deal with the gravediggers — and paid them well for their cooperation — that when they arrived at the cemetery with their employers to look about for a suitable plot, they would start digging only on a certain sign from him.

Then, late at night, in the pouring rain, he accompanied the heads of the burial society through the mud and clay of the cemetery as they searched for a place to bury the Chozeh. At every turn he would say: "What difference does it make where you bury him? Any place will do."

When they arrived at a certain point, Reb Naftali sensed that they had lighted upon a place of heightened sanctity. He turned to the head of the burial society: "As far as I am concerned, even here would be satisfactory."

He gave the agreed sign to the gravediggers, and they immediately started their work. The head of the burial society soon observed that this was the most favored spot in the whole cemetery, next to the grave of the famed scholar Rabbi Shachna of Lublin, and protested at the top of his voice that this plot he could not give at any price. By the time they had finished arguing, the gravediggers had finished their work. The question was brought to the rabbi, who ruled that since the grave had been dug nothing could now be done — and the Chozeh was buried there.

The townspeople found this to be significant, because whenever there had been a time of woe, the Chozeh had always directed people to pray at the burial place of Rabbi Shachna, and had explained that all the tzaddikim who had ever lived in Lublin had spent their last years in *Eretz Yisrael*, where after their passing they had been laid to rest. Rabbi Shachna alone had remained in the city, and was buried there, in order to protect its townsfolk through his intercession in the World of Truth.

☙ *Made in Heaven (i)*

מֵה׳ יָצָא הַדָּבָר
This thing comes from Hashem (24:50)

The Torah teaches us that God destines a woman for a man, as it is written: 'And Lavan and Besuel answered and said, "This thing comes from the Lord"' *(Talmud, Tractate Moed Katan).*

A young unmarried chassid once took his leave of Reb Dov Ber, the Maggid of Mezritch, after having spent the festivals in the court of the rebbe, and complained that because of his poverty no one ever proposed him a match.

"Go in peace," said the rebbe, "and accept the first marriage proposition that is put before you."

On his way home the young man spent the night in a village inn, where he found a group of empty-headed loafers who wasted all their time on eating and drinking and foolish jesting. Being cold from his journey he found a seat in a corner next to the stove, but these mischief-makers spotted him, and asked him where he was from and what was his business. He gave them the name of his home town, and told them that he had just visited the Maggid of Mezritch.

They asked him again: "What did you want from the rebbe, and what did he answer you?"

He replied: "I asked the rebbe to pray that the Almighty arrange that I meet my marriage partner, and he told me that I should agree to the first *shidduch* that was proposed to me."

At this, one of the party jumped up and exclaimed: "Excellent! I've got a first-class match for you. My sister is a young divorcee, and she has a hundred silver rubles — and she's here right now. If you're agreeable, we can shake hands on it."

Now in fact this good-for-nothing was in no way related to the young woman: she was the daughter of the innkeeper, who was not at home at the time.

The young man answered: "Very well; I'm agreeable."

The band of scoffers thereupon ordered vodka with which to treat the young man on the occasion of his unconventional engagement, and sniggered all the while behind his back. Then one of them came up with a further suggestion: "Why don't we arrange the marriage ceremony straight away?"

One of his friends objected: "But none of our crowd knows how to draw up the marriage contract and run the ceremony."

The young man promptly volunteered: he could do both. This gave them even more cause for mirth. They first found a *tallis*, spread it out like a canopy, and held it up over the heads of the couple as a *chuppah;* the young man wrote out the *kesubah* document; and then he duly sanctified the young lady as his lawful wedded wife according to the rites of Moses and Israel.

His companions now enjoyed their practical joke so much that they tugged at his hat from all sides, made fun of him without any restraint, and even struck him. Seeing how things were faring for him, the young man managed to get away, and spent the night in the cottage of one of the gentile villagers. In the morning he ventured out as far as the door of the inn, but was afraid to enter lest he be beaten up again. Just at that moment he heard one of the servants saying: "Here comes the boss at the front door!"

The young man approached the innkeeper, and said, "How do you do, father-in-law!"

The poor fellow was somewhat taken aback: "Who is this?" he asked.

His daughter, who had come out to greet him, explained: "This young man has been providing us with a little entertainment, and last night we had a whole marriage ceremony, just for fun!"

Her father did not like the sound of what he heard, and plied her with questions in order to find out exactly what had happened. When he heard her answers, he shouted furiously at the young man: "Dolt! What's the idea of marrying this young lady? Didn't you realize that they were making fun of you?"

And, to make his point clearer, he slapped the hapless young man across the face. Soon enough, however, he had second throughts on the subject, and told himself: "Since I'm already tied up with this dope, I'll have to speak to him gently in order to be able to get out of this mess. If I get him angry, he'll take no notice of me."

He therefore changed his tone, asked the young man to give his daughter a bill of divorce, and promised him twenty silver rubles for his trouble.

"I'll tell you the whole truth," said the young man. "My rebbe told me to agree to the first *shidduch* that was proposed to me, and that's what I did. This crowd may have treated the whole matter as a joke — but I took it seriously. If you don't agree to the match, let us both go to visit the rebbe, and we'll let him decide."

The reluctant father-in-law had no option but to travel with the young man to Mezritch, and when they arrived he put his plaint to the Maggid: "One day while I was away from home, along came this pauper, believed a band of jokers who told him that my daughter was their sister, and married her. I am now willing to offer him one hundred silver rubles, so long as he gives my daughter a divorce."

"If you would like to retire to your lodgings," said the Maggid, "I would like to have a few words with the young man on this subject."

When the innkeeper returned a few hours later, the Maggid told him: "I discussed the divorce with the young man, and he is agreeable — provided that you give him a thousand silver rubles. I will then propose a fine and respectable match for your daughter, and the new bridegroom will give you a thousand silver rubles, so that you will lose nothing at all."

"I am willing to do whatever you say, Rabbi," said the innkeeper.

"Very well," continued the Maggid. "I would only like to add that this young man comes from a family of refined lineage, and is himself a man of outstanding character. His only fault was his poverty. Now, thank God, he has a thousand silver rubles. You could do no better than to carry on with this match: I assure you, it is a match made in heaven — and may you both journey home with joyful hearts."

The innkeeper took the rebbe's counsel to heart, went home happily with his son-in-law, and the young couple lived their life together in harmony.

☙ *Made in Heaven (ii)*

The Rav of Skole once spent *Shabbos* at the home of Reb Baruch of Mezhibuzh, the grandson of the Baal Shem Tov. While they were at table, Reb Baruch asked his guest to retell a story of the Baal Shem Tov, for he was one of the last surviving disciples of the founder of Chassidism. And this is the story he recounted.

It once happened that while he was deep in conversation with the Baal Shem Tov, the latter was visited by two men from a certain town — the local rabbi, and one of the householders. The rabbi had come to ask the Baal Shem Tov whether he should marry his son to the daughter of this man, who begged for the match so persistently.

"And why not?" asked the Baal Shem Tov.

The rabbi explained that this householder was a very ordinary fellow; in fact he had once been a water carrier, and in the course of time had become wealthy. When he had first conceived the idea that this was a desirable marriage, he had hired a certain schoolmaster for fifty rubles to visit the rabbi every day in order to propose the match; he was to be deterred by no refusal, but was to carry on with his proposal day by day. On his first visit the rabbi had refused outright to hear of such an idea, but the schoolmaster never forgot what he was being paid for, and persisted faithfully in his daily mission. On one occasion he conveyed a new message of persuasion to the rabbi: his principal was prepared to give a dowry of two thousand silver rubles to the young couple, and a gift of one thousand silver rubles to the rabbi. At this stage the rabbi saw that he stood very little chance of shaking off these unwelcome advances, and decided that the time had come to travel to the Baal Shem Tov, together with his importunate congregant.

The Baal Shem Tov asked: "Is this householder a God-fearing man?"

"He is," answered the rabbi.

"If so," said the Baal Shem Tov, "then this is a fine match."

So saying, he took out a kerchief, and each of the parties in turn took hold of it, according to custom, in confirmation of the transaction. He then wished them both *Mazel Tov*, and gave them his blessings for the journey home.

As soon as they had left, the Baal Shem Tov turned to the Rav of Skole, who had witnessed the whole episode, and said: "The world of scoffing can make a fine matchmaker."

So baffled was the Rav of Skole by these cryptic words, and so curious was he to learn what the tzaddik was hinting at, that he decided then and there to seek out the visiting rabbi in his lodgings in order to get to the bottom of the matter. When the rabbi heard from his mouth what the Baal Shem Tov had said, he was overawed, and exclaimed: "Now I know where I was!"

He then proceeded to tell the Rav of Skole that he had once dreamt that he was doing the rounds of the villages around his town, according to a widespread custom in those days, collecting the gifts of farm produce which the Jewish peasants offered him. On his way through one township, he came to the door at the back of a synagogue which was filled with learned folk of all ages, who were deep in scholarly discussion. As he listened in more closely, it seemed to him that the particular Talmudic argument which they all apparently found so problematic presented no real difficulty at all. He offered his explanation of the subject to the young men who stood nearby, and they passed it on to the older scholars, until it reached the most venerable sages who occupied the places of honor in the front row. They approached him and scrutinized his face, and one of them said: "Is this the ignoramus who mixes in scholarly argument?"

The rabbi left the synagogue forthwith, and said to his wagon-driver: "It is clear that we have no more business in *this* place. Let us move on."

When they reached the next township the rabbi entered the synagogue, and in his imagination lived through exactly the same episode a second time. They drove on to a third township, where the whole of the same spectacle presented itself once again — except that this time the rabbi was approached by the oldest of the sages, who looked him in the eye, and then said to his colleagues: "And this ignoramus still refuses to marry off his son to the daughter of that householder!"

The rabbi awoke from his dream with a troubled spirit, and decided at once to journey to the Baal Shem Tov. And at this moment, when the Rav of Skole had brought him the pregnant words of the rebbe, it became clear to him that heaven had ordained that he be cast into the scoffing and imaginings of the world of dreams in order that he should consent to this *shidduch*, since it was a match made in heaven.

◌§ *Made in Heaven (iii)*

In the town of Mezhibuzh there lived a chassid of the Baal Shem Tov called Reb Wolff Kitzis, who was so poor that he was unable to marry off his daughter. Once the Baal Shem Tov asked him: "Why don't you arrange a match for your daughter?"

"Rebbe," said Reb Wolff, "I haven't even enough bread to eat. With what will I marry her off?"

The Baal Shem Tov told him sternly that he should find a match for her immediately, and when Reb Wolff again showed hesitation, he said: "I would like you to know that now is the right time for her match to be made. Here, send a special emissary at my expense to the city of Jassy, and let him tell the matchmakers there that you are willing to give a dowry of two thousand silver rubles, provided that the bridegroom is a scholar and of good family."

Reb Wolff carried out this instruction immediately, and his agent set out and described him to the matchmakers of Jassy as a pious chassid, who had promised to give a dowry of two thousand silver rubles. The matchmakers promptly put forward their various propositions, none of which the agent found satisfactory — except for a certain scholarly young man, who was the son of a wealthy and respected citizen of good family. He therefore drew up and signed a betrothal agreement, and in this *tenaim* contract it was specified that the father of the bride would give a dowry of two thousand silver rubles.

Reb Wolff was pleased to hear of his agent's work — but now, with a heavy heart, he made his way to the Baal Shem Tov concerning the dowry that he had promised. Whence would come his salvation?

As soon as he arrived the tzaddik wished him *Mazel Tov,* and reassured him that he need not worry in the slightest, for help would soon come from above, and he would be able to honor his promise.

A few weeks after the agreement had been signed, Reb Wolff received a letter which expressed the surprise of the bridegroom's father that the customary gift to the bridegroom had not been sent. When he showed the letter to the Baal Shem Tov, the tzaddik again put him at his ease, promising him that salvation was near at hand. When a similar letter arrived a few weeks later, Reb Wolff was so certain of his rebbe's reassurances that he answered not a word. Seeing that his earlier letters were producing no tangible results, the father of the bridegroom wrote once more, but in quite a different tone: if he would receive no reply this time, he would return the betrothal agreement. With a melancholy spirit Reb Wolff took this letter too to his rebbe.

"Write to him," said the Baal Shem Tov, "and tell him that the bridegroom should arrive at the time set for the wedding, and, God willing, everything will be ready, including the dowry, and gifts for his son."

Reb Wolff wrote accordingly, and because he was reputed to be a pious and upright man, the bridegroom's father took him at his word and began his preparations for the wedding. As the date approached Reb Wolff visited the Baal Shem Tov once more, and was told to write again, inviting his correspondent to arrive three days before the wedding, because he wanted to spend those few days rejoicing together with him. Reb Wolff wrote in this vein, and several days before the wedding received a letter from the bridegroom's father, saying that he and his family were on their way to Mezhibuzh for the happy occasion. But it was with a sad face that Reb Wolff set out to show this letter to his rebbe. On his way there he met a stranger who asked him where the Baal Shem Tov lived.

"I'm on my way there myself," replied Reb Wolff. "Here, come along with me."

When they arrived the Baal Shem Tov greeted the guest, and said: "I would like to tell you a true story. There was once a prosperous timber merchant who used to float logs in large rafts to Prussia. For one such consignment he received some forty thousand silver rubles. Now this merchant owned a splendid carriage with fine horses, which was driven by a gentile wagon-driver. On his way home with his wallet of money, the merchant fell asleep as they entered a forest. The driver directed the carriage off the road into the wild thickets, woke the merchant, and wielding an ax over his head, demanded all his money. Trembling in terror, the merchant begged to be allowed to keep half of his earnings. His driver was unequivocal: if he did not receive the entire sum, he would kill his supplicant on the spot. Seeing the way things stood, the merchant asked only that his life be spared, and handed over the forty thousand rubles.

"As soon as the wallet was in his grasp, the wagon-driver said: 'How can I let you stay alive? You'd go and tell the whole story. I'll have to kill you.'

"The merchant implored and entreated from the bottom of his heart, but the driver was adamant: he would have to kill him at once. The poor man then begged to be given a few minute's grace, so that he could at least confess before his death. This request the driver agreed to. He tied him to a tree, and left him to recite his last confession. The merchant poured out his soul before his Maker, and made a solemn vow: 'Master of the Universe! If I am saved from the hands of this murderer, I will give a tenth of all of this money to charity.'

"At that very moment, his bitter weeping reached the ears of the watchman of the forest. Musket in hand, he flew to the spot where the wretched man stood bound, and in a trice freed him of his bonds. The merchant had barely managed to tell him what had happened, when the wagon-driver reappeared. The watchman seized him by surprise, bound him up, and led him off to the nearest post of the gendarmes. After interrogation the wagon driver was compelled to return the money, and was thrown into prison. As for the merchant, he made his way joyfully home, singing praises all the way to Him Who had saved his life from the very hands of a murderer.

"When he arrived home, however, the weeks passed by, and he utterly forgot the vow which he had made in his hour of woe. Not the merest kopek did he give to charity out of all that tithe he had promised. Now that merchant had one only son and one only daughter. The little girl was suddenly stricken by cholera, and died, but this did not set him thinking, and he did not remember to pay his debt to the poor. A little later his young son fell suddenly ill. The greatest physicians despaired of saving him. Then he was told that in the town of Mezhibuzh there lived a Baal Shem who was able to work wonders, so he set out to visit him, in order to ask him to pray and intercede for the life of his only son..."

❦ ❦ ❦

Needless to say, the guest who had accompanied Reb Wolff to the home of the Baal Shem Tov was none other than the selfsame timber merchant who had come to ask the tzaddik to pray for his son. When the Baal Shem Tov came to the end of his story the merchant was deeply shaken, for he now recalled his unfulfilled promise.

"Rebbe," he said, "at this very moment I want to give away that money — to whomever you name."

"In that case," said the Baal Shem Tov, "weigh out four thousand silver rubles, and give them to Reb Wolff Kitzis."

The merchant complied, and with a happy heart Reb Wolff hastened to arrange the wedding. He bought gifts for the bridegroom, gave the dowry as promised, and detained his benefactor so that he could take part in the festivities, which were conducted in grand style. As for the merchant, before leaving Mezhibuzh he received a letter from home with the welcome tidings that his son had recovered, and was well on his way to robust health.

◆§ *The Light of Liberated Sparks*

וַיֵּצֵא יִצְחָק לָשׂוּחַ בַּשָּׂדֶה

And Yitzchak went out to speak in the field (24:63)

Speech connotes prayer (*Talmud, Tractate Berachos).*

In his younger days Reb Moshe of Sambor used to earn his livelihood as a peddler, making his way on foot from village to village, and selling his wares to the gentiles who lived in various parts of the Ukrainian countryside. One day he asked his brother and teacher, Reb Zvi of Zhidachov: "Why is it that when I come in from the fields and the villages and say the afternoon prayers, my every limb is suffused with a powerful and wondrous light? From where could I have attained it? Perhaps I am mistaken, and it really derives from the unholy forces in the universe; and in that case, God forbid, my service of my Maker is all based on a mistake."

"Why are you so surprised?" replied Reb Zvi. "For when you walk about among the fields and the gentile villages thinking holy thoughts, all the sparks of sanctity that lie dormant — in the realm of the inanimate, and in the plant, animal and human kingdoms — having no other place to cling to, cleave to you; and you separate them from their material husks and elevate them. These liberated sparks of sanctity then draw down upon you a taste of divine light, the like of which you have never savored before."

סדר תולדת
Sidra Toldos

◆§ *The Mask of Piety*

וַיְהִי עֵשָׂו יֹדֵעַ צַיִד
And Esav was a cunning hunter (25:27)

A cunning hunter: He used to ensnare and deceive his father with his mouth, by asking him questions of spurious hyper-piety; for example: "Pray, father, how does one tithe salt and hay?" *(Rashi).*

A woman once came to Reb Avraham Yehoshua Heschel of Apta, who is known as the *Ohev Yisrael,* with the following query: Since before Purim she had washed her laundry with starch made of potato flour, was she permitted during Pesach — considering the laws prohibiting the use of leaven *(chametz)* — to use the room in which the clothes had hung to dry?

"I will tell you a story," said the tzaddik. "Please listen carefully. In a certain village there once lived a Jewish leaseholder, who conducted a tavern and sold vodka to the gentile peasants, according to the custom. The local priest, who was a violent anti-Semite, made it known that he would not receive for confession any parishioner of his who patronized the Jew's tavern — and his threat was effective. Seeing his livelihood taken from his very mouth, the leaseholder asked his neighbors what he had done to stop them from frequenting his hostelry. When he was told the reason, he said: '*I* will receive you all for confession, and will take all your sins upon myself.'

"Being by nature practical men, the peasants were quick to appreciate the advantages of this suggestion, and immediately exploited both its spiritual and its spirituous benefits to the full. Business flourished for the little Jew as never before. One day a peasant approached his tavern; he stood on the threshhold, but did not enter.

" 'You, there,' called out the innkeeper, 'why don't you come right in?'

" 'I want to confess,' murmured the peasant, 'for I have sinned.'

"The following conversation then took place:

Innkeeper: Tell me, my good man, what is your sin?

Peasant: I stole a rope.

Innkeeper: Return the rope to its rightful owner.

Peasant: I don't know who it belongs to.

Innkeeper: Give charity for whatever it was worth, and your sin will be atoned.

Peasant: But I have another sin.

Innkeeper: What is your other sin?

Peasant: I wanted to steal the rope, but two oxen were tied to it.

Innkeeper: And what did you do with the oxen?

Peasant: I slaughtered them.

Innkeeper: Then give the value of the oxen as well to charity.

Peasant: But when I wanted to steal the oxen, I saw that they were harnessed to a wagon, so I stole the wagon as well.

Innkeeper: And what did you do with the wagon?

Peasant: I broke it up for firewood.

Innkeeper: In that case, give away the value of the wagon, too, and your transgression will be expiated.

Peasant: But when I wanted to steal the wagon, I saw that there was a child lying in it.

Innkeeper: And what did you do with the child?

Peasant: I killed him."

And as the tzaddik of Apta repeated these words of the peasant, he grasped his head in his hands, and cried out aloud: "Killed! Killed!"

At the sound of this outcry the woman fell to the ground, broke down in bitter weeping, and sobbed out her story to the tzaddik: she had given birth to an illegitimate child, and had killed him, and now wanted to know how she could repent.

The tzaddik first reproved her for coming to him so sanctimoniously with tritely pious queries involving starched laundry, instead of asking about what really needed to be asked. Then, seeing that she was now truly contrite, he taught her a way of repentance, and she became a sincere penitent.

◆§ *Keeping a Kosher Mouth*

צַיִד בְּפִיו
Venison in his mouth (25:28)

Reb Yaakov Yitzchak of Pshischah, who is known as the Yid HaKadosh, once instructed Reb Simchah Bunem — in later days his successor as rebbe — to make a certain journey, without telling him its purpose. Reb Simchah Bunem took several chassidim with him, and set out. When the time came for them to eat in one of the cottages in the hamlet of their destination, their host told them that he had no dairy food for them, but could offer them a meat meal. The chassidim thereupon began to question him, paying the most scrupulous attention to all the detailed laws relating to kosher meat — who was the ritual slaughterer; whether the lungs of the animal were found on examination to be utterly free of any blemishes; exactly how the meat was salted and rinsed in order to drain it of all traces of blood, and so on.

Their investigations were interrupted by the voice of an individual who had been sitting quietly next to the fireplace, and who was dressed like an itinerant beggar.

"My dear chassidim!" he cried. "Concerning what you put *into* your mouths you conduct the most meticulous cross-examination; but on what you bring *out* of your mouths — your words — you make no halachic queries at all!"

When Reb Simchah Bunem heard these words, he felt certain that he had now lighted upon the reason for which his rebbe had sent him out on his journey — simply to learn this lesson — and promptly returned to Pshischah.

⌘ *The Wellsprings of Salvation*

מָצָאנוּ מָיִם *We have found water* (26:32)

A villager came to Reb Yitzchak Aizik of Zhidachov for advice. His local squire was prepared to give him the lease on his inn, which would provide him with a reasonable livelihood since it was situated on the highway used by the dealers in oxen. It had one drawback: since there was no water there for their livestock, they had to make a long detour through a different road. If only water were to be found near this inn, he would be a prosperous man. What should he do?

"Take the lease," advised the rebbe, "and start digging a well there. When you have dug a few feet, come to me for a *Shabbos*."

The villager did just this, and when he came to Zhidachov for *Shabbos* the rebbe told him to dig a little deeper, to write the following words on a slip of paper — 'And the servants of Yitzchak dug a well, and they came and told him, "We have found water" ' — and to throw it into the well.

The innkeeper followed these instructions, and the well immediately filled with spring water, to the delight of the passing gentile merchants. He meanwhile grew rich, because he had taken the lease on this unwanted inn at a very cheap rate.

Now another Jew went along to the squire, and pointed out that he was not earning as much as could be expected on his lease, considering how much the present tenant was obviously prospering; in fact, he could better the offer. In a word, the first leaseholder found himself soon displaced, and without any means of income. He set out at once for Zhidachov, and told his rebbe his tale of woe.

"This time," said Reb Yitzchak Aizik, "these are the words which you should write on the note which you are to throw into the well: 'And all the wells which his father's servants had dug, the Philistines stopped them up, and filled them with earth.' "

The villager did as he was told; the well dried up; and the disappointed gentiles went to the squire with a complaint: he had leased this concern to a new tenant — but for some reason the water supply had expired with the first lease. The squire called back the first tenant, but when he proposed that they renew their former arrangement, the tenant stipulated that he would first have to consult his rebbe. Reb Yitzchak Aizik advised him to agree only if the terms were the same as heretofore, and told him that the slip of paper which he should throw into the well this time should bear these words: 'And they dug another well, and did not quarrel over it; and he called that place Rechovot, saying, "For now God has made room for us, and we shall be fruitful in the land." '

The squire agreed to the earlier terms; the Jew threw in his note; and the spring came back to life. And that same inn on the highway provided a respectable livelihood for the man, and his children, and his children's children — without any unfair interference — for many long years thereafter.

◆§ *Eyes that See Not*

וַיְהִי כִּי־זָקֵן יִצְחָק וַתִּכְהֶיןָ עֵינָיו

When Yitzchak was old and his eyes grew dim (27:1)

His eyes grew dim: From the smoke of the fires in which the wives of Esau used to burn incense to idols *(Rashi).*

Reb Pinchas of Korets was once approached for advice and a blessing by a German Jew who hailed from Danzig: his daughter had suddenly become blind, and no doctor could fathom the cause.

"The reason," said Reb Pinchas, "is that her father is also blind, and this is a hereditary disease."

"But my eyes are perfectly healthy," protested the German Jew. "Why, I don't even wear spectacles!"

"The man who is really blind," explained the tzaddik, "is the sinner. Thus we find that Yeshayahu (Isaiah) admonishes 'the blind people that have eyes,' and the Mishnah says: 'Samson followed his eyes, therefore the Philistines gouged out his eyes.' "

The tzaddik went on to warn his visitor that all the members of his family who looked at him were also in danger of losing their vision; in the words of the Talmud: 'If a person gazes upon the face of a wicked man, his eyes grow dim.'

At these words the unfortunate man wept, and undertook at once to conduct his life according to the Torah. The tzaddik then told him that if he kept his promise, his daughter would regain her sight, and instructed him to give her honey from the Land of Israel for, in the words of the Talmud: 'Honey and other sweet things add light to one's eyesight.' This the Sages derived from the verse spoken by Yonasan: 'See, I pray you, how my eyes have brightened, because I tasted a little of this honey.'

The visitor returned to Danzig and made his entire household kosher in all respects. And when his daughter was cured, she traveled to Korets to see the tzaddik, and while there donated money for the writing of two Scrolls of the Torah.

☙ The Grapes of Wrath

לֹא יָדַעְתִּי יוֹם מוֹתִי
I know not the day of my death (27:2)

After falling from a window on the eve of the festival of Simchas Torah, Reb Yaakov Yitzchak, the Chozeh of Lublin, was grievously ill. Some of his antagonists were certain that he would never recover, and went so far as to express their glee by drinking wine.

When word of this reached the rebbe, he said: "On the day I leave This World they won't even be able to drink water."

At first no one understood his meaning, until the day he died — on the Fast of Tishah B'Av.

☙ A Time to Die

Reb Yitzchak of Neshchiz was married to the granddaughter of Reb Levi Yitzchak of Berditchev, who supported the young couple — according to the custom prevalent among fathers-in-law at the time — for four years. When the arrangement was first made the tzaddik was asked whether he could possibly undertake a longer period, but he claimed that under no circumstances was he able to make a promise for anything beyond four years. People were of course somewhat surprised by this refusal, for quite some time. Then, on the couple's fourth wedding anniversary, the tzaddik passed away.

◈§ Gathered unto his Fathers

In the summer of 1827 Reb Dov Ber of Lubavitch traveled to Haditch in order to pray at the graveside of his father, Reb Shneur Zalman of Liadi. Throughout the journey he was stern and uncommunicative, neither delivering chassidic discourses, nor desiring the company of his chassidim. When he wished to commit his teachings to writing, various obstacles presented themselves, and on several occasions his pen fell from his hand. This he took to be a sign that the divine attribute of lovingkindness was at that moment being overshadowed by the attribute of strict justice. He said that he was apprehensive at the approach of the year 5588 (1827-1828), which he sensed was destined to bring harsh tidings.

At one point he made the following observation: "My late father, of blessed memory, was fifty-four years old when he was arrested and taken to St. Petersburg for the second time. He was then presented from heaven with a choice — to undergo suffering, or death. He chose the first alternative; it seems that he left me the second."

Reb Dov Ber arrived in Haditch in time for the Days of Awe that heralded the year 5588, and many chassidim who gathered there from all the surrounding provinces heard from his mouth the wealth of chassidic discourses that he delivered in the House of Study that he had built near his father's resting place. On one occasion he went out to pray at the graveside, and stayed there longer than usual. When he returned his face was radiant with joy, and he said: "I have persuaded my father to promise that I will be relieved of my position as rebbe."

His chassidim took this to mean that he now intended to travel to the Holy Land — a pilgrimage which he had long yearned to make — and asked him: "Why should our rebbe speak thus? How could you leave us like a flock without a shepherd?"

"But you have my son-in-law, Reb Menachem

 Mendel," he reassured them, referring to the Tzemach Tzedek, who was to succeed him. "In him you will have a faithful shepherd."

He then journeyed on by way of the town of Niezhin, where he fell seriously ill. He died on the ninth of Kislev in the year 5588 (1827), when he was fifty-four years old, to the day.

☙ The Golden Fleece

וְאֵת עֹרֹת גְּדָיֵי הָעִזִּים
And the skins of the young goats (27:16)

In the days of the Baal Shem Tov there was a God-fearing Torah scholar who earned his livelihood as an *arendar* — that is, by leasing a tavern, or tax-collecting rights, or whatever — on one of the estates of Count *(Graf)* Pototzki. Fortune did not smile kindly on the little man. After he had not managed to pay his lease for two consecutive years, the Count warned him that if he did not liquidate his debt in the third year, he and his family would soon taste the barbaric vengeance that was common among the local squires in those days. The entire household of the poor man was plunged into misery: there seemed to be no hope for them.

Then one day his good wife said: "Listen to me. I've heard it said that not too far from our province there lives a holy rabbi who has brought salvation to many people in distress. He is known as the Baal Shem Tov, and many of the great men of our time travel long distances to be near him. My advice to you is that you travel there likewise, and tell him all about the fix we're in. Do exactly whatever he tells you to do, and the Almighty will surely help us through him."

Now this leaseholder was no chassid, and did not regard the Baal Shem Tov as being a particularly holy man who could bring people salvation, so he refused to follow his wife's advice. She, however, was not one to be refused lightly; so eventually, under the relentless pressure of sheer torrents of words and tears, he capitulated. He set out with a heavy heart to the Baal Shem Tov, and described his intolerable situation.

The Baal Shem Tov advised him: "Go for a stroll in the street on Sunday morning, and when you are approached by a gentile villager who offers to sell you something, buy it at once. Take absolutely no notice of what the object is, or whether it is worth the price the villager asks for it. Then come to visit me again, and I will tell you what to do with your purchase."

This sounded like a bitter jest to the poor fellow, who had never been one to believe in wonders and miracles, and besides, he had certainly not intended to carry out the instructions of the tzaddik. But when he reported on his visit at home, his wife forced him to go out to the street for a stroll on Sunday morning, in compliance with the instructions of the Baal Shem Tov. Having no alternative he did so, and immediately saw the words of the tzaddik coming to life: a villager approached him, and offered to sell him the fleece of a sheep. He asked for its price: it was one gold ruble. In his pocket he had exactly one gold ruble; and so astonished was he at what was happening that without a second thought, he handed over the last gold ruble he owned, and took the fleece. At that moment the villager disappeared.

Now it is true that the leaseholder was overawed at the time by this amazing encounter, and had bought the fleece without hesitation, but, being (as we have said) anything but a staunch believer in the powers of the Baal Shem Tov, he regretted the transaction immediately, and went home vexed and disgruntled. His wife, of course, was the prime butt of his ire.

"Look what I've earned by listening to your advice," he complained. "What on earth can I possibly do with a fleece? And I went and spent my last gold ruble on it! What will come of us now?"

His wife, though, had a way with words. "How long can one persist in not recognizing a man of God? Haven't you seen with your own eyes that no word of his is said in vain? What you should really do now is to go back and visit the holy man again, just as he told you to. God will surely come to our help."

After words like these, her husband felt he had to go. The Baal Shem Tov heard his account of what had transpired with the villager, and said: "My son, you did the right thing by buying that fleece. Now take note of what I tell you. In a few days' time a great number of nobles will be coming to visit your Count for his birthday celebration, and each one of them will bring a gift. You go along on the same day, and present him with that fleece as a birthday gift."

Was the Baal Shem Tov making fun of him in his misery, with such a preposterous suggestion? The wretched listener did not have the effrontery to express his thoughts aloud in the presence of the tzaddik, so he left and hastened home. There, with bitter tears, he let his wife know how he felt.

"Just picture it. On the big day, when all the worthies from all around will knock at the Count's door, bringing him costly tributes of gems and the like, I'll come along and insult him with *my* gift — the fleece of a sheep! Why, his henchmen will take up their muskets and shoot me on the spot; and whoever hears the story will justify them, too, because they'll say that the Jew came along in order to poke fun at the Count. And who can tell what pogroms might break out on all our fellow Jews because of me!"

His wife knew her own mind. "Does it not say in the holy books that you should not try to figure out things that are beyond the reach of our humble mortal understanding? All you should do is carry out whatever the Baal Shem Tov tells you to do, and to be strong in your faith in God, who works through the tzaddik."

And so it was, that when the Count's birthday came around, the leaseholder's wife bustled him out of the house, with the fleece over his shoulder. His heart was heavy with foreboding, and his steps trembled with terror, as he made his way towards the Count's castle, which was full of nobles and other fine folk who had come to celebrate their host's birthday. He paused at the massive door: should he go inside, or turn home? He had just about decided to go home when the door creaked open, and one of the Count's bodyguards sized him up, and roared: "Jewboy! What are *you* doing here? Don't tell me you've brought the Count a birthday present!"

In his bewilderment the unwilling guest held out the fleece. The bodyguard grabbed it from his hand, hurried inside with it, and displayed it to the Count and all the assembled notables.

"This," he announced, "is the gift of the miserable

Jew who holds a lease on milord's estate!"

The Count duly took offense, and in his pique had the Jew locked up until he would have time to solve this riddle: how could it have occurred to him to insult his master so blatantly?

He continued to think aloud to the nobles surrounding him: "Is it not unthinkable that this man should have the nerve to insult me in the middle of my festivities? Didn't he know that he would be killed at once? Surely no man hands himself over to be killed!"

With that he rose from his table, the fleece still in his hands, and secluded himself in his room, where he would better be able to examine this strange gift. Perhaps there was something special about it, after all. And, as he gazed upon its locks, he saw that they had arranged themselves into the shapes of letters; the letters added up to words; and the words were — his own name, his father's name, and his family name, and the year, the month, and the day on which he was born! He was so overawed by this wondrous sight, and so filled with joy, that he strode back to the reception hall, and went from table to table with his prize possession, asking each of his guests whether they thought this was the work of some gifted craftsman, or whether it was an uncanny product of nature. They were all of one opinion: all the craftsmen in the world could not contrive such a wonder. It must be a miracle from heaven.

The Count immediately had the trembling leaseholder released and brought before him. From all sides he was asked the same question: where did he get hold of such a fleece?

The poor fellow was now convinced that death was indeed near at hand. In his desperation he hurled himself to the floor at the feet of the nobles, and with bitter tears told them his whole sad story. They all listened attentively, and when he fell silent the Count spoke up: "Do not fear, my good man, for the holy man sent you here for a blessing."

He then showed him the wonder of the fleece that he himself had brought. The visiting nobles meanwhile decided that the Count should make himself a fur hat out of this fleece, and should celebrate every birthday thereafter by wearing it, and by presenting the Jew with gifts worthy of a Count's generosity. To start the tradition, all those present gave him gifts of gold and silver, and the Count announced that he would forego the entire debt of the preceding years.

The leaseholder was escorted from the castle with due pomp, and from that day till the end of his years he prospered in all his ways.

☙ *The Flavor of the Garden of Eden*

וַיָּבֵא לוֹ יַיִן וַיֵּשְׁתְּ
And he brought him wine and he drank (27:25)

From where did Jacob have wine? — The Archangel Michael brought him wine from the Garden of Eden *(Midrash Tanchuma Yashan)*.

Reb David of Lelov once came to the house of his friend who lived in a nearby village, intending to travel with him to visit the Chozeh of Lublin, as was their wont. This friend, who was as poor as he was pious, hastened to ask his wife to prepare a meal in honor of the worthy guest who had just arrived. The good woman did not know which way to turn. The house was bare, except for a little flour, nor was there any firewood. How could she prepare a meal?

She went out to the forest and gathered some dry twigs for firewood, then mixed her bit of flour with water, having neither oil nor spice to improve the taste, boiled it, and served this unpretentious dish to the two tzaddikim. They finished their meal, and set out for Lublin.

When Reb David eventually came home, he told his wife: "When I was at my friend's house in the village, I ate some kind of delicacy, and in it I really tasted the flavor of the Garden of Eden."

The *rebbitzin* knew how far removed her husband was from delighting in the pleasures of This World, so she set off at once to that village, to find out from the woman who lived there just how she had prepared the meal which her husband had praised so highly.

The woman told her of her circumstances, and how she had been utterly without anything which could add flavor or fragrance to the sorry dish. While she was preparing it, therefore, she had addressed the Almighty as follows: "Master of the Universe! You know full well that I would not have spared the rarest delicacies in order to provide a meal worthy of the visiting tzaddik; but what can I do when I have nothing in the house? But You, Master of the Universe, You have a Garden of Eden. So please, won't You add a touch of the flavor of the Garden of Eden into this thing I'm cooking, so that the tzaddik will enjoy what I've prepared?"

And the woman concluded: "It seems that the Almighty heard my prayer, and that's why the tzaddik tasted the flavor of the Garden of Eden."

◆§ *A Whiff of the Garden of Eden*

וַיָּרַח אֶת־רֵיחַ בְּגָדָיו וַיְבָרְכֵהוּ

And he smelled the scent of his garments, and blessed him (27:27)

And he smelt the scent of his garments, and blessed him: For Yaakov was accompanied by the fragrance of Paradise *(Rashi)*.

Reb Yaakov Yitzchak, the Chozeh of Lublin, was once the guest of Reb Baruch of Mezhibuzh, the grandson of the Baal Shem Tov. On Friday afternoon Reb Baruch set out to immerse himself in a river in honor of the approaching Sabbath, and took his guest with him in his carriage. As they traveled along the road, Reb Baruch meditated intensely on the Kabbalistic secrets of Creation and, soaring aloft into mystical worlds, he examined his companion to see whether he too sensed this elevation of the spirit.

As they arrived at a cerain point in the fields Reb Baruch asked: "What does the *Chozeh* from Poland sense now?"

The Chozeh (Seer) answered: "The air of the Land of Israel."

A little later Reb Baruch asked: "And now?"

The Chozeh replied: "The spirit of Jerusalem."

"And now?"

"The site of the Sanctuary."

When they were immersing in honor of the Sabbath, Reb Baruch asked once again, and the answer was: "The mystic pure stream that flows from the Garden of Eden."

Reb Baruch was well pleased with these answers. "A

 true Seer," he said of his guest, "never missing his target."

◆§ *A Whiff of the Garden of Eden (ii)*

Every time Reb Zelig of Shrintzk (the disciple of Reb Simchah Bunem of Pshischah) used to come to Kalisz, he stayed at the home of a certain chassid. Reb Zelig was accustomed to spending many hours over his prayers, and out of respect for him his host would always wait at the synagogue until he too was ready to go home. On one Sabbath, however, the host felt too weak to be able to wait so long, and decided to go home and recite the *Kiddush* over a goblet of wine and to partake of some light refreshments. Before leaving, he asked his son to wait in the synagogue for Reb Zelig to finish his prayers and to accompany him home, where the family would be waiting with their Sabbath meal.

Reb Zelig was old and blind, and as he and his young companion passed through a certain street on their way home, he suddenly stood still, and said: "At this very place I suddenly feel a fragrance so beautiful that I cannot go on."

The young man marveled at this remark, for he smelled nothing whatever. They stood still at this place for some time, until Reb Zelig decided that it was time to move on. When the host heard of this incident from his son, he too wondered as to its possible meaning. They tried to get to the bottom of it, and in the course of their investigations discovered that at that very spot, over a century earlier, had stood the house of Reb Avraham Abele Gombiner, the saintly author of *Magen Avraham*.

It was his piety, then, that had left the fragrance that Reb Zelig sensed.

◆§ *A Whiff of the Garden of Eden (iii)*

On his travels, Reb Chaim of Zanz once passed through a remote little village called Makali. He suddenly asked the wagon-driver to halt, climbed down, entered the inn which stood nearby, and asked if there were any old men or women on the premises. The innkeeper's mother was ninety years old, and when she was brought to see the distinguished guest, he asked her: "Do you recall any tzaddik ever having stayed in this inn?"

The old woman recounted that once Reb Levi Yitzchak of Berditchev had passed through their village on his way to Hungary, and had spent two weeks in this very inn.

Reb Chaim turned to his chassidim: "As we passed by, I felt the aroma of a tzaddik — but how could it have reached here? After what I heard this moment, though, there is no longer anything surprising about it."

סדר ויצא

Sidra Vayeitzei

◆§ *Timely Deliverance*

כִּי לֹא אֶעֱזָבְךָ *For I will not forsake you (28:15)*

Reb Menachem Mendel of Vizhnitz once told the story of a chassid who came to Reb Levi Yitzchak of Berditchev with the sorry account of his financial misfortunes. He had been extremely wealthy, but because of a number of calamitous investments had fallen deep into debt, though no one yet knew of it.

"My advice," said the tzaddik, "is that you should buy a lottery ticket, and, God willing, you will be helped thereby."

Replied the chassid: "I do not doubt for a moment, God forbid, whether your promise will be fulfilled — but who knows when? For it may take years to win with lottery tickets, and in the meantime my creditors will be after me. Besides, my daughter is not getting any younger, and I must marry her off."

Reb Levi Yitzchak thereupon promised him that the Almighty would soon make money come his way, even before he won the lottery.

The chassid, of course, immediately bought a lottery ticket. On the way home, he stayed the night at a wayside inn; so, too, did a certain powerful noble, who had been riding about in his carriage. In the dead of night the noble dreamt that in the very same inn there was a Jew who owned a lottery ticket that was destined to win; he should therefore find a way of exchanging his own worthless ticket with the one that was bound to bring riches to its bearer. The noble awoke, and behold, it was but a dream — but when he fell asleep again, exactly the same dream repeated itself. This time he got out of bed, and ordered his servant to investigate whether there was any Jewish stranger about, and if there was, to bring him at once. The Jew was found soon enough, and brought to the rich man's room.

The noble asked whether he held a lottery ticket, and then said: "I also have one of those tickets. Let us exchange tickets, and I will add a few gold rubles to whatever it cost you."

The Jew refused: "Even if you give me that number of rubles several times over, I will not exchange tickets with you."

The noble was so eager to settle his transaction that he kept on increasing his offer until it reached one thousand rubles, but the Jew would not budge. By this time the noble was fuming. He ordered his servant to seize the ticket by force — which he did, and handed the ticket to his master.

Then, thinking better of it, the noble said: "Look, I don't want to really rob you altogether. Here, take the thousand gold rubles that I offered you before, as well as my lottery ticket."

The Jew reluctantly accepted the money and the ticket from the noble, but soon resigned himself gladly to the workings of Providence, thinking: "This, too, is for the best" — and continued his journey home, where he married off his daughter in grand style. Not long after, the ticket which the noble foisted upon him against his will won a vast sum of money, and the chassid decided it was time to set out to visit his rebbe.

When he arrived, Reb Levi Yitzchak said: "I saw that your luck was running low indeed, so I had to send along the angelic Master of Dreams to persuade the noble to exchange tickets with you; I could see that his ticket was going to win, not yours. As for the thousand gold rubles that he gave you in addition, that is because you said you had to marry off your daughter soon; and that is why you were granted a little salvation first, then later a great salvation."

And when the chassid returned home, he became more prosperous than he had ever been before.

❦ ❦ ❦

When Reb Menachem Mendel of Vizhnitz finished recounting this story, he said: "This is what the Almighty meant when he said to the Patriarch Yaakov, 'For I will not forsake you until I have done that which I have spoken of to you.' Why '*until* I have done'? Would he forsake him *after* having fulfilled His promise?! For no man could remain alive even one moment without the Almighty's constant vigilance. The meaning of the verse is, rather, that He promises Yaakov that even *until* the great salvation comes He will not forsake him, and in the meantime will grant him a little salvation."

☙ *The Body Sleeps; the Soul Soars (i)*

וַיִּיקַץ יַעֲקֹב מִשְּׁנָתוֹ
And Yaakov awoke from his sleep (28:16)

And Yaakov awoke from his sleep: Do not read מִשְּׁנָתוֹ, *from his sleep,* but מִמִּשְׁנָתוֹ, from his meditation on the Torah (*Midrash*).

When Reb Meir, the great-grandfather of Reb Hillel of Paritsh, was a youth he studied together with a dear friend called David. Eventually each of the young men married in their hometown, and both were supported by their wealthy fathers-in-law, according to custom, in order to enable them to continue their studies, which they did together. After some years had passed, Reb David suddenly disappeared. Word soon arrived that he had been "kidnapped by the Sect" — that is, he had joined the outlawed brotherhood of the chassidim of the Baal Shem Tov.

His father-in-law was horrified. He set out to speak to his errant son-in-law, and tried in vain to persuade him to leave his new path. Returning home, he first attempted to convince his daughter to ask for a divorce, promising her a husband who would be better by far. The young woman would not hear of such a suggestion, for she knew what a saintly individual her husband was. Indignant, her father promptly disowned her of all his possessions, and drove her out of his house. She accepted her change of fortune with fortitude, and patiently endured a few years of penury — until one day two men arrived in a wagon to take her to Nikolayev, where her husband had just been appointed rabbi.

Meanwhile, Reb Meir's father-in-law had passed away, leaving him his business interests, and he now divided his day between Torah study and merchandising. Thus it happened that he once had to travel to a fair in a far-off city. Entering the inn where he was to stay, he saw a group of people who were exceedingly happy.

"What is the occasion for your joy?" he asked them.

"Why," they answered, "Reb David of Nikolayev is staying here!"

Assuming that this was his boyhood friend, Reb Meir asked where he was at the moment, and was told that he was in his room, finishing his morning prayers. He went upstairs eagerly, and as soon as the door opened, the two old friends embraced each other.

"Tell me the truth," said Reb Meir. "What gave you the urge to go to see the Baal Shem Tov?"

"I'm sure you recall," answered his friend, "that in the days when we used to study together we once came to the conclusion that though we studied a great deal, we did not feel that this was a devotion to the Torah *for its own sake*. A little later I heard that in the brotherhood of the Baal Shem Tov they do achieve this — so I decided to join them."

"But why did you not tell me of your plan?" asked Reb Meir.

"I was afraid you might not agree," answered Reb David, "and then I would not be able to go either."

"One more question," asked the visitor. "I know you well. Tell me, please, what was it that made you stay with the Baal Shem Tov?"

"When I first came to the Baal Shem Tov," replied

Reb David, "I did not find what I was looking for, but the chassidim there wanted me to stay near him anyway. They started by telling me that if I would stay there until Friday, the eve of *Shabbos*, and make the effort to be in his presence while he recited the Song of Songs, then I would find what I had come to seek. I made the effort, and the chassidim helped me manage to do what they had suggested — and you may be sure that I heard something sublime that was a delight to hear. Why, his words set up a clamor in all the supernal worlds! But even through this he did not capture my soul. The chassidim then said that I should wait until the day on which the rebbe observed *yahrzeit* after one of his parents. On the eve of that day, they said, he walks up and down in his room all night long, reciting the whole of the *Mishnayos* by heart. This, they assured me, would certainly captivate me. I waited until the eve of the *yahrzeit*, and hid in his room, and what I saw was of course remarkable indeed. But still this wasn't it. Then the chassidim told me that I should wait until the following night, for all that day he fasted, and at nightfall invited his elder disciples for a mystic meal. At that meal, they assured me, it was impossible that he should not draw out my soul. They forewarned me earnestly that I should see to it that I not fall asleep there, because for some reason slumber often overcame those who were at the table on that occasion. I prepared myself by day by means of sleep and other devices in order to ensure that I would not fall asleep at the table, and took my place at the gathering.

"The Baal Shem Tov sat at the head of the table, with his chassidim all around him, and began to expound upon the kabbalistic meditations which accompany the ritual immersion in the *mikveh*.

" 'Rebbe,' one of his chassidim addressed him. 'Does not the Ari, of sainted memory, explain these meditations otherwise?'

"The Baal Shem Tov leaned his head back. His face, which had been like a fiery flame, suddenly grew pale. His eyes stood out, prominent. He looked like one who had left this life. At that moment I was overcome by a deep slumber which no amount of effort could ward off.

In my sleep I saw myself in some city, which was filled with people who were all hurrying in one direction. I asked them whither they hastened so urgently, and they told me that the Baal Shem Tov was soon to deliver a discourse, and they were eager to hear it. I ran with them, until we came to an imposing edifice, inside which stood two chairs.

" 'For whom?' I asked.

"'For the Baal Shem Tov and the ARIzal,' I was told.

"I managed to stand near the chair of the Baal Shem Tov, who soon began to expound the Kabbalistic meditations of the *mikveh*. When he had completed his discourse the Ari asked him a series of questions, each of which the Baal Shem Tov answered, until it was clear that the Ari wholly accepted the exposition that had been given. At that point I awoke from my sleep, and saw that I was sitting at the table of the Baal Shem Tov with all of his disciples. The color was returning to his face, and it was becoming fiery once more. Again he began to deliver the discourse on the meditations of the *mikveh*, and again the same disciple asked him: 'Rebbe! Does not the Ari, of sainted memory, explain these meditations otherwise?'

"The Baal Shem Tov turned to me, and said: 'David! Stand up and testify to what you have seen!'

"And at that moment," Reb David concluded his story, "the Baal Shem Tov captured my soul."

When Reb Meir heard these words, he dispatched his assistant home with all his merchandise, journeyed straight from the fair with his friend to see the Baal Shem Tov, and in due course became one of his outstanding disciples.

◆§ *The Body Sleeps; the Soul Soars (ii)*

Late one Friday night the holy brotherhood of the disciples of Reb Dov Ber, the Maggid of Mezritch, convened according to their custom to reconstruct from memory the latest discourse of their teacher. One of the greatest of that brotherhood, Reb Aharon of Karlin, was alone in his room at that time, whispering something. He was interrupted by a knock on the door, and the voice of the Maggid's messenger: "Is Reb Aharon around here somewhere? The rebbe says he should stop reciting the *Song of Songs*, because with his *Song of Songs* he creates such a tumult in the spiritual worlds above that our rebbe can't sleep."

When Reb Hillel of Paritsh recounted this story, his eyes streamed with tears, and he added: "From this we can gain a tiny inkling of the stature of the Maggid. Even though Reb Aharon's recitation of the *Song of Songs* set up repercussions in the spiritual worlds above, the way the Maggid served his Maker during his *sleep* was even loftier."

◆§ *Only a House of God*

מַה־נּוֹרָא הַמָּקוֹם הַזֶּה
How dreadful is this place (28:17)

Reb Meir of Premishlan once went to pray in a certain synagogue in Galicia which was in a deplorable state of disrepair. He opened the ragged door, gazed inside upon the gaping signs of neglect that met his eyes, and, in the words of the Patriarch Yaakov at Bethel, cried aloud: 'How dreadful is this place! This is no other than the house of God!'

The chassidim who surrounded him did not grasp his intention, and assumed therefore that their rebbe doubtless had in mind some awesome mysteries which, unbeknown to them, lay hidden in these words. Seeing that they had not understood him, he explained his words himself: " 'How dreadful is this place!' — Indeed, it is literally dangerous to walk inside. 'This is no other than the house of God' — for I see it has no owners to look after it, unlike the other houses in this town, which all seem to be kept in a fine state of repair."

◆§ *Keeping Body and Soul Together*

לֶחֶם לֶאֱכֹל וּבֶגֶד לִלְבֹּשׁ
Bread to eat, and garments to wear (28:20)

At the "great wedding" at Zhlobin — the marriage of the grandchildren of Reb Levi Yitzchak of Berditchev and Reb Shneur Zalman of Liadi — the festivities were graced by the presence of both illustrious grandfathers.

In the course of the wedding breakfast, Reb Shneur Zalman drank a toast to Reb Levi Yitzchak: "*LeChaim*, *mechutan!* May the Almighty help us materially and spiritually!"

Reb Levi Yitzchak protested: "Material blessings before spiritual blessings, *mechutan*?"

Replied the Alter Rebbe: "For this we have a precedent in the words of the Patriarch Yaakov: 'If He will give me bread to eat, and garments to wear,... then the Lord will be my God' — placing the material before the spiritual."

Reb Levi Yitzchak was not satisfied: "But can we compare the material life of the Patriarch Yaakov with our own?"

Answered the Alter Rebbe, "And can we compare our spiritual life with that of the Patriarch Yaakov?"

◆§ *Homeward Bound (i)*

וְשַׁבְתִּי בְשָׁלוֹם אֶל־בֵּית אָבִי
I will return in peace to my father's house (28:21)

Once Reb Shmelke of Nikolsburg was voyaging on the high seas in the company of his close disciple, Reb Moshe Leib of Sasov. A violent storm suddenly whipped up the waves, and all those on board were almost certain that their vessel was about to capsize and founder in the terrifying turbulence. In their anguish people on all sides cried out to their Maker, desperate for deliverance.

In the midst of this tumult Reb Shmelke was amazed to perceive his disciple, all alone in a quiet corner, dancing from sheer joy.

"My dear Moshe Leib," he said. "What are you doing at a time such as this? What is the meaning of your joy right now?"

His disciple's reply was simple: "How can my heart not be glad, when soon I will return to my father's house?"

"If so," rejoined his teacher, "rejoice, my son, and my heart too will be glad."

The tempest soon after subsided, and their ship came in peace to its haven.

◆§ *Homeward Bound (ii)*

After the passing of Reb Menachem Mendel of Lubavitch, who is known as the Tzemach Tzedek, he was succeeded by several of his sons, each of whom became a rebbe in his respective town. They included Reb Shmuel in Lubavitch, Reb Yehudah Leib in Kopust, Reb Yisrael Noach in Niezhin, and Reb Chaim Shneur Zalman in Liadi. Reb Chaim Shneur Zalman was wont to serve his Maker with ecstasy, and his prayers melted the hearts of all those who overheard them. While his father was yet alive he delivered discourses on the teachings of Chassidim, and on his father's instructions sometimes answered the questions that chassidim brought to the rebbe, giving guidance on both spiritual and temporal matters.

In 1869, when he settled in Liadi, the town made famous by his great-grandfather and namesake, the author of *Tanya,* he quoted the verse, apropos of himself: 'The fourth generation shall return here.'

In fact his chassidim pointed out a series of parallel circumstances. Their rebbe, who was born in 1814, within a year of the passing of his illustrious great-grandfather, and bore his name, like him spent exactly eleven years in Liadi, and like him lived exactly sixty-six years.

One *Shabbos* in 1879 he delivered a chassidic discourse on a verse occurring in that week's Portion of the Torah: 'I will return in peace to my father's house.' At the close of that *Shabbos* he suddenly took ill and, after ailing for four weeks, passed away on the eve of *Shabbos,* the fourth of Teves. The last discourse of his lifetime had been the one that opened with the words: 'I will return in peace to my father's house.'

To Thee, with Love (i)

וְכֹל אֲשֶׁר תִּתֶּן־
לִי עַשֵּׂר
אֲעַשְּׂרֶנּוּ לָךְ
And of all that You shall give me, I will surely give a tenth to you (28:22)

The grandfather of Rabbi Mordechai HaKohen of Birzan, Reb Shalom by name, supported himself all his life by working as a goldsmith. As to his spiritual life, Reb Mordechai of Kremenets and Reb Meir of Premishlan testified that he was a hidden tzaddik. By day, while his hands were busy with his craft, his mind would be concentrating on Kabbalistic mysteries. And by night, shunning sleep, he spent the quiet hours studying Torah.

In the manner of the pious, Reb Shalom was accustomed all his days to set aside a tenth of his earnings for charity. It so happened that he once sustained a heavy financial loss while refining a certain quantity of gold. He thereupon calculated one tenth of that loss, and gave it away to charity. His rationale for this came straight from the Mishnah: "A man is obliged to bless his Maker for evil tidings just as he is obliged to bless his Maker for glad tidings." Therefore, he argued, just as he was accustomed to giving away a tithe from his profits, surely he should give away a tithe from his losses.

◈§ *To Thee, with Love (ii)*

When Reb Meir of Premishlan was a young man, before he became a rebbe, his livelihood came from one milch cow. Even then, he always lived as modestly as possible, in order to have the wherewithal to buy meat to distribute to the poor in honor of *Shabbos*. This practice he maintained into old age, supplementing his own meager savings with alms which he himself collected.

One Wednesday, seeing that he had not a single copper coin with which to buy meat for the poor, he sat down to think of what could be done — until the solution dawned upon him. He would have his cow slaughtered, and give away its meat to the poor. In the dead of night he led his cow off to the *shochet* and had it slaughtered, and managed to distribute all its meat to the poor while it was yet dark. Early in the morning his wife went out to milk the cow, and was amazed that it was nowhere to be found. When all her searches were in vain, she ran in, all alarmed, and gasped the bitter news to her husband: the cow was lost!

The tzaddik was quick to reassure her: "The cow isn't lost, God forbid. It has ascended to heaven."

◈§ Bless This House

וַיְבָרְכֵנִי ה׳ בִּגְלָלֶךָ
Hashem has blessed

Reb Shneur Zalman of Liadi and his father, Reb Baruch, both lived for some time in the town of Liozna. Whenever Reb Baruch came to visit his son, the latter would rise in his honor, in fulfillment of the Fourth *me for your sake (30:27)*

Commandment. The father could not bear this, and once expressed himself as follows: "Is it proper that a man from whose throat the Divine Presence speaks should rise in my honor?"

He decided therefore to leave Liozna, and wandered from town to town, in each place finding his way to the local synagogue. Wherever he went the congregants saw that he was no common pauper, and everywhere they would invite him respectfully to their homes to eat with them. In this way he one day reached a town in Hungary called Pulat. He entered the local synagogue, as was his wont, and a wealthy householder invited him to his home, where he ate at midday and again in the evening. This man owned a liquor distillery, and that day his business transactions succeeded exceptionally well. It crossed his mind that perhaps his house was being blessed by virtue of his pious guest. His wife therefore urged him to invite the guest to stay on for another day. Once again business flourished as never before, so the householder drew his conclusions and said to Reb Baruch: "I see, sir, that you are not journeying about in order to grow rich. Allow me therefore to ask you to stay always in my house, and all your expenses will be borne by me."

Reb Baruch accepted this offer, and for some years lived and studied in the room which his host set aside for him. When at length he lay on his deathbed, the scholars and notables of the town all gathered about him, for they regarded him highly, and asked whether he had children, and where they lived, so that they could write to them according to need.

"In Russia," replied the ailing scholar, "I have four sons, all of them rabbis. Two of them need to be notified, one of them needs only a hint, and one does not need to be told at all, for he will know by himself."

After his passing he was buried with due respect, and the burial society set up a suitable gravestone over his resting place.

When Reb Shneur Zalman of Liadi came to know of his father's passing, he dispatched a special emissary to Hungary with a large sum of money with which to compensate the householder for the expenses of his hospitality, and the burial society for the cost of the plot and the tombstone. Since neither party would even consider accepting payment, the emissary warned them: "My rebbe is a man of God, and a man of principle. You would be well advised not to cross him."

They agreed to allow the matter to be arbitrated by a rabbinical court, which ruled that the burial society — though not the host — was obliged to accept the payment offered.

At the time of his passing, the householder's wife was heavy with child, and Reb Baruch had requested that the son whom she would bear be given his name. His wish was granted, and with the passage of the generations that Baruch's grandchildren were also named Baruch, and were known by the townsfolk as "the grandchildren of our rabbi Reb Baruch."

◆§ *Learning from Primary Sources*

וַתִּגְנֹב רָחֵל אֶת־הַתְּרָפִים אֲשֶׁר לְאָבִיהָ
Rachel had stolen her father's images (31:19)

Rachel had stolen her father's images: Her intention was to wean her father from idolatry *(Rashi).*

Troubled by a strange dream which was repeated nightly with increasing intensity, a man came to seek the advice of Reb Zusya of Hanipoli. The man's father, who had passed away not long before, appeared to him each time and ordered him to baptize, God forbid. The first dream he had ignored, but the second time the demand was repeated, and the third time it was accompanied by threats.

The tzaddik said that no doubt there was a crucifix or something similar in his father's grave. If he were to open the grave and remove it, his father would be enabled to rest in peace. Sure enough, when the grave was opened, it was discovered that a few coins which bore the sign of the cross had fallen into the grave by accident during the burial. They were removed, and the deceased father never appeared in his son's dreams thereafter.

It so happened that someone repeated this episode to Rabbi Eliyahu, the Gaon of Vilna. The Gaon, who was celebrated as the arch-antagonist of chassidism, remarked that there was nothing miraculous about Reb Zusya's reply, for this matter is mentioned in the Talmud Yerushalmi; the only wonder was that a chassidic rebbe should be familiar with a source as scholarly as the Talmud Yerushalmi ...

This gibe was reported back in due course to Reb Zusya, who said: "True enough, I did not see that statement in the Talmud Yerushalmi. I saw it instead in the same Source that the Talmud Yerushalmi saw it in."

◆§ *A Lifeline from Heaven*

וְצַדִּקִים יֵלְכוּ בָם וּפֹשְׁעִים יִכָּשְׁלוּ בָם

Just men walk in them (the ways of God), but sinners stumble in them (Haftarah)

In the winter of 1903, Reb Shalom Ber of Lubavitch spent several months in Vienna for medical treatment. He was accompanied by his son, Reb Yosef Yitzchak, who was later to succeed him as rebbe. From time to time he would take along his son and visit one of the *shtiblach*, or informal prayer houses, and sit quietly in the company of the chassidim from Poland who gathered there, in order to hear from their mouths some fresh morsel of chassidic ethical lore, or the story of an exemplary life.

One evening on the Fifteenth of Shvat they went together, father and son, to one of these *shtiblach*, and found a little group of aged chassidim sitting around a table, exchanging their favorite stories about Reb Meir of Premishlan. One old man related that the *mikveh* for ritual immersion was situated high up on the slope of a steep hill on the outskirts of Premishlan, and when the road leading up to it was slippery, people had to take the long way around the hill, for to walk uphill was dangerous. Reb Meir alone always took the direct route up, irrespective of the state of the road, and was never known to stumble or slip. One snowy day, when the icy mountain paths were hazardous in the extreme, Reb Meir walked uphill to the *mikveh* as usual. Two guests were staying in the area, sons of the rich who had come somewhat under the influence of the "Enlightenment" of the Haskalah movement. These young men did not believe in supernatural achievements, and when they saw Reb Meir'l that day striding with sure steps uphill as usual, they convinced themselves and each other that the road up there was no doubt perfectly safe, and not in the least dangerous. And in order to bolster their theory by empirical proof, they waited until Reb Meir had entered the *mikveh* building, and set out confidently up the hillside road. After only a few steps they stumbled and slipped, and needed medical treatment for their injuries. One of them was the son of one of Reb Meir's close chassidim, and when he was fully healed he mustered the courage to approach the tzaddik with a question: Why was it that no man could negotiate that slippery uphill road, while the rebbe walked with such sure steps, never stumbling?

Reb Meir replied: "If a man is tied up on high, he doesn't fall down below. Meir'l is tied up on high, and that is why he can take even a slippery hill in his stride."

❦ ❦ ❦

Reb Shalom Ber of Lubavitch was under orders from his Viennese doctors to go outdoors for a certain period for a daily constitutional. One cool, fresh evening the rebbe and his son went out to stroll in one of the avenues of the city, in the middle of which there was a municipal garden. As they walked side by side, the rebbe became so deeply absorbed in thought that he unwittingly drew the attention of many passers-by. He walked on in this manner for a long time, until his son became embarrassed. For him each minute seemed to last an hour, until at length a deep sigh inadvertently passed his lips.

His father paused, being grieved to hear that any circumstance could reduce his son to becoming morose or distressed, and said: "Why do you sigh? If a man is tied up on high, he doesn't fall down below."

◆§ *Of Saints and Sinners*

Rabbi Yechezkel Landau, the erudite author of *Noda BiYehudah,* was on friendly terms with the Baal Shem Tov, but did not believe in him as a holy man and a miracle worker. Whenever the Baal Shem Tov was in his city he would stay in his house, and the famous scholar would personally serve him tea, in fulfillment of the *mitzvah* of hospitality. When the guest saw that he was thereby disrupting the studies of his host, he ceased staying with him, and thereafter took up more modest lodgings in the communal House of Study. The wife of Rabbi Yechezkel, who did believe in the Baal Shem Tov as a tzaddik, used to visit the House of Study with her sons in order to ask after his welfare, and he, in turn, would interest himself in the wellbeing of her husband.

Rabbi Yechezkel was altogether opposed to the ways of the newborn chassidic movement, though he did not combat it publicly. Prominent in one of his responsa, however, is a violent attack on the new practice of introducing certain prayers in the chassidic editions of the prayer book by the words *LeSheim Yichud,* which bear Kabbalistic connotations. This he considered presumptuous, and bitterly decried "those whose hearts raise them aloft, each of them saying: '*I* am he who sees, and for me have the gates of heaven opened, and for my sake the world exists.' ... It is to this orphaned generation that I would apply a paraphrase of the words of the prophet Hosea: 'For the ways of God are right; just men walk in them, but chassidim stumble in them.' I have much to add on this subject, but our Sages have taught us that 'Just as it is a mitzvah to say that which will be hearkened to, so is it a mitzvah not to say that which will not be hearkened to.'"

Many years later, when one of his grandchildren prepared a new edition of this work for the press, he wanted to remove this gibe, and replace the word *chassidim* with the word *sinners* — in accordance with the actual words appearing in the Book of *Hosea* — in order to make his grandfather's attack less blatant.

Ironically, it was a chassidic rebbe who advised him otherwise: "Leave the sentence alone, and change nothing. Your grandfather made *chassidim* out of *sinners;* would you want to make *sinners* out of *chassidim?!*"

סדר וישלח
Sidra Vayishlach

◆§ A Haven for Holiness (i)

עִם־לָבָן גַּרְתִּי
I sojourned with Lavan (32:5)

I sojourned with Lavan: And observed the 613 Commandments *(Rashi)*.

The Baal Shem Tov once had occasion to spend a little while in the home of a heathen who kept an icon in his house. He came out very happy, and said to his disciples: "I have good cause for joy, for in one hour I observed the entire Torah. For the law forbids one to meditate on the words of the Torah in any filthy place, and idolatry is considered the same as any other obscene or repulsive thing. The fact that I controlled my mind from considering even a *single* thought from the Torah may be accounted equal to having observed the *whole* of the Torah."

Commenting on this statement of the Baal Shem Tov, Reb David of Dinov once said: "Rashi's words (quoted above) on the 613 Commandments are problematic, since obviously the Patriarch Yaakov could not have observed those Commandments which can be fulfilled only in the Land of Israel. This story about the Baal Shem Tov, however, solves the problem. Lavan's house, too, was full of icons and idols, and when Yaakov entered it he was forced to guard his thoughts from dwelling on even a *single* idea from the Torah, since the prohibition on thinking of holy matters in inappropriate places applies to the *whole* of the Torah. Hence, since he was vigilant about any and every thought involving Torah, it could well be said of him that he observed *all* of the 613 Commandments of the Torah."

◆§ A Haven for Holiness (ii)

A chassid of Reb Yisrael of Ruzhin, whose business involved transporting timber to Danzig for sale, was once asked by his rebbe: "Where are your thoughts purer — when you are at home, or when you are visiting Danzig?"

"I am always surprised," answered the chassid, "that when business brings me to Danzig — a city without the traditional virtues of modesty, where most of the community is made up of irreligious German Jews, and where the fear of heaven is not common — it is there that my thoughts are purer than when I am at home."

"The reason is simple," explained Reb Yisrael. "Holiness finds itself there to be an unsought-after stranger. When, therefore, it finds some Jew — whoever he may be — to cling to, it holds him tight."

◆§ Humility (i)

קָטֹנְתִּי *I am unworthy (32:11)*

The Baal Shem Tov instructed a certain group of chassidim that after his passing they should appoint for themselves as rebbe only such a tzaddik who, when asked how one could rid oneself of conceit, would answer that he did not know the answer to their question. If anyone were to offer them an answer, this would indicate that he had not yet plumbed the innermost depths of his heart, and for that reason was not aware of the crumbs of conceit still lingering there. By way of explanation, the Baal Shem Tov expounded a verse in the Book of *Psalms:* 'God reigns; He is clothed with majesty.' Since majesty is, figuratively speaking, the garment of the Almighty, it is infinite. And since the impure "opposite side" of Creation mirrors everything that exists in the "holy side" of Creation, so too the pretensions and conceit that stem from impurity are also infinite.

After the Baal Shem Tov had passed on to the World of Truth, that group of chassidim went about from one tzaddik to the next, asking each one in turn how they could rid themselves of conceit. Each one offered them sage counsel, which they heard out — and then went their way, saying: "This is not the rebbe for us."

At length they came to visit Reb Pinchas of Korets, and posed their question.

"But I stand in fear of the same danger," he confessed, "and I know no way out."

And him the chassidim installed as their rebbe.

◂§ *Humility (ii)*

They were hard times for Reb Noach of Lechovitch, and he sank so deeply in debt that he was forced to visit the various towns where his chassidim lived, and they were pleased to be able to help him in his hour of need. When he arrived in Minsk, all the famous names of that scholarly city came out to honor him, for he was renowned even in non-chassidic circles for his erudition.

Reb Noach saw this welcome as being addressed to him almost on false pretenses and later commented: "The sages of Minsk came out to do me honor; but I only set out on my travels because I am in debt and have to pay my creditors. After all, it is only money that I owe, not honor. I did not set out to travel because I was in need of *honor.*"

One of his favorite sayings was the following: "A man is often called a microcosm — a small world. If he is a whole world in his own estimation, then he is small; if he is small in his own eyes, then he is a whole world."

◂§ *Humility (iii)*

Reb Menachem Mendel of Kotsk once shared with his brother-in-law and disciple, Reb Yitzchak Meir of Ger, a legal query which was bothering him. His own *rebbitzin,* he argued, had no doubt agreed to join him in marriage on the understanding that he was a rebbe. Yet he felt in his own heart that he was not really a rebbe. It followed, therefore, that his marriage, being based on a mistaken assumption, was invalid.

His brother-in-law reassured him: "In fact it makes no difference to the *rebbitzin* whether her husband is really a rebbe or not — though she does derive satisfation from the fact that her husband is popularly esteemed as a rebbe. And in this there is no mistake whatever, for you will always be known as 'the rebbe of Kotsk.' "

◈§ Unity in Diversity

הַכְזוֹנָה יַעֲשֶׂה אֶת־אֲחוֹתֵנוּ *Should he deal with our sister as with a harlot? (34:31)*

A debate once sprang up between Reb Yaakov Yosef of Ostrow and Reb Pinchas of Korets as to which was the most common transgression in their day. Reb Yaakov Yosef held that the most widespread offense was the habit of indulging in idle conversation during prayer services in the synagogue. His friend held that greater danger lay in the practice then common whereby the daughters of poor Jewish families would knock on the doors of the gentile squires, selling them fish and chickens and the like, thus leaving themselves open to the risk of being left alone with them. And so they debated away, each trying to convince the other by all manner of proofs and arguments that he was right, until they finally agreed on a means of arbitration: they would open a *Chumash* at random, and the first Scriptural verse to catch their eye would indicate who won the argument. They opened a copy of the Book of *Genesis* that happened to be near at hand, and their first glance fell upon the indignant words of Shimon and Levi, the brothers of Dinah: "Should he deal with our sister as with a harlot?"

What an outright victory for Reb Pinchas!

"Wait a moment," said Reb Yaakov Yosef. "Let us see how the classic Aramaic translation of Rabbi Yonasan ben Uziel understands this verse."

And this is what they read: "It is not proper that it be talked about in the synagogues of Israel that ... idolators defiled the daughter of the Patriarch Yaakov."

The worst part of the offense would thus seem to be that people would talk about it in synagogue — so that both scholars won the argument. Or, in the words of the Talmud, "Both these and those are the words of the living God."

◈§ The Secret Weapon

וַיְהִי חִתַּת אֱלֹקִים עַל־הֶעָרִים *The dread of God was upon the cities (35:5)*

Late in 1856, Reb Menachem Mendel of Lubavitch (known as the Tzemach Tzedek) sent his son Reb Shmuel — who was later to succeed him as rebbe — to St. Petersburg on matters of communal concern.

On the eve of his departure he told him the following: "When I was summoned in 1843 to the rabbinical conference in St. Petersburg, I went to pray at the resting place of my saintly mother at Liozna, and she told me that by virtue of her self-sacrifice for chassidim and for Chassidism she had been privileged to be granted entry to the palace of the Baal Shem Tov in heaven. She had requested the Baal Shem Tov to pray on my behalf, and had asked him to give her some *sgulah* that would enable me to withstand the opposition of the antagonists of Chassidism. The Baal Shem Tov had answered: 'Your son knows — by heart, and letter perfect — the Five Books of the *Chumash,* all the psalms in the Book of *Tehillim,* and the book of *Tanya.* Now we read in the Torah that the sons of the Patriarch Yaakov were not harmed by the Canaanites, because *the dread (חִתַּת) of God was upon the cities around them.* The three consonants of this word are the initial letters of the Hebrew names of these three books: *Chumash, Tehillim, Tanya.* He who is thoroughly acquainted with every letter in them is granted the spiritual strength to shatter all the obstacles that prevent the revelation of holiness.'

"Therefore," Reb Menachem Mendel instructed his son Reb Shmuel, "wherever you may be, whether in government institutions or with ministers of state, recite a chapter of *Chumash,* a psalm from the Book of *Tehillim,* and a chapter of *Tanya.*"

Many years later Reb Shmuel recounted this episode to his son, Reb Shalom Ber, and added: "It was a wonderful prescription. With the first three chapters of the *Chumash,* three psalms from the Book of *Tehillim,* and three chapters of *Tanya,* all the plans of the *maskilim* collapsed, and the Children of Israel, true to the Torah, came out triumphant."

◆§ You *Be the Candlestick*

הוּא עֵשָׂו אֲבִי אֱדוֹם
He is Esav, the father of Edom (36:43)

Reb Shlomo HaKohen of Radomsk, the author of *Tiferes Shlomo*, used to bring back into the fold, as penitents, those who turned to him after having forsaken the path of the Torah. Many were those whom he brought back through harsh words of rebuke, and many were those whom he brought back by words of kindly persuasion.

He was once visited by a man of means from Chenstochov, who remembered him from their childhood days in the town in which they had both been born, Vloshchov. The wealthy guest handed the rebbe a note, which was accompanied, according to custom, by a certain sum of money as a *pidyon*. The rebbe took the note, refused to accept the money, saying he had no need of it, and went on to ask his guest how things fared with him and with his children. Now, this man had forsaken the ways of the Torah and, influenced by the "Enlightenment" movement, had educated his sons in the spirit of the Haskalah, and in secular schools.

He therefore replied: "I lack nothing, and in addition I derive satisfaction from my sons. The first is a doctor, the second a lawyer, the third an engineer, and so on."

"This week's portion of the Torah also lists all the chiefs," replied the rebbe. "It says 'the Chief of Knaz, and so on, and concludes: 'He is Esav, the father of Edom.' "

And as Reb Shlomo quoted those concluding words of the verse, he pointed at his guest.

When the latter returned to his lodgings, he sent for a few of Reb Shlomo's chassidim, told them of his encounter with their rebbe, and shared with them his fear of repercussions arising out of the rebbe's displeasure. The chassidim first advised him to try to appease the rebbe by sending him a gift of tall silver candlesticks with which he could honor the *Shabbos*. He forthwith sent such a gift to the *rebbitzin*, and she gave them a place of honor on the rebbe's *Shabbos* table. When the rebbe was told where they had come from, he gave orders that they be returned to their sender as soon as the holy day came to an end.

Seeing that his gift was not accepted, the visitor called together the same chassidim again, and asked for their advice. This time they explained him that the way to smooth over his relations with the rebbe was not to offer him money and gifts; the answer lay in repentance and good deeds. He took their advice to heart, and lived out the remainder of his years in conscientious observance of the mitzvos. And, in the course of his repentance, he had a prayer house built at his expense for the chassidim of Reb Shlomo whose advice had directed his steps back to the right road.

סדר וישב

Sidra Vayeishev

☙ *The Dandy with a Destiny*

And he was a lad: He used to act as lads do — grooming his hair ... in order to look handsome *(Rashi).*

וְהוּא נַעַר
And he was a lad (37:2)

Reb Moshe Leib of Sasov once encountered a band of empty-headed young rascals who were standing about and idling away their time on all manner of vanities. The rebbe's eye singled out one of them, for he sensed that he was possessed of a lofty soul, which he dearly wanted to ignite with a love for its Maker.

He called the young fellow to him, and said: "If you repent, all your transgressions will be transformed into merits."

The lout answered with a jest: he would best concentrate on accumulating more transgressions, in order to have more merits to his credit. And with that, ignoring the words of the tzaddik, he rejoined his snickering gang.

That night, however, before he fell asleep, the words of the tzaddik found their way into his heart, and thoughts of repentance turned over in his mind. The dandies of those days obeyed the current fashion whereby after they had groomed and set their locks as desired, they would enclose them in a casing especially designed to protect the waves and curls from being crushed during their sleep. The thought now entered his mind that if he were to die in the course of the night, then the members of the burial society who would come in the morning would no doubt see the casing which protected his curls, and would probably laugh out loud at the sight ...

Anyway, for whatever reason, thoughts of repentance gave him no rest, until he left his band of cronies. Whenever they met him thereafter, they taunted him for his metamorphosis, but he found the strength to withstand their gibes, and steadfastly grew in learning and in character until he became a man of spiritual stature.

◆§ Dream Stuff

מָה הַחֲלוֹם הַזֶּה אֲשֶׁר חָלָמְתָּ *What is this dream that you have dreamt? (37:10)*

Reb Shlomo Zalman of Kopust, who is known as the author of *Magen Avos*, once said: "No night passes in which my late grandfather (Reb Menachem Mendel of Lubavitch) does not appear to me in my dreams. Every night he delivers a discourse for me on the philosophy of Chassidism, and I always remember it afterwards as well. But I have never repeated those discourses when addressing my chassidim. After all, a dream is — a dream."

◆§ The Staff of Life

אַל־תִּשְׁפְּכוּ־דָם *Shed not blood (37:22)*

Every passer-by would find an open door at the house of Reb Yitzchak of Kalush, the brother of Reb Meir of Premishlan. One day a gentile came past and asked for a slice of bread, at a time when the only bread in the house was the whole braided *challos* which the *rebbitzin* had baked in honor of the Sabbath. When her husband saw that she was reluctant to break open the whole loaves, he said: "Slice up a loaf; no blood will be lost because of it."

The *rebbitzin* obliged, and gave the gentile enough to sate his hunger.

One day Reb Yitzchak had occasion to travel to Hungary, and the craggy roads across the Carpathian Mountains were infested with bloodthirsty brigands. A band of such highwaymen seized the tzaddik, stripped him of all his belongings, and led him off to their chief, who was to decide whether to kill him, in order that he should not reveal their whereabouts, or to set him free in the mountainous wilds.

Now this robber chief was the very same gentile for whom the *rebbitzin* had sliced her bread. Recognizing the tzaddik, he turned to his henchmen: "This Jew once saved my life. Let him live, and give him back all his bundles as well."

His word was law. The tzaddik was released, and eventually found his way home, safe and sound. When he saw the *rebbitzin*, he said: "Do you remember that I told you to slice up the loaf, and no blood would be lost because of it? Well, because of it, the blood that wasn't lost — was mine."

◈§ *The Price of Disgrace*

הִיא מוּצֵאת
She was brought forth
(38:25)

She was brought forth, and she sent to her father-in-law: For she did not want to shame him ... From this example our Sages taught: Let a man allow himself to be cast into a fiery furnace rather than disgrace his comrade in public *(Rashi).*

It would be difficult to find a man as charitable as Reb Chaim of Zanz. He provided for the needs of tens of thousands of poor folk, while his own home was sore pressed for the most basic necessities. He would exert himself in particular to marry off poor orphans, supplying them with dowries and clothes, and rejoicing at their weddings as if they were his own flesh and blood.

It so happened that one day his son, Reb Yechezkel of Shiniva, was involved in scholarly discussion with the Rav of Libichov at the table of Reb Chaim. The door opened, and in walked one of the local schoolmasters. When Reb Chaim asked him whether he was soon going to marry off his daughter, the guest replied that he did not know.

"And why don't you know?" asked Reb Chaim.

"Because I can't afford to buy a *tallis* and *shtreimel* for my future son-in-law," replied the schoolmaster.

"Father, this is strange indeed!" blurted out Reb Yechezkel. "Only a day or two ago I myself happened to see this very gentleman buying a *tallis* and a *shtreimel!*"

Overcome with shame and confusion, the schoolmaster hastily left the house. Reb Chaim, seeing this, grasped his beard in horror and exclaimed: "How could you do such a thing, to disgrace a fellow Jew! For all we know, perhaps he hasn't yet paid for the *tallis* and the *streimel* that he bought; or perhaps he has to find money to buy clothes for his wife, and was too embarrassed to say so, so he said instead that he had to buy things for his future son-in-law. And you shamed him in public! What answer will you have for the Heavenly Court when the time comes to account for your actions?"

Reb Yechezkel heard this rebuke in silence, and ran out to look for the schoolmaster. Finding him standing alone in the street, he sought to placate him and to beg his forgiveness, but the injured party would not hear of such a thing. He insisted instead that they present their lawsuit to be heard at once by Reb Chaim. Re-entering the house, and standing before his father, Reb Yechezkel now redoubled his efforts to appease the fuming plaintiff — but to no avail.

Reb Chaim thereupon turned to the schoolmaster and said: "Listen to my advice: do not forgive the Rav of Shiniva until he agrees to buy you a *tallis* and a *shtreimel,* and covers as well all the expenses of the wedding, down to the last shoelace."

Reb Yechezkel undertook at once to do so, and the schoolmaster, for his part, forgave him.

☙ *True Self-Sacrifice*

In 1843 the Czarist government of Russia called a rabbinical conference which was to discuss various matters affecting the religious life of the Jews. The delegates chosen were Reb Menachem Mendel of Lubavitch (known as the Tzemach Tzedek), the renowned scholar Reb Yitzchak of Volozhin, a magnate from Berditchev by the name of Reb Yisrael Heilprin, and Betzalel Stern, the headmaster of the school in Odessa.

When Reb Menachem Mendel returned to Lubavitch, he heard that chassidim were saying he had sacrificed himself at St. Petersburg for the sake of the House of Israel.

He wept bitterly, and said: "Woe is him concerning whom the world errs! Is this self-sacrifice, that a man sacrifices himself for the sake of the House of Israel — perhaps even with a motive of self-interest, for he knows that he is thereby increasing his reward in the World to Come? There is nothing worthy about *that* kind of self-sacrifice. True self-sacrifice is the kind of action I heard was exemplified by Reb Baruch of Mezhibuzh, who sacrificed his life *and* his share in the World to Come for a solitary Jew; no, not for the life of that solitary individual, but for saving his property!"

Reb Menachem Mendel then told his chassidim what happened to Reb Baruch: "It so happened that one of Reb Baruch's close disciples, a God-fearing chassid, was a merchant who used to deliver wine to distant towns. He did not possess the capital needed to pay for his wares at the outset, but because he was known to be a trustworthy man, the wholesalers used to give him wine on account. One night, while he was staying at some wayside inn, the thought entered his mind that there was a certain matter for which he had not yet repented as fully as he should have. So eager was he to set this right that he left his wagons loaded with wine at the inn, and set out at once to see his rebbe at Mezhibuzh. When he arrived, Reb Baruch asked him about his business affairs, so he told his whole story.

"Hearing that he had left his whole stock of wine unattended at the inn, Reb Baruch surprised him with an avalanche of scolding and abuse: 'Fool that you are! How did the thought ever enter your head that you should abandon the property of others over a matter of no consequence?'

"This encounter took place on Friday afternoon, before the approach of *Shabbos*. But later in the evening, and again by day, there was no end to the same kind of rebuke, which was even carried on in the presence of others. One of Reb Baruch's guests that *Shabbos* was his relative by marriage, Reb Avraham of Chmielnik, who could not refrain from protesting: '*Mechutan!* Does the Talmud not say something about he who shames his fellow in public?'

"Replied Reb Baruch: 'Don't I know that he who

shames his fellow in public has no share in the World to Come? But I decided to abandon my share in the World to Come in order to do this poor fellow a favor. You see, his gentile wagon drivers had already conspired to rob him of all his wine and leave him penniless. But the distress that I put him through with my abuse will save him, for the anguish of public shame has been reckoned in the Heavenly Court as an ample substitute for the anguish of monetary loss which had been ordained for him.'

"This," concluded Reb Menachem Mendel, "is true self-sacrifice: that a person should be prepared to abandon his share in the World to Come in order to spare a fellow Jew some monetary loss!"

☙§ *Intent*

וְאֵת־כָּל־אֲשֶׁר עֹשִׂים שָׁם הוּא הָיָה עֹשֶׂה *Whatever they did there, he used to do (39:22)*

In his younger days, before he became known as a tzaddik, Reb Moshe Leib of Sasov used to study Torah until deep into the night, then steal across to the house of entertainment where the sons of the squires wasted away their hours in eating, drinking, and making merry. Dressed for the occasion like any one of them, he would join in their dancing, singing away in his pleasant voice until dawn — when he would return to his house, change back into his usual clothes, and embark upon his morning prayers. This he did several times, thereby saving those young people by his mere presence from immoral conduct.

Many years later, when as a renowned tzaddik he was visited every *Shabbos* by hundreds of people, one of those youths joined the throng, recognized the rebbe from his younger days, and mused: "What an expert he is at fooling them all! I remember him dancing and laughing with me. He's nothing more than I am!"

But when he heard his wisdom, and sensed the sanctity that encompassed him, he had second thoughts, and decided: "His intent in those days must have been to save us from sinking in sin."

He quickly rose from his place, bowed deeply before the tzaddik, and said: "A thousand thanks to you, my master, for saving me long ago from the depths of depravity."

◆§ A Trust That Wavers Not (i)

וַיִּשְׁכָּחֵהוּ *And he forgot him* (40:23)

When Reb Aharon of Titiev — the grandson of the Baal Shem Tov — was a young man, and not yet a rebbe, he lived in grinding poverty. Things came to such a pass that one *Shabbos* there was literally nothing in the house to eat. In his distress he was unable to refrain from speaking his mind, and he addressed his plaint to his fellow worshipers in the synagogue that *Shabbos:* "Is it not unthinkable that a grandson of the Baal Shem Tov should be so utterly neglected by his townsmen that he should not even have the barest portion of bread and water?"

Their consciences aroused, the worshipers immediately undertook to set aside a certain sum weekly as *maamad* for his support, and decided to meet after *Shabbas* in order to organize the matter properly, by appointing collectors, and so forth.

No sooner had they all gone home than Reb Aharon was overcome with remorse: What had he done? All his days he had made a point of never requesting favors of flesh and blood, placing all his trust in Him Who would no doubt come to his aid. And now, had he not forsaken that trust, and turned instead to seek salvation from the hands of mortal man? Worse still, he had even used the name of his saintly grandfather, the Baal Shem Tov, for this purpose.

So overcome was he with anguish that he finally poured forth his entreaty to God in prayer — that his townsmen should completely forget about him and about their promises, and should do nothing whatever for him.

His prayer was granted, and no one recalled a word of their noble intentions.

❀ ❀ ❀

Reb David Moshe of Chortkov — the son of Reb Yisrael of Ruzhin — used to recount this story, and was wont to add that it enables one to understand the meaning of the Midrash which speaks of Yosef and Pharaoh's butler in prison. The Midrash applies to Yosef the verse in *Psalms:* 'Blessed is the man who makes God his trust, and turns not to the proud.' This is problematic, for the fact is that Yosef did turn to the butler with the request that he mention him to Pharaoh. It will be noted, though, that the verse describing the result of this request is worded curiously, in dual form, as follows: 'And the butler did not remember Yosef, and he forgot him.' The reason for this is that Yosef soon after regretted having placed his trust in mortal man, and therefore prayed that the butler would forget him.

Hence, concluded Reb David Moshe, the Midrash is able to say of Yosef that he placed his trust in God.

◆§ *A Trust That Wavers Not (ii)*

Reb Yitzchak of Vorki used to illustrate the above-mentioned Midrash with a different story.

Reb Elimelech of Lyzhansk once walked to the *Tashlich* ritual of atonement, accompanied by a learned chassid by the name of Reb Zev Wolff, the author of *Leshon HaZahav.* As they concluded reading the appropriate passages, Reb Elimelech stepped aside a moment in order to carry out the custom of symbolically shaking out the sins from one's garments. Reb Zev Wolff followed him, saying: "Rebbe, let me see where you throw your sins, so that I can pick them up and keep them for myself, for what a rebbe regards as a sin, relative to other people is a mitzvah."

"So it was," said Reb Yitzchak of Vorki, "with Yosef. His trust in God was perfect at all times — except that on this occasion he wanted to have it operate through natural causes, rather than supernaturally. For Yosef this was regarded as a sin, but relative to other people, it would be meritorious. When the Midrash says that the verse in *Psalms:* 'Blessed is the man who makes God his trust, and turns not to the proud' — refers to Yosef, its intention is as follows: 'Blessed is the man who is as trusting as Yosef, whose sin lay only in his desire to utilize the opportunity of the butler's release to have his trust in God clothed in natural agencies.' "

סדר מקץ

SIDRA MIKEITZ

◈ The Days of Our Years

וַיְהִי מִקֵּץ שְׁנָתַיִם יָמִים
And it came to pass at the end of two years (41:1)

Reb Meir of Presmishlan related that once, when his father's soul — during his lifetime — had ascended for a little space to experience a higher spiritual life, he saw two men being brought to the World Above, first a young man, then an old man. The first they called "old man," and the second they called "child."

"Is this not the World of Truth?" he asked, much surprised. "Why, then, do you jest?"

And the answer came that this was indeed the truth, for the young man in his few years had accomplished a great deal, so that each day he lived was reckoned as a year, whereas the old man, having nothing to show for his eighty years, was in fact a child.

To make his point, Reb Meir then took the liberty of punning on the phrase in Scripture: 'And it came to pass at the end of two years.' (In the Hebrew original, the two words meaning *two years* are שְׁנָתַיִים יָמִים; the former, שְׁנָתַיִים, brings to mind the word שָׁנִים, meaning *years*, and the latter, יָמִים, literally means *days.)*

"Thus," punned Reb Meir, "it sometimes *comes to pass at the end* of a man's lifetime that he realizes that his *years* have been but *days.*"

◈ An Exercise in Decoding

יֶשׁ-שֶׁבֶר בְּמִצְרָיִם
There was corn in Egypt (42:1)

When Reb Shneur Zalman of Liadi, the author of *Tanya,* was arrested on a capital charge, his brother-in-law, Reb Yisrael Kozik, hastened to ask him what he should do.

The rebbe answered: "You should set out immediately

for St. Petersburg, and someone else should travel at once to Berditchev with a *pidyon nefesh*, with the request that Reb Levi Yitzchak intercede in heaven on my behalf."

Reb Levi Yitzchak was so distraught at the tidings, that he fell to the floor with a bitter cry. He then asked the messenger whether his rebbe had been distressed by the brutal arrest.

"He was," answered the messenger.

"Was he distressed externally, or internally?" asked the tzaddik.

"Only externally," replied the messenger, "for I noticed that he forgot to take his slippers, but not his *tallis* and *tefillin.*"

The tzaddik was well pleased with this answer, saying: "He's perceptive, this Lithuanian."

He then asked the man for the name of Reb Shneur Zalman's mother, as is customary with a *pidyon*. The man said that he had forgotten to ask before he set out, and when the question had come to mind on the journey he had decided not to return, since he had wanted to fulfill the rebbe's instruction that he set out at once.

Reb Levi Yitchak thereupon opened at random a *Chumash* which was on his table, and his eyes lighted upon the verse: 'And Yaakov saw that there was corn in Egypt.' Now the three consonants that make up שֶׁבֶר, the Hebrew word for corn, are the letters ש, ב, and ר.

"Do you see?" said the tzaddik. "Here we have the initials of the name Shneur ben Rivkah."

And, indeed, Rivkah was the name of Reb Shneur Zalman's mother.

◌§ *Man or Meat*

וְהֵם לֹא הִכִּרֻהוּ
But they did not recognize him (42:8)

One *Shabbos*, at the *tish* of Reb Moshe of Kobrin, scores of people who were unable to find seats at the long table crowded around, standing on the surrounding benches, and straining to catch a glimpse of the rebbe and to hear his words. The rebbe took a look at one of these young men, who used to attend the *tish* regularly, and asked his attendant: "Who is that young man?"

When he was told his name, the rebbe said: "I don't know him."

The attendant was surprised: "But he is the son of chassid so-and-so!"

But the tzaddik repeated his words — "I don't know him" — until the attendant gave him a number of unmistakable marks of identification, and only then did he finally recall who he was.

At this point he called across to the young man and said: "Do you know why I did not recognize you? You see, the essence of a man is his thought, and wherever he focuses his thoughts, that is where he is. Now your thoughts have been wandering in all kinds of undesirable places, and that is why I saw before me not the face of a man, but a chunk of meat."

◆§ *A Case of Mistaken Identity*

Reb Yitzchak of Vorki had a friend who was a rabbi of repute, but a great antagonist of Reb Yitzchak's rebbe, Reb Simchah Bunem of Pshischah. He always had hard words to say about him, even in the presence of his friend, who never answered a word.

This attitude astonished Reb Yitzchak's chassidim, who asked him how he found it possible to hear such harsh language about his rebbe, and yet to hold his peace.

"I will tell you about an incident that happened to me," replied Reb Yitzchak, "and then you will understand. I was once traveling in a certain city when a stranger approached me, looked at me for a moment, and exclaimed: 'That's him!' A second man did the same thing soon after, and then a third, and I had not the slightest notion what it was all about. Then I was approached by a deserted woman in need of a bill of divorce, an *agunah,* who was accompanied by a noisy little group of men, including the three who had approached me earlier. All in a chorus they showered me with curses and abuses, the gist of which was: 'You are the man who all these years has left this poor woman as an *agunah!*' They were so convinced that they knew who I was, that no amount of explanation on my part could persuade them that I was not the irresponsible gentleman they were seeking. In the end I had to go along with them to the local rabbinical court, which accepted my evidence of identity.

"Now while they were busy abusing me I was not in the slightest angry at them, because I knew that it was not at *me* that they were directing their complaints and their curses. They thought I was her husband, and had they known me better they would not have abused me. In a word, whatever they did, they did to someone else.

"So, too, with this rabbi. When he says unpleasant things about my rebbe, Reb Simchah Bunem, I don't get excited, because I know that he talks this way only because he doesn't know my rebbe. If he knew him, he wouldn't say a thing. In a word, he talks about someone else, not about my rebbe."

◆§ *Remote Control*

מְרַגְּלִים אַתֶּם *You are spies (42:9)*

During the Austro-Hungarian War in 1848, a chassid by the name of Reb Yisrael from the town of Skoli in Austria happened to find himself on business in the Hungarian city of Debrecen while it was besieged by the Austrian army. Finding himself thus confined, he bought some plums, wine, and other provisions, and settled down to wait until the storm blew over, spending his days in no other business than prayer, study, and the reading of *Psalms* in the local synagogue.

A squad of Hungarian soldiers stopped him in the street one day, and asked him where he was from. When he answered that he was from Austria, they arrested him on suspicion of espionage, and handed him over for a military trial. The atmosphere of siege and crisis was hardly conducive to dallying on legalistic niceties, such as determining his possible innocence, and the military tribunal promptly sentenced Reb Yisrael to death. This was on a Thursday, and the execution was scheduled for *Shabbos*. Throughout those few days Reb Yisrael fasted, and recited the Book of *Psalms* without respite, from beginning to end, time after time. On *Shabbos* morning, after he had finished saying his prayers, soldiers entered his cell, and led him off in the direction of the place of execution.

On their way there they met a high-ranking officer who looked at the prisoner and exclaimed: "Srulke! Where are you going to?"

And Reb Yisrael, even though he did not know this officer, answered that he was about to be executed.

"But why?" asked the officer.

Reb Yisrael told him that he had been suspected of espionage.

"You — a spy?!" cried the stranger. "Never! I know you as an honest and innocent Jew."

Then, turning to the soldiers, he gave the order: "Return the Jew to the lockup!"

The soldiers protested that they were under orders to convey him to a certain place. They could not disobey.

"If so," said the officer, "let me ask you at least to wait here for a little while until I bring you new orders from high up."

The soldiers agreed to wait, and the officer went off to wherever he had to go, returning after a few minutes with new orders from the requisite authority that the Jew was to be returned to his cell. The soldiers complied.

And in the afternoon of that very same day, the Austrian army captured the city.

When they unlocked the prison doors, they found Reb Yisrael sitting quietly, reading his Book of *Psalms*. They asked him what he was doing there, and he answered that he had been arrested because of his espionage for Austria. They freed him at once, and as a mark of admiration asked him: "What can we do for you?"

Reb Yisrael could think of only one request: "The plums and the wine that I bought, and put away in such-and-such a place... Do you think I could have them back?"

The order was duly given, and a light task force was dispatched forthwith to the destination indicated. Its mission, however, proved a failure: there was no sign left of the provisions named. The invading army therefore made a quick estimate of the loss, and then and there gave the injured party full financial reimbursement.

Reb Yisrael first returned home, and from there set out to visit his rebbe, Reb Meir of Premishlan.

As soon as he entered, Reb Meir turned to his *gabbai*, Reb Aryeh, and said: "Aryeh, do you remember that *Shabbos* when we ate the pears that Reb Yisrael gave us?"

For Reb Yisrael was fond of bringing dried pears to his rebbe as a gift, and on that *Shabbos* when he was about to be executed in Debrecen and was saved by that mysterious officer, Reb Meir had said to his chassidim: "Please bring to the table those pears of Reb Yisrael of Skoli, and we'll eat some."

And now Reb Meir turned to his chassid and said: "If you only knew, Yisrael, who was the personage from up there whom I troubled to come and save you..."

⸎ *Envy (i)*

וַיִּשְׁתּוּ וַיִּשְׁכְּרוּ עִמּוֹ

And they drank and were merry with him (43:34)

A certain tzaddik passed away, and was succeeded by another rebbe. One of the chassidim, however, entertained the notion that he was better suited to fill the position of his late rebbe. He decided, though, that he should first travel to visit the new incumbent, to see what kind of stuff he was made of. When he arrived, he took a seat at the table together with the other chassidim, and throughout the *Shabbos* meal observed his fill. Then the new rebbe invited him to share some insight on the Torah with those present.

"We find," he said, "that when Yosef's brothers are reunited with him, though as yet not realizing it, the Torah says, 'And they drank and were merry with him.' On this verse Rashi comments that from the day they had sold him until this moment they had not drunk wine. Now this is difficult to understand. It is easy to see why Yosef should drink now, since he already knew that they were his brothers. But they, who had not yet recognized him, why should they drink already?

"Now all their hatred of Yosef, and the reason for which they had sold him, was based on their envy of his coat of many colors. Therefore, when they later regretted their action, they no doubt made efforts over the years to eradicate the despicable trait of envy from their hearts.

 Still, not being certain that they had completely succeeded in this, they did not yet allow themselves to drink wine. But now that they had seen Yosef giving their brother Binyamin five times as many gifts as they had received, and they saw that they themselves were not at all envious of him, it was apparent to them that they had succeeded in their self-imposed task. They therefore allowed themselves to drink wine."

"And therefore," continued the chassid, "since after visiting your table I find that I am not envious of your having been chosen rebbe, I too am in turn for a cup of wine!"

❧ *Envy (ii)*

A man came to complain to Reb Meir of Premishlan that a certain fellow was depriving him of his livelihood.

"I am sure that you've noticed," explained Reb Meir, "that when a horse drinks from a river, it stamps its hooves in the edge of the water. Tell me now: Why does the horse do this? And if you don't know the answer, Meir will tell you. You see, the water is like a mirror, and as soon as the horse lowers its head to drink, it sees another horse down there, which is also lowering its head to drink. He can't bear seeing the other horse drinking so much. Envy makes him angry, so he stamps away at the other horse so that it shouldn't drink up his water."

"But you, my friend, surely realize that there is enough water in the river for any number of horses. Or, in the words of our Sages, no individual ever subtracts anything from the livelihood which has been foreordained for his fellow man."

❧ *No More Police*

וְאֵיךְ נִגְנֹב *How could we steal? (44:8)*

Reb Yehudah Aryeh Leib of Ger, the author of *Sfas Emes*, related after his first visit to Kotsk that on his arrival there he had found that the rebbe's household arrangements were disorganized and unsupervised. Articles would be missing through theft, and Feivl, the odd-job man, would complain loudly to the *rebbitzin*, saying: "And why *shouldn't* they steal, when everything around here is such a mess, and nothing is supervised?"

Reb Menachem Mendel of Kotsk overheard that remark, and shouted at the top of his voice: "But Feivl, the Torah says *Thou shalt not steal!*"

❦ ❦ ❦

The visitor from Ger averred that when he heard those words of the rebbe, it seemed to him that it was quite impossible for anyone to steal anything in the whole world — because of that Commandment: *Thou shalt not steal!*

◈ *Elementary, My Dear Beadle!*

A woman once deposited with Reb Chanoch Henich of Alexander for safekeeping the three hundred rubles which she had saved up for her daughter's dowry. He left it for a short while in his coat pocket, and discovered soon after that it had all been stolen. Sorely distressed, he told his beadle what had happened, and the beadle took the liberty of rebuking him: "Who leaves money in a coat pocket? The place for money is a trouser pocket."

"I have never put my hand in the pocket of my trousers," said the tzaddik. "And besides, watch how I get all the money back."

With that, he called for a certain young man, and on his arrival ordered him to return the money. The young man first protested his innocence, but finally confessed, and returned the money in full.

"Now don't start imagining that I worked a miracle," said the rebbe to the startled beadle, after the young man had left the room. "It is all really very simple. When this young man was a small boy I once examined him orally on the subject of the relative liability of the various kinds of custodians discussed in Tractate *Bava Metzia* in the Talmud. And this child asked me the following question: 'When a custodian claims that the missing article deposited with him was stolen or lost, what is the point of obliging him to swear that it is not in his possession? For he could have stolen it himself and deposited it with a friend, and then he could swear truthfully that it was not in his possession, even though he was in fact the thief.'

"As soon as I heard his question, I knew he was going to grow up to be a thief."

סדר ויגש

Sidra Vayigash

⋄§ *Two Men — One Soul*

וְנַפְשׁוֹ קְשׁוּרָה בְנַפְשׁוֹ
Their souls are bound up with each other (44:30)

Four times a year Reb Pinchas Reizes (the son of Rabbi Henich Schick, a prominent scholar from Shklov) would journey to his rebbe, Reb Shneur Zalman of Liadi — in the months of Elul, Tishrei, Nissan, and Sivan. One Tishrei he fell ill and was unable to travel. On the festival of Shemini Atzeres, which falls in that month, while he was dining in his *sukkah*, he was suddenly shaken, and stood up and cried: "Oh, Rebbe!"

Then, turning to those at the table, he said: "The rebbe just now thought of me."

And the rebbe, who at that moment was also in the middle of his festive Shemini Atzeres meal, said to those at his table: "Pinchas Reizes is now in need of a bodily cure. What I cannot give him I do not give him — but a bodily cure I can secure for him."

Those of Reb Pinchas's townsmen who were present on that occasion hastened back to Shklov after the festival, called on Reb Pinchas, and invited him to treat them to vodka. When he obliged, they told him of the incident at the rebbe's table — and only later did they find out that at the very same moment he had cried out: "Oh, Rebbe!"

In good chassidic tradition, they now took to teasing him in a good-natured way: "Tell us, where did you pick up your new tricks? Don't tell us you now regard yourself as some spiritual giant!" — and the like.

"It's not me!" protested Reb Pinchas, and proceeded to tell his listeners how, stage by stage, he had entrusted the various levels of his soul to the rebbe's guidance when he had first spoken with him at *yechidus,* the private interview at which a chassid shares his spiritual burdens and aspirations with his rebbe, and in return is given direction and encouragement.

"The first time I was closeted with the rebbe for *yechidus,*" he said, "I entrusted to him my *nefesh;* the second time I visited, I entrusted him with my *ruach;* and at the third *yechidus,* I handed over my *neshamah.* Now that all the levels of my soul are handed over to his guidance, it is not he that knows nor I that feel..."

☙ *Melancholy (i)*

וְעַתָּה אַל־תֵּעָצְבוּ
And now, be not grieved (45:5)

When Reb Dov Ber of Lubavitch was a boy, he came from school one evening and dropped into the room which the chassidim of his father — Reb Shneur Zalman of Liadi — used to call "the Lower Garden of Eden" (that is, the waiting room adjoining the study in which the rebbe received chassidim for *yechidus,* the latter room being known as "the Upper Garden of Eden"). There he found a number of elder chassidim conversing soberly, as each awaited his turn to be received in private. Among those present were Reb Shmuel Munkes and Reb Shlomo Raphaels of Vilna, and they were soon joined by Reb Yosef of Shklov, a wealthy merchant and philanthropist.

Reb Shmuel Munkes was fond of playing with the rebbe's little boy, who ran straight to him as soon as he caught sight of him, and overheard him asking Reb Yosef why he was so downcast.

He and Reb Shlomo, who was also wealthy, answered together: "Times are bad, and business is slow."

Hearing this, the child sat up and said punningly to Reb Shmuel: "Why do you need to ask them for the reason for their melancholy (in Hebrew: עַצְבוּת)? Your question is answered by an explicit verse in the Book of *Psalms:* 'Their idols (עֲצַבֵּיהֶם) are silver and gold, the work of men's hands...' "

◆§ Melancholy (ii)

The fickle wheel of fortune had brought him down with a thud — Zalman Senders, the prosperous merchant from Shklov, had not only lost his wealth through a variety of enterprises which had failed, but owed formidable debts to his business associates. To make things worse, he had promised — in happier days — to marry off the daughters of his poor relatives. Even his own two daughters of marriageable age would be more of a financial burden than he could carry.

Being a chassid, he decided to pour out his bitter heart to his rebbe, Reb Shneur Zalman of Liadi. At *yechidus,* he told the rebbe what had befallen him, and said: "If it has been ordained in heaven that I be a pauper, then I accept the divine verdict. But if I do not pay my debts, nor keep my promises to my poor relatives, nor marry off my own daughters to suitable young men, then this would all add up to a desecration of the divine Name; and why should the Almighty punish me as at present, if it is going to bring about such a *Chillul HaShem?* I ask only that the Almighty enable me to honor my debts and my promises. Once that is attended to, even if I am destined to live thereafter in poverty, I will not doubt the wisdom of the divine judgment."

Then he added one more sentence: "Rebbe! I need to pay my debts, and I need to marry off my poor relatives and my daughters!"

All this time, the rebbe was leaning on his elbows, listening. Then he said: "You only know how to talk about what you need. You are not even interested in knowing about what you are needed *for.*"

Like an arrow these words struck the man's heart, and he fell in a faint. The chassidim in the waiting room heard him fall, and rushed in to help bring him to. But when he awoke he was a new man. Forgetting all his worries and all his needs, he remained in Liozna, devoting himself assiduously to study and prayer in the local synagogue. He missed no lecture, whether on the legalistic or the mystical aspects of the Torah, and whether he was at study or at prayer one could now see the face of a man who rejoices in the performance of a mitzvah, and who is happy with his lot.

On that *Shabboas* Reb Shneur Zalman delivered a learned discourse which not only discussed the esoteric Kabbalistic concepts of *tohu* and *tikkun*, but served at the same time as a prayer of intercession on behalf of the contrite listener from Shklov, who found that he was now given the strength to rehabilitate himself, both spiritually and materially.

Some days later the rebbe instructed him to return to his home, and assured him that the Almighty would come to his aid. And, indeed, as soon as he arrived home his business interests began to thrive, so that he not only honored his debts and his promises, but became wealthy once again.

Apropos of this man's metamorphosis, Reb Shneur Zalman cited a passage from Chapter 31 of his own classic work, *Tanya:* "When one is in any case troubled by mundane worries, ... then is the appropriate time to transform the sadness by becoming one of the 'masters of account' (a reference to moral stocktaking), ... and to act on the counsel of the Sages 'constantly to excite the Good Inclination against the Evil Inclination.' ... Thereby will he rid himself of the dejection occasioned by mundane affairs, and following this he will attain true joy."

In the life of his chassid Zalman Senders, commented the author, he saw this passage realized in practice.

◆§ *Melancholy (iii)*

A chassid of stature by the name of Reb Shlomo of Dvort once told his fellow chassidim who were gathered in their *shtibl* that late at night, while he was poring alone over his studies, he suddenly became aware of someone seated next to him. Alarmed, he had extinguished his candle and gone to bed.

"How did you dare to do that?" asked the chassidim. "Perhaps it was the Prophet Eliyahu, of blessed memory."

"It wasn't," answered the man of stature. "The Prophet Eliyahu is always happy, and this fellow was deep in melancholy. From this I knew that he was (God forbid!) some personage from the Other Side — an envoy from the forces of impurity."

☙ *The Problem of Honor (i)*

וְהִגַּדְתֶּם לְאָבִי אֶת־כָּל־כְּבוֹדִי
And you shall tell my father of all my glory (45:13)

While Reb Moshe of Kobrin was once staying with Reb Moshe Zvi of Savran, his host was invited to spend *Shabbos* at a town six *viorst* distant. It so happened that a post office was situated halfway there. Since Reb Moshe of Kobrin had to go the same way they set out together, the host in his impressive carriage, and the guest in his workaday wagon.

All the townsfolk of Savran thronged the highway to wish their rebbe well on his departure, and they could be seen all along the way to the post office. From there on he was greeted by crowds of well-wishers from the town that had invited him: they had walked all the way there in spontaneous expression of their welcome. And there he was, the rebbe of Savran, in the middle of it all, receiving the adoration of crowds from this side and from that.

Reb Moshe of Kobrin stopped his wagon for a moment and climbed down: he was curious to see for himself just how the rebbe of Savran sat in his carriage while all these honors were being heaped on him. His host sensed the purpose of his glance, and said: "Reb Moshe, what are you looking to see — whether I am *able* to receive honor? I know *how* to receive honor."

☙ *The Problem of Honor (ii)*

Someone told Reb Yisrael of Ruzhin that as Reb Moshe Zvi of Savran had once neared a certain city, he was greeted with outstanding marks of honor. And when he sat in the carriage drawn by fleet-footed horses which was sent ahead for his convenience, he sought to be repelled by all this seeming glory, thinking: Where does all this honor come from? Is it not from the carriage, a thing drawn by horses? And what is a horse? — an unclean and repugnant thing, which smells vilely when its carcass is skinned. And so he continued contemplating the vanity of mortal glory, until he began to vomit.

When Reb Yisrael of Ruzhin heard this story, he exclaimed: "*Nebbich*, poor fellow! Couldn't the rebbe of Savran find any other way to deal with honor?! There is a straightforward method: to receive all the honor, and nevertheless not to be at all impressed by it."

And Reb Yisrael went on to make his point with a parable: "Imagine a high-ranking courtier — superior to all the other courtiers, who bow in deference before him. One day this courtier goes strolling with the king. The petty courtiers don't know what the king looks like, but when they see this important courtier walking with some man, they immediately bow in deference to the important courtier as usual. Now it is easy to guess how distressed this courtier felt about all the glory he was getting while he was walking with the king himself, and how shamefaced he was in the presence of the king about all that glory..."

◆§ *The Problem of Honor (iii)*

When many of the luminaries of the generation, headed by Reb Avraham Yehoshua Heschel of Apta, gathered at the "great wedding" at Ostila, the opponents of Reb Simchah Bunem of Pshischah found the occasion opportune for waging a campaign against the chassidim of Pshischah and their conduct. They planned to muster all manner of arguments and proofs in order to persuade the scholars and tzaddikim attending to declare that the ways of Pshischah were not in harmony with the teachings of the Torah.

Reb Simchah Bunem had intended to attend the wedding, both out of respect for the illustrious families involved, and out of a desire to demonstrate the validity of his chassidic teachings by answering any objections that might be raised. His disciple, however, Reb Menachem Mendel — later famous as the rebbe of Kotsk — disagreed violently, and said to his teacher: "Rebbe, even if you are seated in your carriage all ready to travel, I will lie down in front of the horses, and will not let you go."

The tzaddik therefore decided to be represented by his

 disciples, and it was agreed that five people should be dispatched: a scholar, a chassid, a clever fellow, a magnate, and a good talker. Those chosen were: Reb Yitzchak Meir (later the rebbe of Ger), as the scholar; Reb Feivl of Gritza, as the chassid; Reb Zusya of Shidlitz, for his brains; Reb Yissachar Horovitz, for his wealth; and Reb Eliezer Dov of Grabovitz, as the good talker.

Reb Yitzchak Meir was the youngest of the group, and on their arrival amazed all those present with his sheer erudition. Even the venerable rebbe of Apta — the doyen of that rare gathering — showed him marks of respect. Finally, after many words had been exchanged between the delegation and the opponents of Pshischah, the chassidim of Pshischah won the day, and their antagonists were forced to abandon their campaign.

After the festive meal, the tzaddik of Apta grasped the belt of Reb Yitzchak Meir, and chose to dance with him — the youngest scholar present — to the amazement of all the wedding guests.

From Ostila, Reb Yitzchak Meir wrote to his rebbe, Reb Simchah Bunem, that the tzaddikim at the wedding had honored him considerably. Reb Simchah Bunem called together his inner circle of chassidim, and told them excitedly: "Just look what this young man writes! He has already reached such a level of self-refinement that he can even receive honor!"

Then, as an afterthought, he added: "This is what we can see too in Joseph's instruction to his brothers: *'And you shall tell my father of all my glory in Egypt.'* "

◆ *The Problem of Honor (iv)*

Reb Menachem Mendel of Lubavitch (the Tzemach Tzedek) once visited Minsk and Vilna, which were known to be the strongholds of the *misnagdim* (the opponents of the chassidim). He was received there with extraordinary respect. Chassidim from the surrounding towns near and far thronged in the thousands around his hotel. The renowned non-chassidic scholars of those cities likewise came to visit him, debated all manner of abstruse subjects with him, and honored him in every way. One of his sons, who accompanied him on this journey, wrote from Minsk to his mother in Lubavitch, mentioning in passing how pleased he was to see what honors were being showered on his father.

When the tzaddik returned home he happened to light upon this letter, which disturbed him so deeply that he called for his son, and rebuked him. The *rebbitzin*, hearing her husband's words, asked him: "Why the rebuke? What has he done wrong?"

Replied the tzaddik: "My blood was being shed mercilessly — and he writes how *pleased* he was!"

◆§ *Posterity*

וּבְנֵי־דָן חֻשִׁים
And the sons of Dan were Chushim (46:23)

A chassid by the name of Reb Yaakov Yitzchak of Brizin once came to see Reb Yissachar Dov of Radoshitz with a bitter plaint: his offspring had all died in their childhood. The rebbe told him that when his wife would next be close to the time of childbirth, he should visit him again. When his wife entered her seventh month, the chassid duly journeyed to Radoshitz. The rebbe asked him for the name of his late father, and when he answered "Yirmeyahu," he told him to call the son who was to be born: Chaim (meaning: *life)* Yirmeyahu.

Before the chassid left town he visited the rebbe once more, according to custom, to receive his farewell wishes. The rebbe offered him his blessing that the son to be born should survive into maturity, and concluded with a verse from the Torah: 'And the sons of Dan were Chushim.' Not being able to muster the courage to ask for the meaning of this strange addendum, the chassid took his leave and returned home, and when his wife gave birth he named the infant according to the rebbe's instructions.

All this time, understandably enough, the chassid was burning with curiosity to discover the meaning of the rebbe's mystifying quotation. He repeated it to every sage and chassid in his town, and they all excelled each other in the ingenuity of their interpretations. None of them satisfied him. He wrote to his brother-in-law who was a rabbi in Pshischah, but he and his learned colleagues were as baffled as the local sages. After a whole year had passed fruitlessly, he posed the riddle afresh to the scholars of his hometown, and this time they agreed to one interpretation, as follows.

Paradoxically, the verse in question employs the plural form — 'And the sons of Dan were' — even though Dan had only one son, Chushim. The Talmud explains that this plural form is a hint at Dan's later posterity, for through the offspring of Chushim, Dan became the progenitor of a numerous tribe. This, suggested the chassidim, was the import of the rebbe's quotation.

They proved to be right. Chaim Yirmeyahu remained indeed an only child, but with the passage of years his seed bore fruit, and the family multiplied and flourished.

◆§ *Sparks Gone Astray (i)*

וַיְלַקֵּט יוֹסֵף אֶת־כָּל־הַכֶּסֶף הַנִּמְצָא בְאֶרֶץ־מִצְרַיִם

And Yosef gathered in all the silver that was found in the Land of Egypt (47:14)

And Yosef gathered in all the silver that was found in the Land of Egypt: Yosef sought out and purified all the sparks of sanctity which were scattered throughout Egypt, separated them from their worldly husks, and elevated them *(Kabbalah).*

In the days before Reb Simchah Bunem of Pshischah became a rebbe he was a businessman, and whenever he was in Danzig he would spend time on discussions with nonobservant freethinkers, with the intention of arousing in them thoughts of repentance.

Once a group of such men said to him jokingly: "Rabbi, if you will come to the theater with us, then we will oblige, and repent of our present way of life."

This was, shall we say, a difficult request to comply with. Reb Simchah Bunem sensed, however, that there was no alternative, and was quite certain that he could succeed thereby in causing them to repent, so he promised to do as they asked. He set out at once for the House of Study and settled down to immerse himself wholly in his books, first leaving word with these men that he would let them know the time at which he would go to the theater. When after several hours he had not arrived, they set out to find him. There he was, still in the *beis midrash*, studying his Talmud in a vigorous singsong, as Talmud scholars have always done. To their question as to why he had not kept his promise, he answered that he had simply forgotten, but he was now ready to join them. So off they went to the theater together, the rabbi and the freethinkers.

As they neared the door he asked them to enter first; he would follow them. They walked right into the theater, which was illuminated by wax candles, and sat back to enjoy a play in which all the actors were dressed in white. Reb Simchah Bunem went as far as the foyer and sat down in a corner, where he broke down in bitter tears, and sobbed out passages from the Book of *Psalms*. His companions inside the theater soon realized that he was not with them. They stole out to look for him, and found him lying prostrate in the foyer, weeping bitterly.

"Rabbi," they exclaimed in astonishment, "why are you lying here and weeping, when inside the theater everyone is singing and dancing so happily?"

Reb Simchah Bunem answered them boldly and loudly: "Let us repent, for today is Yom Kippur, the Day of Atonement — complete with wax candles and white robes!"

So vigorously did he address them that they were terror-stricken, and fled from the theater. The tzaddik followed them, and then directed them to the *beis midrash*, where his words of admonition permeated their hearts, renewing their bond with their Maker. And a short time later they were all guiding their steps — treading more surely from day to day — along the path of the Torah.

◆§ *Sparks Gone Astray (ii)*

And Yosef gathered in all the silver that was found in the Land of Egypt: In the Kabbalah, the word *kesef* [silver] connotes lovingkindness and love. Yosef's spiritual mission was to seek out and elevate all the loves of Egypt *(Torah Or).*

While Reb Leib Sarahs was in Russia he sensed that in a certain town in Hungary there was a lofty soul which had to be cultivated, in order to enable it to reach the level of spiritual growth which its source made potentially possible. He therefore told his wagon-driver to harness his horses in preparation for a long journey. The simple fellow knew from experience that when the rebbe said "a long journey," they would no doubt find that the distance was miraculously shortened for them. And so it was. The driver held the reins until they reached the outskirts of the town, where he handed them over to the rebbe's charge, and dozed off. Just as in a dream one imagines towns and villages flying by before one's very eyes, so too he could half see the distance of the journey vanishing away before him. When their destination came in sight the tzaddik roused him, and he resumed control of the reins.

It was dawn when they reached the township they sought, and after morning prayers the tzaddik went for a stroll in the nearby woods. There he saw a boy of about eight, whose lean frame was only half clothed with rags and tatters, looking after a gaggle of geese. The tzaddik struck up conversation with the little waif, and soon learned that he was the son of a poor widow, whose name he gave. Forthwith the tzaddik went to seek out the lonely woman, and asked her to entrust him with her son. He promised to bring him up, and train him to be a respectable businessman. The widow consented. Before leaving, Reb Leib gave her a certain sum for her own sustenance, then set out with the boy for a long journey, to the house of Reb Shmelke of Nikolsburg.

When at length they arrived, Reb Leib said to his host: "I have brought you a lofty soul whose source in heaven is the Palace of Melody; I hope that you will make of it what it needs to become."

And so the little gooseherd grew up in the home of Reb Shmelke, and all the melodies and shepherd songs that he knew, he made holy. The books of Kabbalah explain that all the tunes in the world originate in the Palace of Melody in heaven. The Other Side — impurity — knows no melodies, nor knows the taste of joy, since it is itself the source of melancholy. Only through the sin of Adam did certain stray sparks fall into the unholy domain of the Other Side, and the task of the tzaddik is to elevate those sparks of melody that have gone astray. And that is exactly what this little gooseherd did with the songs he had known from the woods.

He recalled, for example, a song that ran like this:

Forest, O Forest, how big you are!
Rose, O Rose, how far you are!
If only the forest was not so vast,
The rose would be nearer to me.
If someone would take me
out of the woods,
Together, O Rose, we'd be.

And now, lilting to the same melody, this is how he sang this ditty:

Exile, O Exile, how long you are!
God, O God, how far You are!
If only the exile was not so vast,
Then God would be nearer to me.
If Someone would take us
out of it soon,
Together, O God, we'd be.

That inspired gooseherd grew up to be a tzaddik celebrated as a sweet singer of Israel — Reb Yitzchak Aizik Taub, better known as the rebbe of Kaliv.

When Reb Naftali of Ropshitz heard the above little song with its silvery tune for the first time, he averred: "Whenever the rebbe of Kaliv sings it, all the Worlds Above resound; the Source of Mercy is roused; and choirs of angels of mercy draw near to the palace on high where dwells Reb Leib Sarahs, to do him honor, and they chant in harmony: 'Blessed be He Who has brought us this precious soul!' "

סדר ויחי

Sidra Vayechi

◆§ A Promise

וְקִבַרְתַּנִי בִּקְבֻרָתָם
And bury me in their place of burial *(47:30)*

Reb Hillel of Paritsh was renowned for his punctilious observance of the *mitzvos*, being prepared to risk his life even for the merest detail ordained by the Sages. The Czarist regime of his day decreed that all Jews were to shave off their *peyos*, and some unscrupulous informer told the local authorities that Reb Hillel's earlocks were still intact. They decided to shear them off by force, but Reb Hillel covered them tightly with his hands so that they would not be able to execute their plan. He was in great distress until a simple Jewish tailor came by, intervened, and saved him. Grateful for his help, Reb Hillel blessed the man, and promised him that "after a hundred and twenty years," when his time came, he would be rewarded by being buried next to him.

Many years passed. Reb Hillel in the meantime became rabbi of Bobruisk, and every year would travel around the provinces and to the cities of Kherson and Yekatrinoslav, teaching Torah as well to the farmers of the Jewish agricultural colonies, by whom he was greatly admired. In the summer of 1864, when he was sixty-nine years old, he suddenly fell ill while staying in Kherson — which is very far from Bobruisk and Paritsh in White Russia — and passed away there on *Shabbos Nachamu*. On the following day, amidst widespread mourning, he was brought to burial, and his disciples and admirers flocked there for many years thereafter to pray at the graveside of this tzaddik.

Some time later, on a bitterly cold and stormy day, an unknown pauper died in the town's communal hostelry. The beadle of the burial society was too lazy to go out on such a wintry day to find out from his superiors just where this anonymous pauper should be buried, so he went to the cemetery himself, and dug him a grave at some free spot — wherever chance would have it — and had the poor man buried. A day or two later it was noticed that the new grave had been dug right next to the resting place of the illustrious Reb Hillel. When the facts came to light a great hubbub arose in town: was it proper that a mere pauper who had died in the communal *hekdesh,* a nobody from the poorhouse, whom no respectable citizen even knew — that such a one should be buried next to the tzaddik?!

It was too late, though, to change things: the Torah would never allow it. At least let them find out just who this individual was. His identification papers disclosed his name and that of his father, and the fact that he came from Paritsh. The communal worthies of Kherson therefore wrote to their counterparts in Paritsh, asking to be told at least whatever they knew about this man.

The answer from Paritsh identified him clearly: this was the same tailor who many long years earlier had been promised by Reb Hillel that "after a hundred and twenty years," when his time came, he would be brought to rest next to his own resting place.

◆§ *Sons and Grandsons*

כִּרְאוּבֵן וְשִׁמְעוֹן יִהְיוּ־לִי

As Reuven and Shimon they shall be mine (48:5)

Reb Mordechai of Chernobyl (known as the Maggid of Chernobyl) was married to the daughter of Reb Aharon of Karlin, who bore him five sons, all of whom became famous scholars. After his wife passed away many years elapsed, and he still did not consider remarrying. In due course he received a letter from his late wife's brother, Reb Asher of Stolin, rebuking him for his undue delay. The writer went on to recommend that he marry the daughter of Reb David Leikes, the Maggid of the Russian town of Bar, and a prominent chassid of the Baal Shem Tov. Reb Mordechai decided to act on his brother-in-law's suggestion, and set out by carriage for Bar.

When he explained the circumstances of his visit to Reb David, he was given a plain answer: "I do not agree to this match."

"Could I perhaps know the reason for your refusal?" asked Reb Mordechai. "If it is a question of my ability to support your daughter according to her station in life, then let it be clear that there is definitely no problem in that direction."

"No, my reason is quite different," said Reb David. "I simply foresee that my daughter is destined to bear five sons, while you, sir, are due to beget only three more sons — which means that my daughter will have to be widowed, then remarry, and only then bear two more sons. Under the circumstances, therefore, I cannot consent to this match."

Reb Mordechai asked for three days during which to wrestle with this delicate problem. This favor he was granted.

He then returned to the young lady's father and said: "I have found a solution, thank God! I consulted the Baal Shem Tov, of blessed memory, who gave his consent to the *shidduch,* and quoted the words of the patriarch Yaakov when blessing his grandsons: 'Ephraim and Menashe, like Reuven and Shimon, shall be mine.' That is, two of our grandsons will rank in saintliness with our sons, and will thus make up a total of five."

Reb David agreed and in due course his daughter bore to Reb Mordechai a family of renowned tzaddikim: Reb Yochanan of Rachmistrivka, Reb David of Tolna, and Reb Yitzchak of Skver — three in number.

And the consensus of opinion among Reb Mordechai's chassidim affirmed that of his many grandsons, the two who were of the requisite stature to make up the quorum of five were Reb David (son of Reb Yochanan) of Zlatopol, and Reb David of Skver. It was they, then, who made their grandparents' marriage possible — albeit retroactively ...

☙ *Awaiting the Messiah (i)*

עַד כִּי־יָבֹא שִׁילֹה

Until Shiloh comes: This refers to the Messiah (*Rashi*).

Until Shiloh comes (49:10)

In 1777 Reb Menachem Mendel of Vitebsk led a large group of Russian chassidim to *Eretz Yisrael*, where they established a community in Tiberias. Some time after his arrival, some enterprising fool climbed up the Mount of Olives unperceived, and blew a mighty blast from his *shofar*. The simple folk who heard it assumed in their innocence that this was the long-awaited *shofar* of the Messiah, heralding the glad tidings of the Redemption. But when the rumor reached Reb Menachem Mendel, he opened the window, looked around at the world outside, and said: "No. I don't feel that there is anything new in the air."

☙ *Awaiting the Messiah (ii)*

Reb Moshe of Rozvidov, the son of Reb Eliezer of Dzikov, was once talking of the Messiah in the company of a group of his chassidim. They came to discuss the different dates, or *kitzim*, which had been calculated by various tzaddikim as the times when — out of all the years remaining until the six thousand years allotted to this world elapse — the Messiah is most likely to come.

"Believe me, my brothers," he said, "that even if the nine hundred and ninety-ninth year of the sixth thousand comes around and we reach sunset of the last day of that year, right before the last minute, and the Messiah has not yet come — I will not despair, God forbid. I will confidently await his coming."

☙ *Awaiting the Messiah (iii)*

Reb Yaakov Yitzchak, the Chozeh (or Seer) of Lublin, discussing these same learned calculators of the date of the Messiah's arrival, once said that even though their predictions — always somehow connected with a verse from the Torah — proved to be unfounded, their intentions may be understood, and condoned.

"The law," he explained, "prescribes that if a son observes that his father conducts himself in a manner which is contrary to the Torah, he is not allowed — because of the obligation to honor one's parents — to say so outright. Instead, he is advised to show him the law, saying: 'Father, thus is it written in the Torah.' Now certain tzaddikim would like to get the message across to our Father that in their opinion it is time for Him to have compassion on His children, and to bring about the Messianic Redemption. How do they go about it? They calculate some date or another, connect it to some verse in the Torah that speaks of the Redemption, and thus hint to the Almighty: 'Father, thus is it written in the Torah...' "

◆§ An Accomplishment

מִידֵי אֲבִיר יַעֲקֹב
From the hands of the Mighty One of Yaakov (49:24)

From the hands of the Mighty One of Yaakov: At that moment Yosef saw in his mind's eye the countenance of his father Yaakov *(Rashi).*

When Reb Yisrael, the Maggid of Koznitz, was once visiting Apta, the townsfolk requested of him to preach in the synagogue on *Shabbos.* He refused, saying: "Did I accomplish anything by last year's sermon?"

Sorely disappointed, they left him, and as word spread of his sharp reply, all of Apta was distressed.

Then an artisan, one of the common folk, called on the Maggid and said: "Rebbe, you said that you accomplished nothing by your sermon last year. Now let me tell you the truth. Last year I heard you say that every Jew has to practice what it says in the Book of *Psalms:* 'I have set God always before me.' Well, since then the Name of God is constantly before my eyes, like black fire written on white fire, and I tremble in awe of it."

"Very well," said the Maggid, "I'll go along on *Shabbos* and preach."

And so he did, succeeding in penetrating the hearts of many who had strayed from the path.

◆§ Equanimity

וַיַּרְא מְנֻחָה כִּי טוֹב
He saw that rest was good (49:15)

Reb Yitzchak of Vorki, who when a young man was wealthy, used to journey to Reb Yitzchak, the Chozeh (or Seer) of Lublin.

On one such visit the Chozeh said: "If a reasonable

opportunity were to come up for taking a job as a schoolmaster, it would be a good idea to take it."

Reb Yitzchak was certain that the Chozeh had erred and in fact had in mind some other person: why should a propertied man like himself be interested in the meager stipend of a *melamed?* Out of respect, of course, he kept his thoughts to himself, and, after taking his leave, entered the rebbe's *beis midrash.*

A moment later a villager from near Ternigrad called on the Chozeh and wept bitterly. His sons were growing up to be coarse because they lacked a good schoolmaster. He was prepared to pay whatever was requested, so long as he had a conscientious teacher for his boys.

"If you can pay forty gold rubles," said the Seer, "then I would suggest that you hire the young man who left this room just now, and your sons, God willing, will do well in their studies."

The villager went out, found Reb Yitzchak, and told him that he would be agreeable to paying the sum the rebbe had stipulated, provided that he would travel back with him at once. Reb Yitzchak was now convinced that the rebbe had not erred and had really meant himself. What he still did not understand was what had prompted the Chozeh to make a schoolmaster out of him. Nevertheless he accepted the rebbe's orders without a second thought, and off he went. Before leaving Lublin, he managed to write to his wife, explaining why he was not yet returning home. After several days he received her reply: he had acted wisely in accepting this modest appointment, because the French, who were then at war with Russia, had marched through their town, and had plundered all their property. Even their fodder was gone.

Reb Yitzchak now began to teach *Chumash* to the villager's sons. Their minds were not active, though, and they grasped not a word. Sorely vexed, he journeyed to Lublin, and told the Chozeh of his difficulties.

"Pray for them," advised the Chozeh.

This he did, and from then on, saw steady progress in his work.

Now, in the village, there was a regular *minyan* of ten men, and it once happened that one of them refused to join the others in prayer because of grievance he had against one of them. One of the other villagers commented: "The Torah says, 'And he saw that rest was good..., and bowed his shoulder to bear.' This suggests that if a man understands that tranquility is a good thing, then he is willing to bear anything, because whoever bears all the vicissitudes of life with equanimity and is never angry at another — has peace."

When the period of his employment came to an end, the villager asked him to stay on, but Reb Yitzchak said: "Since I came here only because of my rebbe's orders, I must ask him about continuing here."

Once in Lublin, he was told by his rebbe that he no longer had to be a *melamed*. The Chozeh added: "Tell me, did you perhaps hear some quotable insight on the Torah out there in the village?"

Receiving no reply, the Chozeh asked again: "Is it possible that in half a year there, you heard nothing?"

Reb Yitzchak then recalled the villager's observation on patience and peace. He repeated it to the rebbe, who said: "If so, then you've heard a great deal."

❀ ❀ ❀

When, after many years, Reb Yitzchak became a renowned rebbe, he recounted this incident, and concluded: "Soon after this happened, I became wealthy once again, and gave away the stipend which I had earned as a *melamed*. As to the observation of that villager on peace and patience — why, I'm still working on it today."

◆§ *Self-Control*

וַיַּעַשׂ לְאָבִיו אֵבֶל
And he mourned his father (50:10)

One Friday in the year 1798, Reb Asher of Pshedborz passed away. Among those who came to his town for the funeral was of course his son, Reb Yaakov Yitzchak of Pshischah, who is better known as the Yid HaKadosh. Since the funeral took place just before sunset, he remained in Pshedborz for *Shabbos*. The whole town was of course eager to honor such a prominent guest, and the *tish* that he conducted at each of the meals that day was attended by all the scholars and chassidim of the community. To their astonishment,

HaYehudi bore himself on that *Shabbos* — only one day after his father's passing — exactly as on every other *Shabbos* throughout the year. The joy of the holy day made his face radiant as he delivered his learned discourses, and he altogether maintained the dignified stance of a rebbe at his own *tish,* as if nothing whatever had happened. This disturbed the local people. Could the great man not have spared a thought for the passing of his own father? Be that as it may, for the Third Meal of *Shabbos,* at twilight, all the chassidim were there again, and the visiting rebbe's joy was still buoyant.

Night fell, someone recited *Havdalah,* separating the holy day from the weekdays, and *Shabbos* came to a close. As the chassidim began, as always, to quietly sing the *HaMavdil* hymn, the Yid HaKadosh fell off his chair, tore his hair, and was overcome by paroxysms of grief. For hours he lay prostrate on the floor, wailing and sobbing, and no words of consolation could calm him.

Only then did the people of Pshedborz realize what stuff he was made of.

☙ No Hard Feelings

לוּ יִשְׂטְמֵנוּ יוֹסֵף
What if Yosef will hate us? (50:15)

Soon after Reb Menachem Mendel succeeded his father Reb Yitzchak as rebbe of Vorki, he sensed that many of those with whom he had been on friendly terms during his father's lifetime had now taken offense because they were no longer able to call on him when they felt so inclined. Instead, they were now obliged to wait for an appointment, and this had to be arranged through a *gabbai,* as is customary with every rebbe.

He therefore called these disgruntled folk together, and spoke to them as follows: "It is written, "And the brothers of Yosef saw that their father had died, and they said, 'What if Yosef will hate us?'" ' Rashi explains their apprehension by saying that 'they had been accustomed to dining at his table, and he had spoken affectionately to them, but since his father Yaakov had died, he no longer showed them these marks of friendship.' Now the question is, Why in fact did he not show them such marks of kinship? And the answer is simple. When the Patriarch Yaakov was alive, he was the rebbe, and when he passed away, Yosef became rebbe. So he closed his door a little, as people in positions of leadership have to do. And his brothers thought that he did so out of hatred, God forbid ... "

◈ A Generation Goes, a Generation Comes

גַּם בְּנֵי מָכִיר בֶּן־מְנַשֶּׁה
Also the children of Machir the son of Menashe (50:23)

Every Channukah Reb Yitzchak Meir of Ger (the author of *Chiddushei HaRim)* would give his grandchildren the pocket money customary on that occasion, which is known as Channukah *gelt.* One year after they had all had their turns and left the room, he told one of them, Reb Shimon Chaim, to call in his older brother, Reb Yehudah Leib, who was later to write *Sfas Emes.* (These brothers were the sons of Reb Avraham Mordechai, who passed away during the lifetime of his father, Reb Yitzchak Meir.) Reb Shimon Chaim called his older brother, and remained standing near the open door to see what he would receive. He heard his grandfather asking: "What would you like me to give you for Channukah *gelt?*"

Came the answer: "What need have I for money?"

"But," rejoined his grandfather, "you do need a son, so let that be your Channukah *gelt*" — for some years had passed since his marriage and no son had yet been born.

And so it was. His wife conceived soon after, but became exceedingly weak, and the doctors warned that she would be in great danger if she did not undergo surgery to abort the fetus. When Reb Yitzchak Meir heard this from his *rebbitzin,* he was displeased that they had consulted doctors.

"I have promised him a son, and, God willing, that is what he will have. Was all my toil in vain?"

He left instructions that doctors should not be consulted further, and again promised that the Almighty would certainly help her, and that she would give birth to a lively male child.

When the time came, she had an exceedingly difficult labor, and the midwife maintained that the lives of both mother and child were in jeopardy if a doctor was not summoned at once. Reb Yitzchak Meir was told of this, and answered that the young woman would give birth to a son, God willing, without the help of doctors. Difficulties continued for two days, and on the third morning, the risks were serious. The old *rebbitzin* and the young woman's mother hastened together to the study of Reb Yitzchak Meir, weeping bitterly, for the midwife had now despaired, God forbid. The rebbe answered that he would not begin his morning prayers until salvation came. After a short while, one of his granddaughters entered his study.

"*Mazel Tov!*" she cried. "It's a girl!"

The rebbe answered: "No! That is not true!"

Moments later word came that the young woman had safely delivered a boy. (This infant grew up to be the Gerer Rebbe who passed away in Jerusalem in 1948.) Reb Yitzchak Meir now said *Mazel Tov*, and began his morning prayers. Immediately thereafter he sat down to write a letter (which is extant) to his *mechutan* Reb Yudel, the father of the young mother. It opens as follows: "With the help of the Almighty, your daughter just now gave birth to a boy — *Mazel Tov!* — after several miracles and acts of lovingkindness on the part of the Almighty. Blessed be He Who is good, and Who does good."

The circumcision was celebrated with due pomp and festivity and the great-grandfather radiated joy and high spirits, gracing the occasion with a wealth of Torah discourses and chassidic insights.

In the course of the festive meal, he said: "Thank God, that I have seen fulfilled in my life the words of the Torah, 'Also the children of Machir the son of Menashe were born on the knees of Yosef.' "

One of the venerable guests, Reb Pinchas Eliyahu of Piltz, rejoined: "The Aramaic translation understands this phrase to mean that Yosef *brought up* his great-grandchildren ... "

The tzaddik heaved a long, deep sigh.

And not in vain. For only a few weeks after this celebration, Reb Yitzchak Meir of Ger passed away.

ספר שמות

exodus

סדר שמות
Sidra Sh'mos

◆§ *Data Processing*

וְאֵלֶּה שְׁמוֹת בְּנֵי יִשְׂרָאֵל
And these are the names of the Children of Israel (1:1)

According to established custom, a chassid once handed Reb Shlomo of Radomsk a *kvitl,* a note bearing his name and his mother's name, with the request that the tzaddik remember him in his prayers.

"On my way here," he told the rebbe, "I met an acquaintance of mine, who asked me to request that you intercede in prayer on behalf of a certain sick person who stands in need of the mercies of heaven. He told me the man's name and the name of his mother, but in my haste I forgot them both. No matter how hard I try, I simply cannot recall them."

"But if you don't know the names, how can I pray for the ailing man?" asked the tzaddik.

The chassid was silent. The tzaddik too was silent for a few moments, then he said: "Perhaps the sick man's name is such and such?"

"Yes, indeed, rebbe!" the chasid exclaimed.

"And is his mother's name perchance so and so?" asked the rebbe.

"Why, of course!" the chassid recalled, overwhelmed.

All those who were present were astounded at the divine inspiration which graced their rebbe. Perceiving their astonishment, he said: "Do you know from where I know the names of the sick man and his mother? We have a *Chumash,* the Book of *Exodus,* which opens with the words: 'And these are the names of the Children of Israel.' There are to be found all the names of the Children of Israel, and amongst them I found the names of the sick man and his mother."

◆§ Still Waters Run Deep

וַיָּמָת יוֹסֵף וְכָל אֶחָיו
And Yosef and all his brothers died (1:6)

Every day during the last half year of his life, Reb Menachem Mendel of Lubavitch (who is known as the Tzemach Tzedek) used to open up a volume of *Midrash Rabbah,* and read out a certain passage to his son, Reb Shmuel, who was later to succeed him as rebbe in Lubavitch. The passage runs as follows: "'And Yosef and all his brothers died, and all that generation' — though Yosef and his brothers died, their God did not die."

At the time Reb Shmuel would show no sign of melancholy; if anything, his face sought as if to smile. But after each day's reading he would retire to his home, and there give vent to his mounting grief.

◆§ The World has a Plan

הַאֵלֵךְ וְקָרָאתִי לָךְ אִשָּׁה מֵינֶקֶת מִן הָעִבְרִיֹּת
Shall I go and call you a nursing mother from among the Hebrew women? (2:7)

From among the Hebrew women: For Pharaoh's daughter had taken the infant to many Egyptian women, but he would not suck *(Rashi).*

The following story was told by Reb Chaim of Kosov.

A childless woman once visited the Baal Shem Tov, and with bitter tears begged him to bless her. The tzaddik assured her that the same year she would bear a son. Soon after her arrival home she became pregnant, and nine months later gave birth to an unusually beautiful baby boy. When he was two years old she brought him to the Baal Shem Tov in order to receive his blessing before he was weaned. As they entered, the tzaddik told his beadle to take the baby from his mother and pass it to him. The tzaddik hugged and kissed him, and told the beadle to return him to his mother's arms. They set out homeward, and on their arrival the child died.

Griefstricken, the woman decided to return and to confront the Baal Shem Tov, and in the bitterness of her heart cried out: "You killed my boy!"

"Weep not," said the Baal Shem Tov, "and listen carefully to what I shall tell you."

"A king who was childless once confided in his veteran adviser: 'You are my counselor on all subjects, even on military strategy. Can you not advise me on this predicament of mine, in which I do not even know who will be heir to my kingdom?'

" 'No one can help you in this,' said the adviser, 'except for the Jews.'

" 'Very well,' replied the king. 'If the Jews help me, I will free them of all their taxes and tributes.'

" 'That will not help you at all,' said the adviser. 'Instead, issue a decree compelling all the Jews in your kingdom to pray to the Almighty that you beget a son this year; if they are unsuccessful, there will be neither sight nor sound of any Jew here thereafter.'

"The king accordingly issued such a decree, and threatened that he would expel every Jew, man and woman, young and old, from his land. Terror seized his hapless Jewish subjects. They fasted, recited *Psalms*, and implored the Almighty that He save them in their distress — and their outcry reached the heavens.

"Now a certain lofty soul in heaven heard this outcry, and hastened to the Throne of Mercy, and spoke as follows: 'I am willing to be sent down to the world below. *I* will be the king's son, and thereby save the people of Israel from peril.'

"And that is exactly what happened. The queen soon became pregnant, and within the year gave birth to a son. The joy of the Jews was boundless.

"When the child was weaned he was introduced to the world of books, and so intelligent was he that he grasped every idea clearly at its first explanation. As he grew up he mastered more and more fields of knowledge, until one day he told his father: 'None of my studies have yet given me pleasure. I yearn to study something in which I can delight!'

" 'If so,' replied his father, 'I will ask the most senior ecclesiastic in my realm to teach you. Learning from him will surely give you pleasure.'

"He thereupon summoned the priest, and asked him to tutor his only son. The priest answered: 'I am of course obliged to fulfill my king's commands, but I have one solitary request. Since I spend two hours every day in solitude — that is when I ascend to heaven — and since the life any mortal who visits me during that time stands forfeit, I would ask you to forbid your son to enter my study at that time.'

"The king undertook to oblige, and within a short period the brilliant young prince was expert in all the subjects that the cleric taught him. Only one thing bothered him: why should he not see for himself exactly what his tutor did during those two mysterious hours? He made himself a set of keys to the study, waited impatiently for the daily period of solitude, opened the door — and to his amazement found the priest sitting in *tallis* and *tefillin*, studying the Talmud! Finding himself taken by surprise, the priest almost fainted from fear, but the young prince solemnly promised that he would divulge to no one the dread secret that he had uncovered.

" 'Now,' said the tutor, 'I will begin to teach you the Torah. Here at last you will be able to relish a study that is sweeter than honey.'

"And indeed, as the young man thirstily drank the waters of the Torah, he sensed that he had finally lighted upon the elixir of life.

"One day he asked the clandestine Jew: 'Tell me, please, why do you deceive everyone?'

" 'Most of my years have passed,' answered the other, 'and I am obliged to remain in my present situation as long as I live.'

" 'Advise me, though,' begged the prince, 'how to convert to the faith of Abraham, for I want to be a Jew; but you know that my father cannot bear to live even a single day without seeing me.'

" 'Then explain to your father,' said the tutor, 'that he asked for a son in order that he should have an heir for the throne. And since you have not yet seen any part of the country, you would like to travel about, and meet the governors of the various provinces. This will not be feasible because you will miss each other so sorely. You therefore propose that for the space of a month you accustom yourselves to meeting only at intervals, and thereafter you will be able to travel throughout the length and breadth of the country.'

"The prince echoed these words when speaking to his

father, who accepted the plan. When a month had passed, the young man set out to visit the cities throughout his father's kingdom, but when the border came within sight he told the driver of his carriage that he could go home, because he would be spending quite some time at the place at which they had arrived. As soon as the coachman had taken his leave, the prince crossed the border, and soon after converted to Judaism. He settled in a certain town, and spent all his days in the House of Study, meditating on the words of the Torah. He lived on the money which he had brought with him from his former home as he studied on, year after year, until he died.

"When his soul ascended to the World Above, the prosecuting angels could not find a single count on which to accuse him. What *could* one say about a soul so lofty that its very descent to This World was born of self-sacrifice for the sake of the Jewish people who were then in peril, about a soul that had spurned a royal crown in order to convert to the faith of Abraham?

"One prosecuting angel nevertheless did open his mouth: 'But for the first two years of his life he was nursed by a non-Jewess!'

"Whereupon the Heavenly Court issued its verdict that this soul must descend to This World once more, and in its new incarnation be nursed by a Jewess for two years..."

The Baal Shem Tov concluded telling his story to the woman who stood before him: "Why should it grieve you, then, that for the space of two years you were found worthy of nursing such a lofty soul?"

◆§ *Why Reb Meir Became a Chassid*

זֶה שְׁמִי לְעֹלָם
This is My Name for ever (3:15)

I am not called by My Name as it is written *(Talmud, Tractate Pesachim).*

At the very height of the war waged against Chassidism, the celebrated Reb Meir Raphaels — one of the elected leaders in rotation *(parnas hachodesh)* of the Jewish community of Vilna, undisputed headquarters of the opposition to "the Sect" — became an enthusiastic disciple of Reb Shneur Zalman of Liadi, the author of *Tanya.* The two stories that explain this change of heart were once told at a chasidic gathering by Reb Shalom Ber of Lubavitch.

In a certain township there lived a chassid, whose daughter was deserted by her husband. When three years had passed and the poor *agunah* had not heard any word of her husband, she set out with her father to seek words of counsel and blessing from Reb Shneur Zalman of Liadi. The rebbe instructed them to travel to Vilna, and to ask the *parnas hachodesh* there to find the missing man.

His chassidim acted on this instruction as on a divine command. In a flash, those who knew the unfortunate family got together the fare which the young woman would need to take her the long distance to Vilna, and made it clear to her that when she arrived at the home of the *parnas,* she was to demand of him insistently that he find her husband. They warned her moreover that even if he would drive her out of his house, abuse her, curse her, or even beat her, she should bear it all quietly, and on no account give him rest until he found her husband for, since the rebbe directed her to him, there was no doubt as to how things would work out.

After a long and tortuous journey, the woman dutifully called at the prosperous home of Reb Meir Raphaels. Since he was at the synagogue just then, she told her story to the lady of the house, who found it an occasion for mirth: how on earth was her husband expected to know the whereabouts of some young gentleman who three years earlier had run away from his wife in some unheard-of little hamlet far removed from Vilna? And when Reb Meir came home, his wife gave it as her opinion that the current persecution of "the sect" was fully justified, for their antics were incredible. Right now they had dispatched some poor unfortunate woman from a remote village with the request that she be given her husband. The *agunah,* undeterred, told Reb Meir in plain terms that she would not budge until she had located her man. The rich man and his wife persisted in explaining to her how absurd her request was — but to no avail. Finally, realizing that she would not be shaken off lightly, Reb Meir said: "Obviously one cannot find your husband in one day. I would suggest therefore that you take up temporary lodgings in the community *hekdesh,* and we'll see how things work out."

The woman took his advice, but he was still far from free of her, for day after day she would come to him, weeping and wailing: "Give me my husband!"

A morsel of gossip like this is not easily foregone. Sure enough, once Reb Meir had passed on to his fellow worshipers the choice details of this latest instance of the inanity of the chassidim, the case of the *agunah* became a favorite conversation piece among the local *misnagdim,* and added fuel to the raging opposition to "the sect."

Not long after, Reb Meir was summoned to the Vilna police station. From time to time groups of convicts without identification papers were brought to the city; Reb Meir would be called in to identify whomever he could, and they would be released. This time, as the prisoners in turn called out their names and places of birth, one of them called out the name of the *agunah's* hometown. As if struck by a thunderbolt, Reb Meir hastened home, pausing only to ask the police officers to wait till he returned. He sent for the *agunah,* cross-examined her as to all possible means of identifying her husband, and sure enough her description seemed to match that prisoner perfectly. She accompanied the *parnas* to the police station, and there recognized her husband at once. Through the good offices of Reb Meir he was released and, in the study of a local rabbi, he finally freed his wife of the marriage bond by handing her a *get,* a bill of divorce.

From that day on, something changed in the attitude of Reb Meir to "the sect": things could not possibly be like they were described here in Vilna. Not that he had developed an unequivocal stand on the issue. After all, this little incident could have been a fortunate coincidence. In the meantime, Reb Meir decided to tell no one of what had happened, pending some future development that might hopefully shed more light on the chassidim and their rebbe.

Now one day a poor man who lived in the Vilna region, a scholar and a chassid, passed through Vilna on foot on his way to visit Reb Shneur Zalman at Liozna. He entered one of the synagogues, took down a large volume of the Talmud, and was soon deep in study. It was Thursday evening, and the wayfarer had decided to spend *Shabbos* in Vilna. The *shammes* sensed that this was no common vagabond. Asking for no alms, he contented himself with the piece of herring and coarse bread that he took out of his pack, and returned to his studies, continuing diligently all night long. On Friday morning the *shammes* asked him where he planned to spend *Shabbos*. When he was told: "Here, in *shul*," the *shammes* said: "Look, in our city we have any number of well-to-do householders who fulfill the mitzvah of hospitality with all their hearts — especially if the guest is a scholar. Why then should you not fulfill the mitzvah of enjoying *Shabbos*, instead of roughing it here in *shul* and making do with coarse bread and herring?"

The guest replied that he would prefer not to go to anyone's house for *Shabbos*; he had his own provisions.

The *shammes* repeated this conversation to a certain learned and wealthy householder who always made a point of gracing his *Shabbos* table with a guest. Hearing that the stranger was a scholar and had refused to accept any invitation, he asked the *rav* of that *shul* to join him in his efforts to persuade the independent stranger to change his mind. In response to their concerted efforts the chassid finally accepted the invitation, provided that he would be able at least to sleep in *shul*.

At the Friday evening meal the table talk was so rich in Torah discussion that the host thanked the Almighty for having brought his way a guest who was a sage and a man of stature. Before the Grace after Meals, however, he uttered a deep sigh, but with no syllable of explanation. His guest wondered at it, but asked no questions. He simply returned to the *beis midrash* after the meal, and resumed his studies. The midday meal was again occupied by lively debate on Talmudic subjects, and again there was a deep, silent sigh before the Grace after Meals. The same story repeated itself at *Seudah Shlishis*, and later in the evening, at *Melaveh Malkah* once more.

By now the guest was more than curious, and he gently asked his host to explain what lay behind those sighs.

The householder told him that he was in serious trouble, for someone had trumped up a slanderous story about himself and his partner, and the local court had sentenced them to three years' exile in Siberia. Their appeal to the regional court was quashed, and the verdict confirmed. The matter was soon to be reopened, for the last time, at St. Petersburg, and heaven alone knew what the outcome would be.

Hearing these words, the guest said: "I have something confidential to tell you. Could we perhaps speak for a moment in private?"

When the door was closed, the guest said: "My advice to you is that you set out at once to Liozna, and ask the rebbe to advise you and to give you his blessing. I am the least worthy of the company of his disciples, and I am headed there myself. Without any doubt you will be helped out of your predicament."

"On a matter such as this I must consult my partner," said the host. "I will call for him at once, and we'll talk it over."

When he was told of the guest's advice, the partner said: "I fear that not only will we find no relief over there, but we will get ourselves into new trouble over here. All that our townsmen have to hear is that we've got ourselves involved in 'the sect' and we'll be persecuted to the bitter end."

They debated the proposal back and forth, and in the end decided to take the advice of Reb Meir Raphaels, who was a friend of them both. Before they gave him any inkling of what they were about to ask, they made him promise solemnly that no matter what the outcome of their discussion, he would treat it in absolute confidence. Reb Meir listened to their query and, with the story of the *agunah* still fresh in his mind, advised them without hesitation: "I agree that you should journey to Liozna."

Losing no time, the partners harnessed their horses, and took their guest with them in their carriage straight to Liozna. Arrived there, they told Reb Shneur Zalman all the details of their woes.

The rebbe said: "Now you are men of some learning. Tell me, then, the meaning of the following Talmudic dictum: מַלְכוּתָא דְאַרְעָה כְּעֵין מַלְכוּתָא דִרְקִיעָא ('The worldly kingdom resembles the heavenly kingdom')."

The partners stood in silence.

"Then I will give you the explanation," resumed the rebbe. "On the verse זֶה שְּׁמִי לְעֹלָם ('This is My Name forever'), the Talmud writes: 'I am not called by My Name as it is written; the first two letters of My written Name are *yud* and *hei*, while the first two letters of the Name by which I am called are *aleph* and *daled.*' Thus the Almighty is not called by His personal Name, as it were. And the same applies to earthly monarchs, who are addressed not by their personal names, but as 'czar'."

With this the rebbe sent them on their way, without having as much as mentioned the matter which had brought them to Liozna.

As they left his room and harnessed their horses, they abandoned once and for all whatever happy illusions they might have harbored about this rebbe and his chassidim and this wayfaring guest — the whole crew. They drove back to Vilna disappointed, and told Reb Meir that this chassidic rebbe was simply not quite normal. He did not even speak to the point.

Told what the rebbe had said, Reb Meir was forced to the same conclusion: he was nothing more nor less than a confused equivocator. The story of the *agunah* must have been a coincidence, after all.

As the months passed, the date for the trial in the Senate at St. Petersburg drew near. No matter how many lawyers they consulted in the capital, things still looked grim; in fact, well nigh hopeless. One advocate recommended that they fall at the feet of the minister of justice and beg him for mercy. He might perchance grant them remission. After inquiring on all sides, they established that it was his habit to take a daily constitutional at a fixed hour in the municipal gardens. They spoke to the guard there, bribed him handsomely in order that he should admit them before the arrival of the minister, and arranged that he should give them some signal so that they should know just who he was.

Now on the day that they were duly admitted to the park, the minister of justice was indisposed and stayed at home. The minister of education, however, happened to be there for a stroll, and the guard approached him to see whether he could be of any service. Fearing that the two Jews might mistake this dignitary for the minister of justice, the guard attempted to signal to them that this was not their man. The Jews understood this instead to be the sign for which they had been waiting so anxiously. They hastened across the park, fell at the feet of the wrong minister, launched into an account of their miserable lot, and pleaded for his help.

"Gentlemen," said the minister, "I am afraid that you have made a little mistake. Your case obviously falls within the domain of my colleague, the minister of justice; I am the minister of education."

Downhearted and disappointed, the two Jews left the park. A few minutes later, however, the minister said to the guard: "Run along and bring back those two Jews who were here a moment ago."

The poor fellow was alarmed. Perhaps the minister wanted them back in order to have them testify against him for having admitted them illegally to the gardens? But there was no way out. He ran off, caught up with them, and passed on the minister's request. They of course shared the guard's fear, but reported back at once to the minister, who addressed them as follows: "I can tell from your faces that you are learned Jews. Now a few days ago the czar asked me a certain question. If you can provide me with an answer that I find satisfactory, I will pass it on in your names to the czar, and at the same opportunity I will request him to give the order to cancel your hearing in the Senate. And here is the question. The following is written in your Talmud: 'The worldly kingdom resembles the heavenly kingdom.' His Majesty found it difficult to grasp in what way the earthly kingdom could be said to resemble the kingdom of heaven. I was unable to enlighten him. Perhaps you have an answer?"

Their hearts surging with relief and amazement, the two partners now well understood the intent of the rebbe's cryptic answer so many months earlier in Liozna. They promptly gave him the interpretation they had then heard, and the minister was well pleased with it, promising to do as he had undertaken. He was as good as his word, and at his next meeting with the czar related all the circumstances in which he had come by this answer. Seeing how well received it was, the minister proceeded to tell the czar of their plight, stressing that there was only one man who could save them — and the czar issued the appropriate decree to the Senate. With happy hearts they drove quickly back to Vilna, and before even going home they went straight to the house of Reb Meir Raphaels and told him all that had befallen them.

As for Reb Meir, he lost no time, set out for Liozna, cleaved with all his soul to Reb Shneur Zalman of Liadi, and became a chassid of repute.

◈§ *A Gift of Speech*

מִי שָׂם פֶּה לָאָדָם
Who makes a man's mouth? *(4:11)*

Reb Dov Ze'ev of Kazivnikov is remembered among chassidim for his surpassing articulateness, for when expounding the philosophical system of Chabad Chassidism he would enchant his listeners with the richness of his language. But this litheness of tongue was no inborn talent: it was granted him through the blessing that chassid received from Reb Menachem Mendel of Lubavitch. And this is how it came about.

Reb Dov Ze'ev was born and brought up in a little township in the district of Chernigov, and the learned chassidim amongst whom he lived instilled in him the ideal that a chassid should be constantly dedicated to seeking the welfare of others. By the age of twelve he had mastered an impressive proportion of the Talmud and was familiar with much of the *aggadah* written by the Sages.

In his township there lived a number of simple folk who were so ignorant that they could not even make out the meaning of the most basic Hebrew texts. The young lad felt so sorry for them that he began to explain to them the contents of the daily prayer book, and to relate to them the *aggados* that he had read in the Talmud and Midrash. This went on for a few years, though with great difficulty, for he suffered from a speech impediment which grew worse with time. When he was seventeen years old he journeyed to Lubavitch, and when he was admitted to *yechidus* told Reb Menachem Mendel of the lessons he gave the ignorant yokels at home, adding that his stammer made this difficult for him.

The rebbe pondered a little while, and said: "Continue teaching the simple folk, and the Almighty will give you a capacity for clear and fluent explanation."

The moment he left the rebbe's room the young man could not recognize himself: he began to talk fluently, and found it a novel experience. On his return home, he repeated three entire discourses that he had heard from the rebbe, to the amazement of his listeners.

"I am the rebbe's *golem,*" he quipped. "The Maharal of Prague made a *golem* of clay, and the rebbe has made a *golem* of flesh."

◆§ *A Blessing in Disguise (i)*

כִּי מֵתוּ כָּל הָאֲנָשִׁים

For all the men are dead (4:19)

For all the men are dead: They have become impoverished, and a pauper is accounted as if dead *(Rashi).*

Not being able to afford the wagon fare, Reb David of Lelov set out by foot to visit his rebbe,Reb Elimelech of Lyzhansk. As he trudged along the highway, he was overtaken by a carriage in which rode a chassid who was a well-known magnate from Warsaw. The coach slowed down, and when Reb David learned that it too was headed for Lyzhansk he asked its owner whether he could travel with him, and was told to climb up. The rich man took Reb David for a tramp, and made fun of him as they traveled, but the passenger uttered not a word. And so it was throughout the journey — the rich man spouted insults and laughed, and Reb David held his peace.

As soon as they arrived at Lyzhansk the rich man went straight in to speak with Reb Elimelech; Reb David preferred to spend a little time meditating and preparing himself spiritually for the encounter with his rebbe. When he finally entered, Reb Elimelech spent some two hours talking with him. Leaving the rebbe's study, he approached the rich man, and said: "You may as well take to the road, for I have yet to stay here for some time. One thing more. When on your way home you hear a voice screaming, follow that voice, and then you will know what you are to do."

Having seen that the rebbe had spoken with Reb David at such length, the rich man had already realized that his passenger was no ordinary person, and now that he heard these words he noted them well.

As he passed by a forest halfway home, he suddenly heard someone screaming out in Polish. Reb David's parting words came immediately to mind. Leaving the highway, he drove deep into the forest until he saw before him a nobleman in a carriage, which was sinking in the mire together with the struggling horses that were still harnessed to it. He tied one end of a thick rope to his own carriage, which he had left standing safely in a dry spot, and the other end to the carriage of the unfortunate stranger, jumped up on to the driver's seat, and whipped his horses into action. Within a few minutes the floundering carriage was drawn up into safety.

The nobleman had spent quite some time in the mire, and was now not only filthy but shivering from cold. The merchant covered him with a warm cloak and gave him food and drink until he felt better. Hearing that the nobleman was from Warsaw too, he offered to take him there in his carriage, and invited him to rest in his home until he had completely recovered. On their arrival he gave the nobleman a warm change of clothes, prepared him hot beverages and a square meal, and then allowed him to sleep off the effects of his ordeal. In the morning, a new man, the nobleman thanked his benefactor and left happily.

A few days later he called for the merchant and asked him: "What recompense can I offer you for all that you have done for me? For if you had not come along and saved me, I would either have drowned in that swamp, or perished of exhaustion."

"I am in need of no recompense," answered the merchant. "It suffices for me that I was able to save a man from death; that alone is my reward."

"Then at least give me your name and address," said the nobleman, "so that I will always be able to remember who my benefactor was."

And he made a note of these details in his diary.

Years went by, and the restless wheel of fortune came full circle. The wealthy merchant found himself so impoverished that he was forced to sell not only his business, but even his mansion, his precious furniture and his costly clothes, in order to provide himself with the most frugal necessities. When he had nothing left to sell, he was reduced to knocking on doors to beg for alms. He tramped from town to town and from village to village, living in this wretched condition for ten whole years, until he quite forgot that he had ever been rich. His long and luckless wanderings eventually brought him back to Warsaw. By now he felt no shame in his fallen estate even in his hometown, whether he was begging from door to door or stopping passers-by in the street.

One day he saw some dignitary riding past in a magnificent carriage. He approached it, as he was accustomed to do, removed his hat, bowed his head, and put out his hand in expectation of alms. The dignitary — who was nothing less than the governor of the Warsaw district — looked at him steadily, and said: "Jew, come here, please."

The poor fellow took fright, and ran away as fast as his weary legs would carry him. The governor told his valet to run after him, and to bring him back by force. When the Jew was duly stationed in front of him, the governor said: "Do not fear, I will do you no harm. I only want you to tell me your name."

This the frightened man did.

"Do you recognize me?" asked the governor.

"No," said the pauper.

"Then let me remind you," continued the other. "Do you recall that many years ago you saved the life of a certain nobleman in the forest outside Warsaw?"

"Yes, I remember, " said the pauper.

"Very well, then: I am that nobleman. I am the man you saved ... But tell me, what brought you to the sorry state you are in?"

The beggar told him all that he had gone through, and the governor promptly wrote him out a check for two thousand rubles.

The former merchant immediately opened a trading business, and Providence smiled upon his enterprises, so that before long he had attained the prosperity that had been his in happier days.

Now in the course of these years Reb Elimelech had passed away and had been succeeded by the celebrated Chozeh of Lublin, and Reb David of Lelov had likewise gained renown as a tzaddik and a leader of men. The merchant decided one day to visit Reb David, without knowing that this was the same penniless passenger whom he had insulted so many years earlier. But the tzaddik recognized him as soon as he stepped over his threshhold, and asked him to recount whatever had befallen him in the course of all those long years.

When he had listened to the merchant's account of all the vicissitudes of his life, Reb David said: "You should know that on the day that you insulted me, the Heavenly Court pronounced a death sentence upon you. Knowing of this verdict, I went in to see Reb Elimelech in order to see how we could have it annulled. We managed to arrange for a compromise — that you become impoverished, since a pauper is accounted as if dead, and your sin would thereby be expiated. However, since you did me a great favor by bringing me to Lyzhansk in your carriage, I made every effort to do you a favor in return — that after a period of ten years had elapsed your misfortunes would come to an end, and you would be restored to your former pedestal."

◆§ *A Blessing in Disguise (ii)*

For some reason things started going badly for a certain chassid, who fell from his prosperous estate and became a pauper. Since he had very wealthy relatives overseas, he consulted with Reb Yitzchak Meir of Ger as to whether he should travel to ask them for help so that he could start up some business with which to support himself. Since the tzaddik did not agree to this proposition, the chassid went on and asked: "Then shall I perhaps write to them and describe the straits I am in, so that they will send me a sum of money to keep me going. I know that they are generous, and I am after all a relative of theirs."

The rebbe answered: "I do not agree to this, either."

These were truly surprising answers. The man went home disappointed, and nothing in his financial situation improved. After some time he traveled once more to Ger, asked the same questions, and received the same answers — and then again, and again.

Things now became decidedly worse. His children asked for bread — but the house was empty, and his wife harassed him for having no pity on himself and his family, by not visiting his relatives. When he next journeyed to Ger he wept profusely as he told the tzaddik: "I see no alternative open to me apart from turning to my overseas relatives for help."

The rebbe answered: "What can I do? I have already given you my opinion."

But the man could restrain himself no longer. He wrote to his relatives, describing the situation in which he found himself, and his letter bore fruit: they sent him a handsome sum and things improved. This they repeated several times, without any further request from him, until he was quite out of his difficulties. But immediately thereafter he became dangerously ill, and his condition deteriorated from day to day until he was utterly bedridden. His distress was intensified by the fact that he was not even able to travel to Ger to offer his apologies, for he attributed his illness to his having ignored the rebbe's advice. The best he could do was to ask one of his friends to make the journey to Ger on his behalf. The friend hastened there, and told Reb Yitzchak Meir that the invalid stood in desperate need of divine mercies.

After a few moments of silence, the tzaddik said: "You see, when a sentence of death is passed on someone, it sometimes happens that the Heavenly Court finds a way of modifying its own verdict by substituting in its stead a measure of suffering. A pauper is reckoned as if dead, and through such a substitution this man could have lived on. But what can I do if he himself pushed away poverty? When his relatives relieved him of his difficulties, his life-force was cut off."

The friend hastened home, but the sick man was no longer alive.

A Cry from the Heart

וַיֹּאמֶר פַּרְעֹה מִי ה׳

And Pharaoh said: Who is Hashem? *(5:2)*

During a visit to Germany, on which he was accompanied by his son, Reb Avraham Moshe, Reb Simchah Bunem of Pshischah was accustomed to deliver discourses on Torah subjects at the *Shabbos* table for the edification of the local Jews who joined him in the festive meal. They were of course utterly unused to East European traditions of chassidic interpretation and style of delivery, and openly made fun of his discourses. Indignant, his son said: "Why should you address your *divrei Torah* to such freethinkers, such *apikorsim?*"

"There is nothing I can do about it, my son," was the reply, "for the moment I am aroused to speak *divrei Torah* I become quite oblivious to my surroundings. Next *Shabbos*, therefore, when you see that I am moved to deliver such a discourse, just give me a sign to remind me, and I will know that that is not the right time to speak."

The next *Shabbos* came round, and when Reb Avraham Moshe saw his father was about to deliver another learned discourse, he reminded him just where they were. Whereupon Reb Simchah Bunem countered: "It is only Pharaoh who may rightly be called an *apikores*, for when God smote him with the Ten Plagues he said, 'Who is the Lord that I should listen to his voice?' But these German Jews cannot possibly be called *apikorsim*, for if one of them has as much as a headache, his first reaction is to cry out *Shema Yisrael!*"

From the Mouths of Babes and Sucklings

לֹא עַתָּה יֵבוֹשׁ יַעֲקֹב ... כִּי בִרְאוֹתוֹ יְלָדָיו מַעֲשֵׂה יָדַי ... יַקְדִּישׁוּ שְׁמִי

Yaakov shall not now be confounded

Reb Shmuel of Lubavitch would often go driving in his carriage in the countryside. On his way he would always pass through a certain village near Lubavitch, though he never stopped off at the inn there which was owned by a Jew. On one occasion, though, he asked the driver to stop the carriage outside it, climbed down, and entered the inn, but found no one there apart from two small children.

"Where are your father and mother?" he asked them.

"They've gone about their business," they replied. "They'll probably be back soon."

"And where is your *melamed?*"

"Our tutor has gone off home," they said, "because now we have the Elul vacation."

"Tell me, what do you learn?"

"I learn *Chumash,*" said the older one.

"And I," said his younger brother, "can read *Psalms.*"

"Very well," said the rebbe, "Then let me test you. Could you bring me a copy of *Tehillim?*"

... when he sees his children, the work of My hands, ... sanctifying My Name (Haftarah)

They at once brought him the Book of *Psalms.* He opened it, and told them to read aloud, and as they read, he read along with them, word by word, and so on through a number of passages.

Meanwhile, on her way home, their mother was surprised to see the rebbe's carriage standing near the front entrance. She entered the house through the kitchen, from where she could hear the rebbe saying *Tehillim* with her children; she did not dare to join them. And as she listened to a strange sadness in the rebbe's voice, her heart was so moved and her spirit so troubled, that without quite knowing why, she broke into tears.

The rebbe closed the *Tehillim* and was about to leave. But when he reached the door he paused there for several minutes, then returned to the table and said: "Children, let us read some more *Tehillim.*"

So they opened the book again, and together read several more passages, as before. Finally, saying "*Shalom,*" he mounted his carriage and drove back to Lubavitch.

This incident left the lady of the house all astir, and she waited anxiously for her husband to come home so that she could tell him all about it.

But her husband was not to be seen. He had gone to a neighboring village to collect debts from a few peasants and was due home at some time in the afternoon — but as the hours dragged on and night fell, his wife and children began to fear the worst. At midnight they were alarmed by a sudden knocking on the shutters, and the terrified woman ran to open the door. Her husband took one step in, and fell to the floor in a swoon.

When he came to, he told them what had happened. He had come to the door of one of his creditors in the village, and was asked to accompany the householder to the barn, so that he could measure out a quantity of the newly harvested grain in payment of his debt, according to the custom of those times. As soon as they were both inside, the peasant closed the door from within, and told the Jew that he was about to kill him. At first the Jew took it to be some kind of a joke, since they had known each other for so long, but he became convinced soon enough that the peasant meant exactly what he said. He fell before his feet and begged for his life. "When I make up my mind," said the peasant, "I don't change it." And he hunted around the barn for his ax, but could not find it. Then he recalled that he had left it in his house, but being afraid that the Jew might escape while he went to fetch it, he took the reins that were hanging on a nail, tied him up tightly hand and foot, closed the door somehow with a stick, and headed for the house.

A moment later, the peasant's wife, who had been working in the fields, opened the barn door, and saw a Jew trussed up in ropes. He told her what had happened, and with tears of desperation pleaded with her to release him. This request threw the poor woman into confusion. "My husband doesn't pussyfoot," she said. "If he figures out that it was I that freed you, he'll kill me."

The Jew was not to be silenced. He begged and implored, and suggested that as soon as she had freed him she should return to the fields, and when she saw her husband leaving the house on his way back to the barn, she should come to meet him, as if she were coming in from the fields to the barn for the first time. Finally, finding herself unable to harden her heart to resist his appeals, she deftly untied his bonds and let him out of the barn, and quickly returned to the fields as he had advised. She advised him in return not to take the main road home, for then her husband, not finding him in the barn, would chase after him and kill him on the highway. Rather, let him hide for a few hours among the loose sheaves in the fields, and find his way home only when night fell.

From his hiding place he soon heard the peasant, panting and fuming, bolting from the direction of the barn in search of him. Terror overcame the poor innkeeper. The peasant, ax in hand, was right next to him. Death was a moment away. But the peasant did not see him through all the grass and sheaves, and after pacing up and down along the highway he saw that his quarry had disappeared, and stomped back to his house in a rage. Trembling all over, the Jew waited for night to fall. He freed himself noiselessly from the sheaves, and clambered through bushes and brambles, slowly, stealthily, until at midnight he finally reached home.

When his wife now told him of the rebbe's visit, they both understood what it was all about: during the first reading of *Tehillim* he had been saved from being killed in the barn, and during the second reading, from death among the sheaves.

סדר וארא

Sidra Va'eira

◆§ *A Time to Remain Silent*

הֵן בְּנֵי יִשְׂרָאֵל לֹא שָׁמְעוּ אֵלַי
The Children of Israel have not listened to me (6:12)

Reb Yisrael of Vizhnitz was in the habit of strolling with his *gabbai* for half an hour every evening. On one such occasion they reached the house of a certain wealthy bank manager who was a *maskil*, a follower of the "Enlightenment" movement — in a word, anything but a chassid of the tzaddik. Reb Yisrael knocked on the door, and when a servant opened it, entered the house. The *gabbai* did not begin to understand the reason for this unexpected visit but, without asking a word, followed the rebbe inside. The host received his distinguished guest with all the marks of respect and politeness dictated by such an occasion; the rebbe for his part took the seat that was offered him, and sat for quite some time without saying a word. Considering that it would be an impertinence to ask the rebbe directly for the purpose of his visit, the host whispered his question to the *gabbai*, but was made none the wiser. At length the rebbe offered him his farewells, and rose to leave. As a mark of respect, the host accompanied him in silence all the way to his home, but at the last minute, when he was about to leave, his understandable curiosity got the better of him, and he turned to the tzaddik: "Rebbe, pardon my question, but it would hardly have been proper for me to ask when we were in my home, so I am taking the liberty of asking now: why did you honor me with a visit?"

"I went to your house in order to fulfill a mitzvah," answered the rebbe, "and thank God I was able to fulfill it."

"Which mitzvah?" asked the bank manager.

The rebbe explained: "Our Sages teach that 'Just as it is a mitzvah to say that which will be heard, so is it a mitzvah not to say that which will not be listened to.' Now if I remain in my house and you remain in yours, what kind of a mitzvah is it that I refrain from telling you 'that which will not be listened to'? In order to fulfill the mitzvah properly, one obviously has to go to the house of the man who will not listen, and *there* refrain from speaking to him. And that is exactly what I did."

"Perhaps, rebbe," said the bank manager, "you would be so good as to tell me what this thing is? Who knows, perhaps I *will* listen?"

"I am afraid not," said the rebbe. "I am certain that you will not."

And the longer the rebbe refused, the greater grew the curiosity of the other to know his secret, and he continued to press him to reveal "that which would not be listened to."

"Very well," said the rebbe at length. "A certain penniless widow owes your bank quite a sum for the mortgage of her house. Within a few days your bank is going to dispose of her house by public sale, and she will be out on the street. I had wanted to ask you to overlook her debt, but didn't — because of that mitzvah of 'not saying.' "

"But how is such a thing possible?" asked the bank manager in amazement. "Surely you realize that the debt is not owed to me personally, but to the bank, and I am only its manager, not its proprietor, and the debt runs into several hundreds, and if so..."

The rebbe interrupted him: "It's exactly as I said all along — that you would not want to hear."

With that he ended the conversation and entered his house.

The bank manager also went home — but the rebbe's words found their way into his heart and gave him no rest, until he paid up the widow's debt out of his own pocket.

◆§ *Of Noble Descent, But of Nobler Ascent (i)*

אֵלֶּה רָאשֵׁי בֵית אֲבֹתָם
These are the heads of their fathers' houses (6:14)

When the Maggid of Mezritch was a child of five, his parents' home caught on fire and was razed to the ground. Seeing how grieved his mother was, he said: "And if the house did burn down, should one be so distressed?"

"God forbid!" answered the pious woman. "I am not distressed over the house, but over our family tree that was inside it, and was destroyed. Our lineage may be traced back to Rabbi Yochanan HaSandlar, the disciple of Rabbi Akiva."

"If so," replied the boy, "our pedigree will start again from me."

◆§ *Of Noble Descent, But of Nobler Ascent (ii)*

Reb Dov Ber of Lubavitch, the son of Reb Shneur Zalman of Liadi, was the son-in-law of a prominent householder who lived in Janowitz. Once, while still a very young man, he met one of the chassidim of his father during a visit there, and in the course of conversation made light of his friend's attainments, both in scholarship and in the service of the Creator.

The chassid retorted: "How do you compare yourself to me? Who is *your* father, and who is *my* father? Your father is our rebbe, and everyone knows what spiritual level he is at. When it was time to bring a soul down to

 This World — I mean, when you were conceived — his intentions were no doubt pure and noble, and he brought down a lofty soul; that is how *you* were born. Then as you grew up they watched you vigilantly from all sides, and so you became what you became. *What* an impressive achievement! But me — you can guess for yourself what my father's mind was concerned with. And as for my soul, he probably swiped it from the storehouse of souls up there. And after I was born, I grew up like an untamed goat. And now, in order to make a living, I supply the local *goyim* with the capital needed to buy grain during the sowing season, and then during winter make the rounds of the villages in order to collect my debts. This has to be done in a certain way. For a start, you have to equip yourself with a bottle of vodka for the road; and you have to travel by night, because in winter these peasants get up while it's still dark. When you finally reach your *goy's* cottage you have to start off by drinking *LeChaim* with him, because without that he won't even begin to talk business with you. And you mustn't forget to fill a glass for his good lady, either, or else the shrew is likely to ruin the whole deal. Then you get around to settling your accounts with him. And so you clatter off with your horse and wagon from house to house, until you've collected your debts from three or four *goyim*. At this point it's time to head for home, to go and dip in the *mikveh*, and to *davven* your morning devotions. So you can imagine what kind of praying one can muster...'

Now in point of fact this chassid served his Maker in prayer with all his might and with all his mind — though, being a humble man, he underestimated his own efforts considerably.

When the young Reb Dov Ber heard his words he was quite overwhelmed. He returned at once to his father in Liozna, and bemoaned his own spiritual attainments: it seemed to him now that his divine service was almost worthless.

And when the chassid from Janowitz next came to Liozna to visit Reb Shneur Zalman, the rebbe told him: "I am indeed indebted to you. You have made a chassid of my Berl!"

◆§ Of Noble Descent, But of Nobler Ascent (iii)

A mixed gathering of rabbis, chassidim and householders of all sorts once heard Reb Naftali of Ropshitz telling of his forefathers, who were sages and tzaddikim of world renown.

"I doubt if there is anyone in the world," he concluded, "who can compete with me as far as distinguished lineage is concerned, whether on my father's or my mother's side. And if there is such a one, I would very much like to meet him."

One of his chassidim, a chassid from Siebenbuergen, took up his challenge: "Rebbe, my genealogy is more distinguished than yours!"

When Reb Naftali asked him to trace his ancestry, the chassid replied: "My *yichus* is that I am the only one in my family who puts on *tefillin.*"

Well pleased with his answer, the rebbe laughed and said: "Gentlemen, our friend from Siebenbuergen is perfectly right. Allow me, though," he went on, being in jovial spirits, "to explain the difference between a person who has *yichus* and a person who is not of noble extraction. Suppose we have a tzaddik who is a great scholar, serving God with both love and awe, who rises at midnight to lament the darkness of the Exile, then makes his way to the *mikveh* to immerse himself for the sake of purity, then returns to study both the revealed and the esoteric treasures of the Torah until daybreak. At dawn, like the spiritual lover celebrated in the *Song of Songs,* his voice is roused and his spirit wakened to an eager flame as he prepares himself for worship — by singing psalms, studying *Mishnayos,* and giving alms. He now joins the congregation for communal prayer, and his soul cleaves to his Maker — devoutly, sweetly. Half the day has passed, and it is time to partake of something, but as he prepares to wash his hands before eating, he sighs bitterly: 'Very well, so I am about to do my body a favor. But what have I done for the good of my soul? What is the real worth of my Torah study and my level of worship?' But then he thinks it over, and consoles himself: 'After all, for the son of a simple man like my father was, it's not too bad' — and he is satisfied.

"But as for me — suppose now and again I happen to rise at midnight, and sometimes study a little Talmud and the legal codes, and perhaps a bit of Kabbalah, or occasionally recite a few psalms, and go off to prayers. Then, as I come home to eat something, I weigh my deeds, and realize that I have not yet done anything worthwhile towards revealing in This World the awesome unity of Him Who gives life to all Creation. To make matters worse, I bring to mind the memory of my saintly father, and my other pious forebears, and I ponder — in the words of our Sages — 'When will my deeds come to equal those of my forefathers?' This though humbles me no end, as I consider how worthless I really am.

"This, then, is the value of *yichus*."

◆§ *Of Noble Descent, But of Nobler Ascent (iv)*

A certain tzaddik, whose antecedents were neither high born nor well known, was accustomed to travel to visit Reb Shalom of Belz. On one such visit it seemed to him that Reb Shalom was giving himself airs of superiority because of his parentage, stemming as he did from a long line of Torah scholars. Sensing at once that his guest harbored a certain grudge toward him, Reb Shalom turned to him with a question: "Who in your opinion is more praiseworthy — a tzaddik who is born to an illustrious family, or one whose parents are simple, honest folk?"

The guest remained silent. Reb Shalom resumed: "Our Sages teach us that every man is obliged to ask himself, 'When will my deeds come to equal those of my forefathers?' Any man whose forebears were celebrated scholars is thereby made to be exceedingly humble of spirit, for he knows without a doubt that his deeds are still far from being comparable to the deeds of his forefathers. Not so him who stems from plainer stock. Such a one can even fall prey to conceit, for he tells himself: 'My deeds have already outshone the achievements of my forebears ...' "

It was now clear to the guest that the rebbe had read what was on his mind. And as the rebbe's *yichus* — far from making him supercilious, his distinguished lineage made him all the more humble.

☙ *Being Impressed by Oneself*

תְּנוּ לָכֶם מוֹפֵת *Show a miracle for yourselves (7:9)*

During the Polish rising against Czarist Russia, a squad of Polish soldiers seized a certain wealthy and respected chassid who lived near Radomsk, and prepared to sentence him to death for having allegedly refused to supply them with the grain and wine that they had demanded of him. His wife and relatives immediately called upon Reb Shlomo of Radomsk, who was renowned as a miracle worker, and told him, with much weeping and wailing, about the chassid who was a mere hairsbreadth away from death.

"There is no need for all this uproar," said Reb Shlomo. "The rebels will not kill him, and the whole episode will end up as no more than a matter of money."

He then told them to seek out the rebel chief and to address their entreaties to him.

Following the camp of the rebels, the relatives found their chief and begged him to spare the life of the prisoner. He received them cordially, and averred that a prisoner such as this, who had refused to provide his fighters with provisions, certainly deserved to be fined thirty thousand gold rubles. In a flash the relatives were off to fetch the required sum in cash, and in minutes they were back to ransom their loved one from certain death.

Their first thought thereafter was to bring the glad tidings to the rebbe: his blessing had been fulfilled. As the family arrived exultant, Reb Shlomo asked the freed man: "In what manner did they let you go?"

When he answered that he had paid a fine of thirty thousand gold rubles, the rebbe commented: "Is it right that they should take such a vast sum from you? No! You will not lose the money either. You will get it back."

All those who were present wondered at the rebbe's

 words. Everyone knew that the rebels never let out of their grasp anything they managed to lay hands on, and who would dare take such a fearsome adversary to court?

A long time passed, and the episode was almost forgotten by all concerned. In the meantime the Czarist regime had quashed the rebellion, and had taken all the loot that the Polish rabble had pillaged — including a bag loaded with thirty thousand gold rubles. A journal entry in the rebel camp informed them that this sum had been received from a certain individual in payment of a fine. They promptly summoned the former prisoner, and returned his money in full.

His friends recalled the assurance of their rebbe, and observed that every word of his had come true — clearly a miracle. They hastened to give him the good news, but when he heard their excited report, he answered angrily: "Away with you! What makes you come and confuse me with stories of miracles? Off you go! I don't want to hear any more of your miracle stories!"

One of the venerable chassidim who was present took the liberty a little later of turning to the tzaddik with a query: "Rebbe, pray enlighten us. Why did you now tell these chassidim so harshly that they should not retell the miracle? For the fact remains that something miraculous did take place. In the first instance you assured this man that he would lose his money but not his life, and that is exactly what happened; then you told him that he would even get his money back — from the very teeth of that pack of wolves — and this also came true. Is there no value in recounting incidents that show what tzaddikim are capable of doing? Why then scold the chassidim and drive them out?"

"Your question is in place," replied the rebbe, "but allow me to tell you a story of the Baal Shem Tov. The Baal Shem once earnestly requested one of his disciples to accept a rabbinical post. The disciple refused. The rebbe spoke to him as if in anger: 'Indeed! Here I am trying to set you up in an easy job, where you will be able to devote yourself to the study of Torah while occupying a position as a rabbi — and you're not interested?! This just goes to show that you don't take the obligation of

Torah study seriously' — and so he continued, with more words of severe reproach in the same vein. The disciple, however, did not swerve from his stance: 'No, I do not want to be a rabbi.' At this point the Baal Shem told him that he had only been putting him through a trial.

"So, too," continued Reb Shlomo, "heaven sometimes shows even great tzaddikim signs of greatness and miraculous exploits, with the intention of putting them to the test, of seeing whether it will make them proud, and cause them to grow lax in the service of their Maker. Even Moshe Rabbeinu was put through such a test. For when he interceded at Sinai for his People who had sinned in worshiping the Golden Calf, the Almighty spoke of destroying them, and said: וְאֶעֱשֶׂה אוֹתְךָ לְגוֹי גָּדוֹל — 'I will make you into a great nation.' Now had he agreed to accept this promise he would have perished, God forbid, for it was mentioned only to test him. He however withstood the test, and answered that if God would not forgive His People, מְחֵנִי נָא מִסִּפְרְךָ 'erase me, please, from Your book.'

"Who knows, then," concluded Reb Shlomo, "what is behind these miracles they are talking about? Perhaps they are brought about only as a test. Why should they make such a fuss about miracles?"

One of the grandsons of Reb Shlomo saw a hint of the same idea in the following verse: "When Pharaoh will speak to you, saying, 'Show a miracle *for yourselves,*' then shall you say to Aharon, 'Take your rod, and cast it before Pharaoh, and it will turn into a snake.' " Why, asked this grandson, does the verse say "for yourselves" (תְּנוּ לָכֶם מוֹפֵת)? The answer, he said, is that Pharaoh well knew that if Moshe and Aharon fell prey to pride they would not be able to redeem the Children of Israel. For the redemption of Israel can come only through a humbled heart. Thus we first find the verse וַיֵּאָנְחוּ בְנֵי יִשְׂרָאֵל מִן הָעֲבֹדָה וַיִּזְעָקוּ ("And the Children of Israel sighed because of the bondage, and they cried out"); and immediately thereafter we read וַתַּעַל שַׁוְעָתָם ("And their cry rose up"). Pharaoh, then, particularly wanted them to show a miracle, in order that they should thereby lose that humility on which the redemption of the Children of Israel depended. This explains why he said: "Show a miracle *for yourselves*" — his intention being that they themselves should be impressed by their miraculous powers.

The grandson of Reb Shlomo went further. This concept, he said, also explains why the Almighty specified that the staff should turn into a snake. This was to remind them subtly of the snake in the Garden of Eden, which endeavored to seduce Chavah to sin through falling into the pride that stems from having miraculous powers. His words to Chavah were וִהְיִיתֶם כֵּאלֹהִים ("Then you shall be like God"): you will be able to create worlds miraculously. Moshe and Aharon were therefore to turn the rod into a snake. This would bring to mind the danger of succumbing to pride through the gift of miraculous abilities.

◆§ *From the Humblest of Mouths*

וַיַּעֲלוּ הַצְפַרְדְּעִים
The frogs shall come up (7:29)

After the passing of Reb Dov Ber, the Maggid of Mezritch, a number of chassidim were sitting together, discussing the ways and habits of their late rebbe. One of that brotherhood, Reb Shneur Zalman of Liadi, posed a question: "Is anyone here able to explain why every morning at dawn our rebbe was accustomed to stroll near the lakes, where the frogs croak?"

Receiving no answer, he continued: "Then let me tell you what our rebbe's intention was in doing this. Do we not read in *Perek Shirah* how every particle of Creation, animate and inanimate, from the loftiest to the humblest, sings its own paean of praise to its Creator? Well, the frogs too have their own song, and the rebbe wanted to hear how these creatures praise their Maker."

◆§ *Otherworldly Help on a Worldly Level*

וּמִמִּקְנֵה בְנֵי יִשְׂרָאֵל לֹא מֵת אֶחָד
But of the cattle of the Children of Israel not one died (9:6)

Reb Yitzchak Aizik of Zhidachov never delivered Torah discourses for the sake of discourses alone. They always had in them something in the nature of a prayer, through which he would bring about tangible salvation, both for entire communities, and for individuals who stood in particular predicaments. Toward the conclusion of a discourse he would always find evidence in the proof-texts that he had been expounding that whoever needed help from heaven — whether with regard to children, health, or livelihood — would indeed be answered. And thus it was that Reb Yehoshua of Belz once asked him why he dealt with only the bodily and financial needs of his chassidim, instead of exhorting them to elevate themselves morally and spiritually.

Replied Reb Yitzchak Aizik: "In the prayer *Ana Bechoach* (אָנָּא בְּכֹחַ) we ask the Almighty every day to do two things for His People: בָּרְכֵם טַהֲרֵם — 'Bless them and purify them,' *in that order.* Let the People of Israel first be helped with a livelihood; the purity will then come of its own accord."

❀ ❀ ❀

On one of his journeys to Zhidachov, Reb Yosef Meir of Spinka passed through a certain village where he was asked to urgently request Reb Yitzchak Aizik to pray on behalf of an individual who had a bone stuck in his throat. On his arrival in Zhidachov he found the tzaddik presiding at a festive meal which was being held to mark the New Moon, Rosh Chodesh. The moment the visitor entered the room, Reb Yitzchak Aizik began to expound the story related in the Midrash about a lion who had a bone stuck in his throat, and who said: "Whoever takes this thing out will be richly rewarded." As soon as he heard these words, Reb Yosef Meir realized that by virtue of the holy spirit that rested upon the tzaddik, he had sensed the purpose of his mission, and that this Midrash had been cited only for the sake of that despairing villager. He took good note of the time, and when he passed through the village on his way home he visited that man, and was told that on the day of Rosh Chodesh, at a certain hour — exactly the hour at which the tzaddik had given his discourse — the patient had finally coughed up the bone.

❀ ❀ ❀

At one time it happened that in a certain region there was an outbreak of a fatal cattle disease. One old farmer who used to fatten cattle for the market saw that several of his oxen showed dangerous symptoms, and decided to set out in order to spend *Shabbos* in Zhidachov. On Friday night, when the time came for the tzaddik to deliver his regular *derashah*, all the chassidim present pressed forward, tense and eager, the better to hear his every word. And this old man, though preoccupied with the troubles that brought him there, and not really interested in the learned words of the tzaddik, nevertheless pushed his way in as vigorously as the best of them — for was this not a time-honored custom? Reb Yitzchak Aizik now began to expound the verse אָדָם וּבְהֵמָה תּוֹשִׁיעַ ה׳: "You, God, will save both man and beast."

As soon as he heard these words the old farmer said to himself: "The rebbe no doubt went to the trouble of explaining this verse only for my sake. For sure, God will save both man and beast!"

Returning to his farm, he found that of all of his cattle not one had died: the epidemic had ceased.

סדר בא

SIDRA BO

☙ *For Thou Art With Me*

בֹּא אֶל פַּרְעֹה *Come to Pharaoh (10:1)*

A chassid called Reb Mottel of Kalshin had extensive business interests in Warsaw, and spoke Polish fluently. One day Reb Yitzchok of Vorki called for him, and asked him to approach a certain powerful minister with a view to having the government retract from its intention of burning all extant copies of the *Shulchan Aruch, Choshen Mishpat*; that is, that part of the Code of Jewish Law which deals with civil and criminal matters. The design of the authorities was to compel Jews to take all their litigation to the secular courts which dispensed justice according to the law of the land, instead of settling their differences before the rabbinical courts. Though no such decree had yet been promulgated, it was known that this was in the offing.

Reb Mottel protested: "But that minister has a raging temper. He threatens to shoot anyone who so much as approaches him on missions of this sort!"

Replied the tzaddik: "When the Almighty sent Moshe Rabbeinu to save his brethren, He did not say '*Go* to Pharaoh' but '*Come* to Pharaoh.' Moshe Rabbeinu was afraid of the Egyptian despot, so God invited him to come along with Him..."

The chassid thereupon set out to encounter the minister, happy and unafraid. The powerful man found himself awestruck in the presence of the chassid who stood thus before him — and granted his request.

◆§ *Burying Their Differences*

וְיָמֵשׁ חֹשֶׁךְ *Darkness which may be felt (10:21)*

A businessman once encroached on his neighbor's source of income by hiring his *arenda*, the business that the other had held in lease for years. When rebuked for this by Reb Chaim of Zanz, the offending party argued: "But that other fellow is nothing less than a wicked sinner. It would be a veritable mitzvah to bury him!"

"And who told you," countered Reb Chaim, "that it is a mitzvah to bury the wicked? Look, I can prove to you from evidence in the Torah that it is not a mitzvah at all. Regarding the Ninth Plague, the Midrash says that the Almighty inflicted darkness upon the Egyptians in order that they should not be able to see the Children of Israel burying those of their own brethren who died for their sins during those three days, and conclude therefrom that the Children of Israel were also smitten by the Plagues. From this we see that the Israelites did bury their wicked brethren — though that is not to say that this was a mitzvah. For, as Rashi comments elsewhere, the time had come for the Almighty to fulfill the oath which He had made to Avraham, that he would redeem his descendants — except that they did not have mitzvos with which to occupy themselves, and which would make them worthy of being redeemed. It is to this lack of mitzvos that the prophet Yechezkel refers when he says of the Children of Israel וְאַתְּ עֵרֹם וְעֶרְיָה — 'And you were naked and bare.' He therefore gave them two mitzvos:

the blood of the Pessach sacrifice — the קָרְבַּן פֶּסַח — and the blood of the circumcision. Now, in the light of Rashi's comment, it is clear that burying the wicked is not a mitzvah; if it were, then our forefathers would not have been lacking in mitzvos, for they had buried so many sinners.

"That being the case," concluded Reb Chaim of Zanz, "go right home and restore the lease to that other fellow, or you will live to regret it."

☙ To Avert a Decree

כִּי מִמֶּנּוּ נִקַּח לַעֲבֹד אֶת ה׳
For we will take some of them to serve Hashem therewith (10:26)

Every Rosh HaShanah, in the dread moments before blowing the *shofar*, Reb Shalom of Belz would address words of instruction and exhortation to the assembled chassidim in inspired ecstasy. On one such occasion, speaking of the miracles wrought for the Children of Israel before the Exodus, he quoted the verses which tell of how God sent Moshe Rabbeinu to bring them out of Egypt. In response to Pharaoh's question מִי וָמִי הַהֹלְכִים — "Who are those who are to go?" — Moshe Rabbeinu answers: "We will go with our young and with our old; with our sons and with our daughters, with our flocks and with our herds will we go." Pharaoh finally calls for Moshe, and says: "Go, serve God; only let your flocks and your herds stay behind. Let your little ones also go with you." To this Moshe replies: "Our cattle too shall go with us: no hoof shall be left behind; for we will take some of them to serve G-d therewith."

Having quoted these *pesukim*, Reb Shalom recited the benediction which precedes the blasts of the *shofar* — לִשְׁמוֹעַ קוֹל שׁוֹפָר — and, this mitzvah completed, he went on directly to the *Musaf* prayer, as usual. The chassidim were of course wonderstruck. No one understood the relevance of those verses to these moments before the blowing of the *shofar* on Rosh HaShanah, but they held their peace, thinking it unseemly to ask their rebbe for an explanation.

Now one of his chassidim, Reb Elimelech of Tlust, was accustomed to journey to Belz every year for Rosh HaShanah, and then to proceed to visit Reb Meir of Premishlan. On this occasion, as soon as he stepped on the threshhold of the tzaddik's room in Premishlan, Reb Meir said: "Elimelech! Please repeat for me the Torah discourse that the Belzer rebbe delivered this year before the *shofar* was blown."

The chassid told him what Reb Shalom of Belz had said, and added that all those who heard it were at a loss to see the connection between Rosh HaShanah and the dialogue that preceded the Exodus.

Reb Meir at once waxed eloquent in praise of the discourse which Reb Shalom of Belz had given: in his profound insight he had penetrated through all the heavens, and had averted ominous decrees that had threatened Israel; through his words on Rosh HaShanah he had proved to the Almighty: "Father! In your own holy Torah it is written that no evil shall hold sway over Israel!"

Seeing that Reb Elimelech had no conception of what he was talking about, Reb Meir added: "Let me explain to you what the intention of Reb Shalom was. You see, on Rosh HaShanah this year, when all of Creation was arraigned before the Heavenly Court, Satan, the Prosecuting Attorney, was most outspoken in his accusations of Israel. In fact, a decree was at the point of being promulgated which would have wrought havoc with the lives of little Jewish children. But the rebbe of Belz argued fervently that these children would grow up and serve their Maker. The next design was a decree of extermination to be issued against the cattle of Israel. The tzaddik of Belz did not let that pass, either, arguing that 'we will take some of them to serve God therewith.' And in this manner he mitigated the verdict, by quoting the verses which spell out the argument between Pharaoh, that is, Satan, and Moshe Rabbeinu, that is, the tzaddik of the generation. Thus the decree against the cattle of the Jews was also averted. However," concluded Reb Meir, "since the tzaddik of Belz made no mention of birds, this year will see an epidemic affecting them, because the decree hanging over them was not annulled."

And so it was. That same year a contagious disease struck the domestic poultry of the Jews of those parts, but neither man nor beast was affected.

◆ Portrait of a Chassid of Long Ago

וְעָבַרְתִּי בְאֶרֶץ מִצְרַיִם
And I will pass through the Land of Egypt (12:12)

And I will pass through the Land of Egypt: I am God — I, and no other *(Haggadah).*

This is not quite a story, but rather four glimpses into the life of an unsung chassid called Reb Yoel of Tshopli. Together they give some notion of the thinking of a chassid of long ago.

Reb Yoel was a disciple of Reb Mordechai of Lechovitch, known as the Old Rav of Lechovitch, who lived not very far away. He was respected by all as an honest and righteous man — even by the gentiles of his village, and even by the local *paritz*, the squire who was master of all the land and livelihoods in the district. His dress was like that of any common peasant: a short sheepskin jacket, with a length of rope for a belt. One day the local *paritz* was visited by many of the squires of that province for some festive occasion and, in the course of their carousing, boasted that among his many *arendars* there was one leaseholder who was a really special person, a gem. His guests of course were curious to see who this was, and pressed their host to call for this Jew. He agreed, and Reb Yoel soon arrived at his door in his usual garb, with the long white threads of his *tzitzis* peeking out here and there under the hem of his sheepskin jacket. Seeing this, the *paritz* asked him to hide his *tzitzis*, for his guests might laugh at him. Unaffected by the prospect of soon having to face the mirth of that tipsy crew, Reb Yoel quietly answered his all-powerful squire: "What do you mean? Do you think I would be ashamed of my *tzitzis?* Why, they are our very life!"

❀ ❀ ❀

Reb Yoel used to carry about with him the little account book in which he recorded the debts that the local gentiles owed him for the vodka they bought at the inn that he leased from the squire. On its front page, and at the top of each of the other pages as well, he had written the following words: "I believe with perfect faith that the Creator, blessed be He, is the Master and Sovereign of all the worlds, and the Root and Source of all the worlds."

❦ ❦ ❦

He kept a little white pony especially for the ride to Lechovitch to see his rebbe. And there were tzaddikim who said that when he paused near a well to let his pony drink, Eliyahu the Prophet used to reveal himself to him.

❦ ❦ ❦

One day, his soul suddenly thirsted to hear from the lips of his rebbe some delectable *vort*, some insightful thought that would help him refine his sensitivity to his service of the Creator. He rode off to Lechovitch, and tied his pony to a peg outside the rebbe's house. Now on that day Reb Asher of Stolin was also visiting Reb Mordechai, but because it was such an extremely hot day, he had gone out for a little while to take some fresh air in the veranda, and had closed the door of the rebbe's house behind him. As Reb Yoel now approached the door he found it closed, and so eager was he to hear some *vort* from his rebbe, that he knocked loudly and called out: "Open up, please!"

Startled by the sudden knocking, Reb Asher turned around and asked: "Who is that?"

Reb Yoel answered: "It is I."

The voice of Reb Mordechai came booming from inside the house: "Where in the whole universe can one find a creature that can say 'I' about itself? אֲנִי ה׳—אֲנִי הוּא, וְלֹא אַחֵר, 'I am God — I, and no other': only God Himself is able to say 'I' — *but no other!*"

When Reb Yoel heard these words through the door, he had no further need to enter the house. He untied his little white pony and trotted quietly home to Tshopli, his soul's thirst quenched.

סדר בשלח

Sidra Beshalach

◆§ Grass Roots Initiative

מַה תִּצְעַק אֵלָי
Why do you cry out to me? (14:15)

Reb Menachem Mendel of Kotsk was once visited by Reb Yaakov David, head of the rabbinical court of Koznitz, and a disciple of Reb Shlomo Leib of Linchna. The rebbe of Kotsk asked him: "And how is your teacher getting on? I really am fond of him; but why is he always crying out to the Almighty, asking him to send the *Mashiach?* If he is so eager to bring about the Messianic Redemption, why doesn't he call out to the Jews, and exhort them to repent? After all, that is what the Almighty told Moshe Rabbeinu at the brink of the Red Sea: מַה תִּצְעַק אֵלָי? דַּבֵּר אֶל בְּנֵי יִשְׂרָאֵל — 'Why do you cry out to me? Speak to the Children of Israel...!' "

◆§ Before the Leap of Faith

וַיּוֹשַׁע ה׳
And Hashem saved (14:30)

A woman came to visit Reb Shalom of Belz and asked him to pray that she be helped from heaven in a certain matter.

"The important thing to remember," said the rebbe, "is to have faith in God."

"But rebbe," protested the woman, "when our forefathers stood in danger on the shore of the Red Sea, *first* we read וַיּוֹשַׁע ה׳ — 'And God saved,' *and only later* is it written וַיַּאֲמִינוּ בַּה׳ — 'And they believed in God.' If salvation comes now, then without a doubt I'll have faith as well."

Said the rebbe: "No one ever got the best of me in argument — except for this woman."

And as for the woman, her plaint was effective, and she was granted all she needed.

◈ Don't Forget the Address בשלח

וַיַּאֲמִינוּ בַּה׳ וּבְמֹשֶׁה עַבְדּוֹ
And they believed in Hashem, and in his servant Moshe (14:31)

A poor man who had to marry off his daughter came to Kotsk to seek the help of Reb Menachem Mendel. The tzaddik gave him a letter addressed to Reb Moshe Chaim Rothenburg, the wealthy brother of Reb Yitzchak Meir of Ger, asking him to extend a helping hand to the indigent bearer, in keeping with the means with which he had been blessed. The poor man trudged from town to town until he finally reached the rich rabbi's house in Chenshin, where he was received warmly. After having rested a little he handed the rebbe's letter to his host, confident in the assurance that Reb Moshe Chaim would hand him immediately everything he needed to cover the wedding expenses. After all, had he not brought him a letter from the rebbe of Kotsk?

Reb Moshe Chaim read through the letter quietly, took some modest donation out of his pocket, say a ruble, and handed it to his guest. The poor fellow was astonished. What of the trouble and expense of the long trek here? What of the wedding expenses he would soon have to cover? But no remonstrations were eloquent enough to change Reb Moshe Chaim's mind. He would add not a penny. The poor man had no choice but to take his leave, if nothing else, and, disappointed and dispirited, set out homeward on foot.

His unpredictable benefactor was now able to proceed with his plans. He hurried out and bought costly clothes, utensils, and whatever else a young couple might need, put together a generous sum of money as well, loaded all the goods on to a number of wagons, set out along the highway to catch up to his penniless visitor — and presented him with all these gifts.

Quite amazed, the poor man said: "If you were going to be so generous after all, why, may I ask, did you have to put me through all that anguish for no reason whatever?"

"Listen, my friend," said Reb Moshe Chaim, "and I will give you the reason. When you came along with a letter safely in your pocket from the great rebbe of Kotsk addressed to some wealthy individual by the name of Moshe Chaim, you quite forgot that we Jews have a God we turn to. So I simply wanted to remind you to place your trust in Him. And now, my good man, have a good ride home."

◆§ *The Power of Faith*

Reb Aharon of Karlin told the following story which he had heard from his relative by marriage, Reb Yisrael of Ruzhin, in order to show the power of belief in tzaddikim.

Two men lived in neighboring villages. One believed in tzaddikim, though his wife did not, while with the other, the opposite was the case: he did not believe in the powers of tzaddikim, but his wife did. The villager who believed once fell ill, and when he saw that no physician seemed able to help him, he asked that someone should take his case to a tzaddik and ask him to pray on his behalf. His wife saw no point in such a journey, but out of deference to her husband's wishes she hired a wagon and set out to see the tzaddik of Ruzhin. On her way through the neighboring village she learned that the man who lived there was also in distress, for the payment for the lease of his tavern was due, and he possessed not a solitary kopek to pay the insistent *paritz* who owned it. His wife, who believed in tzaddikim, saw that her friend was on her way to see Reb Yisrael, so she took a seat in the wagon beside her, and off they went to Ruzhin. As soon as they arrived they sought out the *gabbai* whose task it was to write out *kvitlach* for the many comers — slips of paper which bore the names of the supplicant and of his mother, and the subject of the request. In their excitement, however, each one took from his hand the other's *kvitl.* When their turns came to see the rebbe, the sick man's wife handed him the note about the lease, and Reb Yisrael answered: "May God help you," while the leaseholder's wife gave him the note about the illness, to which the tzaddik reacted by advising the application of cupping glasses and leeches ...

So strong was this woman's faith that she believed in her innocence that the tzaddik's advice came in answer to her request, and that the Merciful One would indeed send His help from Above through the agency of leeches and cupping glasses. When she arrived home, her husband's first question, understandably enough, was: "What did the rebbe say?" He was more than a little surprised to hear that the rebbe had recommended such an uncoventional *sgulah* as a remedy for his financial embarrassment but, though he had never been a believer in the powers of tzaddikim, he told himself: "Something is better than nothing."

The final date for payment fell due, and his pockets were as empty as ever. It was time to try the rebbe's suggestion. He lay down in bed, covered himself with blood-sucking leeches, and dutifully applied to his body the heated cupping glasses which our great-grandparents in Eastern Europe called *bankess,* and which were confidently used as the ultimate remedy for all ailments. While he was lying there, bleeding from all sides, one of the henchmen of the local squire banged on the door, and brought the warning from his master that if payment was not made that very same day, the Jew would be evicted from the village forthwith. He then returned to the *paritz,* and reported that he had seen the Jew in bed, bleeding profusely. The squire could hardly be expected to believe this kind of story, for only the day before, any number of people had seen the Jew, hale and hearty as always. He gave the order to have the lessee brought to his house, in bed, and his underlings jumped to carry out his wishes.

As they brought him inside, the squire's wife saw the sorry state he was in, wounded and bleeding, and felt pity for the poor fellow. She clapped her hands in anguish and cried: "Tell me, tell me! Whatever happened to you?'

And in his desperation he came up with the following story: "Yesterday I rode off to town in order to find some way of getting together the money I owe for the lease. It cost me unbelievable effort, but I finally managed to scrape up the sum through borrowing from all kinds of friends and acquaintances. It was time to go home, but since no wagon was going in the direction of our village so late at night, I was forced, dark as it was, to set out to make all that long distance on foot. Just my luck, and a vicious gang of brigands and highwaymen attacked me violently. They robbed me of all my money, beat me up true and proper, and only by the grace of God am I alive today, more or less ..."

Deeply touched, the squire's wife said to her husband: "Look, Piotr, it's clear that *we* are responsible for this man's wounds, and it's our job now to pay for a doctor to make him well again."

Turning to the Jew, the good woman added: "As for the rent that you owe us for the lease, well of course we'll forget about it. But you must have got yourself deeply into debt by borrowing from everybody yesterday, so don't worry: we'll let you lease the tavern for the next three years for nothing."

Finding her logic irrefutable, her husband assented to every word she had said.

❦ ❦ ❦

Reb Aharon of Karlin came to the end of his story, and added: "When the tzaddik of Ruzhin finished telling me this story, he said, 'Believe me, *mechutan,* that when that woman stood before me and made her request about the lease, I knew no way of drawing down help for her. She alone, through the intensity of her faith, drew her salvation down from heaven.' "

✤ *The Song of the Sea*

אָז יָשִׁיר מֹשֶׁה
Then Moshe sang (15:1)

In the days of Reb Shmelke of Nikolsburg a cruel decree was drawn up against the Jews of the city. Accompanied by his disciple, Reb Moshe Leib of Sasov, the tzaddik set out for the imperial court in Vienna in the hope of having the statute annulled before it came into effect. It was thawing season, and no boatman would dare to navigate the width of the Danube for fear of the treacherous chunks of ice which jostled their way down the torrents of the swollen river. Time was short: the decree would soon be implemented. Seeing a boatman with a rowboat barely big enough to hold two, Reb Shmelke hired it, boarded it together with his disciple, and began to recite the Song of the Sea, the exultant paean of praise and thanksgiving that the Children of Israel sang after crossing the Red Sea. And, as he sang its words, with Reb Moshe Leib repeating them after him, verse by verse, the little skiff flitted across the river between the blocks of ice, hampered by no obstacle.

The Viennese burghers who watched all this from the banks could hardly believe their eyes, and word of what they had seen soon reached the palace. When the kaiser and his advisers realized what manner of man they were dealing with, they granted his request, and the Jews of Nikolsburg were allowed to live on unharmed.

◈ *A Song for All Seasons*

אָז יָשִׁיר
Then will he sing (15:1)

Then will he sing: Whoever sings God's praises in This World will surely be privileged to sing His praises in the World to Come *(Talmud, Tractate Sanhedrin).*

Reb Moshe Leib of Sasov once married off at his own expense a young couple who had neither relatives nor means, and at the ceremony took the place of the parents of both sides. As the bride was led in to the *chuppah* to the accompaniment of musical instruments his joy was visible, and he said to those standing beside him: "If only when my time comes I could be brought to my resting place to the strains of that same melody!"

Years passed, and the comment was forgotten.

In due course his time came — on the fourth of Shvat in the year 1807 — and on that same day a band of musicians set out with their instruments to play at a wedding in Brody. The horses suddenly began to gallop up hill and down dale, and could not be restrained, until they arrived at the fence of the cemetery of Sasov, where they stopped. Seeing thousands of mourners there, the musicians realized that this must be the funeral of some distinguished personage. They were told who it was who had passed away, and the mention of his name brought to mind the words that they themselves had heard from the mouth of Reb Moshe Leib at a wedding long ago. Even the melody stole its way back into their memories, for it was they who had gladdened the hearts of that fatherless bride and groom. Three sages were consulted as to whether it would be proper to allow the musicians to play their melody at that time and place. It was decided to respect the wish of the departed, and all those thousands stood in silence as the musicians honored the memory of the tzaddik by playing a wedding dance at his funeral.

☙ *This is* My *God*

זֶה אֵלִי וְאַנְוֵהוּ
This is my God, and I will glorify Him (15:2)

A schoolmaster from the town of Bilgoraj (or Goray) often used to travel the short distance to visit Reb Yaakov Yitzchak, the Chozeh of Lublin. On one such occasion the tzaddik told him: "In your town there is a certain holy spark. Please try to locate it and bring it to me."

When he came home he considered his townsmen one by one, but was unable to identify the person who would meet the rebbe's description. There was in fact a youth called Mendel, the same who was to become famous as Reb Menachem Mendel of Kotsk, and it was him indeed that the tzaddik had had in mind — but it never occurred to the *melamed* that this was the spark he was seeking, for this youth behaved somewhat oddly, and was never seen studying.

Continuing his search, therefore, the schoolmaster decided to spend a few nights in the local *beis midrash:* the House of Study seemed to him to be a likely place in which to find the saintly, scholarly individual he sought. In the dead of night he watched from a corner as Mendel entered alone, opened a volume of the Talmud and, full of enthusiasm, studied aloud — while standing on one foot. The schoolmaster began to wonder whether he had at last found his spark, or whether this was an exceptional occurrence. He returned the following evening, and discovered that night after night this youth maintained the same schedule. One night, however, the schoolmaster yawned and coughed. Sensing that he was being watched, the youth closed his *Gemara* at once, strode suddenly to the stove, clapped his hands loudly, and in general acted in a way that would make him appear odd.

The schoolmaster stood up, approached the youth, and said: "I know full well that your outlandish behavior is intended only to delude people. But your acting cannot fool me, for the Chozeh of Lublin told me to bring you to him."

The youth lost no time and set out for Lublin. When his father, who was a *misnaged,* found out that his son was on his way to the court of a famous chassidic rebbe, he rode off there in hot pursuit, and remonstrated with him: "Why do you forsake the tradition of your fathers?"

Replied the youth: "*First* it is written זֶה אֵלִי וְאַנְוֵהוּ – 'This is *my* God, and I will glorify Him'; only *later* is it written אֱלֹהֵי אָבִי וַאֲרֹמְמֶנְהוּ – 'the God of my *father,* and I will exalt Him' ... "

◆§ With Himself at War

כִּי מָרִים הֵם

For they were bitter (15:23)

There once lived a *shochet* who was a devoted chassid of Reb Yisrael of Ruzhin, and unusually hospitable. Some time after the death of his wife he remarried, but his second wife would not allow guests into the house. Word of this reached his rebbe, and when the chassid came to visit Ruzhin as usual, the tzaddik asked him what had come of his attitude to guests.

The *shochet* replied: "What can *I* do? My wife simply doesn't agree to being hospitable. Surely I am not expected to divorce her over this issue!"

In response the tzaddik simply simply quoted a verse from *Exodus,* stressing two words: כִּי מָרִים **הֵם** עַל כֵּן קָרָא **שְׁמָהּ** מָרָה – "For *they* were bitter, therefore he called *her* name Marah."

In the original context, "they" refers to the waters of Marah, and "her name" refers to the name of the place Marah, which means bitter, and which in Hebrew requires a feminine pronoun. But the chassid understood that his rebbe was in fact subtly rebuking him, by making these words refer respectively to himself (or his fellow chassidim) and his wife: "For *they* were bitter, therefore they called *her* name Marah ..."

❀ ❀ ❀

◆§ Bread for the Wise

וַיִּמְתְּקוּ הַמָּיִם
And the waters were made sweet (15:25)

And the waters were made sweet: Mortal man heals bitterness with sweet things — unlike the Almighty, who heals bitterness through bitterness *(Yalkut).*

In the course of the imprisonment of Reb Shneur Zalman of Liadi in the dreaded Peter-Paul Fortress in St. Petersburg, it once happened that for days on end he ate nothing, because no kosher food was provided. Assuming that he refrained from eating as a means of suicide, the warders resorted to force, but the tzaddik held his mouth firmly closed and they were unable to open it. The hubbub caused by his desperate struggle attracted the attention of the cross-examining official. He strode across to the cell to investigate, and told the warders: "A man like this should not have food forced into his mouth. He should be spoken to until he consents to eat."

And he proceeded to take the matter in hand himself. "Why don't you eat?" he asked. "There is a chance that you will be acquitted, in which case you will live; if you do not eat, you will certainly die. Besides, surely you know that a person who suicides has no share in the World to Come."

The tzaddik answered: "I do not eat because there is no kosher food here, and I would not touch *trefah* food even if it meant doing without the World to Come."

"And if I were to get hold of kosher food for you, would you trust me?" asked the official.

"For the moment," answered the tzaddik, "there is no need for any food, for my stomach has become very weak. What I do need is some medication from the apothecary to strengthen it. And if someone could get me some marinated radish salad from a Jewish household, I would eat that. After all, marinated radish salad exemplifies the sweetening of bitterness, and I could certainly do with some of that right now ..."

"And if you got such a salad," asked the official, "would you take my word about it?"

Reb Shneur Zalman answered that if the Russian

would take it personally from the Jew who prepared it, and no other person touched it until it reached him, then he would eat it.

Now at that time a wealthy chassid called Reb Mordechai of Liepli, who was on close terms with various government authorities, was in St. Petersburg on business. The prison official therefore sent him a message requesting that he send him at once — by the hand of a Jew — a jarful of good, kosher, marinated radish salad. Reb Mordechai found it hard to believe that this was intended for the official's private consumption: something made him think that it was for his rebbe. He sent the salad, and hid a tiny signed note in it: "I would like to know who it is who is eating my salad, and where." The official kept his word, and brought the dish personally to the tzaddik without having tampered with it at all. The latter found the note, and when the food was finished he asked the official to bring him some more. He left a little in the bottom of the vessel, however, and explained: "A little of the food has to be left there, so that the blessings of heaven will have something to rest on." And under that morsel he hid a miniscule signed note in return, which said: "I am the one who is eating this salad, and in such-and-such a place" — and went on to ask that a man be dispatched at once to Vilna.

This time too the official passed on the vessel unopened, and when Reb Mordechai found the note and passed on the glad tidings that the Alter Rebbe was alive and well, a wave of relief and joy refreshed the anxious brotherhood of his chassidim. Reb Mordechai sent some more of the same dish to the fortress, and a man was sent out at once to Vilna. Truth to tell, no one had any notion of what he was to do on his arrival, but, trusting in the superior insights of a tzaddik, they were confident that the aim of the urgent journey would become clear to the emissary once he was there — as indeed events later proved.

But that is another story.

❀ ❀ ❀

◆§ The Professor of Hanipoli

כִּי אֲנִי ה׳ רֹפְאֶךָ *For I, Hashem, am your healer* *(15:26)*

A desperately ill chassid, whose visits to dozens of doctors seemed unable to help him, sought out Reb Mordechai of Neshchiz in quest of a blessing and sound advice. The tzaddik's counsel was simple enough: "Consult the professor in the town of Hanipoli. *He* will cure you."

Now in those days, of course, there was no railway line in the backwoods of the Ukraine, but the ailing chassid spared no effort, and hired a wagon-driver for the long and arduous journey across the marshes to Hanipoli.

"Where does your professor live?" he asked the townsfolk on arrival.

"A professor?" they mused. "In Hanipoli?!"

"Then your doctor: where does your doctor live?"

"But we've never had a doctor in Hanipoli," they assured him.

"Then at least a nursing attendant, perhaps?"

But even a nursing attendant was not to be found. The chassid was dumbfounded. How could the saintly tzaddik of Neshchiz have uttered words so far removed from the truth? But then again, what was there to do? So, full of regrets about his waste of time, trouble and expense, he journeyed all the long way back to Neshchiz, and told the rebbe his doleful tale: that in all of Hanipoli there was no professor, no doctor — nothing.

"Tell me, then, my good man," asked the tzaddik, "what do these people in Hanipoli do if one of them (God forbid) falls sick?"

"Do? What *can* they do? I suppose they have no option but to trust in the Almighty, and ask Him to be merciful and heal them from heaven."

"That's him!" exclaimed the tzaddik. "That's the professor of Hanipoli that I referred you to! ... And He Who helps the townsfolk of Hanipoli will surely help you, too."

And so it was. No sooner did the chassid leave that room, than he felt his health returning to him, and after some time he was completely cured.

⤜ In God We Trust

An epileptic from a far-off town near the Prussian border came to visit Reb Yitzchak of Neshchiz, the son of Reb Mordechai, and requested that the tzaddik promise him that he be cured. Reb Yitzchak declined, and the poor man pleaded, until the tzaddik finally told him: "It is possible that you will be cured, but I certainly cannot give such a promise — and the fault lies with you, for you have forgotten to place your trust in the Almighty, Who alone can help. You no doubt heard from afar that in Neshchiz there lives some rebbe who can work wonders, and you placed your trust in me alone. Your salvation will be forthcoming, therefore, when you revert to trusting in the Almighty."

The tzaddik then told him about a villager and his wife who, having been robbed of a large sum, called on Reb Yisrael of Koznitz to ask for his help. The Maggid of Koznitz protested: "*I* didn't steal anything from your house: I was at home that day. My family can testify to that."

They entreated him to do something, and gave him a gold ruble as a *pidyon* to be given to charity. The Maggid said: "But I want more."

They placed two more rubles on the table, but the Maggid would not agree. They added more and more, until the Maggid told them that he wanted them to give him no less than sixty gold rubles for charity. This was too much for the peasant woman. She briskly collected all the gold coins from the table, tied them up in her kerchief, and turned to her husband: "Let's leave this place. I'm sure God can help us without all this."

Hearing these words, the Maggid told them: "I think you should know that your request was hard to fulfill, because you forgot the Almighty, and came only to me, with the request that *I* should help you. You did not stop to think that salvation comes only through the power of the Almighty — and that is why I refused whatever you offered me. But now that you have brought Him to mind, your salvation is just around the corner ... And one more thing," concluded the Maggid, "if you don't mind: could you please give me back that gold ruble that you first gave me for charity?"

◆§ *A Reminder to Heaven*

לֶחֶם מִן הַשָּׁמָיִם
Bread from heaven (16:4)

A man's sermons in the course of an entire rabbinic career may be expected to vary considerably, both as to content and as to purpose. This was not the case with Reb Menachem Mendel of Rimanov. In the introduction to his master's book, *Menachem Tziyyon*, his disciple, Reb Menachem Panet, writes as follows: "It is well known that for twenty-two consecutive years my illustrious mentor, Reb Menachem Mendel of Rimanov, delivered discourses every *Shabbos* on the subject of the manna with which our forefathers were sustained from heaven during their forty years' wandering in the wilderness. And for those twenty-two years, through these very discourses, he drew down from heaven spiritual and material blessings in plenty for all the House of Israel."

◆§ *Blessings for the Undeserving*

הֲיֵלֵךְ בְּתוֹרָתִי אִם לֹא
Whether they will follow My Torah, or not (16:4)

In a year of severe drought a group of unlettered Jewish peasants came to Ruzhin to ask Reb Yisrael to give them his blessing for rainfall. The tzaddik answered: "But the Torah says, *'If you walk in the way of My statutes,* ... I will give you your rains in their season.'"

One of the coarser yokels spoke up: "Rebbe, what's all this fancy talk about what it says in the Torah? Torah yea, Torah nay — we need rain!"

Hearing this outburst the tzaddik said not a word, but turned to leave them and to retire to his study. But one of the other peasants, who had more simple faith than scholarship, ran after him and protested: "Rebbe, but in the Torah it also says לְמַעַן אֲנַסֶּנּוּ הֲיֵלֵךְ בְּתוֹרָתִי אִם לֹא."

Now this verse in fact means: "In order that I may put them to the test, as to whether they will follow My Torah, or not." This well-meaning ignoramus, however, understood it otherwise, taking אֲנַסֶּנּוּ to stem from the word נֵס, meaning banner. He therefore innocently explained his quotation to the tzaddik as follows: "Come now, rebbe! Anyone who can read knows what *that* means! Why, it's a promise from God Himself, and it means: 'I will raise them aloft like a banner, *whether they follow My Torah or not ...* '"

The tzaddik was moved by these naive words that came straight from the heart of a simple Jew. He returned to the waiting villagers and blessed them: "May the Almighty listen to your requests, and grant you rains in their season!"

Shabbos in the Air

וְהָיָה בַּיּוֹם הַשִּׁשִּׁי וְהֵכִינוּ
On the sixth day they shall prepare (16:5)

From midday on Friday Reb Elimelech of Lyzhansk would feel the impending sanctity of *Shabbos* ringing in his ears like a bell, and would stop them up because of its intensity. Terror and trembling seized everyone in his home. His housekeepers were obliged to complete all their preparations before noon, because if any one of them did a workday chore from that time on, whatever was in his hands would fall or spoil.

◆§ *By Invitation Only*

The daughter of the celebrated scholar Rabbi Meir of Constantine (who was the son of the renowned Rabbi Yaakov Emden) was a woman of unusual righteousness, and her husband was a man richly blessed both in wealth and in learning.

One Friday morning she rose very early and went to the market, basket in hand, together with her maid. There she was offered an enormous live fish, and immediately bought it in honor of *Shabbos*. Seeing this prize catch lashing about in her basket, she prayed in joy and gratitude: "Master of the Universe! Just now You have given me the opportunity to buy such a fine fish in honor of the holy day. Won't You now send me along some pious guest for *Shabbos*, so that he too can enjoy this fish?"

Some time after midday an unfamiliar carriage drew up in front of her house. The personage of distinguished appearance who stepped out was none other than the saintly Reb Yitzchak of Drohovitch, the father of Reb

Michel of Zlotchov. No one in the family knew who he was, nor did he introduce himself, but his very countenance whispered to them that this stranger was a holy man. They greeted him with eager respect, and asked him to spend *Shabbos* with them.

The day passed all too quickly, and after the Third Meal at dusk Reb Yitzchak retired to his room to rest a little. While alone, he asked heaven to enlighten him as to the reason for which he had been sent to this house. What sparks of hidden sanctity needed to be revealed or elevated in these parts? And answer came that there was nothing waiting here to be set right by him. It was only that the lady of the house — scion of devout and scholarly forebears, and righteous in her own life — had prayed on Friday morning that a guest of stature be sent her way, so that he too could partake of the fish that she had bought. Her request had been granted, and since he, Reb Yitzchak, was one of the loftiest souls of his generation, heaven's voice had guided him there on the eve of the Day of Rest.

Night fell, and for one last time the visiting tzaddik graced the family's table — this time, for the mystic repast of *Melaveh Malkah* which bids farewell to the departing *Shabbos* Queen. The tzaddik too had to go on his way, and the family all rose to see him out to his carriage. But before he climbed up he asked to see the lady of the house. He turned to her and said: "My good woman, I have a favor to ask of you. Please do not offer the same prayer again to heaven. You see, I was at a great distance from your town, and they made me come this long, long way to spend *Shabbos* in your home — all because of your prayer..."

◆§ *The One that Nearly Got Away*

וְהֵכִינוּ אֵת
אֲשֶׁר יָבִיאוּ

And they shall prepare that which they shall bring (16:5)

Rav used to salt the fish in honor of *Shabbos* *(Talmud, Tractate Shabbos).*

Reb Yaakov Yitzchak was visiting Mezritch for the first time. He was still a very young man, not yet renowned as the Chozeh of Lublin, and his intention was to study at the feet of Reb Dov Ber, the Maggid of Mezritch. As soon as he arrived, on a Friday afternoon,

he went straight into the kitchen, and told those who were busy cooking the *Shabbos* meals: "I am accustomed to personally taking some part in the preparation of the fish that I am to eat on *Shabbos*. With your permission, I would like to maintain that custom today too."

He then took up a piece of fish, salted it, put it down, and went his way.

The disciples of the Maggid who had watched this little incident were somewhat surprised, and asked each other: "What makes this young man think that precisely this piece of fish is going to be served to him? Obviously, it will be mixed up among all the other pieces. They are all being cooked together, and will all be divided up and served by the waiters to the various people who will be sitting at the rebbe's table!"

And so they dismissed the callow newcomer's action as bizarre or, worse, pretentious.

Now one of these disciples was a young man known affectionately by his colleagues as Zalmanyu — the same who was later to become famous as Reb Shneur Zalman of Liadi, the author of *Tanya*. This young man tied a short piece of thread to that chunk of fish, in order to be able to trace it — as is done with certain other species of migratory fish — to its precise destination at the table. The newcomer, of course, having left the kitchen, knew nothing of this unobtrusive sign.

At the *Shabbos* table Zalmanyu watched the waiters closely, and, sure enough, the marked piece was being served to some stranger who was seated next to the newcomer. But no sooner did he take it up than he was overcome by a feverish trembling, and was unable to eat. He pushed his plate aside — right in front of the newcomer, who duly ate it.

And that is how Zalmanyu removed all doubts as to the stature of his new colleague.

◆§ *Learning Nothing*

וְנַחְנוּ מָה
And what are we? (16:8)

Returning from one of his many visits to the Maggid of Mezritch, Reb Aharon of Karlin was pressed by an eager throng of friends and chassidim: "Tell us! Tell us!

What did you gain from this visit to the Maggid?"

Replied Reb Aharon: "Nothing."

"Then why do you bother to travel there?" they asked.

So he explained himself: "I gained the knowledge that I am worth nothing."

◆§ *A New Soul, a New Face*

וַיֹּאמְרוּ אִישׁ אֶל אָחִיו מָן הוּא
They said to each other: "It is manna" *(16:15)*

A chassid once met Reb David of Lelov on his return from a visit to Reb Yaakov Yitzchak, the Chozeh of Lublin, and asked him what Torah discourses he had heard. The Chozeh, he was told, had expounded the verse which speaks of the wonderment of the Children of Israel in the wilderness when they were sent food from heaven: וַיֹּאמְרוּ אִישׁ אֶל אָחִיו מָן הוּא כִּי לֹא יָדְעוּ מַה הוּא — "And they said to each other, 'It is manna,' for they did not know what it was." (That is — to take one of various possible interpretations — they gave the unfamiliar food the name manna, מָן, because of its similarity to the Hebrew word for "what," מַה.) The Chozeh had explained this verse on a mystical level. The manna, he said, being food from heaven, provided nourishment for the soul, and so rapidly did those who ate it grow in spiritual stature that from one day to the next they did not recognize each other. They therefore asked, with reference to *each other*, מָן הוּא — "What (or who) is he?"

The Chozeh had then added: "Here in our midst, for example, we have a young man who goes walking among the trees. No one is aware of his true stature, but a day will come when people will ask: 'Who is this?' "

Reb David now concluded his report of his visit to Lublin: "So I went along to see for myself who this was who went walking among the trees. It turned out to be some young man called Simchah Bunem."

The unknown young man in fact grew up to be a tzaddik of renown — Reb Simchah Bunem of Pshischah.

❀ ❀ ❀

◆§ Food for the Soul

וַיֹּאמֶר מֹשֶׁה אִכְלֻהוּ הַיּוֹם כִּי שַׁבָּת הַיּוֹם
And Moshe said: "Eat it today, for today is Shabbos" (16:25)

For today is Shabbos: Since that day's portion of food from heaven had become sanctified by being set aside for *Shabbos*, it would not be proper to eat it on a weekday *(Sifsei Kohen on the Torah).*

Reb Nechemiah Alter recollected: "I once traveled to Piltz on a Thursday evening to spend *Shabbos* there at the home of Reb Pintchi. After we had eaten supper together the tzaddik favored me with a wealth of expositions and insights on passages in the Torah, and altogether he was in a most joyful frame of mind. When I later went to bed, I overheard my host walking up and down in the next room, praying away: 'Master of the Universe! The kugel that my wife is now cooking in honor of the holy day — please make it come out tasty, for I have a very special guest for *Shabbos.* And when the holy day comes in, grant me that its sanctity should permeate my body, and my house, and the food prepared in its honor. And please give the food the flavor of the sanctity of *Shabbos!*' "

"This, then, was the prayer of Reb Pintschi of Piltz on a Thursday night."

◆§ Only a Penny for Your Thoughts

הֲיֵשׁ ה׳ בְּקִרְבֵּנוּ
Is Hashem among us? (17:7)

Is God among (or within) us? The Children of Israel said: "If He knows our thoughts, we will serve Him, and if not, we will rebel against Him." Said the Almighty: "Then let the wicked one come and test you!" And at once Amalek came *(Midrash).*

When Reb Yisrael Yitzchak of Radoshitz, as yet an unknown figure, first succeeded his famous father as rebbe, two chassidim set out to visit him, just as they had been wont to visit his late father, the Grand Old Man of Radoshitz. On the way they had second thoughts as to whether it was worth going to all the trouble of traveling so far to see a new rebbe. For does a rebbe not have to be a man possessed of a holy spirit who can know what thoughts lurk in the heart of his chassid? For all that, since they had already covered more than half of their journey, they decided to go ahead and spend one *Shabbos* in Radoshitz. The new incumbent was, after all, the son of their dearly-remembered rebbe.

They no sooner stepped on his threshhold than the new rebbe stepped forward to greet them with a smile: "Now suppose someone *does* know what thoughts cross the mind of a chassid on his way here. Does that alone make him worthy of being called 'rebbe'?"

☙ *Fellow Feeling*

וִידֵי מֹשֶׁה כְּבֵדִים
And the hands of Moshe were heavy (17:12)

And the hands of Moshe were heavy, so they brought a stone and placed it under him: He did not sit on cushions and quilts, for he said, "The Children of Israel are in distress; I, too, will be with them in their distress" *(Rashi).*

A fire broke out in Breslov on Rosh Chodesh Adar, 1810, and the house of Reb Nachman was gutted with all the rest. The very same week he moved to Uman. In this circumstance his chassidim saw evidence of supernatural perception, for only one week earlier he had sent a man to Uman to find out on his behalf whether he could settle there, and the very day after the fire the emissary had returned with the news that the townsfolk there would be very happy to have the tzaddik live in their midst.

When Reb Nachman left for Uman he said: "The fire gives me an additional reason for leaving Breslov, for it would not be proper that the townspeople here should be in a state of anguish, while I was happy."

He went on to explain his paradox: "If the fire had not touched my house I would of course have been distressed, for when my brothers all around are suffering, how could I not share in their pain? Since, however, my house and all my possessions were in fact destroyed, then of course I accept this — like all tribulations — joyfully; indeed, with the greatest of joy. For we have before us the instruction of the Mishnah: 'A man is obliged to utter a blessing over evil as over good,' and this the *Gemara* explains to mean 'to accept evil tidings joyfully.'

"Do you not see that it would not be proper for me to remain here among all my suffering townsfolk, while I am so full of joy?"

סדר יתרו

SIDRA YISRO

⌘ *Forever in His Presence*

לֶאֱכָל לֶחֶם עִם חֹתֵן מֹשֶׁה
To eat bread with the father-in-law of Moshe (18:12)

Reb Levi Yitzchak of Berditchev held Reb Baruch, the Maggid of Rika, to be a man of exemplary purity, and hired him as *melamed* in his household to tutor his children. When the contracted period had expired Reb Levi Yitzchak said: "I would like you to continue tutoring my family, but only on condition that you eat with me out of the same plate."

Replied the Maggid of Rika: "I would like to think it over."

Just at that time Berditchev was being visited by Reb Elimelech of Lyzhansk and his brother Reb Zusya of Hanipoli, so the Maggid decided to ask their advice. Going up the staircase which led to the attic where they were lodging, he heard Reb Elimelech saying to his brother: "In the Torah it is written, 'And Aharon and all the elders of Israel came to eat bread with the father-in-law of Moshe in the presence of God.' On this the Talmud comments as follows: 'Why does the Torah say that they ate in the presence of God? Was it not in the presence of Moshe that they ate? The intention of these words is to teach us that whoever partakes of a meal in which sages take part is like him who enjoys the radiance of the Divine Presence.' "

"Now, brother," Reb Elimelech went on, "something here is problematic. How could the Talmud question whether or not they ate in the presence of God? It is obvious that they ate in the presence of God, for the whole universe is full of His glory. And the answer appears to me to be as follows — that because they stood in awe of the tzaddik, something was lost in their fear of heaven. This is what the Talmud is hinting at when it says וְכִי לִפְנֵי אֱלֹקִים אָכְלוּ וַהֲלֹא לִפְנֵי מֹשֶׁה אָכְלוּ. The Talmud is really querying whether the Children of Israel in fact remained fully conscious that they were eating in the presence of God, since they were at the same time eating in the presence of Moshe Rabbeinu.' "

The Maggid realized that he had already received the answer to the question which he had wanted to ask: it is not such a good thing to be always eating out of the same plate as a tzaddik.

◆§ *A Lesson in Prudence*

וְהוֹדַעְתָּ לָהֶם אֶת הַדֶּרֶךְ יֵלְכוּ בָהּ

And you shall make them know the way in which they should go (18:20)

Reb Meir of Premishlan was a dear friend of Reb Yisrael of Ruzhin. His household, furniture and all, was a picture of dire poverty. No penny was ever allowed to spend the night in his tumbledown cottage: all the large sums that people used to give him he would immediately give away in charity. The household of Reb Yisrael, on the other hand, was conducted in a manner befitting royalty. Reb Meir used to make the following comment: "What is the difference between the tzaddik of Ruzhin and me? To him one may apply the words of the Psalmist: 'Treasure and wealth are in his house; his righteousness (or charity) endures forever.' To me the other verse applies: 'He distributed alms freely to the poor; his righteousness (or charity) endures forever.' "

The two friends once met as they were both preparing to set out on their respective journeys. Reb Meir was sitting on a simple cart drawn by one lean horse, while Reb Yisrael was climbing into his shiny carriage to which four proud stallions were harnessed. Said Reb Yisrael to Reb Meir: "I always travel with four horses, so that if my carriage should get stuck in the mud, they will be able to pull it out quickly. As for yourself, if I may ask, why do you take only one horse?"

Replied Reb Meir: "Since my cart is drawn by only

one horse, and I know that I will not be able to drag it out of the mud, I am forced to take the precaution of not getting myself into trouble in the first place..."

◆§ *Farewell, Dear Friend!*

ומשה עלה אל האלהים
And Moshe went up to God (19:3)

On the *Shabbos* that Reb Moshe Zvi of Savran passed away, Reb Yisrael of Ruzhin was seated at the head of his table surrounded by chassidim, expounding the verse "And Moshe went up to God..." When he had completed his discourse he said: "There were once two watchmen in a forest, and when one of them would call out to his friend, the other would call out in return. Now one day the second watchman left the forest. When the first watchman called out and heard no voice in return, he knew that his friend had gone far away, and was no longer to be found."

◆§ *Actions Speak Louder*

וְגַם בְּךָ יַאֲמִינוּ לְעוֹלָם
And they will believe in you, too, forever (19:9)

The following story was told by Reb Shmuel of Lubavitch.

There were once two chassidim who remembered the Maggid of Mezritch from their youth, and who were now disciples of Reb Shneur Zalman of Liadi. They were neighbors, both wealthy, and used to give the rebbe generous sums for the chassidic colony in *Eretz Yisrael* and for the other communal causes in which he was involved. They both served their Maker earnestly, though each had his own style. The first ordered his spiritual life in the manner that chassidim call מִלְּמַטָּה לְמַעְלָה — starting from the bottom, and working upwards; that is, first seeing to the actual performance of his religious duties in a spirit of self-sacrifice, and only later taking off the time to digest intellectually their spiritual connotations. The other favored the pattern known as מִלְמַעְלָה לְמַטָּה — starting from the top, and working downwards; that is, first working through each spiritual challenge intellectually, and only then bringing it to fruition in its physical fulfillment.

Reb Shneur Zalman, who at that time was living in Liozna, once sent an emissary to ask them for funds for some worthy cause. He came to the first chassid and said simply: "The rebbe needs money."

"How much?" he asked.

"I don't know," said the emissary. "The rebbe didn't say."

The chassid left the room for a moment, and returned with all the money he had in the house at the time.

From there the emissary proceeded to the second chassid, and here too said: "The rebbe needs money."

"How much?" the chassid asked.

"I don't know," said the emissary as before. "The rebbe didn't say."

The chassid decided: "I will travel to Liozna, ask the rebbe how much he needs, and give it to him."

The emissary returned to Liozna and gave the rebbe the wallet which he had received from the first man. When asked what he had brought from the other chassid, he repeated the answer he had been given. For a few moments the rebbe meditated, then said: "Before the event, or after the event?"

At dawn the next day the *first* chassid came to Liozna, and the rebbe told him: "You should move your place of residence."

Without a moment's delay he returned home, sold whatever household items were saleable, hired a wagon for his family, and took to the highway. Not that he knew where he was headed or why he was traveling — but the rebbe had said he should move, so he moved. Arriving at Liozna, he left his family at some suitable place, and went off to *shul* to pray.

The second chassid got up in the morning and thought: "Why should I hurry and leave right now? I'll *davven* first, then after prayers have some breakfast, and set out for Liozna about midday."

In the meantime a violent storm broke loose. In the midst of the thunder and lightning his whole street caught on fire, and he barely succeeded in saving his family, though nothing else.

❦ ❦ ❦

His story completed, Reb Shmuel commented: "That is the difference between obedience — and obedience.

Both men obeyed, except that the first started with the practical execution of the rebbe's instruction, while the second started by thinking it over."

☙ The World is Too Much With Us

אָנֹכִי
I am (20:2)

One of the grandsons of Reb Menachem Mendel of Lubavitch was observed to be in low spirits. His friends asked: "What makes you so morose?"

"The *aleph-beis,*" he replied.

"What do you mean?" they asked.

"The א of אָנֹכִי and the ב of בְּרֵאשִׁית," he replied.

[The former word means "I", while the latter is the first word of *Genesis,* and means "In the beginning." Two challenges, then, this young man found difficult to cope with — the natural tendency to self-centeredness, and the unspiritual demands of This World.]

☙ An Act of Faith

זָכוֹר אֶת יוֹם הַשַּׁבָּת לְקַדְּשׁוֹ
Remember the Sabbath day (20:8)

Reb Zvi Hirsch of Rimanov was known as Reb Hirsch the Beadle, because in earlier days he had acted as messenger and odd-job man in the household of his predecessor, Reb Menachem Mendel of Rimanov. He was once asked the meaning of a certain comment by Rashi which appears to be somewhat redundant, and hence puzzling.

In the passage in the Torah which speaks of the Priestly Blessing, God instructs Moshe to convey the following command to the *kohanim* who are to pronounce the blessing over their fellow Jews: כֹּה תְבָרְכוּ אֶת בְּנֵי יִשְׂרָאֵל אָמוֹר לָהֶם — "Thus shall you bless the Children of Israel, saying to them ..." On the verb אָמוֹר ("saying"), Rashi comments: אָמוֹר כְּמוֹ זָכוֹר וְשָׁמוֹר. Taken on their simplest level, these words merely explain the grammatical structure of the verb אָמוֹר by pointing out that it is analogous to the structure of the verbs זָכוֹר and שָׁמוֹר, which appear respectively in two commandments referring to *Shabbos:* זָכוֹר אֶת יוֹם הַשַּׁבָּת לְקַדְּשׁוֹ; שָׁמוֹר אֶת יוֹם הַשַּׁבָּת לְקַדְּשׁוֹ ("Remember the Sabbath day to keep it holy"; "Observe the Sabbath day to keep it holy").

Reb Hirsch, however, chose to see Rashi's comment

 from a less prosaic perspective, and told the following story:

In the days when I served as attendant to Reb Mendel it once happened that Thursday arrived, and there was not a single coin in the house with which to buy the barest necessities for *Shabbos.* The *rebbitzin* requested that I ask her husband what to do. I went across to his study, but as soon as I saw the intensity of his inspired concentration in the service of God I could not bring myself to disturb him, so I tiptoed out. Thursday evening came, and the *rebbitzin* made it clear to me — somewhat insistently — that it was high time that I go and remind the tzaddik that there was nothing whatever in the house for *Shabbos.* So I went, but exactly the same thing happened as before. On Friday morning, when there was still neither fish nor meat nor anything else, I again entered the rebbe's study, but he spoke first: "Please take the saucepan in which we always cook the fish, fill it with water, and put it on the fire. Do the same with the pot which we use for meat, and the same again for all the other things we usually cook for *Shabbos.*"

"But rebbe," I protested, "what will we cook in those pots? There is no sign of fish or meat in the house."

The rebbe answered me as follows: "Concerning the manna in the wilderness which fell from heaven on Friday and was to be eaten on *Shabbos,* God commanded our forefathers through Moshe Rabbeinu: 'And on the sixth day they shall *prepare* that which they shall bring.' That is to say, we are obliged to make the *preparations:* the holy day itself will bring whatever is needed."

And that is exactly what happened. We took out the saucepans, filled them with water, and left them simmering away on the fire. After a little while we were surprised by a knock on the door. It was a villager who said he had to spend *Shabbos* in our town for some reason or other, and asked whether he could spend the holy day in our household. He assured us that wherever he traveled he took along ample supplies of food — fish, meat, and whatever else one could need. We of course were very pleased to have him stay with us, and we were all blessed with a happy *Shabbos* together.

"So it is," concluded Reb Hirsch, "with the Priestly Blessing. It is obvious that the *kohanim* themselves are unable to grant blessings, for it is written: וְשָׂמוּ אֶת שְׁמִי עַל בְּנֵי יִשְׂרָאֵל וַאֲנִי אֲבָרְכֵם — 'And they shall set My Name over the Children of Israel and *I* will bless them.' All the Almighty commands the *kohanim* to do is to go ahead with all the preparations they are capable of — taking off their shoes, washing their hands, raising them, saying the words of the blessing, and so on. At this point the Almighty comes into the picture and says וַאֲנִי אֲבָרְכֵם — 'And *I* will bless them.' And this is what Rashi meant when he wrote אָמוֹר — כְּמוֹ זָכוֹר וְשָׁמוֹר, comparing the 'saying' of the Priestly Blessing to 'remembering' and 'observing' the Sabbath day. He was not simply giving us a lesson on the structure of verbs. He was teaching us something about the nature of the Priestly Blessing — that, just like the preparations we made for the *Shabbos*, it is an act of faith."

◆§ *Generation Gap*

כַּבֵּד אֶת אָבִיךָ וְאֶת אִמֶּךָ
Honor your father and your mother (20:12)

The renowned chassid Reb Avraham Sheines of Shklov, who had long been one of the foremost antagonists of Chassidism, became attracted in the course of time to both its ideology and its exponents, and became a devoted disciple of Reb Shneur Zalman of Liadi, who lived at this time in Liozna. When his father and family discovered that he had been "kidnapped by the Sect," and that he and his friends were to be found at that little stronghold of Chassidism, they rent their garments, and solemnly observed all the rites of mourning that are prescribed in the Code of Jewish Law for the loss of a loved one. So deep was their sense of bereavement that his father dispatched a letter to Reb Shneur Zalman demanding that he send his son home immediately, on pain of dire consequences. The son answered that he would be prepared to return to his home only on condition that his family give their word of honor to their local *rav*, Rabbi Henich Schick, and confirm it with a handshake, that they would do him no harm. If he received such a letter from their *rav* confirming that he had been given such a handshake, he would trust them and set out for home. The letter duly arrived and he returned to his family. They and all their *misnagdisher* colleagues were faithful to their promise in that they did him no harm; on the other hand they showed their distaste by utterly ignoring his existence, so that he spent his days in isolation, studying Torah in the attic. After some time the father relaxed his sanctions somewhat, because Rabbi Schick had meanwhile given it as his learned opinion that straying to the chassidic fold could not be unequivocally termed defecting (God forbid!) from the faith ...

When the young man traveled again to Liozna with his wife a number of friends accompanied him, and together they rejoined the brotherhood of the disciples of Reb Shneur Zalman. In Liozna his wife died, and after some time the rebbe offered him his daughter in marriage. Reb Avraham answered that he was certainly agreeable, but he would first like to ask his father's opinion — which he did.

His father's letter in reply ran as follows: "From what I know of you, you are so taken by any word of your rebbe that even if he had suggested that you marry his maidservant you would be eager to agree. How much more so now that he is offering you his daughter's hand in marriage — when according to your lights she would qualify to be called the daughter of a *talmid chacham*, a genuine Torah scholar. Besides, the fact is that you are not obliged to obey me in this matter, so why should I try to prevent you from going ahead, and thereby have you ignore my instruction, God forbid? So I hereby give you my consent. May God grant you good fortune."

After receiving this letter, Reb Avraham was privileged to be the son-in-law of the tzaddik for five years.

❀ ❀ ❀

◆§ Silence is Golden

Reb Avraham of Sochatchov was taught as a child by his father, Reb Ze'ev Nachum of Biala. One day the father posed an involved query in Talmudic legalistics which he considered to be particularly knotty, but the gifted child instantly proved that the seeming problem was in fact no problem at all. The learned father rejected his argument, pointing out wherein lay its fundamental fault and he smacked him lightly on the cheek, saying: "You'll have to get out of the habit of answering quickly before you've had a chance to think more deeply."

Decades passed, and the father was visited in his ailing old age by his son, who was now hailed as one of the luminaries of age. The old man reminded his son of that little episode, and told him that when he had again looked into the classical commentaries on the subject then discussed he had discovered that his son's solution was in fact perfectly acceptable. He had not told him this at the time, however, lest he become conceited. Now, after all these years, he wanted to ask his son's forgiveness for the smack of gentle reproach that he had then given him without justification.

Reb Avraham answered: "Believe me, father, that I knew at the time that I was right and that the little smack was undeserved, and of course I forgave you for it at once. I just didn't say anything, because of the mitzvah of honoring one's father."

Just for Fun

לא תִגְנֹב *You shall not steal (20:13)*

You shall not steal: Even if your intention is only to vex; even if your intention is to pay the prescribed fine *(Talmud, Tractate Bava Metzia).*

With joy respectfully restrained, long lines of venerable chassidim followed the Baal Shem Tov on their way to the wedding of one of his grandchildren, at which Reb Yaakov Yosef of Polonnoye had been asked by the rebbe to officiate. On their way they encountered an unfamiliar Jew traveling in a wagon. The

Baal Shem Tov left those who were accompanying him, whispered a few words to the stranger, and resumed his place. The members of that holy brotherhood were left bemused, and decided that this stranger was most likely some hidden tzaddik. They would have to find out just what he was up to. It would hardly be proper for the older and more dignified sages amongst them to leave the Baal Shem Tov and his immediate company, so they motioned to some of the younger scholars that they should find out what this mysterious encounter was all about.

Two young men promptly volunteered, and followed the man in the wagon into the courtyard of one of the local inns. At this point they approached him, and greeted him with due deference: "*Shalom Aleichem*, rebbe!"

"What's this talk of rebbe?" asked the stranger in wonderment. "I am neither a rebbe nor the son of a rebbe!"

"Sir, there is no point in trying to hide your identity any longer," they said. "We *know* that you are a tzaddik, and we beg you to make yourself known to us."

The poor fellow did not know what they were talking about, and gave them his word of honor that at no time in his life had he ever been a tzaddik or a rebbe. They assured him, though, that since their rebbe had approached him and spoken to him as soon as he had seen him, there was no doubt about it: he was a hidden saint, and they would give him no rest until he revealed his true identity, and spoke to them in the manner that tzaddikim may be expected to speak.

Seeing that he would never get rid of them, the Jew on the wagon said: "For a start, I am a plain, ordinary Jew. But since you are so persistent, I see I have no option but to tell you what your rebbe said to me. In the meantime you will see what a great man your rebbe is. So — here is my story.

"I live in a little township, over the road from my friend. Since childhood we've been like brothers. There are no secrets between us, and each of us shares in the other's joys and woes. This friend buys up flax, honey, wax and other produce from the villagers all around, and takes it to the city to be sold. With the profits he brings home he pays up his debts, leaving some money for his family to live on, and sets out on another round.

"Now on one of these occasions when he returned from the city with his earnings, all of his friends and relatives dropped in to his home to greet him, as always, and to join in the joy of his family on his return. I was there too, of course. I felt like smoking, and since we always made ourselves completely at home in each other's house, I went straight to the cupboard where he kept his tobacco. As soon as I opened the cupboard door, I saw the wallet of money that my friend had brought back from his long itinerary. His carelessness amazed me. I decided that I would have to teach him not to leave such a valuable item in so accessible a place. I would quietly take the wallet so that he would be shaken up when he saw that it was missing, and then I would return it to him. That would certainly teach him to take more care with his valuables. I did exactly that, and took the wallet home, with the intention of returning it after an hour or so.

"When the poor man opened the cupboard he was alarmed. He asked his wife if she had put it away somewhere. She of course was as dumbfounded as he was, and the whole household was soon in turmoil. They turned the whole place inside out, but of course they found nothing. Hearing all the hubbub, the neighbors ran in. And the more people shared their panic, the greater it grew, until my friend fainted; his wife did, too,and their children ran around desperately, crying at the top of their voices. When I heard all this uproar coming from my friend's house over the road, I gathered what it was all caused by, and went straight across in order to return the 'lost property.' But as soon as I walked inside and saw all the tumult, I couldn't bring myself to own up right them and there, in the presence of all those friends and relatives, that I had taken the money. The best thing, I thought, would be to wait a little until they all went home, and then, when the two of us were left alone, I would return to him his wallet.

"But you know how news of any calamity spreads like wildfire through a township where everyone knows everyone. The house filled up more and more, and the greater the pandemonium, the harder was it for me to own up and say: 'I did it.' If I had returned the wallet as soon as I had come in, people would have accused me of causing my friend all that anguish — but nothing more. Nobody would have suspected me of stealing, God forbid. But if I had come forward at this point — now that hours had gone by, and the whole town was simmering with shock and indignation about the damage that had supposedly been done — people would have suspected that my original intention had in fact been to steal the wallet, and that now, because I could not bear the sight of what was going on, I had changed my mind and decided to return it after all. So, very late at night, I went home, vexed by the tears of despair. My family of course knew nothing of my escapade, and assumed that I was simply upset at the misfortune that had struck my best friend. And upset I certainly was, for I knew that I had caused all that misery and mess, but did not know how to extricate myself from it.

"More serious complications started the next day. My friend had dozens of creditors, and they began to suspect that he had staged this theft in order to evade their claims. They started off speaking in whispers, then spoke openly on the subject, until finally they walked into his kitchen, thumped on the table, and shouted: 'Cheat! Robber! We want our money!'

"And the more complicated the story became, the harder was it for me to return the money. Several days dragged by. Now the Evil Inclination stepped into the picture. He argued as follows: 'You can see with your own eyes that you have absolutely no possibility of returning the money now. For the time being, you might as well use it yourself. Invest it somehow, make some profit on it, and in the course of time you're bound to think up some means of returning it to your friend.'

"I was beginning to find this argument convincing. The problem was that in my hometown I couldn't possibly do any business that required capital, because everyone would start suspecting me. This hadn't happened till then, and my family were still blissfully ignorant of what I had done. But if I suddenly started throwing around sums of such unaccustomed proportions ...

"The *yeitzer hara* came to my aid once more with his evil counsel: that I travel to some remote town, at first alone, and later bring out my family to join us. From that distance no one in my hometown would know if I had money or not, and even if they did find out after some time, they would assume that business was looking up and I had struck it rich. And besides, once I was well established in a far-off town, I surely wouldn't take to heart what my former townsmen had to say about me behind my back.

"So I hired a horse and wagon, and off I went. I let out word that I was going to try my luck wherever I happened to find it — in a job, or business, or whatever. And even my family knows no more than that.

"And just now, half an hour ago, I encountered your rebbe, the Baal Shem Tov, and all your colleagues, apparently on your way to a wedding. As soon as he saw me — and he has never in his life laid eyes on me before — your rebbe came across to me and said: 'My dear friend, take my advice! Go back home and return the money to your neighbor. I promise you that I will personally appear before the rabbinical court in your hometown and testify that you had no evil intentions when you took it.'

"And now" — the stranger heaved a sigh as he neared the end of his story — "I feel as if a heavy stone has been rolled off my heart. I'm now going to return straight home, with God's help. I'll give my friend his money, and the Baal Shem Tov will no doubt fulfill his promise and testify before the court that when I took the wallet I was acting in good faith. You'll see! Everything will work out well in the end, after all!"

◆§ *The A-B-C of Success*

Two prospective business partners once called on Reb Meir of Premishlan to request that he bless their joint enterprise with success.

"Have you written out your partnership contract yet?" he asked.

"No," they said.

"If so," said the tzaddik, "I'll write one out for you."

He took out a clean sheet of paper, wrote on it the first four letters of the Hebrew alphabet — א, ב, ג, ד — and handed it to them, saying: "Very well, here is your partnership contract."

Seeing that they were utterly perplexed, he explained: "In these four letters the secret of your success is hidden. The letters א,ב,ג,ד are the initials of אֱמוּנָה—בְּרָכָה; גְּנֵבָה—דַּלּוּת. If your transactions are *Above-board*—then *Blessing* will light upon them; if you *Cheat* — then you may expect to be *Destitute*."

All's Well that Ends Well

In Leipnick there lived a Jew by the name of Yossel who earned a meager livelihood by peddling merchandise among the surrounding villages. As he was preparing one day to set out with his humble wares he saw how downcast his wife looked, and asked her what was bothering her.

"Look, Yossel," she said, "things with us are pretty grim: even the most basic necessities are missing. That's what is bothering me."

"Don't worry," he reassured her. "The Prophet Eliyahu who has blessed so many people can bless us too!"

And off he went. On the way out of town he met the mail coach on its way towards Leipnick, and just as it passed him he saw that two envelopes fell out of it. Picking them up, he saw that one of them was marked with the information that it contained thirty thousand marks in cash, and it was to be delivered to some squire or other whose address was written there. The other was a perfectly ordinary addressed envelope. Without thinking much Yossel popped the fat envelope into his coat pocket, and at the top of his voice shouted out to the coach driver that he had dropped something. The mailman heard him and returned, thanked Yossel for the plain envelope, and continued on his way.

Not so Yossel. Instead of continuing towards the villages, he turned around and headed for home. By way of answer to his wife's wide-eyed surprise at seeing him as soon, he said: "Well, what did I tell you? Blessings have already been sent our way!" And he blithely told her the whole story.

The good woman was flabbergasted. "How could you ever have come to do such a thing? Don't you realize that it's plain and simple robbery? Are we suddenly going to become common thieves?!"

Yossel tried to calm her: "In the first place, the addressee isn't one of us. Secondly, he won't suffer any loss anyway, because the post office will have to pay him, and that belongs to the government, not to a private individual. So what's all the noise about?"

"Look here, Yossel," she persisted. "I'm just a plain ordinary housewife, and I don't know from clever words and fancy talk. All I know is that the money isn't ours, and we're not allowed to use up somebody else's! What will our children say when they wake up tomorrow morning and find out all of a sudden that their parents are thieves?"

But when she saw that all her words made no impact whatever on her husband, who was listening to all her rebukes in relaxed tranquility, and obviously was not even considering the possibility of returning his find, she tried another tack: "The people from the government will come and search through our house, for sure, because the mailman knows that you found one letter, and he'll guess that you found the other one, too."

Now this was an argument of a more convincing kind. Yossel got up quickly, moved the wardrobe from its corner, tore up one of the floorboards, hid the envelope under it, returned the plank, and pushed the wardrobe safely back into place. Sure enough, only a few hours later they had two callers — a gendarme, and the mailman. They cross-examined Yossel as thoroughly as they could, and he stoutly denied having seen any envelope apart from the one which he had so faithfully returned. His wife sat in silence. She was certainly bitterly disappointed with this husband of hers — but that was hardly any affair of their visitors... After an unsuccessful search of the house the policeman renewed his cross-examination, until the mailman spoke up: "Look, the letter which he found he passed on to me at once, which surely means that he found nothing else. Just because he's an honest man, and returned me the letter that he found, does that mean that we should suspect him without cause?"

Unexpectedly, the policeman flared up at these words, and turned on the mailman: "So you're putting in a good word for him, are you? It's obvious that this is a carefully-planned inside job! I'll have to arrest the two of you!"

And so Yossel was hauled off to jail. Word spread fast enough, and since his townsfolk all knew him as a simple, honest peddler, they assumed that he was the innocent victim of a vicious libel, and vied with each other in expressing their sympathy to his sorely embarrassed wife. Day by day they brought her food and drink, and delicacies in plenty for her defenseless little ones, who had been so cruelly separated from their sinless breadwinner...

In the meantime the postal authorities plastered the city with notices: whoever returned the lost envelope to the post office would receive a reward of five hundred rubles. Not surprisingly, the reward remained without a claimant.

One day the resourceful woman thought up a plan. She would take the bundle of notes to the local *rav*, and he in his wisdom would devise some means of returning it to the post office. In this way the whole matter would be dropped, and her Yossel would be freed. No sooner thought than done. She dragged the wardrobe from its corner, pulled up the floorboard, took out the envelope, and walked quickly to the home of the local *rav*, who was the celebrated Reb Baruch Frenkel-Teomim, the father-in-law of Reb Chaim of Zanz. As she approached the rabbi's house, however, she saw through the window that he was in the midst of teaching a group of Talmud scholars. She could hardly bring herself to walk in and confess the whole truth in the presence of a number of people, so she saved the situation simply: she threw the envelope through the open window into the rabbi's study, and promptly and anonymously left the scene.

The rabbi picked up the flying object, and to his

amazement identified it as a fat envelope with "30,000 Marks" written on it. This must clearly be the lost item that poor, innocent Yossel was imprisoned over — but who was the individual who had thrown it in incognito, and why had he not returned it to its proper address, the post office?

"Now this *is* a tricky business," thought the rabbi. "I'll have to consider my steps very carefully indeed."

His students had fortunately not seen what was written on the envelope that he had picked up as soon as it had fallen near his chair. He cut the lesson short, and walked up and down his room, deep in thought.

"If I go straight to the post office and return the money," he told himself, "that will only cause a *Chillul HaShem.* Who would ever believe such an alibi, that an anonymous stranger threw the object through the open window of the local rabbi's study ? The Name of Heaven would be disgraced. They will assume that the rabbi together with his community originally planned to lay hands on the government's money, but later changed their minds for some reason."

In the meantime he deposited the envelope in his drawer and locked it, and went out to stroll. That way, he would have a clear mind and be able to think his way out of his dilemma. When he was only a short distance from his home he checked himself: "Now that wasn't very clever of me, locking the envelope up in the drawer! Who knows — perhaps it was thrown into my house by some anti-Semite as the first step in a trumped-up libel? The money has got to be found right on the floor where it first landed. Any gendarme who comes to search the house will realize that no thief leaves his loot lying around on the floor!"

With that he went back, took the envelope out of the drawer, put it on the floor, and resumed his stroll. On and on he walked, turning over all the possibilities in his mind, until he found that he was on the outskirts of the city. There he was suddenly greeted by the bishop of Leipnick, who was out on his daily constitutional. The bishop had always respected him as a learned and holy man, and now asked him what made him look so preoccupied. A novel idea flickered in the rabbi's mind.

"Could you please tell me," he asked, "whether you are obliged to keep in strict confidence whatever you are told in confession?"

"Most certainly," intoned the cleric. "Secrets from such a source are divulged to no man."

"Another question," continued the rabbi. "Are you permitted to receive confessions from persons who are not of your faith?"

"I am indeed," returned the other.

"In that case," said the rabbi, "I would like to make confession to you, on condition that this take place in your home and not in your place of worship."

The bishop was dumbstruck: the rabbi was coming to him for confession?! But when he saw that this was no joking matter, and the rabbi was speaking in perfect seriousness, he answered that at home too he kept a special chair for confessions.

"I'm afraid not," said the rabbi. "I could really do without a special chair. What I had in mind was that we should both sit together on ordinary chairs next to the table, and there I would give you my confession."

The bishop was at a loss for a moment. "Reverend sir," he said, "I must point out that ecclesiastical statutes *are* ecclesiastical statutes."

Then he thought the better of it, and decided that out of deference for the rabbi he could allow an episcopal dispensation in this case, and suspend the conventional forms. He would receive the rabbi's confession without any of the trappings of churchly ceremonial.

"Very well," said the rabbi, "let us go home, and in about an hour I will call on you at your residence."

He went home to collect the envelope and took it to the bishop, who received him with all the politest marks of respect. It was now time to tell the bishop the whole story. When he had concluded, he explained his dilemma and his apprehensions, and requested that the cleric take the money from his hands, pass it on to the postal authorities, and tell them that someone had given it to him during confession. Under these circumstances no questions would be asked. The bishop listened carefully, and consented.

The next day the whole of Leipnick was agog with the

exciting news: the money had been found, and Yossel was free! The innocent little man had been arrested for nothing.

Overjoyed at his unexplained good fortune, Yossel yet had to face a tribunal of a different sort... As soon as he came home his wife told him how she had thrown the envelope into the house of the *rav*, who, being such a righteous and holy man, had immediately passed it on to the postal authorities in order that he, Yossel, be freed. "In which case," she concluded, "the right thing for you to do now is to go along to the *rav* to thank him — and to tell him the whole truth."

He had no option but to agree, and off he went to do his duty. As soon as the *rav* laid eyes on him he uttered the benediction מַתִּיר אֲסוּרִים, which praises Him Who frees the bound, and, his heart swelling with honest sentiments, expressed his joy that one so innocent and so righteous as Yossel had at last been saved from such a foul miscarriage of justice.

"No, rabbi, no!" Yossel insisted. "I am neither innocent nor righteous. I am a sinner!" — and the unwilling martyr told his whole story, expressing as well his profound regret at what he had done. And the *rav* for his part did his best to console him with the thought that the wrong had at last been rectified.

At this point they were joined by the bishop, who had come to pass on to the rabbi the reward of five hundred gold rubles that he had received from the postal authorities. The rabbi refused to accept the money. "You are the one who deserves it," he said, "for your trouble in conveying the envelope to its rightful owner. Moreover, I am deeply indebted to you for getting me out of a fix."

The bishop was not readily convinced. "No," he said, "the reward is not due to me, because I did not find the money. And if indeed you refuse to accept the five hundred rubles for yourself, you might perhaps like to distribute it instead among the poor."

"Even that," said the *rav*, "is your prerogative, for it is you who did the good deed."

In the course of this discussion the *rav* suddenly recalled — Yossel. "Look here, my friend," he said to the bishop. "Here before us stands Yossel. *He* is the innocent victim of this whole unpleasant affair, and he is poor into the bargain. Wouldn't it be proper to give *him* the reward?"

The bishop was much impressed with the rabbi's ingenuity. "How is it that this didn't occur to me until now?" he mused.

Yossel was at first unwilling, not seeing himself as exactly deserving of a reward, but the *rav* insisted that he accept it and use it to open a shop. He even undertook to send him customers. And so it was that Yossel took the reward, opened a business, prospered exceedingly, and gave charity with an open hand to all comers until the end of his days.

◊§ *An Uncommon Thief*

Before Reb Yitzchak of Vorki became a rebbe, he was employed as a clerk in the timber business of Tamar'l, a woman who is affectionately remembered for the generosity with which she distributed her wealth among needy chassidim. In the course of conversation with a fellow clerk in the office in the forest, Reb Yitzchak once said: "You know, one is allowed to steal just a little from one's employer. In fact, I do it myself."

"So you do too?" said the other. And he went ahead to tell what he himself had stolen, and what he yet planned to lay hands on.

Reb Yitchak was aghast. "Do you think that's what I meant?" he cried. "Don't you realize that you're just a common thief? All I meant was that when one is not actually needed on duty, one is allowed to steal a little time for the study of Torah — not plain thievery!"

These were strong words. They found their way into the man's heart, and he lived the rest of his life as a sincere penitent.

◊§ *Not by Bread Alone*

לֹא תַחְמֹד
You shall not covet (20:14)

"Why are most of your chassidim so poor?" a visiting tzaddik once asked Reb Uri of Strelisk, nicknamed הַשָּׂרָף, the fiery angel, on account of the rapturous fervor of his prayers.

"My chassidim haven't the slightest desire to be rich," he replied.

And, to support his assertion, he called across one of his chassidim and said: "Right now, while this righteous guest and I are sitting together, is an auspicious hour in heaven. Whatever you ask of us will be yours."

"Very well," said the chassid. "My single wish is that every morning it be granted me to utter the prayer בָּרוּךְ שֶׁאָמַר ('Blessed be He Who spoke') just like you do, rebbe!"

On another occasion the *rebbitzin* said to her husband: "Your chassidim spend so much time with you. Why don't you do something to better their material situation?"

Replied Reb Uri: "Watch what happens tomorrow, and you will be convinced that my chassidim are not interested in riches."

At prayers the next morning, when his chassidim had reached the phrase וְהָעֹשֶׁר וְהַכָּבוֹד מִלְּפָנֶיךָ — "Wealth and honor come from You" — he took the corner of his frockcoat in his hand, approached his chassidim, and said: "Whoever wants money, let him put his hand into the hem of this coat, and he will be rich."

But not one man was interested.

סדר משפטים
sidra mishpatim

To Live Forever

וַעֲבָדוֹ לְעֹלָם *And he shall serve him forever (21:6)*

Reb Yaakov Yitzchak, the Chozeh of Lublin, once said to his disciple, Reb Zvi of Zhidachov: "So long as I am alive I am not afraid that you will slip from your present spiritual level. But afterwards — who knows?"

Said Reb Zvi: "I don't want to live longer than you, rebbe."

"How can you say such a thing?" protested the Chozeh. "You are still a young man, and I am old."

"Rebbe," replied Reb Zvi, "I will pray that you live forever."

"But does mortal man live forever?" asked the Chozeh.

"I meant, rebbe," explained Reb Zvi, "that you should live one hundred and twenty years, as Moshe Rabbeinu did."

"Come, now Reb Zvi," said the Seer. "Just a moment ago you said 'forever', and now you're saying 'one hundred and twenty years.' A hundred and twenty years is not forever."

Replied Reb Zvi: "I came across the idea in some book that Moshe Rabbeinu lived one hundred and twenty years, corresponding to the number of jubilee years during which the world will exist. For in the Talmud it is written that שִׁיתָּא אַלְפֵי שָׁנֵי הַוָה עַלְמָא – 'The world will exist six thousand years' – and in six thousand years there are a hundred and twenty *yovel* years. In the Torah, furthermore, the jubilee year is sometimes called עֹלָם, meaning 'forever,' as in the phrase וַעֲבָדוֹ לְעֹלָם, literally 'and he shall serve him forever,' and in fact meaning 'until the jubilee year.' In brief, one hundred and twenty years can be called לְעֹלָם, 'forever.' "

The Chozeh was well pleased with this answer from his disciple.

"And in what book did you see this idea?" he asked.

"Well, actually," answered Reb Zvi, "it could have been mine..."

◆§ In Search of the Truth

שְׁאֵרָהּ כְּסוּתָהּ ... לֹא יִגְרָע
Her food and clothing ... shall he not diminish (21:10)

When Reb Uri of Strelisk first visited Reb Shlomo of Karlin as a young man the tzaddik gave him his hand in welcome and wished him *Shalom*. Such an awe overwhelmed the young man that he understood at once that Reb Shlomo was in fact his true rebbe – for is it not written that "The awe of our rebbe shall be like the awe of heaven"?

From then on he was a devoted disciple of Reb Shlomo, and throughout the time that he spent at Karlin, his pious young wife was a househelp in the home of Reb Chaim Kohen Rapaport, the president of the rabbinical court of Lvov (or, according to another tradition, in the home of Reb Naftali Herz Suchstvir). Be that as it may, when Reb Uri came home for the festival of *Pessach* he was obliged to join in the *Seder* of his wife's employer. When that rabbi saw the holy rapture with which he participated in the *Seder*, he addressed a question to him: "Since, Sir, you are a righteous man — and it is written: 'And You fulfilled Your words, for You are righteous' — why, then, do you not fulfill what is written in the *kesubbah*, where the marriage contract specifies, 'And I will work...and sustain you and provide for you?' "

Replied Reb Uri: "You will note that the same passage goes on to say, 'according to the custom of Jewish husbands who provide for their wives *in truth.*' And that is why I first traveled to my rebbe in Karlin — in search of the truth."

Healing the Whole Man

וְרַפֹּא יְרַפֵּא
And he shall surely heal him (21:19)

The patient was so weak that he could not even utter a syllable, and his doctor despaired of saving his life. It so happened that the Baal Shem Tov passed through his town, and was asked to visit the man, who was fast sinking. He saw the patient and asked the lady of the house to prepare him some meat broth; after drinking it, the patient began to speak. The Baal Shem Tov thereafter continued attending to him until he was completely restored to health.

The doctor was amazed, and asked the Baal Shem Tov to explain what he had done. "For I know," he added, "that the poor man's blood vessels were diseased beyond cure."

Said the tzaddik: "You comprehended the patient physically; I comprehended him spritually. Every man has 248 organs and 365 blood vessels, corresponding to the 248 positive precepts of the Torah and the 365 negative commandments. When a person disobeys one of these commands, the organ or blood vessel corresponding to that mitzvah is affected. When, for example, he trangresses a large number of prohibitive commandments, a large number of vessels are impaired, and when the circulation of the blood is hampered, the man's life is in danger. So I spoke to the soul of this patient, appealing to it that it repent. It agreed to do so, so all the man's organs and blood vessels became viable again, and then I was able to heal him."

◆§ A Sinful Silence

כָּל אַלְמָנָה וְיָתוֹם לֹא תְעַנּוּן
You shall not afflict any widow or orphan (22:21)

The following story of the Baal Shem Tov was told by Reb David of Tolna.

One *Motzaei Shabbos*, after the Sabbath had passed, the Baal Shem Tov took three of his distinguished disciples with him in his wagon — Reb David of Milkiev, Reb David Sirkis, and Reb David Leikes. As was his custom, the tzaddik sat the Russian wagon-driver, Alexei, with his back to the horses, and, within moments, miles and miles of highway vanished under their wheels.

On the second day they lost their way, and found themselves in the trackless maze of a forest so dense that the very light of day barely filtered through to them. The tzaddik was dismayed. Such an experience was foreign to him, and he could not fathom the meaning of this strange situation. To make matters worse, he found that he had been deprived of that heightened spiritual sensitivity which is the gift of heaven to tzaddikim. For the moment he was as uninspired as the plainest man in the street. Things were no better by Friday. When the Baal Shem Tov saw that the eve of *Shabbos* was approaching, and they were nowhere near a settled place of any kind, he was so grieved and dispirited that he fell asleep. His disciples hoped that heaven's voice would tell him in a dream what they should do, but he awoke unenlightened. Deep was their anguish — when suddenly, at midday, they saw a light flickering in the distance. At long last, they thought, the Almighty had directed them to some inhabited spot where they could spend the holy day.

Heading for the light, they came upon a cottage which stood alone in the midst of the forest, its doorway darkened by the hulking silhouette of a vulgar and barefoot Jewish peasant dressed in clothes as coarse as his visage. When they asked him if they could spend *Shabbos* with him he growled: "Who needs you and your *Shabbos?* I could tell just by looking that you are a bunch of chassidim and preachers, and I could never stand the likes of you, just like my father and grandfather before me. Move away from here! I don't even want to look at you!"

The disciples of the Baal Shem Tov asked him whether there was any village that they could reach before sundown, but he said that the nearest one was as far away as whatever place they had come from. Only after they had begged him again for permission to spend *Shabbos* in his cottage and had offered him an exorbitant sum in return for the favor, did he begrudge them his consent. Even then, he had a list of conditions: they were not to say their prayers aloud, lest the gentiles who came to buy vodka from him take fright and leave him; they were to complete their prayers hastily, because he was a man with a ravenous appetite who did not like being kept waiting for his meals, whether morning or evening; and they were not to bother him with detailed questions as to how perfectly kosher the food was, in the fussy manner of chassidim and other fools ...

After they had rested a little, the Baal Shem Tov asked their host whether there was a river nearby in which they could immerse themselves in spiritual preparation for *Shabbos*. This innocent request triggered a barrage of curses. He accused them of being thieves, and threatened to throw out all their belongings and to drive them out of his house — which he would have done, had they not all entreated him to allow them to stay.

It was a bare dwelling, with neither table nor chair nor bench, except for four short poles driven into the earth, supporting a plank. There seemed to be no sign of habitation, and whatever rooms could be seen around appeared to be equally desolate. Nor was there any man in sight, whether gentiles buying vodka as the man had led them to expect, nor any other; nor was there as much as a cat or a bird to lend a sign of life to the bleakness that chilled the air and made the newcomers tremble in terror. The afternon was passing, but their host, instead of busying himself with the necessary preparations in honor of *Shabbos*, strode up and down the house, biting into chunks of melon, or whistling away to himself in the manner of the gentiles of those parts. As sunset neared, he covered what served for a table with a length of black homespun cloth, poked his thumb into a lump of clay and stuck a candle in the hole, and lit it. They did not see him saying the afternoon prayer, but they observed how he galloped his way through the twilight hymns and prayers that welcome the Day of Rest, mispronouncing the words in his irreverent haste like the coarsest yokel. His guests were likewise forced to read through the beloved words at this unaccustomed pace, in order that he not be kept waiting, for this was one of his conditions. Prayers over, they turned to wish him *Gut Shabbos*. His answer: "A wretched year upon you all!" Following universal custom, they next began to sing *Shalom Aleichem*, the hymn of welcome to the ministering angels which come to bless every Jewish home on Friday night with peace and tranquility. But peace was not to be theirs: their host's abuse cut short their pensive harmonies.

It was time to express the sanctity of the day by reciting *Kiddush*. The peasant poured himself a mug of vodka, and told them that they would have to fulfill this obligation by listening to him. Guessing what his *Kiddush* would sound like, they begged to be allowed to recite it themselves, and offered him extra payment for the modest amount of vodka needed, but they were obliged to content themselves with listening to his maltreatment of its words. When he had given them the few drops that he had left in the mug he brought to the table a loaf of coarse bran, and silenced them when they asked for the two loaves with which *Shabbos* is traditionally honored. Nor were they to touch his loaf, for he said their hands would contaminate it. Instead, he himself carved them each a chunk, and on this they whispered the benediction of *HaMotzi* over bread. The meal consisted of a bowl of lentil stew. Each man was given a spoon, and they had no choice but to eat out of the same bowl, together with the master of the house. If they could not nourish their bodies in a manner befitting the holy day, at least their souls could be warmed by the singing of *zemiros*, the lyrical mealtime hymns of Friday night — but this too was denied them.

It was barely daybreak when they woke up the next morning, but their host was already striding barefoot up and down the house, gobbling up the words of the morning prayers with brutal indifference. Once again they were forced to forgo the leisurely meditation which customarily accompanied their prayers. When the time came for the mystical Third Meal at dusk, he scoffed at them as if their only interest in it was food, so they made do by exchanging Torah thoughts in a whisper, having learned to be wary of arousing his ire.

"What is this that God has brought upon us?" they asked each other. But even from their rebbe they could have no reply, for his clear vision had been dimmed for the while, and his soul was now too dull to ascend and discern the secret ways of heaven.

For most of the night the master of the house kept them awake with his insults. After snatching an unsteady nap they rose early to say their prayers, and prepared to leave. Their host slammed the door, and told them that he had already prepared them breakfast. They were only too willing to pay him for the meal without staying to eat it, but he shouted: "Would you make a robber of me, to have me take your money for nothing?"

And so it was that by day he detained them, and by night it was impossible to set out in the forest — until Wednesday, when he laid hands on all of their possessions by way of fee for his hospitality, and they prepared to leave. At that moment a door was opened by a woman richly dressed and bejewelled. She approached the Baal Shem Tov and said: "Rebbe! Please stay with us for *Shabbos.*"

The tzaddik was wonderstruck. Then he said: "Two things are beyond me. Firstly, what makes you think I am a *rav?* And secondly, if you know me to be a *rav*, why did you allow my *Shabbos* to be so disturbed, and not appear earlier?"

"But rebbe," said the woman, "don't you recognize me?"

Since the Baal Shem Tov could not recall who she was, she continued: "Perhaps, rebbe, you remember that so-

 and-so many years ago I was a little orphan maid in your house. I came to your household with lice in my hair, and every Friday your *rebbitzin* used to scrape and rub my scalp. Once I cried out and would not let her continue, so she slapped me on the cheek. You were sitting nearby and kept silent. Not a word did you say in protest. At that moment the Almighty's ire was aroused by this transgression of the commandment: כָּל אַלְמָנָה וְיָתוֹם לֹא תְעַנּוּן — 'You shall not afflict any widow or orphan.' You were sentenced in the Heavenly Court to being denied your portion in the World to Come. Years later, when I married this man — a hidden tzaddik — our hearts bled when we learned what was written in your verdict. We prayed that you be forgiven, and it was granted that your tranquility would be marred on one *Shabbos* — for *Shabbos* is a foretaste of the World to Come — and through this exchange your sin would be mercifully atoned. But then we saw that there was no one in the whole world who was prepared to disturb your *Shabbos*, so we took this duty upon ourselves. And now, rebbe, you may rest in the assurance that your share in the World to Come is awaiting you, as it was in earlier years."

At that moment a holy spirit returned to repose upon him. With eyes now illumined as in happier times, it was now given him to see the truth in every word that the woman had spoken. He thanked her for her invitation, and together with his disciples stayed on in the home of the hidden tzaddik for a *Shabbos* made happy by the comradely exchange of chassidic insights into the secret ways of heaven.

⸎ *Refinement of Taste*

Reb Avigdor Halberstam, the brother of Reb Chaim of Zanz, was once the honored *Shabbos* guest of one of the prominent citizens of some township. The custom in those parts was that the householder would pass the whole pot of *cholent* to his distinguished guest, who would be asked — by way of compliment, as if he were the host — to apportion the steaming stew into the plates of the members of the family. As the *cholent* was passed to him, Reb Avigdor caught a whiff of it, tasted it, then tasted it again, and again — until bit by bit he finished it all, leaving nothing for the others at the table. Then he asked: "Is there perhaps a little more *cholent?*" And this, too, he finished, down to the last spoonful.

The host and his family were dumbfounded — but it was known that tzaddikim see a spiritual mission in eating, revealing the sparks of sanctity that are hidden in the things of This World. And who would be so bold as to pretend to guess at the hidden things that tzaddikim relish...?

But some of his disciples were present, and in all the time they had known him they had never observed him serving his Maker in *this* manner. So they gathered up courage and after some time asked him to enlighten them as to the hidden things that he had relished in that *cholent.*

"I am sure I can trust you with the explanation," he said. "By mistake, the maid in that household flavored the *cholent* with kerosine instead of vinegar. I could smell it and taste it. I gathered that if our host and hostess would find out, the defenseless girl would never hear the end of it, and possibly lose her job as well — and she's a penniless orphan, poor thing. So I ate up the *cholent,* and let them think of me whatever they please. Why should an orphaned waif have to suffer abuse?"

◆§ *The Torah is Not in Heaven*

וְהָיוּ נְשֵׁיכֶם אַלְמָנוֹת
And your wives will be widows (22:23)

And your wives will be widows: Wives will be bound like living widows for lack of evidence of their husbands' death, and therefore unable to remarry *(Rashi).*

An *agunah* — a wife in this predicament — once came to Reb Yitzchak of Neshchiz, and told him of her husband whose whereabouts were unknown.

"Go in peace," said the tzaddik, "and the Almighty will soon help you while you are on your way."

Heading for home, she passed through the nearby village of Zaprudy, and stopped to rest on a bench outside the local inn. A Polish militiaman rode up on his horse, went inside for a drink, and returned to take a seat next to the *agunah*. The modest custom of Jewish women bade her move away a little, whereupon the soldier scoffed: "We used to be closely related once; why do you move away now?"

"Why, if it isn't my husband!" she cried.

And, to the astonishment of a number of onlookers who heard every word of that strange conversation, he mentioned the names of all their relatives, described their former dwelling in detail, and, in brief, identified himself beyond any shadow of a doubt. They were interrupted by the approach of another armed militiaman, who likewise rode up for a drink, and came out to join them. In no time the two soldiers were arguing angrily over which horse had first disturbed the other. The newcomer lost his temper, grabbed his musket, and shot the other dead — in full sight of the circle of onlookers, whose evidence in due course was to release the woman from her state of doubt and enable her to remarry, in accordance with the legal procedure laid down in the Torah.

The tzaddik later explained that her husband had in fact died long before, but no rabbinic court of law is permitted to pronounce an *agunah* free to marry on the strength of knowledge granted by the gift of heavenly inspiration. It was therefore necessary that her husband be clothed in such a form and circumstance, in order to enable such a pronouncement to be made according to the due processes of Torah law.

◆§ *A Promise for a Promise*

A chassid who was a *shochet* in Odessa once traveled with his wife to the mineral springs which were to be found at some distance from their city. The owner of the village in at which they stayed on their way was an exceedingly old woman. In fact even her grandchildren, who also lived there together with their numerous progeny, were already advanced in years.

Sensing that her guests from Odessa were chassidim, the wizened old woman told them her story: "I was only twenty-five years old when I was left an *agunah*. The Baal Shem Tov was still alive in those days, and I desperately wanted to visit him so that he could help me out of my troubles. After a great deal of effort I finally reached him, and told him that my husband had disappeared, and that I was left with our little boy. The Baal Shem Tov rested his head on his hands, then looked up and told me with a heavy heart: 'My daughter, I am unable to help you. Your husband is dead, but there are no witnesses to testify to his death, so you will have to remain an *agunah* all your life.' Then he added: 'My daughter! If you promise me that throughout your life you will conduct yourself in a manner befitting a virtuous Jewess, I will give you my blessing that you live to see generation upon generation of descendants from this little boy, and that you be well provided for always.' I gave him my word of honor — and here I am, a hundred and five years old, with five generations of descendants all around me!"

☙ *The Little Things that Count*

אִם כֶּסֶף תַּלְוֶה אֶת עַמִּי
If you lend money (22:24)

If you lend money: Every "if" in the Torah refers to a voluntary act, except for three, which introduce mandatory mitzvos — and this is one of them *(Rashi).*

Whether awake or in his dreams, Reb Menachem Mendel of Lubavitch would often see his grandfather, Reb Shneur Zalman of Liadi, who had passed away from his life in This World, and who brought him solutions from the World of Truth to the learned problems which troubled him in both the overt and hidden areas of the Torah. On one occasion he was closeted in his study, profoundly immersed in his books, and in doubt as to how to resolve certain scholarly questions. He yearned to see his grandfather — but this was not granted him, and he was deeply distressed.

A long time passed, and one morning Reb Menachem Mendel rose early to go to pray in the *shul* of his father-in-law, Reb Dov Ber of Lubavitch. On his way through the market place he was stopped by a simple pious Jew who made a living from his petty transactions there. It was market day, and the man asked for the loan of three rubles until the evening, or until the next morning. Reb

 Menachem Mendel asked him to call on him at home after he had returned from the *Shacharis* service, and then he would give him the loan.

Arriving at *shul* he prepared himself for prayer, and had already taken out his *tallis* and put it over his shoulder in readiness to wrap himself in it, when the request of that man came to mind. It had not been right on his part to defer the loan: today was market day, and in the meantime that dealer could possibly have earned something. He laid down the *tallis* at once, went home, took five rubles, and set out to find the man — which he eventually did, though with great difficulty, for the market place had filled by now with hundreds of peasants with their wagons and merchandise from the surrounding villages. The little deed done, he returned to *shul*.

No sooner had he wrapped himself in his *tallis* and put on his *tefillin* than he saw before him the joyful countenance of his grandfather, who answered his scholarly questions and then added: "When a man gives a loan to a fellow Jew with all his heart and without any untoward motives, and does a favor lovingly, in fulfillment of the command וְאָהַבְתָּ לְרֵעֲךָ כָּמוֹךָ — 'Love your neighbor as yourself,' — for such a man the portals of all the palaces of heaven are opened wide."

◆§ *The Tyranny of the Majority*

אַחֲרֵי רַבִּים לְהַטֹּת
To incline after a multitude (23:2)

Reb Shlomo of Radomsk felt uncomfortable with the document presented to him by a multitude of chassidim in which they made him their rebbe. On one occasion he scolded a large number of chassidim who had foregathered in his *beis midrash* for one of the festivals: "What do you want of me? Have I not told you time and again that I am neither a rebbe nor a tzaddik?"

The chassidim, however, did not budge, and quietly waited for him to receive them. Only one of them spoke up in answer, an old and respected sage.

"Rebbe," he said, "we who are facing you here are a multitude, and we, the many, hold that you are our rebbe. And it is a well-established legal rule that where there is a conflict of opinion between a single view and a view held by many, the law is laid down according to the majority. According to the views of Torah law, therefore, you are obliged to obey us, the many; and — as our rebbe — to teach us the way in which we should live, both spiritually and materially."

To which Reb Shlomo answered: "This, then, is what King David had in mind when he wrote in *Psalms:* אַתָּה יָדַעְתָּ לְאִוַּלְתִּי וְאַשְׁמוֹתַי מִמְּךָ לֹא נִכְחָדוּ אַל יֵבֹשׁוּ בִי קֹוֶיךָ ... אַל יִכָּלְמוּ בִי מְבַקְשֶׁיךָ — 'You know my folly, and my sins are not hidden from You. Let not those who trust in You be ashamed because of me ...; let not those who seek You be confounded on my account ...' That is to say: 'You, Master of the Universe, know my faults and limitations — that I am neither a sage nor a tzaddik. But people do know this, and they insist: 'Rebbe, help us!' And according to their lights they are right, for the view of the majority always prevails over the opinion of an individual. But that leaves me with a request to You, Master of the Universe: 'Let not those who trust in You be ashamed because of me ...; let not those who seek You be confounded on my account!'"

◆§ *The Mystic and the Minister*

In 1843 the Jews of Russia were ordered by the Czarist government to choose rabbinical delegates whose task would be to answer various questions to be posed by the educational authorities. Those chosen were Reb Menachem Mendel of Lubavitch; the renowned Lithuanian scholar Rabbi Yitzchak of Volozhin, representing non-chassidic circles; a learned chassidic magnate from Berditchev called Reb Yisrael Heilprin; and Betzalel Stern, a headmaster from Odessa, representing the "Enlightenment" views of the *Maskilim.* The conference, held at St. Petersburg, was chaired by a government minister by the name of Count Ubarov, and all the religious problems raised by him were resolved in the spirit of the Torah.

When the question arose of permitting the instruction of the mystical teachings of Kabbalah and Chassidism, the affirmative view was of course supported by Reb Menachem Mendel of Lubavitch and Reb Yisrael

 Heilprin; Betzalel Stern opposed it; and Rabbi Yitzchak of Volozhin remained silent. In the course of this session, which took place on a Friday, the minister said to Reb Menachem Mendel: "In this matter we will follow the advice of your Torah, and 'incline after the majority.' Heilprin and yourself say Aye, Stern and I say Nay, and the rabbi from Volozhin holds his peace. Since his silence implies agreement with our view, we are in the majority."

The rebbe was electrified by these words. "No matter what happens," he said, "the study of Kabbalah and Chassidism must go on!"

The minister merely motioned to his attendants, and the rebbe was led away to a cell in the same building for solitary confinement. The delegates who remained in the conference room were alarmed, because the minister strode back and forth in a rage.

After a little while the rebbe started reciting the *Minchah* prayer of Friday afternoon in the singsong of his grandfather, Reb Shneur Zalman of Liadi — that well-loved singsong that expresses the yearning of a soul in This World to cleave to its Source. After lingering on the verses of thanksgiving in Psalm 107, he went on to the passage from the *Zohar* which begins *Pasach Eliyahu,* describing the links which make up the mystical bond between the Creator and all things created. And his words, proceeding from the heart, found their way into the hearts of all those who heard him.

"What is that he is saying?" asked the minister.

"*Minchah,* the afternoon prayer," he was told.

"And on what subject is he reading?" he asked further.

"The very subject we spoke of — a passage of Kabbalah from the *Zohar,*" they said.

The minister sat for some time, entranced. When the rebbe had completed his prayer, the minister called out: "Schneersohn! Come out of your cell!"

The rebbe was released, and resumed his place at the conference table. The minister now changed his tune: "Now let us see. Heilpern and yourself say Aye, and the rabbi of Volozhin is silent, which may be understood to indicate his agreement with your stand. Since you are thus in the majority, your view must be upheld."

Since, however, *Shabbos* was nearing, the session had to be suspended without any policy decision being formally recorded.

The anguish of that day took its toll of the rebbe's health, and the last remaining session had to be deferred until he was well. When the other delegates had already met in the conference room, Betzalel Stern left them for a moment to take a breath of fresh air in the adjoining garden. At that moment the rebbe was on his way to the meeting place, accompanied by his son Reb Yehudah Leib (later rebbe in Kopust). There were two ways of reaching it — along the road, or through the garden. The rebbe chose the latter, and on the way they met Stern. His eyes streaming with tears, the rebbe took his hand in his, and began by quoting a famous dictum from the Talmud: "Rabbi Judah HaNasi wept and said, 'There are such as earn their portion in the World to Come in a single hour.' You are now given the possibility of doing exactly that, if you support the cause of Kabbalah!"

His words made their impact, and Stern, a changed man, spoke out in support of the rebbe's cause. The matter was duly recorded and registered by the Czarist authorities, and confirmed by the Imperial seal, and the rebbe journeyed home to Lubavitch with joyful thanksgiving.

☙ *Ends and Means*

מִדְּבַר שֶׁקֶר תִּרְחָק
Keep yourself far from a lie (23:7)

In the course of the self-appraisal that accompanies the bedside prayer, a wealthy chassid from Janowitz decided that for everything he uttered that smacked of a lie that he would donate twenty-five rubles to charity.

He mentioned his undertaking to his *melamed*, the tutor whom he retained in his household.

"Then lie!" advised the *melamed*. "You will be providing sustenance for needy Jews."

But when that *melamed* later visited Lubavitch, Reb Shmuel reprimanded him for his advice.

◈§ Integrity

Reb Yechezkel of Shiniva, the son of Reb Chaim of Zanz, was widely known as a lover of truth and a detester of falsehood. His father testifies in one of his responsa: "You could give him everything this world has to offer, and he would not go back on his word."

A tailor had once been hired to make up a garment for one of his grandchildren, and when he brought it to be tried on, the little boy absolutely refused to take it off. Only when the tailor promised him that he would make him pretty pockets did he agree to part with the new garments. The tzaddik thereupon insisted that the tailor make up pockets exactly as promised — "for I do not want the child to become accustomed to telling lies."

At another time he spent *Shabbos* in the home of one of his chassidim, and in his honor the host bedecked the table with a new, silver-plated candelabrum, acquired especially for the occasion.

"Both falsehood *and* conceit!" said the rebbe, and asked that it be removed from the table.

◈§ The Power of a Seudah

וַיֶּחֱזוּ אֶת הָאֱלֹהִים וַיֹּאכְלוּ וַיִּשְׁתּוּ
And they beheld God, and ate and drank (24:11)

Reb Pinchas of Korets once circumcised an infant, but could not stop the bleeding. At that moment the company was joined by Reb Zusya of Hanipoli, who instructed all those present to wash their hands immediately in preparation for the *seudas mitzvah*, the festive meal, which they were to partake at once. The bleeding stopped.

Reb Zusya explained himself as follows: "It is written: וַיֶּחֱזוּ אֶת הָאֱלֹקִים וַיֹּאכְלוּ וַיִּשְׁתּוּ — 'And they beheld God, and ate and drank.' When one sees the attribute of stern justice which is indicated by the particular Name of God used in this verse, one should eat and drink and be joyful, for thereby one can temper the sternness of a divine verdict."

And when Reb Zusya himself was ill and bedridden, he used to arrange to have a *seudah* made for his sake, in which pious scholars would participate. In support of this custom he was wont to quote the phrase from

Psalms: סְעָדֵנִי וְאִוָּשֵׁעָה—'Support me and I will be saved.' By playing on the similarity between סְעָדֵנִי and סְעוּדָה, Reb Zusya found another meaning in this phrase from *Tehillim:* "Make a *seudah* for me, so that I shall be healed."

◆§ *Of Tea and Eternity*

During the mystical Third Sabbath Meal — *Seudah Shlishis* — it was the custom of Reb Chaim of Zanz to quietly share some of his rare Torah insights with his disciples, and then to linger with them in the stillness of dusk, while his soul roamed free in a higher, more spiritual world. On awaking from his trance of *dveikus,* he would pensively sing his favorite *zemiros,* including *Kel Mistater* ("God Who conceals Himself").

It once happened that while he was singing this hymn he began to cough violently, but tried to continue singing nevertheless. His son, Reb Baruch, quickly rose and brought his father a cup of tea. Reb Chaim declined to drink: "What do you expect me to do with this? In the spiritual sphere of *Atzilus,* you know one doesn't drink tea."

"I know, father," rejoined his son, "but in the spiritual sphere of *Atzilus* one doesn't cough, either."

And the tzaddik drank up his tea.

◆§ *Seeing and Believing*

A chassid of Reb Mordechai of Lechovitch by the name of Reb Meir had a business partner who was a *misnaged* called Reb Gershon, and no matter how earnestly he was asked, he would never agree to joining Reb Meir on any of his numerous visits to his rebbe. On one occasion, however, since their joint business interests brought them both to Lechovitch in any case, Reb Gershon consented to accompany his partner to visit his rebbe.

The tzaddik was at his table when they arrived, and Reb Meir observed that his *misnagdisher* partner was enthralled by what he saw. As they left he asked: "What made you so excited on your very first visit to the rebbe?"

The *misnaged* answered: "I saw that the tzaddik eats in such sanctity that his very eating resembles the priestly service of the *Kohen Gadol* in the Temple!"

Reb Meir thereupon brought his plaint to the tzaddik: "Rebbe, is it right that this fellow, on his very first visit here, is privileged to perceive the way in which you serve the Creator, while I, who always come here, do not see the same things?"

Replied the tzaddik: "He is a *misnaged*, and has to see with his eyes; you are a chassid, and have to believe."

סדר תרומה
sidra terumah

✥ One for the Misnagdim

וְיִקְחוּ לִי תְּרוּמָה
Let them bring Me an offering (25:2)

After the passing of Reb Moshe of Kobrin most of his chassidim became followers of Reb Avraham of Slonim, until then the head of the yeshivah of Slonim, and appointed him their rebbe. The head of the city's rabbinical court at the time was Rabbi Yitzchak Aizik of Slonim, and this *av beis din* was an outspoken *misnaged*.

When they once met on some festive occasion Rabbi Yitzchak Aizik asked the newly-appointed rebbe: "What is the meaning of this, Reb Avraham? Not so long ago we knew you as a man like other men — so how does one suddenly turn into a tzaddik, with people all around proclaiming how holy you are?"

Replied the tzaddik: "What is so surprising about that? We have a precedent for this in the Torah. Supposing there is a heap of ordinary grain, and along comes a Jew and sets aside a certain portion of it as a tithe, then that *terumah* becomes holy; it may not be eaten by non-priests or those who are unclean, and it may be eaten only in a state of ritual purity. The same applies to an ordinary man. When the Jews of a whole community set him aside for a holy task and call him their rebbe, their very act causes a measure of sanctity to light upon him."

❀ ❀ ❀

To be fair to all parties, it should be recorded that the *misnagdim* tell the identical story — except that they add a retort which Reb Yitzchak Aizik is alleged to have made on the spot: "To that, my friend, the Mishnah has an explicit answer. 'If a deafmute, imbecile, or minor set aside *terumah,* their tithe cannot be considered a tithe. . .' "

☙ With All Your Heart

מֵאֵת כָּל אִישׁ אֲשֶׁר יִדְּבֶנּוּ לִבּוֹ
From every man whose heart prompts him (25:2)

Whose heart prompts him: The verb יִדְּבֶנּוּ comes from the word נְדָבָה, and expresses goodwill *(Rashi).*

A wealthy individual who was known for his miserliness once wanted to give Reb Shlomo of Radomsk a large sum of money as a *pidyon,* but the tzaddik absolutely refused to accept it. When asked his reason — for he could certainly have put it to good use — he replied: "If you had seen with what glee he took the money back, you would not have asked why I did not want to receive it."

❀ ❀ ❀

On another occasion, according to the custom on festivals, his chassidim were taking turns at placing bottles of wine on the rebbe's table, the names of the donors being announced by the *gabbai.* At one point Reb Shlomo asked an attendant to remove a certain bottle from the table, and explained himself by quoting a Mishnah which says that a liquid whose current location is at first desired by its owner (שֶׁתְּחִלָּתוֹ לְרָצוֹן), but which is later unwanted there (שֶׁאֵין סוֹפוֹ לְרָצוֹן), renders objects susceptible to contracting impurity. In fact this Mishnah refers to the detailed laws governing the transmission of ritual impurity, but Reb Shlomo — for this occasion — took it to mean the following: "This liquid was also 'at first desired by its owner.' At this moment, when he asks to have his bottle of wine placed on the table, he does so willingly; but it is 'later unwanted there,' for after the festival he will have to pay up his account for what was taken on credit. This he will do unwillingly, thus making it clear that the gift was not made wholeheartedly *in the first instance* — and that is why I would rather not accept it."

◈ *Patience for the Imperfect*

וְעָשׂוּ לִי מִקְדָּשׁ
And they shall make Me a sanctuary (25:8)

And they shall make Me a sanctuary that I may dwell among them: The Torah does not say בְּתוֹכוֹ — "within *it*," but בְּתוֹכָם — "within *them*" *(Shlah).*

After the passing of Reb Menachem Mendel of Kotsk his chassidim took upon themselves the leadership of Reb Yitzchak Meir of Ger, who lived at the time in Warsaw. After a few years there he thought it preferable that he move to a small town, because the numbers of disciples coming to visit him and to hear his teachings snowballed from hundreds to thousands, and he did not think it advisable that the younger scholars should spend long periods in a big city.

The word spread like wildfire, and from all directions came requests from representatives of communities that he become their spiritual leaer. None of these were accepted, until an invitation came from the small town of Ger (Gora Kalwaria) near Warsaw, and this the rebbe accepted at once. When the good news arrived, many of the townsfolk accompanied their communal leaders to Warsaw to hand the rebbe the traditional letter of rabbinic appointment, and he promised to move to their township within a short time. This he did, despite the repeated requests of the communal leaders of Warsaw that he remain in their city. At first he lived in the house which the people of Ger kept for the local *rav*, and his chassidim studied and prayed in the community's *beis midrash.* Seeing, however, that this building could not accommodate the thousands of disciples who streamed there from all parts of Poland, the more prosperous amongst them undertook to build a fitting residence for the rebbe, and next to it a spacious *beis midrash* for his chassidim.

At the festive dedication of the House of Study the rebbe entered the grand edifice for the first time, surrounded by huge crowds of chassidim, and his joy at the completion of the mitzvah was beautiful to see. His address for the occasion spoke of what entering a *beis midrash* can do for a man.

He began with the text of a Mishnah: "On that day (that Rabban Gamliel was deposed from the office of *nasi*), they removed the guard from the door of the House of Study, and permission was granted to all scholars to enter. For Rabban Gamliel had been wont to announce: 'That student whose internal integrity does not match his external appearance — let him not enter the House of Study.' On that day many benches were added in the House of Study, and Rabban Gamliel was in distress."

"Rashi," continued Reb Yitzchak Meir of Ger, "explains this last phrase by saying that Rabban Gamliel was apprehensive lest he be punished for not having allowed those scholars to enter while he was in authority. The question, though, still stands: what changed Rabban Gamliel's thinking? What made him relent from his earlier policy of refusing admission to scholars who were not inwardly as they appeared outwardly? And the answer is as follows. He watched what happened to these latter scholars as they entered the *beis midrash*: their very entry there made them rectify their moral inconsistencies at once. And this explains his distress. He regretted not having admitted them earlier, for then they might have undergone this moral metamorphosis long ago."

◆§ *A Shul with a Soul*

As soon as Reb Shalom of Belz began building his synagogue, a local gentile noble began to build a place of worship directly oposite it. To make his point clearer, he sent a message to the rebbe saying that he was a second Haman; the rebbe replied that his end would resemble that of his Biblical namesake.

On his way to *shul* one day Reb Shalom was stopped by the son of that same *graf* who held up a piece of pork and said: "Eat this, rabbi!" No sooner had he uttered these words than he began trembling convulsively. Panic spread through the bystanders, and the young man's father came running to ask the tzaddik to forgive him and pray for his son — but he refused, and the young man died. From that time on the *graf* was ten times more furious than before.

Reb Shalom built his *shul* in such a way that it should stand higher than the other edifice over the road. The *graf* thereupon made his steeple taller — but one day Reb Shalom told him: "With the Almighty's help you will not be able to beat me, nor will you ever complete your building."

In the course of time it became known that the land on which that building stood belonged to a family of orphans, and had been held by the noble unlawfully. One thing led to another, until the courts advertised the block of land for public sale. The noble promptly made it known that any Jew daring to buy it would be killed at once by his sword, no matter what consequences he himself would later have to face. Now Reb Shalom was on friendly terms with a Christian medical specialist in Vienna, to whom he now dispatched a courier with a message asking him to come to Belz for the auction, and to buy the land for whatever price was named. This he did, and in due course buildings belonging to the *rav* were constructed there.

The *graf* now began to build his house of worship on a different street, but still opposite the *shul*, and once again the two buildings were competing for prominence. At this point the festival of *Pessach* was approaching, and the noble — who was the lord of Belz and owned most of its property — decided to issue a new decree forbidding the baking of *matzos* in the town, ostensibly for fear of outbreaks of fire. Reb Shalom had been accustomed year by year to distribute his many students among the householders of the surrounding towns and villages for the duration of the festival. Though his own household could provide meals for them throughout the year, the special needs of *Pessach* meant that the burden had to be shared out. This year, however, he gave the order that they should all remain with him for the festival, for he trusted in the Almighty that there would be ample *matzos* for all comers.

And so there were. Only a few days after the decree was issued the noble was out riding on his horse on a narrow track, where he encountered the *graf* of the nearby town of Hubnov. An argument flared up as to which of them was going to make way for the other, and in the course of the duel which followed, the *graf* of Belz was killed — to the relief of the Jews of the town, who were now able to bake *matzos* as in earlier years.

❀ ❀ ❀

When Reb Shalom laid the foundation stone of the *shul* in Belz, he requested heaven that the prayers of all persons entering it be heard On High.

❀ ❀ ❀

One day he took up a bucket of mortar, wanting to have a share personally in its construction. A chassid who saw him hastened to help by taking the bucket from his hands, but his pious *rebbitzin* urgently motioned to the chassid through the window that he should not dare to touch it, for fear of confusing the rebbe in his inspired concentration.

❀ ❀ ❀

There is a tradition among the Belzer chassidim that this *shul* will continue being built until the coming of the *Mashiach*, and that Reb Shalom did not complete it intentionally, in order that the worshipers of each succeeding generation should add to it — and to this day the building is not quite finished, though additions are made from time to time. On one occasion the tzaddik was offered a large sum of money to enable him to complete its construction, but he refused it, saying: "I would like *all* of Israel to have a share in this synagogogue."

❀ ❀ ❀

It is told of his *rebbitzin* that for a thousand nights she stayed awake with her husband, holding the candle for him as he studied in preparation for the attainment of the lofty spiritual insights involved in the building of his *shul.* If he fell asleep for more than half an hour he could depend on her to wake him up. On the thousandth night he was overcome by a deep sleep, but the *rebbitzin* did not let him succumb, for on that night he finally attained the exalted level of spirituality to which he had for so long aspired and toiled.

When his devout helpmate passed away, Reb Shalom said: "Almighty God, You know that it was the *rebbitzin* who made a Jew of me! If I were able to revive the dead I would bring her back to life — but I cannot. But You, Master of the Universe, are able to raise up the whole House of Israel. Why then, do you not raise her up...?"

❧ *Best of Both Worlds*

וְעָשׂוּ אֲרוֹן עֲצֵי שִׁטִּים
And they shall make an ark of cedar wood (25:10)

The Ark occupied no space *(Talmud, Tractate Yoma).*

In the days of Reb Dov Ber, the Maggid of Mezritch, there lived in his town a householder who was both rich and scholarly — and a little proud. He spent his entire day in Torah study in the *beis midrash,* joining his wife in their shop for only two hours daily. Being a *misnaged,* he never once went to see the Maggid.

Early one Friday morning he happened to see several young strangers who were studying together in the *beis midrash.* When he asked them what brought them to his town they answered that they had come from afar to visit the rebbe. This set him thinking: "Here we have people coming from all distances to see the Maggid, and here am I, living in his very town, and I have not even once set eyes upon him! I certainly will not interrupt my regular hours of study for this purpose, but just for once, instead of going to the shop I will go out and visit him."

Arriving at the court of the Maggid he was overawed at the reflection of the Divine Presence which illuminated his face. From then on he began to forgo his periods of private Torah study in order to listen to the discourses of the Maggid, and altogether he became a devoted disciple of his like any other chassid.

But from that time on the wheel of fortune turned sharply, and the sales in his shop declined, until he became quite simply a poor man. He could not restrain his puzzlement forever, and finally took his question to the Maggid: "Why is it, rebbe, that since I made this step in the direction of holiness my material situation has deteriorated?"

"Being a scholar," replied the Maggid, "you are no doubt familiar with the advice of our Sages: הָרוֹצֶה שֶׁיַּחֲכִּים — יַדְרִים; וְשֶׁיַּעֲשִׁיר — יַצְפִּין; וְסִימָנְךָ — שֻׁלְחָן בַּצָּפוֹן וּמְנוֹרָה בַּדָּרוֹם. That is to say: 'He who wishes to grow wise should face southwards when praying; he who wishes to grow rich, let him face northwards in prayer. And your mnemonic for this: in the Temple, the table of the showbread (signifying material blessings) stood to the north, while the candelabrum (signifying spiritual enlightenment) stood to the south.' My question to you," said the Maggid, "is as follows: what direction should be faced by the man who wants to be both wise and rich? — for great indeed is the distance between north and south..."

The man had no answer, so the Maggid continued: "If a person makes nothing of his own ego, he becomes spiritual; and since spiritual things occupy no space, he can be both here *and* there."

Those words found their quiet way into the man's heart. He became humble of spirit, and success became his lot once more.

◆§ *Where the Tablets Lie*

Through all the throngs of chassidim who were jostling each other in their efforts to press nearer to hear his discourse, Reb Shlomo of Radomsk perceived one of his most devoted disciples, Reb Aharon by name, standing quietly in a corner, and listening from there without attempting to push his way closer.

When he had concluded his exposition, Reb Shlomo added: "The Talmud teaches that 'the Ark occupied no space.' Though all the other furnishings and vessels in the Temple occupied space, it was the Ark (אָרוֹן: *Aron)* that was chosen to be the repository of the Tablets of the Law. And so it is too with our Reb Aharon. He does not push himself ahead, nor occupy space, but nevertheless he understands the discourse I just delivered better than many others."

◆§ *An Honest Penny*

מִקְשָׁה אַחַת זָהָב טָהוֹר
One beaten work of pure gold (25:36)

The candelabrum in the Tabernacle, as is known, was to be מִקְשָׁה אַחַת – "one beaten work," and made of זָהָב טָהוֹר – "pure gold." Playing on the similarity between מִקְשָׁה and קָשֶׁה ("difficult"), Reb Mordechai of Neshchiz used to render the Biblical verse punningly as follows: "There is *one difficult thing* (מִקְשָׁה אַחַת) in This World, namely, the ability to earn *clean money* (זָהָב טָהוֹר)." And he would add that a person who succeeded in doing this was, in heaven's eyes, a luminous candelabrum.

❀ ❀ ❀

Three tzaddikim were once seated together – Reb Leib Sarahs, Reb Pinchas of Korets and the *Rav* of Shipitovka – and it was agreed upon between them that if any one of them owned some perfectly kosher money, it would be his prerogative to go out and buy *tikkun* (that is, the comradely bottle of liquor over which chassidim exchange morsels of Torah teachings, stories of tzaddikim, and candid mutual criticism).

The first to speak was the *Rav* of Shipitovka. "I have honestly-earned money," he said, "for today two litigants paid me for a case which they brought before me and which I decided according to the law of the Torah. There cannot be any slur on my ownership of *that* money."

"Not necessarily," said Reb Pinchas of Korets. "It could well be that one of the litigants had no desire or intention to give you the amount he actually gave, and did so only because the other did. No, I wouldn't call your money absolutely untainted. But I have honest earnings. A man came along and asked me to pray for him. I interceded for him and my request on his behalf was granted, thank God; and in gratitude he gave me a gift of money as a *pidyon.*"

"But your right to this payment can also be questioned," Reb Leib Sarahs pointed out. "For it could easily be that if the man had prayed himself, or asked some other honest man to pray on his behalf, their prayer might have achieved exactly the same result — in which case there would be no justification for giving you the *pidyon* money. But I will buy *tikkun* for us all with money that is absolutely pure. How? You see, I don't own a solitary penny. I'll go out and *borrow* the amount needed to buy the vodka, and that simple loan, given to me in good faith, will be the most kosher transaction imaginable, giving me an unquestioned title to the money."

And it was agreed by all present that Reb Leib had won the day.

סדר תצוה

sidra tetzaveh

◆§ *A Lifelong Link*

וְהָיָה עַל מִצְחוֹ תָּמִיד
And it shall be on his forehead always (28:38)

And it (the gold platelet which bore the Name of God) shall be on his forehead always: That he should never divert his attention from it *(Talmud, Tractate Yoma).*

When Reb Yaakov Yitzchak (later renowned as the Chozeh of Lublin) first arrived in Nikolsburg to begin his long years as a disciple of Reb Shmelke, his new rebbe imposed a certain task upon him. Whenever the young scholar saw him becoming so intensely involved in the legalistic arguments of his Talmudic studies that he momentarily forgot the bond of spiritual rapture by which he cleaved to his Creator, he was to remind him of this by touching the rebbe's gloves.

The Chozeh later recounted that never did the need arise for such a reminder, for not even for a moment did Reb Shmelke ever lapse from his state of *dveikus*. On one occasion he became so involved in the thrust and parry of Talmudic debate that his disciple thought there was a need to touch his glove by way of reminder, but Reb Shmelke turned to him and said: "Just now, my son, I recalled it myself."

☙ *Showing Who's Boss*

וְעָשִׂיתָ לָהֶם אַבְנֵטִים
You shall make them girdles (28:40)

The girdle of the *kohanim* atones for sinful thoughts *(Talmud, Tractate Arachin).*

A man once came to Reb Dov Ber of Mezritch with the complaint that he was unable to clear his mind of the sinful thoughts that bothered him constantly. By way of reply the Maggid told him to go and visit Reb Ze'ev of Zhitomir.

By the time he arrived at the village in which Reb Ze'ev was the leaseholder of an inn, it was late at night, and the building was locked. He knocked, and knocked again, but with no response. It was in the height of a Ukrainian winter, and he cried out, begging whoever was inside to open up for him. Seeing that still no response was forthcoming, he shouted angrily: "How can you people have no pity on a fellow Jew who is stranded here outside?"

Not a word in return. No one unbolted the door.

At daybreak the door opened as always. He entered and stayed at the inn for a few days, but Reb Ze'ev asked him no questions whatever. The man was puzzled: "Why on earth did the Maggid of Mezritch send me all the way here?"

Before he rose to leave he brought his riddle to his host: "Our rebbe, the Maggid, sent me to visit you — but I don't know why."

"I'll tell you why the Maggid directed you here," said Reb Ze'ev. "He wanted you to learn from me that a man is the master of his house, and whomever he does not want inside he simply does not admit."

☙ The Rebbe and the Shtreimelmacher

תצוה

וְשַׂמְתָּ הַמִּצְנֶפֶת עַל רֹאשׁוֹ
And you shall place the miter on his head (29:6)

On his head: On the head of Aharon alone, for he is the anointed High Priest *(Ibn Ezra).*

In the *shul* of Reb Shneur Zalman of Liadi the custom was that any man called to the Reading of the Torah was obliged to wear the furbrimmed hat known as a *shtreimel,* and a spare one was kept by the *shammes* to be worn by any person who did not have one of his own.

It once happened that just when the spare one was needed it was nowhere to be found, so that the resourceful *shammes* took the rebbe's *shtreimel* down from its hook and lent it to the stranger, and when the Reading of the Torah was over he returned it to its place.

The rebbe finished his prayers and took down his *shtreimel,* eyed it keenly, and called for the *shammes.*

"Did someone wear this?" he asked.

The *shammes* told him exactly what had happened.

The rebbe straight away summoned the local *shtreimelmacher* and said: "Please take this home, undo all the seams, stitch all the parts together again, and return it to me."

With reverent care the hatter did exactly as he was told to the rebbe's own *shtreimel,* and when it was finished just like new, and ready to be dried, he placed it gingerly in the oven, as all good *shtreimelmachers* do. But instead of taking it out after an hour, he forgot it there all night. Early the next morning he jumped out of bed in consternation, ran to the oven — but all that was left of the rebbe's noble *shtreimel* was a pathetic cinder.

What would he tell the rebbe? This was no trifling matter: the great man had personally entrusted him with his own *shtreimel* — and he had let it burn! Wracked by shame and self-incrimination, he considered over and again the two possibilities open to him — either to go to the rebbe and tell him of the calamity, or not to go at all. But how could he not go? He decided ultimately that he would have to face the consequences. With trembling knees and a troubled spirit he made his way to the rebbe's home, opened the door of his study — and stood there, unable to utter a word.

"What is the matter, my good man?" asked the rebbe. "The *shtreimel* has burnt, no doubt?"

"Yes, rebbe," he muttered.

"Don't worry," said the rebbe gently. "You can go home in peace."

◆§ To Save a Jew

וְאָכְלוּ אֹתָם אֲשֶׁר כֻּפַּר בָּהֶם
And they shall eat those things with which atonement was made
(29:33)

And they shall eat those things with which atonement was made: From this we learn that the *kohanim* eat the offering and the owners are granted atonement thereby *(Talmud, Tractate Pesachim).*

The men of a little township in Lithuania once came to Mezhibuzh with the request that the Baal Shem Tov send them one of his disciples to serve as the local *rav*, whom they promised to pay in keeping with the respect due to his position. The disciple chosen by the tzaddik was received warmly, and devoted himself from the beginning to civic needs, in particular to securing steady sources of income for the community's charitable funds which he administered conscientiously.

Now in that township, there lived a certain scholar of good family who devoted his whole time to Torah studies, and was supported by the stipend which the local householders set aside for him week by week, through the good offices of one of their number who collected their contributions towards it. The *rav* was displeased with this arrangement, which worked to the detriment of the communal charities, for when the local citizens were asked to contribute to these causes they always had a ready answer: they were helping support that gentleman, and more than that was beyond their ability. He therefore told such people that it would be preferable to give a little less to an individual, rather than to overlook the needs of the many. The result of his words was that the contributions toward the stipend of the scholar dwindled to the point that the volunteeer who had formerly collected them decided that it was hardly worth his while to carry on, and discontinued his rounds. The scholar's wife came to visit him in the *beis midrash* on Thursday, as was her custom, to ask him for money to buy the family's provisions for *Shabbos*, and he had to answer that he had nothing to give her. She left for home emptyhanded, and he was so distressed that he wept.

His tears stole their way into heaven, and spoke as eloquent witnesses for the prosecution of the *rav* who had brought about the end of his livelihood. In fact another charge had been brought against the *rav* in the Heavenly Court only a few days before. Two litigants in his town had appeared before him in a case involving trespass by one of them into the legitimate rights of the other in the leasing of some business from the local squire. Had the *rav* protested energetically against his foul play, the guilty party would have obeyed his ruling and backed down. Finding the *rav* guilty on both charges, the Heavenly Court now ruled that he be sentenced on both counts cumulatively, and decided that he be handed over to the jurisdiction of Satan.

The Prosecuting Angel was summoned, and asked if he feared the Baal Shem Tov. When he answered that he did, the Heavenly Court addressed him as follows: "We hereby hand over to you the *rav* of that town, a disciple of the Baal Shem Tov, to be dealt with as you see fit. Do not fear his teacher, for the *rav* is now leaving his jurisdiction and entering yours."

Filled with vengeful glee, Satan hit upon a fate for the *rav* which would be worse than death: he would lure him into becoming an apostate!

It had always been the *rav's* custom on *Shabbos* to recite the *Shacharis* prayer in the undisturbed privacy of his home which was near the synagogue, and then to be called there to hear the Reading of the Torah with the congregation, whom he would also join in the concluding *Musaf* service. After prayers all the worshipers would be invited to his home where they would exchange *Shabbos* greetings and partake of the light refreshments which accompanied the *Kiddush* recited over a goblet of vodka — though he personally never tasted more than a sip of any strong drink.

Now on the *Shabbos* immediately following the incidents of the trespass and the scholar, his heart was suddenly set on fire with a burning desire to convert to Christianity. In fact, he had already wrapped himself in his *tallis* in readiness for morning prayers. But as if crazed by an insane lust, he impetuously cast it off, and drained the beaker of vodka which had been prepared on the table for his congregants. Still dressed in his dignified *Shabbos* garb, he bolted unbridled to the house of the parish priest which stood on the outskirts of the town. The priest asked him respectfully what he could do for him. When the *rav* told him what had brought him there the priest was speechless with astonishment — but rejoiced quietly. Afer all, not every parish priest landed a fish of this size...

"I am afraid that right now I am occupied with important guests," he said. "Allow me to show you to a room where you can wait until they have gone, and then I will call you and we will arrange our little business."

He instructed his servant to show the rabbi to the room where he was to wait, and to provide him there with ample food and drink. Left alone, the *rav* helped himself freely to the large bottle of vodka that stood on the table, but so unused was he to liquor of any kind that he soon vomited and fell asleep on the floor. When he awoke a few hours later the priest was still engaged, but the conflagration in his heart had not abated. He drank even more, and once again lay drunk on the floor, until sundown.

Anxious for his welfare, his congregants visited his house after prayers to pay their respects as always. Not finding him there they asked about him in the town, and learned to their horror that their *rav* had suddenly gone out of his mind, and was last seen running like a madman in the direction of...

The women wailed. The men were dumbstruck, and their hearts froze.

❦ ❦ ❦

There is one hour that is less earthbound than all other hours — the hour of *Seudah Shlishis*, the mystical twilight meal at which *Shabbos* reveals to some few stalwart climbers the rarefied atmosphere of its peak. During that hour the soul of the Baal Shem Tov would soar aloft, and, from beyond the bounds of vision, gaze on all the farflung hamlets in which his disciples were scattered, to see how they fared in the secret battles of the soul. And on that *Shabbos*, when that disciple came into his ken, he saw him sinking in the murky forces of evil. The Baal Shem Tov was perplexed: how could such a man fall so mightily?

He began to sing *Bnei Heichala*, the kabbalistic hymn written by Reb Yitzchak Luria, the saintly Ari *zal*, but stopped unexpectedly when he reached the words לְבַטָּלָא בְּכָל קְלִיפִּין — "It is His will to annul all the powers of impurity." His restless soul was questing, climbing, seeking a voice in the Upper Worlds that would tell him for what sin his disciple had been abandoned to such a wretched fate. At every rung in heaven he asked in vain — until in one awesome supernal palace it was revealed to him that these two sins were the reason for his punishment. The tzaddik now appealed with all his might to the Heavenly Court. He recounted in defense of his disciple all the noble and selfless deeds that he had wrought before his fall, but even these did not suffice to nullify the verdict. At the last moment the Baal Shem Tov recalled that his disciple had always been punctilious in celebrating his *Melaveh Malkah*, the *seudah* at which the *Shabbos* Queen is escorted, reluctantly but lovingly, from every Jewish home after her weekly visit draws to an end. Could his past observance of this one last mitzvah not save him now? The Heavenly Court conceded that this mitzvah could indeed save him — provided that he would this very night fulfill it again, and eat in honor of the *Melaveh Malkah*.

With this ruling of the Heavenly Court still echoing in his ears, the Baal Shem Tov opened his eyes, and took a slice of the *challah* over which he had made a blessing at the beginning of his *Seudah Shlishis*, and one of the twelve loaves which were always baked in his house in honor of *Shabbos*, and gave them to one of his saintly chassidim, with these words: "Take these and go. God will help."

The emissary neither asked his rebbe where he was to go, nor what he was to do with the whole *challah* and the slice. If he would faithfully follow an instruction from his rebbe, the Almighty would doubtless lead him to his proper destination and show him there what he was to do. The Baal Shem Tov remained at the table, surrounded by all the holy brotherhood of his chassidim, and repeated over and over in a voice of desperate entreaty: לְבַטָּלָא בְּכָל קְלִיפִּין — "Annul all the powers of impurity!" No man of those present could grasp the meaning of their rebbe's conduct — but it was apparent that something awesome was afoot.

The emissary had meanwhile reached the outskirts of Mezhibuzh. Darkness had fallen, progress was slow, and his destination was still unknown to him. To make things worse, the road was now strewn with gravel, an unaccustomed hindrance in those parts. The emissary understood that this was an obstacle especially contrived by Satan to hamper him, so he walked right on for some two miles, undaunted. After a short stretch of smooth road, he felt his footsteps drag, toiling in immeasurable sand. Again he had to muster superhuman determination, and yet again a third time. He cried out to God and begged to be helped to carry out the orders given by his rebbe, and to fulfill the mitzvah whose nature was still hidden from him. On he strove and did not yield, until he sensed that not only was the road now smooth, but that within seconds, miles and miles of it were disappearing miraculously under his feet.

After some time he saw a lantern shining from a window in the distance. He approached, and entered an open door in order to rest a little. But there before him on the floor lay a dishevelled Jew asleep, his black *kapote* soiled by his own vomit. The newcomer asked a watchman outside who this was, and was stupefied to hear that this was the local rabbi who had come to the parish priest in order to apostatize.

The purpose of his mission was now clear! He returned to the room and sat down to rest, his heart brimming with gratitude to the Almighty Who had lent him the strength to overcome all the obstacles on the way, and had brought him to his destination in peace.

The drunkard soon awoke and reached out for his bottle, but the messenger of the Baal Shem Tov took his hands in his own and said: "My friend! What will be, will be — but in the meantime wash your hands, and later you can drink as much as you like."

The dazed man raised no objection. He washed his hands, and wanted to return to his tippling. But the messenger spoke to him again: "What will be, will be — but first eat a piece of bread. Drinking without eating is not good for you."

At his request, the other mumbled the words of *HaMotzi*, the blessing over bread, and took a bite from the whole *challah* as well as from the slice as they were offered him. And as he began to eat, the sanctity that clung to those remnants of the tzaddik's meal permeated his whole being, and the forces of impurity released their clutch on him. He was a man newborn — and contrite.

"What have I done?" he cried out in anguish. "Did I really intend to part with the faith of the God of Life? Woe is me, and woe to my soul!"

And he tore his hair in his distress.

"Nothing can help me," he went on, "except for a talk with the Baal Shem Tov. He alone will be able to guide me to complete *teshuvah*, and make a true penitent of me. But how far away he is! How can I reach him now? Would that I could fly like a bird and stand now before our rebbe!"

The emissary could see that the *rav's* regret came from the very depths of his heart.

"My friend," he said, "for your own sake listen to me. Let us go out of here and set out directly for Mezhibuzh, and I trust that the Merciful One will help us get there."

So assured was he of the holiness of his rebbe, after all that had happened thus far, and so certain was he that the Merciful One would save the *rav*, after such an earnest regret, that he added: "Take hold of my belt and we will leave this place."

The leader and the led stepped out into the pitch blackness of the night, and began their trek. They saw nothing whatever around them until, after a few short moments — the vast distance having sped wondrously under their feet — they found themselves in Mezhibuzh. They opened the door, and at the sight of the Baal Shem Tov and his chassidim still seated around the table at their *Melaveh Malkah*, the *rav* fainted. When he came to, he wept the bitter, humble tears of the true penitent. The Baal Shem Tov taught him how to atone for his past, and thereafter set his feet on the path of unswerving piety.

◆§ *Food for Thought*

A serious-minded chassid once came to visit Reb Elimelech of Lyzhansk, who sensed that his guest had not yet learned to refine and elevate his appetite for food. He decided therefore to invite him to join him at breakfast. The chassid felt honored indeed. The table was set with rye bread, salt, and a breadknife, and they washed their hands and pronounced *HaMotzi*, the blessing over bread.

The rebbe bit off a little from his slice, and had not yet swallowed it when he began to complain to himself, addressing himself by the diminutive Yiddish form of his name: "Melech, Melech! Just look how you're eating, and with what ugly desire you're chewing the bread. Why, you want to swallow up all the bread at once! You really are worse than an animal."

But then he answered himself as follows: "No, I don't eat out of animal desire, but simply to satisfy my hunger, for if I don't eat I won't be able to study Torah and serve my Maker."

He cut himself another morsel of bread, and again, before swallowing it, chided himself in a harsh undertone: "Melech, Melech! Whom do you think you're fooling? Whom are you trying to convince that your only intention in eating is to keep your soul alive so that you can serve your Maker? It's all a bunch of lies! Just look — every part of you is fraught with animal desire, and if you could, you would swallow your whole meal in one gulp. How could you bring yourself to lie, and say that you eat for the sake of heaven?"

After a thoughtful pause he again answered himself in a sober whisper: "No, in fact it is not an animal urge that impels me to eat. But what is there to be done? I am fashioned of physical matter, a creature of flesh and blood, and I am obliged to pay this material body its due, otherwise it won't want to serve me. So I do have to eat bread — though I won't eat it for the sake of sensual gratification, but simply because of the necessity of keeping myself alive."

And with that he gave himself another slice.

Overhearing the muttered monologue, the guest's heart was humbled within him. He would make a fresh start! Reb Elimelech thereupon rounded off his breakfast by reciting the Grace after Meals, confident that his novel prescription had accomplished its purpose.

◈§ *My Body, Too, Sings to You*

Three tzaddikim were staying in the home of Reb Yisrael, the Maggid of Koznitz: Reb Yaakov Yitzchak of Pshischah, better known as the Yid HaKadosh ("the Holy Jew"); Reb Fishele of Strikov; and Reb David of Lelov. Being weak at this time, the Maggid sat up in bed, with his table drawn up next to it. For the simple meal that he asked to have prepared for his guests, he seated the Yid next to himself, while the other two guests sat opposite each other on either side of the table. The Maggid and the Yid exchanged whispered secrets on the treasures hidden in the Torah, while Reb Fishele pricked his ears in an attempt to share in the source of their delight. But Reb David did his own thing: he ate a slice of bread and butter.

Said the Maggid to Reb Fishele: "Why don't you learn from this young man? He's sitting and eating bread and butter. *There's* divine service for you! What he is doing is accounted a veritable sacrifice in the Temple. Another slice of bread and butter — and there you have another Temple sacrifice!"

◈§ *Rain Check*

Reb Naftali of Ropshitz once shared a meal in Lublin with Reb Yaakov Yitzchak of Pshischah and Reb David of Lelov — but there was barely a morsel to eat. A rich young man came past and offered them a gold ruble with which to buy food, and as they ate and drank together, they gladdened their hearts by delving into the mysteries of the Divine Plan.

Years later, when all three had established themselves in their respective pastoral posts, they happened to meet again in a countryside inn. As they reminisced over their student days in Lublin, they recalled the joy that they had shared at that meal together, a joy that had come to them thanks to the kindliness of the young man who had given them a gold ruble. Where was he now? Their souls took wing as they sought him high and low, in This World and in the Next — but he eluded them. Never despairing, they plumbed all the depths of Creation, until they finally found him: the young man had forsaken the path of the righteous!

"We owe him a favor," they said to each other.

And through toil of the soul and exertion in prayer, the three tzaddikim succeeded in arousing in his heart an urgent desire to return to the fold, and the young man became a sincere penitent.

◆§ *The Horse with His Head in the Clouds*

Reb Simchah Bunem of Pshischah once asked a question: "How is it possible nowadays for a man to offer a sacrifice to a pagan god?"

And he answered his own question: "If a man withholds himself from eating because of anger; or if a man is commonly considered to be a scholar and a tzaddik, and though he is hungry he refrains from eating in order that those around him should consider him saintly and abstemious — then such a man is offering a sacrifice to a pagan god."

❧ ❧ ❧

A man once came to Reb Simchah Bunem with a problem: "The holy books all say that if a man fasts so-and-so many days, the Prophet Eliyahu in person reveals himself to him. Now I have fasted all those days — and no one appeared."

"Let me tell you a story," said the tzaddik. "The Baal Shem Tov once had to make a long journey. As you know, the whole length of the highway used to contract miraculously as he approached it; the horses and the wagon were there only for the sake of appearances. Now from their experience at drawing other people's wagons, the horses were accustomed to being given fodder and water at every village stop. But now that the distance was covered miraculously, by *kfitzas haderech,* and they had the sensation of flying from one place to the next, there was no need to rest at any of the usual stops on the way, and of course no one stopped to feed them. So the horses started philosophizing: 'Who knows? Perhaps we aren't horses after all. Perhaps we are really people, and when we arrive at night at some town, where people are accustomed to eating, they will feed us too.'

"But when they saw that even when they passed by the places where *people* usually ate they did not stop to rest, nor were they fed, they came to the conclusion that they had been mistaken in considering themselves to be *people:* in fact, they must be *angels,* for angels neither eat nor drink!

"At length, the Baal Shem Tov arrived at his destination. The horses were led to a stable, bags full of chaff were placed under their noses, and they attacked their food like real horses ...

"And so it is," concluded Reb Simchah Bunem, "with a person who fasts, and already imagines himself to be an angel worthy of being visited by Eliyahu the Prophet. What counts is that when he has completed his fasts, and is confronted by food, he should not attack it like a horse, because then he remains the same horse that he always was ..."

◈ *A Joint Account*

Rabbi Enzil of Staria, a well-known and scholarly *misnaged,* once asked a chassidic rebbe: "If, God forbid, someone in the family is sick, the custom among you chassidim is to drink *LeChaim* and to wish the patient a speedy recovery, even though he is not present. Even if we assume that drinking *LeChaim* is a *segulah* which acts as a supernatural remedy for the ailment, then surely any such *segulah* should be taken by the patient himself. How do you explain a situation in which Reuven drinks and Shimon is cured?"

"There is nothing remarkable about that," replied the

rebbe. "In fact one could even derive this principle from an explicit statement in Tractate *Sotah* of the Mishnah. Concerning the waters of the ordeal which are to be drunk by a woman suspected of unfaithfulness, we are told there that 'Just as they test *her*, they test *him*.' Now, if in relation to punishment we learn that *she* drinks and *he* is tested thereby, then how much more so will such a transference be effective in the context of a blessing!"

סדר כי תשא
Sidra Ki Sisa

◆§ *A Policy for Economic Betterment*

זֶה יִתְּנוּ *This they shall give (30:13)*

A visiting *rav* once asked Reb Mordechai of Nadvorna: "Whatever is to be done about the material state of our fellow Jews? People are finding it really hard to make a living, and things are going from bad to worse."

"The only solution," said the tzaddik, "is for everyone to do *teshuvah*, to repent. You see, under the Divine Throne there lies a great treasury of money. How do we know? Because when the Children of Israel each had to contribute half a shekel, God wanted Moshe Rabbeinu to know exactly what this coin looked like. So, the Midrash teaches, He showed him a coin which He had taken from under the Divine Throne, and said: כָּזֶה יִתְּנוּ — 'Such a one shall they contribute.' Now in praise of repentance the Talmud says גְּדוֹלָה תְּשׁוּבָה שֶׁמַּגַּעַת עַד כִּסֵּא הַכָּבוֹד — 'Exalted indeed is *teshuvah:* it reaches right up to the Divine Throne.' The rest is easy. Once our brethren repent and are already way up there, *right next to the Divine Throne*, I'm sure they'll have no difficulty in getting hold of a little money from the treasury that is hidden underneath it ..."

◆§ We're In This Together

וְעַתָּה אִם תִּשָּׂא חַטָּאתָם וְאִם אַיִן מְחֵנִי נָא
And now, if You will forgive their sin —, and if not, erase me (32:32)

The rebbe of Sadigora, who was the son of Reb Yisrael of Ruzhin, once told the following story.

Whenever the Baal Shem Tov paid his annual visit to a certain township, he always stayed at the home of the same householder, who was one of the more prosperous of the local townspeople. One Friday he arrived in town during the season when he was least expected, and settled in for *Shabbos* in the synagogue. His usual host asked him to be his guest as always, but the tzaddik declined to join him. All the townsfolk were soon assembled in *shul,* and after evening prayers the Baal Shem Tov instructed them all to stay on and recite *Psalms* together. As midnight approached he asked to have the *Shabbos* evening meal brought for himself, and told the worshipers to join their families for the mitzvah of eating the *Shabbos* meal, then to return. And so the whole congregation continued reciting *Tehillim* in unison right through the night. After they had completed the morning prayers the tzaddik told his former host that he would now be pleased to accept his invitation for the midday meal.

After *Kiddush,* when all those around the long table were feeling refreshed by the joyous spirit of *Shabbos,* a gentile suddenly entered the room and asked for a drink of vodka. The Baal Shem Tov requested the host to oblige, and asked the gentile to tell what he knew.

"Yesterday," said the *goy,* "just before evening, the squire who owns this estate summoned all the gentiles from the surrounding villages, gave them armfuls of weapons and ammunition, and told them to go out and wipe out all the Jews of this township. All night long they waited impatiently for the order to go ahead. But just before dawn along rolled a carriage, and out came some important-looking official who sat and talked with the squire, and when they finished the squire told all the villagers to go home."

The Baal Shem Tov now addressed the company around the table: "This *paritz* is so wealthy that he is never in a hurry to sell his grain, and no price offered is high enough for him. In this way the harvests of many years piled up in his granaries until they began to rot. Some of his anti-Semitic friends managed to convince him that his Jewish sales agents were to blame for this, by dissuading customers from buying his produce. Duly incensed, he decided to wreak vengeance on them by wiping out all the Jews in the town. I therefore had no option but to bring back an old school pal of his who has been dead these forty years, though the local *paritz* did not know this because they had lived so far apart. The newcomer's first question was about the dangerous-looking villagers whom he had seen on all sides on his way: why were they armed? And the *paritz* told him that he was about to avenge himself on the Jews who had maliciously caused his grain to accumulate and rot. 'You don't say!' exclaimed the important-looking visitor. 'Why, I constantly deal with Jews and I've always found them to be honest. You try summoning them to you tomorrow, after their Sabbath, and you'll see that they will sell even the rotten grain for you.' And that's when the *paritz* went out and told the waiting peasants to disperse."

❀ ❀ ❀

The rebbe of Sadigora finished telling the story, turned to his brother, Reb Mordechai Shraga of Husyatin, and said: "There remains something problematic here. Why did the Baal Shem Tov have to go to the trouble of traveling to that township? After all, he could have done what he did without moving from home. But the Baal Shem Tov thought as follows: 'If my plan works — well and good; but if it doesn't, then I want to be there together with all the Jews of that township.'"

◆§ *Finding One's Soul Root*

מְחֵנִי נָא מִסִּפְרְךָ
Erase me from Your book (32:32)

While yet a child, Reb Yitzchak Meir of Ger was widely looked upon as a prodigy of scholarship and piety. After the death of Reb Yisrael of Koznitz, whom he had regarded as his rebbe, chassidim of all persuasions endeavored to convince him to visit their tzaddikim, but to no avail. For three years he continued traveling to Koznitz, to visit Reb Moshe, the son of his rebbe. On one such visit, when he was preparing to resume his journey there after having stopped to rest at a wayside inn, he was spotted by Reb Simchah Bunem of Pshischah, who at that moment had alighted from his carriage. As soon as he set his eyes on him he said: "Young man, what is your name? And from where do you come?"

Reb Yitzchak Meir gave his name, and told the unfamiliar tzaddik that he lived in Warsaw.

Asked Reb Simchah Bunem: "And why don't you come to visit me in Pshischah?"

The young man replied: "I am on my way to Koznitz, and the chassidim over there say that it is a religious obligation for every man to say every morning, 'Blessed art Thou, Who has not made me a chassid of Pshischah ...' "

To which the rebbe of Pshischah replied: "A time will yet come when you will come to me in your socks!"

After three years of visiting Reb Moshe at Koznitz, Reb Yitzchak Meir suddenly ceased going there. In Warsaw there lived a large group of learned chassidim of Reb Meir of Apta, who made every effort to persuade the young prodigy to visit their rebbe, and he finally agreed. Reb Meir was overjoyed — as was the whole district — with the news that this young man was about to come to Apta, and when Reb Yitzchak Meir arrived there, he showed him every mark of respect and affection.

But Reb Yitzchak Meir chose not to remain in Apta. In that town there lived a sizeable concentration of Pshischah chassidim, including several men of stature who had earlier been disciples of Reb Yaakov Yitzchak, the Chozeh (or Seer) of Lublin, and of another tzaddik of the same name, Reb Yaakov Yitzchak (the Yid) of Pshischah. These chassidim were among the many who flocked to his hotel to exchange Talmudic and chassidic discourse with him, and in the course of their conversations they quoted many of the teachings of their rebbe, Reb Simchah Bunem. When *Shabbos* had passed he told them that he had decided not to stay in Apta, but to travel directly from there to Pshischah. They were of course overjoyed at his decision, and chose from amongst themselves a small delegation who were to accompany him there.

Reb Yitzchak Meir now called on Reb Meir, together with one of the Pshischah chassidim, to receive his parting blessings. Reb Meir sensed what the young man's intentions were, and immediately penned a letter which he asked the Pshischah chassid to pass on to his rebbe, and added the following words: "They say that Reb Simchah Bunem is a man of intellectual and spiritual attainments. Please tell him in my name that my prayer to the Almighty is identical with the prayer of Moshe Rabbeinu: מְחֵנִי נָא מִסִּפְרְךָ אֲשֶׁר כָּתָבְתָּ. [This verse in fact simply means: "Erase me from the book that You have written." Reb Meir, however, treated it punningly as follows.] By this I mean: מְחֵנִי נָא — Grant me מוֹחִין, *that is, intellectual and spiritual attainments, but only* מִסִּפְרְךָ אֲשֶׁר כָּתָבְתָּ — that is, only such as are derived from the study of Your Torah, and not from business and theaters in Danzig..." [Before Reb Simchah Bunem became rebbe, he used to arrange for the transport of timber from Warsaw to Danzig, where he would sometimes stay for months at a time, dressing in the modern garb of the assimilating German Jews amongst whom he mixed, so that he could bring some of them back to the fold of tradition.]

The messenger faithfully passed on these words, and was promptly instructed as follows: "Please tell Reb Meir of Apta that I am afraid he is in the wrong. For King Solomon wrote in the book of *Koheles:* טוֹב לִשְׁמֹעַ גַּעֲרַת חָכָם מֵאִישׁ שֹׁמֵעַ שִׁיר כְּסִילִים — 'It is better to hear the reprimand of a wise man *than* [*to be*] *a man who hears the song of fools.'* Now the wording presents a problem, for surely he should have said מִלִּשְׁמֹעַ שִׁיר כְּסִילִים, *than to hear the song of fools.* But the meaning is as follows: 'From whom is it good to hear the reprimand of a wise man? מֵאִישׁ שֹׁמֵעַ שִׁיר כְּסִילִים, *from a man who hears the song of fools,* but is unharmed by it, and remains a wise man — from such a man is it good to hear a reprimand!'"

Reb Simchah Bunem then opened the letter from Reb Meir of Apta, which expressed his disappointment that Reb Yitzchak Meir was leaving his hoped-for tutelage because of the pretensions of some other spiritual leader

— so keenly did these two scholars vie with each other for the privilege of nurturing this choice spirit. This letter in turn drew from the pen of Reb Simchah Bunem a witty retort (still extant) which was couched in equally learned phrases — and was equally uncomplimentary.

As soon as the word spread through Pshischah that "the prodigy from Warsaw" had arrived, people of all ages thronged excitedly around their rebbe's house in the hope of catching a glimpse of him. The hero of all this adulation was still a very young man whose beard had barely started to appear, and amidst all the jostling he was lost in the crowd — who did not know what he looked like. As he found himself pressed forward by the waves of people who wanted to greet their rebbe, his shoes fell off, and so cramped was he by jubilant chassidim from all sides that it was quite impossible to bend down and pick them up. When he found himself directly opposite Reb Simchah Bunem, the rebbe greeted him cordially, then glanced down at his feet and saw that the celebrated guest of honor was in socks ... A good-natured smile flitted across his face, for he recalled his remark to the young man at their first meeting outside the village inn: "A time will yet come when you will visit me in your socks!"

Then he said to his new disciple: "You know, it was no easy matter laying hold of you! It has cost me a great deal of self-sacrifice to finally bring you here."

But he retained the loyal devotion of the young man for the remainder of his life.

◆§ *Charity is Not Charitability*

וְחַנֹּתִי אֶת אֲשֶׁר אָחֹן

And I will be gracious to whomever I will be gracious (33:19)

And I will be gracious to whomever I will be gracious: Even to the undeserving *(Talmud, Tractate Berachot).*

Reb Zusya of Hanipoli had a wealthy chassid who saw it as a privilege to give him something towards the maintenance of his household whenever he visited him, and indeed attributed his success in business to his generosity.

One day he visited Reb Zusya and found that he was

 not at home. So he asked the *rebbitzin:* "Where is the rebbe?"

"Why, he's gone to see the rebbe," she said.

The chassid was stupefied: "Do you mean to say that the *rebbe* has a rebbe?"

"Why, of course!" she replied.

"And who is that rebbe?" he asked.

"The Maggid of Mezritch," she told him.

On the way home that businessman did some practical thinking, along the following lines: "If when I visit *my* rebbe things prosper so well for me, then how much more will my business flourish if I visit instead my *rebbe's* rebbe!"

And, persuaded by his own irrefutable logic, he paid no more visits to humble Hanipoli, and thereafter set his sights only on Mezritch. After a time, though, he saw that his accustomed prosperity was waning, and decided that by ignoring Reb Zusya he must have done the wrong thing after all. So once again he took the familiar road to Hanipoli, and said: "Begging your pardon, rebbe, but there is a question bothering me. Why is it that when I used to visit you my business throve, but when I started visiting *your* rebbe — who is presumably a greater rebbe — success deserted me?"

"It's all very simple," explained Reb Zusya. "You see, in fact I'm not a tzaddik at all, and that is why when you used to give me money, *even though I was unworthy of receiving it,* the Heavenly Court was not particular with you, either, and you were granted prosperity even though you did not really deserve it. But the moment you started being particular about evaluating people precisely, and decided to visit the Maggid of Mezritch — who is really a tzaddik — the Heavenly Court decided to start being particular about evaluating *you;* and when they found that you weren't in fact deserving of all that prosperity, they withheld it."

◆§ *What the Undeserving Deserve*

Reb Yehudah Zvi of Rozla was once visited by a man who gave him a *kvitl* which bore his name and that of his mother, and the subject of his request. This note was accompanied by a *pidyon*, the traditional gift of money to be used by the rebbe for his own living expenses or for distribution to charitable causes, as he saw fit.

Said the tzaddik: "In giving me this *pidyon* you are assuming that I am a *guter Yid* [literally: a good Jew; the popular Yiddish term for a chassidic rebbe]. But where will I turn in the World to Come when you discover that I am not a *guter Yid* at all, and you'll demand your money back? Where will I find the wherewithal to repay you with? And besides, since I know the truth about myself, how do I allow myself to accept your *pidyon* in the first place?

"We can find our answer by examining an analogous situation in the Torah. The Talmud tells us that Yirmeyahu the Prophet cursed the people of Anasos by wishing upon them that whenever they would be stirred to give charity, they would be confronted with undeserving recipients. Now surely the Prophet Yirmeyahu was not such an anti-Semite! The explanation to his words is simple. He saw that according to the letter of the law of the Torah the people of Anasos stood no chance whatever of being saved. The only possible source of salvation for them was the attribute of divine mercy through which God is gracious 'even to the undeserving.' But the dynamics of the universe are governed by the principle explained in the Kabbalah: — אִתְעָרוּתָא דִלְתַתָּא אִתְעָרוּתָא דִלְעֵילָא. This is, in order to set in motion this flow of divine grace, the recipient has to first bring himself to be magnanimous to some other mortal recipient *who is just as undeserving as he is himself.* Only then will the mercies of heaven be aroused toward him, measure for measure, and — though undeserving — he will be granted the blessing of indiscriminate divine grace.

"This explains why the Prophet Yirmeyahu prayed that whenever the people of Anasos felt like being generous, only *undeserving* objects of charity should present themselves. By thus enabling them to practice charity on the undeserving, he was in fact giving them their one last chance to be saved; he was thereby making them qualify to be *themselves* the recipients of that divine grace which is granted 'even to the undeserving.' "

The tzaddik concluded: "And now, my son, that you are giving me a *pidyon* even though I am in fact unworthy of receiving it, it is only right that you yourself should be helped from Above in the matter you request, by virtue of God's promise: 'I will be gracious — even to the undeserving.'"

◈§ *A Question of Priorities*

פְּסָל לְךָ *Engrave for yourself* (34:1)

A comradely company of chassidim, sitting around a table on which stood vodka and refreshments, were surprised by the entry of their rebbe, Reb Yisrael of Ruzhin. Perceiving from his unsmiling face that he did not approve of what he saw, one of them took the liberty of remarking that Reb Pinchas of Korets had said that the camaraderie of chassidim at such a gathering could be likened to the mitzvah of studying Torah.

"Far be it from me to contradict the words of the tzaddik of Korets," said Reb Yisrael, "but nonetheless, all depends on how a thing is done. Thus in the Torah we find a word which is used sometimes for a sacred end, and sometimes for a profane. Take the words פְּסָל לְךָ — Engrave for yourself,' which refer to the Tablets of the Law. We find exactly the same root in the verse לֹא תַעֲשֶׂה לְךָ פֶסֶל — 'You shall not make yourself a graven image,' which refers to idolatry. The difference between them is as follows: When that root signifies something sacred, then the word לְךָ, *'yourself'* comes *after* it; but when the word לְךָ, *'yourself'* comes *before* it, then it signifies something profane.

"When a man does something positive *with no thought of self-interest* — that is, when 'yourself' comes last — then he is indulging a sacred activity. If, however, he does exactly the same thing, but with his own benefit foremost — that is, putting 'yourself' first — then his otherwise positive deed transgresses the commandment: 'You shall not make yourself a graven image.'"

◈§ *Philanthropy without Plaques*

וְאִישׁ לֹא יַעֲלֶה עִמָּךְ

And no man shall ascend with you: There is nothing more beautiful than modesty *(Rashi).*

כי תשא
And no man shall ascend with you (34:3)

On his way to visit the Baal Shem Tov, Reb Michel of Zlotchov passed through a place in which a certain Jew held a three-year lease on the tavern, and allowed no fellow Jew to stay in the whole village. It was Friday, and when the tzaddik's wheel broke, his wagon-driver took it on his shoulder back to the village and had it repaired. They had barely resumed their journey and another wheel broke. This time, since the sun was beginning to decline, Reb Michel said: "Whatever happens, we cannot desecrate the holy day: we will have to spend *Shabbos* back in that hamlet."

He gave a sum of money to the local guard in order to secure permission to enter the village, but as soon as they entered, the Jewish tavernkeeper shouted at them: "Who brought you here?"

The tzaddik answered calmly: "We ask for neither food nor drink, just to spend *Shabbos* here."

The tavernkeeper consented — but only on condition that they did not spread the word about his hospitality: he didn't want people to get him into the bad habit of being hospitable ...

When Reb Michel arrived at Mezhibuzh the Baal Shem Tov asked him where he had spent *Shabbos*, and he told him. On his way home he was surprised to see that man's wife standing on the wayside near the approach to the village, next to a wagon in which her husband lay dead. He heard that some people from the neighboring town were even pleased that he had died, such was his reputation, and the regional burial society there was demanding a high fee for his burial. The woman whispered to Reb Michel that her husband was in fact one of the hidden tzaddikim, and out of his pocket had financed all the renowned hospitality of a certain householder in the neighboring town. This was only one of the many acts of charity that he had done in the same self-effacing manner. He had requested in his will that no one should occupy himself with his burial, except for the two strangers who would come out to meet the wagon which bore his body, as it approached the nearby town.

Reb Michel immediately conveyed the dead man's wishes to the people there. Sure enough, as the wagon approached the town, two strangers went out to meet it, and it was they who prepared the body of the self-effacing tzaddik for burial.

One of those two men, averred Reb Michel, was the Prophet Eliyahu.

◆§ *Not* Too *Much Truth, Please!*

וְרַב חֶסֶד וֶאֱמֶת
Abounding in lovingkindness and truth (34:6)

Reb Meir of Premishlan once found himself facing a sanctimonious individual who was decked out grandly in all the rabbinic garb and trappings of a self-styled saint. Perceiving that this was mere window-dressing, while the man behind it all was somewhat base, the tzaddik said: "In the Biblical verse which lists the Thirteen Attributes of Divine Mercy, we find the word 'truth'. This is somewhat surprising, for truth surely characterizes the Attribute of Strict Justice (מִדַּת הַדִּין) rather than the Attribute of Mercy (מִדַּת הָרַחֲמִים). Indeed, if God were to judge us by the criterion of uncompromising truth, demanding of us an absolute degree of truth in our performance of the mitzvos, who would survive such a test?

"Fortunately, though," explained Reb Meir, "the attribute of truth is sometimes itself an attribute of mercy. Let us suppose the Almighty sees a man who passes himself off as a saint, flaunting the cloak of a sage, and garments of purest white. One might expect the Almighty to judge such a man according to the exacting standards demanded of tzaddikim. In fact, though, He judges him only according to the measure of truth — according to such a man's *truthful* measure — for He sees what goes on inside his heart, and knows that in fact he is nothing more than a simple, base fellow.

"And this answers our question as to what 'truth' is doing in a list of merciful attributes. For what greater demonstration of mercy and lovingkindness could there be, than the fact that God judges such a man according to his *true* measure? ... "

◆§ *Vision Tests for Visionaries*

וּבְבֹא משֶׁה לִפְנֵי ה׳ ... יָסִיר אֶת הַמַּסְוֶה

In his later years Reb Menachem Mendel of Kotsk suffered from aching eyes, and was advised by a Warsaw oculist to wear spectacles when studying in order to spare his vision. The tzaddik refused outright, saying: "I am not going to have anything intercepting between my eyes and the Torah!"

His disciple, Reb Eliyahu of Viskit, had a similar problem, and was given the same advice about spectacles for study. Quoting with approval the rationale of his rebbe, he also made a point — until the day of his death — of never wearing his spectacles when studying. Out of deference to the oculist from Warsaw, however, he duly wore them at all other times...

כי תשא
And when Moshe went in before Hashem ... he removed the veil (34:34)

◆§ *With Malice Towards None*

It was clear from his face that one of the chassidim listening to Reb Yitzchak Meir of Ger disapproved of some point the rebbe had just made to the credit of Achav, the wicked king of Israel.

The rebbe thereupon turned to that chassid and said: "My attitude is confirmed by logic. You, for example, only imagine that your rebbe is such a man to whom Eliyahu the Prophet perhaps reveals himself, and yet that is sufficient reason for you to travel all this way to visit him. How much more should we look positively upon a king who in fact saw the Prophet Eliyahu face to face, and even had the courage to speak harshly to him; how much more so should we endeavor to give him the benefit of the doubt, by finding non-literal ways of understanding what his sin was!"

לֵךְ הֵרָאֵה אֶל אַחְאָב
Go, appear before Achav (Ahab) (Haftarah)

◆§ *Those That Have Eyes to See*

The disciples of the Baal Shem Tov repeatedly requested that he show them the Prophet Eliyahu, until he finally agreed. Once they all went out to the fields together, according to their custom every Friday midafternoon, in order to hear words of Torah from the mouth of their rebbe and to greet the incoming *Shabbos*.

Suddenly he said: "I would like to smoke a pipe."

His disciples spread out in all directions in the hope of finding someone willing to lend his pipe, but saw no one and returned emptyhanded. The tzaddik stood up and said: "Here, I can see a Polish squire walking along.

וַיֵּלֶךְ אֵלִיָּהוּ לְהֵרָאוֹת
And Eliyahu went to appear (Haftarah)

Perhaps you could go across and see if he has a pipe I could borrow?"

They went over to ask him, and not only did he agree to lend it, but followed them back to the rebbe so that he would give it to him personally. He filled it with tobacco and lit it with a spark from two stones, and while the Baal Shem Tov smoked, he asked the stranger whether that year's harvest was coming up well all over the countryside, whether during threshing it yielded an ample measure of grain, and so on. His disciples took no notice of the stranger, and spent the time repeating and memorizing the most recent teachings of their rebbe.

After the stranger had taken his leave, the Baal Shem Tov said: "Very well, I have kept my promise: I have shown you the Prophet Eliyahu."

His disciples were stupefied, and protested: "Rebbe, why did you not tell us that this was Eliyahu, so that we could ask him to teach us?"

The Baal Shem Tov answered: "If you had understood yourselves and asked who this was, I would have revealed him to you, but if you did not understand, I was not permitted to do so. I can however tell you what I said to him. When I asked him if the new crop was sprouting satisfactorily, my question meant: 'Has there been a widespread אִתְעָרוּתָא דִלְתַתָּא? Have our brethren taken the initiative in turning their souls toward their Father in heaven?' And when I asked whether the harvest yielded ample grain, my question meant: 'Has this spontaneous awakening of our brethren resulted in an arousal of divine grace, an אִתְעָרוּתָא דִלְעֵילָא, bringing all manner of blessings upon their heads?'

"And what he answered me, he answered me."

◆§ *A Revelation in Disguise*

When Reb Yitzchak Meir of Ger was a child of three and all those who saw him were amazed at his precocious talents, his mother took him with her to visit Reb Yisrael, the Maggid of Koznitz, who showed his delight at seeing the young prodigy.

On the road leading home the child took ill with sunstroke. After carrying him as far as her strength would allow, his mother sat down exhausted on a stone, and wept bitterly as she saw what a state he was in. Suddenly she caught sight of a passer-by who was dressed like a German Jew, with something like a traveler's bag around his neck. When he asked her for the cause of her distress and she told him, he said: "I'll give the child some medication and he will feel well right away."

Taking a bottle out of his pocket, he poured a few drops of its contents on to a lump of sugar which he had, and gave it to the child. The toddler's color at once reverted to normal as his temperature dropped, and the mother resumed her way homeward to Magnishov, accompanied by the stranger. On her arrival she told her story, and in no time word of it spread through the town.

The house soon filled with people eager to bring their ailments to this remarkable physician — but the stranger vanished.

Reb Yitzchak Meir recounted this episode when he was an adult, and added: "That 'German Jew' was Eliyahu, but my father did not recognize him, because the leather girdle which he always wears around his waist was for the purpose of this occasion worn around his neck."

סדר ויקהל
Sidra Vayakheil

◆§ *"Funny, Isn't It?"*

וּבַיּוֹם הַשְּׁבִיעִי יִהְיֶה לָכֶם קֹדֶשׁ
But on the seventh day you shall have a holy day (35:2)

In his youth, Reb Shmelke of Nikolsburg had a friend who was pious, talented and studious, but by nature so obstinate that he never conceded that another man's viewpoint was right.

Many years later, when this young man had grown up to be the *rav* of Yanov, he invited the dignitaries of his town to travel with him to the wedding of his son which was to be held at some distance. A whole caravan of carriages, carrying all the most prominent and scholarly citizens, set out in honor of their *rav*. He himself led the way, accompanied in his coach by the bridegroom, the lay leader of the community, and a certain gifted young scholar. When the time came to recite the afternoon prayers they all got down from the carriage to find a quiet spot in the forest in which to pray, the *rav* choosing to stand under a tall tree at a little distance from the others. The other three waited respectfully in the carriage for his return, but even when the sun had set there was no sign of him. They set out to look for him amongst the trees, expecting to find that he had tarried over the *Minchah* prayer, and became increasingly anxious as night fell. Returning to the highway they found that the rest of the caravan had caught up to them, and when they explained what had detained them, their newly-arrived townsmen reassured them: "A little while ago one of the worthies of our town drove past us alone in his coach on his way to the wedding. He must have invited the *rav* to join him for some reason."

This assumption sounded plausible enough, and off they all went, much relieved. On their arrival at their destination, though, they were stricken with consternation: the father of the bridegroom was not there. Guesses of all kind were proposed, and finally, the wedding ceremony was solemnized in the most dismal spirit imaginable. All the way home the guests asked passersby whether they had seen the *rav* — but in vain. Nor did they find him at home at Yanov, nor did the messengers sent out to various other places bring back any clue.

Actually, the *rav* had lost his way in that endless forest. Wanting to return to the highway, he had become confused by the roundabout tracks leading in all directions, and in fact walked on in the dark for several miles, ever deeper into the wilds. As the sun rose he paused to rest, and was obliged to recite his morning prayers with neither *tallis* nor *tefillin*. On he wandered for weeks on end, surviving on whatever fruit he could find. And so distressed was he by his tribulations that he lost track of time, and honored *Shabbos* in whatever humble ways his predicament allowed — one day early.

By virtue of his Torah study over the years the Almighty protected him from harm, until at long last, after all manner of adventures, he found his way back to Yanov, and recounted his unenviable story to a family wild with joy.

Came Thursday afternoon, and the *rav* busied himself with all the traditional preparations for the fast-approaching *Shabbos*. When he expressed his puzzlement that his family did not do likewise, they explained that his calculations had become confused: Friday was only the next day. But all the suffering he had undergone must have left its somber mark on him. No matter how earnestly his relatives and townsmen debated and argued the subject with him, nothing could make him budge from his irrational fixation: he alone was right in his calculations. They became secretly worried about his sanity — but what could be done? On Friday he desisted from travel, and did not put on *tefillin* at morning prayers, as if the holy day had already arrived. *Shabbos* he treated like a weekday, and reprimanded his family for their stubbornness — while their buoyant joy shriveled into dismay.

In the weeks that followed, rabbis and sages from all around tried to convince him, by entire batteries of invincible scholarly arguments, that this time he was in the wrong — but to no avail. Though rational in all other respects, his harsh experiences in the forest had further toughened his innate obstinacy.

When word of this bizarre impasse reached Reb Shmelke of Nikolsburg, who was then the *rav* of Shiniva, he immediately set out for Yanov, arriving on Thursday. Overjoyed at seeing his boyhood friend, the *rav* of Yanov asked his guest: 'Would you do me the honor of staying with me for *Shabbos*?''

''Why, of course,'' said Reb Shmelke. ''In fact I was hoping for such an invitation.''

He then took aside his host's family and told them to prepare for *Shabbos* that same evening, and to bring to the table a good bottle or two of strong, old wine. On Thursday afternoon all the menfolk duly went off to immerse themselves in the *mikveh*, dressed up in their fur *shtreimels* and black silk *kapotes*, and proceeded to the synagogue for evening prayers. The local folk were stupefied: surely their *rav* had not won over Reb Shmelke! The guest saw to it that his host served as *chazzan* for the prayers of welcome to *Shabbos*, while Reb Shmelke himself and all the other congregants quietly recited the weekday evening service.

As if it were Friday night, the *rav* and his family returned joyfully home, where they were joined by a great many guests who had come in honor of Reb Shmelke. They sang *Shalom Aleichem*, welcoming the ministering angels whose appointed time is Friday night; they recited the *Kiddush* of Friday night over goblets of wine; and in between courses of *gefilte fish* and other delicacies not normally reserved for Thursday nights, they exchanged favorite gems of Talmudic lore, as Jews all around the world are wont to do — on Friday night.

In the course of the festive meal Reb Shmelke remarked to his host that it would be only right to turn this occasion into a *seudah* of thanksgiving for his miraculous survival — by serving a few extra bottles of wine, for example. He then saw to it that his host drank a considerable quantity of the kind of old wine that throws a person into the extended stupor of deep sleep. When the *rav* duly fell asleep at the table, Reb Shmelke asked that a pillow be placed under his head so that he should be able to slumber on, undisturbed. Finally, taking up his pipe and puffing happily away, he turned to the townsfolk who were at the table: "You can now all go off and rest. Everyone can go ahead with his usual occupations, and with the help of the Almighty, everything will work out well. And tomorrow night, on *Shabbos* eve, at this same hour, I would ask you all to come here again."

Reb Shmelke personally stood on guard all that night and throughout Friday, maintaining his patrol around the house as well as within it, lest the slightest noise disturb the *rav* in his sleep. On Friday night he did not even go to the synagogue, but prayed alone in the house of the *rav*. After prayers, the townsfolk came to the *Shabbos* table exactly as they had done the night before, and found the *rav* still sound asleep. Reb Shmelke partook of the *Shabbos* meal joyfully, delighting his listeners with discourse after discourse until midnight — and then woke up his host.

"Rabbi of Yanov," he said, "please join us for the Grace after Meals."

"Funny, isn't it?" yawned the *rav*. "I feel as if I've been sleeping for hours on end!"

He washed his hands, joined in the end of the learned table talk, and then together they all recited the Grace after Meals.

After *Shabbos* all the local dignitaries came to offer Reb Shmelke their whispered thanks, to which he responded by making them give their solemn promise never to make the slightest mention of the whole episode.

And until the day of his death the *rav* never discovered what had happened. On the contrary, he was proud of the fact that so many people had finally seen the light and were now observing *Shabbos* according to the way he had argued all along.

"Mind you," he would add, "one must always give credit where credit is due. It took none less than my esteemed friend from way back, Reb Shmelke of Nikolsburg, to do the trick. Funny, isn't it? Some people can be *incorrigibly* obstinate!"

◆§ *The Lifesaver in Spite of Himself*

Reb Levi Yitzchak of Berditchev was once out on a journey, accompanied by his *gabbai* and his *shammes*. On Friday they arrived at a small township, and since the tzaddik made a point of never traveling on Friday afternoon they decided to stay there for *Shabbos*.

It so happened that over the months before their arrival, this township had been visited by a whole series of charlatans. These resourceful gentlemen had in turn provided themselves with the retinue of *gabbai* and *shammes* expected of a visiting tzaddik, and through carefully-studied theatricals had managed to dupe the simple folk who lived there, until with understandable alacrity they had left, even more full of resources than they had come... The townspeople therefore suspected Reb Levi Yitzchak too, and to make matters worse, one of their number claimed to have once seen the *Rav* of Berditchev, and his memory told him that the newcomer did not resemble him in the slightest. His cronies therefore decided that in synagogue the next day, on *Shabbos*, they would call this scoundrel to the Reading of the Torah, and then and there abuse him and beat him up so heartily that he would be lucky to get out of their town alive.

The two attendants of the tzaddik smelled a rat, and begged him to set out in time to reach some other township before *Shabbos*. But he was insistent: he had never traveled on Friday afternoon, and he was not going to relax his principles now.

Dusk settled in over the township, and Reb Levi Yitzchak made his way to the local *shul* in order to join the congregation in welcoming *Shabbos*. Unable to contain the rapture and ecstasy that fired him in prayer, he prayed as he always did — with violent gesticulations and the voice of one possessed. Having made up their minds about him before they had as much as seen him, the congregants marveled: "Now this one is a *real* expert at making an impression on people!"

The unaccustomed sounds proceeding from the *shul* were overheard by a gentile who was passing by the doorway on his way through the township to a village some miles away. He asked the nearest Jew: "What's all the noise about?"

"We've got some character visiting our town," said the local Jew, "who says he's the rabbi of Berditchev. That's him shouting his way through the prayers."

The gentile continued on his way until he arrived at the village of his destination. After his first drink the Jewish tavernkeeper there asked: "Well, what news did you pick up on the way?"

"I passed through a little town," said the new arrival, and heard the weirdest screaming coming out of the synagogue. So I asked one of your people what it was all about, and he said they have some rabbi visiting them, and that's how he prays."

"Any idea where the rabbi comes from?" asked the tavernkeeper.

"Berditchev, I think they said," answered the gentile.

Now this conversation was heard by the resident *melamed* who was maintained by the tavernkeeper at his expense in order to tutor his children. He had once met the tzaddik, and his heart was instantly kindled with a desire to see him again. It was unthinkable that Reb Levi Yitzchak of Berditchev in person was actually in the neighboring town, and he would not visit him there! There was only one thing to do: he would set out at once.

After he had already made some headway, a thought that crossed his mind suddenly stopped him in his tracks: "What on earth am I doing? Today is *Shabbos!* It's absolutely impossible to walk the whole distance to that town without exceeding the permissible limits. Would I go ahead and desecrate *Shabbos?"*

So he stood, giving this objection weighty consideration — and finally decided: "No matter what! If the tzaddik is so near, I just *have* to go ahead and greet him!"

After having gone a little further he stopped again.

"Come now," he told himself, "you're acquiring a mitzvah by paying with a sin. Where does it say you're allowed to desecrate *Shabbos* in order to be able to earn the mitzvah of paying your respects to your rebbe?"

He stood stock still, thought this way and that, and decided: "Straight ahead!"

And so right through the night he strode and stopped, stopped and strode, until by daybreak he was on the outskirts of the town. By the time he found the synagogue the congregation was ready for the Reading of the Law, and as he peered eagerly through the window he saw the tzaddik himself, making his way towards the Torah. Just as the long-awaited moment arrived for the irate townsfolk to teach their newest impostor a lesson he would never forget, the back door burst open, and the *melamed*, who was known by them to be some kind of scholar, ran in a frenzy up to the tzaddik, and wailed: "Rebbe! *Oy*, rebbe! I've desecrated *Shabbos!"*

"No, my son," the tzaddik assured him quietly, "you have not desecrated *Shabbos*, because your coming right now can truly be called a life-saving mission. If you had not arrived at this very moment, I would have been in real danger."

And the townsfolk, realizing that they had suspected an innocent man, asked his forgiveness.

◆§ The Life of an Hour

It was midwinter, and the dirt roads were treacherous, when Reb Yitzchak Meir of Ger set out to visit Reb Menachem Mendel of Kotsk. The wheels of the coach broke time and again so that the journey took longer than usual, and on Friday morning they were still quite some miles from their destination. The tzaddik was distressed by this, as were the chassidim who accompanied him, for he was not accustomed to traveling on Fridays, and was considering the possibility of spending *Shabbos* at some wayside village. But first he asked the Jewish wagon-driver if they stood any chance of arriving at Kotsk at least a few hours before sunset; he dearly wanted to spend *Shabbos* there, and would repay him well for his effort.

Seeing how much it mattered to him, the simple fellow said that he would do his very best. And indeed, he drove the horses so fast that halfway there one of them collapsed of exhaustion and died. The tzaddik and his chassidim were grieved to see what had happened, and decided to stop and spend the holy day by the wayside, but the wagon-driver begged them to allow him to drive on. Nothing would make him happier than to enable the tzaddik to reach Kotsk for *Shabbos*, as he had originally planned to do, and he was certain that this was still possible. Reb Yitzchak Meir allowed himself to be persuaded, and in fact they reached Kotsk well before sunset. On Friday night, however, the driver's remaining horse died. The moment the tzaddik heard this he sent word to the wagon-driver that he should not worry, for immediately after *Shabbos* the chassidim would give him whatever it would cost to buy a new pair of sturdy horses. But the incident was too much of a trauma for the little man to bear. He pined away, and died there in Kotsk.

The tzaddik later told his chassidim that when that wagon driver presented himself before the Heavenly Court to stand trial for his actions in This World, a long line of prosecuting angels ranged themselves opposite him, for he had almost no record of good deeds to his credit. One angel, though, spoke up in his defense: it was because of the observance of a *Shabbos* that the accused had lost his property, then his life; and he had exerted himself beyond the call of duty to enable others to reach their destination before the Day of Rest. The verdict was, therefore, that by virtue of *Shabbos* he would be exempted from undergoing all the punishments which his sins warranted. On the other hand, it was impossible to reward him by spiritual bliss in the Garden of Eden, because his was well-nigh bare of any good deeds. It was therefore decided that he should be dispatched to the World of Imagination. There he would live in the illusion that he was in This World, forever sitting in the driver's seat of a handsome carriage to which four sleek stallions were harnessed, and galloping lustily along a smooth broad highway. This illusion he would find more pleasurable than all the spiritual delights that could be offered.

"And now," added Reb Yitzchak Meir, "a certain quotation in the Talmud has finally become clear to me. We read that Rabbi Yehudah HaNasi wept and said: 'There are such as earn their portion in the World to Come in a single hour' (יֵשׁ קוֹנֶה עוֹלָמוֹ בְּשָׁעָה אַחַת). The classical commentaries ask why he wept. If anything, surely he should have rejoiced that it is possible for men to earn a reward in heaven by the efforts of a single hour. And the answer is as follows: Rabbi Yehudah HaNasi wept for people like our wagon-driver, who are without good deeds, but who through one great mitzvah have earned a share in the World to Come. But *because his tastes are coarse* the only rewards such a man can be given are the pleasures of This World, the world whose life the Sages call חַיֵּי שָׁעָה — literally, 'the life of an hour,' that is, a world of ephemeral pleasures. It is true to say of such a man יֵשׁ קוֹנֶה עוֹלָמוֹ בְּשָׁעָה אַחַת: such a man, it is true, may earn a world *in* an hour — but the world he earns is the world *of* an hour, a world of transient vanity. And over this Rabbi Yehudah HaNasi wept."

Reb Yitzchak Meir ended on a personal note: "I should add that I didn't remain an ungrateful debtor. I was fortunate in that my prayers were the instrument through which our wagon-driver's spiritual eyes were opened. He finally realized that he was dead, and that his reward was one without substance. Having got that far, he could then be granted the spiritual bliss of the Garden of Eden."

◆§ *The Anguish of Shabbos*

It is *Shabbos*, when one may not cry out; healing will come soon *(Talmud, Tractate Shabbos).*

Reb Hillel of Paritsh used to spend a substantial part of every year traveling through the towns of the southern parts of Russia in order to give instruction in the applied ethics of Chassidism, and to arouse people to repentance wherever the need arose.

He once arrived in a town where the Jewish tavernkeepers kept their businesses open on *Shabbos.* Reb Hillel was shocked to hear this, and invited them all to meet him. When he had explained to them what a serious matter this was they all undertook to oblige — though on one condition: that he persuade a certain wealthy tavernkeeper, whose turnover was the highest in town, to do likewise, for otherwise they would not be able to survive competition with him. The tzaddik thereupon sent for that man — once, twice, three times — but he ignored the invitation. Reb Hillel stayed on in the town for *Shabbos*. In the morning the wealthy tavernkeeper suddenly suffered increasingly severe pains in the stomach, and his wife, fearing that they were brought on by the disrespect her husband had shown the tzaddik, hastened to seek him out so that he should intercede on his behalf. While Reb Hillel was at the *Shabbos* midday meal surrounded by a large company of chassidim, she burst into the room, and with tears in her eyes implored the rebbe to give her husband his blessing for a speedy recovery.

The tzaddik remained silent.

His chassidim were dismayed: "Rebbe, at least give the blessing that is traditional in such cases on the holy day — 'It is *Shabbos*, when one may not cry out; healing will come soon!' "

But the tzaddik said not a word.

The woman left bitterly disappointed, and her husband's pains grew worse.

On *Motzaei Shabbos*, when night fell and the holy day had passed, the tzaddik was discoursing with his chassidim at a table on which stood a samovar, in fulfillment of the Talmudic dictum: "Hot beverages at the close of *Shabbos* serve as a cure." In ran the same woman, weeping and wailing, begging the tzaddik to have pity on her husband and to pray for him.

Reb Hillel simply said: שַׁבָּת הִיא מִלִּזְעוֹק וּרְפוּאָה קְרוֹבָה לָבֹא ('It is *Shabbos*, when one may not cry out; healing will come soon')...

The chassidim were amazed. On *Shabbos* itself the tzaddik had said nothing — and now, when the holy day was over, he said these words?!

The tzaddik continued: "שַׁבָּת הִיא מִלִּזְעוֹק — If *Shabbos* itself will no longer have cause to cry out *against him,* then healing will come soon. Go along and tell him that if he gives a solemn handshake in the presence of three witnesses that he will close his business on *Shabbos*, then he will be cured."

Three chassidim hastened to his bedside to convey the rebbe's words — and he earnestly gave his word of honor.

His illness passed, and the sanctity of *Shabbos* was upheld in that town.

Sight Subtler than Light

לֹא תְבַעֲרוּ אֵשׁ ... בְּיוֹם הַשַּׁבָּת *You shall kindle no fire ... on the day of Shabbos* (35:3)

Reb Nachum of Chernobyl once spent *Shabbos* at the home of Reb Shimon Shlomo, the father of Reb Moshe of Savran. In accordance with the custom of the household a long candle was lit before sunset which was to last until morning, in order to give light to anyone wanting to rise and study Torah before daybreak.

A little after midnight, the host and his family saw Reb Nachum groping his way about the house like one moving in absolute darkness, and were afraid lest he bump into something and hurt himself. Hearing that they were also awake, Reb Nachum asked them: "Why did you not light a candle to last through the night?"

This they could not fathom: that very room was in fact illuminated by the candle they had lit. They investigated, and found that it had earlier blown out, and the gentile maid had relit it. But because it had been lit on *Shabbos*, the tzaddik was able to see nothing by its light.

◆§ *Tzaddikim Work Hard*

מַרְבִּים הָעָם לְהָבִיא
The people bring too much (36:5)

During the time that Reb Avraham Yehoshua Heschel (better known as the Ohev Yisrael, the "lover of his fellow Jews") was the *rav* of Apta, the community began to build an imposing edifice — the new synagogue. A table and chair were set up for the *rav* on the construction site, and word was given out in *shul* that he was sitting there ready to accept contributions towards the costs of building. Immediately after prayers all the congregants hastened to the site and gave their generous donations with willing hearts. After some time, since he was exhausted, he was taken to a nearby house for rest and refreshment, but before he left he asked his son Reb Yitzchak Meir to take his place until his return.

When after an hour the tzaddik returned his son asked him: "Why is it, father, that so many people brought money while you were here, and during the hour you were away there were so few contributors?"

Replied the tzaddik: "In connection with the nationwide appeal for materials for the Tabernacle constructed in the wilderness we read the following: 'And all the wise men who carried out all the work of the Sanctuary ... spoke to Moshe, saying, The people bring more than enough for the service of the work ... And Moshe gave the order, and they caused it to be proclaimed throughout the camp, saying, Let neither man or woman *do any more work* for the offering of the Sanctuary. So the people refrained from bringing.' Now this is strange. If the problem was that 'the people bring more than enough,' then surely all Moshe had to do was to proclaim that they stop bringing their materials. Why did he find it necessary instead to give the order that no one was to 'do any more work'? And the answer is as follows: So long as the people heard the clanging of the workmen's hammers, they were filled with the desire to bring their contributions, and they would have ignored a simple announcement telling them to stop. But once people are no longer aware that *someone is working hard* — on their personal construction site — they lose interest, and contribute no longer ..."

◆§ *Her Value Exceeds that of Gems*

בְּמַרְאֹת הַצֹּבְאֹת
The mirrors of the women assembling (38:8)

The daughters of Israel had mirrors which they used when adorning themselves; these, too, they contributed toward the building of the Sanctuary *(Rashi).*

Soon after Reb Shneur Zalman of Liadi became rebbe, there lived in Vitebsk a chassid by the name of Reb Gavriel, who was persecuted by his father and brothers and other relatives for having joined "the Sect." He even ignored their concerted efforts to ruin his sources of income, and continued periodically to visit Liozna, where the rebbe lived at that time.

Not once did he complain to the rebbe about the deteriorating financial situation of his shop; on the contrary, he always contributed generously to all the causes for which the rebbe turned to his chassidim, such as support of the needy scholars in *Eretz Yisrael,* and the ransom of captives. Nor did he ever complain to the rebbe about another cause for heartache: twenty-five years after his marriage he and his wife had not yet been blessed with a child. But He Who engineers all circumstances brought about a circumstance through which Reb Gavriel was granted a triple blessing — children, long life, and livelihood. And this is how it happened.

A large sum was once needed for the ransom of captives, and Reb Shneur Zalman — as was his custom — named the amount that Reb Gavriel was expected to contribute. When he told his wife of this she observed that he was not happy, which he always was in such circumstances. In answer to her query, he let her into the secret that as a result of his family's activities they had been reduced to poverty, and he simply did not possess the amount that the rebbe had named.

"Haven't you told me many times," said his wife, "that our rebbe says that one should always trust in God and be constantly joyful? So why be unhappy? The Almighty will surely help, and enable us to contribute the amount the rebbe expects of us!"

She then went ahead and quietly sold whatever jewelry and gems she had, and brought the money they had fetched to her husband, saying: "Look, here we already have the whole amount."

And she suggested that he set out at once, and take her little bundle directly to the rebbe. Reb Gavriel reminded her that the rebbe usually sent out an emissary to collect such moneys, and it would be preferable to wait this time too. But since within a short time his brothers caused him another serious loss, he was afraid that if the money would be needed he might be tempted to use it for some other purpose, and decided after all to set out with the bundle to Liozna.

Arriving there, he placed the bundle on the rebbe's table, and explained that since his financial situation was not as comfortable as it had once been, he preferred not to wait until some emergency made him divert this money to another end, in which case he might not have it ready for the emissary; he had therefore come now. The rebbe thereupon told him to open the bundle and to count the money. He did so, and was surprised to see that the coins shone as if they had come directly from the mint.

The rebbe leaned his head on his hands, then raised his head and said: "The contributions to the Sanctuary in the wilderness included gold, silver and copper, but the only metals to shine were the mirrors of the women, from the copper of which the laver and its pedestal were made. The laver and its pedestal by the way, were the last items to be made, but the first to be used, in the service in the Sanctuary ... Tell me, where did this money come from?"

Reb Gavriel told the rebbe that he had suffered persecution by his family for ten years, and went on to tell of how his wife had secured the money.

Once again, in a state of *dveikus,* the rebbe leaned his head on his hands for some time, and then said: "בַּת דִּינָא, בַּטֵּל דִּינָא — Your harsh trials are over. May God grant you and your wife sons and daughters, and long life to see the offspring of your offspring; may God grant you over and again prosperity wherever you turn, and favor in the eyes of all those who see you ... Close your shop and start dealing in gems."

With a happy heart Reb Gavriel hastened home to bring his wife the good news — and asked her why the coins shone.

"I rubbed them for a long time with sand," she said, "until they glistened and sparkled like stars in the sky. By virtue of that, may our fortunes start sparkling too!"

Reb Gavriel closed his shop and began dealing in gems. God made his way prosper, so that he found favor in the eyes of the local nobles and squires who soon became his regular customers. His clientele widened from day to day. Moreover, within a year his wife gave birth to a son.

Within three years he had become wealthy, prospering in whatever he applied himself to, and finding favor in the eyes of whoever saw him, until he was nicknamed "Gavriel the Likeable." After forty years he handed over his business to his sons, and spent his retirement in the study of Torah, in prayer, and in acts of charity. Indeed, in his philanthropy the growing community of chassidim in Vitebsk found a source of constant blessing.

◆§ *A Woman of Valor Who can Find?*

Reb Shalom of Belz arranged a match for his son Reb Yehoshuale with the granddaughter of Reb Avraham Yehoshua Heschel, the Ohev Yisrael of Apta. The *shidduch* was finalized without anyone of the bridegroom's family having seen the bride.

The bridegroom's mother was displeased with this way of doing things, and asked her husband, the tzaddik: "Is it right to arrange a *shidduch* without anyone having seen the bride?"

Reb Shalom reassured her: "In heaven there is a palace which is named after the מַרְאֹת הַצֹּבְאֹת, the mirrors of the pious women who assembled outside the Tabernacle with their gifts born of self-denial, and there are listed the names of all the young women of valor. I saw her there, and you may be certain that she is truly virtuous and worthy of our son."

סדר פקודי

SIDRA PEKUDEI

☙ *Two Dialogues with God*

In this verse the word for *Tabernacle* (מִשְׁכָּן) appears twice, hinting at the Temple which was, as it were, pawned (נִתְמַשְׁכֵּן) into foreign hands, after each of the two Destructions *(Rashi).*

אֵלֶּה פְקוּדֵי הַמִּשְׁכָּן *These are the accounts of the Tabernacle (38:21)*

Reb Yisraël of Ruzhin recounted that the Shpoler Zeide used to bring this plaint to the Almighty: "Master of the Universe! Is it right that in order to allow Yourself to win some small point Your People should have to suffer such a long exile? For you have a long-standing argument with them. *They* say: הֲשִׁיבֵנוּ ה׳ אֵלֶיךָ וְנָשׁוּבָה – 'Return us, O God, unto You, and we will return!' *You* say: שׁוּבָה אֵלַי וְאָשׁוּבָה אֲלֵיכֶם – 'Return to Me, and I will return to you.' And because of this deadlocked argument You withhold the Redemption, and are waiting until the Children of Israel return to You in repentance. Very well, then: By the sanctity of my beard I swear to You that Israel will not repent before the Redemption!"

And Reb Yisrael of Ruzhin added: "I hold the same – but one thing I can promise for sure. When the *Mashiach* comes the Children of Israel will certainly repent, for until then they have a justifiable claim: 'We say in our festival prayers, וּמִפְּנֵי חֲטָאֵינוּ גָּלִינוּ מֵאַרְצֵנוּ – *Because* of our sins we were exiled from our Land. But מִפְּנֵי really means *before:* even *before* we sinned exile was decreed upon us, for when You made Your covenant with Avraham You decreed four exiles upon his descendants.'

"Therefore, Master of the Universe," continued Reb Yisrael of Ruzhin, "just as You decreed exile upon Your children before they sinned, so should you redeem them before they repent!"

Therefore, Master of the Universe, [illegible] Yisrael of Shushan. Just as You decreed [illegible] upon Your children [illegible] should you redeem them [illegible] they repent.

ספר ויקרא
Leviticus

סדר ויקרא
Sidra Vayikra

A Man Like Any Other

וַיִּקְרָא אֶל מֹשֶׁה *And He called to Moshe (1:1)*

וַיִּקְרָא: the first word of this Book appears in the Torah with a small *aleph (Mesorah).*

At a tender age Reb Menachem Mendel of Lubavitch, who is known as the Tzemach Tzedek, lost his mother, the daughter of Reb Shneur Zalman of Liadi, and was brought up thereafter by his illustrious grandfather, who on the day after Yom Kippur, 1792, brought the child to the *cheder* to begin his Torah lessons. Reb Shneur Zalman had prayed at daybreak, which was not his custom, and had led the prayers and read the Torah himself. It was a Thursday, in the week in which the Portion of *Haazinu* was read from the Torah, and he read the passage "Remember the days of old" in a way that stirred the minds and hearts of all his listeners. When he came to the verse — "He led him about, he instructed him, he watched over him like the apple of his eye" — his eyes brimmed over with tears, and a shudder passed through the congregants.

After prayers he had the toddler enveloped in a *tallis* so that he could see nothing around him, and asked to have him carried to his mother's burial place. They arrived at the cemetery together with the child's father, Reb Shalom Shachna, and approaching the gravestone the rebbe said in a loud and cheerful voice: "*Mazel Tov* to you, Devorah Leah the daughter of Sterna! Today I am introducing your son, Menachem Mendel the son of Devorah Leah, to the study of the Torah. Give him your blessing that just as he has been brought to the study of the Torah, so too should he be led to the *chuppah* and to the performance of good deeds; and bless him too with long life."

And all those who stood with them responded warmly: "Amen!"

When they came home the child was brought to the courtyard of the synagogue, where the rebbe asked the boy's *melamed* to teach him the opening passage of *Vayikra,* the chapter of *Leviticus* with which young children traditionally begin their Torah studies. Throughout the lesson the rebbe leaned his head on his arms in the wordless ecstasy of *dveikus,* and when it came to an end he asked that the child be given a cake of oil and honey and a hard-boiled egg, on both of which verses from the Torah were inscribed.

At this point the youngster asked his grandfather: "Why is the *aleph* of the word *Vayikra* small?"

For some time the rebbe remained silent in a state of *dveikus,* then he opened his eyes and said: "Adam was created by God's hands, and in understanding he surpassed the ministering angels. He was aware of his own stature, and thereby erred in the sin of the Tree of Knowledge. Moshe Rabbeinu was also aware of his own stature, but not only did this not cause him to wax proud: on the contrary, he was humble of spirit, thinking that any other man — who was not the son of Amram, nor seventh in direct line of descent from the Patriarch Avraham — if he were granted a soul like his, and the spiritual advantages of an ancestry like his, would have been far greater than he. The Torah itself testifies to his modesty: 'And the man Moshe was very humble, more so than all the men on the face of the earth.' Now the Torah is comprised of large letters, letters of intermediate size, and small letters. This is to teach us that every man should strive through the study and practice of the Torah to attain the spiritual level of a *beinoni* [the so-called "intermediate" man, whose consistently successful struggle for mastery over his Evil Inclination is described in Reb Shneur Zalman's classic *Tanya,* which is also known as the *Sefer shel Beinonim*]. The name of Adam, who stumbled because of his awareness of his own greatness, appears in the Book of *Chronicles* with a large *aleph;* Moshe Rabbeinu, who was led by this awareness to an unparalleled degree of humility, is addressed in the Torah by the word *Vayikra,* which is written with a small *aleph*".

The rebbe then delivered a chassidic discourse based on the verse: "If any man among you brings an offering to God," and asked all those present to partake of the *seudas mitzvah*. He left the synagogue, and those remaining washed their hands in preparation for the festive meal, and took their places at the table. Some of the elder chassidim sat the child on a chair, placed it on the table, and asked him to repeat the answer which his grandfather had given to his question. This he did, in the unfaltering voice of a little boy who had just turned three.

Hearing his words, one of the oldest chassidim present rose and said: "May the Almighty fulfill all the blessings with which our rebbe blessed his grandson, Menachem Mendel the son of Devorah Leah!"

And all his friends responded: "Amen! Amen!"

◆§ *Guard Your Tongue*

וְנֶפֶשׁ כִּי תֶחֱטָא וְשָׁמְעָה קוֹל אָלָה
And if a person sins, and hears the voice of an oath (5:1)

When he was a young man, recalled Reb Yitzchak of Vorki, he suffered a great deal of anguish from his wife, but no matter how bitterly she berated him he bore everything in silence. When he saw, however, that she was making life a misery for their servants as well, he was unable to decide whether for the sake of peace he should make no comment, or whether he was under a moral obligation to speak up — not, indeed, for himself, but in defense of the downtrodden servants. He decided that this was a question for his rebbe, Reb David of Lelov.

The tzaddik, listened, and said: "Why do you tell me? Tell yourself!"

Reb Yitzchak was baffled by this response — until after some time he came across a teaching of the Baal Shem Tov: If a person is remiss in the realm of action, he suffers anguish caused by his cattle and his servants; if he does not rule his tongue, he has to undergo distress caused by the harsh words and curses of his wife and other people; and if he is careless as to what kinds of thoughts are allowed to occupy his mind, his children will be the cause of his heart-ache. Moreover, taught the

Baal Shem Tov, if a person succeeds in setting aright these three areas of his life — his thought, speech, and action — then the three corresponding sources of distress are transformed to sources of happiness. Pondering over this teaching of the Baal Shem Tov, Reb Yitzchak of Vorki came to understand his rebbe's sharp reaction: "Tell yourself!"

A certain scholar saw a hint of this teaching in the verse: "And if a person sins, and hears the voice of an oath." If a person sins, he said, then he is bound to hear oaths and curses from his wife and from others.

◆§ *Exchange of Energy*

וְלֹא אֹתִי קָרָאתָ יַעֲקֹב כִּי יָגַעְתָּ בִּי יִשְׂרָאֵל:
You have not called on Me, O Yaakov, for you have been weary of Me, O Yisrael (Haftarah)

Ridden by illness and pain, Reb Yisrael of Koznitz was confined to his bed for long periods, but when the time came for prayer, or for the study of the Torah, or for the performance of a mitzvah, he rallied with the strength of a lion, and appeared to be perfectly fit and robust.

One of his chassidim took the liberty of asking him for an explanation of this phenomenon, and the Maggid answered: "We read in the Book of *Isaiah*, וְקֹוֵי ה׳ יַחֲלִיפוּ כֹחַ — 'Those who trust in God will renew (literally: *exchange)* their strength.' Now we often see laborers who work hard as porters and the like for six days of the week, and when *Shabbos* comes they are so exhausted that they almost fall asleep during their prayers. Where has their strength disappeared to? Simple — during that time they exchange their strength with those who trust in God, so that the latter will have the strength to serve their Maker in prayer and study. And when their prayers are over, those who trust in God return the strength to those who lent it, thus enabling them to resume their new week's hard work."

סדר צו
Sidra Tzav

◆§ Dressed for the Occasion

וּפָשַׁט אֶת בְּגָדָיו וְלָבַשׁ בְּגָדִים אֲחֵרִים
And he shall take off his garments, and put on other garments (6:4)

Reb Uri of Strelisk was once told of the seemingly pretentious conduct of Reb Yisrael of Ruzhin, who used to have musical instruments played before him. The Saraph of Strelisk wanted to know what the tzaddik of Ruzhin looked like when he was listening to his musicians, and was given a picture of inspired ecstasy.

"Concerning the Prophet Eliyahu," he said, "we are told that 'the girdle of his loins was a girdle of leather.' This really means that in his case his very loins, his very body, was like a leather girdle, which he could put on and take off at will. And so it is with the tzaddik of Ruzhin: when he so desires, he can divest himself of his body, and when he wills it otherwise, he can clothe himself in his body."

◆§ In Another Man's Shoes

It once happened that Reb David Zvi Chein, the *rav* of Chernigov, arrived late for his *yechidus* with his rebbe, Reb Shmuel of Lubavitch. He decided to wait in the room adjoining the rebbe's study, and to ask a certain question of the rebbe as he passed, for he had to return home within a short time. He was joined there by the rebbe's attendant, who had brought the change of clothing which the rebbe would soon need, for by the time he had received a long series of chassidim for private interviews he always perspired heavily.

"Would you happen to know," the attendant asked Reb David Zvi, "why he perspires so much when he grants *yechidus* in there? The whole thing lasts only an hour, but does he perspire!"

The chassid remained silent, so the attendant asked again: "Why, in heaven's name, does he perspire so much?"

The door to the study opened at once, and the rebbe addressed the questioner: "I am dismissing you as of today. Please go home, and I will send you your wages there every week. And by the way, why is it so hard to understand why I perspire? In the course of this past hour I received twenty-five people for *yechidus*. If I am to counsel each man well, then I must experience his distress exactly as he himself experiences it: I must divest myself of my own garments and clothe myself in his. When the time comes for me to offer him advice, I cannot do this while I am still dressed in his spiritual garments — just as he was unable to advise *himself* while in that condition. I therefore have to get out of his clothes and dress myself again in my own. In brief, for every person who comes in with a question, I have to undress and dress twice. Now work it out for yourself: if in the course of one hour a man has to undress and dress fifty times over, how can he not perspire?"

◆§ *A Prayer by Any Other Name*

לֹא יֵחָשֵׁב לוֹ פִּגּוּל יִהְיֶה
It shall not be accounted to him; it shall be an abomination (7:18)

Prayer substitutes for the sacrificial offering. Let the worshiper therefore take heed not to admit any alien thought — just as an improper thought renders a sacrifice invalid *(Shulchan Aruch).*

On their way through Ruzhin, a group of *misnagdim* from Sanik decided to call on Reb Yisrael of Ruzhin in order to enjoy a little argument with him on the ideology of Chassidism.

"We, at least, walk in the path of God," they began. "We set aside times for the study of Torah; we pray with a *minyan* at daybreak; and when prayers are over, while we are still wearing our *tallis* and *tefillin,* we settle down to learn *Mishnayos.* But the chassidim — not only do they pray after the statutory time, but when they have done with their prayers they sit down to drink vodka together. And then they call themselves chassidim, which means 'pious ones,' and us they call *misnagdim,* their antagonists. Why, it should be the other way round!"

The rebbe's *shammes,* who happened to be present,

could not contain himself, and came out with his own jocular reply: "You *misnagdim* serve the Creator frigidly — you are as lacking in warmth as a corpse, God forbid. And everyone knows that after a death the traditional custom is to study *Mishnayos*. But when chassidim serve their Maker, be it ever so little, at least they do it with enthusiasm, and their heart is on fire, just as a living man is full of warmth — and doesn't a living man need a drop of vodka now and again?"

The tzaddik commented: "This answer, of course, was not to be taken seriously. But the fact is that from the day on which the Temple was destroyed, it is prayer that substitutes for the sacrifices which can no longer be offered, as it is written: וּנְשַׁלְּמָה פָרִים שְׂפָתֵינוּ — 'And our lips will compensate for oxen.' Moreover, the Sages teach us that the daily prayer services were timed so as to correspond to the daily sacrifices. Just as a sacrifice is rendered invalid by an improper thought, and becomes an abomination which is not acceptable On High, so too is a man's prayer invalidated by the admixture of an alien thought. The Evil Inclination therefore devises various stratagems by which to introduce all manner of alien thoughts into the mind of the worshiper in order to distract him. And that is why the chassidim invented a counter-strategy of their own. After their prayers they sit down to drink vodka together, and wish each other *LeChaim*; and as each man gives expression to what he most needs, his friend says: 'May God grant your request!' Now according to the law of the Torah, prayer may be uttered in any language, so these informal words are of course reckoned in heaven as prayer. Here, however, the Evil Inclination has no say, for when he sees people eating and drinking and speaking in their everyday language, he thinks that this is a mere bodily activity and does not even realize that this is prayer!"

☙ *Enemy Aliens*

A man called on Reb Yaakov Yitzchak, the Chozeh (or Seer) of Lublin, and complained that alien thoughts bothered him during prayer.

"*Alien* thoughts?!" queried the Chozeh. "Concerning

tzaddikim, whose thoughts are always holy and revolve around the Torah, one may describe the thoughts that seek admission to their minds as alien. But with you — why, these unholy thoughts are not *alien:* they are all your very own!"

סדר שמיני
sidra sh'mini

◆§ Smiling Through One's Tears

וַיִּדֹּם אַהֲרֹן
And Aharon held his peace (10:3)

The son-in-law of Reb Shlomo of Radomsk, a chassid by the name of Reb Lipman of Radomsk, once came to visit Reb Menachem Mendel of Kotsk, who asked him to repeat some teaching of his famous father-in-law. Reb Lipman obliged, and said: "The tzaddik once pointed out that when Aharon was rebuked, the Torah records in his praise, וַיִּדֹּם אַהֲרֹן — 'And Aharon held his peace' — and this shows what a high spiritual level he had attained. But King David surpassed him and reached a yet higher rung: לְמַעַן יְזַמֶּרְךָ כָבוֹד וְלֹא יִדֹּם — 'In order that my soul may sing praise to You, *and not be silent'* — for even in times of distress he would still sing God's praises."

Reb Menachem Mendel was delighted with this *vort* and thanked his guest warmly for conveying it to him.

◆§ All Ears and Eyes

וַיִּשְׁמַע מֹשֶׁה וַיִּיטַב בְּעֵינָיו
And Moshe heard, and it was good in his eyes (10:20)

Reb Yaakov Yitzchak, the Yid HaKadosh ("the holy Jew") of Pshischah, was a tutor in his younger days in a certain household. After some years the son of his former employer was stricken by some eye ailment, and no doctor was able to help him. When the boy's father heard, therefore, that the former *melamed* had in the meantime acquired a name as a tzaddik, he took his son, who was called Moshe, to visit him.

On their arrival the tzaddik discussed various Torah subjects with the boy, and then said: "Moshe, do you hear?"

"Yes," answered the sightless boy.

שמיני

Said the Yid HaKadosh: "It is written, וַיִּשְׁמַע מֹשֶׁה וַיִּיטַב בְּעֵינָיו — 'And Moshe heard, *and it was good in his eyes.*' "

And the boy immediately regained his vision.

◆§ Of Hosts and Guests

מִמַּעֲלֵי הַגֵּרָה וּמִמַּפְרִסֵי הַפַּרְסָה
Of those that chew the cud, or that divide the hoof (11:4)

Two chassidim whose rebbe had passed away traveled to visit Reb Meir of Premishlan in order to decide whether or not to choose him as rebbe for themselves and for their fellow chassidim. They arrived at Premishlan just in time for candle-lighting, on the eve of a *Shabbos* on which the weekly Portion of *Shemini* was read. They did not even have enough time to order meals for *Shabbos* at a hotel, but went straight to the *beis midrash* of the rebbe. After prayers each of them was invited to the home of one of the local householders. One of the hosts was accustomed to eating very little, so his guest, though ravenously hungry, could hardly bring himself to eat a square meal in his presence. The other host ate, but did not slice the *challah* that was on the table, and since his guest did not take the liberty of slicing it for himself, he too remained hungry. After the meal they both came to the *tish* of the tzaddik at which he presided until after midnight. When it was over, they went to one of the local hotels and asked the proprietor if he had anything for them to eat. He explained that he only had a place for them to sleep, but since they were hungry he would give them some leftovers that required no preparation.

After *Shacharis* prayers in the morning they went home with the same hosts, and exactly the same story repeated itself. In the afternoon they came to the *beis midrash* of the rebbe for *Minchah*, but Reb Meir was not yet there. Assuming that he was doubtless studying Torah in his room, they went to his house, but his *gabbai* told them that he was out in the courtyard. They went out and, sure enough, Reb Meir was there — telling his attendant to feed the geese and chickens. When that was done, he said: "Let us go and *davven* the *Minchah* prayer."

The guests were stupefied: throughout the entire

Shabbos they had not heard a solitary word of Torah from his mouth. To make things worse, they had now seen what kind of spiritual preparations he made for his afternoon prayer. Besides, they were hungry, so they decided not to go to the *Seudah Shlishis* of the rebbe, and to try their luck once again at the homes of their respective hosts. Their hosts were not at home, though: they had gone to the *tish* of the rebbe, so their would-be guests had no option but to go there too.

As soon as they arrived the rebbe said: "Where are the two young men who are seeking a rebbe who is possessed of the holy spirit?"

There was no answer.

Again the rebbe asked: "Where are they? Why are they hiding from me?"

Not a word in reply.

The third time he said: "If they don't come before me at once, they will regret it."

The two guests approached him shamefacedly, and he greeted them and asked: "Where did you eat your *Shabbos* meals?"

When they named their hosts, Reb Meir called them to him and said: "The Torah gives us a mitzvah of hospitality — but one has to know how to conduct oneself when one has guests. When one invites a guest, the host should slice bread generously on the table so that his guest should not be obliged to do so or be too embarrassed to help himself. And even if a host does this, if he himself does not eat, his guest will not feel comfortable eating in his presence. There is a hint of this in today's Portion of the Torah: אֶת הַחֲזִיר כִּי מַפְרִיס פַּרְסָה הוּא — the pig, for he does slice the bread [actually, "divide the hoof," but here punningly mistranslated: פַּרְסָה means "hoof"; פְּרוּסָה means "slice"]; וְהוּא גֵּרָה לֹא יִגָּר — but he does not chew the cud, that is, he himself does not eat; טָמֵא הוּא לָכֶם — he is unclean unto you; אֶת הַגָּמָל כִּי מַעֲלֵה גֵרָה הוּא וּפַרְסָה אֵינֶנּוּ מַפְרִיס טָמֵא הוּא לָכֶם — the camel does chew the cud, but does not 'slice the bread'; he is likewise unclean unto you. Only one that does *both* is a kosher creature!

"And now," added the tzaddik, "these two young men are no doubt very hungry. We should really give them something to eat."

With that, he gave each of them a slice of *challah* with a piece of fish on it.

He went on to deliver a discourse, in the course of which he intimated to the two guests the mystical explanation for his having fed the poultry during the afternoon. None of those present understood his references to the cloven hoof and the chewed cud, nor his abstruse discourse — except for the two hosts and their guests.

And on *Motzaei Shabbos*, when the holy day had drawn to a close, the two visitors to Premishlan recounted the whole story, and concluded: "Here we have found a rebbe on whom rests *ruach hakodesh*, the spirit of God."

◆§ *Sensitivity*

וּבֵין הַחַיָּה הַנֶּאֱכֶלֶת וּבֵין הַחַיָּה אֲשֶׁר לֹא תֵאָכֵל

Between the creature that may be eaten and the creature that may not be eaten (11:47)

Reb Yitzchak Meir of Ger, the author of *Chiddushei HaRim,* was possessed of a remarkable ability to identify whether any item of food that was placed before him was tainted by the merest suspicion of a prohibition, even if strictly speaking it was legally kosher. It once happened that a *she'elah* arose in the kitchen of his household, so the maid duly took along the chicken involved to the local *rav* to have the query clarified, and he ruled that it was kosher. The *rebbitzin,* who knew that her husband was accustomed not to eat of any food over which such a query had arisen, was not at home, and since the maid was new and unaware of this, she saw no reason to report to anyone what had happened. When the *shammes* served the rebbe the cooked chicken, he looked at it and asked to have it removed from the table without so much as tasting it. The *shammes* went to the *rebbitzin* to find out what had happened; then the two of them went to see the maid, who told them of her visit to the local *rav.*

This kind of story repeated itself quite frequently, and the tzaddik once said: "You no doubt think that this is some special prerogative of a rebbe. This is not so, for every Jew who so desires can develop the sensitivity to discern whether his heart allows him to eat a particular dish or not. And this is hinted at in the verse: וּבֵין הַחַיָּה

הַנֶּאֱכֶלֶת – 'between the creature that allows itself to be eaten' (literally, 'that may be eaten'), וּבֵין הַחַיָּה אֲשֶׁר לֹא תֵאָכֵל – 'and the creature that does not allow itself to be eaten' (literally, 'that may not be eaten')."

On another occasion he told his chassidim: "You should realize that this is not a feat that demands any great spiritual achievements. In fact any one of you can easily attain this sensitivity, by following the tried and tested advice which Reb Simchah Bunem of Pshischah taught us: before a person takes any food or drink into his mouth, let him undertake, decisively and wholeheartedly, that if (God forbid) it is forbidden in any way, he would prefer to choke on it rather than swallow it. And then, if need be, they tell him from heaven, in a way that he feels clearly, that he should not swallow a particular mouthful."

◆§ *Secrets from an Unknown Land*

When Reb Meir of Premishlan was a child of about ten, he was taught by a chassid by the name of Reb Dov of Podheits. Every Thursday, which was market day in Podheits, the boy would collect donations and distribute them to the poor in time for them to buy their provisions for *Shabbos*. In the course of his rounds he once came to a butcher by the name of Shimon and asked him for his weekly donation of one *kreutzer* for the poor.

"I'll give you two," said the butcher, "on condition that you tell me whether this ox that I want to buy is going to turn out to be kosher or not."

"Very well," replied the boy. "If you give me half a *fertziger* – that is, ten *kreutzer* – then I'll tell you."

The butcher thought it over for a moment, and gave it to him, whereupon the boy told him: "This ox cannot be eaten; it is *trefah*."

Pointing to another ox, the butcher asked: "And what about this one?"

"If you give me another half-*fertziger*," said the boy, "then I'll tell you."

And when he received the coin, he said: "About this ox there aren't even any queries about possible blemishes in its lungs: it is *glatt* kosher."

The butcher had his doubts as to whether there was any substance to all this, but he paid up his two half-*fertziger* all the same, because the boy was born of holy parents, and he was a likable child — and besides, everyone knew that the alms he collected was for the paupers. And so it was that Shimon bought the second ox, while the first was bought by some other butcher. Sure enough, Shimon's ox was in fact *glatt* kosher, and the other was found after slaughtering to be *trefah*.

The following Thursday, when the boy came to the ox market to collect his donations from the dealers, Shimon the butcher called him aside and said: "Meir'che, I will give you a whole *fertziger* if you tell me whether each one of the oxen up for sale is kosher or not."

"If you give me half a *fertziger* for each ox," said the boy, "I'll tell you."

The butcher paid in full without hesitation, and the boy told him: "This one is kosher, this one is *trefah*" — and so on.

Young Meir was of course delighted with the way things had worked out, for he now had a considerable sum to distribute to the poor without having to lose valuable study time in trudging for hours from one donor to the next.

The butcher, for his part, seeing that the child never missed his target, approached him on the third week with a new proposition: "I would like to make a contract with you, and I will pay you weekly for each ox according to your request — provided that our little transaction remains a secret."

"I am not interested in contracts and secrets," said the boy, "but if you give me half a *fertziger* for each ox, I'll give you the answer."

This went on for a few months, and no one knew of it. Week by week the butcher paid in advance for his information, as a result of which he prospered exceedingly, because he bought nothing but kosher animals, while the other butchers grew poorer. His competitors banded together and brought their bitter complaint to the local *rav*: it was clear that the *shochatim* were receiving bribes from Shimon in exchange for which they pronounced his animals kosher, while in the course of slaughtering they either caused or pronounced *their* animals to be *trefah.*

"But you can see for yourselves in the slaughterhouse," said the *rav,* "that all of Shimon's cattle are in fact *glatt* kosher, without any room for the slightest doubt — and what is to be done if he has such good fortune?"

To this the butchers had no answer. Nevertheless, they started watching Shimon's movements very closely: what could he be doing to ensure that all his animals without exception were in fact kosher? The following Thursday they watched him walking the length of the market place in the company of little Meir, who was pointing at each of the oxen in turn. When Shimon finally left him, they approached the child and said: "Meir'che, pray for us, too, just like you pray for Shimon; or please do for us whatever you do for Shimon."

"I don't do anything," he assured them. "If you give me half a *fertziger* I'll tell you what I tell him."

"Well, what is it that you tell him to do?" they asked. "Tell us, too, and then we'll do whatever he does."

"He asks me which ox is kosher and which is not," said Meir, "and I tell him."

So they gave him a half-*fertziger,* and pointed at an ox that stood near them.

"That one is *trefah,*" said the boy.

When they pointed at another ox, he said: "But you have given me only one half-*fertziger,* and Shimon gives me that much for every single ox."

"So *that's* his secret!" said the butchers to each other. And from that Thursday on, they gave Meir in partnership the amount he stipulated for charity, and walked with him up and down the market place, while he told them which oxen were kosher and which were not.

When word of this reached the boy's *melamed,* Reb Dov, he scolded him and told him that in future he should not tell anyone things revealed to him through *ruach hakodesh.*

Now Reb Dov was a chassid of Meir's father, Reb Aharon Leib of Premishlan, and when he went to visit him he told him the whole story, adding that he had scolded the rebbe's son.

"Well done," said the father. "A boy must learn not to divulge privileged information."

◆§ *The Bear and the Ballroom Dance*

וְדָוִד מְכַרְכֵּר בְּכָל עֹז לִפְנֵי ה׳
And David leaped about before God with all his might (Haftarah)

After the Friday evening prayers of welcome to the Sabbath Queen, Reb Aryeh Leib of Shpola, who is known as the Shpoler Zeide, would often dance in ecstasy, wheeling and turning at a remarkable speed, while his chassidim sang their rhythmic accompaniment.

One *Shabbos* he had as a guest the son of the Maggid of Mezritch, Reb Avraham, who because of his piety was nicknamed "the *Malach*" ("the angel"). Reb Avraham observed every dance-step closely, then approached his host and said: "Sir, you certainly dance well! Until now I did not know how one dances before the Bride, the *Shabbos* Queen — but in every single dance-step tonight I saw a heavenly *yichud*, a sublime feat of divine worship."

"This ability," returned the Shpoler Zeide, "I have by virtue of a blessing I received from the Baal Shem Tov."

Reb Avraham was not satisfied: "But even as far as plain dancing and rhythm are concerned you dance like an expert. Where did you learn this?"

"It was the Prophet Eliyahu who taught me how to dance like this," answered the Shpoler Zeide, "and there is a story behind it all. Listen!

"In the days when I used to wander about in remote regions, it came to my ears that in a certain village a Jew had been arrested by the local squire because he had been unable to pay him what he owed on his lease. The squire, who held the title *graf,* was not a particularly villainous type, but the manager of his estates, who had the last word on everything that went on in the village, was a great anti-Semite, and he incited the *graf* to imprison the Jew who had defaulted. Now in those days each squire ruled his village like an absolute monarch, even sentencing people to death, and in cases like this one they would cast a Jew into a deep dungeon, and once a week lower him his provisions of bread and water. There he would languish until the squire's birthday, when he would make a raucous feast for all his cronies, and when they were tipsy with wine they would drag out the Jew to entertain them. Their tradition was to prepare a bearskin which they would dry on a wooden dummy, until when it was ready it almost looked like a live beast. They would dress the hapless Jew in this bearskin and lead him into the ballroom where the landlords tippled and made merry, and there he was told to dance to whatever tune the musicians played. One of the servants was appointed to lead in the fearsome creature by the kind of iron chain that is used for real bears, and to take charge of him during the dancing. The servant would dance to the music, and the Jew in the bearskin was obliged to keep up to the pace of his dancing partner. But before they started, someone would announce in a loud voice: 'Listen, bear! If you dance nicely before us and keep up with your partner, you will be freed today; if you dance better than he does, you will be allowed to attack him and beat him up, just like a bear attacks a cow; but if you don't dance well, then your partner will lead you off to dance with the dogs!'

"The squires in those days used to keep large numbers of big, ferocious dogs, and when they were thrown a man who had been sentenced to death, they would tear him to pieces.

"After all that time in the dungeon, with his wretched rations of bread and water, the Jew of course could barely walk straight, let alone dance in a bearskin.

"At this point I was given the order by the Prophet Eliyahu to go to that village, where I was to hire myself out as a *melamed* in the household of one of the local Jews, so that I would able to find out all the details of how to go about saving that poor fellow from the teeth of the squire's hounds. For I was to replace him in the bearskin, and dance better than my partner, and eventually attack him and beat him up.

"So I said to Eliyahu: 'But I don't know the first thing about dancing. I don't even know the names of the dances!'

"And he answered: 'I shall teach you how to dance.'

"So it was that every time we met he taught me some other kind of dance, until I became quite an expert. In the meantime, while I worked as a tutor in the village, I investigated all the ins and outs of the garden in which the dungeon was located. I found out, among other things, that it was possible for a man to lower himself down into the dungeon by a rope through an aperture at the top, though it would be very difficult to climb out of there by rope.

"One night before the night of the birthday party, I crept stealthily through a hole under the fence into the garden, and found the dungeon. With the aid of a rope, several staves, an iron peg, and a sledge-hammer that I brought with me, I managed to lower myself down into the pit.

"The poor Jew was of course alarmed. 'Have no fear!' I reassured him. 'I have come to save you.'

"I revived his spirits with a drop of vodka that I had brought, and with words of encouragement: God would surely come to his help. We then exchanged clothes. I put on his moldy and foul-smelling rags, and he dressed in my clothes. Then I told him that when the iron trap-door covering the dungeon would be opened, I would go out instead of him. Only after I was at some distance from the garden was he to climb out; the door would probably be left open, because he was the only prisoner there.

"Around midnight we heard rude laughter resounding over our heads. The iron trap-door creaked open, and a half-drunk voice bellowed out the name of my companion, and ordered him to get out. I clambered out on all fours in order that I should not be recognized, and groaned and tottered as if I was unable to walk. They immediately threw the bearskin over me and tied it firmly around my body, put an iron chain around my neck, and led me along to the tune of their loud guffaws. Before they had opened the door the prisoner had told me that he recognized the laughter up there as belonging to the manager of the squire's estates, the same man who had persuaded his master to imprison him. I asked him to describe his appearance precisely, which he did.

"When they led me into the ballroom, all that merry crew laughed and clapped their hands with glee. I could tell at once by the prisoner's description that the man designated to be my dancing partner was none other than the manager of the squire's estates, who was now looking forward to seeing his project through to the finish by personally throwing his victim to the dogs.

"A voice was now heard, asking all the guests to take their places and to listen to the sentence which was to be read out. A man dressed from head to foot in red, like a hangman, duly stepped forward in front of me and read from a sheet of paper. He announced what was promised me if I equalled my partner or bettered him, and warned me that if I did not perform well enough he would lead me straight out to the kennels, where the dogs would soon teach me how to dance. This was greeted by an outburst of laughter. When it subsided, the signal was given to the musicians to start playing a Cossack dance.

"My partner immediately pranced into action, then they motioned me to join in as his opposite number. Seeing that I was outshining him, the audience laughed and clapped. The band was told to stop playing. I could clearly tell that my partner was terror-stricken: he had never thought such a defeat possible. The master of ceremonies then announced that the band was to play a mazurka, and as it started, my partner took me by the hand. As I twirled my way through the steps of the dance, I sensed that my drunken partner was about to fall — which he did. I at once jumped upon him, and gave him a choking bearhug and a sound beating. There was an immediate uproar from all sides. Some of the guests egged me on, for I was doing what the rules of the game entitled me to do, but two squires ran up and begged that I spare the man's life. Since I was now free, I had better go home and gladden the hearts of my wife and family. I took their advice, and released my hold. They hurried to do whatever they could for the estate manager who lay in a faint on the floor; and I, bearskin and all, ran as fast as I could to the house of the prisoner. There, as you may well imagine, I found a household bursting with joy."

Having come to the end of his story, the Shpoler Zeide turned to his guest and said: "Well, Reb Avraham, do you understand now how it is that I can dance so well?"

"After such a story," replied the *Malach*, "it is clear that your dances are loftier than my prayers."

◆§ An Opportunity for Joy

וְשִׂחַקְתִּי לִפְנֵי ה׳ וּנְקַלֹּתִי עוֹד מִזֹּאת
I will play before God, and be even less esteemed than this (Haftarah)

Looking through the window, Reb Zusya of Hanipoli once saw a wedding procession passing his house. He went straight out, and danced in the street before the bride and groom with the greatest of joy. When he came in again, his family remarked that it was neither seemly nor dignified for him to dance out there in the street for some wedding or other.

"Let me tell you a story," said Reb Zusya. "In my youth I was a pupil of Reb Yechiel Michel, the Maggid of Zlotchov, and it once happened that he scolded me severely. He later came around to clear up any hard feelings, and said: 'Reb Zusya, forgive me for my harsh words.'

" 'Rebbe,' I answered, 'I forgive you.'

"Before I went to sleep he came again, and said: 'Reb Zusya, forgive me!'

"I reassured him again: 'Rebbe, I forgive you.'

"And when I lay down to sleep, but was still awake, my rebbe's father, Reb Yitzchak of Drohovitch, appeared to me from the World Above, and said: 'One only son I left after me in the World Below, one precious son — and do you want to destroy him because he insulted you?'

" 'Rebbe!' I protested. 'But I have already forgiven him with all my heart and soul! What else should I do?'

" 'This is not yet a perfect forgiveness,' he said. 'If you come along with me, I will show you how to forgive.'

"I got out of bed and followed him, until we came to the local *mikveh*. There he told me to immerse myself in it three times, and to say each time that I forgave his son. Coming out of the *mikveh*, I saw that Reb Yitzchak's face radiated a light so bright that I could not look at him. When I asked him what it came from, he said that all his life he had been careful to observe the three things to which the Talmudic sage Rabbi Nechunyah ben HaKanah attributed his longevity: 'I never gained honor at the expense of the degradation of my fellow; I never went to sleep without forgiving everyone for the day's vexations; and I have been generous with my money.'

 Reb Yitzchak added that what he had attained through these three things could also be achieved through joy.

"Therefore," concluded Reb Zusya, "when I saw the wedding procession passing by our house, I hurried out in order to participate in the joy of a mitzvah."

◆§ *Verses and Curses*

In 1777 a large group of chassidim settled in *Eretz Yisrael*, and Reb Shneur Zalman of Liadi established the Rabbi Meir Baal HaNess Fund for their support. One of his chassidim, Reb Yitzchak Aizik of Homil, thereupon began to hire himself out as a jester at weddings, where he would entertain the guests, according to the old custom, by improvising jocular verses. All the earnings he would give to the Fund.

It so happened that there was once a wedding involving a well-known chassidic family from Homil, and a respected family from Slutsk, which was an uncompromising center of hard-boiled *misnagdim*. The *mechutan* from Slutsk watched Reb Yitzchak Aizik versifying happily away, and commented: "Woe is to accursed Belorussia! Where *we* come from, a wedding like this is an occasion for scholars to vie with each other in the complexity of their learned discourses; here, people fill their heads with doggerel ... "

His chassidic counterpart from Homil sought to correct him. "*Mechutan*," he said, "would you perhaps like to discuss Torah scholarship with this jester of ours?"

The *misnaged* did so, and was stupefied to discover that the jester — better remembered as the author of *Chanah Ariel* — was in fact a scholar of repute. He turned to his chassidic *mechutan*, and exclaimed: "Villains, *that's* what you are! Here you have such a sage in your midst, and you allow him to earn his living as a jester!"

And he was appeased only when he was told that this was not the jester's occupation: he was simply doing a good deed to benefit charity.

סדר תזריע
Sidra Tazria

⁂ A Hidden Tzaddik

וּבַיּוֹם הַשְּׁמִינִי יִמּוֹל
And on the eighth day shall he be circumcised (12:3)

When the Baal Shem Tov was a young man, soon after his marriage, and his saintliness was still known to no man, he used to eke out a meager livelihood by the toil of his hands. With his horse and cart he would bring loads of mortar and sand which would be sold in town. His pious wife, having been brought up in a wealthy household, was unused to the rigors of harsh labor; nevertheless, feeling sorry for her husband, she too went out with him with a spade and helped him load his cart. Sometimes they traveled from town to town for weeks on end, but no one took much notice of them, taking them for just another couple of itinerant beggars.

In time the Baal Shem Tov's horse grew so weak that it was unable to draw a load. The tzaddik was distressed: he could not afford a new horse, yet without one he had no way of earning his daily bread. He mentioned his plight to some other poor folk whom he met on the road. They advised him to set out for a certain village near Uman, to the home of a Jewish landowner called Reb Baruch who was known for his hospitality. Whenever a pauper drove his wagon into his estate in order to buy bones or rags or whatever, Reb Baruch always offered to exchange his guest's old hack for one of his spare horses that was no longer capable of drawing a plow, but could still be useful for lighter work. And so it was that the Baal Shem Tov and his wife undertook the long and arduous journey to that village.

Reb Baruch had fled to Russia from the pogroms in his native Bohemia. He was certainly no Torah scholar: just an ordinary householder, but he was upright and God-fearing, as was his wife Rachel. Of all their many charitable and neighborly acts, they exerted themselves in particular for the mitzvah of hospitality. For this purpose they set aside a separate house which was made up of many small rooms, each furnished with two beds and a table. Here any needy wayfarer was welcome to stay for a week. He was given two meals daily, and on *Shabbos* joined all the other paupers at Reb Baruch's table. When a poor man came together with his wife and children, the couple was assigned a separate room; if a man and a woman came without children Reb Baruch would not give them a room together, for fear that they were not man and wife. And before any of their penniless guests left, their hosts gave them gifts of money — Reb Baruch to the men, Rachel to the women.

It was in this house that the Baal Shem Tov and his wife rested when they finally arrived at their destination. After they had been offered a meal the Baal Shem Tov told his host about his horse, and Reb Baruch immediately instructed his servants to replace it. The gift was of course much appreciated, but since the tzaddik and his wife were exhausted after their journey, most of which they had been obliged to make on foot, they stayed to rest for a few days until after *Shabbos*. Reb Baruch nevertheless did not give his guests a joint room, and explained that this was a principle of his, unless he knew for sure that his guests were a married couple. The Baal Shem Tov was pleased with his answer. And throughout the entire *Shabbos* there was nothing about his conduct that could suggest that here was a man who was somewhat different from the general run of paupers.

On *Motzaei Shabbos*, after the holy day had come to a close and Reb Baruch was preparing to retire for the night, he was surprised to see a bright light shining through his window. He got up to see where it came from, and observed that its source was one of the rooms occupied by the paupers. Bestirred by wonderment and the fear of fire, he dressed in haste and went out to investigate. He tiptoed stealthily to the door of the room, peeked through the keyhole, and saw the new arrival sitting on the floor, and reciting in holy dread the midnight lament on the Destruction of the Temple and the exile of the Divine Presence — *Tikkun Chatzos*. He strained and heard the piteous words: "Why do You forget us for all eternity, and forsake us for so long?" The arms of the supplicant were stretched out toward heaven, his countenance was radiant, and tears were in his eyes. Nor was he alone, for by his side there stood a white-garbed figure, tall and gaunt, a long beard flowing from his luminous countenance. Terror struck at the heart of the man at the keyhole; he tottered, and collapsed on the floor in a faint.

Hearing the thud at his door, the Baal Shem Tov quickly rose to open it, and saw his host prostrate before him. He massaged him until he came to, then brought him into his little room to rest. Realizing by now that his guest was no ordinary man, Reb Baruch fell at his feet, and with tears in his eyes begged forgiveness for not having given him one of the rooms for married couples. The Baal Shem Tov raised him up to his feet, and solemnly adjured him never to breathe a word of what he had seen, all the days of his life. He then blessed him that he should be granted a son who would grow up to be a tzaddik, and added that his wife should take care to nurse this child herself, instead of hiring a wetnurse, as she had done for each of her infant daughters in turn. Reb Baruch listened to the blessing and responded fervently: "Amen! May this be His will!"

Ever so humbly, he then added: "Pardon me, Sir, for my daring, but I have one question. Who was that aged one, robed in white?"

"Since it was granted you to see him," said the Baal Shem Tov, "I shall reveal this secret to you. This was the soul of the saintly Maharal, Rabbi Yehudah Leib ben Bezalel of Prague, from whom you are descended. The time has come for his soul to live another life in This World, in order to set it right by accomplishing awesome *tikkunim,* and it is your privilege to have this lofty soul find its new abode in the body of the son whom you will beget. To this infant you are therefore to give the name 'Leib'. I am certain that I will see him, and I will then bless him."

Reb Baruch wept for joy, for he had never had a son.

"My saintly master," he said. "I beg you not to be angry with me, but I have one more question. I would dearly love to know your name and where you hail from, and I ask you earnestly to allow me throughout my life to provide for all your needs, so that you will no longer know the pain of privation."

"Pray do not ask me these questions," responded the Baal Shem Tov, "for the time for me to be known in the world has not yet come. Your son likewise will not be known early in life. He will first live a life of poverty and want, and his righteousness will later shine forth like the radiance of the sun. Further than this ask me no questions and reveal to no man what you have seen and spoken of with me. Show me no special honor in anyone else's presence, but treat me exactly as you do all the other poor folk. And tomorrow I will be on my way."

Reb Baruch took his leave and went home, and the next day the Baal Shem Tov drove off in his wagon which was now harnessed to the new horse that he had been given. Not a soul knew a word of what had transpired that night, but Reb Baruch recorded every detail of it in his diary.

In due course the blessing of the tzaddik was fulfilled: Reb Baruch's wife gave birth to their first son, and their joy was boundless. The father sent word to all the neighboring townships inviting all their poor to attend the circumcision, and because, as the Talmud says, "Your friend too has a friend," the message spread in no time, and throngs of eager paupers converged on his village, often accompanied by their wives and little ones. Nor were any disappointed, for each needy visitor was provided with a warm bed and ample meals.

The great day arrived, and the faces of hundreds of friends were beaming with joy — all faces, in fact, except for the face of Reb Baruch himself, which divulged a hint of anxiety. He walked back and forth among the crowds of poor people, earnestly looking for that hidden tzaddik whose blessing was the fount of everyone's joy that day. And there he was indeed, with his staff and knapsack, in the thick of that same crowd. Reb Baruch ran to greet him, but did not manage to give expression to his joy before the Baal Shem Tov motioned him to remain silent, adding: "Please take care not to speak to me, nor to honor me in any way. Simply treat me like all the other poor people here."

The circumcision was carried out after morning prayers, and the infant was named Aryeh Leib. According to the custom then current, the *kvater*, followed by the father, carried the baby past the standing guests, each of whom would lay his hand on the infant's head and bless him and his father. Reb Baruch made sure that the godfather carried the baby all the way through the crowds of poor folk, too, because he was eager to have the baby receive their blessings — in particular, the blessings of one unknown stranger who stood obscurely in their midst ... Slowly, silently, they neared his presence. The Baal Shem Tov placed his two hands on the baby's head, and said in a loud and happy voice: "Look, I'm only an ignoramus, and don't know how to give blessings in the Holy Tongue. But I do remember what my father taught me about the verse in the *Chumash:* וְאַבְרָהָם זָקֵן — 'And Avraham was old.' He said that the Hebrew word אָב *(av),* which is the beginning of the name Avraham, means 'father,' and the second word — זָקֵן — means *'zeide'* (Yiddish for 'grandfather'). That is to say, the Patriarch Avraham became the grandfather of us all. And now I would like to give this baby my blessing that he grow up to be a grandfather for all Israel, just as Avraham Avinu was."

Many were amused by this commentary and blessing, and the child was called thereafter Zeide — first jokingly, then affectionately. "How's your Zeide?" people would ask his parents, and they themselves would call him "our little Zeidele."

Indeed, this nickname stayed with him throughout his entire life. Reb Aryeh Leib became known as a tzaddik who helped his brothers through acts of kindness in This World and through intercession in the World Above. But he was loved in his time, and is remembered to this day, as the Shpoler Zeide — may his memory be a blessing!

◆§ *No Questions Asked*

At the festive meal following a circumcision, Reb Yitzchak Meir of Ger once asked a certain chassid to tell a story he knew concerning Reb Levi Yitzchak of Berditchev.

"One of the disciples of Reb Levi Yitzchak," began

the chassid, "was a dealer in oxen. It so happened that the price once dropped at a time when he had many head of cattle to sell, so, anticipating heavy losses, he traveled to Berditchev to ask Reb Levi Yitzchak for advice and a blessing.

" 'Is there one particular mitzvah that you especially engage in from time to time?' asked the rebbe.

" 'Yes,' answered the dealer, 'I am a *mohel.*'

" 'And what do you do,' resumed the rebbe, 'if (God forbid) the bleeding does not stop after you have circumcised an infant?'

"The *mohel* duly enumerated the various kinds of medication he used.

" 'I will give you a certain herb,' said the tzaddik. 'If (God forbid) you should again be confronted by such a situation, then apply this herb to the source of the bleeding and, with the Almighty's help, it will heal at once.'

" 'And what shall I do about the cattle business?' asked the merchant.

" 'But I've already told you,' answered the tzaddik, 'that whenever a newly circumcised child bleeds profusely you should apply this herb, and with God's help the incision will heal immediately.'

"The merchant took his leave and traveled home."

At this point in the chassid's story Reb Yitzchak Meir stopped him for a moment, and said: "From this it is clear that this merchant was a chassid, for he did not persist with his query about the oxen, believing instead that his rebbe's words no doubt included an answer to the question that had brought him there, even though he did not understand how this could be the case."

The chassid continued with his story. "Now on his way home this dealer stopped at an inn, and found out incidentally that the innkeeper's infant son was not circumcised. He therefore approached him and asked: 'Why have you not yet had your son circumcised?'

"The father answered that two earlier sons of his had died as a result of their circumcision (Heaven forfend!), because the bleeding could not be stopped. Recalling the words of the tzaddik of Berditchev, the merchant asked his host: 'What would you give if a solution were to be found to this problem?'

" 'If it were possible to circumcise my son without danger,' he answered, 'I would be prepared to pay four hundred silver rubles.'

" 'I will circumcise him on my responsibility,' said the merchant, 'and will deposit with you four hundred silver rubles of my own, to be forfeited in case (God forbid) of misfortune.'

"The innkeeper agreed, provided the *mohel* remained on the premises for four weeks, until the child was sure to be out of danger. The circumcision in fact caused the infant to bleed heavily, but the *mohel* applied the herb which he had been given, and the bleeding stopped immediately. After some days news reached the village that the price of oxen had risen, and the *mohel* wanted to hurry home to sell his livestock, but his host held him to his promise to stay in the village for four weeks. Several days later he heard that the price was soaring even higher, but the innkeeper ignored his pleas. Only after the full four weeks had reluctantly moved on did he allow the merchant to get back to his business, not forgetting to pay him first his fee of four hundred silver rubles and to return him his deposit of another four hundred. Arriving home, the merchant sold his oxen for a price that exceeded his wildest hopes and made a handsome profit.

"It was now time to visit his rebbe. He rode off to Berditchev, and said to Reb Levi Yitzchak: 'Rebbe, the fee of four hundred rubles belongs to you without a question, and a certain proportion of the profit I made on the sale of my livestock rightly belongs to you likewise.' "

Reb Yitzchak Meir of Ger turned to the storyteller: "Why tell that part too?"

◈ *Who Wants to be Cured?*

נֶגַע צָרַעַת כִּי תִהְיֶה בְּאָדָם וְהוּבָא אֶל הַכֹּהֵן
If the plague of tzaraas is in a man, he shall be brought to the kohen (13:9)

Reb Asher of Stolin disapproved of those chassidim who, when visiting their rebbe, would give prominence to their more commendable traits, and conceal their less attractive side.

"When I used to visit my rebbe," he recalled (that is, Reb Shlomo of Karlin, and he kissed his own fingers at the mention of the cherished name), "I would hide whatever good there was in me — for did the rebbe have God's task of handing out reward and punishment? — and would show him the evil that was in me. For what the Torah commands a man to show the kohen is the symptoms of the *plague* within him ..."

סדר מצורע

Sidra Metzora

◌§ Speaking Up

וּבָא...וְהִגִּיד לַכֹּהֵן...: כְּנֶגַע נִרְאָה לִי בַּבָּיִת

And he shall come...and tell the kohen...: Something like a plague seems to be in the house (14:35)

With three daughters to marry off, and not one wretched kopek in the cottage with which to begin to put together dowries and weddings, the wife of Reb Mordechai of Pintchov nagged him incessantly to describe their woeful situation to his rebbe, the Chozeh of Lublin. Time after time he would travel to Lublin, but never once did he mention his troubles to the rebbe, because on arriving there he would forget them completely. Being a practical woman his wife decided to say nothing more, but to make the journey there by a separate wagon immediately after he had left home. When Reb Mordechai arrived at Lublin, he was confronted by the fact of his wife's presence. There was no way out — and he told the rebbe what the state of affairs was at home.

"Why did you never mention this until now?" asked the Chozeh.

"Rebbe," answered the chassid, "I assumed that my situation would be known to you through *ruach hakodesh,* through the holy spirit that rests upon you."

"Not so," answered the rebbe. "In the case of plagues of the soul the Torah says: 'A man in the skin of whose flesh there shall be ... a plague of *tzaraas* shall be brought to Aharon the *kohen* ... and the *kohen* shall see the plague.' That is to say: As soon as the ailing man is brought before him, the *kohen* will discern the malady himself, without being told. In the case of plagues that affect houses, however, the Torah teaches us otherwise: 'And he who owns the house shall come and tell the *kohen*, saying: Something like a plague seems to be in the house.' From this we see that with plagues affecting houses — the needs of a household — one is obliged to come to the *kohen* and speak up and *tell* him of them ..."

סדר אחרי
Sidra Acharei

◆§ *In Good Company*

הַשֹּׁכֵן אִתָּם בְּתוֹךְ טֻמְאֹתָם
That dwells with them in the midst of their impurity (16:16)

Two lodging places were prepared in a certain city for the forthcoming visit of Reb Avraham Yehoshua Heschel of Apta, who is known as the Ohev Yisrael ("the lover of his fellow Jew"). On arrival he was to choose between them. The two hosts were both wealthy, their kitchens were both impeccably kosher, and their houses were both spacious enough to accommodate the prominent guest comfortably. The reputation of one of them, however, was marred by whispers about certain indiscretions of his, and he, acknowledging the truth to himself, was of a humble spirit and a complaisant temperament. The other host was not only far removed from sin, but was one of those who are known in Yiddish as *"a sheiner Yid"* (a fine, dignified Jew) — and he was not a little proud of the fact. The Ohev Yisrael chose to stay in the home of the former.

When his closest chassidim asked him later to explain his choice, the tzaddik answered: "It is perhaps true that the other host is free from sin. But if he is conceited — why, we learn in the Talmud, regarding the arrogant man, that the Almighty says: אֵין אֲנִי וְהוּא יְכוֹלִים לָגוּר בָּעוֹלָם — 'He and I cannot dwell together in the world.' And if the Almighty, as it were, cannot find any room in such a house, then surely I cannot. But this fellow, even though he has certain transgressions on his account, is not arrogant, and about such folk we read in the Torah, in connection with the Sanctuary: הַשֹּׁכֵן אִתָּם בְּתוֹךְ

 טֻמְאֹתָם — 'that dwells with them in the midst of their impurity.' And seeing that the Divine Presence, as it were, was able to find a lodging place in the home of such a man, I moved in too."

◆§ *Unwarranted Pride*

In the course of a stroll with his son in the Zaksi Gardens in Warsaw, Reb Yechezkel of Kozmir once asked him whether he felt anything special. Surprised that the answer was negative, the father said: "Whoever wants to feel the taste of sanctity has better prospects here than elsewhere, for in a place of impurity, holiness finds no nook in which to rest; and since in truth 'The whole world is full of His glory,' and it must find a place *somewhere*, anyone who wants to cleave to the sanctity of the Divine Presence can do so most readily in this very place. Here, let me tell you a story.

"In the days before Reb Simchah Bunem of Pshischah became known as a tzaddik, whenever he came back from seeing to his affairs in Danzig, he would spend the first *Shabbos* with the Chozeh, Reb Yaakov Yitzchak of Lublin. On one occasion he arrived at Lublin, but the rebbe did not give him the usual greeting of *Shalom*. Taking this for an oversight, he returned to see him some hours later, but again the same thing happened. There must be something in it. So he scrutinized in retrospect every detail of his conduct in Danzig, but could recall nothing in which he could be found wanting. If anything, he noted with satisfaction that this visit was definitely of the kind that he liked to nickname 'a good Danzig', for he had brought many of the assimilated German Jews there back to the path of the Torah.

"After Reb Simchah Bunem had puzzled over his cool reception for some time, a familiar teaching of the Talmud came to mind. The Sages of the Talmud, as you know, advise a person beset by tribulations of unexplained source to scrutinize his actions. They then go on to say: פִּשְׁפֵּשׁ וְלֹא מָצָא, יִתְלֶה בְּבִטּוּל תּוֹרָה — 'If he sought and did not find, then let him ascribe his woes to the sin of losing time from Torah study.' Taking this advice to heart, Reb Simchah Bunem recalled that in the course of his travels he had in fact lost time from Torah study. This he now decided to set right. Opening his Talmud, he sat down and studied earnestly all that day and all that night. At this point, a novel light on that familiar Talmudic teaching dawned on him. He turned the words over in his mind once more: פִּשְׁפֵּשׁ וְלֹא מָצָא, יִתְלֶה בְּבִטּוּל תּוֹרָה. Perhaps what the Sages really meant by their advice was that if a person examined his past and failed to find any blemish in himself, he should *ascribe this failure* to his inadequate study of the Torah. For surely, if a man immersed himself in this as he should, he could not overlook his faults. And what of himself? ... Now that he had once again steeped his mind in the Torah, Reb Simchah Bunem became aware of his sin: he must have been a little *too* pleased with what he had accomplished in the course of his 'good Danzig.' It was time to repent.

"And when in due course he went to see the Chozeh once again, the rebbe greeted him warmly, and said: 'Danzig, as you know, is an impure place. There the Divine Presence is in exile, and clings to any man who desires to cleave to it. If, while you were there, the Divine Presence rested upon you, this was no great feat accomplished by your efforts. You see, there was no justification for your pride.'"

סדר קדושים
Sidra Kedoshim

◆§ *Chassidic Logic*

לֹא תָלִין פְּעֻלַּת שָׂכִיר
You shall not withhold the laborer's wages overnight (19:13)

Penniless as always, patient as always, Reb Zusya of Hanipoli knew no rest — and now his wife was nagging him for a new dress. In the end he had no option but to somehow put together the money needed; he bought the material, and handed it to his wife to give to the tailor. Now, surely, he would enjoy some peace and quiet. But when Friday came, he saw clouds gathering over the features of his *rebbitzin*.

"What is troubling you?" he asked. "After all, you now have a new dress, thank God, haven't you?"

The *rebbitzin* told him that when the tailor had brought her the finished garment, he had let out a deep sigh. When she asked him what lay behind it, he had told her that when the young man who was to marry his daughter had seen him sewing a dress he had assumed that it was for his bride; when he had discovered that it was not, he was so angry that the poor tailor was sorely distressed.

"So," concluded the *rebbitzin*, "I immediately took the dress and gave it to the tailor as a gift for the bride, poor thing."

"But did you pay him for his work?" asked Reb Zusya.

"No," answered his wife, "but I gave the whole dress as a gift!"

"How on earth could you ever consider cheating the man of his wages?" protested Reb Zusya. "The whole week long this pauper has been working for you, and for you alone, not for his daughter. He has been waiting anxiously, eagerly, to finish this job, so that he will be able to receive his payment and buy bread for his little ones. What is the poor man going to do now? Is it *his* fault that you decided to give the dress to his daughter?"

And the *rebbitzin* set out at once, borrowed a little money, and paid the tailor his wages.

⊲§ *Where There Is Smoke*

לא תֵלֵךְ רָכִיל
You shall not go about talebearing (19:16)

The chassidim of Reb Baruch of Mezhibuzh were ill at ease: their rebbe was marrying off one of his daughters to the son of a man whose name was often whispered by the local gossipmongers. Since none of them would dare proffer advice to the rebbe, they decided to ask his jester, Herschele Ostropolier, to drop him the hint jokingly. Being a resourceful young man, Herschele contrived to refer to the tzaddik and to his apparently mismatched counterpart by borrowing two nicknames from the prayer book: וְהוּא רַחוּם ("And He is compassionate") and עַל חֵטְא ("For the transgression"), respectively. Walking straight into the rebbe's study, he quipped: "They say that וְהוּא רַחוּם has just made a match with עַל חֵטְא ... "

In response to this jest, Reb Baruch called for his chassidim and asked them what they had heard about his *mechutan*, whereupon they repeated the not very moral episode that was being passed around behind his back in Zhitomir.

"And would one of you happen to know what comment Reb Ze'ev of Zhitomir made on this story at the time?" asked Reb Baruch.

At this point one of them indeed recalled seeing Reb Ze'ev standing at his window when this story reached his ears, and he had said: "If this is a lie, he will make a match with the family of the greatest man in this generation."

These words brought reassurance to the chassidim of Reb Baruch, and whatever doubts they may have harbored about their rebbe's judgment were dispelled.

◆§ *How To Stand Corrected*

הוֹכֵחַ תּוֹכִיחַ אֶת עֲמִיתֶךָ
You shall surely rebuke your neighbor (19:17)

Reb Hillel Lichtenstein of Kolomya used to travel about among the Jewish towns and villages, rebuking his listeners, and exhorting them to live their lives piously. Arriving at Zanz one day, he was greeted warmly by Reb Chaim of Zanz, who exchanged Torah thoughts and chassidic insights with his honored guest, and then turned to him with the following remark: "You seem, sir, to be rebuking the whole world. Why don't you rebuke me, too?"

"Quite so," answered Reb Hillel. "The fact is that I am surprised that in this house I do not see the area of a cubit square which is left unpainted in many Jewish houses, in commemoration of the Destruction of the Temple."

His request granted, Reb Chaim asked for a ladder, climbed up, marked off the requisite area on the wall opposite the entrance, as the law requires, and with a knife peeled off all the paint from that square. When that was done, he thanked Reb Hillel for being so candid.

◆§ *Take It from a Friend*

As he walked up and down the *beis midrash* of Reb Yehudah Aryeh Leib of Ger, all that could be heard from his mouth was an uncomplimentary barrage of rebukes, all of which were addressed at no less a personage than — himself, Reb Pinchas Eliyahu of Piltz. Words like these one would hardly hurl at the most unworthy individual, and when they were heard by the speaker's uncle, Reb Avraham of Parisov, he approached him and said: "Young man, if you don't mind, please don't say such harsh things about our Reb Pintchi, for round these parts we consider him to be a man of some stature. In particular, I would advise you to watch out for the wrath of our younger chassidim, because if they get to hear you saying unpleasant things about our Reb Pintchi, they'll want to break your bones ... Besides, if *I* were to say this kind of thing about you, you would no doubt be angry with me, so who gives *you* the right to talk this way about yourself?"

"True enough," said Reb Pintchi. "If anyone else were to say these things about me, I would probably regard him as an enemy. But when *I* talk about myself this way — why, I'm my own friend."

◆§ *Forgive and Beget*

וְלֹא תִשָּׂא עָלָיו חֵטְא
Nor cause sin to come upon him (19:17)

Bustling throngs of chassidim were crowded just outside the door of the study of Reb Yitzchak Meir of Ger, and it was the task of Reb Bunem the *shammes* to try to keep order. There was one individual there who impatiently refused to take notice of him. He tried to force his way in ahead of his turn, and when he was refused admission, he slapped the *shammes* across the cheek. Those around him were shocked by his shameful conduct, and the poor *shammes* went straight in and put his complaint before the rebbe: "If I serve you so faithfully, why do I deserve this?"

But he did not give the rebbe the name of the man who had struck him.

The chassidim continued to take their turns at their

private interviews with the rebbe, and when this individual entered for his *yechidus* the tzaddik sensed at once who it was who stood before him. Instead of listening to him, the rebbe addressed him sharply: "Why did you do it?"

The man shed bitter tears, not only because he regretted his action, but also because, being childless, he had come to ask for a blessing, and now, instead of awakening the rebbe's compassion, he had aroused his ire. And the tzaddik was adamant: he would hear no word from him until he had made amends with the injured party and been granted forgiveness.

Off he went to speak to the *shammes*, and when they then entered the rebbe's study together, the *shammes* said: "Rebbe, I am willing to forgive this man, but only on one condition."

"And what is that?" asked the tzaddik.

"My condition, rebbe, is that you give this man your blessing that he be blessed from Above with children."

The rebbe was agreeable, and in due course his blessing was fulfilled.

◆§ *Mine and Thine*

וְאָהַבְתָּ לְרֵעֲךָ כָּמוֹךָ
Love your neighbor as yourself (19:18)

"How can you claim that I am a tzaddik," Reb David of Lelov used to say to his chassidim, "when I know that I still love my children and grandchildren more than I love my other fellow Jews?"

It once happened that his son fell seriously ill. Anxious for his welfare, all the townsfolk assembled in the local synagogue to pray for his recovery, visited his bedside frequently, and spared no exertion in securing the services of the most expert physicians and apothecaries. When in due course he recovered, they of course expected to see their rebbe rejoicing — instead of which they found him weeping bitterly.

Reb David sensed their amazement, and said: "When my son fell ill, everyone was concerned, and prayed, and did whatever could be done until he was well. And if any other person is sick, no one makes such a stir about it, and people do not pay nearly that much attention to him. Now isn't that something to weep over?"

◆§ *As Yourself*

It once entered the head of one of the chassidim of Reb Menachem Mendel of Kotsk to hide behind his rebbe's door in order to hear how he read through the weekly Portion of the Torah when alone. It was the *Shabbos* on which the *Sidra Kedoshim* was to be read — the passage which includes the words וְאָהַבְתָּ לְרֵעֲךָ כָּמוֹךָ: "Love your neighbor as yourself." As he listened, the rebbe came to this phrase, which he read as follows: וְאָהַבְתָּ לְרֵעֲךָ־הָא? כָּמוֹךָ?! ("Love your neighbor — how? *As yourself?!"*). And after a few moments the rebbe repeated the conclusion of the phrase, not as a startled question, but as a placid statement: כָּמוֹךָ ("as yourself").

This query and its response threw the chassid into a turmoil. He hastened to consult Reb Hirsch of Tomashov, an elder chassid who was close to the rebbe, and he explained the incident as follows: "The rebbe asked himself, 'How can the Torah command a man to love his neighbor *as himself?* Why, is a person allowed to love *himself?'* Surely you know that Kotsk teaches that self-love brings on dishonesty, and deception, and intellectual sloth, and so on and on. Then he answered his own question: 'As yourself. Just as you are obliged to hold yourself in unqualified disfavor, so are you obliged to love others with unqualified love.' "

◆§ *Loving the Unlovable*

Before he left This World, Reb Shlomo of Karlin told his disciples that after his passing they should visit Reb Mordechai of Neshchiz and accept him as their rebbe. Reb Uri ("the Saraph") of Strelisk arrived soon after in Karlin, and learning there of the passing of the tzaddik, asked his colleagues what instructions he had left. He then set out by foot on the long trek to Neshchiz.

Of all the many guests who were standing about in the rebbe's antechamber there, waiting to receive his blessing, the individual who caught Reb Uri's eye was a certain prosperous merchant who had come to consult the rebbe on some forthcoming transaction and to request his blessing for its success. Reb Mordechai soon came out, and greeted this individual warmly — as was his wont with all comers, for in this direction his divine service was in fact outstanding. But Reb Uri, as he looked upon the face of this merchant, could tell that only recently he had sinned, seriously, vulgarly. He was incensed: why should the tzaddik of Neshchiz extend such a cordial welcome to such a creature?

Quick to read his thoughts, Reb Mordechai walked over to Reb Uri: "Please leave this place right away. What do you want here in my room?"

Weary, distressed and disappointed, Reb Uri found his way to the local *beis midrash.* But no sooner had Reb Mordechai concluded his conversation with the merchant than he went out to seek his visitor from Strelisk, found him, and said: "What you knew, brother, I also knew — but do you know why your rebbe of Karlin sent you here? In order to learn that the man in whom the love of a fellow Jew is not so entrenched in his heart that he is unable to love and embrace even a grievous sinner — such a man has not accomplished even half of his divinely appointed lifelong task. For if you bring such a sinner close to your heart, then without a doubt he will return to God with all his heart, and, being a *baal teshuvah,* a sincere penitent, he will rank higher than a perfect tzaddik — that is, unless you know him to be one who transgressed wilfully."

Reb Uri stood silent: he had found a rebbe from whom he would have much to learn in the years to come.

◆§ *Where It Really Hurts*

> *Love your neighbor as yourself:* Let your love and solicitude for your brother be like your love and compassion for yourself *(Maimonides, Sefer HaMitzvos).*

The doctors had decided that there was no other way to treat the painful sore on the back of Reb Mordechai Dov of Hornisteipl than to cauterize it — and the tzaddik gave his consent. In keeping with the medical techniques of those days they heated three metal rods, and prepared to apply them. On the rare occasions when the patient did not react to the first, they would apply a hotter one, and if he appeared not to feel even this, they had a yet hotter one in readiness.

Having accustomed himself to accepting all suffering in silence, the tzaddik gave no indication of what he was going through, so the doctor proceeded to apply the second instrument. Again the same, and the doctor went on to the third. Even now the tzaddik accepted his agony with uncomplaining love. Stupefied, the doctor exclaimed: "I don't know whether this is an angel or a demon!"

Reb Mordechai Dov hardly understood Russian, and asked a bystander: "What did the doctor say?"

When he was told, he answered: "Please tell him that if a fellow Jew comes along and presents me with a *kvitl* on which his woes are recorded, and asks me to pray on his behalf, and I see that I won't be able to bring him help, — it hurts much more, and then too I have to keep silent ..."

◆§ *Someone Else's Child*

While Sarah, the daughter of Reb Menachem Mendel of Vizhnitz, was newly married, and still living with her young husband at the home of his father, Reb Yehoshua of Belz, she fell seriously ill. One day, when for the first time her father received neither letter nor telegram informing him of her condition, he was exceedingly distressed. His son, Reb Baruch, reassured him that there was no cause to fear the worst: there was no doubt simply a postal delay. Sure enough, a telegram arrived that very afternoon from Belz, informing them that Sarah had recovered.

Seeing his father's joyful spirits returning, Reb Baruch asked: "How is it, father, that a man of your stature should allow his spiritual equilibrium to be jarred simply because he has not had news of his daughter for a few hours? What, then, is to be expected of humbler folk?"

"My son," answered Reb Menachem Mendel, "one by one, without great difficulty, I have managed to elevate and sanctify all the traits and attributes of my nature. The one task which I found harder than all the rest was to bring myself to fulfill the commandment to love my neighbor *as myself,* literally. And there came a time when it seemed to me that I had in fact reached the level at which I did not distinguish between that which affected me personally and that which affected any other Jew in the world. This morning, however, when the usual mailtime passed without news, I was alarmed — and realized at once that I had in fact not reached that level. For how many notes and letters reach me daily, hourly, bearing news of all the maladies and misfortunes that burden the People of God! But does my heart quite bleed for them as it did for my own daughter? My failure to fulfill the mitzvah in its entirety was twice as hard to bear as my daughter's illness, and that explains why I was so downcast."

◆§ *The Food was Heavenly*

לֹא תֹאכְלוּ עַל הַדָּם
You shall not eat anything with the blood (19:26)

You shall not eat anything with the blood (הַדָּם also implies *lifeblood):* You shall not eat before you pray for your lives *(Talmud, Tractate Berachos).*

Bereft of his rebbe, an elderly chassid was unable to decide whom to accept in his place. At this time he happened to be visiting a relative who was the aunt of the *rav* of Torchin, the same who was later to be renowned as the saintly Reb Yechiel of Alexander.

"My nephew is due to be here today," she told him one morning, "and if you see him, that will suffice to put an end to your search."

The old man did not take her assurance seriously, for the *rav* of Torchin was still a very young man, and certainly not yet a rebbe. In the meantime he arrived, greeted the other guest, and embarked on the morning prayers — until nightfall. The elder chassid, listening all those hours, was touched by the sanctity that warmed the words that welled from this young man's heart. When the prayers were over, he approached the younger man and said: "Does the Torah not command us to guard our health? Why do you pray at such length that you are unable to eat all day long, at the expense of your physical well-being?

"You can look at it either way," replied the *rav*. "If with God's help one manages to pray the way one should, who needs to eat? And if not, God forbid, who *can* eat?"

Hearing these innocent words, the chassid thought: "The time will come when thousands will flock here to learn Torah from this young man's mouth!"

סדר אמור
SIDRA EMOR

The Tzitzis-Jew

אֱמֹר...וְאָמַרְתָּ
Speak...and say *(21:2)*

Speak ... and say: The adults are obliged to instruct the young *(Rashi).*

The custom in the household of Reb Yisrael of Ruzhin was to clothe each baby boy in a tiny four-cornered garment fringed with *tzitzis* from the age of thirty days. It once happened that one of his infant sons — famous decades later as Reb David Moshe of Chortkov — worried his mother by crying without end, refusing to suck, and being unable to fall asleep, despite all her motherly efforts at soothing her baby by fondling and dandling him. She did not want to call a physician without first telling her husband, but Reb Yisrael only laughed: "Someone has no doubt forgotten to put on the baby's *tzitzis*," he said.

The *rebbitzin* hastened to check. She clothed him in his little garment, the baby stopped crying — and from that day his brothers nicknamed him "the *tzitzis*-Jew."

וּפְאַת זְקָנָם לֹא יְגַלֵּחוּ
They shall not shave off the corners of their beard (21:5)

☙ *For the Sake of a Principle*

Polish Jewry was in turmoil. The year 5611 (1851) was approaching, by the advent of which — so the government had ordained — all Jews were to divest themselves of their distinctive garb, and were to shave off their earlocks and their beards. The decree was to apply in the first instance to Warsaw, and only later to the rest of the country. Seeing that it was for the most part ignored, the municipal police were ordered to seize any Jews in the street and to shave off their beards and *peyos* by force. They often encountered stout resistance, which led to blows and imprisonment, and the streets echoed with the wailing of the wives and children of those who had been dragged off brutally to jail.

The rumor now spread that the government had designs to lay hands on Reb Yitzchak Meir of Ger, who then lived in Warsaw, for certain *Maskilim* — Jewish advocates of the "Enlightenment" movement — had advised the authorities that if they could impose the requirements of the new law on this distinguished leader of men, the rest of Warsaw Jewry would conform without objection. Word of this conspiracy reached the tzaddik in time to allow him to find a temporary haven in the house of a sympathizer. At the same time, a delegation of local worthies succeeded in securing a promise from the minister in charge of the police force that no harm would befall the rebbe. Though Reb Yitzchak Meir now returned home, he changed his name for good measure from Rothenburg to Alter, which has remained the name of his descendants to this day.

As the decree was gradually proclaimed in more and more Polish cities, the rabbis who were consulted for guidance pointed in either of two opposite directions. Those who took the more stringent view argued that in times of religious persecution — when the aim of the authorities is clearly to stamp out Judaism — the Torah obliges every Jew to be prepared to surrender his life for any observance which is distinctively Jewish, be it ever so peripheral, even a distinctive way of tying one's shoestraps. Other rabbis argued that the government's intention was not necessarily anti-religious, in which case a person would be obliged to give his life for three prohibitions only: idolatry, incest and murder.

The first party was headed by Reb Avraham of Chechanov, who made his view known in all the synagogues of the town, and instructed the scholars in his own *beis midrash* to prepare themselves for the imminent self-sacrifice of *Kiddush HASHEM* by carefully studying all the learned sources on the subject. For, throughout the ages, have Jews not always prepared themselves for the Pessach festival by studying all the laws relating to *that* religious obligation?

The authority of Reb Avraham, however, was questioned by certain reputed scholars of Chechanov, who approached him as follows: "Is it proper that questions of life and death should be decided by one person, singlehanded? For we hear that other respected scholars take a more lenient view on the subject."

Reb Avraham answered that his was not a solitary view, for he had heard from Warsaw that Reb Yitzchak Meir took the same stand.

"But does hearsay suffice for a question like this?" one of them objected.

"Granted," said Reb Avraham. "I will set out at once for Warsaw in order to consult with Reb Yitzchak Meir, after which we will be able to issue a clear statement jointly."

His *rebbitzin* and family implored him to change his mind: the journey to Warsaw was plainly dangerous, since policemen now loitered about the streets unrestrained, waiting for the opportunity to abuse any Jewish bypasser. The worthies of Chechanov likewise entreated him not to leave his flock without a shepherd at such a time, but his answer was clear: he simply had to travel to Warsaw. Then he added: "After all, I am not going to settle [the Yiddish *avekzetzen-zich* could also mean 'to sit'] in Warsaw; I'll be coming straight back home, with God's help."

Accompanied by a chassid by the name of Reb Abba, he set out the same day for Warsaw, where Reb Yitzchak Meir greeted him warmly and offered him a chair. The guest refused the offer once, twice, and again, to the wonderment of all those present, and out of respect for him the host remained standing too.

"I have come here," opened Reb Avraham, "to hear your respected view on the new decree. What do you think is the government's intention?"

"It appears to me," replied his host, "that they simply

want our brethren to desert their Judaism."

"Thank God!" exclaimed Reb Avraham. "The conclusion at which I arrived coincides with your own learned view."

After discussing the laws governing *Kiddush HASHEM* for some two hours, Reb Yitzchak did his guest the courtesy of seeing him off. On the way back to Chechanov, when Reb Avraham spoke highly of Reb Yitzchak Meir, his traveling companion seized the opportunity, and took the liberty of asking the obvious question: "If you think so highly of Reb Yitzchak Meir, why did you not accede to his repeated request that you seat yourself? Does the Talmud not teach us that 'It is not proper to stand on ceremony in the presence of one's superior'?"

"Before I left home," explained Reb Avraham, "I assured my family that I was not going to *avekzetzen-zich* in Warsaw. What I meant, of course, was that I had no intention of *settling* in Warsaw, and would not tarry there. At the same time, however, I did not want to go back on my word, even in its literal sense."

❀ ❀ ❀

Rumor had it that Reb Menachem Mendel of Kotsk took the lenient view on the burning question of the day. Reb Abba was due to leave now for Kotsk, and on the assumption that on his arrival there he would be asked what stand Reb Avraham took, he asked his rebbe for a prepared answer when he went to receive his farewell blessings.

"As you no doubt recall," said Reb Avraham, "Reb Yitzchak Meir and I agreed in Warsaw that the Torah prescribes that in these circumstances a Jew is obliged to give his life rather than submit."

In Kotsk, as expected, the first question from Reb Menachem Mendel was: "What is news in your district as regards the new law? And what does your *rav* have to say on the halachic question involved?"

"Our *rav*," answered Reb Abba, "traveled to Warsaw for the express purpose of discussing this issue with Reb Yitzchak Meir."

"And if two such great scholars met to confer on this

halachah," said his host, "then we may be certain that they arrived at some conclusion. What then, did they decide?"

When the chassid quoted their joint view, Reb Menachem Mendel grasped his beard in consternation and cried out: "And is that how they decided the *halachah*? Do you mean to say that they studied the subject, and then decided the law *this* way?! I, too, have opened a book on odd occasions; I, too, have some familiarity with the scholarly small print. But I have certainly not come across the law that says that in this case our brethren are obliged to surrender their lives rather than submit! Is it not unthinkable that two great men should treat their people's blood so cheaply? Better by far if great men like themselves were to exert all their influence on our fellow Jews, so that they should all repent wholeheartedly, and in that way bring about the Messianic Redemption! ... "

❦ ❦ ❦

As the months passed, the policemen of Warsaw realized that most of the Jews of the city would not observe the requirements of the law without the application of brute force. Growing weary of violence, the police force gradually became lax in the execution of its duties. Such a situation could not be tolerated — by sundry Jewish assimilationists and *Maskilim.* They presented themselves promptly before the Russian commissioner, and drew his attention to the fact that certain officials on the government's payroll were turning a blind eye to the recent decree, and thereby making a laughing-stock of it; they were no doubt receiving bribes from certain wealthy chassidim. His best course of action, therefore, would be to force Reb Yitzchak Meir to issue a manifesto instructing his fellows to conform to what was required of them, and explaining that this was their religious duty, under the circumstances. They led him further to believe that Reb Yitzchak Meir, alone among all the rabbis, held this intransigent view — a view which could no doubt be changed by a brief period of imprisonment.

In order to avert a furor in the middle of the day, the

local police chief and his assistant arrested Reb Yitzchak Meir at midnight, and took him in their carriage to the lock-up which adjoined the town hall. The high officials who were waiting for him there proposed that he issue a manifesto, and when he refused, they threatened that if he did not oblige within a day or two, they would shave off his own beard.

"Not a hairsbreadth will I give in," he said. "You are wasting your words, for in my view the Torah forbids every Jew to obey this order. Even if you do to me whatever it is in your power to do, I will not cause others to transgress."

Realizing that words alone would achieve nothing, the officials decided to have the tzaddik transferred to a cell which was occupied by coarse-grained criminals of every description. And the indignities which he there underwent for the sake of his principles are recounted by Gerer chassidim to this day.

❧ ❧ ❧

Who in all of Warsaw could sleep that night? The news of the rebbe's imprisonment spread in the darkness like wildfire, and the city was seething with shock and indignation. The chassidim of Reb Menachem Mendel dispatched a delegation to Kotsk, but the rebbe received the news with equanimity, instructing his faithful elder chassid, Reb Hirsch of Tomashov, to write in his name to the chassidim in Warsaw, reassuring them that there was nothing to worry about. Not only would the police officers not be able to touch the beard and *peyos* of the tzaddik, but by virtue of his righteousness all of Jewry would find their salvation, and the decree would be rescinded.

In Warsaw, in the meanwhile, the uproar was growing by the hour, and daybreak found the streets crammed with groups and crowds of distraught Jews, including as well many *Maskilim* and assimilationists who deplored what had been done, seeing it as an insult to Jewry at large. Tens of thousands of Jews, some shouting, others weeping, jostled in the vast square that fronted the town hall, where they were joined in their protest by a number of Polish citizens. Passing government officials saw it as their duty to report what they saw to the responsible ministers, until the message even reached the ears of the Russian commissioner. His advisers warned him that this could well spark off a popular revolt. A moment later he was confronted by a delegation of leading Jewish citizens, accompanied by a few Polish nobles, who pointed out that Warsaw had never seen treatment of this kind meted out to a man of such stature as Reb Yitzchak Meir. The commissioner gave them his word that he would be freed at once, and indeed the rebbe was back at home before midday.

This arrest nevertheless left a somber imprint on the lives of Warsaw's Jews. People were already pointing their fingers at certain *Maskilim* who were known to be the informers, and there were those who made it their task to track them down and wreak vengeance on them. They, for their part, flew to the government for protection, and the populace was splintered by disputants and informers on all sides.

Reb Yitzchak Meir came to the conclusion that the only way for him to bring some peace to the city was to leave it. His followers and admirers begged him not to go, especially since the Pessach festival was only two weeks away, but he left nevertheless for Novidvor, leaving word with his distressed chassidim that he would not return until the decree was annulled. After baking *matzos* in readiness for the festival he wrote a letter to his chassidim in Warsaw, entreating them not to engage in disputes for his sake, nor to speak harshly with any man — "for we are all the sons of Avraham, Yitzchak and Yaakov; and there would be no need for the Torah to exhort us to love our neighbors, nor to warn us against harboring hatred in our hearts, with regard to those who are our loving friends and brothers ... "

Over a week later, after *Shabbos HaGadol,* the decree was rescinded. The leading lights of Warsaw hastened to bring the good news to Novidvor, and soon after, Reb Yitzchak Meir joined them in their carriage for the joyful homeward journey. It was one day before the eve of Pessach when he neared the outskirts of Warsaw, where he was given a hero's welcome by jolly, jubilant crowds of bearded chassidim.

◆§ A Guide for Gourmets

וּטְרֵפָה לֹא יֹאכַל
He shall not eat ... trefah (22:8)

Watching the pranks of Reb Shmuel Munkes, you would take him for a rather light-headed chassid, something of a jester. His rebbe, however, Reb Shneur Zalman of Liadi, who knew of his rich spiritual life, respected him highly.

One day he and his friends were sitting around a table *farbrengen* together, as chassidim are accustomed to do — discussing the teachings of their rebbe, exchanging stories of great men, and now and again sipping vodka and nibbling whatever refreshments happened to be on the table. One of the brotherhood, a *shochet,* now came in with a dish of cooked meat which he had brought from home for all those present. Reb Shmuel promptly took it and held it firmly under his arm, allowing no one else at the table to touch it. They demanded that he place it within reach of anyone who wished to help himself, and when he refused to oblige, some of them even tried to snatch it from him by force. Seeing that they would soon succeed, he raised the platter aloft, danced around with it to the corner of the room where a garbage pail stood, and threw it right in.

The other chassidim were dumbfounded by his odd behavior, and would have given him a piece of their mind — but at that moment they were interrupted by the arrival of a breathless messenger from the house of the *shochet:* they were not to eat from that dish! The meat that had been brought by mistake was *trefah!*

The elder chassidim now turned on Reb Shmuel with a different complaint altogether: "Tell us, our budding young tzaddik! Since when has the voice of divine inspiration been whispering secrets in *your* ear?"

Seeing that he would have no respite from their good-natured teasing, he was forced to explain: "Years ago, during the period when I was preparing myself to enter the rebbe's study for my first *yechidus,* I resolved that I would abstain from any physical thing that I desired unduly. Today, when I took this meat dish in my hands, I felt a strong urge to eat it — and that is why I didn't. Then when I saw with what eager eyes our little brotherhood looked upon it, I threw it out."

◆§ Worth the Sacrifice

And I will be sanctified amongst the Children of Israel: Surrender your life and sanctify My name *(Rashi).*

וְנִקְדַּשְׁתִּי בְּתוֹךְ בְּנֵי יִשְׂרָאֵל
And I will be sanctified amongst the Children of Israel (22:32)

This story used to be told by Reb David Zvi Chein, a distinguished chassid who was the *rav* of Chernigov.

A rare manuscript book of chassidic philosophy, bound with *two* spines, was kept in the house of Reb Shneur Zalman of Liadi, and its cover bore the inscription: "The ban of Rabbeinu Gershom respecting the secrecy of documents is hereby invoked — in This World and in the Next — on anyone who looks inside this book."

Fire broke out in his home one day, destroying his entire library and all his manuscripts, including this one. With tears in his eyes he asked his son, Reb Dov Ber of Lubavitch, if he had perchance ever glanced at it. Tne answer was of course negative, but the father persisted: "If you were perhaps to recall even one chapter, one discourse, you would restore my spirits!"

"But could I ever have looked at it?" protested Reb Dov Ber. "Didn't you invoke the ban both in This World and the Next?"

Even this explanation did not satisfy his father, who objected: "But isn't the discovery of fresh manuscripts of chassidic philosophy worth the sacrifice?"

◆§ One Moment of Ecstasy

The following account of the passing of Reb Yaakov Yitzchak, the Yid HaKadosh of Pshischah, was given by Reb Avraham of Sochatchov.

Reb Yaakov Yitzchak had always hoped that his life would come to an end while he was at prayer; he yearned to attain such a degree of *mesirus nefesh* that in a moment of ecstasy his soul would fly home and cleave to its Maker. His sons, however, used to see to it that this should not occur. On one occasion nevertheless he was left alone in his room while he was immersed in his morning prayers, and when he came to the verse:

"Redeemers will go up on Mount Zion" — those who were in the adjoining room heard a thud. The Yid HaKadosh had fallen to the floor. They ran in, just in time to hear him whisper the words יְחִידָה לְיַחֲדָךְ — "My soul proclaims Your unity" — and the tzaddik was no more.

◈§ *An Honest Epitaph*

After the passing of Reb Uri of Strelisk, his son, Reb Shlomo, journeyed to visit Reb Yisrael of Ruzhin. On his arrival, his host asked him to repeat some quotable saying or to tell of some noteworthy practice of his father, who was nicknamed "the Saraph" — the fiery angel — on account of the ecstatic nature of his prayer. Reb Shlomo thereupon told him two things: firstly, every morning before Reb Uri went off to his prayers he used to go to the kitchen in order to exchange farewells with his *rebbitzin* and children, being fearful lest his soul break loose from his body in the ecstatic *dveikus* of prayer; secondly, on each such occasion he used to say: "Keep in mind that the manuscripts in that chest were authored by my teacher, Reb Shlomo of Karlin, and not by me, and the Talmudic novellae appearing there should not be attributed to me."

Reb Yisrael was well pleased, and said that he valued the second statement even more than the first.

◈§ *A Boy at a Picnic*

It was too much for the simple householder from Tomashov to comprehend.

"This Reb Menachem Mendel of Kotsk," he would declare, "was born right here in Tomashov, and he and I went to *cheder* together when we were little. And do you mean to say that now he is a rebbe?!"

A number of chassidim of Kotsk heard this statement, and made it their business to ply this fellow with questions about the conduct of their rebbe in his childhood. He insisted that there was nothing to tell: their rebbe had been a child like all the other children. But when they persisted further, he recalled one incident: "One day our *melamed* took all the children from his *cheder* to celebrate Lag BaOmer by a picnic in the high mountains beyond the town, as all schoolmasters do. We had all returned home before we realized that one boy — that's the Kotsker rebbe — was missing! We hurried back to look for him, and found him lying with arms and legs outstretched on the mountainside. Someone bent over him, and heard him murmur: לִבִּי וּבְשָׂרִי יְרַנְּנוּ אֶל אֵל חָי — 'My heart and my flesh sing praises to the living God.''

◈§ *The Voice of the People*

אֵלֶּה מוֹעֲדֵי ה׳ ... אֲשֶׁר תִּקְרְאוּ אֹתָם *These are the festivals of God ... which you shall proclaim (23:4)*

These are the festivals of God ... which you shall proclaim: Do not read אֹתָם (them) but אַתֶּם (you); by *your* decision shall they be determined, even if you err unwittingly, or misjudge intentionally *(Talmud, Tractate Rosh HaShanah).*

It is the custom among certain groups of chassidim to mark the visit of a tzaddik to their town by omitting the Tachanun prayer from the morning and afternoon service, as is in fact done by all congregations on festive days. So it was that when Reb Yechezkel of Shiniva spent a few weeks in Militz, the whole town took this liberty throughout his entire stay.

''The reason that chassidim omit *Tachanun* when their town is visited by a sage,'' commented Reb Yechezkel, ''is that a *talmid chacham* is akin to the spirit of *Shabbos* and the festivals — days on which one never recites the penitential prayers. This rationale, however, holds good only for you chassidim here, who choose to regard me as a *talmid chacham.* But as for myself, who knows my own real worth, and who know that I am neither sage nor tzaddik, — why do *I* not say *Tachanun?*

''The explanation is as follows: We read: 'These are the festivals of God ... which you shall proclaim.' On this the Sages comment: אַל תִּקְרֵי ''אֹתָם'' אֶלָּא ''אַתֶּם'' — 'Do not read אֹתָם (them) but אַתֶּם (you): by *your* decision shall they be determined, even if you err unwittingly, or misjudge intentionally.' It follows, therefore, that even if the chassidim here are mistaken in their assessment of my worth, I am nevertheless still akin to *Shabbos* and *Yom Tov*, and am hence exempt from reciting *Tachanun*."

סדר בהר
Sidra Behar

◆§ No False Pretenses

אַל תּוֹנוּ אִישׁ אֶת אָחִיו
You shall not defraud one another (25:14)

He was the grandson of Reb Avraham of Chechanov, and he was engaged to be married to one of the prominent burghers of Polotzk — but he was an immature youngster, and one day while his celebrated grandfather took off his coat and left the room, he subtracted a few small coins from his pocket and dropped them into his own. As soon as Reb Avraham returned to the room he sensed what had happened, and was pained by the fact that his own flesh and blood had thus faltered. He sat down at once at his desk and dispatched a letter to the *rav* of Polotzk, asking him to instruct the father of the bride to set out immediately for Chechanov. The poor fellow received the message and trembled in apprehension. Was it possible that at this late stage the tzaddik of Chechanov had decided that he was unworthy of being his *mechuten* after all?

He entered the rebbe's study, and Reb Avraham opened exactly as he had feared: "Now you have been thinking all along that you are about to join your family in marriage with the *rav* of Chechanov." But then he went on: "Well, sir, it is my obligation to inform you that such and such has taken place. I would certainly not want our arrangements to be based on a mistaken assumption."

Much relieved, the *mechutan* said: "Rebbe, I'll go ahead with the match, all the same."

The tzaddik repeated his statement again, and again — but the *mechutan* stood by his first answer.

"If that is the case," said the tzaddik finally, "then the responsibility no longer rests on me. I have done my part."

◆§ A Mitzvah for Mortals

וְהֶחֱזַקְתָּ בּוֹ
You shall support him (25:35)

Hundreds of chassidim from all around converged on Kosov for *Shabbos*, for their rebbe, Reb Menachem Mendel of Kosov, was to be visited by his brother-in-law, Reb Uri of Strelisk. Among them was one Reb Moshe, an *arendar* who had been wealthy and generous, but had now fallen from his fortunes to such an extent that his local squire was threatening him with imprisonment and other humiliations if he did not pay up the rent on his leased business.

When *Shabbos* was out the distracted debtor told his story to his rebbe, Reb Menachem Mendel, who recommended that he recount his woes to Reb Uri as well.

"I certainly feel sorry for you in your troubles," said Reb Uri. "I am now going to immerse myself in the *mikveh* for your sake, and the merit of the *mikveh* will no doubt stand you in good stead and protect you."

When the *arendar* reported this reply back to his rebbe, Reb Menachem Mendel advised: "Please go back to my learned brother-in-law, and tell him that you can't pay your creditors with a *mikveh*."

Reb Uri's reply to this was: "Very well, my son. Then in addition I am prepared to give you the credit of an even greater mitzvah — the *tefillin* that I am about to don this morning."

When Menachem Mendel was told of this answer, he said: "Now tell Reb Uri, please, that you cannot placate your creditors with *tefillin*."

The *arendar* had no choice but to obey his rebbe. Once again he went off to Reb Uri, who listened, and then reassured him: "If that is the case, then you may have as well the *zechus* of my prayers this morning. Without a doubt, the merit of all these three mitzvos together will bring about the salvation you require!"

This assurance, too, was relayed to Reb Menachem Mendel, but he remained unconvinced. "Go back and tell Reb Uri," he said "that even with all these three mitzvos together you will not be able to pay a single debt."

Reb Uri realized that it was time to clarify what was

going on. He went along himself, and asked his brother-in-law what he was driving at.

"All I am suggesting," said Reb Menachem Mendel, "is that you and I should spend the next few weeks traveling about the countryside, knocking on the doors of our brethren, collecting whatever amount the poor fellow needs. That we can fulfill a mitzvah which is written in the Torah: 'And if your brother grows poor, ... then you shall support him.' "

And so they did. The *arendar* settled all his debts, and soon after the Almighty again gave him the means to become an open-handed philanthropist, just as he had always been in earlier times.

◆§ *Telegraphic Accounting*

An upstanding householder once came to pour out his troubles to Reb Menachem Mendel of Kosov: he needed a large sum with which to marry off his daughter, and did not have a penny to start with.

"The best thing for you to do," advised the rebbe, "is to travel to Jassy, and there you will do well."

"But how can I cross the border to Rumania without a passport?" asked the chassid.

"I will give you a letter to a certain person who lives near the border," said the rebbe, "and he will get you across."

Everything went as planned, and before dawn the chassid was in Jassy. There was no one in sight who could tell him where he could find a hotel, so he stood with his belongings out in the street, waiting for daybreak. One of the first citizens to be seen was an impressive-looking individual who by his modern garb would seem to be an assimilationist, a "Deitsch". He approached the chassid and asked him where he came from, and was told that he had just arrived and did not yet know where he would be lodging.

"Come along with me," said the stranger.

"Why, do you own a good lodging place?" asked the chassid.

"I certainly do," said the stranger. "But it's not for payment: it's for nothing."

The visitor was somewhat surprised. They had never met before, and here was this total stranger inviting him to his home.

"Come along with me," resumed the stranger, "and I'll tell you what it's all about.

"A few years ago we had a visit here from some rebbe from Galicia by the name of Reb Menachem Mendel. Through his intercession and blessing, heaven granted me the gift of a baby boy, and I vowed at the time that I would give him a certain large sum of money. But I didn't have his address over there, so I never repaid my debt to him. I kept on hoping that one day either I would be in Galicia, or else he would visit us again here, and then I would settle my acount once and for all. Then last night he appeared to me in a dream and said: 'Do you recall that debt that you owe me? Well, I'm sending you now a man of such and such a description, and I would like you to hand him the whole amount. You will know that you have found your man if you go out and find him right away in the street.'

"I woke up with my mind in a whirl. I could rest no longer, and at daybreak I went straight out to the street. I looked around until I caught sight of you — and your description tallies exactly with what the rebbe told me."

His story completed, the stranger gave the visitor the whole sum that he had resolved to give the rebbe, and added to it by asking friends to join in the mitzvah. They then exchanged farewells and parted company, each turning to wend his thoughtful way homeward.

◆§ *The Apple-Vendor*

A poor woman of good family once came to Reb Chaim of Zanz and complained that she did not even have the wherewithal to buy food for *Shabbos*.

"But don't you sell apples?" asked the rebbe.

"I do," she said. "But people say my apples are no good, so I haven't sold any."

The venerable tzaddik, resplendent in his fur hat, black silk *kapote* and white stockings, strode immediately out to the market place, took up his stand next to the poor woman's apple-cart, and cried out: "Apples! Beautiful apples! Who wants to buy first-class apples?"

Crowds of customers jostled with each other in their eagerness to buy the apples that the rebbe was selling. The price did not matter: they offered far more than they needed to, and in no time the entire stock was sold out at an enormous profit.

As he turned to leave the market place, the rebbe said to the woman: "You see, your apples are fine! It's only that our townsfolk didn't know it ..."

סדר בחקתי
Sidra Bechukosai

◆§ *Head and Heart*

אִם בְּחֻקֹּתַי תֵּלֵכוּ
If you walk in the way of My statutes (26:3)

If you walk in the way of My statutes: You shall *toil* in the study of the Torah *(Rashi).*

When Reb Avraham of Sochatchov was a very young man, Reb Menachem Mendel of Kotsk once told his father: "Your brilliant son is a great worshiper, with an unusual gift in prayer. I am only afraid lest it impair his intellectual power."

This was not an easy comment to understand. In the first place, no one had observed the young man exert himself particularly in prayer, and secondly, what did that have to do with his intellectual power?

An uncle of Reb Avraham decided to ask the young man himself, and was given the following innocent explanation: "I once had a watch that I was very fond of, for it used to tell me the time for Torah study, prayer, and so on. One day its wheels stopped, but I couldn't afford to have it repaired by a watchmaker. I wept before the Almighty in my distress — and straight away its wheels started to work, even though it had not been repaired. Now when I saw that my tears were heard Above, every time I was confronted in my studies by a particularly problematic passage I would cry again, asking God to illumine my eyes. And each time I found I could immediately solve the problem at hand.

"Now the rebbe of Kotsk evidently sensed this, and that is why he said that I have 'an unusual gift in prayer.' That also explains why he said that he was fearful that my intellectual powers should be impaired, because what is demanded of us is that we should come to master the Torah through toil of the brain, not by means of prayer."

◈§ *By the Sweat of Your Brow*

I encountered this story in a manuscript written by the hand of Reb Raphael Wolf of Skoli, Galicia, who died in Jerusalem early in 1929 at the age of some ninety years. Reb Raphael heard it from a chassid of repute by the name of Reb Alter of Yazlivitz, who heard it from the mouth of the tzaddik Reb Meir of Premishlan (who died in 1850), son of Reb Aharon Leib, the protagonist of this story.

A certain merchant who was a chassid of Reb Aharon Leib of Premishlan had occasion to pass through Lyzhansk in the course of business. It would be a pity, he thought, to be so far away from home and not to utilize this opportunity to visit one of the towering figures of the generation, Reb Elimelech of Lyzhansk. In order to be able to do this in an untrammeled frame of mind, he first settled his various business affairs in the district, and arranged to be back in town for *Shabbos*. On Friday morning, after immersing himself in the *mikveh*, he went to greet the rebbe.

Reb Elimelech welcomed him, and then said: "Are you not one of the chassidim of Reb Aharon Leib of Premishlan? Tell me, now, why is your rebbe so conceited?"

And Reb Elimelech repeated the phrase in the hearing of all those who happened to be present: "So conceited! So conceited!"

And not only then, but again and again at each of the *Shabbos* meals — until the merchant's joy at the privilege of meeting the celebrated personage turned to distress.

Nor did his departure from Lyzhansk lighten his

burden, for when he came to Reb Elimelech to receive his parting blessings, he was told: "When you come home, please tell your rebbe in my name that he should not be so conceited."

His arrival home threw him into a quandary. Reb Aharon Leib was certain to ask him, as he always did whenever his chassidim came home from a journey, whether he had anything of interest to report. He would have to say that he had met Reb Elimelech. Reb Aharon Leib would then ask, naturally enough, whether he had seen or heard anything noteworthy or quotable. He would then have to say ... — but how could he ever bring himself to mouth such words? At length, realizing that there was no way out of fulfilling the explicit instruction of Reb Elimelech, he spoke to his rebbe and withheld nothing.

"Woe is me!" said Reb Aharon Leib. "Who knows how I have sinned in the sight of God, and what blemish the tzaddik has discerned in me? Indeed, I am in such a sorry state that I do not even sense what my sin is, and therefore do not even know how to go about repenting!"

Calling in his *rebbitzin,* he said: "The tzaddik of Lyzhansk sees that I am a sinner. I must journey there at once to find out from him in what way I have transgressed, otherwise I will not know how to repent. But the road to Lyzhansk is a long, long road, and even when I finally arrive there I know I no longer have the strength to look after myself."

The *rebbitzin* assured him that she would share the rigors of the journey with him and see to his needs. They hired a wagon, trundled along for six whole days, and arrived at Lyzhansk just in time for *Shabbos.* A sinner such as himself would certainly not be granted admission to the Friday night table of the tzaddik, so Reb Aharon Leib asked his *rebbitzin* to go out to the market place to buy a bottle of wine and two loaves of *challah,* while he himself went off to find the local *mikveh,* so that he could immerse himself for purity's sake in honor of the holy day.

Entering the rebbe's house, he found himself among hundreds of chassidim who were also waiting to receive his greeting of *Shalom.* He made his way through the crowd and extended his hand to receive the rebbe's handshake, being careful to keep his head bowed so that the tzaddik should not see his face. Reb Elimelech sensed at once that this was Reb Aharon Leib, and wanted to call him back, but the guest had already hurried off to his lodging place. From there he went to a nearby *shul* for evening prayers, then back to his modest little room, there to sing the *Shalom Aleichem* that welcomes the ministering angels who accompany every Jew on his way back from *shul* to whatever nook he calls home.

At the same time, Reb Elimelech asked his *shammes* and his chassidim to search through the whole town until they found the guest from Premishlan. When they returned without having found him, Reb Elimelech stood up and protested: "A guest of the stature of Reb Aharon Leib is here with us in our town, and will I not have him at my table for *Shabbos?!*"

He again gave the order that his chassidim were to search through the whole of Lyzhansk, from house to house, room by room, until they found this same Reb Aharon Leib, and to inform him that he himself would not sit down to conduct his Friday night *tish* until this guest joined him there.

Again they set out, and searched once more, until they found him at his lodgings in the low-roofed cottage of some penniless *melamed* on the outskirts of the town.

They gave him the message and brought him to the rebbe's table, where Reb Elimelech expressed his delight at his arrival by giving him a seat of honor by his side. Surprisingly, though, several times in the course of the meal he said: "Who would believe that Reb Aharon Leib should be so conceited!"

And, as before, not once, but at every one of the *Shabbos* meals he repeated this comment in public.

When the day of rest was over Reb Aharon Leib called on the rebbe in order to take his leave — but first to find out just what was the conceit that he had perceived.

"Why, is there any conceit greater than this?" answered Reb Elimelech. "On many occasions Eliyahu the Prophet has come to me with the complaint that you do not want to learn Torah from his mouth. He, the Prophet Eliyahu, wanted to teach you Torah, and you refuse! Think how many tzaddikim have longed and yearned for this privilege — and you decline the offer! In any case, I promised Eliyahu that I would try to persuade you to change your mind."

"I am afraid that even after your persuasion," answered Reb Aharon Leib, "I cannot agree."

"Why so?" asked his host.

"Because my desire," said the guest, "is to do my own hard work in the study of the Torah. For how does the Psalmist express it? 'When you eat of the labor of your hands, happy shall you be, and it shall be well with you.' And the same lesson we learn in the Talmud: 'The Torah truly becomes the possession only of him who gives his very life in the effort of its study.' For this reason I have not been taught by him, nor will I be taught by him. I will only pray to the Almighty that he give me the strength to toil always in the study of His Torah."

The tzaddik gave him his blessing, and Reb Aharon Leib made his way back to Premishlan, where he continued to serve his Maker by an honest day's labor, day by day.

☙ *Judging by Appearances*

וְנָתַתִּי גִשְׁמֵיכֶם בְּעִתָּם
And I will grant your rains in their season (26:4)

A *Chabad* chassid of the Slonim family traveled to White Russia over a hundred years ago to visit his rebbe and relative, Reb Shmuel of Lubavitch. The rebbe was eager to hear news of the welfare of the Jews in *Eretz Yisrael,* and the chassid in the course of his report, commented: "I cannot understand the claim which is made in many sacred books that in *Eretz Yisrael* there are to be found people with lofty souls. I know the Jews over there, and I have not seen amongst them any more individuals with lofty souls than are to be found in other countries."

"And do you understand exactly who it is who has a lofty soul?" queried the rebbe. "Let me tell you a story that I heard from my father, Reb Menachem Mendel, of blessed memory, and you will see to what heights a simple Jew in the Holy Land can sometimes aspire.

"In a village just beyond the outskirts of Jerusalem there lived a very simple peasant, who had studied neither *Chumash* nor Mishnah, and did not even understand the meaning of the words of the daily prayers. Not only that, he could not even find his way around the *Siddur*, so that he was unable to work out for himself which prayers were to be said on any particular day. When he drove his donkey cart up the winding road to Jerusalem once a week to sell his fruit and vegetables, he would call on a certain *rav*, who would jot down for him the order of prayers for the coming week. It might have been simpler to explain the subject in general terms — to tell him that all weekday prayers are identical, except for the Daily Psalm, and except for the additional passages on Mondays and Thursdays, and so on — but this was out of the question. The poor fellow was so utterly ignorant that he would only flounder in all those unmanageable details. The *rav* was therefore obliged to write down each day's order of service in full, day by day.

"Once he came to the *rav* in the rainy month of Cheshvan, and asked him to write out the daily lists that would be needed for several weeks ahead, for the roads were likely to become muddy and impassable. As things worked out, however, a week or so later he found that he had to make the trip to town after all. He arrived in Jerusalem, but was amazed to find that all the Jewish shops were closed. Perhaps he had made a mistake, God forbid, and today was in fact *Shabbos*? As he stood next to his donkey, straining to puzzle this out, he saw a man walk past with his *tallis* and *tefillin* under his arm. That was a relief, for everyone knows that one doesn't don *tefillin* on *Shabbos*. But what kind of day could it possibly be? He asked the same bypasser, who told him that that day was a public fast.

"The villager could not begin to understand how his *rav* could have neglected to note this down in his list. In the first place, he had thus eaten on a fast day; and secondly, he had omitted the special prayers which he should have been told about. He left his donkey and wagon in the market place and ran off to the house of the *rav*, where he was told that the man he sought had gone to the local synagogue. He hurried there in confusion, went straight over to the *rav*, and broke down in bitter tears: 'Tell me, rabbi! Do you think that's fair? How could you ever do such a thing to me?'

"The *rav* was nonplussed, and asked gently: 'What is the matter, my son?'

" 'What do you mean *What is the matter?*' returned the villager. 'Today is a public fast day, and you didn't write down any mention of it. So now I've eaten when I shouldn't have, and I haven't prayed what I should have!'

" 'Do calm down, my son,' the *rav* replied. 'Today is not a regular fast day, but a fast that we decreed just now in Jerusalem especially for today, because of the drought that is threatening. We are all fasting here, and asking the Almighty to send us rain.'

" 'Do you mean to say that for this you have to decree a *fast?*' mused the villager.

" 'Then what, in your opinion, should one do?' countered the *rav*.

" 'Simple,' said the villager. 'I know that when I don't get enough rain on my fields back at home, I go outside, and I say to God: *Father, I need rain!* And the rain starts to fall.'

" 'Very well,' said the *rav*, 'then try to do the same thing here.'

"The simple fellow went out to the courtyard of the synagogue, was overcome with tears, and said: 'Father! Is it possible that Your children in the Holy City should perish of hunger? Can't you see that they need rain?'

"And the Holy City was blessed at once with rain."

❀ ❀ ❀

His story concluded, the rebbe asked his guest: "Tell me, are you still able to judge exactly who in *Eretz Yisrael* is possessed of a lofty soul?"

⸎ *Every Custom Tells a Story*

וְחֶרֶב לֹא תַעֲבֹר בְּאַרְצְכֶם *Nor shall a sword pass through your land (26:6)*

The little town of Rimanov, for as long as it survived, had a custom all of its own. Every *Shabbos* eve before the late afternoon prayer the congregants used to chant together the verses of Psalm 144, which opens with the words: בָּרוּךְ ה׳ צוּרִי הַמְלַמֵּד יָדַי לַקְרָב אֶצְבְּעוֹתַי לַמִּלְחָמָה —

"Blessed be God, my Rock, Who teaches my hands for battle, my fingers for war" — and proceeds to express the gratitude of the Psalmist to Him Who repelled His enemies, leaving His People to dwell unafraid. The custom originated with Reb Menachem Mendel of Rimanov, who died in 1815. This is its story.

The fury of a violent peasants' revolt at the time focused on Rimanov. When the authorities at Dukla heard that even bridges were being smashed, they dispatched troops forthwith in order to restore law and order to the best of their ability. The peasants fled in all directions, and the troops, unwilling to lose valuable time in the dispensation of justice, let loose with their clubs and muskets on whomever happened to be in sight. The townsmen, including the Jews of Rimanov, locked and barred their houses, and no one dared to step out into the terrors of the street.

Before daybreak on Friday morning, Reb Menachem Mendel did not hear the communal *shammes* doing his accustomed rounds of the cobblestoned alleys to wake up the *shomrim* whose turn it was to go to *shul* for early morning devotions. Asking his attendant for the reason, he was told that the militiamen had come to town, and people were afraid to go out of doors.

"They won't spend the night here," said the rebbe. "Of that I am certain."

When sunset was drawing near, and the rebbe went to his *beis midrash* for the afternoon prayers, he found the building deserted, apart from his own family and attendants.

"Where is the holy congregation?" he asked.

And he was told that the worshipers were afraid to leave their wives at home alone, because of the soldiers who were still roaming the streets.

Reb Menachem Mendel stepped forward to lead the *Minchah* service, but before starting it, he began to recite Psalm 144. He had not even managed to read its fifteen verses, when his companions were startled by a raucous clarion call, summoning the militiamen to parade at their colors. And in a matter of minutes, still before nightfall, the unwelcome regiment had galloped out of sight and hearing.

And from that Friday on, Reb Menachem Mendel instituted the custom of chanting Psalm 144 every Friday afternoon before the afternoon prayers, in remembrance and gratitude to Him Who repelled the enemies of His People, leaving them to dwell unafraid.

◈§ *Real Trust*

בָּרוּךְ הַגֶּבֶר אֲשֶׁר יִבְטַח בַּה׳
Blessed is the man who trusts in God (Haftarah)

While traveling in distant parts with the Baal Shem Tov, Reb Mendel of Bar was once parched with thirst.

Said the Baal Shem Tov: "If you will truly trust in God, you will certainly come across water."

And so it was. They encountered a gentile, who asked them whether they had perhaps seen the horses which he had lost and for which he had been searching for three days. They then asked him whether he had any water with him, and he allowed Reb Mendel to drink some.

When he had passed, Reb Mendel asked the Baal Shem Tov: "Since Providence evidently ordained that this gentile should come past here especially for my sake, why, then, should he have spent three days on the road?"

Replied the Baal Shem Tov: "The Almighty had him prepared earlier, so that if you were to have *real* trust in Him, your need would have been satisfied at once."

◈§ *No Worries*

The Baal Shem Tov was once instructed by a voice from heaven to make the journey to a certain village in order to learn a lesson in how to trust in God. Arriving there with his disciples, he took up lodgings with the local *arendar*, an innkeeper who held his hostelry on lease from the squire of that region. Their host was an elderly and dignified gentleman, and was obviously happy to be able to extend a warm welcome to guests such as these.

The next morning, as they were preparing for their prayers, a sheriff in the service of the squire strode into the inn, struck the table three times with a hefty rod, and strode out. The guests asked no questions, but searched the face of their host for an explanation. His cheerful equanimity had not been ruffled in the slightest. Half an hour or so later, after their prayers, they witnessed the same odd visit, repeated exactly.

The Baal Shem Tov asked the innkeeper what was going on, and received the following answer: "This is a warning that today I am obliged to pay his master the annual rent on the inn. He does this three times. If, after the third visit, the squire doesn't get his money, he comes along and throws the leaseholder and his family into his dungeon."

"It is clear, just from looking at you, that you have the necessary sum in hand," said the Baal Shem Tov. "I would therefore suggest that you go along now to the squire, before breakfast, and pay up your lease. We will wait till you return, and then we will all be able to sit at the table at leisure."

"At the moment, though," said the *arendar*, "I haven't even got a single penny — but the Almighty will no doubt bring some money my way. Let us therefore sit down, please, and eat and drink without haste, for I still have three hours grace."

They took their time over their meal, and one would never be able to tell from the host's face whether he needed the money or not. As they finished eating, in came the sheriff on his third visit and hammered his threefold warning into the table — but the innkeeper did not stir. When they had all recited the Grace after Meals with unhurried devoutness, the inkeeper rose from the table, donned his best *Shabbos* coat, belted it with his broad girdle, and said: "Gentlemen, I must now be on my way to pay the squire his lease."

The Baal Shem Tov repeated his earlier question: "But do you have enough money?"

"I haven't got a single penny of it yet," answered the innkeeper, "but the Almighty will no doubt see to that."

Taking his leave of them he went on his way, while the Baal Shem Tov and his chassidim went up to the balcony overlooking the highway, to see him off from afar as he set out on his unpredictable mission. From out of the distance they could discern a wagon rumbling dustily along to meet him. Now it stopped, and they could tell that its driver was exchanging a few sentences with their innkeeper. He then continued walking further away from them as before, and the wagon likewise continued in its own direction, coming towards the inn, but more slowly than before. After a moment or two the wagon stopped, its driver called out to the innkeeper asking him to retrace his steps, and when he reached the wagon they could see that money was changing hands.

The innkeeper thereupon resumed his previous direction and was soon out of sight, but when the wagon finally arrived at the inn, the Baal Shem Tov and his chassidim asked its driver: "Tell us, please, what was this little incident with our host, whom you called back after he had already walked away, and then gave him money?"

"I proposed a business offer," said the driver. "I would buy up the vodka that he is due to make next winter. At first we couldn't agree on a price. But later, when I saw that he stood his ground, and was prepared to wait for his price, and even walked away — and I know him to be an honest man — I had to give him the price he asked. But I couldn't spend much time talking with him, because he said he was on his way to the squire to pay up his lease."

"Just look," said the Baal Shem Tov to his disciples, "how mighty is the power of a man's trust in God!"

◆§ *Faith without Trimmings*

While explaining the beauty of faith and trust to his chassidim, Reb Noach of Lechovitch told the story of a simple Jew who arrived at the level of pure, uncomplicated faith, and prospered thereby.

This simple fellow, Hirschke by name, used to earn his living by bargaining with the gentile farmers over the merchandise that they used to bring to town on market day — hides, honey, wax, milk, boar bristle, and so on. Stallholders at the market, like himself, were accustomed to go out to the countryside two or three hours before daybreak in order to meet the *goyim* on their way to the market, in the hope of clinching their deals before the merchandise arrived in town.

Now one day an itinerant preacher came to spend *Shabbos* in town, and he held forth in the synagogue on the virtues of living with perfect trust in God. He explained the teaching of the Talmud that the world is so ordered that in the final analysis no man ever trespasses on the earnings that have been divinely ordained as the particular livelihood of another. This *darshan* was a God-fearing man, so it is not to be wondered at that his words found their way deep into Hirschke's heart. The next day, Sunday, was market day, but instead of rising hours before daybreak in order to meet the gentile farmers before his competitors did, he decided that this time he was not going to do so. Whatever Providence had set aside for him he would be able to buy at home — for is it not written that "no man ever trespasses on the earnings" and so on? His wife, seeing him lying snugly in bed at a time when he was normally up and about, urged him to get up and start moving.

"I'd like you to know," he answered, "that I myself heard the preacher say that no one can take away the earnings that have been set aside for someone else. Why, then, should I rush out in the freezing snow on the lookout for these *goyim?* For nothing is stopping God from seeing to my needs right here in my house."

His wife was not one to submit meekly. She buried him in abuse, and then declared: "This preacher of yours will be paid for his sermon, that's for sure! And you? You'll sit home idle — and starve!"

Hirschke did not answer a single word — but neither did he step out of the house.

After a little while they heard the loaded wagons of the gentiles creaking past their house. They could even hear Hirschke's friends slapping their hearty handshakes with the gentiles as they settled their deals.

This was too much. "Tell me, Hirschke," she pleaded. "Are you stark crazy, or just a fool? Can't you see that your friends will buy up every last ounce of merchandise?"

"Those uncircumcised *goyim* can jolly well come in here, if they like!" he retorted. "Why should I go out to them in this bitter cold?"

Then, right under their very shutters, they heard the

insistent voice of one of the gentile farmers: "We're not selling any more stuff until Hirschke turns up!"

One of Hirschke's competitors gave a quick reply: "Hirshcke's dead!"

"A bunch of lies!" shouted the gentiles, and began thumping with their fists on the shutters. "Hirschke, get up!"

Hirschke obliged. He got dressed, and opened the door, and the farmers with whom he was accustomed to do business came right inside, and he bought up whatever merchandise he had always bought from them, without even having to bargain. From that day on he never had to leave his house, for the farmers used to bring him their goods, and he made a respectable livelihood to the end of his days.

Reb Noach had finished his story. "Now this worked for him," he added, "because he was a simple fellow whose faith was whole and uncomplicated. Things would hardly be the same for someone who tried to improve on Hirschke's kind of faith by adding the sophistication of reason."

◆§ *From Your Hand*

Before he was known as a rebbe, Reb Yitzchak of Vorki used to live in a village where he was responsible for the timber interests of Tamar'l, a prosperous lady who invested her wealth in acts of charity. He was once asked to use his influence on her for the benefit of a chassid who was related to her, and who was hoping that she would help him bear the expense of marrying off his daughter. At first Reb Yitzchak would not hear a word of the chassid's request, but finally told him to come back the next day.

When he paid his second visit, Reb Yitzchak not only received him warmly, but asked him in a voice loud enough to be heard by Tamar'l, who was standing nearby: "So how much is it that you say you are short of? Was it three hundred gold rubles for a dowry and another two hundred for the wedding? You are related to Tamar'l, aren't you, so I am sure she will help you out."

Tamar' took the hint, and acted on it. But the chassid

could not understand why the tzaddik should have rejected his request so firmly the day before, if in the end he was to consider it so compassionately. He decided to ask him point blank.

"I only wanted to teach you," said Reb Yitzchak, "not to rely on mortals, but only on God alone."

ספר במדבר

NUMBERS

סדר במדבר
SIDRA BAMIDBAR

☙ A Labor of Love

לַעֲבֹד אֶת עֲבֹדַת הַמִּשְׁכָּן

To do the work of the Sanctuary (3:7)

The story of how Reb Shalom of Belz built his famous synagogue has already been told — but once his older brother, Reb Leibish Rokeach, came to Belz to visit their mother, and encountered the tzaddik working with bricks and mortar together with the construction laborers. This sight rather displeased him, and he sought to correct his brother: "Surely you are familiar with the teaching of our Sages, that 'Once a man is appointed a leader of the community he is forbidden to engage in menial tasks in public.' Why, then, do you do otherwise?"

"My dear brother," answered Reb Shalom, "when I used to live in Skohl I had two close friends with whom I used to study Torah. At that time it was intimated to me from Above that if one were to remain awake for a thousand nights, one could aspire to the level at which Eliyahu the Prophet reveals himself. The three of us resolved to stay awake every night and to study together. One of my friends left us after a few hundred nights, and after eight hundred nights the other friend could manage no more. I remained alone. On the thousandth night there raged such a furious tempest that it shattered all the windows of the *beis midrash* and extinguished all the lamps. Only the violent wind held me back from going home. I staggered in my anguish through the darkness towards the Holy Ark, and wept there. God took pity on me, the storm subsided, and an old man appeared before me. He began to speak and to teach me Torah, and the very last law that I heard from his lips was a law regarding the synagogue. How, then, could I possibly part with this work, and leave it to be done by others? Believe me brother, that if I only had the strength I would build this whole *shul* myself, from the foundations to the rafters — but God knows that I no longer have the strength for such an undertaking. At least what I am able to do, I do myself."

Concerning this *shul* Reb Shalom once said that he had located it at such a point that if one were to draw a straight line between its site and Jerusalem, one would encounter neither symbol nor image of idolatrous worship all the way.

◆§ *Longsightedness*

As a number of merchants were passing through Belz on their way home from Lvov to the nearby town of Krasnopoli, Reb Shalom of Belz sent them a message through his *gabbai* requesting them to stay in his town a little while, and to help the construction workers build the local synagogue. Now these men were not chassidim of his, and besides, they were in a hurry to reach home. Nevertheless, they did not feel easy about ignoring his request, so they went along and helped out as he had asked — though every little while they sent one of their number to ask him whether they could finally be on their way. The answer each time was that they should continue in the meantime; he would inform them himself when it was time for them to leave.

A few hours later, when he had finally released them from their task and they were out on the highway on their way home, they encountered a stranger who told them breathlessly: "The river which you have to cross on your way suddenly flooded over its banks. Only an hour or two ago the parish priest, being unprepared, tried to cross, and was drowned."

The impatient merchants now saw the tzaddik's insistence in a different light.

◆§ *Lifeline*

בְּנֵי אֵל חָי
You are the children of the living God (Haftarah)

Reb Naftali of Ropshitz had spent a year studying at the feet of the aged tzaddik Reb Mordechai of Neshchiz, when his teacher one day told him, suddenly: "It is time for you to return to your home."

Since his own entreaties were ignored, Reb Naftali

decided to ask his teacher's *rebbitzin* to try to persuade her husband on his behalf. His answer to her was brief: "I have always taken your advice, and I shall do so now. I only hope that we shall have no cause for regret."

A few days later, while the tzaddik was at *shul*, a stranger visited his home and entered his study. Reb Naftali was there at the time, and no sooner had he laid eyes on this stranger than he perceived that he was besmirched with sin. He was unable to restrain himself, and blurted out: "Get out, you impure fellow! How dare you step over the rebbe's threshold!"

The stranger fled, but Reb Mordechai, sensing what had happened, hastened home and asked: "Who was here?"

When Reb Naftali described the visitor, the tzaddik rebuked him: "Whatever have you done? Quick, quick! Hurry out and bring him here!"

When the stranger was brought in, Reb Mordechai gave him a warm, smiling welcome, and asked him why he had not called on him for so long. The visitor assured the tzaddik that in future he would come more frequently, offered him gifts of his own farm produce, and took his leave.

The tzaddik then explained to Reb Naftali that this man had once been close to him, and the tzaddik had been able to help him keep his distance from evil. Lately, however, various circumstances had combined to prevent him from visiting Neshchiz, and the link between them had been severed. At first he had become sullied with lesser transgressions, but since, as the Sages teach, "One sin brings on another in its train," he reached the point where he asked himself: "How am I going to end up? After all, I am really neither a Jew nor a *goy*. I can hardly go off to Neshchiz to visit the rebbe, for he will recognize at once that I am utterly enslaved to the Evil Inclination. On the other hand, if I don't go, I will simply become more and more deeply entangled in sin." And so he had continued to ponder the possibilities open to him, until finally he had decided to break his ties with his faith, and to become an apostate, God forbid.

But at that point a new idea had entered his head: "Let me make one more trial. I will make the journey to

Neshchiz, and there I will see: if he receives me warmly, that shows that there is hope for me yet; I'll put my life in order, be a good Jew again, and visit the rebbe often, just like I used to do. But if he doesn't, then I'll make a clean break with him and with Judaism altogether."

The tzaddik, understandably enough, had not wanted all his hard work on behalf of this struggler, in speech and in prayer, to be imperiled by Reb Naftali's impetuous tongue. And that was why, some days earlier, he had asked him to go home.

סדר נשא
Sidra Nasso

◆§ *Putting in a Good Word*

וְהִתְוַדּוּ אֶת חַטָּאתָם
And they shall confess their sin
(5:7)

The disciples of Reb Yisrael of Ruzhin once told him that one of his outstanding chassidim had passed away. The tzaddik had known him well, for all his life he had been an eager disciple, and those who had now delivered these tidings hoped that the tzaddik would be moved to intercede on his behalf in the Heavenly Court. How great therefore was their surprise when instead of that, he uttered a deep sigh, and said: "Oh, but he was a great sinner!"

Their hair stood on end. What could the tzaddik mean by such talk? Why should he choose to join the prosecution in the World Above?

They sought an explanation from his son, Reb Avraham Yaakov, who in later years succeeded his father as rebbe in Sadigora. He spoke as follows: "The whole of creation, as you know, may be perceived in three dimensions — עוֹלָם (literally 'world,' that is, space); שָׁנָה (literally 'year,' i.e. time); and נֶפֶשׁ ('soul,' i.e., the spiritual dimension). The choicest *place* in the world is *Eretz Yisrael;* the loftiest spot within the Holy Land is Jerusalem; within the Holy City, the Temple Mount; on the Mount,the Temple courtyard; within it, the site of the Temple; and within that site, the Holy of Holies. The holiest *times* of the year are the days of *Shabbos* and the festivals; and the most elevated of the holy days is Yom Kippur, the Day of Atonement. The loftiest *souls* are those of Israel; within the House of Israel, the Tribe of Levi; within Levi, the *kohanim;* and of all the priestly clan, the *Kohen Gadol,* the High Priest. Now when this High Priest enters the Holy of Holies on the Day of Atonement, what does he say there? 'Your People, the House of Israel, have sinned and transgressed' — for he is the one chosen to confess on behalf of all Israel.

"Unfortunately, the chassid you spoke of did not manage to confess before he passed away. Who, then, is more fit to confess on his behalf than my father?"

☙ *Returning a Favor*

They had already mounted the wagon for the long-awaited journey to Belz — the village leaseholder, with his daughter and future son-in-law — for it was the custom of Reb Shalom of Belz to reserve his blessings for young women until the day of their marriage. As they were about to set out, the leaseholder's wife called out: "And don't forget! Ask the rebbe to pray that we earn a decent living! And that we should bring up our children without problems!"

The horses were already straining in their harness, but she ran after the wagon and reminded her husband: "And another thing! Don't forget to ask that the cows should give plenty of milk! And the harvest — don't forget to ask him to pray that we sell the next harvest at a good profit!"

The wagon rolled out of sight and they soon arrived in Belz, where the father of the bride began to set out his list of requests — a blessing for the young couple, a request for their own livelihood, and so on — faithful to his instructions word for word.

Said Reb Shalom: "The right thing for a man undertaking a journey would be to confess his sins."

The leaseholder did not allow this remark to disturb him, and proceeded as before — the cows, and the milk, and the harvest, and ...

The tzaddik again reminded him that he should confess his sins, whether committed intentionally or unwittingly. When he saw that even now the leaseholder resumed his list unperturbed, the tzaddik assumed that he did not know what confession meant, so he began to translate for him the words of the *Vidui*, one at a time: "אָשַׁמְנוּ – We have transgressed; בָּגַדְנוּ – We have acted perfidiously" – and so on. Even this did not convince the visitor that it was time to react to the rebbe's words, and he took his leave.

On their way home the travelers lost their way in a dense forest, and eventually slithered – horses, wagon, and all – into a deep swamp. They tried to climb down, but sank in the quagmire up to the waist. The man now recalled the words of the tzaddik and they all confessed, each of them knowing his own account, and "from out of the depths," as the Psalmist says, they cried out to God. Suddenly they heard a gentile wagon-driver urging on his horses, and as soon as he reached them – without saying a word – he dragged them all, with their wagon, out of the mire. When he had brought them to a nearby inn they uttered a prayer of thanksgiving for their salvation, and asked the gentile how it was that he had suddenly come to their help.

"Then let me tell you my story," he said. "I was employed by a squire to drive his carriage and to take charge of his stables. Just my luck, and one day his two favorite horses were stolen. He immediately concluded that I had made off with them and sold them, and threw me in his dungeon for a long time. Then he decided he would do better by freeing me, so that I could search for his horses in all the markets and fairs in the district. Not that he sent me alone. I was trailed everywhere by two of his servants whose job it was to make sure I didn't run away. On the way I asked them to let me go to visit the holy man of Belz, for I had heard that he works miracles. They agreed, and came along with me. When I told him my whole sad story, he said: 'If you promise that you will always be friendly to Jews, then in a few days you will find your horses in next week's fair in such-and-such a town.' I gave him my promise, and sure enough I found my horses, just as he had said. I took them home to my master, and he not only compensated me generously for everything he had put me through, but even freed me! With the money he gave me I bought a wagon and horses of my own, and besides that I do some farming on the side. So altogether I can say that I've definitely come up in the world.

"Now just last night the holy man of Belz came to me in my dream and reminded me of my promise. Then he told me to get up quickly and to save a number of Jews who were sinking in the mud at a certain spot. To tell the truth I was a little lazy, and I didn't feel like getting out of bed in the middle of the night to go and help some Jews. But a little while later I dreamed a second time, and he said: 'Why didn't you go as I told you to? Soon they will perish out there!' So I answered: 'Right away, rabbi! I'll go right away!' But I only curled up under my quilt-cover, even more cozily than before. This time, though, when he appeared to me again in my dream, he seized me by my hair, and didn't let go until I had dressed, and harnessed the horses. I galloped off to the place he told me of, looked around for the mire — and there you were!"

◆§ *For Good Measure*

After lighting the Channukah candles, it was the custom of Reb Chaim of Zanz to take his seat next to the fireplace, where he would sit for some time, motionless, in the rapt state of *dveikus*. In awesome silence his chassidim stood about and waited — and then he would give a discourse on the mystical meanings of the festival, and finally pour wine for each of the listeners.

It once happened that during one such holy trance his son Reb Baruch, being weak, fainted. Those around hastened to splash him with water in order to help him come to, but his father remained unaware of all the excitement in the room. When his son returned to his place, pale and drenched, his father finally saw him and asked what had happened, and was told.

Then, with reference to *Vidui*, the confession which is uttered on the approach of death, Reb Chaim asked: "Did you say the confession? When I was young I also fainted several times, and each time, as soon as I began to feel unwell, I said *Vidui.*"

◆§ Grand Finale

A thousand miles south of his native Odessa, the once-famous *chazzan* Betzalel Shulsinger lay waning on his deathbed in Jerusalem for three whole days. As the evening of the third day drew near, he suddenly rallied, opened his eyes, and asked for his student cantors, his choir of *meshorerim.*

"Listen,' he said, "and I will tell you a true story. I was one of the close disciples of Reb Meir of Premishlan. On one occasion I approached him, expecting the usual greeting of *Shalom.* Instead of that, however, he quoted a phrase from a Mishnah — not as quotation, but as an expression of wonderment: בֶּאֱמֶת אָמְרוּ הַחַזָּן רוֹאֶה? [In its context of the laws of *Shabbos,* this phrase refers to the duties of a schoolteacher, the Mishnaic word for which is *chazzan.* In the way it was spoken by Reb Meir, however, it meant: 'Did the Sages really mean that the cantor can see?!'] I understood what he was hinting at. He had no doubt been told that at one stage I had sung in a theater like a common actor, and had thereby defiled my vision through having used my eyes in undesirable directions. I heard his words, and wept in repentance. So the tzaddik turned to me and said: 'Very well, then, I promise you that you will not die before you repent.'

"It seems that I was unable to die before this incident came to mind. They must be waiting Up There for my confession. In that case, my dear choirboys, please prepare yourselves to sing *Vidui — Ashamnu, Bagadnu* — with me.

And in solemn remembrance of the majestic chords to which the old *shul* in Odessa had echoed on Yom Kippur in years gone by, the *chazzan* sat up to sing his tremulous solo while the choirboys around his bed intoned their hushed harmonies. The last magical cadence rose, and then faded. Reb Betzalel bowed deeply to the great Conductor, and returned his soul in peace.

◈ One Account to Settle

A simple fellow who lived in Jerusalem suffered such agony while in the prolonged throes of death that he begged his callers to pray that God take his soul, and spare him from his misery. For a moment it would seem that welcome death was near at hand — but then it would withdraw.

Among his visitors was one who asked him to recount the story of his life. There was much that he could not recall, but he mentioned in passing that he had once been in Lyzhansk. This set his questioner thinking.

"And did you go to visit the burial place of Reb Elimelech of Lyzhansk?" he asked.

"And is it possible to visit Lyzhansk and not to go to pray at the grave of that tzaddik?" returned the ailing man.

"If so," said the other, "everything is clear. For Reb Elimelech wrote in his will that whoever passed by his grave to pray there could rest assured that he would not die without first having repented. You would be well advised to say *Vidui,* my friend, and to repent."

The sufferer did so, and died thereafter.

◈ The Soul Sees what the Law Decrees

וְאִם לֹא שָׂטִית
And if you have not strayed (5:19)

Two men once traded in partnership with the help of their wives, one of whom was more expert and active than the other. One day this woman asked her husband: "Who needs this partnership? I am livelier than that other woman, and I have a better business head than she will ever have. She is the kind who will never succeed in any sort of enterprise. Who needs her kind of help?"

Her husband acted on her advice, the partnership was dissolved, and each couple traded separately from then on.

After some time, the merchant whose wife had assumed that כֹּחִי וְעֹצֶם יָדִי עָשָׂה לִי אֶת הַחַיִל הַזֶּה — "My power and the might of my hand have acquired me this wealth" — found that his income was declining, while his former partner was growing wealthy. His wife became so obsessed with envy that she even went to the length of hiring two witnesses to testify falsely that the other woman had been unfaithful to her husband, in order that he should be obliged by law to divorce her. Everything went according to plan — except that its victim, knowing that the court's ruling was unwittingly founded on a cruel lie, asked her husband to accompany her to visit Reb Avraham Yehoshua Heschel of Apta.

Now the *rav* of Apta — who is known as the Ohev Yisrael, "the lover of his fellow Jew" — saw by divine inspiration that the poor woman who stood before him was telling the truth. But was it possible, on the strength of one's *ruach hakodesh* alone, to undo a ruling arrived at by a duly constituted rabbinical court, after it had accepted testimony which was *prima facie* valid?

He called in his son, Reb Yitzchak Meir, and said: "Working on the assumption that I am a tzaddik, people have always been giving me their *pidyon* contributions for charity. Now go out and announce that they should stop at once. Not one penny more! For my *ruach hakodesh* contradicts the laws of the Torah as laid down by a *beis din* — in which case it is not *ruach hakodesh*."

Now as soon as he uttered these words, the malicious woman and her false witnesses were seized by such a fearful trembling that they too were moved to make the journey to Apta, where they assured the tzaddik that they had conspired to ruin an innocent woman's life because of spiteful jealousy.

The tzaddik of Apta turned to his son: "Now go out and announce that people may indeed give me their *pidyon* offerings, for my *ruach hakodesh* is in harmony with the laws of the Torah."

◆§ *Inspired Efficiency*

וְכִפֶּר עָלָיו
And he shall make atonement for him (6:11)

And he shall make atonement for him: The Nazirite sinned by abstaining from wine. And if such a man is called a sinner, how much more will this be true of one who causes himself anguish by refraining from other things *(Talmud, Tractate Taanis).*

Reb Elimelech of Lyzhansk had come to Nikolsburg to spend some time at the feet of his teacher, Reb

Shmelke. He was walking down the street on *Shabbos*, when he heard someone studying Torah with the voice of one who experiences both the love and awe of Him Who gave the Torah. Entering the house quietly, he stood and watched for an hour, while the young man who was seated there — it was Reb Mordechai Bennet — was so utterly concentrated on the volume of Talmud before him that he did not even notice the presence of a stranger.

At length he paused, and Reb Elimelech approached him: "Repent, brother, repent! Return to the ways of your Maker!"

The scholar was taken aback, and answered nothing; in fact he knew that his rebbe — Reb Shmelke — was very fond of him. He therefore called on Reb Shmelke a little later, and told him that Reb Elimelech had said this thing even though he had seen him doing nothing but studying Torah.

"Let me explain," said Reb Shmelke. "You fasted this whole week through; this must have weakened you, and in some degree hampered your Torah study. And the task of a scholar such as yourself is to study — unhindered!"

◆§ *A Mission of Peace*

וְיָשֵׂם לְךָ שָׁלוֹם
And grant you peace (6:26)

David of Lelov, accompanied by his disciple Reb Yitzchak of Vorki, set out for a certain town in order to settle a dispute that had brought discord among the townsmen. The moment they arrived they said their prayers, and as soon as they had concluded, Reb David had the horses harnessed so that they could return home immediately.

"Rebbe!" asked Reb Yitzchak in amazement. "Didn't we come here in order to bring peace to this town? Why are we going home now?"

"In the course of our prayers," answered Reb David, "I said ... עֹשֶׂה שָׁלוֹם בִּמְרוֹמָיו — 'He Who makes peace in His heavens, may He make peace for us and for all Israel.' And that sufficed to bring peace upon this town."

◆§ A Burden to Shoulder

בְּכָּתֵף יִשָּׂאוּ
They shall bear it on their shoulders (7:9)

For several hours Reb Yitzchak of Vorki had been closeted with Reb Yechezkel of Kozmir, and when he came out, tears were streaming down his cheeks — but he revealed the cause to no one. Only after his passing was the following account of this meeting given by his son, Reb Yaakov David of Amshinov.

His father had come to Kozmir to consult with Reb Yechezkel as to the choice of his own final resting place. Should it be Vorki, where for many years he had served his Maker, and fired his brethren with the awe of heaven? — Or Warsaw, which he had frequently visited in the course of his many contacts and intercessions with the authorities on behalf of the Jewish community? They had agreed that when his time came he should be buried at Vorki, leaving Warsaw for his son.

And indeed, in 1868 his second son, Reb Menachem Mendel of Vorki, was stricken by a grievous illness. He was brought to Warsaw for treatment, but died there.

Now the custom in that city was that the deceased were not carried to the cemetery by shoulder, but were brought on a special wagon. Now Reb Yechiel of Alexander, one of the disciples of the tzaddik of Vorki, would not agree to this on any account. He went straight to Rabbi Beirish Maisels, the head of the local rabbinical court, and requested that he sanction the carrying of his rebbe by shoulder. The rabbi at first refused to allow such a departure from the established local custom, but when the tzaddik of Alexander begged him again to change his mind, he asked him at least to offer some hint in the Torah that would affirm that the practice he sought implied respect for a sage.

Reb Yechiel was quick to answer. "With regard to one of the Levite families we read in the Torah: כִּי עֲבֹדַת הַקֹּדֶשׁ עֲלֵהֶם בַּכָּתֵף יִשָּׂאוּ. Literally, of course, this means: 'For the sacred work devolves upon them; they shall bear their burdens by shoulder.' But we could also read these words so as to mean something else: 'Those upon whom the sacred work devolves shall be carried by shoulder...'

And the rabbi of Warsaw granted his request.

סדר בהעלתך
Sidra Beha'aloscha

◆§ Spiritual Symbiosis

עִמְדוּ וְאֶשְׁמְעָה מַה יְצַוֶּה ה׳ לָכֶם
Stand still and I shall hear what God will command concerning you (9:8)

Each of the prayer services rises to its hushed crescendo in the *Shemoneh Esreh,* and on this prayer the Baal Shem used to linger for hours on end. The other worshipers in his *beis midrash* found it difficult to wait until he completed his inspired meditations, so they used to go home to take some refreshment, and on their return they could be sure to find him standing in the same place as before. But the chassidim of stature — his closest disciples who made up the holy brotherhood which was known as the חֶבְרַיָּא קַדִּישָׁא — would wait in deference for their rebbe.

It once happened, though, that even they felt so weak that they too found it necessary to go home to eat something. They were certain that they would come back in good time — hence their surprise to find on their return that the tzaddik had already concluded his devotions. Some of the elder chassidim allowed themselves the liberty of asking him to explain why that day was so different, and he answered: "I will give you a parable. A few men were standing next to a tall tree, and one of them, whose sight was unusually keen, saw an exquisite bird at the tip of the tree. Though he very much wanted to reach up there and catch it, he had no ladder. What did he do? He stood a couple of his friends on top of each others' shoulders, with himself uppermost, reached out, and caught the bird. The men underneath him, though they had helped him catch it, knew nothing of its surpassing beauty — but without them he could not have reached it. Indeed, if the man at the bottom had decided to walk away, they would all have fallen, and the man with the keen vision would not only fail in his aspiration, but would no doubt fall and break his neck.

"Now when I say *Shemoneh Esreh,* it so happens that all manner of hidden things are revealed to me, and my consuming desire is to ascend to the level which the *Zohar* calls 'the palace of the bird's nest' — the palace in the World Above which is the abode of the Messiah. But I cannot aspire to such a lofty height unless I first stand you, my disciples, on each others' shoulders. The entire feat is thus accomplished thanks to yourselves, when you are with me in my *beis midrash,* even though you may not be aware of it. Today, when you left, I fell; having nothing more to do in *Shemoneh Esreh,* I finished off."

A chassid once commented that in the light of this explanation one can understand the verse עִמְדוּ וְאֶשְׁמְעָה מַה יְצַוֶּה ה׳ לָכֶם (literally: "And Moshe said to them, Stand still, and I shall hear what God will command concerning you"). For the verse may be taken as well to suggest that Moshe requests his disciples: "Stand here next to me, and then, by virtue of your merits, I shall be able to hear what God will command."

◆§ *Desiring Mastery vs. Mastering Desire*

הִתְאַוּוּ תַּאֲוָה
They fell a-lusting (11:4)

By no stretch of the imagination could Rabbi Enzil of Staria be termed a sympathizer of Chassidism. Once he tossed the following gibe in the direction of Reb Yehudah Zvi of Rozla: "It seems to me that to be a chassidic rebbe is just a desire like all other desires ... "

The chassidic rebbe was quick with his retort: "You are right — except that one cannot fulfill this desire before one has learned to master all one's other desires.

◆§ *Charity Begins at Home*

הֶאָנֹכִי הָרִיתִי אֵת כָּל הָעָם הַזֶּה
Did I conceive all this People? (11:12)

The son of a certain chassid came to visit Reb Yehudah Aryeh Leib of Ger, the author of *Sfas Emes,* with the complaint that his father gave him no financial support whatever. At his next visit the father was duly asked for an explanation, and he answered that he had no money.

"We read," said the tzaddik, "that Moshe Rabbeinu says to the Almighty: מֵאַיִן לִי בָּשָׂר — 'Whence should I have meat to give all this People?' But in the same breath he has just said הֶאָנֹכִי הָרִיתִי אֵת כָּל הָעָם הַזֶּה אִם אָנֹכִי יְלִדְתִּיהוּ — 'Did I conceive all this People? Did I beget them?' Now this is difficult to understand. For if the speaker wishes to argue that he has no meat, then surely it is immaterial whether he did beget the hungry People, or did not beget them. Either way, will he not still be without meat?

"But this passage proves that if a person says 'I conceived him' and 'I begat him,' then the claim of 'I have not' is insufficient. One is obliged to take pains and find ways and means to support one's son!"

☙ *It's Only Me*

וְהָאִישׁ מֹשֶׁה עָנָו מְאֹד
And the man Moshe was very humble (12:3)

Hearing that the chassidic book *Noam Elimelech* was written by a disciple of Reb Dov Ber of Mezritch, a certain prominent *misnaged* chose to give unmistakable expression to his sentiments toward "the Sect" by depositing it under the bench he sat on. Nevertheless, when he was once visited by Reb Shneur Zalman of Liadi, he asked his guest to describe for him the character of its author, Reb Elimelech of Lyzhansk.

"Rabbi," said the guest, "even if you were to put the author himself under your bench, he would not say a word."

❀ ❀ ❀

Reb Elimelech once said that he was without a doubt assured of a place in the World to Come. For when his time came to go up to the World Above and he would be asked if he had studied Torah to the best of his ability, he would answer "No"; if he had served God fully through worship, he would say "No"; if he had done his quota of mitzvos and good deeds, he would say "No". Then they would say: "If so, then you are telling us the truth — and in that case you deserve to be rewarded in the World to Come."

❀ ❀ ❀

"Do you know," he would ask, "why people are always coming to me with all kinds of requests, whether for a cure for their children, or for a livelihood for themselves, or whatever? It is because through my sins I have brought suffering into the world. That is why they cry out to me: 'Melech, give us a livelihood! Melech, give us children! It's all your fault that we are lacking these things, so it's up to you to make good what you've spoiled!"

◆§ *Camouflage*

In his youth, Reb Menachem Mendel of Vitebsk studied under Reb Dov Ber, the Maggid of Mezritch. By the time he was ten years old his mastery of the legal intricacies of the Talmud amazed all who saw him, and the Maggid was very fond of him. One *Shabbos* morning he was standing at the door of his study, holding it open for a moment, and as he looked out he saw his young pupil walking up and down the adjoining room in the highest of spirits.

"Mendel!" he called. "How many pages of *Gemara* have you studied today?"

"Six," answered the prodigy.

The Maggid spoke on as if he were thinking aloud: "Let us see. If after six pages of *Gemara* one is so excited that one's hat slips like that over one ear, how many pages does it take for a hat to topple off altogether? ... "

Weeping in remorse, the boy ran to the rebbe's room, knocked on the door, and said: "Rebbe, advise me what to do, for it is true that my studies have made me a little conceited."

"Have no fear," the Maggid reassured him. "Let us travel, you and I, to the Baal Shem Tov, and he will teach us both the path in which we should walk."

They set out on a Tuesday for Mezhibuzh, and arrived on Friday, in good time before *Shabbos*. The Maggid went straight to the Baal Shem Tov to receive his greeting of *Shalom,* while his pupil tarried until he had washed and tidied himself — and indeed he maintained this habit into adulthood, being meticulous about his outward appearance at all times. The Baal Shem Tov, as always, was ready to receive the *Shabbos* with its lyrical prayers of welcome some hours before sunset, but though he stood in his place in the *beis midrash,* he waited some two hours until the boy arrived.

He did not greet him, though, until *Shabbos* had passed. After marking the conclusion of the Day of Rest by the recitation of *Havdalah* he sat down with his pipe, called for young Mendel, and told him a story. But this was no ordinary story, for every episode in it contained a hint of the events which befell its young listener from the moment of his birth until the time of his death many years later in *Eretz Yisrael.* The boy did not listen alone, for both the Maggid and Reb Yaakov Yosef of Polonnoye stood with him. One of them later said that he had understood the whole story while the other confessed that he had understood only half — and the traditions among elder chassidim are divided as to which of these statements is to be attributed to which of these venerable disciples of the Baal Shem Tov. The boy, at any rate, said that he understood that part of the story which related to his life until that day.

The Baal Shem Tov later commented to the Maggid that his pupil appeared to be truthfully humble. And, in fact, to the end of his days Reb Menachem Mendel was to sign הַשָּׁפָל בֶּאֱמֶת — "he who is in fact lowly."

When he reached adulthood, he said that he now comprehended the whole of that story. It happened once while he was still in Vitebsk that he became so ill that he utterly lost the faculty of speech. The wailing of the chassidim, who were fearful that they were about to lose their rebbe, aroused him, and he said: "Have no fear! From the story that the Baal Shem Tov told me I know that one day I am still going to be in *Eretz Yisrael.*"

And so it was. He recovered, and set out for the Holy Land. Passing through Polonnoye, he took up lodgings in an inn, lit up his pipe, removed his *gartl* — the belt which is worn by chassidim for prayer and as an expression of reverence on certain other occasions — and went off to pay his respects to the celebrated tzaddik who lived there, Reb Yaakov Yosef. When the local chassidim saw with what a free and easy air he seemed to be making this awesome visit, they felt it to be their duty to warn him: "Rebbe, we think you ought to know in your own interest that Reb Yaakov Yosef is likely to express his displeasure when he sees such a lack of deference!"

The visitor ignored their advice, and when he spoke to Reb Yaakov Yosef he was received warmly, and was asked whether he understood the story that he had heard from the mouth of the Baal Shem Tov. When he answered that he did, the next question was: "And which part of the story are you up to now?"

Reb Menachem Mendel sighed: "I have already used up more than half of the story."

"And do you know," asked his host, "that there is a hint in the story that you would be visiting me?"

"I do," replied Reb Menachem Mendel, "and that is why I passed through Polonnoye, so that I should have the honor of calling on you."

At length, after a free and cordial exchange of ideas, Reb Yaakov Yosef walked his younger guest to his lodgings.

The local chassidim were curious, so finally some of the elder disciples of Reb Yaakov Yosef broached the question: "What kind of a man is this who dared to pay a visit to you, rebbe, without his *gartl,* and with a long pipe in his mouth, and with silver-threaded shoelaces in his shoes?"

"Come and hear a parable," said the tzaddik. "Once upon a time there was a king who owned a priceless gem, but he lived in constant fear lest thieves discover his best hiding places. What, then, did he do? He hid it in the toilet, for he knew that it would occur to no one to expect to find a treasure *there.* And so it is with Reb Mendel. He is most lowly in his own eyes, and is afraid that whatever visible expression he gives his humility may be misinterpreted in this world of falsehood, thereby nourishing the evil in the cosmos instead of the good. And that is why he has chosen to conceal his humility in a place of filth, namely — pride!"

◆§ *A Vision Earned*

בַּחֲלוֹם אֲדַבֶּר בּוֹ
In a dream do I speak to him (12:6)

Reb Eliezer of Dzikov, the son of Reb Naftali of Ropshitz, dreamed once that he was being shown to the Garden of Eden. He was taken up a luminous hill and found himself in a splendid courtyard, wherein stood a palace built of scintillating jewels. Asking who was the man looking out of the window of the house, he was told that this was Reb Elimelech of Lyzhansk, and to him all of this opulence belonged, though he was master of much besides. Reb Eliezer gazed upon his face, the face of an angel, and experienced a rare moment of spiritual bliss.

Early in the morning he went off to tell his father of his wondrous dream, but Reb Naftali was loath to believe him — until he described the features of the face that he had seen.

"My son," he said, "it is true that it is my rebbe Reb Elimelech that you have described. But a man has to have reached a very lofty level before he is able to see Reb Elimelech."

"What does 'level' mean if not serving God through prayer and the study of Torah?" countered his son. "Then what *do* I do?"

"True again, my son," said Reb Naftali, "that you have reached a certain level. Still, in order to see Reb Elimelech one has to climb even higher. Could it be, for example, that you did someone a great favor, and because of that you were granted this beautiful gift?"

Reb Eliezer recalled that a few weeks earlier he had encountered one of the grandsons of Reb Elimelech making his rounds to collect alms, and he was sorely in need of a warm garment. Reb Eliezer had then taken off his own fine fleece coat and had given it: a dual gift — for while it gave the body warmth, it gave the man esteem.

"Now," exclaimed his father, "it is clear that you did in fact see Reb Elimelech, and that you deserved to see what you saw! For Reb Elimelech asked the Almighty that his descendants should be reduced to begging, so that they should remain righteous, and he retains a liking for anyone who helps them without indignity."

◆§ *Leaving it to His Discretion*

בְּכָל בֵּיתִי נֶאֱמָן הוּא
For he is trusted in My house (12:7)

Reb Nachum of Stefanesti, the son of Reb Yisrael of Ruzhin, once said of his brother, Reb David Moshe of Chortkov: "As soon as he opens his Book of *Psalms* and starts reading *Tehillim,* the Almighty says to him, 'David Moshe, my son! I am now entrusting the whole world into your hands; do with it as you will.' Now if that were to happen to me, then I would most certainly know what to do with the world. But my brother is such a faithful servant that he returns it to the Almighty exactly as he was given it ..."

☙ To Give Each Man His Due

וּמַדּוּעַ לֹא יְרֵאתֶם לְדַבֵּר בְּעַבְדִּי בְמֹשֶׁה
Why then were you not afraid to speak against my servant Moshe? (12:8)

Rabbi Aryeh Leib Heller, the author of *Ketzos HaChoshen,* was an opponent of Chassidism, and it so happened that a great number of chassidim of Reb Yaakov Yitzchak of Lublin lived in his hometown, Staria. If the truth were to be told, there was no great love lost between the two sides, and the chassidim did not show him the respect that is due to a *mara de'asra,* the local rabbinic authority. The rabbi, for his part, was in the habit of reproving these nonconformist townsfolk for their chassidic customs, which he held to contravene the dictates of the Code of Jewish Law. He felt that it was improper that his rulings should be ignored, and eventually pronounced a ban of temporary excommunication on them, which was to last thirty days. Obedient to this *shamta,* the bulk of the local population promptly severed all contact with them. The chassidim put their heads together, and decided to set out to Lublin, there to spend the few weeks in the heartwarming company of their rebbe, until with the passage of time they would find themselves a little less unwelcome in their own hometown.

Now the custom in Lublin was that the *shammes* would bring the rebbe — who is known as the Chozeh, or Seer, of Lublin — a list of all the recent arrivals who were waiting to be greeted by him; the rebbe would then indicate who was to be invited to enter his study for a private *yechidus.* When the group from Staria arrived, the Chozeh told the *shammes* that they would have to wait to receive their greeting for two weeks and so-and-so many days — exactly as long as it would take for the *shamta* to expire ...

When the time finally passed, they came together to speak to the Chozeh, who said: "We read in the Torah that the Almighty rebukes Aharon and Miriam with the question, 'Why then were you not afraid to speak against my servant Moshe?' Since these words appear to be repetitious, Rashi comments: *'Against My servant —*

even if he were not Moshe; *against Moshe* — even if he were not My servant.' Now the first half of this comment is understandable. But such a Moshe who is not 'My servant' — why should one stand in awe of *him?*

"And the answer is as follows. The House of Israel is made up of two categories of people: those whose main concern is to be expert and punctilious as regards every word in the Code of Jewish Law, and those whose first love is to cleave to God in devoted *dveikus*, serving him not only in prayer, but also — as is explained at length in *Duties of the Heart* — in the manner of their walking and sitting, lying down and rising, their eating and their drinking. This, then, is what Rashi means. One is commanded to stand in awe of Moshe — the great legalistic scholar — even if he is not 'My servant' in the sense of having unceasing communion with God; likewise in awe of 'My servant' — who delves rather into the mysteries of the Torah, in order to draw closer to his Maker — even though he may not be a Moshe in his mastery of the legalistic side of the Torah. Both are to be held in awe.

"And if this be the case, consider now the *rav* of your town, who is a veritable pillar of the revealed Law. *Why were you not afraid to speak against him?*"

סדר שלח

SIDRA SH'LACH

◆§ *Unfinished Symphony*

שְׁלַח לְךָ אֲנָשִׁים וְיָתֻרוּ
Send men to spy out (13:2)

Reb Yaakov Yitzchak (the Yid HaKadosh) of Pshischah once fell violently ill while on a visit to his rebbe, Reb Yaakov Yitzchak (the Chozeh) of Lublin. His son hurried to the Chozeh to ask him to intercede in heaven on his father's behalf, and received the following answer.

"In connection with the twelve spies whom Moshe Rabbeinu sent to the Land of Canaan, it is written: 'Send men to spy out.' Now it sometimes happens that the Heavenly Court sees that a certain Jew has completed the tasks which were divinely allocated for him during his stay in This World, that he has elevated whatever it was his duty to elevate. In such a case, the Almighty *sends* him willing disciples, men who are eager to *spy out* the way in which they should go. When a person is thus given a fresh task, he is enabled thereby to continue living in This World."

And so indeed it was. The Yid HaKadosh was immediately restored to health, and from that time on he became the spiritual mentor of thousands of his fellows.

☙ *The Wondrous Ways of Heaven (i)*

וַיָּבֹא עַד חֶבְרוֹן
And he came to Hebron (13:22)

And he came to Hebron: Caleb went there in order to pray at the graves of the Patriarchs *(Rashi).*

An upright young merchant once set out from his home in Vilkomir to buy up stocks of tobacco in Niezhin. Though not a chassid himself, he was on very friendly terms with a celebrated chassid by the name of Reb Yaakov Kaidaner, so before he left he called on Reb Yaakov, who said: "My friend! Even though you are not one of our chassidic brotherhood, I would still ask you to visit the grave of a renowned tzaddik who is buried in Niezhin, Reb Dov Ber of Lubavitch, the son of Reb Shneur Zalman of Liadi."

The young man gave his promise, was bidden farewell, and set out for a journey that was to take six months, for in those days there was not yet any railway train that could clatter its way all the distance from Vilkomir in Lithuania to Niezhin in White Russia. While he was far away trying to do business, his wife became so desperately ill that the doctors despaired of her life. One evening she lost consciousness, and though three expert physicians sat by her bedside all night, there was nothing they could do to help her. Then at ten in the morning her illness loosened its hold on her, she began to regain her strength, and within a month, without the aid of doctors or medicaments, she was strong and robust. Her friends were amazed, but not nearly so much as were her doctors.

When her husband finally came home, he barely

managed to put his nose inside the door when he ran off in agitation to the home of his friend Reb Yaakov, without so much as stopping to take off his overcoat.

"Now I ask you," said Reb Yaakov, "is this the way to do things? After you have been away from home for over half a year you don't even stay there a little while to gladden the hearts of your wife and little ones, but off you run to say hello to me?! There must be something behind your behavior, something remarkable."

"And indeed," affirmed the other, "something remarkable did bring me to you, something of a marvel. You see, my business dealings out there fell through, and I not only lost everything I owned, but as well got myself deep into debt through all kinds of unfortunate circumstances that befell me on the way. To make things worse, throughout all that time I was in a state of fear: I seemed to imagine that my wife was desperately ill. When I arrived in Niezhin I recalled my promise to you, and went to the local *mikveh* to immerse myself in preparation for my visit to the holy resting place of the tzaddik. Though all the way there my warm clothes had sufficed to keep out the bitter cold, as soon as I came close to where he lay I was overcome by an awesome fear, the like of which I have never experienced. My hair stood on end, and despite my warm clothes I trembled in a feverish cold. It even occurred to me to flee from that fearful place, but then I thought: 'No evil is going to befall me on account of the tzaddik who lies here. Why should I flee from the presence of the tzaddik?' So I began instead to read the quotations from the *Zohar*, and the chapters from *Psalms*, and other passages from *Maavar Yabok*, which are inscribed there on a tablet, on the wall of the enclosure which is built around the grave. And while I read, I wept rivers of tears. Then I wrote out two notes which expressed my special requests — one *kvitl* bearing a prayer for the welfare of my family and myself, and the other especially for my wife, for my heart was uneasy. The moment I put those two *pidyonos* on the grave, I was overcome with a most exquisite joy, the like of which I had never known before. It was just as I imagine the flavor of the Garden of Eden to be. It took me two full hours to tear myself away from that bliss, and to depart from there with a heart full of gladness and peace.

"That joy accompanied me all the way home, and when I arrived, I was told the whole story of what my wife had been through, including the events of that long, long night that ended only at ten in the morning. I asked what date this had been. Sure enough, it was the very day on which, at ten o'clock in the morning, I had placed the *pidyonos* on the resting place of the tzaddik. You cannot be surprised, therefore, that when I heard all of this, I did not even take off my greatcoat, but ran as fast as I could to tell you, my friend, of the wondrous ways of heaven.

"I have only one thing to add. If your rebbes are so alive and luminous *after* they have departed from This World, then they must be even greater and even holier in their lifetime!"

"Not so," answered Reb Yaakov. "For our Sages have taught: 'Tzaddikim are greater in their death than in their life.' "

◈ The Wondrous Ways of Heaven (ii)

Reb Moshe Teitelbaum of Ujhely, the author of *Yismach Moshe,* saw that his nine-year-old son was so ill that he was in mortal danger. He prayed to heaven for mercy, and sent a number of righteous men to Lyzhansk to do likewise at the resting place of Reb Elimelech. He instructed them that when they arrived at the entrance to the cemetery they should say: "We hereby promise to give a copper coin to charity for the benefit of the soul which will go and inform the soul of Reb Elimelech that we have come to his resting place to pray to the Almighty." Then, he went on to explain, "All the souls that are then in the vicinity will hasten to pass on the message to the tzaddik, for it is not at all times that a man's soul is to be found near the place of his burial; and the souls of the departed are always eager to 'earn' the coin which is given in the World Below for the greater elevation of their souls. You are then to approach his grave, where you will pray for my son. And mark well what time it is that you pray there."

The chassidim of course followed their rebbe's instructions exactly.

Meanwhile, back in Ujhely, the little boy suddenly sat up out of his feverish stupor and said: "Father! With God's help I'm going to be well now! For just this moment I was visited by a venerable old man" — and the description he gave exactly matched the appearance of Reb Elimelech — "and he blessed me, and promised me that I would get better!"

His father looked at his watch, and saw there — as it transpired some days later when his chassidim returned — exactly the same time that they had seen on their watches that day in far-off Lyzhansk.

◌§ *To be Cruel to be Kind*

וַיֹּצִיאוּ דִּבַּת הָאָרֶץ
And they spread an evil report of the Land (13:32)

From the example of the spies sent by Moshe Rabbeinu we may observe how great is the power of slander *(Talmud, Tractate Arachin).*

Before he became renowned as a tzaddik, Reb Yisrael of Koznitz was a tutor in a well-to-do household. As Pessach drew near, and it was time for him to go home, his employer approached him with a suggestion.

"I would advise you," he said, "to come with me to Chenshin for the *Shabbos* before the festival, and there we will be able to hear the discourse which will be given in honor of *Shabbos HaGadol* by the rabbi there. They say he is quite a scholar. Besides, the rabbi's *mechutan* will be there, and you will be able to ride back to your hometown in his carriage, instead of having to plod all the way on foot."

Reb Yisrael thanked him for his suggestion, and on the eve of *Shabbos HaGadol* they called on the rabbi of Chenshin to pay their respects, as too did all the worthies of the town. The householder mentioned to the rabbi that his *melamed* was outstanding in both scholarship and piety. But when the host took one look at the *melamed* — a man of unprepossessing presence, short of stature, though with a pleasant face and kindly eyes — he disdained him. When he had nevertheless given his hand in greeting, he asked the newcomer where he came from.

 Reb Yisrael answered that he came from Apta, and his employer whispered to the rabbi that his *melamed's* father was Reb Shabsi the bookbinder.

The rabbi could not restrain the offensive jest that immediately sprang to his mind, and at the expense of his guest's self-respect he allowed himself to pun on the similarity between קֹרַח (Korach, the rebel who was swallowed up by the earth) and כּוֹרֵךְ *(korech,* which means "bookbinder").

"In that case," he said expansively, "we are related! For I am Levi, and the descendants of Korach are Levites, too. And didn't you say this fellow's father is a *korech?"*

The *melamed's* face dropped, and he left.

Now the time-honored custom in learned Torah circles is that when a scholar advances a legal hypothesis before an academic audience, any listener who finds a fallacy in his reasoning is allowed to interject and challenge him. The next day, then, the *melamed* went along to the *beis midrash* to hear the same rabbi's discourse. But every novel deduction that he proposed, the young visitor refuted. Whenever the rabbi attempted to reconstruct his thesis, the stranger rebutted him again — until the rabbi lost his dispassionate objectivity, took offense, and left in a huff. It was clear that he held his congregants to be at fault for allowing this young upstart to show up his failings in public. And Reb Yisrael, seeing the vengeful way the wind was blowing, promptly left the *beis midrash,* and hid.

On *Motzaei Shabbos,* though, when the Day of Rest had passed, he called on the rabbi alone in order to make the peace — but the rabbi refused to forgive him. At this point the future Maggid of Koznitz was forced to reveal to him that he had acted as he had during the discourse for the rabbi's own good. For when he had offended him and insulted him the day before, the Heavenly Court had sentenced him to death, and only through the efforts of the Maggid had the Court agreed to avert the decree — by substituting the punishment of being shamed in public.

⸎ Some are More Equal

A God-fearing young scholar from Apta, the son of an honest workman, was conscripted to serve in the ranks of the brutal battalions of those times. On Friday afternoon, when Reb Avraham Yehoshua Heschel (the Ohev Yisrael) was resting on a seat just outside the local bathhouse before returning home, he turned to the prominent citizens who were sitting around him, and appealed to their finer feelings: perhaps they could find a way to ransom this young man from the violent fate that awaited him?

They were all convinced readily enough — until one of their number spoke up: "I sure don't know why you, rebbe, should exert yourself so much to ransom this young fellow, what's-his-name's son. After all, if what's-his-name's son is missing from our town, won't our town be a town any more?"

And that comment was enough to cool off the enthusiasm of the little group.

The tzaddik was taken aback. He rose and re-entered the bathhouse, while the speaker headed for home. On his way there, however, he was gored by an ox, and was carried home in a critical state. When his family heard from bystanders that it seemed that he had offended the rebbe, they hastened to appease him, and met him as he came out of the bathhouse.

The Ohev Yisrael assured them: "I did not punish him, God forbid, nor did I pray that he be punished — especially since I have been in the bathhouse all this time, and as you know one may not say a single word of prayer in there. To tell you the truth, though, when he made his comment — 'If what's-his-name's son is missing from our town, won't our town be a town any more?' — the thought occurred to me: 'If *this* citizen is missing from our town, won't our town be a town any more?' I made every effort to prevent that thought from occupying my mind, but I had no choice in the matter. It was heaven's will that it be there."

And a short time later, as a result of his wounds, that citizen was in fact missing from the town.

◆§ A Venomous Tongue

It once happened that the sons of Reb Yaakov Yitzchak (the Yid HaKadosh) of Pshischah were afraid to leave Lvov, because they had no passports. One night a certain rich merchant introduced himself to them and put himself at their service — he invited them to his home for *Shabbos* and offered to conduct them without fear or hindrance to wherever they needed to go. And, in the course of their conversation, he recounted an incident that involved their father many years earlier.

"I was once a tutor in a household not far from Lublin," he began. "During one of my visits there to see Reb Yaakov Yitzchak, the Chozeh of Lublin, I encountered another visitor, Reb Kissele by name, who said all kinds of slanderous things to the Chozeh about your father. And how did I come to hear this *lashan hara?* Well, they were closeted together in a room, but I hid behind a wardrobe in order to overhear the conversation. I was so overwrought by what I heard there that I couldn't restrain myself. I bounded out from my hiding place, grasped the *tefillin* of the Chozeh which were then on the table (for he was wearing the *tefillin* of Rabbeinu Tam at the time), and I said: 'I hereby swear, as I hold this sacred object in my hand, that every word this man is saying is an unspeakable lie!'

"Reb Kissele left the room in a hurry, and the Chozeh thanked me for my rude interruption. Then he went on: 'For the last forty years Satan has been guarding Reb Kissele from even thinking an improper thought, so that his credibility should be such that I should now be prepared to believe what he said about the Yid HaKadosh!'

"Now your father saw all of this through Divine Inspiration, and in a few minutes the word spread that he had arrived. I ran ahead and told him the whole story, and he gave me his blessing for success. And indeed, from that day on I am a rich man, for God prospers whatever enterprise I put my hand to.

"And now tonight your father appeared to me in a dream and told me that you were here in my town,and that you were in a fix. Do come to my home for *Shabbos*,

I beg you; all your needs I will take care of, with God's help, and then I will see you safely on your way."

◆§ Rose-Colored Spectacles

טוֹבָה הָאָרֶץ מְאֹד מְאֹד
The Land is very very good (14:7)

Year by year Reb Shmuel Abba of Zichlin would send many thousands of rubles to *Eretz Yisrael* for the paupers there, and in addition, a separate sum every three months for a family for which he retained a particular affection — the children of Reb Moshe of Lelov.

One of his chassidim once returned from the Holy Land with a letter for his rebbe written by Rabbi Meir Auerbach, the author of *Imrei Binah,* who had formerly been head of the rabbinical court in Kalisz, and was now a prominent *rav* in Jerusalem. In the letter this sage expressed surprise that money should be sent especially for a family that did not seem to invest their time in holy pursuits.

The tzaddik of Zichlin read the letter and said: "It will all become clear to Rabbi Meir in due course ... "

Some time later a wealthy chassid called Reb Leib Koshmirk made the voyage to *Eretz Yisrael.* When he visited Rabbi Meir, he was asked to call in again in order to take a letter to his rebbe on his return home. When he duly came again, Rabbi Meir told him that this letter was an expression of regret and apology for his earlier remarks.

Reb Leib was curious: "If I may ask, rabbi, what did you think then, and what makes you now think otherwise?"

The scholar explained: "A few weeks after I had written my first letter, an old man appeared to me in a dream and rebuked me. 'How dare you,' he demanded, 'write slanderous comments to a tzaddik about the holy children of Reb Moshe of Lelov?' So I protested in my dream: 'But I see various faults in them!' He answered: 'That is only because you are lacking in humility. Ifyou manage one day to acquire that attribute, you will find all kinds of positive qualities in them. For after the other spies had slandered the Holy Land, Yehoshua and Caleb insisted: טוֹבָה הָאָרֶץ מְאֹד מְאֹד. Literally, this means *The Land is very, very good.* But at the same time that verse reminds one of a Mishnah which says מְאֹד מְאֹד הֱוֵי שְׁפַל רוּחַ — *Be very, very lowly of spirit.* You see, when a person reaches the level of humility, the מְאֹד מְאֹד, of which the Mishnah speaks, then he sees only מְאֹד מְאֹד טוֹבָה הָאָרֶץ — he sees only that the Land is very, very good, and sees no evil there, God forbid!'

"I awoke from my dream," concluded Rabbi Meir Auerbach, "and recalled the letter I had written to the tzaddik of Zichlin. I then worked steadily on myself for a long time with the aim of becoming more and more humble — and now, in the very same children of Reb Moshe of Lelov, I can see all kinds of positive and attractive qualities."

◆§ *How to Spell the Name of God*

וַיֹּאמֶר ה׳ סָלַחְתִּי כִּדְבָרֶיךָ
And God said: I have forgiven according to your word (14:20)

The Yid HaKadosh of Pshischah once related the following episode from his childhood.

"When I was a little boy, still being taught the *aleph-beis* by my *melamed*, I learned a lesson to last a lifetime: that when two people sit together over a glass of vodka, and each of them is willing to play down his ego for the sake of his friend, and neither of them considers himself higher than the other — then the Almighty forgives them all their sins.

"You see, one day I asked my *melamed:* 'What is one dot?' And he answered: 'The letter *yud.*' I asked again: 'And what about two dots?' So he said: 'Two *yuds* spell out the holy Name of God.'

"Some days later I saw a colon in a book, and asked him whether this too spelled the Name of God. So he answered: 'There is an easy way to tell. If you see these two *yuds* on a level, neither trying to raise itself up over its comrade, then you have the holy Name of God. But if you have the same two dots on *top* of each other, that is definitely no holy Name.'

"From that I gathered that two Jews who meet over a glass, neither of them considering himself superior to the other, together constitute the Name of God. For the word for glass, כּוֹס, is made up of the initial letters of וַיֹּאמֶר סָלַחְתִּי כִּדְבָרֶךָ — 'And He said: I have forgiven according to your word.' But the second word of the verse is still missing — the Name of God. However, when these two Jews meet over their glass of vodka in the way we've been talking about, then *they* make up the Name of God, as we said before. And now we have the verse in full: וַיֹּאמֶר ה׳ סָלַחְתִּי כִּדְבָרֶךָ — 'And God said: I have forgiven according to your word.'

"You see, then, how it is that when two Jews meet the way they should, the Almighty forgives them all their sins!"

◈§ *A Perceptive Eye*

רֵאשִׁית עֲרִסֹתֵכֶם
The first of your dough (15:20)

Reb Meirke of Mir, one of the chassidim of Reb Mordechai of Lechovitch, once interrupted a journey in order to enter an inn to say his prayers. While he was there a whole caravan of wagons arrived, full of itinerant paupers with their wives and little waifs. Reb Meirke saw one man in their midst, of old and venerable appearance, whose face bespoke a rare purity of mind. As he watched him closely, the inkeeper's wife placed bread and other food on the table, and while the other poor folk all grabbed their slices to allay their hunger, that old pauper walked deliberately over to the water basins, and examined a dipper carefully to see if it was suitable for *netilas yadayim.* Before washing his hands, however, he took up the slice of bread over which he was due in a moment to say the blessing *HaMotzi* — but he immediately laid it down, took instead some other bread that was there, and sat down to eat.

The paupers all left the inn soon after, and this old man left with them. But throughout his prayers and his evening meal, Reb Meir could not stop thinking about that aged beggar. *Why did he not eat that slice of bread?*

He had to find out. He approached the landlady and asked: "Excuse me, but when did you bake that bread?"

"Why yesterday or the day before," she replied.

"And do you recall," he continued, "whether you remembered at the time to separate the tithe of *challah* from the dough?"

"Woe is me!" exclaimed the woman. "I forgot to take off the tithe!"

It was now clear to Reb Meirke that this old man was

 divinely inspired. He immediately harnessed his horses and made all haste to catch up to that ragged crew, whom he found soon enough — though his man was nowhere to be seen.

"Where is that old man who was with you?" he asked.

"Why should you ask after that crazy old fellow?" they answered. "He tagged on to us a few weeks ago, and he travels wherever we travel, and sleeps wherever we sleep — but he behaves as if he was out of his mind. Look, sometimes he leaves us for a while and stands alone for some time among the bushes in the forest. And once, in midwinter, when he saw a lake frozen over, he broke the ice and went for a dip in that freezing cold water."

When Reb Meirke now followed the direction in which they pointed, he came upon this strange man standing under a tree, entranced in his thoughts, his face burning like a brand.

"Rebbe, bless me!" he exclaimed.

The pauper asked him for a copper coin, and then gave his blessing.

When in due course Reb Meirke again visited Lechovitch to see his rebbe, Reb Mordechai, and told him the whole story, the tzaddik said: "How fortunate you are! For the man who gave you his blessing was none other than the saintly Reb Leib Sarahs!"

❀ ❀ ❀

This same Reb Meirke once lost his way while traveling alone through a forest. As evening fell he spotted a house with a stable next to it, and on entering the house found no one at home but a woman who was busy cooking.

"Is there room here to lodge for the night?" he asked.

"Most certainly," she said.

But when the owners of the house came home later at night, he saw at once that they were a gang of murderers. Nor was he at all reassured to overhear the women telling them: "We have a very worthwhile guest ... "

There was no chance to escape; every door and every window was locked. He therefore found himself in a quiet corner, and as he recited *Vidui,* wept over his con-

fession with the honest tears of a man who is nearing his end. When they had finished their rude meal, they pounced on him from all sides and bound him hand and foot, ready for the slaughter.

"Open up, there!" a raucous voice snarled at the window.

The murderers were so alarmed by the insistent battering on the shutters that they were afraid to oblige. But the cold was bitter outside. The impatient callers broke down the door, and a noisy crowd of sturdy Russian merchants, who had also lost their way, burst their way in. In a flash they gathered what was going on before their eyes. A couple of them unbound the poor victim, while the others seized the murderers and trussed them up. At daybreak they lifted them on to their wagons and drove off to the nearest town, where they handed them over to the local gendarmerie.

"You wont't believe this," they said to Reb Meirke, "but we often take this road, and know it well. In fact we have never lost our way around these parts. But today for some funny reason we somehow got mixed up and strayed from the highway, until we landed here. It is clearly the finger of God, so that we should be able to save you from death."

When Reb Meirke next visited Reb Mordechai of Lechovitch, no sooner had he appeared in the doorway than his rebbe said: "It's all because of you that I couldn't sleep that night. But thanks to the fact that you once gave a coin to Reb Leib Sarahs, and received his blessing, those merchants lost their way and arrived out there just in time to save you."

☙ *Memory and Piety*

לְמַעַן תִּזְכְּרוּ
In order that you may remember (15:40)

A scholarly chassid once came to Kotsk and complained to Reb Menachem Mendel of weakness of memory in his studies.

"Why, the Torah itself gives us a *sgulah* to improve the memory," said the tzaddik. And he went on to quote excerpts from two adjacent verses in the *Shema*, omitting the words that follow them in order to make his point. "It is written ... וְלֹא תָתוּרוּ אַחֲרֵי לְבַבְכֶם וְאַחֲרֵי עֵינֵיכֶם

 !לְמַעַן תִּזְכְּרוּ — 'You shall not stray after your hearts and after your eyes ... *in order that you may remember!"*

◆§ *Memory and Modesty*

It was an ordinary weekday, but Reb Yitzchak Meir of Ger — then still living in Warsaw — had invited all of his closest chassidim to a festive meal, and he sat radiant at the head of the long table in his *Shabbos* garb. When asked for an explanation, he said: "In my childhood I once visited Reb Yisrael, the Maggid of Koznitz. There were all kinds of learned folk there, and he asked whether anyone present could clarify a certain problematic commentary by *Tosafos* on the Talmudic tractate *Bava Metzia.* No one was able to answer. I jumped up and said: 'This passage means so-and-so.' The Maggid gave me a gentle slap on the cheek and said: 'When no one else knows the answer, one doesn't jump forward and give it!' I immediately forgot the explanation I had just given, and was never able to recall it — *until today.* And that is why I am celebrating."

◆§ *An Unforgettable Memory*

The sons of Reb Menachem Mendel of Lubavitch, who is known as the Tzemach Tzedek, were once sitting with a group of chassidim, exchanging reminiscences of their father. Reb Shmuel, later his successor in Lubavitch, recounted the following, for example: "A certain scholar and I were once wrestling with a complex Talmudic problem when my father, who had been sitting in the adjoining room, joined us, and explained it so beautifully that we thought he had just been working on it himself. When he had completed his exposition he mentioned that it was thirty-five years since he had last thought over this problem."

Another son, Reb Yehudah Leib, later rebbe in Kopust, rejoined: "Why, do you folk think that the marvel is that he remembered what he had thought thirty-five years earlier? Not at all! The marvel is that he remembered that in the course of those thirty-five years this thought had not occupied his mind. From this we see that all his thoughts of thirty-five years were preserved in his memory to the point that he was able to say what he had thought and what he had not thought in the course of that period."

סדר קרח
sidra korach

An Unintentional Compliment

ומדוע תתנשאו
Why do you raise yourselves up? (16:3)

The chassid who served as the *shammes* of Reb Yitzchak of Vorki once recalled that when he had accompanied the rebbe on one of his many missions to Warsaw for the public good, they had returned in the evening only to find their hotel door besmirched from top to bottom with all manner of insults and abuse against the rebbe. From sheer embarrassment the *shammes* did not know which way to look, but the rebbe reassured him: "Do not allow this to dampen your spirits. For I learned a lesson on this subject from the *Ilui* ['genius' — so was Reb Yitzchak in the habit of referring to his teacher, Reb Avraham Moshe, the son of Reb Simchah Bunem of Pshischah]. My teacher used to point out that those who foment controversy always slander that very attribute of character about which their victim is most vigilant. In support of this observation he used to cite the case of Korach, whose complaint to Moshe Rabbeinu was: 'Why do you raise yourselves up over the congregation of God?' — as if he were arrogant — whereas the Torah itself testifies that 'The man Moshe was very humble, more so than all the men on the face of the earth."

A Painful Paradox

Though he was emphatically anything but a chassid, a certain sage was so bothered by his problem that he decided to pose it to Reb Yaakov Yitzchak, the Chozeh of Lublin.

"Why, rebbe," he asked, "should so many thousands flock to you from all sides? What can they see here? And why don't they come to me? For am I not a greater scholar than yourself?"

"To tell you the truth," confided the Chozeh placidly, "I am quite as amazed as you are. For I know my true worth. Who am I, what am I, that people should come to me in search of ways to approach their Maker? And why, in fact, should they not go to visit yourself, whom I know to be a scholar of unquestioned repute, a veritable Mount Sinai in the knowledge of Torah?

"But perhaps here lies the catch. Because I am surprised that people come to me, that is *why* they come to me; and because you are surprised that they do not come to you, that is why, rabbi, they do not come to you ... "

◆§ *I Cannot Tell a Lie*

During the time that Reb Yaakov Yitzchak (the Chozeh) was rebbe in Lublin, the city's rabbinical seat was occupied by Rabbi Azriel Horovitz, whose logical acumen was so invincible that he was nicknamed "the iron-headed." He made it his business to constantly bother the Chozeh with all kinds of questions, but especially with the charge that though he himself knew that he was not really a rebbe, he nevertheless continued to draw a large following after him and to teach them his ways.

"But what can I do about it," argued the Chozeh, "if they all make the journey here of their own accord?"

"Simple," said the rabbi. "Next *Shabbos* announce to your followers that you are not a rebbe, and then they will leave you alone and stop coming to you."

Sure enough, the tzaddik faithfully took his advice. The very next *Shabbos* he stood up meekly before his congregation, and told them in plain, quiet words that he was really a man of very poor worth indeed. The effect, though, was not as expected. His chassidim were so moved by the genuine self-effacement of their rebbe that they made every attempt to emulate his humility, and cleaved to him more ardently than ever.

When the Chozeh next met the *rav*, he told him that

he had followed his advice, but to no avail.

The *rav* now had an alternative suggestion: "Your chassidim love humility and spurn arrogance. Tell your followers, therefore, that you are a true tzaddik. Then they will be *sure* to go home and leave you in peace."

"I may not be a rebbe," returned the Chozeh, "but neither am I a liar. How, then will I be able to get up and say that I am a true tzaddik?"

⸙ A Searching Question

וַיִּשְׁמַע מֹשֶׁה וַיִּפֹּל עַל פָּנָיו
And Moshe heard and he fell on his face (16:4)

A *misnaged* once came to Reb Shneur Zalman of Liadi and expressed his antagonism to the chassidic movement by confronting him with allegations of pride — for did he not have an attendant at his door, and so forth? The tzaddik rested his head on his arms, just as one does during the penitential *Tachanun* prayer, and after an interval of silence replied: "The expression the Torah uses for the leaders of the People is רָאשֵׁי אַלְפֵי יִשְׂרָאֵל — 'the heads of the thousands of *Yisrael'* — from which we see that our leaders are known as 'heads'. Now even though the head and body are joined to each other, nevertheless they are clothed separately, and differently. Why so? Because the head must be distinct from the body, just as the heads of any generation must be separate from the people."

The questioner found the answer satisfactory, and went on his way. But the rebbe's son, later to be renowned as Reb Dov Ber of Lubavitch, was left with a different question: "In order to give that answer there was no need to rest your head in your arms. Why did you not give him his answer immediately?"

Replied his father: "In the episode of Korach, first we read 'Why, then, do you raise yourselves up over the People of God,' then we read 'And Moshe heard, and he fell on his face.' Only later did Moshe give his answer — that in the morning God would make the matter clear. The same question could be asked there. Why did Moshe first fall on his face, before giving his answer? But Moshe Rabbeinu suspected for a moment that perhaps this question was really being asked of him from Above, while Korach was no more than a messenger. If this were so, and he were to give an answer at once, then some other questioner would no doubt be summoned from Above to pose the same query afresh. He therefore fell on his face first, in order to meditate a while as to whether there really was any fragment of pride in himself. After he had found that this was not the case — as the Torah itself avers: 'The man Moshe was very humble' — he knew now that this was no divine messenger confronting him, but simply quarrelsome Korach. Only then could he go ahead and give his answer.

"And a similar thing happened here today ... '

❧ *In Defense of the Living*

וַיַּעֲמֹד בֵּין הַמֵּתִים וּבֵין הַחַיִּים
And he stood between the dead and the living (17:13)

An epidemic had broken out in Vloshchov, and a respectful delegation of householders came to ask Reb Shlomo of Radomsk to return with them to his hometown to pray for its stricken residents. He was greeted on his approach by the venerable sages of the town, headed by the local *rav*, and behind them the whole eager populace, men, women and children, all decked out in their *Shabbos* best, with music and dancing and firebrands.

"How great is the *ruach hakodesh* of the Yid HaKadosh of Pshischah!" exlaimed Reb Shlomo as he saw the sight before him. "For I recall that when he once visited this town — I was then a little boy — all the townsfolk came out to greet him with due pomp. My father, Reb Hirschele, who was the respected lay head of the community, traveled with the Yid HaKadosh in his carriage, and sat me on his lap. When the tzaddik saw me there next to him, he tweaked my cheek in a grandfatherly way, and said: '*Nu, nu* ... When you come here, you'll be honored more!"

The next day the tzaddik instructed all the townsfolk to walk with him around the edge of the local cemetery, and then he began as follows: "Concerning Aharon the High Priest we read, 'And he stood between the dead and the living, and the plague was stayed.' Now reason dictates that there should be only living people, not dead — for what use does the Almighty have from the dead? Even if they are righteous and dwell in the Garden of

Eden, what benefit does he have from them as they sit there, basking in the soothing warmth of Paradise? But living people thank, and pray, and praise, and bless! Besides, they drink *LeChaim* now and again! [And here Reb Shlomo indulged in a fanciful play on the similarity between לְחַיִּים – the toast *To Life!* that accompanies a convivial sip of vodka, and לְחָיַיִם – the jowls of the sacrificial animal offered as a reminder of *prayer*, which is breathed and mouthed by the worshiper.] When Pinchas prayed to God that he remove the plague, he pointed out to the Almighty these two advantages of the living over the dead: first, that they pray; and secondly, that they say *LeChaim*. And so we find, indeed, that 'he stood [in prayer] between the dead and the living *(hachaim)*.' And through the strength of this argument the plague was indeed banished.

"Now, you good folk," concluded Reb Shlomo, "would you please learn from Pinchas, and bring a drop of vodka here, so that we can all say *LeChaim?*"

A few of the townsfolk hurried home to bring some spirits and refreshments, and right where they were, just outside the cemetery walls, they drank *LeChaim*, and in loud and happy voices wished each other *To Life!*

From there they went home with happy hearts, and the epidemic vanished from their town.

◆§ *A Sense of Perspective*

וַיִּקְחוּ אִישׁ מַטֵּהוּ
And each man took his staff (17:24)

From time to time Reb Yaakov of Moglenitz would visit Reb Yisrael of Ruzhin. Once, on a *Shabbos* on which the weekly Portion of *Korach* is read, he came to see him at Sadigora, where he was then living. From the day he had come to settle in Sadigora, Reb Yisrael was in the habit of isolating himself in his study for *Seudah Shlishis*, the mystical Third Meal which is held at sunset. On this *Shabbos*, therefore, the tzaddik of Moglenitz arranged to have his own *Seudah Shlishis* at his lodgings, where a number of chassidim foregathered to join him at his modest table.

On that occasion he taught as follows: "We read in the Torah this morning that the Almighty told the princes of the Tribes that they should each place their staffs in the Tabernacle, and among them the staff of Aharon, in order that the people might see for themselves whom God had chosen for the office of High Priest. The Torah goes on to say that the staff of Aharon blossomed, 'and they saw, and each man took his staff.' Now the question is: Why does the Torah tell us that they each took their staffs? Aharon, of course, had to take his staff, in order that the rebellious Levites should see what God had made clear. But to whom does it matter whether the other heads of the Tribes took their staffs or not?

"But the Torah here teaches us how great was their humility — that they each hastened to show those around them that their staffs had not blossomed, as if to say: 'Look! God chose not me, but Aharon.'"

Those sitting around the table of the quietly-spoken rebbe understood the relevance of his message.

◆§ *Higher Hurdles Ahead*

הַאִם תַּמְנוּ לִגְוֹעַ
Are we to perish utterly? (17:28)

Are we to perish utterly? Have we reached the level of utter perfection (תְּמִימוּת) that a person must reach during his lifetime so that he should be ready to pass away *(Tiferes Shlomo)*?

When Reb Avraham of Sochatchov was a little boy he once fell dangerously ill, and his father, Reb Ze'ev Nachum of Biala, set out at once to Kotsk to ask Reb Menachem Mendel to intercede in heaven on his behalf. When he arrived there, he began to tell the tzaddik of the intense desire and assiduity with which his brilliant son studied Torah.

"You call *that* studying?" the tzaddik said, half to himself.

The father was alarmed. Why should the rebbe seek to utter such a negative appraisal of his son in the hearing of the Heavenly Court? And why especially now, when the child stood in mortal danger?

By the time he arrived home he found his son on his cheerful way to recovery. But when he asked his father exactly what the tzaddik had said when he had asked for his blessing, the father was at a loss for an answer. Then when the boy begged him repeatedly, he could only say: "Believe me, my son, I too do not understand what he said."

Finally, when he had persuaded his father to repeat the words of the tzaddik, the prodigy said: "What is difficult to understand in that? For what he said is exactly parallel to what we find in the Talmud Yerushalmi. We learn there that when Rabbi Tarfon was ill, his mother said to the Sages who came to visit him: 'Pray for my son Tarfon, who honors me even more than one is obliged to do.' And when they asked her: 'Why, what does he do?' — she told them that one *Shabbos,* when she was about to return to her house after strolling in the courtyard, he had gone out and put the palms of his hands under her feet, moving them step by step so that she could walk on them, until she reached her bed. The Sages then retorted: 'Even if he does that a thousand times a thousand, he still will not have reached one half of the respect which the Torah commands children to show their parents.'

"Now, father," concluded the young boy, "surely we should ask the same question here. Could it possibly be that the Sages wanted to play down Rabbi Tarfon's merits in the eyes of heaven at the very moment that he stood in need of mercy? Is it not likelier that they were apprehensive lest his task on earth had thus reached its fulfillment? If so, he would now have nothing to do in This World. And just as they wanted to remind the Heavenly Court that there were even higher levels at which that mitzvah could be fulfilled, in order that he should live on, so too with the rebbe of Kotsk. When you told him how well I study, he was fearful lest I had already completed my life's work. So he too wanted to make it clear that there were many challenges still waiting for me in This World, in the field of Torah study."

Amazed at his son's perception, the father repeated his explanation to Reb Menachem Mendel when he was next in Kotsk.

"Now, now!" said the tzaddik. "Do you mean to say that he already guesses at what I have in mind?"

◆§ My Brothers Do I Seek

כִּי לֹא יִטֹּשׁ ה׳ אֶת עַמּוֹ
For God will not abandon His People (Haftarah)

Before making the long voyage to *Eretz Yisrael,* Reb Wolff Kitzis called on the Baal Shem Tov to receive his farewell blessings. As they parted, the tzaddik told him: "Reb Wolff! Be careful with your words, and know what to answer!"

The chassid (who is also known by his Hebrew name, Reb Ze'ev) set out, and on the way his ship dropped anchor near an island in order to have its provisions replenished. While the crew was thus occupied, he found himself a quiet spot on the island where he could commune alone with his Maker. But so rapt was he in his holy thoughts that he quite forgot about his ship, and when he came out of his inspired trance he found that it was already quite out of sight. He was in very serious trouble. As he turned around he stumbled upon a path and followed it, until he reached a house, where an old man greeted him, and asked: "Reb Wolff, why are you so worried?"

"How should I not worry," he said, "when my ship has gone, and I am left alone?"

"Be composed, Reb Wolff," the old man reassured him. "Stay with me for *Shabbos,* and then next week you can travel from here with one of the ships that pass by. We have a *minyan* here for prayer, and a *mikveh* for immersion."

When the time came for him to board ship, the old man turned to him: "Reb Wolff, I forgot to ask you something. How are the Jews making out where you come from?"

The chassid was preoccupied with his imminent departure, so he replied briefly: "The good God does not abandon them."

And he boarded ship, and sailed on his way.

When he had time to think things over, the old man's question came to mind. He could not forgive himself, and tormented himself with accusations: "What did I answer him? Did the Baal Shem Tov not tell me that I should know what to answer? Why, then did I not tell the old man how wretched is the plight of our persecuted brothers?"

So overcome was he with remorse that he decided to change his direction at the first opportunity, and to speak with the Baal Shem Tov.

As soon as he walked into the familiar room, the tzaddik greeted him and said: "Day after day Avraham Avinu presents himself before the Almighty and says, 'Master of the Universe! My children — *where are they?*' and the Almighty assures the Patriarch: 'I do not forsake them. And look,' he adds, 'here you see Reb Wolff on his way to *Eretz Yisrael.* Now there is a fine Jew. Ask *him* how they are faring!'"

The Baal Shem Tov concluded: "Now if you had told Avraham Avinu how intense is the suffering of the Children of Israel throughout this long exile, then the Messianic Redeemer would have come! But you did not heed my warning ... "

סדר חקת
Sidra Chukas

◆§ Of Books and Bookmen

This is the Torah: a man ... : A man is a living Scroll of the Torah *(Traditional).*

זאת הַתּוֹרָה אָדָם
This is the Torah: a man (19:14)

One *Shabbos* in the year 1840 Reb Yitzchak of Vorki was visiting Lublin, where a circumcision was to take place in the very *beis midrash* in which Reb Yaakov Yitzchak, the Chozeh, had taught and inspired thousands until his passing some twenty-five years earlier. The table around which all the local dignitaries were ranged was the same table at which the Chozeh used to sit, and it was expected that the tzaddik of Vorki would now occupy the seat of honor, on its east side.

Reb Yitzchak declined, though, saying: "When our rebbe was alive, I never stepped forward more than half the length of the *beis midrash* out of sheer awe."

But as soon as he took up a place on the west side of the table, scores of chassidim jostled their way eagerly towards him.

Reb Yitzchak turned to them and remarked gently: "Every Jew, you know, is likened to a holy book; that is why you mustn't lean on him or push him around ... '

"But isn't one allowed to stack one holy book on top of another?" countered Reb Getzel, the grandson of the celebrated Rabbi Zvi Hirsch Ashkenazi.

Replied Reb Yitzchak: "Yes — but every Jew should consider himself as not being a holy book."

This remark was overheard by the *rav* of Lublin, Rabbi Meshullam Zalman Ashkenazi, who later commented: "If I had come only to hear that remark, that would have been sufficient."

One way and another the table talk continued on the subject of books, and on the *mitzvah* involved in making Torah works available for public use. And when the *rav* of Lublin left the gathering, he wrote a will that bequeathed his entire scholarly library to the *beis midrash* for the continued edification of his townsmen after his passing.

☙ A Crumb of Comfort

זֹאת הַתּוֹרָה אָדָם כִּי יָמוּת בְּאֹהֶל
This is the Torah: a man who dies in a tent (19:14)

This is the Torah: a man who dies in a tent ... : The Torah truly becomes the possession only of him who gives his very life in the effort of its study (Talmud, Tractate Berachos).

Reb Yitzchak Aizik of Komarna recalled that his father, Reb Alexander Sender of Komarna, was so utterly entrenched in his studies that he would sometimes forget to eat or drink for four or five days at a time. Though he lived in grinding poverty, he never seemed to notice the fact.

"Once," recounted his son, "when I was a boy, I hadn't had a slice of bread to eat for almost two days. On the second day, in order to allay my suffering, my father taught me a Mishnah from the Tractate *Nedarim,* and then introduced it to me afresh with all its mystical meanings, according to the Kabbalah of the ARI*zal.* By then I was very weak, and close to fainting. So my father said: 'Go along to the woman next door; she will give you something to eat.'

"I was surprised to hear this, for I knew that she would not give me food without payment. But I trusted in his every word, and stood at her door. There was an old gentile sitting there, and as soon as he saw me he said: 'My son! Would you like some vodka? How about some bread?'

"And he gave me as much as I needed. All the bystanders looked on in wonderment, but I was so hungry that I didn't take time off to pay close attention to anything in particular. But — because I am such a worthless sinner — I later understood from my father's words that I had been allowed to see Eliyahu the Prophet only in this garbled guise."

◆§ A Five-Wheeled Carriage

בַּמְסִלָּה נַעֲלֶה
We will go up by the highway (20:19)

Reb Aizik of Safrin was the father of five celebrated sons: Reb Zvi Hirsch of Zhidachov, who was the teacher of all his younger brothers; Reb Moshe of Sambor; Reb Alexander Sender of Komarna; Reb Beirish of Zhidachov; and Reb Lipa of Sambor.

Their father never occupied a rabbinical position; he earned an ample livelihood by the toil of his hands, and was a great philanthropist. His oldest son used to quote a Talmudic metaphor when referring to himself and his less famous father: "I am like vinegar the son of wine" — and was fond of repeating some of the ways in which his father's character excelled. His father, he affirmed, never spoke of another man; every single meal in his home was graced with learned table talk — his sons took daily turns at preparing a scholarly discourse to be delivered at the table; and he always made a point of eating together with his servants out of sheer love for his fellow Jews.

When he was already well advanced in years, he once woke up in the middle of the night, and uttered a long, deep sigh.

"Why do you sigh?" asked Hinda, his pious *rebbitzin*.

"And why should I not sigh?" he countered. "We are now well on the way to old age — and how will we go up to the World Above?"

"Don't worry," she said, "for בַּמְסִלָּה נַעֲלֶה!" [Literally, "We will go up by the highway" — but her meaning was: "We will go up (נַעֲלֶה) by virtue of our sons, whose initials make up the word בַּמְסִלָּה — namely: בֵּירִישׁ, מֹשֶׁה, [י". סֶנְדֶר, לִיפָּא, הִירְשׁ

An Envoy to the World Above

וַיִּרְאוּ כָּל הָעֵדָה כִּי גָוַע אַהֲרֹן
And all the congregation saw that Aharon had passed away (20:29)

And all the congregation saw that Aharon had passed away: On a hint from the Almighty, the angels raised aloft the coffin of Aharon, and it floated in the heavens *(Yalkut).*

It was in Mezhibuzh, on the night of the fifth of Nissan, 1829, that Reb Avraham Yehoshua Heschel, the Ohev Yisrael of Apta, departed This World. On the very same night, in the holy city of Tiberias, people heard a knocking on the windows of Kollel Vohlin. The beadle inside, alone, was the one who held the keys to the gates of the cemetery. The voice from outside said: "Go outside, go outside, and follow the bier of the *rav* of Apta!"

He ventured outside and was chilled by terror, for the bier was being followed by a grim retinue of a myriad human forms from the Other World. One of these followers intimated to him that this was the funeral procession of the tzaddik of Apta; he had died in Mezhibuzh, and angels from Above had borne his coffin here for entombment in the soil of the Holy Land.

The beadle repeated his story in the morning. People refused to believe him, until on the suggestion of an elderly sage they went together to the cemetery, where they found a newly-covered grave.

Letters from Apta later confirmed that the tzaddik had indeed passed away on that very day. Before his passing he had cried out to heaven in bitter protest over the length of the exile. Why was the Messiah tarrying so long? And in his heartache he had wept and said: "Before Reb Levi Yitzchak of Berditchev left This World he promised that he would not rest, nor allow the tzaddikim in the World of Truth to rest, until their insistent pleas would bring about the Messianic Redemption. But when he arrived there, the saintly souls in the Garden of Eden found spiritual delight in his company, and ascended with him to the palaces of supernal bliss — until he forgot his own promise. But I will not forget!"*

❦ ❦ ❦

When Reb Chaim Eleazar of Munkatsch visited the holy sites in *Eretz Yisrael* in 1930, he asked about among the oldest citizens of Tiberias as to whether any of them knew where the *rav* of Apta was buried. They led him to a certain stone slab in the old cemetery which their hoary elders, who were now in the World of Truth, had shown them — the place where the Ohev Yisrael had been brought to rest.

◆§ *Antics with Skeptics*

וַיְדַבֵּר הָעָם בֵּאלֹקִים וּבְמֹשֶׁה
And the people spoke against God and against Moshe (21:5)

If one entertains doubts regarding his rebbe, it is as if he entertained doubts regarding the Divine Presence, as it is written: "And the People spoke against God and against Moshe" *(Talmud, Tractate Sanhedrin).*

Reb Moshe of Kobrin was once visiting Reissin, in Belorussia, where he lodged in the *shtibl* of the local chassidim. At the festive evening meal which was arranged in his honor, all the leaders and citizens of the community listened respectfully to the learned discourse which he delivered — except for one chassid at the end of the table, who kept up a whispered conversation with his neighbor.

* When it was granted me some years ago to leave the Vale of Tears which is known as the USSR on my way to settle in *Eretz Yisrael*, and I had to visit Moscow in order to arrange the formalities, my fellow chassidim there arranged a farewell gathering. On that occasion, on the eve of my departure, they told me the above story, and then added the following words: "We do not have to tell you, rabbi, that here in this wretched exile we live a life of torment and anguish. We are supported only by the hope that our Father will one day deliver us too out of this dungeon, and bring us to the Holy Land. But all our friends from here who were fortunate enough to go there, and who promised that from the moment they arrived they would never rest until they found some way of getting us out of here, — when they arrived, the same happened to them as happened to Reb Levi Yitzchak of Berditchev in the World Above: they savored the spiritual delights of the palaces of bliss, and forgot us completely. But on you, our friend, we rely. You will not forget us!"

By reason of my imperfections, no doubt, the hope they placed in me bore no fruit. They probably assumed that I too spent my years in the Holy Land disporting myself in the quest of spiritual or other delights ... My heart bleeds for them.

S.Y.Z.

"Sh!" said his companion. "It's not right to talk during a *tish."*

The talker said nothing, but he thought to himself: "Why, he's not *my* rebbe!"

Suddenly, in the middle of his discourse, Reb Moshe said: "כָּל הַמְהַרְהֵר אַחַר רַבּוֹ ... — If one entertains doubts regarding his rebbe, it is as if he entertained doubts regarding the Divine Presence!"

None of those present knew whom the rebbe was referring to. As to the talker, he thought: "Could he really mean me? Why, my rebbe is someone else!"

Reb Moshe spoke again, this time playing on the similarity between אַחַר ("regarding") and אַחֵר, ("someone else"): "כָּל הַמְהַרְהֵר: אַחֵר רַבּוֹ ... — If someone thinks his rebbe is אַחֵר, someone else, it is as if he entertained doubts regarding the Divine Presence!"

This time the talker felt that Reb Moshe must really mean himself — but then he found solace in the thought that perhaps after all the rebbe had someone else in mind, for he did not know him at all.

Reb Moshe now spoke a third time: "כָּל הַמְהַרְהֵר: אַחֵר רַבּוֹ ... — If someone thinks that the rebbe is really thinking of אַחֵר, of someone else, it is as if he entertained doubts regarding the Divine Presence!"

The chassid — at last — got the message.

❀ ❀ ❀

This story has also been handed down among chassidim in an alternative version.

Two chassidim had occasion to pass through Vilednick in the course of a business trip, so one suggested to the other: "Since we are already here, let us drop by and see Reb Yisrael Dov of Vilednick, the famous wonder-worker."

His friend reacted with a contemptuous grunt. Nevertheless, when *Shabbos* came they both went along to *Seudah Shlishis* — just out of curiosity, let us say. The little hall was so packed that these two merchants found themselves jostled into a spot right behind the chair of the rebbe, where, of course, he was unable to see them.

In the midst of his exposition of some other learned topic, this tzaddik, too, interrupted himself by quoting the above Talmudic teaching — once, twice, three times, as before — except that he then quoted it a *fourth* time: "... כָּל הַמְהַרְהֵר אַחַר רַבּוֹ — If one entertains doubts מֵאֲחוֹרֵי רַבּוֹ, while standing *behind* (מֵאֲחוֹרֵי) his rebbe, it is as if he entertained doubts regarding the Divine Presence!"

סדר בלק
Sidra Balak

◆§ A Visual Restriction (i)

לֹא הִבִּיט אָוֶן בְּיַעֲקֹב
He sees no iniquity in Yaakov (23:21)

Reb Yisrael of Ruzhin recounted that Reb Zusya of Hanipoli was once present in the home of his rebbe, the Maggid of Mezritch, when a man entered and proceeded to recite his list of requests. With the penetrating perception which accompanies the divine gift of *ruach hakodesh,* Reb Zusya saw that this man's sins were grave indeed. He was indignant. How dare the man stand so fearless and unpenitent before the holy Reb Dov Ber of Mezritch!

"A man who has committed such-and-such!" he exclaimed. "Is such a man not ashamed to stand there before the tzaddik without at least a glimmer of *teshuvah?"*

After the man had left Reb Zusya expressed his profound regret at having spoken thus in the presence of his rebbe, whereupon the Maggid gave him his blessing that from that day on he would never see evil in a fellow Jew — only good.

◆§ A Visual Restriction (ii)

At a gathering on the festival of Simchas Torah, Reb Yosef Yitzchak of Lubavitch recalled a childhood dialogue with his father, Reb Shalom Ber of Lubavitch.

"When I was four years old," he said, "I asked my father: 'Why is man created with two eyes, but only one mouth and one nose?'

"'Do you know your *aleph-beis?'* he asked.

"When I answered that I did, he asked again: 'And what is the difference between the letter שׁ *(shin)* and the letter שׂ *(sin)*?'

"'Why, the שׁ has the dot on the right, and the שׂ has the dot on the left,' I answered.

"'And that is why you have two eyes,' my father explained. 'There are things that one should look at with the right eye, and there are things that one should look at with the left eye. A fellow Jew one should always look at with one's right eye, and a candy and a toy — with one's left eye.'

"And it was from that time," concluded Reb Yosef Yitzchak, "that it became a principle deeply rooted in my heart — that one must look at any Jew, whoever he may be, and in whatever spiritual state he may be, with a kindly eye."

◈ *Evil Be to Him who Evil Thinks*

כִּי לֹא נַחַשׁ בְּיַעֲקֹב *For there is no sorcery in Yaakov (23:23)*

In a town near Liadi there lived a promising young scholar whose father-in-law supported him for a few years after his marriage so that he would be able to advance his Torah studies. After some time, however, the fluctuations of business were such that the young man had to go out and try his own hand at merchandising in order to provide for himself. So it was that once, on the way back from a fair where he had bought up a good deal of merchandise, he passed through a forest near Liadi. It was a day or two before Shavuos, and as he recalled how it had always been his custom to spend the Festival of the Giving of the Torah in the company of his rebbe, Reb Zalman of Liadi, he was so overcome with nostalgia that he decided to leave the wagon with its costly load in the forest and to make his way on foot to Liadi.

He arrived in *shul* just in time for the afternoon prayers, and when the rebbe saw him he commented to his son: "This young man may well be called a chassid of *mesirus nefesh*, a man of self-sacrifice."

The son was surprised to hear this, for his father had not exchanged a word with the young stranger. He later went to speak with the visiting chassid himself, until he eventually understood where lay his self-sacrifice.

When the visitor went to speak to the rebbe after the festival, he was assured: "You will find the wagon and the merchandise untouched, with God's help."

And when the chassid told the rebbe that his business took his mind away from his study and his devotions, the rebbe said: "I would suggest that you find yourself some inn with a tavern in a village. That kind of livelihood will not bother you unduly. Your wife will be able to help out in the business, and you will be left with time for study and prayer."

As the chassid reached his wagon in the forest soon after, untouched as expected, a certain nobleman passed by, and asked him how he had left a loaded wagon unattended.

The chassid laughed heartily. "Good sir," he said, "this wagon of mine has been standing unguarded for three whole days!"

The nobleman was so amazed to hear the young man's story that he said: "Young man, I see that you are straight and honest: I would like to make you a business proposition. In my village there stands a fine inn. You could make a decent living out of it, and I am willing to lease it to you."

"But I haven't got a penny to my name," protested the young man. "I haven't even got what it takes to buy fodder for the horses, let alone vodka, beer, or whatever."

"Very well, then," said the other, "I shall lay out all that is needed now, and in the course of time you will repay me."

It was a deal. The chassid went home, sold his stock, and took over the inn as arranged — despite the friendly warnings of his new Jewish neighbors, who told him that even though one could make a living out of the inn, the people next door were a malevolent old Russian couple who wielded the mysterious threats of the black arts. No Jew living in that inn had ever survived one whole year.

"I'm not afraid of witches," he answered them, "for my rebbe told me that I would make a living out of this place. Now tell me: would my rebbe direct me to a living from which I would die, God forbid?!"

Within a few months his little business had done so well that he was able to return his entire debt to the nobleman. A little while later, however, he began to feel weak. An ominous malady seemed to be taking hold of him. He was barely able to walk. Suspecting the dread influence of the sorcerer next door, he hastened to make the journey to his rebbe, and arrived at Liadi on the eve of the *Shabbos* on which the weekly Portion of *Balak* was to be read. On Friday evening he could not muster the strength to go to synagogue, but in the morning, with great effort, he managed to walk to the *shul* where his rebbe was wont to pray.

Reb Shneur Zalman of Liadi was accustomed to reading the Torah himself, and when it was time for a fifth congregant to be honored by being called up to the public reading, he asked that this young visitor be so honored. The other worshipers were somewhat surprised, for the rebbe never gave instructions as to who should be called forward to the reading; besides, he could not have seen the stranger coming in, because he had arrived when the prayers were already under way. At any rate, the stranger made his way forward to where the Torah Scroll was being read, and the rebbe proceeded to intone the next passage with especial intensity, which came to a climax in the verse: "For there is no sorcery in Yaakov, nor any divination among Israel." He threw his head back, his face burned like a brand and his eyes blazed — for such was his way when his soul ascended to a higher realm — and while still in a state of *dveikus,* read the same words again and again.

After *Shabbos* the young man felt his health returning, but before leaving Liadi he went to tell the rebbe his whole story.

"Do not worry," the rebbe reassured him. "With God's help you will be well, *for there is no sorcery in Yaakov*" — and again the rebbe repeated the *pasuk* several times with the same impassioned intensity as before.

On his way home the young man felt hale and hearty, and as he approached the outskirts of his village a few of the Jewish villagers ran up to him excitedly: "Have you heard what happened right next door to your inn? That malicious old peasant died suddenly, and so did his wife!"

"When?" he asked.

"On *Shabbos* morning," they said.

"I sensed it in Liadi," he said, "when I was called up to the reading of the Torah."

◆§ *When He Wills It*

אֶרְאֶנּוּ וְלֹא עַתָּה
I see it, but not now (24:17)

Soon after the passing of Reb Shneur Zalman of Liadi, his grandson Reb Menachem Mendel of Lubavitch happened to be in a certain town for a wedding. There he overheard a few chassidim in the adjoining room lamenting the state the world was now left in: God alone knew when the Messiah would finally come.

He opened the door and said: "But that is what the gentile prophet Bilam said concerning the Messianic Redemption — 'I see it, but not now; I behold it, but it is not near.' We Jews, though, should hope and look forward to the coming of the *Mashiach* every day! And in this connection I heard from my grandfather that his teacher, the Maggid of Mezritch, had the ability to cause even a day-old child to experience the loftiest levels of the awe of God; *his* rebbe, the Baal Shem Tov, could have fired even an inanimate object with the same. Why did they not do this, and thereby — since the whole of creation would then be fired by an awareness of the Divine Presence — cause the *Mashiach* to come at once? The answer is that God did not yet will it. And if the arrival of the *Mashiach* depends on the Divine Will, then how is the situation altered by the passing of our rebbe, my grandfather? When the propitious time comes, and God so wills it, the *Mashiach* will surely appear."

◆§ *Incognito (i)*

וְהַצְנֵעַ לֶכֶת עִם אֱלֹקֶיךָ
And to walk humbly with your God (Haftarah)

After having consulted one physician after another to no avail, the father of an eleven-year-old boy who had lost the power of speech came to visit Reb Shneur Zalman of Liadi.

"Make the journey to Metz, in Germany," advised the rebbe, "take up lodgings in the house of a certain timber merchant who lives near the hill at the entrance to the city, and wait there until the Almighty sends a cure for your son."

"And what am I to do there in Metz?" asked the man.

"Don't do anything," answered the rebbe. "Just stroll about the market places and the streets, until salvation comes."

Now the poor fellow could not afford anything approaching the costs of traveling to Germany, but as soon as his fellow chassidim heard what the rebbe had said, they collected amongst themselves all that was needed and sent him off with his son, perfectly confident that the rebbe's words would be fulfilled.

After an arduous journey the chassid finally arrived in Metz, and discovered soon enough that there was in fact a hill near the approach to the city, next to which there lived a Jewish timber merchant. He was well received by his host, and then spent day after day walking about the streets and the market places with his unfortunate son — but his long journey seemed to be quite pointless. Nor only to himself, for one day his host said: "Excuse my asking, but what business brought you here? For you have been here quite some time now, and you do not appear to be occupied with anything."

When he was told the whole story, he was amazed: How did the rebbe know of his existence from such a great distance? And what connection could there possibly be between a cure for the boy and — himself? But an idea crossed his mind.

"Listen here, my friend," he said. "It seems to me that the person your rebbe had in mind was my son-in-law. Let me tell you *my* story.

"A certain youth used to sit in our local synagogue all day, studying Torah. I felt sorry for him, and invited him to be my regular guest. He agreed, but after some time he said: 'I have one request of you. I don't want to eat unearned bread, and you could probably do with a watchman for your timber yard. Why don't you build me a little cabin out there, and I'll look after your yard for you.'

"And that is exactly what we did.

"Once, though, I woke up in the middle of the night.

What do I see through the window? — A huge fire raging in my timber yard, right where I built the cabin for this watchman of mine! In my imagination I could already see it racing through my stacks of timber, and I felt angry at the young man who was no doubt sleeping soundly, quite unaware of what was going on around him. I ran out to wake him up, and to put out the fire. But what fire? When I got there I was astonished to see that there was no fire at all. And when I told my wife of this odd illusion she only laughed and said: 'You only saw it in your dreams!'

"A few days later, though, I again saw the same thing in the middle of the night — and in the same place. But this time I made a point of waking up my wife, so that she should see the thing with her own eyes.

"'Run out there and put it out!' she screamed.

"But again I arrived there breathless only to find that there was no fire to put out. We talked over this weird occurrence, and came to the conclusion that this was no ordinary young man. We decided not to breathe a word of it to a soul, as if we knew nothing and had seen nothing.

"Some time later I asked this young man whether he would like to become my son-in-law. He agreed, but on one condition: that I would build a house at the other end of town for himself and his wife — though I was never to visit them there on any account. He promised that they would come to visit us in our home, and said the he would support himself and my daughter by baking bread, a craft at which he was expert. But the condition was an absolute one. I accepted it, and we both did as we had undertaken to do. They visit us from time to time, and my daughter says she is very happy with her young husband.

"It would seem, then," concluded the timber merchant, "that the man your rebbe had in mind is this hidden tzaddik, my son-in-law."

The guest heard him out, and decided to pay a visit to this unusual baker, whom he addressed as follows: "The rebbe of Liadi sent me to you so that you should cure my son here of his dumbness."

"So he has found me here too?" said the young man,

stupefied. "Tell him that I am now going to move to some place where he will not find me any more!"

He blessed the boy, nevertheless. His prayer was heard, and the child was healed.

◆§ *Incognito (ii)*

The waiting room of Reb Simchah Bunem of Pshischah was once occupied by the venerable inner circle of elder chassidim, whose hushed deliberations were interrupted by the entry of a young man dressed in the modern garb of a "Deitsch'l" (for this was the nickname given to assimilationists and *Maskilim).* His request: to be allowed to speak with the tzaddik. Now this was a most unusual phenomenon. People like this did not normally believe in tzaddikim nor mix with chassidim. There was no doubt about it: this stranger was here only to pester their rebbe with vexatious questions. They therefore made him unwelcome.

The man only answered meekly: "So what can I do? I'll have to go somewhere else" — and he went on his way.

His quiet answer, though, affected them, and they decided to tell the rebbe of his visit. The tzaddik trembled to hear their report, and expressed his displeasure at the fact that they had allowed him to leave. He even ordered them to go out at once in search of the stranger, and to bring him back.

They caught up with him on the highway and explained themselves, but when he had returned with them they were flabbergasted to hear the question he put to the rebbe: "Two *shidduchim* have been proposed to me. One match is with a beauty, though she is not of noble birth; the other is of distinguished ancestry, but is not a beauty. Which should I choose?"

Surprised as the chassidim were that this should be the question he had brought to the rebbe, they were far more surprised to see with what earnest deliberation the rebbe weighed his question before answering: "Beauty! That really is beauty!"

As soon as the stranger left, the tzaddik turned to his

chassidim: "This 'Deitsch'l' asked me whether he should study the Kabbalah according to the school of Rabbi Moshe Cordovero or according to the teachings of Rabbi Yitzchak Luria, the Ari*zal;* I told him that he should follow the teachings of the Ari*zal.*"

◆§ *Incognito (iii)*

Though he was the son of the celebrated tzaddik Reb Yitzchak of Vorki, young Menachem Mendel always managed to give the impression — to a superficial observer — that he was merely a mischievous lad who enjoyed strolling in the open fields. Few men indeed knew that this was no more than a mask. So it was that when his father passed away, and the chassidim installed him as their rebbe, dissident whispers could be heard from various quarters.

Once, for example, a famous sage called on Reb Beirish of Biala, who was one of the first chassidim to cleave to the new young rebbe, while he was visiting Warsaw.

"Does the Talmud not teach us," he queried, "that לֹא יָגַעְתִּי וּמָצָאתִי אַל תַּאֲמִין? 'If someone tells you, *I have not toiled, but I have found — do not believe him!'* Let's face it: we have never seen Reb Menachem Mendel exerting himself in the study of Torah or in divine service generally. Why believe in him?"

"You don't even know what that Talmudic quotation means," replied Reb Beirish, "and you dare to speak thus about a tzaddik from whom tens of thousands of our brethren draw inspiration! It is time you understood the meaning of this phrase *Do not believe him.* Why, is this question a matter of *belief?* Not at all! All you have to do is to open up the scholarly literature with him and you will be able to see for yourself whether he has *found* or not. What the Talmud is teaching us here is something else altogether: 'If someone tells you, *I have not toiled* — do not believe him!' Our rebbe has toiled well and truly toiled — but has kept his exertions hidden modestly from sight."

◆§ Incognito (iv)

Reb Betzalel of Ozoritch, a chassid of Reb Menachem Mendel of Lubavitch, once lodged at the home of a certain Jewish villager whom he had encountered in the course of his travels. His host told him that he employed a youth to shepherd his flocks all day long. At night he would come home and lie down to rest in his favorite nook high up on the huge stone fireplace, and early in the morning he would go out to the fields. True enough, he was a trustworthy young man, but his host said that he had never once seen him washing his hands before a meal or saying the words of a blessing.

Approaching the fireplace, Reb Betzalel found the shepherd eating beans.

He asked him gently: "Why do you not wash your hands and say a *berachah* as one should?"

"What difference does it make to you?" the young man answered.

Since his further questions all received the same response, Reb Betzalel left the fireplace disappointed.

When he had occasion to be passing through that region a year later, his host said: "Let me tell you something remarkable about that young man whom you met a year ago. One day I decided to go out to see for myself just what that young man did out there in the fields, to see whether he was looking after my flocks, at least. I found myself a hiding place under a bush, where he could not possibly see me. And as I listened, I heard him reading the words of the Book of *Psalms*, one melodious phrase after another, in a measured voice that gradually rose in holy ecstasy. This was clearly not the ordinary peasant that I had imagined him to be. I revealed nothing of what I had seen to anyone, but from the greater respect that I now showed him, he must have sensed that I had discovered what manner of man he was.

"Then one Friday night soon after, ten gentiles burst into my house to take this young man off for military service. They said that they were acting on orders issued by the conscription authorities in the neighboring town. I begged them to give him a reprieve at least until the end of our Day of Rest. You see, I thought that I would then be able to speak to the leading Jewish citizens of that town, and tell them about this young man, and perhaps induce them to make efforts to have him released. But those ten *goyim* took absolutely no notice of my entreaties, and took him away.

"Distressed at my failure to save him I waited impatiently for *Shabbos* to pass, and then, as soon as I had recited *Havdalah,* I set out for that town to see what I could perhaps still do for him. But when I spoke of this case to the regional conscription authorities there, it turned out that they didn't know what I was talking about. They had never sent anyone to my village, and they had never heard of this young man!"

Reb Betzalel wept on hearing this story, and said: "How gross and unspiritual are our eyes, that we sensed nothing and knew nothing!"

◈ *Incognito (v)*

Reb Yechezkel Halevi, the son-in-law of Reb Yisrael of Koznitz, repeated the following story which he had heard while visiting his uncle, who was a scholarly *rav* in a certain town in Hungary.

"Many years ago," recalled this uncle, "two men came to me and testified that they had seen one of the common villagers in the district — he held the franchise on the sale of milk from the local squire — committing a certain vulgar sin. I immediately gave out word that all the peasants in the villages in my district should come to town for *Shabbos* in order to hear a *derashah* from me. My sermon was of course full of moral exhortation, with particular reference to the heinous nature of the sin in question, though of course I did not mention the man's name. So earnestly were those good people aroused to true feelings of penitence, that they were even brought to tears — except, that is, for that peasant, whose face I watched intently as I spoke. It was clear that my *derashah* had made absolutely no impression on him: he remained utterly unmoved.

"I couldn't contain myself. 'Villain that you are!' I thundered out at him. 'At least you owe us a word of thanks! It's because of you that I made all this fuss, because people have testified thus and thus about you!'

"'It wasn't me that committed the sin,' the villager answered quietly.

"I tried again, but received the same reply.

"'Very well,' said I to the assembled villagers. 'You had better all go back to your lodgings and eat your *Shabbos* meal, for today is the holy Day of Rest, and tomorrow I will somehow find a way of punishing this fellow.'

"That night, though, my father appeared to me in a dream and said: 'My son! What have you done? For today you shamed publicly one of the hidden tzaddikim of our generation, one of those who fulfill the teaching of the Prophet Michah, to walk humbly with God. Go out at once and beg his forgiveness — but beware not to reveal his identity.'

"Now when I woke up I told myself: 'Dreams are neither one way nor the other.' Nevertheless, just to be sure, I decided not to go ahead with the punishment that I had contemplated giving that man. But then the next night the same dream appeared again, and once more on the third night. So first thing the next morning I hired a wagon and headed for his village. I found his wife, but when I asked her where her husband was, she told me that he had just left the house.

"After waiting all day I went home, and tried again the next day — but with no better results. I kept on trying, once a week, week after week, then once a month, for months on end — but every time his wife tells me that he has just left the house. For ten long years I have been calling at his house, but it has not yet been granted me to meet that tzaddik; and I am not allowed to mention his name publicly, by order of my late father. It seems to me that he is hiding from me because he senses through Divine Inspiration that I want to beg his forgiveness, and once that has happened he knows that the Heavenly Court will want to punish me. But so long as he does not forgive me, he knows what torments of self-incrimination I undergo — and he knows that this spiritual anguish suffices to ward off the severer punishment which would otherwise be my just desserts."

סדר פינחס
sidra pinchas

◆§ Shall Your Land be My Land?

לָאֵלֶּה תֵּחָלֵק הָאָרֶץ
For these shall the Land be divided (26:53)

Evening fell while the Baal Shem Tov was on a journey with a few of his disciples, so they stopped to spend the night in a village inn. The little building soon echoed to the revelry of a wedding party, but the Baal Shem Tov and his companions spent the night quietly in their room. In the morning, when the families of the bride and groom were standing outside, ready to make the journey home, the Baal Shem Tov was also there, for he too was preparing to leave. While they were waiting for their wagons a little bird chirped away on a tree, right in front of the bride and groom.

"Do you know what the bird is saying?" said the Baal Shem Tov to his chassidim. "It is saying לָאֵלֶּה תֵּחָלֵק הָאָרֶץ: 'For these shall the Land be divided.'"

They did not understand his meaning, of course, but neither did they ask him to explain himself.

Decades later, after this couple had lived a good life together and had raised children and grandchildren, the husband decided that come what may, he was going to spend his old age in *Eretz Yisrael.* Since his wife refused to leave her children, and they could find no way out of their dilemma, they brought their case before a rabbinical court. The *beis din* ruled that the wife would receive a bill of divorce: she was not allowed to prevent him from going, nor could he force her to join him. After their monetary matters had been settled according to the court's ruling, the husband departed for *Eretz Yisrael,* and the wife remained with her children.

Word of this incident spread far and wide, until it reached the disciples who had accompanied the Baal Shem Tov to that village inn.

"So this was what the rebbe meant," they said in wonderment. "לָאֵלֶּה תֵּחָלֵק הָאָרֶץ: Between these shall the Land divide!"

◆§ Soul vs. Soul

וַתִּקְרַבְנָה בְּנוֹת צְלָפְחָד
And the daughters of Tzlafchad drew near (27:1)

The passage concerning inheritance should rightly have been written through Moshe Rabbeinu. It was the daughters of Tzlafchad, however, who were thus privileged, for merits are brought about through the meritorious *(Talmud, Tractate Bava Basra).*

Reb Yisrael of Ruzhin once went for a stroll with one of his elder chassidim who was a grandson of Rabbi Yechezkel Landau, celebrated both as the illustrious author of *Noda BiYehudah,* a classic work of halachic responsa, and as a determined opponent of Chassidism. Said Reb Yisrael: "Since you are a grandson of the *rav* of Prague, let me tell you what I heard from Reb Avraham Yehoshua Heschel of Apta, who in turn heard it from Reb Yechiel Michel of Zlotchov, at the time that the tzaddik of Zlotchov was suffering from the antagonism of your grandfather.

"And this is what Reb Yechiel Michel said: 'I harbor him no grudge, for God commanded him to oppose the chassidim. You see, when the Heavenly Court decided that it was time for the soul of the Baal Shem Tov to descend to This World, the voices of all kinds of prosecuting angels spoke up, arguing that if this were to be allowed the Messianic Redemption would be brought about before its time. But at that moment whole choirs of kindlier voices chimed in, so it was decided that the soul of the Baal Shem Tov would indeed be sent down to This World — but at the same time another lofty soul would be dispatched down here, to dwell in a man who would also be a leader of his generation, but an antagonist to the teachings of the Baal Shem Tov and his disciples. That man was your grandfather, the sage of Prague.

"It thus works out that it was Reb Yechezkel Landau who caused the soul of the Baal Shem Tov to come down here; without him this would not have taken place. For, as our Sages say: Merits are brought about through the meritorious.'"

◆§ Leadership (i)

יִפְקֹד ה׳... אִישׁ עַל הָעֵדָה
Let God... appoint a man over the congregation (27:16)

The Baal Shem Tov passed away on the festival of Shavuos in the year 1760. The mantle of leadership was immediately assumed by his son, Reb Zvi, who was accepted by all the chassidim of the day as his father's rightful successor.

On the same festival exactly one year later, in the presence of all the disciples who were seated around his table, he rose, turned to Reb Dov Ber, the Maggid of Mezritch, and said: "This night my father appeared to me, and told me that the Divine Presence, together with all the hosts of heaven, has now passed over and now rests upon you."

With that he removed the white gown which had been his, and placed it around the shoulders of Reb Dov Ber. The Maggid did not decline, but agreed to occupy the seat of leadership.

❦ ❦ ❦

When Reb Shalom Ber of Lubavitch recounted this incident he added: "Reb Zvi was renowned for his self-effacement. But still, what greatness of spirit does a man need in order to do what he did! For we find examples in the Talmud of sages who did not want to be thrust into positions of greatness — but once they were already there ... "

◆§ Leadership (ii)

A group of chassidim from Reissin once came to Reb Dov Ber of Mezritch with a problem. On the one hand it was such a long way to Mezritch that they were unable to visit him for spiritual guidance as often as they would wish; on the other, they did not want to remain without a rebbe for long periods of time.

The rebbe gave them one of his cloaks, together with a black silk belt and a staff, and said: "Take these things and give them to a man by the name of Mendele who lives in Vitebsk. Whenever you find it difficult to come here, you will be able to draw inspiration in your divine service from him."

Off the chassidim all went to Vitebsk in search of a man called Reb Mendele. The tzaddik whom we know as Reb Menachem Mendel of Vitebsk was not yet renowned, so most of the townsfolk whom they asked simply answered: "There isn't any Reb Mendele of that kind around here!"

In the course of their investigations, however, they encountered a woman who asked: "Gentlemen, whom do you seek?"

"We are looking for Reb Mendele," they said.

"There is no Mendele around here of the kind who is called rebbe," she said, "but there *are* plenty of people called Mendele — my son-in-law, for example."

Surmising that this was perhaps the man whom they were seeking, they entered her house, met her son-in-law, and handed him the articles that they had received from the hand of the Maggid of Mezritch. Reb Menachem Mendel garbed himself in the cloak, wrapped the *gartl* around his waist, and took the staff in his hand. And from that moment the chassidim did not recognize him: he was a man transformed, and they stood before him in awe.

◆§ *Leadership (iii)*

After the passing of Reb Dov Ber of Lubavitch, the son of Reb Shneur Zalman of Liadi, the chassidim all decided at once to appoint as his successor his son-in-law, Reb Menachem Mendel, better known by the name of one of his works as the Tzemach Tzedek. Reb Menachem Mendel, who was also the son of Reb Shneur Zalman's daughter, was unwilling to accept the appointment. His first argument was that in point of seniority the next rebbe should rightly be his uncle, Reb Chaim Avraham, the son of Reb Shneur Zalman of Liadi, and he sent the chassidim to speak to him.

Reb Chaim Avraham told the delegation that came to him: "Go and tell him that he should stop deluding people. Everyone knows that he is fully suited to the position of rebbe, to support and lead the People of God. I will soon follow you and back your words."

Soon after they had returned to speak again with Reb Menachem Mendel they were joined by Reb Chaim Avraham, and as he entered, his nephew rose as a mark of deference.

"Please keep your seat," requested the visitor. "I am the uncle, but you are the rebbe."

"But how can I be a rebbe," argued Reb Menachem Mendel, addressing himself to the group at large, "when a rebbe must be familiar with the secrets of the Torah?"

One of the chassidim answered: "In enumerating the gifts which mastery of the Torah bestows upon its devotees, the Mishnah in Tractate *Avos* first says וְנוֹתֶנֶת לוֹ מַלְכוּת — 'it grants him kingship' — and only *thereafter* says וּמְגַלִּין לוֹ רָזֵי תּוֹרָה: 'the secrets of the Torah are revealed to him.'"

Reb Menachem Mendel spoke again: "If I should have been rebbe, I would have heard some hint of this from my grandfather, Reb Shneur Zalman."

"Rebbe, you have most certainly heard," the chassidim insisted, "And one of the hints was the dream you had not long ago."

For Reb Menachem Mendel had cried out in his sleep while ill, about a week before the passing of his grandfather, the author of *Tanya.* When Reb Shneur Zalman had asked him why he had cried out, he had answered: "I dreamed that a Torah Scroll fell to the ground. No man could pick it up. I ran towards it as fast as I could, raised it up, and returned it to its place."

"That is right," his grandfather had answered. "You raised it up."

And everyone had understood the meaning of his words.

In due course, at any rate, in response to the earnest entreaties of large numbers of chassidim, Reb Menachem Mendel undertook to lead the multitudes of followers of the school of *Chabad.* It was then that he began to light them along the path in which they were to progress in the service of God, and to spread his teachings far and wide in both the revealed and the hidden sides of the Torah — a task which he was to maintain, unwearied, for some thirty-eight years.

◆§ Leadership (iv)

The chassidim were perplexed. Their rebbe, Reb Yaakov Yitzchak of Pshischah, better known as the Yid HaKadosh ("the holy Jew"), had passed away, and they did not know where to turn in search of a successor.

At length they consulted one of the giants in their midst, Reb Simchah Bunem, who answered them with a parable: "A shepherd once fell to the ground, and was soon fast asleep. At midnight he awoke, and saw that the moon was shining, and the air was cool, and there was clear drinking water before him. As for his sheep, there was not one missing, and they were all pasturing contentedly. His heart surged with gratitude and joy, and he cried out: 'O my beloved God! How can I thank You for all your kindness to me? If You entrust me with Your sheep, I will guard them like the apple of my eye!'"

Reb Simchah Bunem concluded: "If such a shepherd could be found, he should be our rebbe."

They listened to his parable, and every single man present savored the same thought: he himself, Reb Simchach Bunem, should be their rebbe.

Now one of those present was Reb Abba'le of Neustadt, who had been the mentor of the departed rebbe, the Yid HaKadosh, in the study of the mysteries of the Kabbalah, and in fact many had earlier assumed that he would be his successor. Reb Abba'le sensed what thought was passing through the minds of those around him, and shared it, too. He thereupon stood up from his place of honor and seated Reb Simchah Bunem there in his stead.

◆§ The Altar and the Table

אֶת קָרְבָּנִי לַחְמִי לְאִשַּׁי
My sacrifice, the bread of My burnt offerings (28:2)

Scholars and sages, the rich and the poor, used to come in their hundreds and thousands to hear Torah teachings from the mouth of Reb Avraham, the Maggid of Trisk, and whether it was *Shabbos* or a festival or an ordinary weekday, he always made a point of providing for them all at his massive table. After each festival, of course, when the greatest multitudes of chassidim had just returned to their homes, he always found himself to be deep in debt. A group of elder chassidim of his inner circle approached him therefore with a suggestion: since the cost of providing meals for all of his chassidim got him so seriously into debt that he was forced to dispatch an emissary to collect contributions from them to cover his losses, would it not be better to dispense with the meals and to be spared the necessity of collecting?

Understanding his silence to imply consent, the same delegation came to speak to him again in order to determine the new arrangements. This time, however, he answered: "Our Sages teach us that so long as the *Beis HaMikdash* stood on the Temple Mount in Jerusalem, the altar conferred atonement on the House of Israel; after the Destruction of the Temple, a man's table grants him that atonement. Now in connection with the daily sacrifice on the altar we read אֶת קָרְבָּנִי לַחְמִי לְאִשַּׁי: 'My sacrifice, the bread of My burnt offerings.' And that is what I say, too: אֶת קָרְבָּנִי — *my* sacrifice is — לַחְמִי לְאִישַׁי: my bread which I give to my people [for here, instead of reading לְאִשַּׁי: "my burnt offerings," he punningly substituted לְאִישַׁי: "my people"]. And just as the burnt offerings on the altar gave rise to a רֵיחַ נִיחֹחַ, a savor pleasing to God, so too the bread I provide for my chassidim brings atonement for me, and for them too."

And the custom in Trisk continued as before.

סדר מטות
Sidra Matos

Words have Weight

או הִשָּׁבַע שְׁבֻעָה
Or swear an oath (30:3)

Or swear an oath...he shall not break his word: He shall not treat his words recklessly *(Rashi).*

Money and merchandise he had in plenty. Only one thing was lacking — children, and he tirelessly plied his rebbe with his request for this blessing. Every time he asked, though, his entreaty was deferred by the rebbe, Reb Aryeh Leib of Shpola, until one day the chassid decided that he would give him no rest, and plead with him with such clamorous urgency that the tzaddik would be forced to give him a blessing which heaven would fulfill. The chassid arrived at a moment when the tzaddik was contemplating secrets of higher worlds, so when he opened with his barrage of pleas, the tzaddik said: "Please leave me for the moment, for I am now involved in a matter concerning the welfare of the House of Israel at large; this is not a propitious time for me to undertake the request of an individual."

"Ah!" thought the chassid. "If this is indeed a propitious hour, and that is why he is occupied with the needs of all of Israel, then I am not going to budge from here until he grants me my request!"

And he simply pestered the tzaddik without interruption so that he was utterly unable to concentrate. The Shpoler Zeide first implored him to give him some peace, and later warned him that he would live to regret his insistence — but to no avail, until in a moment of anger he said: "I swear that you will never have children!"

The chassid was terror-stricken. "My soul-root does not belong *here*," he concluded, and, taking his leave from the rebbe, he left Shpola with a heavy heart.

Some time later his business interests brought him to Korets. One day, his transactions over, he retired to the *beis midrash* in which Reb Pinchas of Korets used to study and pray. Now although Reb Pinchas was as yet unknown as a tzaddik, this chassid had any eye for these things; he perceived that he was a man with a lofty soul, and surmised that he was probably inspired as well by *ruach hakodesh*. He interested himself in his material situation, and was told by neighbors that Reb Pinchas was quite penniless. To make things more acute, the month of Nissan was already underway, and the festival of Pessach with its extra household expenses was just around the corner. On top of that, as the guest heard from some of the townsmen, what bothered Reb Pinchas most was that he would be losing precious time from his Torah studies through the preparations which had to be made at home for the approaching festival.

"This could be my lucky hour," thought the visiting chassid.

He went straight to the home of Reb Pinchas, and asked his wife whether she had whatever was needed for Pessach. When she told him that she did not have so much as a single copper coin, he took out his wallet and gave her enough money to enable her to buy the flour which was scrupulously guarded against contact with moisture; to pay the baker who made the *matzos*; and to buy fish and meat and all manner of dishes in honor of the forthcoming *Yom Tov*. He then went out himself and bought a table and benches, and a bed as well, and asked her to arrange everything in the most generous style possible, for he wanted to be their guest for Pessach. He asked her besides to keep these preparations from her husband's attention until Pessach eve. To this she agreed, and day by day he would call at her home to see whether there was anything lacking.

Reb Pinchas, for his part, was somewhat surprised that his wife was not bothering him with requests for money to cover the expenses of the festival. He did not raise the subject, however, and continued with his studies in the *beis midrash* as before, night and day.

Before sunset on the eve of the festival, when the tzaddik was already at prayers, the chassid paid one last visit to his house to give it his finishing touches. When the tzaddik came home and opened the door of his humble dwelling, he was greeted by a table decked with all manner of dishes and delicacies, and a room lit up on all sides by tall white candles. He was overjoyed, and asked his wife where all this festive joy had come from.

"Our guest who stands here before you — he prepared it all," she said.

The tzaddik greeted his guest warmly, but asked him no questions, for they sat down at once to the *Seder* service, which Reb Pinchas conducted with joy and with fervor. Later on in the evening, in the course of the meal, he turned to his guest: "What brings you here? Do you have a request?"

The chassid finally told him all that had passed between himself and the Shpoler Zeide, begged him to undo the oath that he had heard, and asked him to give his blessing that his wife would bear a child.

Reb Pinchas thereupon said: "If any good deed I have

ever done carries any weight in heaven, I swear to you that this year your wife will bear a son."

And his blessing was fulfilled within the year.

❦ ❦ ❦

When Reb Yisrael of Ruzhin recounted this story he added: "At that moment, when Reb Pinchas of Korets made his oath, the entire Heavenly Court was thrown into upheaval: whose oath would give way to whose? And the verdict was that the oath of him who had never made an oath in his life before, even a truthful one, was to prevail. The records were searched, and the Heavenly Court accordingly honored the oath of Reb Pinchas."

But the tzaddik of Ruzhin had one further comment: "From this episode we see how one should not be obstinate in the face of the decree of a tzaddik. For the grandson of that chassid, who came into the world through the oath of Reb Pinchas, grew up to be a treacherous enemy of Israel who slandered his own grandchildren — the saintly brothers from Slavita — to the barbarous authorities."

◆§ *A Blissful Anger*

וַיִּקְצֹף מֹשֶׁה
And Moshe was angry (31:14)

Reb Baruch of Mezhibuzh had a distinctive manner of teaching: he would impose his authority on his disciples with a heavy hand, and would gruffly rebuke all those who came to hear him teach. He was fond of quoting, as a kind of proof-text for his unique style, the verse which speaks of the gentiles whom Avraham and Sarah taught a belief in One God: וְאֶת הַנֶּפֶשׁ אֲשֶׁר עָשׂוּ בְחָרָן. Literally, this means "The souls which they made in Charan," but Reb Baruch would read the place-name not as חָרָן but as חָרוֹן, which means "anger," as if to say: the Patriarchs accomplished their holy task by the exercise of anger...

In 1811 Reb Baruch — whose name means "blessed" — breathed his last, and by his bedside his chassidim found a volume of the holy Zohar. It was open at the passage which says: "There are two kinds of anger. There is one kind of anger which is blessed both in the World Above and in the World Below. Its name is Baruch..."

◆§ Keeping One's Head

Reb Mordechai of Neshchiz of course already owned at least one *tallis katan* — the four-cornered garment, worn like a tunic and with a hole for the head, that carries the fringed *tzitzis* at its corners. But he yearned to have a *tallis katan* that came from *Eretz Yisrael*. After all kinds of strenuous efforts, therefore, his chassidim finally managed to grant him his wish, and to bring a suitable length of white lambswool cloth all the way from the Holy Land. One of his disciples asked for the privilege of cutting it to size and sewing its hems. In his enthusiasm, however, he made a false fold and discovered to his horror that while cutting a hole for the head he had made another gaping hole right in the front of the garment! What would the rebbe say? After waiting for this cherished object for so long, and after all the exertion that had gone into acquiring it, it was now irreparably ruined.

When the rebbe next saw him, and asked him whether the garment was ready, he stammered out his story in the utmost consternation.

"My good man, why are you afraid?" said the rebbe. "Don't you realize that a *tallis katan* really needs two big holes? One, as usual, to *put* one's head through; and the other — to test whether Mordechai will *lose* his head..."

◆§ A Soft Answer

After the death of the first wife of Reb Yaakov Yitzchak (the Chozeh) of Lublin, he summoned Reb Yaakov Yitzchak (the Yid HaKadosh) of Pshischah, and told him that he was responsible: he had made her liable to punishment at the hands of heaven by causing her to speak evil of him to her husband, the Chozeh. (Her remarks were evidently in sympathy with the grudge that was borne by many of the disciples of the Chozeh against the Yid HaKadosh, because he had cultivated a following of chassidim of his own during the lifetime of the Chozeh, their rebbe.)

"God forbid!" said the Yid HaKadosh. "I know nothing of it."

"Then what did you do at the time [that chassidim started following you]?" demanded the Chozeh.

"I read *Psalms*," said the Yid HaKadosh.

"And is that nothing in your eyes?" the Chozeh persisted.

"Well, what could I have done?" asked the Yid HaKadosh.

"At least you should have been angry," said the Chozeh.

"Rebbe," said the Yid HaKadosh, "please look into my heart and see whether I am able to be angry."

The Chozeh leaned forward, looked into the deepest recesses of his heart, and said: "True! The Yid is incapable of becoming angry!"

◆§ *Near Now, Nearer Hereafter*

וּמִקְנֶה רַב *An abundance of cattle (32:1)*

A chassid by the name of Reb Peretz of Pshischah very much wanted to make the journey to *Eretz Yisrael*, but when he came to ask his rebbe for permission, the Yid HaKadosh withheld it. A few days later Reb Peretz fell ill, and his rebbe, who had come to visit him, asked him whether he still wanted to go to the Holy Land.

Reb Peretz answered: "We read in the Torah וּמִקְנֶה רַב הָיָה לִבְנֵי רְאוּבֵן וְלִבְנֵי גָד — the men of the Tribes of Reuven and Gad had an abundance of cattle. Now why does the Torah tell us this? Is this a compliment worthy of such tzaddikim as they were? Their argument, rather, was that they had מִקְנֶה רַב [to be read as if to mean קִנְיָן בְּרַבָּם]: they had acquired a share in their *rav*, Moshe Rabbeinu. And since he was to be buried on the east side of the Jordan, they wanted to be allocated their tracts of land there, for they did not want to part with him. And we see that their argument was accepted. So it is with me. I can see that my rebbe will soon be leaving This World, and that is why I no longer desire to leave for *Eretz Yisrael*. I want to remain together with my rebbe, for I have acquired a share in him."

And indeed, in the course of that illness Reb Peretz departed for another world, where he was joined very soon after by his rebbe.

Early Inklings

בְּטֶרֶם אֶצָּרְךָ בַבֶּטֶן יְדַעְתִּיךָ
Before I formed you in the womb I knew you (Haftarah)

When Reb Baruch of Mezhibuzh, the grandson of the Baal Shem Tov, was a little boy, his *melamed* at school introduced him for the first time to the study of *Gemara.* Perceiving that the first page of the text was numbered ב, the second letter of the alphabet, the child asked: "And where is page א, the first page?"

The *melamed* duly explained that page א was the title page, which bore the name of the tractate.

"Then I will start with the first page," announced the young pupil. "Here it says בָּבָא קַמָּא. Do you see? The name of this tractate makes up the initials of six words: בָּרוּךְ בֶּן אָדִיל, קָדוֹשׁ מִבֶּטֶן אִמּוֹ — Baruch the son of Adel, holy from the womb of his mother."

סדר מסעי
Sidra Mas'ei

Reprieve

וְנָס שָׁמָּה רֹצֵחַ מַכֵּה נֶפֶשׁ בִּשְׁגָגָה
That the person who kills unawares may flee there (35:11)

In a village near Zanz there lived a God-fearing Jew who owned a tavern and an inn. One day a wayfarer came by, dressed in rags and tatters; the innkeeper gave him a square meal, and after the Grace after Meals offered him money. Since the visitor declined the offer the host assumed that it was less than he expected to receive, so he prepared to increase the amount, but the pauper said: "Please do not insist that I accept a donation from you, for I am quite a rich man."

The innkeeper was so stupefied to hear this statement that he asked the stranger to explain why he wandered about in this state. And this is the story he was told.

"I live in the city of Pest, near which I own several villages, fields and vineyards. Once a large sum of money was stolen from me, and I did not know who the thief was. We had a maid — an orphan — and since we suspected that this was her doing we took her along to the local authorities. The police there beat her in order to induce her to confess, but she insisted she had stolen nothing, and they sent her home to us. The harsh treatment that she had endured left its mark. For some days she languished in bed, and then died. Two weeks later the thief was found. I was stricken by terror: I had suspected an innocent person, and through my doing this orphan had met her death!

"I set out to speak to Reb Meir of Premishlan, hoping that he would teach me some way of repenting, and atoning for my sin.

" 'Choose one of these three,' he said. 'Either you die, though you will be granted a place in the World to Come; or you will be ill and bedridden for three years, while the suffering you undergo will cleanse you of your sins; or for three years you will wander about as a vagabond, as the law prescribes for an unwitting manslaughterer.'

"I couldn't bring myself to agree to any one of these three alternatives, and returned home. For several days I suffered headaches, but mentioned this to no man. Pain gradually spread over my whole body, I was confined to my bed, and the doctor who was summoned by my family almost despaired of my life. 'The rebbe,' I told myself, 'has evidently chosen death as my means of expiation without waiting for my consent.' I immediately sent off a telegram to Premishlan, accompanied by a *pidyon* contribution for charity, asking him to pray that I be restored to health and promising that I would then call on him and accept upon myself whatever he would tell me to do. And that is exactly what happened. He prayed on my behalf, I recovered, and as soon as I was strong enough I set out for Premishlan.

"When I went in to speak to him he said: 'You still have ample time to die; and you have already been ill; so choose the exile of a vagabond.'

"As soon as I expressed my willingness to proceed with my punishment, he said: 'Let me teach you now how one goes about *praven galus*, living the life of an exile. First of all, leave everything you have with you at the moment — clothes, money — with me, and leave my house wearing some tattered old garment. Do not spend any day in the place where you found lodging for the night. If you are hungry, ask no man for money or for food, but if people offer you something out of compassion, you may accept it. Throughout the three years you are not to visit your home. This alone I will permit you to to do: at the end of a year you may visit your hometown and stand outside the city limits, while you send a messenger to your wife to bring you the account books of your business. If you see that your business is running at a loss, I allow you to return to your home — but I promise you that your business will not flounder. Throughout these three years you are not to ride in a wagon, but to make your way from place to place only on foot. And when the three years have elapsed you are to come to me. I will return all your possessions to you, and teach you how to conduct your life thereafter so that you will be able to set your soul aright.'

"I took my leave of the tzaddik, and took to the road, exactly as he instructed me to do — a trek of two years so far. Now I heard very recently that Reb Meir had passed away, and since he told me to come to speak with him when three years had elapsed, I didn't know what to do. But then I heard that in Zanz, not too far from here, there lives a tzaddik called Reb Chaim. In fact I'm heading in that direction now, in the hope that he will guide me. And that is why I will not accept your donation, thank-you, because at the moment I am not setting out on another leg of my trek as an exile: I am on my way to visit Reb Chaim of Zanz."

The innkeeper was so curious to know what the end of the story would be that he set out to Zanz with his ragged guest. The vagabond did not even manage to put his question to Reb Chaim, when the tzaddik said: "Return to your home, traveling by way of Premishlan. Find the grave of Reb Meir, and tell him that the *rav* of Zanz says that two years are enough for you, for you observed them with the true self-sacrifice of *mesirus nefesh.*"

ספר דברים
deuteronomy

סדר דברים
Sidra Devarim

⊷ Jesting in Earnest

וַחֲצֵרֹת וְדִי זָהָב
And Chatzeros and Di-Zahav (1:1)

It was a sad story that this penniless chassid brought to his rebbe, Reb Shlomo of Radomsk: his daughter was of marriageable age, and he did not know where to begin to find all the money needed for a dowry and a wedding. All this was written out in the *kvitl* which he handed the rebbe.

The tzaddik read it through, and exclaimed: "What is this I read here about your being 'a poor man'?! You had better leave my house at once, for our Sages teach us that 'a pauper is accounted as if dead,' and I am a *kohen*, one of the priestly family, who may not be defiled by such contact!'

The man ran out from sheer fright, but the tzaddik called after him: "Come now, come now! This must surely be a case of a *mes mitzvah*, a dead body which can be attended to by no one else, in which case a *kohen* is allowed to defile himself."

Those present laughed at the seeming jest, and the tzaddik addressed himself once more to the poor fellow: "You are worrying about marrying off your daughter. Tell me: do you have bread to eat?"

"To tell the truth," stammered the pauper, "I haven't."

"But you do say the *HaMotzi* benediction over bread every day, don't you? So where do you get the bread for that?"

"Most of it comes from my wife; she works, and earns a little."

'What a fine business!" cried the rebbe. "His wife supports him! Shouldn't we be warned by the example of Adam, whose wife gave him something to eat? ... And this fellow says that his wife supports him! Tell me: in what way does your wife earn her income?"

"She goes to all the courtyards [in Hebrew: חֲצֵרוֹת] of the squires in the area, sells vegetables and whatever, and earns a little from that," the pauper replied."

"If so," said the tzaddik, "we have a verse in the Torah which lists place-names, and there it says וַחֲצֵרֹת וְדִי זָהָב: that if she goes to חֲצֵרוֹת, she will no doubt encounter דִּי זָהָב [literally, "ample gold"]. Go home in peace, my good man, and the Almighty will help you, and your wife will prosper with דִּי זָהָב."

But when he came home and his wife asked him what he had brought back from the rebbe, he did not know what to answer.

After some time his wife came home with a package, and said: "Look here. Today I found this thing lying about in the mud."

They opened it, and found three hundred rubles — quite a sum in those days. Half of it they set aside for their daughter's dowry and the wedding expenses, and with the rest the happy man set up a little business in which he prospered for the rest of his life.

❧ ❧ ❧

After the passing of Reb Shlomo of Radomsk, this chassid came to visit his son and successor as rebbe, Reb Avraham Yissachar, and told him the above episode.

"My father," said the tzaddik, "was a remarkable man. Every expression of his supernatural powers and his *ruach hakodesh* he managed to clothe in jests and witticisms, so that no one should detect that there was anything extraordinary afoot."

◆§ *Not Far from the Tree*

יֹסֵף עֲלֵיכֶם כָּכֶם
May He increase you...as you are (1:11)

Seated at his *tish* one *Shabbos*, Reb Yaakov Yitzchak (the Chozeh) of Lublin began rebuking himself in such merciless terms that his disciples could bear it no longer, and one by one they slipped out of the room.

Perceiving this, he changed his tone and said: "May God grant you all sons no worse than myself!"

Relieved, the chassidim returned to their places around the table.

On this incident Reb Leibl Eger of Lublin commented:

"We find a similar situation with Moshe Rabbeinu. When he began to rebuke the Children of Israel — as Rashi explains on the opening verses of the Book of *Devarim* — he no doubt perceived that they had fallen into melancholy. He therefore changed his tone suddenly and said: "יֹסֵף עֲלֵיכֶם כָּכֶם אֶלֶף פְּעָמִים — 'May God increase you a thousand times *as you are*'; that is to says, 'For all that, may Israel be blessed with many more people *like yourselves!*' And then their hearts too were cheered."

◆§ The Summons

לֹא תַכִּירוּ פָנִים בַּמִּשְׁפָּט
You shall not respect persons in judgment (1:17)

When Reb Aryeh Leib, the Shpoler Zeide, had been rebbe for three years, a fearful famine descended on the region. The tzaddik, who had always found ways of providing for the needy and the widows and the orphans like a devoted father, now could find no rest, for he had no way of allaying the suffering of the thousands of paupers on all sides. So great was his anguish that for weeks on end he could bring himself to partake of nothing more than bread and tea.

As the famine extended over the furthest provinces of Russia, rebbes from the starving communities wrote to Shpola, begging Reb Aryeh Leib to clamor On High to have the decree rescinded — for was he not a tzaddik who was accustomed to working wonders? The Shpoler Zeide thereupon dispatched letters to ten of the mightiest tzaddikim of the day — Reb Zusya of Hanipoli, Reb Yaakov Shimshon of Shipitovka, Reb Ze'ev of Zhitomir, and others — asking that they come at once to Shpola.

When they arrived he sat them around his long table and addressed them in the following words: "My masters, I am taking the Almighty to a lawsuit. You are to be the judges. It is true that according to the law of the Torah the plaintiff is obliged to take his suit to the place where the defendant is to be found, but since 'there is no place devoid of His presence,' and since, more particularly, 'wherever ten are assembled the Divine Presence rests,' we shall conduct the court case here."

That holy congregation then prayed in unison — their supplications would melt a stone — and the Shpoler

Zeide instructed his beadle to announce: "By order of the assemblage here foregathered, I do hereby proclaim that Reb Aryeh Leib the son of Rachel summonses the Almighty to a lawsuit, to be duly conducted in this room in three days' time!"

Those three days they spent in fasting and prayer, and no man was permitted to interrupt them in their devotions. On the fourth day, when their morning prayers had come to an end and they were still enwrapped in their *talleisim* and adorned by their *tefillin*, the Shpoler Zeide solemnly signalled his *shammes* to announce that the court case was now to begin.

"In the name of all the women and children of the Jews of Russia," opened the tzaddik, "I hereby state my claim against the defendant. Why does the Almighty not provide them with food, decreeing instead that they perish (God forbid) by famine? Does the Torah itself not say: כִּי לִי בְנֵי יִשְׂרָאֵל עֲבָדִים עֲבָדַי הֵם — 'For unto Me are the Children of Israel bondmen: they are *My* bondmen'? And do we not further have His promise, delivered to us by the Prophet Yechezkel, that even if His children should want to walk in the ways of the nations of the earth, this will never come about? It follows, then, that the Children of Israel are the Almighty's servants for all eternity, in which case at worst they should belong to the category of Jewish bondmen. And does not the law as set out in the *Mechilta* and the Talmud oblige the master to provide for the wife and children of his bondman? How, then, can the Almighty disregard his own Torah so blatantly, God forbid?

"Now I know well that some prosecuting angel will argue in the Almighty's defense that these servants do not serve their Master as perfectly as they should. To this I have two answers. Firstly, where is it written that if a bondman is somewhat lazy his wife and children are to be deprived of their daily bread? Secondly, if these bondmen are slack in their service, their Master has no one to blame but Himself. For who else loaded each bondman with an Evil Inclination which tries its best to dampen their enthusiasm and loyalty? I am even willing to swear that if not for this Evil Inclination which the Master Himself imposed on them, they would render the most faithful service imaginable!"

His case stated, the Shpoler Zeide resumed his seat, and the bench of ten venerable judges consulted their volumes of Torah law. After some moments they rose to their feet, and declared their unanimous verdict: "This court finds that justice lies on the side of Reb Aryeh Leib the son of Rachel. The Almighty is accordingly obliged by whatever means are possible to provide for the women and children of His People. And may the Heavenly Court concur with the verdict of this court in the World Below."

So they declared three times. The Shpoler Zeide then asked to have vodka and refreshments served. They drank *LeChaim* and ate together with happy hearts, and when evening fell they all went their separate ways.

Five days later the government announced that they would soon bring thousands of tons of wheat and other grain from Siberia, where it was abundant and inexpensive; the roads had been impassable, but now a new route had been hit upon. Whatever grain was already available suddenly dropped in price, for all the dealers were eager to dispose of their stock before the new consignments arrived. A month later the new grain was available, and for the whole of that year there was bread in plenty for the humblest purse.

◆§ *A Man of Principle*

אִם תֹּאבוּ וּשְׁמַעְתֶּם... וְאִם תְּמָאֲנוּ וּמְרִיתֶם...
If you are willing and obedient..., but if you refuse and rebel (Haftarah)

Late last century the Russian Imperial Government decreed that none of the rebbes of the Twerski family, who belonged to the chassidic dynasty of Chernobyl, were to leave the bounds of the various towns in which they lived. Reb Mordechai Dov of Hornisteipl was one of those compelled to sign their assent to this decree, for he too was a scion of this dynasty.

One day Reb Mordechai Dov found himself faced with a dilemma. His son, Reb Baruch David, was soon to be married in Homil. How could he attend? But then again, how could he not attend? ... He quickly disguised himself as a merchant, and smuggled himself out of town.

On the way he encountered a chassid who gazed at his

face very intently, and then said: "*Shalom* to you, rebbe!"

"You're a fool yourself!" retorted the rebbe.

But nothing would help. By the time he arrived at the *chuppah* under which the bridal couple were soon to be led for the wedding ceremony, thousands of people from all the towns and villages around had converged on Homil, if not to receive his greeting of *Shalom* then at least to catch a glimpse of the unassuming nobility which rested on his features. But for the rebbe this was a grim prospect: who could know where the Evil Eye of the authorities might be lurking? He asked that a wagon be prepared so the he would be able to leave immediately after the ceremony. Someone secured the services of the first wagon-driver who happened to pass by, and the rebbe hastened away.

As they passed through a forest on their way, the wagon-driver suddenly called the horses to a halt, and turned to his lone passenger: "I would like you to know that I am a professional robber. What I ask of you is that you give me your blessing that I should succeed in my work. If you don't, I will kill you on the spot."

The tzaddik was not alarmed, and answered calmly: "Here, let me tell you something. You know, a very similar thing once happened to Reb Zusya of Hanipoli. He was traveling out on some highway when he met a gang of robbers. They too asked him to bless their work with success, and threatened to kill him if he would not oblige. So Reb Zusya said: 'A wealthy squire is soon going to come past your way. You won't have to kill him, because he is going to die anyway while he is quite near you. This *paritz* will leave a considerable sum of money behind him. Now if you satisfy yourselves with that amount, and become penitent, and abandon your present careers completely, then I promise you that you will prosper in all your ways. But if (God forbid) you persist in your evil ways, then you will most certainly fall into the hands of the authorities, and the day will come when you will be led in fetters before the very door of my house.' And that is exactly what happened. Some of that gang repented, and followed the straight road, and did well; others continued to rob and murder until they were eventually caught, and they were in fact led in chains past the cottage of Reb Zusya in Hanipoli.

"Now as far as I am concerned," concluded Reb Mordechai Dov to his wagon-driver, "I don't promise you any fat squire. But this much I can tell you: that if you decided to abandon your crooked ways and follow the straight road, good for you. If you don't, then you will certainly come to a bitter end. I have warned you!

"And now, if you want to kill me — kill me."

But the wagon-driver accompanied him home in peace.

סדר ואתחנן
sidra vaeschanan

◆§ *Prompt and Impromptu*

וָאֶתְחַנַּן אֶל ה׳ בָּעֵת הַהִיא לֵאמֹר
And I pleaded with God at that time, saying (3:23)

In their younger years Reb Beirish of Alisk and, to a lesser extent, Reb Uri of Strelisk had both been close disciples of Reb Mordechai of Neschiz. With time, as the true stature of the Saraph ("the fiery angel") of Strelisk became apparent, his former friend came to regard him as his rebbe. So it was that Reb Beirish once hastened to spend *Shabbos* in a certain town because he heard that Reb Uri would be there.

At the *Shabbos* table, Reb Uri turned to his chassid: "*Rav* of Alisk! Could you perhaps honor us with a Torah thought, a *dvar* Torah, but without any preparation?"

Reb Beirish answered at once: "It is written, וָאֶתְחַנַּן אֶל ה׳ בָּעֵת הַהִיא לֵאמֹר — 'And I pleaded with God at that time, saying.' You see, in order to be able to *say* something *at that time*, unprepared, one has to *plead with God* ... "

◆§ Seeing is Believing

וְיָדַעְתָּ הַיּוֹם
And you shall know this day (4:39)

Returning home from his first visit to Reb Shmelke of Nikolsburg, Reb Levi Yitzchak of Berditchev was challenged by his father-in-law: "And what did you learn there?"

"I learned that there is a Creator of the universe," was the answer.

The father-in-law called for the maid and asked her: "Do *you* know that there is a Creator of the universe?"

"Why, of course!" she answered.

Returned Reb Levi Yitzchak: "She says; I know."

◆§ Each Servant has his Style

וְיָדַעְתָּ הַיּוֹם וַהֲשֵׁבֹתָ אֶל לְבָבֶךָ
And you shall know this day, and consider it in your heart (4:39)

Two towering figures had come to Lubavitch at the same time to stay for a few weeks and to hear the teachings of Reb Menachem Mendel, who is known as the Tzemach Tzedek: one was Reb Yitzchak Aizik of Homil, the author of *Chanah Ariel*, and the other was Reb Hillel of Paritsh, the author of *Pelach HaRimon*. According to the custom among chassidim, these two elder disciples used to repeat the many discourses on ethics and *Chabad* philosophy that the rebbe had delivered publicly, as a means of refreshing the memory. Following the instructions of his father, whom he was later to succeed as rebbe, Reb Shmuel of Lubavitch was one of those who used to listen attentively to these repetitions.

On one occasion the Tzemach Tzedek asked his son to repeat one of these discourses as he had heard it from the mouth of these two chassidim, for he wanted to know how they went about their task. When Reb Shmeul had completed his piece, his father said: "Reb Aizik is a *maskil*, and Reb Hillel is an *oved*." [Among Lubavitcher chassidim these two words have special meanings of their own, quite distinct from their usual connotations. In *Chabad* circles a *maskil* is one whose chief aim is the intellectual comprehension of the teachings of Chassidism on subjects such as the relationship of the Creator to the cosmos; the prime goal of the *oved* is self-refinement — in thought, word, and deed.]

"What is the difference between a *maskil* and an *oved?"* asked Reb Shmuel. "For is not a *maskil* also an *oved,* and an *oved* also a *maskil?"*

The rebbe gave no answer. A week later, however, he delivered a learned discourse especially for his sons and for these two elder chassidim. That night, some two or three hours after midnight, he called for his son and told him to go and see for himself what these two chassidim were doing ... He was not to disturb them by entering their lodgings, but was simply to take a peek through the window.

Accompanied by an attendant, Reb Shmuel went off to find where Reb Aizik was staying. He saw him plunged in thought, his head thrown back, his eyes closed, his face ablaze, and in his hand — a pipe.

From there Reb Shmuel proceeded to the lodgings of Reb Hillel. There he sat, crouched forward, looking even smaller and leaner than he looked at any time, a finger in his mouth — a sign of profound concentration, his face pale, and apparently worried.

The Tzemach Tzedek listened to his son's report of what he had seen, and said: "They are both meditating on yesterday's discourse. Reb Aizik is contemplating the mysteries of the supernal Crown *(Keser Elyon)* which were elaborated there; Reb Hillel is reflecting on the subject of self-effacing obedience *(kabbalas ol)* which was discussed there, and is applying it to himself."

❦ ❦ ❦

Reb Shmuel was succeeded in turn by his son, Reb Shalom Ber of Lubavitch, who repeated this story, and added: "The difference between a *maskil* and an *oved* is that for the first, his starting point is intellectuality, and from this he labors to find himself tasks in the *avodah* of self-refinement that are in harmony with what he has studied. The *oved* starts with his tasks of *avodah,* and only then seeks the teaching that explains their place in academic terms."

◆§ Silent Partner

שָׁמוֹר אֶת יוֹם הַשַּׁבָּת
Observe the Sabbath day *(5:12)*

A certain shopkeeper complained to Reb Yisrael Yitzchak of Alexander, the author of *Yismach Yisrael,* that his shop did not provide him with a livelihood. The tzaddik gathered that the shop was open seven days a week, and made a proposal: "If you agree to accept me as a partner in your business to the extent of fifteen percent, though without any investment on my part, then I will promise you a proper income."

The shopkeeper agreed at once and they drew up a legal partnership contract. But the rebbe still had something to add.

"Since I now own one seventh of the business," he said, "the share I am choosing as mine is *Shabbos*. The profits of that day are to be mine, while the profits of the other six days are to be yours. You will therefore close the shop on *Shabbos*, for that is my day. And now, my good man, go along — and prosper!"

And the merchandising policy of the shop's new joint management quickly showed tangible results.

◆§ Bad Examples

Reb Meir Yechiel of Ostrov used to fast a great deal. "A person is obliged," he would say, "to change his very nature and to accustom his digestive system not to demand its needs. When a perfect tzaddik eats and drinks," he would add, "by this very activity he comes closer to God. But I, not being a tzaddik, must as far as possible abstain from food." And in fact he reached a point where he fasted even on *Shabbos*.

It once happened that he summoned to his study a Jew who had desecrated the Day of Rest publicly, and rebuked him for his shamelessness.

"But rebbe," retorted the sinner, "you also desecrate *Shabbos!*"

"I — what?" asked the startled tzaddik.

"Rebbe," explained the other, "you fast on *Shabbos* — surely a mark of disrespect for the Holy Day!"

"You are right, my son," conceded the tzaddik. "But still, my desecration of *Shabbos* is not quite the same as your desecration of *Shabbos*. You see, from your example people will learn; from my example, that is not so likely..."

◆§ *A Share in a Mitzvah*

כַּבֵּד אֶת אָבִיךָ וְאֶת אִמֶּךָ
Honor your father and your mother (5:16)

Reb Yaakov Yitzchak of Pshischah, who is known as the Yid HaKadosh ("the holy Jew"), used to conduct a daily Talmud class for a group of his disciples, one of whom was a local youth who had lost his father. During one such class the tzaddik encountered an extremely problematic text, and was soon plunged deep in thought in an attempt to untangle it. The youth knew from experience that when this kind of thing happened, the rebbe could be depended on to be so carried away in his concentration that he would have time to slip out to his mother's house and take some light refreshment, for he was feeling somewhat faint.

Having eaten, he quickly rose to return to the house of his rebbe — but then he heard his mother calling after him, to climb up to the attic in order to bring down a bundle of fodder. At first he continued on his hurried way, for he was afraid that the rebbe had perhaps resumed his exposition by now. But then he thought again: "Isn't actual performance the ultimate goal of my study? If, then, the mitzvah of honoring my mother has presented itself, how can I not fulfill it?"

He ran back home to do the little chore that his mother had asked of him and then hastened off to the house of the rebbe. Exactly as he opened the door the Yid HaKadosh sat up alert, then stood up in his place and asked the youth: "What mitzvah did you perform now?"

The youth recounted the events of the previous few minutes, and then the tzaddik explained himself: "When you came in, young man, I saw that you were accompanied by the soul of Abbaye, the Talmudic sage — and I immediately had my answer. You see, the Talmud tells us that Abbaye was orphaned as an infant. Indeed, his very name — אַבַּיֵי — is made of the initials of the words from the Prophet Hoshea: אֲשֶׁר בְּךָ יְרֻחַם יָתוֹם — *'for in You the orphan finds mercy.'* Since he knew no father nor mother of his own, it is Abbaye's custom to accompany anyone who fulfills this mitzvah of honoring his father and his mother, in order that he too should have a share in the mitzvah. And once he was already here, and found me grappling with that text in which his arguments figure, he gave me the answer..."

◆§ *Spoonfeeding a Penitent*

וְלֹא תִּגְנֹב
You shall not steal (5:17)

Reb Baruch of Mezhibuzh, who was accustomed to speaking harshly of Reb Levi Yitzchak of Berditchev, once made an announcement at his Friday night table: "If anyone here is willing to speak evil of the *rav* of Berditchev, I hereby promise that he will be rewarded by receiving a portion in the World to Come."

Now there was one young man present who wanted to step forward at once and oblige, but the elder chassidim who stood near him dissuaded him.

"God forbid that you should do such a thing," they said. "Our rebbe has no doubt some profound intention in saying what he did; his words are not to be taken at face value!"

The next day, at the *Shabbos* midday meal, the same offer was repeated, and again no chassid present dared say a bad word about Reb Levi Yitzchak — except for the same young man, who again seemed intent on earning his reward effortlessly. His friends once more appealed to him to hold his peace, and he heeded them, because he was certain that he would be given one more chance to do what he wanted, at the late afternoon meal of *Seudah Shlishis.* This opportunity in fact came, and as soon as Reb Baruch repeated his strange announcement, this impetuous young man broke loose from the entreaties of his friends, and burst his way forward towards the rebbe.

Seeing his efforts at pressing his way through the

crowd, Reb Baruch called to him: "Come near, my son, come near, and tell me what you know of the *rav* of Berditchev."

"I once traveled to Berditchev for a fair," said the young man, "and it occurred to me that this would present me with a fine opportunity to drop in to his *shul* to watch him at his prayers, for I had been told that this was a wonderful sight. So I took off time that morning in the middle of my business affairs and found my way to his synagogue. When I arrived there and heard the sound of his ecstatic prayers I did not dare to walk in; I just remained standing at the entrance. But when he reached the passage... יוֹצֵר מְשָׁרְתִים וַאֲשֶׁר מְשָׁרְתָיו — 'He creates ministering angels who stand in the heights of the universe' — the tzaddik suddenly burst across towards me in a passion of anger, and in the middle of his prayers, when one is least allowed to interrupt oneself by speaking, and demanded of me: 'What will the Angel Michael say? What will the Angel Gavriel say?' And he ran back to his place.

"Now whichever way you look at it," concluded the young man, "this episode sounds crazy. How was he allowed to speak in the middle of the morning prayers? And on top of that to be angry? And what do those strange words about the angels mean? And what did he want altogether?"

Reb Baruch of Mezhibuzh heard the young man out to the end of his story, and then addressed him in the hearing of that entire assemblage: "You should know that Reb Levi Yitzchak is an advocate for all of Israel in the Heavenly Court, speaking up in defense of his fellow Jews even when they have sinned. When in the course of their morning prayers Jews in This World reach the passage that speaks of the ministering angels who stand in the heights of the universe, that is the moment at which Michael and Gavriel and all their hosts speak in defense of the House of Israel, seeking to have them acquitted of the charges that have been laid against them. And when the *rav* of Berditchev reaches that passage, he joins them in their noble endeavors and reinforces their arguments. Now when he suddenly saw you standing there before him, besmirched with the sin that you had committed that very morning in your inn — for did you not pocket a silver spoon that caught your fancy at breakfast? — he was enraged, because he could find no mitigating circumstances to submit to the Court in your favor. You were not pressed into theft by hunger or dire need: you are a rich man, lacking nothing. Why then did you steal that silver spoon? *This* was what made the tzaddik ask in desperation: 'What will the Angel Michael say? What will the Angel Gavriel say?' "

The young man was shaken to his very foundations. His entire being surged with shame and regret for his conduct. He begged his rebbe to guide him to repentance, but Reb Baruch declined: only the tzaddik of Berditchev could teach him how to atone for his sin, and only by following his instructions would his repentance be found acceptable in the Court in the World Above.

The young man complied, and in the fullness of time found peace for his soul.

◆§ *What is Thine is Thine*

Reb Zelig of Shrintzk happened to be in the house of his rebbe, Reb Shmuel of Karov, who was taking a nap, when a certain wealthy chassid came in with a gift which he had intended to present to the rebbe: a fine set of tableware to be used on festive occasions. He had bought two sets, one for himself and one for the rebbe, and he left them both on the table so that the rebbe could make his choice between them. Now in fact when he had bought them he had already made up his mind which he wanted for himself and which he would give the rebbe. Later though, thinking it over, he had decided to leave the matter to the rebbe's choice, and he left a message with Reb Zelig to that effect.

Reb Shmuel woke up, received the message from Reb Zelig, and chose the set which the wealthy chassid had in fact intended to give him. Perceiving that Reb Zelig was most impressed by his choice, the tzaddik assured him: "Do not assume for one moment that this was a divinely-inspired feat of *ruach hakodesh*. Nothing of the sort! But there is a story that I would like to tell you involving myself and my brother, who is a *rav* of standing and — a *misnaged.* My brother once invited me to the marriage of his son with the daughter of some magnate, and when I arrived, my brother began to show me all the magnificent clothes which his *mechutan* had prepared for his daughter, the bride. Among these was a splendid gown, embroidered from head to foot in gold and studded with precious stones. Now as soon as my brother stepped forward with this thing in his hand so that I should see it more clearly, I shrank from it and could not approach him; it smelt, I told him. Seeing how he laughed aloud and scoffed at my reaction, I asked that his *mechutan* be requested to join us. When he came I began asking question after question, in an endeavor to establish exactly how he had come by this resplendent garment. It transpired that he had received it as a gift from a prominent gentile nobleman; more precisely, as a token of appreciation — for the twelve thousand gold rubles which this *mechutan* had caused him to earn at the expense of some other Jew.

"My brother was awestruck — but that does not mean that I was making use of the supernatural gifts of *ruach hakodesh.* It simply means that if a man is uncompromisingly meticulous about the boundary between his own property and that of his fellow, then whatever object has proceeded in the subtlest degree from theft *becomes revolting in his eyes* — though he may not know the reason — to the point that he cannot even step near it."

☙ *O God, Israel Hears! (i)*

שְׁמַע יִשְׂרָאֵל
Hear, O Israel
(6:4)

Reb Zusya of Hanipoli once came to Nikolsburg and asked Reb Shmelke to teach him.

"Very well," said Reb Shmelke. "If you teach me the esoteric works of the Kabbalah, then I will teach you the revealed aspects of the Torah — the Talmud and the legal codes."

Seeing that his visitor was agreeable to this arrangement, Reb Shmelke asked him what text he would like to start with. Reb Zusya's reply, true to his custom, was in the ego-effacing third person: "Zusya is a great ignoramus and simply has to be taught *Mishnayos,* with every word explained to him in Yiddish."

Reb Shmelke thereupon turned to the first Mishnah of the Talmud, in Tractate *Berachos,* which opens with the question as to when in the evening one is obliged to read the passage *Shema Yisrael,* the Jew's daily profession of faith. Intending, as requested, to translate the text word for word, he began: "מֵאֵימָתַי — *From when,* קוֹרִין אֶת שְׁמַע — *does one read the Shema ...* "

Reb Zusya fell to the floor in a paroxysm of terror.

"And what makes you think that מֵאֵימָתַי means *From when ...?*" he asked, still trembling. "Perhaps it means *Out of dread does one read the Shema!*" [The word אֵימָה means dread, or awe.]

"Perhaps," suggested Reb Shmelke, "you had best learn by yourself, the way *you* understand."

◆§ *O God, Israel Hears! (ii)*

Reb Yosef Yitzchak of Lubavitch, who passed away in New York in 1950, once delineated the personality of a certain ordinary chassid — not a figure of towering stature, just one of the chassidim of the rebbe's grandfather, Reb Shmuel of Lubavitch.

This Reb Pessach lived in Homil. He was no Torah scholar, nor for that matter was he schooled in worldly matters, but he made a comfortable living by buying various kinds of merchandise in Homil and selling it to the shopkeepers in the hamlets round about.

Just before Rosh HaShanah in the year 1866 he joined a group of chassidim which was led by a chassid of renown by the name of Reb Mordechai Yoel, and they journeyed together from Homil to Lubavitch in order to spend the Days of Awe at the court of their rebbe, Reb Shmuel. When his turn came for *yechidus* — his first private interview with the newly-inducted rebbe — he handed him a *kvitl* in which he had written, amongst various personal details, the manner in which he made his livelihood.

The tzaddik blessed him and said: "You can always fulfill the words of the prophet, שְׂאוּ מָרוֹם עֵינֵיכֶם — 'Raise your eyes heavenward.'" And then he added: "*Shema* is *Yisrael.*"

Reb Pessach went straight from the rebbe's study to find Reb Mordechai Yoel, who would no doubt be able to explain what the tzaddik meant.

"Every synagogue," began Reb Mordechai Yoel, "is built with large windows: not only in order to admit light, but also to enable people to look out at the sky. For the heavens, we read, are reminiscent of the Throne of Glory, and looking skyward inspires a man with the awe of heaven. And this is what the rebbe told you. Since you spend much of your time on the road, and see the sky not only when you are seated in *shul*, you are thus able at all times to fulfill the instruction of the Prophet Yeshayahu: שְׂאוּ מָרוֹם עֵינֵיכֶם וּרְאוּ מִי בָרָא אֵלֶּה — 'Raise your eyes heavenward, and behold Who created these.' Now the word שְׁמַע is made up of the initial letters of the first three words of this verse, and when a person says the *Shema* with every fiber of his being, he is elevated thereby to the level of *Yisrael*. For as you may know, the name *Yaakov* denotes a Jew when he is at the stage where his service of God is that of a servant, motivated by awe; the name *Yisrael* is reserved for him who serves like a son, for the Jew who has reached the stage where his service is prompted as well by his love of the Creator. And that is what the rebbe meant when he said '*Shema* is *Yisrael*': through making the *Shema* a living experience, one can become worthy of being called a *Yisrael*."

Reb Yosef Yitzchak of Lubavitch continued his account of Reb Pessach with the following reminiscence of his own childhood: "Twenty-five years later, in 1891, when Reb Pessach paid a visit to Lubavitch for the Rosh HaShanah season — as he did every two or three years — he told me in detail all about that first *yechidus* in 1866, and added: 'When Reb Mordechai Yoel explained me what the rebbe Reb Shmuel had told me, I felt my soul lighting up, and from then on I yearned to understand the Torah. My neighbor, a chassid whom we knew as Hirschel the Watchmaker, taught me every so often, so that within a few years I was able to study a few lines for myself out of *Tanya, Likkutei Torah,* and various other classic texts. The rebbe's words put me on my feet!'

"The pleasure and the liveliness with which Reb Pessach recalled this experience were striking," recounted Reb Yosef Yitzchak.

As the years rolled by Reb Pessach became a rich man and he moved to Lodz, where he dealt in manufactured goods. Then in 1928, when he was about ninety years of age, he again repeated to Reb Yosef Yitzchak what he had heard from the mouth of the rebbe's grandfather, Reb Shmuel — and still with the same excitement and delight, as if this encounter had happened the day before. This time he concluded his recollection as follows: "From the time I first set out to try my own fortune on the road, I have always sought lodgings with large windows, and I always take a seat near a window, so that I will always be able to fulfill those words: שְׂאוּ מָרוֹם עֵינֵיכֶם — 'Raise your eyes heavenward.' Sixty-two years have now passed since I was privileged to hear from the rebbe, your grandfather, that *Shema* is *Yisrael*. Throughout all those years, whenever I say *Shema Yisrael*, at whatever point in the prayers — whether it be in the obligatory daily reading, or while the Torah Scroll is being brought out of the Holy Ark, or during the responses of *Kedushah*, or in the additions to the penitential *Tachanun* prayer on Monday and Thursday mornings, or during the climax of Yom Kippur at the conclusion of the *Ne'ilah* service — I always recall that *Shema* is *Yisrael*.

"One request I have yet to the Almighty: When the time comes for me to return Him the soul which He has entrusted in my keeping, and I am to breathe *Shema Yisrael* for the very last time, I pray that He grant me a clear mind, so that then too I will be able to recall those words the rebbe told me — *Shema* is *Yisrael!*"

"Such," observed Reb Yosef Yitzchak, "was one of the ordinary chassidim of my grandfather, Reb Shmuel."

◈ *The Password*

וְאָהַבְתָּ אֵת ה׳
And you shall love the Lord (6:5)

"I hear that you have a *segulah* for a great variety of needs, and that these spiritual remedies and talismans that you dispense actually bring results," said a certain non-chassidic *rav* to Reb Avraham of Stretyn.

"In fact I would like you to give me a *segulah* for being God-fearing."

"I am afraid that for the fear of heaven I do not have a *segulah*," replied the tzaddik, "but for the love of heaven I do."

"That's fine with me," said the visitor, "for is not the love of heaven a loftier thing than the fear of heaven? Let me have such a *segulah*, please."

"A great *segulah* for the love of heaven," said the tzaddik, "is the love of one's fellow Jew. Whoever has attained this can readily arrive at the love of heaven."

☙ *Equal Time*

בְּכָל לְבָבְךָ *With all your heart (6:5)*

With all your heart: Love Him with both your Good and your Evil Inclinations *(Mishnah, Tractate Berachos).*

The day before Reb Yisrael of Ruzhin arrived at the age of *bar-mitzvah* he was called to his father, Reb Shalom Shachna Friedmann, who asked him: "Do you know, my son, that tomorrow an important guest is coming to you, and that you should prepare yourself to receive him well so that he will agree to stay with you always? Receive him cordially, as befits a guest of such standing."

"I know full well, father," was the reply, "that tomorrow the Good Inclination will come to me; I made my preparations for his arrival a long time ago, when the Evil Inclination wanted to join me. This is what I told the Evil Inclination: 'You and the Good Inclination are partners in the heart of each man, and it is not proper that one partner should arrive before the other. I would ask you therefore to wait until the Good Inclination comes, and then you can come along too.'

"And in that way," concluded the boy, "I prepared to receive them both together!"

☙ *In the Eye of the Beholder*

וּבְכָל מְאֹדֶךָ *And with all your might (6:5)*

A man is obliged to utter a blessing on hearing evil tidings just as he does on hearing good tidings, as it is written: וּבְכָל מְאֹדֶךָ ... — "and with all your might," teaching us that we are obliged to thank Him בְּכָל מִדָּה וּמִדָּה – *"for whatever measure He metes out to us" (Mishnah, Tractate Berachos).*

Reb Shmelke of Nikolsburg asked his rebbe, Reb Dov Ber of Mezritch: "How is it possible to fulfill the injunction of our Sages, that 'A man is obliged to utter a blessing on hearing evil tidings just as he does on hearing good tidings'?"

"Go along to the *beis midrash,"* advised the Maggid of Mezritch, "and there you will find my disciple Reb Zusya of Hanipoli. He will explain the Mishnah to you."

Now throughout all his life Reb Zusya lived in utter poverty. When he was now told what brought Reb Shmelke to him he said: "I am most surprised that our rebbe should have sent you with this question to me, of all people. A question like this should surely be put to a man who at some time has experienced something evil, God forbid. *I* can't be of any help to you: nothing evil has ever befallen *me,* even for a moment. Thank God, I have had only good things happening to me from the day I was born until today. How could *I* know anything about how to accept evil joyfully?"

Reb Shmelke had his answer. This obligation – to bless God on hearing evil tidings just as one does on hearing good tidings – was now clear. All a man has to do is to rejoice in his lot to the point that he is not even aware of harsh experiences.

◆§ *Yea, though I Walk ...*

And with all your might: וּבְכָל מְאֹדֶךָ – teaching us that we are obliged to thank Him בְּכָל מִדָּה וּמִדָּה – "for whatever measure he metes out to us" *(Mishnah),* whether it be a measure of benevolence, and whether it be a measure of suffering *(Rashi).*

A certain chassid once visited Reb Menachem Mendel of Lubavitch, who showed him frequent marks of friendly encouragement. The rebbe's son, Reb Shmuel, noticed this and was curious to know what manner of man this visitor was. The *gabbai* of the rebbe could not enlighten him, for he of course did not accompany the chassid when he entered the rebbe's study for *yechidus*. None of the other chassidim could add much: he was no one of particular repute, they said — just an ordinary chassid. Reb Shmuel then asked the man himself where he came from and was told he came from Paritsh, but through talking to him he could not discern any indication of unusual spiritual stature. He decided at length that he would ask his father, the rebbe.

"It would be hard to find a man who has undergone such suffering and abject poverty," said Reb Menachem Mendel, "but he accepts it all with faith and equanimity. And this is what our Sages mean when they say לְקַבּוּלֵי בְּשִׂמְחָה, that suffering is to be accepted joyfully — for joy does not necessarily mean rollicking and dancing. Another thing. This man is an accomplished Talmud scholar and well versed in the philosophy of Chassidism, but you will not detect in him any sign of holy aloofness. People treat him lightly and to him this simply does not matter. A man like him," concluded the rebbe, "deserves to be granted heaven's blessings of the visible and revealed kind."

For three years thereafter the visitor was not seen in Lubavitch — but when he next came he was accompanied by a *minyan* of ten chassidim whom he had brought at his own expense. The rebbe's blessing had been fulfilled, and he was now a man of means.

◆§ *Bending the Twig*

וְשִׁנַּנְתָּם לְבָנֶיךָ
And you shall teach them diligently to your children (6:7)

One day when Reb Yosef Yitzchak Schneersohn of Lubavitch was a child of seven he was given a watermelon by his grandmother, the widow of Reb Shmuel of Lubavitch. He gave a piece to a little friend, but as soon as they had sat down together on a bench in the courtyard to eat they were suddenly disturbed by a voice. It was the rebbe, Reb Shalom Ber, calling his son inside.

When he went in his father said: "It is true that you gave part of your watermelon to your friend — but you did not give it wholeheartedly."

The rebbe went on to explain the various levels that may be attained in the attribute of kindliness, as well as the nature of the opposite attribute, and the child wept in remorse to the point that he even felt unwell.

The boy's mother, seeing what was going on, asked her husband: "What do you want of the child?"

"Everything is in order," the rebbe reassured her. "This way he will have acquired a positive character trait."

Reb Yosef Yitzchak repeated this incident when he had already grown to be rebbe himself, and concluded with the words: "*That* is education!"

❀ ❀ ❀

At the *Seder* table, on the first night of the Pessach festival in 1943, Reb Yosef Yitzchak of Lubavitch recalled another childhood incident which had taken place fifty-three years earlier, when he was ten years old.

"In honor of Pessach 1890," he said, "I had been bought new clothes and new boots. The custom in Lubavitch was that after the *chametz* had been burnt in the morning of Pessach eve we would go off to immerse in the *mikveh,* and then, dressed in our best festive clothes, we would bake the *matzah* that was to be eaten at the *Seder* that evening. From that we would proceed to the other preparations that had to be made for the evening. One of my tasks was to remove the seals from the wine bottles, especially those on which letters were imprinted, and to ease out the stoppers, being careful not to let the corkscrew touch the wine inside. This job I did in my father's study, and as he watched my painstaking care not to soil my new clothes in any way, and especially my anxiety lest my new boots lose their shine, he said: 'Among the commentaries which Reb Shneur Zalman of Liadi wrote on the prayers in his edition of the *Siddur* we find a parable. A nobleman sits at the head of his sumptuous table which is laden with all manner of choice delicacies. His dog is busy under the table, gnawing bones. Could one picture this aristocrat forsaking his table and chair, and sitting under the table, gnawing bones?'

"This parable spoke to me so eloquently that I was ashamed to look at my new clothes. *That* is education!"

◆§ Words Worth Saying

וְדִבַּרְתָּ בָּם
And you shall speak of them *(6:7)*

And you shall speak of them: Of *them* shall you speak, and not of other things *(Talmud, Tractate Yoma).*

Reb Naftali of Ropshitz walked into his kitchen one morning before prayers, and complained to the womenfolk who were busy there: "And for all my efforts don't I deserve a little bit of milk?"

At that time Reb Asher, his son-in-law, had not yet learned to plumb the profundity of the rebbe's words, and it bothered him that his father-in-law should become so irritated over matters so paltry as food and drink.

"I'll have to rebuke him about this some day," he thought to himself.

Just at that moment a woman came along to the tzaddik and sobbed out her plaint: "Rebbe, I am a poor widow, and I haven't enough milk with which to nurse my twin babies!"

"Go back to your home, my good woman," he answered, "and the Almighty will help you."

Reb Asher in the meantime forgot to rebuke him because his mind was occupied with his studies, and besides, his father-in-law distracted his attention from the little incident.

A few weeks later Reb Naftali entered the kitchen with another angry complaint: "And I'm already given a bit of milk, it's all watery. Haven't I earned some good, *nourishing* milk?"

"This time," thought Reb Asher, "I will not keep silent. In fact I will rebuke him twice. A holy man like himself losing his temper over such trifles!"

Again his thoughts were interrupted by the bitter weeping of the same widow.

"Rebbe!" she cried to Reb Naftali. "Thank God I now have milk to given my little one — but it's like water, and the babies are as skinny as sticks! Won't you pray and ask the Almighty to bless me with good milk?"

"My good woman," said the tzaddik, "return home to your babies. God will help you and you will have *good* milk."

Reb Asher now began to follow the way in which the tzaddik worked, and from then on harbored no doubts as to his saintliness.

☙ *Early Warning System*

From childhood it was a principle with Reb Shlomo Leib of Linchna — a disciple of both the Chozeh of Lublin and the Yid HaKadosh of Pshischah — to be scrupulously careful not to listen to idle talk; it goes without saying that he for his part never wasted a word.

As a youth he rented a room in a house which was also occupied by a tailor and various other people, and he always made a point of returning to his lodgings after the other boarders had retired for the night. It once happened that the *beis midrash* was closed early for some reason, so that the young scholar had no option but to return to his room. But as he approached the house he looked through the window and saw the tailor plying his needle as usual, surrounded by his apprentices, all of them bubbling their time away in empty-headed jests. In keeping with his principle he stood at a distance, but it was so bitterly cold that he had to try to keep himself warm by walking back and forth. Even this was not effective, and though he felt that it was almost going to cost him his life he still decided to remain outside until, weak and frozen, he lay down on the ground to rest. Had the hand of heaven not intervened he would have met his death soon after — but the lamp in the house suddenly went out, the tailor and his young helpers had to go to sleep, and the young Reb Shlomo Leib got up and entered the house.

"In order to avert a repetition of that incident," he later confessed, "from that time on I learned to give myself advance warning by developing the faculty of hearing even whispered conversations *while still at a distance.*"

☙ *Torah by Telex*

וּכְתַבְתָּם
And you shall write them (6:9)

And you shall write them: With a perfect script [In the original: uksavtam — ksivah tamah] (Talmud, Tractate Shabbos).

In the script used for writing Scrolls of the Torah, *tefillin* and *mezuzos*, there are subtle differences of usage between various schools of thought as to the precise shapes of certain letters.

Now when Reb Shneur Zalman of Liadi was a very young man he left Liozna, his birthplace, to study at the feet of Reb Dov Ber, the Maggid of Mezritch. One day the rebbe summoned his disciple and told him that the Heavenly Court was displeased with the lack of agreement regarding the script between those authorities whose legal decisions were based on the revealed aspects of the Torah – the *poskim*, and those scholars whose teachings were flavored as well by the mystical dimension of the Torah – the *mekubbalim*. He therefore charged the young scholar with the task of mastering both doctrines, with a view to proposing a mode of scribal writing which would answer to the minutest requirements of both schools of thought. The Maggid was pleased with his disciple's work when he saw it completed and thanked him for it, and revealed to him that at that moment a voice in the Heavenly Court had proclaimed that thus indeed should be the shapes of the letters.

The next day Reb Shneur Zalman came to the Maggid to receive his farewell blessings before setting out on a journey, in the course of which he passed through Hanipoli, the hometown of his friend, the tzaddik Reb Zusya. It was late at night, and since a light was to be seen in only one house, he directed his steps towards it in the hope that he would be able to spend the night there. It was the house of Reb David, the local scribe. Not wishing to disturb him while he was engaged in the holy task of writing a Scroll of the Torah, Reb Shneur Zalman slipped noiselessly in through the open door, peered over the shoulder of the scribe, and admired the deft discipline with which his goosequill sanctified the white parchment. But as he looked more closely he was stupefied: the letters being written under his very eyes were identical in every particular with those he had drafted only the day before as the original product of a wealth of scholarly toil! And it was clear that Reb David had not been in Mezritch when the letters had been shown to the Maggid.

After some time the scribe stood up from his work and was delighted to discover that he had such an honored guest. And when Reb Shneur Zalman asked him where he had learned to write his script in exactly this mode he answered: "I really know nothing about it. All I know is that today Reb Zusya told me that a voice in the World Above had proclaimed that this was how the letters should be written, since this style accords both with the *poskim* and the *mekubbalim*, and he gave me an exact copy of each letter."

Reb Shneur Zalman was overwhelmed by this new evidence of the sanctity of Reb Zusya. He called on him in the morning to pay his respects, and after they had refreshed each other's soul by sharing the sweet secrets of the Torah, he went on his way.

◆§ *Asleep, but Alert (i)*

וּכְתַבְתָּם עַל מְזֻזוֹת בֵּיתֶךָ
And you shall write them on the doorposts of your house (6:9)

When Reb Pinchas of Korets was still living in Ostrov, Reb Baruch of Mezhibuzh grew up and was educated in his house, and after his marriage he continued to visit his rebbe frequently. He was once taking a nap in his rebbe's room, when Reb Pinchas said to the people who were with him at the time: "If you stand around my disciple's bed, I will show you something novel."

With that he approached the doorpost of the bedroom, and with his hand covered the tiny parchment scroll — the *mezuzah* — which was affixed to it. Reb Baruch began at once to stir as if about to wake up, but the moment his rebbe removed his hand from the *mezuzah* he again fell soundly asleep.

After Reb Pinchas had repeated this a few times over, he said: "You have now seen a man of true holiness. Even when Reb Baruch is asleep his soul is not diverted from continuous cleaving to his Creator!"

◆§ *Asleep, but Alert (ii)*

Among the spiritual giants who gathered at Mezritch to pay their last respects to the departed Maggid, Reb Dov Ber, were the brothers Reb Elimelech of Lyzhansk and Reb Zusya of Hanipoli. After the burial was over the chassidim of the Maggid considered together the question of a successor, and after some deliberation a large number of those present agreed to appoint Reb Elimelech as their rebbe. He was duly inducted into office, and after they had all cried "Long live our rebbe, Reb Elimelech!" they set out together with him on the highway.

When night fell they stopped at an inn where Reb Elimelech, weary from the day's journey, slept soundly for several hours in the separate room which the chassidim had arranged for him. His new disciples were dismayed. Was it proper that the successor of the Maggid of Mezritch should sleep for hours on end? Some of them even had second thoughts as to their choice of rebbe, and went so far as to ask Reb Zusya, since he was his brother, to wake him up. Reb Zusya simply covered the *mezuzah* scroll on the doorpost with his hand, and Reb Elimelech awoke at once. The chassidim were amazed, and asked Reb Zusya to explain what they had seen. What connection was there between a *mezuzah* and — sleep?

"As we have all learned," said Reb Zusya, "every man is obliged to constantly keep before his mind's eye the four-letter Name of God, in fulfillment of the verse שִׁוִּיתִי ה׳ לְנֶגְדִּי תָמִיד — 'I have set God always before me.' When a man is asleep, however, and cannot fulfill this obligation, he must fall back on the Name of God that is inscribed on the outside of the *mezuzah*. Accordingly, when I covered that Name with my hand he could no longer sleep, and he had to wake up at once in order to resume his task of constantly setting God's Name before him."

The chassidim were overcome with relief and gratitude, and exclaimed: "Blessed be He Who did not leave us like a flock without a shepherd!"

◆§ *Instant Returns, Instant Return*

וּמְשַׁלֵּם לְשֹׂנְאָיו אֶל פָּנָיו
And repays those that hate him to their face (7:10)

To their face: He repays them their due rewards in their lifetime, thereby depriving them of the spiritual rewards of the World to Come *(Rashi).*

Reb Menachem Mendel of Kotsk was on his way by foot to see his rebbe Reb Simchah Bunem of Pshischah, when he was overtaken by a magnificent carriage drawn by well-fed horses. When it slowed down and stopped, he recognized its owner as a childhood friend who in the course of the years had forsaken the path of the Torah. The tzaddik accepted his invitation to join him in the carriage, and in the course of their conversation on various moral questions he asked: "And where is your *This* World?"

"Why, don't you see?" smiled the rich man complacently. "I own all manner of good things in my house and in my fields, and do not lack even the luxuries of royalty."

"But all of these things are substitutes for what should have been your World to *Come*," the tzaddik corrected him. "My question was: Where is your *This* World?"

The materialist listened well. The words of the tzaddik found their way into his heart, and he became an earnest penitent.

◆§ *Instant Returns*

A freethinker once approached Reb Yitzchak Meir of Ger, the author of *Chiddushei HaRim*, and taxed him with a question: "In the *Shema* it says, 'Take care lest your heart be lured away, and you turn astray...for then God's wrath will flare up against you, and He will close the heavens so that there will be no rain...' — and so on. Now I observe the exact opposite to be true: the saintly folk have a hard life, while I, a freethinker, have everything I want!"

"Since you base your question on a verse in the *Shema*," said the tzaddik, "I assume that you have no doubt read that passage at least once in your life."

"That is so," said the freethinker.

"In that case," said the tzaddik, "in return for the mitzvah of a single reading of the *Shema* whatever you own is insufficient. You deserve more!"

◆§ Of Cows and Cards ואתחנן

שְׂאוּ מָרוֹם עֵינֵיכֶם וּרְאוּ מִי בָרָא אֵלֶּה
Raise your eyes heavenward, and behold Who created these (Haftarah)

Reb Simchah Bunem of Pschischah was fond of saying that in three things he had been granted immediate success. Two of them he revealed.

He was once in the company of a group of "Deitschen" — the assimilationists and *maskilim* of the self-styled "Enlightenment" movement — who were drinking coffee with milk. He did not take milk, and when they made an issue of it, and insisted that he explain, he gave his reason, namely, the apprehension discussed in the Talmud — lest the milk provided by a gentile contain an admixture of milk from a forbidden animal. They ridiculed him from all sides: "The peasant woman from whom we buy our milk has fifteen perfectly kosher cows. Why worry about such unlikely admixtures?"

He breathed a silent prayer, asking heaven to vindicate the stand he had taken. Within a moment in walked the peasant woman and asked the little group: "Well, did you find the coffee unusually delicious today?"

"First class!" they chorused.

"And why do you ask only today?" asked the tzaddik.

"Why, because today I improved it with a touch of fresh pig's milk," she replied.

And from that day on the scoffers spoke of the words of the Sages with more respect.

The second episode involved the gifted son of one of the merchants with whom Reb Simchah Bunem used to do business before he became a rebbe. Seeing that his efforts at bringing this young man to an appreciation of Torah and chassidic thought were fruitless, the tzaddik decided to accompany him as a comrade in whatever activities he was engaged. Perhaps *that* would further his purpose. When the young man went to play cards, Reb Simchah Bunem went with him and even joined in the game.

In his own words: "Heaven is my witness that I had not the slightest notion of how to play cards — but I had the most extraordinary success, and won every time. At first I did not even know that I had won, but when I saw that no one else took the money that was on the table I assumed that it was mine, and took it. The young man longed to know by what clever secret I succeeded, because card-playing was more important to him than all the wealth and merchandising in the world. The more I deferred my answer the more curious he grew, until one day I took him for a stroll beyond the city limits, and he was certain that the precious secret would soon be his. But instead, I suddenly cried: שְׂאוּ מָרוֹם עֵינֵיכֶם וּרְאוּ מִי בָרָא אֵלֶּה — 'Raise your eyes heavenward, and behold Who created these!'

"The young man was of course taken by surprise. I told him the truth — that I knew absolutely nothing of card-playing, and that my extraordinary success had been granted me from Above only in order to enable me to bring him to an awareness of the Divine Presence. I went on to explain the vanity of such pastimes, and in response to words proceeding from the heart he became a penitent in all his ways."

סדר עקב

SIDRA EIKEV

◈ The Worth of a Worshiper

וְהָיָה עֵקֶב תִּשְׁמְעוּן *If you listen...then as a result (7:12)*

During the height of the controversy that flared up in Vilna over the chassidic movement in the years 1796 to 1802, one of the mainstays of the *Chabad* school of Chassidism was Reb Baruch Mordechai, a disciple of the founder of the movement, Reb Shneur Zalman of Liadi. This scholar was the son-in-law of the last *av beis din* of Vilna, the celebrated Rabbi Shmuel, and despite his chassidic loyalties he was highly respected among the antagonists of the movement, the *misnagdim* of that city. In 1851 he made his home in Jerusalem, where after some time he passed away.

Late in 1801, while still a young man, Reb Baruch Mordechai was appointed *rav* of Bobruisk, where his repute as a Torah scholar spread throughout the nonchassidic communities of Shklov, Slutsk and Minsk.

When he left Vilna to take up his new position he was accompanied by dozens of families.

Among the chassidim of Vilna there was a scholar by the name of Reb Chaim Zelig who engaged in the study of chassidic thought. He earned his livelihood by hiring coachmen who drove his horse-drawn wagons from town to town with passengers and parcels, and one of his *shmeissers* — the Yiddish word for "wielders of the whip" — was a simple young man by the name of Reb Zalman Leib. He had grown up without a father and without education, until a *melamed* in the chassidic community gave him work as an assistant, his daily task being to bring the small children to and from school. Though he was a simple fellow he was upright and God-fearing, and taught himself with effort to read the basic sacred texts, so that he was able for example to read the weekly passage of the Torah twice over with its Aramaic translation, according to custom. Since, however, he could not understand the Hebrew texts that he read, he pored over their Yiddish translations, and derived pious inspiration from such folk classics as *Tzennah Urennah*. In the course of time he joined up with the brotherhood of chassidim in Vilna, praying with them and adopting their distinctive customs. His humble heart made him prone to tears, especially over his own ignorance of Torah, and when he poured out his soul to his Maker, the very sound of his prayers would arouse the tender emotions of those who stood around him — the more so since his voice had a tone of mellow pleasantness. The *misnagdim*, however, used to poke fun at him, and as he passed by they would jeer: "There goes our chassid, Reb Zalman Leib the *shmeisser!*"

When Reb Baruch Mordechai and his companions moved to Bobruisk, Reb Zalman Leib went with them, and taking the advice of the new *rav* he leased a vegetable field, from which he made a comfortable livelihood. He was happy in his new situation, and hired the services of a *melamed* who taught him Torah at a fixed hour every day.

Now it once happened that Rabbi Avigdor — the *rosh* yeshivah of Vilna, and the son of Rabbi Shmuel of the rabbinical court — was on a visit to Minsk. From the moment he had discovered his brother-in-law belonged to "the Sect" he had severed all relations with him, but when he saw how highly the *misnagdish* sages of Minsk spoke of him he sat down at once to write to Reb Baruch Mordechai, informing him that he intended to visit him in Bobruisk at a certain time. The dignitaries of the local council, presided over by the Seven Good Townsmen, decided at once to extend their expected guest the ultimate honor which was reserved for Torah luminaries – a deputation of venerable scholars would be sent in advance to greet him in a nearby township before he even arrived at Bobruisk. In addition they prepared a public welcome for him at one of the town's largest synagogues, at which he would deliver a learned Talmudic discourse.

On his arrival the guest was respectfully brought to the synagogue, but in order to enable him to rest a little from his journey he was first ushered into the antechamber. This tranquil nook was frequented by those devout worshipers who meditated at length over their prayers, according to the custom honored by the veteran chassidim of the *Chabad* school. From some corner behind him Rabbi Avigdor heard a voice in prayer so soulful that it tugged at his heartstrings. Knowing Bobruisk to be a town of chassidim, he asked his brother-in-law when he entered who this was who was still so enveloped in his morning devotions though it was now past noon.

"Why," answered Reb Baruch Mordechai, "that is Reb Zalman Leib the *shmeisser*."

"And do you mean to say," scoffed the visiting pedant, "That Reb Zalman Leib the *shmeisser* is one of your lengthy worshipers? Why, he is only the *heel* of a worshiper!"

Reb Baruch Mordechai was silent. Soon after, Rabbi Avigdor delivered himself of a discourse that bristled with evidence of his impressive erudition. This he rounded off with eloquent words of *derush*, and he sat down a happy man. Just at that moment he caught sight of Reb Zalman Leib. He succumbed to temptation and repeated his jest aloud: "There goes the *heel* of a worshiper!"

Seeing this repetition as a deliberate public insult to chassidim and Chassidism, Reb Baruch Mordechai returned with a comment on the word "heel," the Hebrew word for which is עָקֵב *(akev).*

"According to the Torah," he began, "the *akev* of a worshiper is something of importance, and brings about three things of benefit."

Accustomed to the quick mind of their *rav*, the scholars of Bobruisk now leaned forward to hear an astute reply.

He continued: "It is stated explicitly in the Mishnah that the *akev* of a worshiper teaches us three things."

This was an amazing statement, and Rabbi Avigdor and his companions waited skeptically to see whether he could substantiate it.

After a relaxed pause the speaker continued: "There is a Mishnah in the *Ethics of the Fathers* which quotes the Talmudic sage Akavya the son of Mahalalel as saying, 'Reflect upon three things and you will not come to sin. Know from where you came, and to where you are going, and before whom you are destined to give an accounting.' Now *Akavya ben Mahalalel* means 'the *akev* of him who is *mehalel E-l,*' the heel of him who praises God. And this *akev*, the *humblest* component of that worshiper, tells us: 'Reflect upon three things and you will not come to sin. *Know from where you came* — and you will not be arrogant; *and to where you are going* — and you will not be lustful; *and before whom you are destined to give an account* — and you will fear sin!' "

❦ ❦ ❦

During a visit to Chicago in 1942 Reb Yosef Yitzchak Schneersohn of Lubavitch told this story, and when it was repeated more widely, objections were raised from various quarters. Surely this *derush* was no more than lighthearted wordplay! For what real connection was there between Akavya ben Mahalalel and the heel of a worshiper?

The answer was given at the time by his son-in-law, the present Lubavitcher rebbe: "The small talk of a sage of the standing of Reb Baruch Mordechai of Bobruisk requires close study." And he substantiated the connection made by that chassid with detailed documentation from the Mishnah, the Midrash, the Torah commentary of *Baal HaTurim*, the writings of the ARI*zal*, and a commentary on *Proverbs* by the author of *Shnei Luchos HaBris*.

The "lighthearted wordplay" of a Torah giant requires very close study indeed!

◆§ *Hidden Earphones*

Among the guests who joined in the festive Purim meal of Reb Shalom Ber of Lubavitch during his visit to Minton in 1902 were a few who had been perhaps a little over-zealous in their fulfillment of the Talmudic injunction to drink wine on this joyous festival. In the course of their uninhibited conversation one of them said to his friend: "I hear you with my heel" — a Yiddish idiom signifying an utter lack of attention to what has just been said.

Overhearing this comment the rebbe said a few minutes later: "Even if this expression were used in a discussion on divine service it would indicate a sense of superiority in the speaker, and one would need to be wary of using it. If however it were to appear in any conversation — particularly to express scorn of another man — then it would bespeak arrogance and vulgarity, which are the exact reverse of the divine intention in sending down souls to dwell in This World."

The tzaddik went on to explain that the divine intention was that a man's heel should indeed attain the level of *listening*, and illustrated his point by recounting the following incident: "In Lubavitch there lived a chassid of Reb Dov Ber, who had heard from his father — one of the inner circle of chassidim of Reb Shneur Zalman of Liadi — that when Reb Menachem Mendel of Lubavitch was a little boy his grandfather examined him on the *Chumash* which he had recently begun to study. They came to the verse עֵקֶב אֲשֶׁר שָׁמַע אַבְרָהָם בְּקוֹלִי — 'Because *(eikev)* Avraham listened to My voice.' Asked to explain it, the child said: "Avraham heard God's command even with his heel!' [As if to say: So utterly permeated was his whole body with an awareness of the divine spark that animated it, that 'with his very *eikev (akev:* heel) Avraham listened to My voice'!] The grandfather, Reb Shneur Zalman of Liadi, was more than pleased with this answer, and said: 'In fact we find this very command in another verse — וְהָיָה עֵקֶב תִּשְׁמְעוּן [literally: 'And it shall come to pass that if you listen, then as a result ... ']. This verse tells us that we should strive to attain a level at which our *eikev (akev:* heel) should listen — that even our *heel* should hear God's command and hasten to fulfill it!'"

עקב

◆§ *Praise from a Stranger (i)*

בָּרוּךְ תִּהְיֶה מִכָּל הָעַמִּים *You shall be blessed more than all the nations (7:14)*

You shall be blessed more than all the nations (or, literally, '*by* all the nations'): Praise by her relatives does not make a woman feel praised — which is not the case with the praise that comes from her less loving co-wives *(Midrash).*

Suddenly, in the middle of leading his congregation in prayer, the Baal Shem Tov walked out to the street, bought a wagonful of firewood from a gentile whose livelihood this was, and asked him to deliver the goods to the *beis midrash,* where his chassidim were waiting for him, dumbfounded. He asked them to pay the gentile for the firewood, and to give him some vodka as well for his trouble in bringing it inside.

"Blessed be the God of the Jews Who has a People like this!" exclaimed the gentile in gratitude. "If one of *my* countrymen had bought this load from me he would have paid me nothing!"

Amazed that their rebbe should have interrupted his prayers for such paltry affairs, the chassidim asked the Baal Shem Tov respectfully for an explanation.

"The voice of a prosecuting angel was just heard in the Heavenly Court," he said, "alleging that certain Jewish villagers have acted dishonestly in their business dealings with the local gentiles. I had to silence that voice by having this gentile praise the Jews — and indeed that prosecuting attorney dropped his charges."

◆§ Praise from a Stranger (ii)

While Reb Shneur Zalman of Liadi was visiting a certain town a fire broke out in the house of one of the local citizens, and he asked to be taken there. When he arrived he stood leaning on his cane for a few moments, and the fire immediately died down.

Some of the soldiers who were encamped nearby had been trying to extinguish it, and when they reported to their officer what the tzaddik had done he ordered that he be brought to the barracks. After asking him to sit, the officer asked him whether he was the son or the grandson of the Baal Shem Tov.

"I am not his grandson in a bodily sense," replied Reb Shneur Zalman, "but I am his spiritual grandson — the disciple of his disciple."

"In that case," returned the officer, "I am no longer amazed at what you did today. Let me tell you a story about my father and the Baal Shem Tov.

"My father was a general, and once, while he was encamped with his troops in the town of Mezhibuzh, he almost went out of his mind with worry because no letter had arrived from his wife for so long. Seeing his extreme anxiety his friends advised him as follows. 'In this very town,' they said, 'lives the Baal Shem Tov, and he reveals things wondrously. Why don't you turn to him?'

"My father therefore sent a message to the holy man asking him to receive him for an interview. This request was denied. My father tried a second time — but again the Baal Shem Tov refused. This time my father sent him word that if he refused to see him he would issue a command forcing all the Jews of Mezhibuzh to billet his troops in their homes. Since this was just at the time when your festival of Passover was about to begin, this would mean that the soldiers would bring their leavened bread into the Jewish houses and wreak havoc with the preparations for your festival. Under the influence of that threat to his fellow Jews the Baal Shem Tov agreed that my father should come to visit him.

"When he arrived at his house together with his aide-de-camp they entered the first room, from which they could see through an open door into the room in which the holy man sat. He was reading a book, which my father was told was the *Zohar*. My father walked up to a mirror in the waiting room in order to tidy his hair before entering — but he was stupefied to see in the mirror a paved road which led to the town where his wife lived. He called his attendant to find out whether he too beheld this amazing sight, and as they stood together before the mirror they saw that the road led to the town itself, and within the town they saw the general's house. And as the door opened before their eyes they saw his wife sitting at her table writing a letter to her husband. Looking more closely they saw the letter itself, in which she explained that she had not written because she had recently given birth to a son; they were both well.

"My father was overwhelmed by this experience, and thanked the Baal Shem Tov from the bottom of his heart. After some time he received the letter which he had already seen at the time of its writing, and then recorded a chronicle of this whole episode in his diary.

"I who stand before you," concluded the officer, "am that infant, and here you may read for yourself my father's own diary."

◆§ *Praise from a Stranger (iii)*

A little before Rosh HaShanah in the year 1883 the Polish count Dravski — who had long ago earned fame as a poet and as a fighter in the battle for independence in 1831 — made the journey to Rimanov, there to pray at the resting place of the tzaddik Reb Menachem Mendel. All the nobility of the region gathered to pay their respects to him, and the eighty-year-old guest of honor explained the reason for his unusual pilgrimage.

"When I was a child of eight," he replied, "I became critically ill. My mother summoned the best physicians available, but none could help. Then one of her aristocratic friends found her weeping in despair over her only son, and told her that in Fristik — for that was where this holy man used to live — there was a rabbi who worked wonders. She had her horses harnessed at once, and by five in the morning the carriage with the two ladies had arrived at the rebbe's house. The household was already awake and active, for this was the time at which they used to bake bread for the needy. A servant informed the holy man of their arrival, and he sent back word that he would receive them at nine, after his morning prayers.

"At the appointed time the noblewoman told him of her friend's request, and he replied in perfect Polish: 'Is it because you think I am a sorcerer that you have come to me?'

"'No,' she replied, 'but your life-style is closer to God than that of most people, and that is why your prayer is heard more attentively.'

"'In that case,' said the rebbe, 'I shall pray for the child.'

"The two women left the room, but through the door, which they had left ajar, they saw him turning towards a corner and then praying with such fervor that beads of perspiration stood out on his face. After three hours of exertion he called for them, just as the clock which hung over his bed struck noon.

"'Right now,' he said, 'just as the clock is striking twelve, the child has felt better. When he has completely recovered bring him to me so that I can bless him.'

"My mother came home, and anxiously asked one of the servants how her child was faring.

"'Nothing has changed,' she was told, 'except that instead of lying motionless as he had been doing the whole time, he woke up at twelve and asked for water.'

"A few weeks later,' concluded the aged count, 'I was completely well. I was brought to the rebbe, who gave me his blessing, and told me that I should always treat Jews with kindness. I have kept my promise, and now, in my old age, I desired to make the journey here to Rimanov in order to pray at his resting place."

Dravski wept profusely at that holy spot, and following the Jewish custom, left there a note — written in Polish.

In 1901 the German scholar Reb Aharon Marcus wrote in his *Der Chassidismus* that he had succeeded in securing that very *kvitl.* (The tzaddik's surname was Turm, and the signature at the end, giving the name of the supplicant's mother, follows the traditional Hebrew wording of such requests.) It reads as follows:

Ye souls of Abraham, Isaac and Jacob — pray for the soul of the late Mendel Turm! And you, Mendel, since you stand already in the presence of the Heavenly Throne, pray for the oppressed nations — the Jewish People and Poland — and pray too for me, for my children, and for my grandchildren!

Miechislav Dravski the son of Victoria

☙ *Praise from a Stranger (iv)*

In Vitebsk, in White Russia, there lived a goodhearted nobleman from whose estates many Jews made their livelihood. The entire town of Chekhov belonged to him, and not only did he forgo the taxes of the poor Jews who lived there, but in addition he allowed the religious functionaries of the community — the *rav*, the *shochet*, the *chazzanim* and the *melamdim* — to pasture their cows and goats without payment.

This *graf*, however, was an ailing man, and as he grew older and weaker he would have to visit Dr. Bertenson in Vitebsk more frequently, leaving the administration of his estates, his castle and all of his business interests in the hands of his manager, who was a sworn anti-Semite. The Catholic parish church stood on the squire's estates, and on the instigation of its zealous new priest the manager began to deprive the local Jews of their livelihoods, and to exact taxes from even the poorest of them. This went on for some two years.

Now most of the Jews of the town were chassidim of Reb Shmuel of Lubavitch. When they visited him for a festival or a *Shabbos* they would listen to a chassidic discourse from his mouth, and when speaking to him individually at *yechidus* they would ask for his blessings for their children, for health and for their livelihood — and then they would travel home, certain that the Almighty would have pity on them. Not one of them thought it would be proper to trouble the rebbe with an account of what was happening to their sources of income, or with stories of some anti-Semitic parish priest.

One of the Jews whose business affairs had been connected for generations with the estates of this *graf* was called Reb Shmuel Isaacs — an honest, respectable and well-to-do merchant, who was moderately learned in both the revealed and the mystical aspects of the Torah, and who was known for his hospitality and generosity. When he visited Lubavitch for the festival of Shavuos in the year 1880 the rebbe asked him detailed questions about the state of the livelihoods earned by the Jews of the town, and the merchant told him the whole truth.

"I know of the condition of the *graf,*" said the rebbe, "for Professor Bertenson has told me that it is precarious. But why did you not tell me all this time about the change in the policy of the administration towards the Jews on his estates?"

The rebbe spent some moments sunk in thought, and then said: "Travel home now, and at the first opportunity at which you see the *graf* tell him in my name that I know that his condition is dangerous, and that his physicians have despaired of saving his life. I promise him nevertheless that if he helps the Jews of Chekhov and the neighboring villages, the Almighty will give him one month's health for each family."

As soon as Reb Shmuel the merchant returned home he began to frequent the squire's courtyard in the hope of meeting him, but for days on end he was not to be seen outside because of his delicate health. One sunny day, though, his doctor advised him to prepare his carriage so that they could take a ride in the fresh air in a nearby forest. Reb Shmuel saw him being led out to his waiting carriage, frail and listless.

The *graf* saw him too, and invited him to join him in his carriage. No sooner did he hear what the rebbe had said than he asked Reb Shmuel to draw up a list of all the Jewish families in the region who could earn their living from his properties, after visiting them all either personally or by proxy — but no one was to know of his mission.

Reb Shmuel duly provided him with a list of more than one hundred and sixty families from the township, with an additional couple of dozen families from the surrounding villages. The Jews were once again enabled to earn a living — and the *graf* was restored to health. Reb

Shmuel became highly regarded around the castle, and every year the *graf* would send with him a *lulav* from his palm trees, together with sprigs of myrtle, as a gift to the rebbe in honor of the festival of Sukkos.

עקב

In this way he enjoyed fourteen years of uninterrupted good health — but then he suddenly felt very weak. He sent for Reb Shmuel and asked him to set out at once for Lubavitch, where he was to visit the resting place of the rebbe — for the tzaddik had passed away in 1882 — and to notify him that the *graf* felt weak, though according to his reckoning he was owed another year and seven months of life. Would the rebbe therefore honor his promise?

☙ *Fellow Feeling*

וְהֵסִיר ה׳ מִמְּךָ כָּל חֹלִי
And God will remove all sickness from you (7:15)

Every night, before going to sleep, Reb Fishele of Strikov would pour himself a drop of vodka. After pronouncing the blessing over it he would taste it, and say: "*LeChaim,* Master of the Universe, Source and Life of all life! A very good night to you, Master of the Universe!"

He once explained that this custom of his was really a roundabout prayer for the speedy recovery of all his ailing brethren, whose suffering usually increased with the approach of night. For since it is written that בְּכָל צָרָתָם לוֹ צָר — "In all their affliction He is afflicted" — it follows that when the sick and ailing have a good night, the Almighty too is caused pleasure, so to speak. This nightly *LeChaim,* then, was Reb Fishele's way of hinting to the Almighty that He should so arrange things for those languishing in This World that He Himself should — in turn — also have a good night ...

☙ *Sources of Income*

לְמַעַן עַנֹּתְךָ לְנַסֹּתְךָ
In order to humble you, to test you (8:2)

There were very few people indeed from whom Reb Menachem Mendel of Kotsk ever agreed to accept money. And the one wealthy and scholarly chassid who did support him was distressed one day to find that the tzaddik refused even *his* accustomed gift. Finding no rest, he finally asked the rebbe directly for his reason.

"Every livelihood," answered the rebbe, "has a cause, and the Almighty is the One Who activates these causes. It sometimes happens that He chooses to put a person to the test — to see whether he places his trust in the cause, or in Him Who *causes* the cause — and so He removes that cause. Now if that man had placed his trust in *it*, then his livelihood is cut off from Above, for by his thinking he made it *in fact* depend on the cause. If however he had placed his trust in Him Who *activates* the causes, then his livelihood continues undisturbed, and the Almighty brings other causes into play, for His emissaries are countless.

"Now in my case," he explained to his chassid, "the immediate cause of my income was — your support. So I thought: What if the Almighty wants to put *me* to the above test, and to remove my cause? Then you will have to become poor, so that you be unable to support me. I would therefore prefer to remove the cause myself, so that you will not have to be impoverished."

"Rebbe," cried the chassid, "I want to continue notwithstanding! And if the Almighty should want to put you to the test, and that involves my being left poor, then I accept that result willingly. Anything, so long as you do not remove the source of your income yourself!"

But only after he had repeated his entreaty many times did the tzaddik finally agree to accept his gifts as he had formerly done.

That same year, through some misfortune, the chassid lost his wealth and became a poor man, and was forced to seek employment as a *rav* and as the head of a rabbinical court in order to support his family.

⊰ *The Vitamins that Count*

לא עַל הַלֶּחֶם לְבַדּוֹ
Not by bread alone (8:3)

Reb Shalom Yosef of Sadigora, the eldest son of Reb Yisrael of Ruzhin, used to eat exceedingly little, and there were times during which he ate almost nothing. One day soon after a meal had been served to him, his daughter Rachel Leah entered his study, and seeing that the food was untouched she began to weep.

"Why are you crying, my daughter?" he asked. "Do

you think that abstaining from food is going to weaken me?"

With that he picked up a heavy chair with two fingers, carried it about the room, and after returning it to its place told her: "If a man provides his soul with all its needs, then he can be strong even without eating!"

☙ The Theory of Relativity

וְאָכַלְתָּ וְשָׂבָעְתָּ
And you shall eat and be sated (8:10)

Reb Dov Ber, the Maggid of Mezritch, once asked a magnate who had come to visit him: "What do you eat every day?"

"Bread and salt, rabbi, like a poor man," was the reply.

The Maggid rebuked him, and told him that he should eat meat and drink mead every day, as wealthy men were accustomed to do. After he left, the disciples of the Maggid asked him to explain his instruction.

"If a rich man eats meat and drinks mead every day," reasoned the tzaddik, "then he will realize that a poor man needs at least bread and salt. If however he himself eats bread and salt, he will think that his poor neighbor can make do with a diet of stones."

☙ A Meeting-Place of Souls

וְאָכַלְתָּ וְשָׂבָעְתָּ וּבֵרַכְתָּ
And you shall eat and be sated, and you shall bless (8:10)

When Reb Yaakov Shimshon Shipitovka came to settle in *Eretz Yisrael* in 1799 he was so distressed by the conditions of famine in which the immigrants from Poland languished, that he decided to travel through Iraq and Egypt and other countries in order to collect contributions for their support. In one of the Oriental communities he came to the house of a *chacham*, the venerable sage who was the spiritual leader of the town. When he heard that his guest came from Poland he asked him if he knew a tzaddik by the name of Reb Baruch of Mehibuzh. Sensing that this *chacham* was a saintly man who knew of Reb Baruch through the gift of *ruach hakodesh*, Reb Yaakov Shimshon replied that he not only knew him, but regarded him as his unquestioned master. But when his host asked him to repeat some teaching that he had heard from his mouth,

Reb Yaakov Shimshon — for the first time in his life — could not recall a word, and they were both distressed at their loss.

Suddenly something came to mind, and he told the sage joyfully: "I have just recalled some little thing I heard from him. In the Grace after Meals we say: 'We thank you, O Lord our God, for having caused our forefathers to inherit ..., and for having brought us out of the Land of Egypt ..., and for Your covenant ..., and for Your Torah' — and so on. After all of this we say: וְעַל הַכֹּל ה׳ אֱלֹקֵינוּ אֲנַחְנוּ מוֹדִים לָךְ — *'And for all of this,* O Lord our God, we thank You.' Now on this passage Reb Baruch of Mezhibuzh commented as follows. We are obliged to thank God for each of the blessings we have listed. But וְעַל הַכֹּל — *more than* all of these reasons for gratitude — *'O Lord our God,* we thank You,' that is to say: We thank you for being the Lord *our* God; we are thankful that we have not strayed from You!"

The sage was overawed at these words.

"And is this what you call 'some little thing'?" he exclaimed. "Why, these are inspired words!"

With that he proceeded to expound them according to the mystical teachings of the Torah. For three whole days they explored these secrets together, divesting themselves of the shackles of the body, and spurning all food and drink. At length Reb Yaakov Shimshon feared that he could survive this ecstasy no more. He rose to leave — but only after he had asked the *chacham* where he had come to know Reb Baruch of Mezhibuzh.

"I saw him in the World Above," he replied, "for he is as familiar with the paths of heaven as he is with the paths of the World Below."

◆§ *On Guard*

הִשָּׁמֶר לְךָ פֶּן תִּשְׁכַּח
Be on your guard lest you forget (8:11)

While speaking to a group of his chassidim Reb Moshe Zvi of Savran once quoted some expression from the Talmud. The head of the local rabbinical court was present, and pointed out that the Talmud never once used such a phrase.

"How much time has passed since you last studied the tractate to which I referred?" asked the tzaddik.

"Why, just half a year," answered the *dayyan.*

"I have not encountered this passage for seventeen years," said the tzaddik, "but allow me to show you that I am in the right."

When he had proved his point by consulting the passage in question, he turned to his chassidim and continued: "There is no cause here for surprise. The Torah, as you know, commands us to sanctify the *Shabbos* in two distinct verses. One tells us to *'remember* (זָכוֹר) the Sabbath day to keep it holy.' This mitzvah is fulfilled by reciting *Kiddush,* the blessing over a goblet of wine which expresses in words the sanctity of the Day of Rest. The other verse tells us to *'Guard* (שָׁמוֹר) the Sabbath day to keep it holy.' Who is obliged to recite or hear *Kiddush?* On this the Sages tell us: כָּל שֶׁיֶשְׁנוֹ בִּשְׁמִירָה יֶשְׁנוֹ בִּזְכִירָה — Whoever is covered by the commandment of *guarding* (שְׁמִירָה) is also involved in the commandment of *remembering* (זְכִירָה).

"And I tell you too: כָּל שֶׁיֶשְׁנוֹ בִּשְׁמִירָה — any person to whom *guarding* applies, who guards himself from the faintest shadow of sin, יֶשְׁנוֹ בִּזְכִירָה — will be one to whom *remembering* applies. Conversely, he who is not constantly aware of this *guarding* will not be blessed with *remembering* ..."

To — or From?

כֹּחִי וְעֹצֶם יָדִי
My power and the might of my hand (8:17)

Reb Levi Yitzchak of Berditchev once saw a man running breathlessly across the market place.

"Why are you running so fast?" he asked.

"What do you mean?" he panted. "I am rushing in pursuit of my livelihood!"

"And how do you know," asked the tzaddik, "that your livelihood is in front of you, and that you are running after it to catch up to it? Perhaps it is behind you, and you are in fact running away from it?..."

Regrets of the Saintly

לֶחֶם לֹא אָכַלְתִּי
No bread did I eat (9:9)

Reb Yaakov Shimshon of Kosov was once in exceptionally high spirits, and kept his chassidim enthralled with a colorful medley of chassidic stories from the conclusion of the morning prayers until the middle of the afternoon. Not a single one of them thought of going home for breakfast.

When his narration had come to an end one of his chassidim rose and said: "There is nothing remarkable about the statement of Moshe Rabbeinu, that while he was on Mount Sinai, 'No bread did I eat, nor water did I drink.' For he experienced such intense pleasure during those forty days in the World Above, with everything that his eyes saw and with the Torah that he heard from the Almighty Himself, that he was sated — just like in the World to Come, in which 'the righteous sit and bask in the radiance of the Divine Presence.'"

Reb Yaakov Shimshon saw the passage otherwise.

"It could be that these words do not express the *satisfaction* that Moshe Rabbeinu had at not eating and drinking, but on the contrary express his *regret*. For he considered how many divine sparks hidden in food and drink he could have liberated and elevated through eating and drinking with lofty intentions — and this food would yet file its claim against him for having thus deprived it from fulfilling its divinely appointed destiny!".

◈ *Two Encounters*

לְיִרְאָה אֶת ה׳ אֱלֹקֶיךָ... וּלְאַהֲבָה אֹתוֹ
To fear the Lord your God...and to love Him (10:12)

Late in 1801, when Reb Shneur Zalman of Liadi was imprisoned for the second time in St. Petersburg, an offer was made to him by Rabbi Nota Notkin, a prominent *misnaged* from Shklov: he would exercise his connections in high places so that the authorities would free him, and in exchange for this, the tzaddik was to undertake to visit three renowned *misnagdish* scholars soon after he was released.

After resolving an exceedingly knotty scholarly problem posed to him by the first of these three opponents of Chassidism, Reb Moshe Cheifetz of Chavs, the rebbe proceeded to his second visit — to Rabbi Yehoshua Zeitlin of Shklov, who received him coolly. Seeing all his questions on Torah subjects handled deftly by his guest, the *misnaged* challenged him on a statement that appears in *Tanya,* the classic text on *Chabad* Chassidism written by Reb Shneur Zalman.

"On what authority do you claim in your book," he asked, "that the Torah must be studied with the love and awe of God, and that the study of the Torah without this love and awe does not rise heavenward?"

"This is an explicit statement in the *Zohar,*" replied the rebbe. "It is written there that 'Torah without awe and love cannot fly upward.' "

Rabbi Yehoshua objected: "But we do not decide according to the *Zohar* — only according to the Talmud!"

"This is to be found explicitly in the Babylonian Talmud as well," Reb Shneur Zalman assured him.

Since his host could not recall such a statement in the Talmud, Reb Shneur Zalman opened Tractate *Pesachim* at the following passage: "Rava pointed out a seeming contradiction. In one verse we read: 'Your lovingkindness is great *unto* the heavens.' In another verse we find: 'Your lovingkindness is great *above* the heavens.' How are we to reconcile these two texts? — The latter verse states the reward of those who study the Torah for its own good sake; the former refers to those whose service is not completely motivated by selfless intentions."

Rabbi Yehoshua was impressed with this reply, and gave his guest a respectful farewell.

From there Reb Shneur Zalman journeyed to Amchislav, where he was surprised at the greeting he was given by Rabbi Yoel: "Shalom Aleichem, my master!"

"And in what way am I your teacher?" asked Reb Shneur Zalman.

"When we were young, and we were both in Vitebsk," recalled Rabbi Yoel, "I asked you a certain question involving the passage I was studying in the Talmud, and you clarified it for me. And that is sufficient cause, the Mishnah teaches us, for me to respect you as my teacher."

"If that is the case," returned Reb Shneur Zalman, "why did you not go to St. Petersburg to ransom me? Is a man not obliged to ransom his teacher of Torah?"

"Believe me," answered Rabbi Yoel, "that if your

release depended on money alone nothing would have held me back ..."

And after a long and friendly conversation and a respectful exchange of farewells, the tzaddik — having fulfilled his promise to be confronted by three famous antagonists of his teachings — went on his way.

◆§ *No More Questions (i)*

וְעָרְפְּכֶם לֹא תַקְשׁוּ עוֹד *And be stiffnecked no more (10:16)*

And you shall circumcise the foreskin of your heart, and your neck you shall no longer make stiff: For homiletical purposes, chassidic tradition is fond of repunctuating this verse, and in addition reading the final verb (תַקְשׁוּ) ambiguously. The verse then gives the following advice. וּמַלְתֶּם אֵת עָרְלַת לְבַבְכֶם וְעָרְפְּכֶם - לֹא תַקְשׁוּ עוֹד: If you wish to circumcise the foreskin of your heart and your neck, then *ask no more questions (Traditional).*

In the first years after Reb Shneur Zalman of Liadi became rebbe, the chassidic interpretations which he gave of Biblical verses and Talmudic quotations were often condensed into one sentence. On one occasion, for example, he took as his text a statement from the Mishnah: כָּל בַּעֲלֵי הַשֵּׁיר יוֹצְאִין בְּשֵׁיר וְנִמְשָׁכִין בְּשֵׁיר. The context defines the restrictions applying to animals on *Shabbos* — under what circumstances may they move freely and be led from a private domain to the public domain. This particular sentence says: "And all animals bearing a chain or ring (שֵׁיר) may go out wearing their chain and may be led along by it." Reading this same text on a mystical level, though, Reb Shneur Zalman gave the following interpretation: "*All the masters of song* (שִׁיר) — that is, the souls and angels who inhabit the World Above — *go out in song and are drawn in song,* that is, they may be either elevated or drawn down into This World through the outpouring of a worshiper's soul in melody."

When one of the chassidim who heard this from the rebbe's mouth repeated this thought to the few chassidim who then lived in Shklov, they are most distressed, in anticipation of the attack which the local *mis-*

nagdim would no doubt make on this seemingly bizarre interpretation of a straightforward legal statement. And in a short time their anxiety proved to be well founded.

In due course Reb Shneur Zalman had occasion to pass through Shklov, but since the local scholars had by now recognized that he was a luminary in the Torah world, many of them visited him and asked him various learned questions which had engaged their attention. He however offered no answers. They therefore decided to convene a gathering of scholars in the communal house of study that was known locally as "the cold *beis midrash*," and at this forum the visiting rebbe would be asked to deliver a learned dissertation, and to answer all the questions that had been put to him. Reb Shneur Zalman accepted the invitation.

Ascending the pulpit he said: "Instead of delivering a discourse and answering questions, I shall sing you a melody. For there is a Mishnah which says: כָּל בַּעֲלֵי הַשִּׁיר יוֹצְאִין בְּשֵׁיר וְנִמְשָׁכִין בְּשֵׁיר — that is, souls and angels from the World Above may be both elevated and drawn down into This World through the singing of a melody."

And with this he began to sing his haunting melody, and they heard in it the intense yearning of a lofty soul. A sweet stillness stole into the heart of every man there. In ways that they could not fathom, the thorny questions and problems that had brought them there all found their sure answers. With his melody lending voice to his *dveikus*, he refreshed their minds from the wellsprings of wisdom, and they could now gaze upon the Torah with a clearer eye.

One of their number, by the name of Rabbi Yosef Kolbo, had spent months of fatiguing exertion in an attempt to solve four near-insoluble problems that not even the sages of Vilna and Polotzk could master. But now, as if melted by the harmony of a soul searching and cleaving to its Source, the toughest of his problems resolved itself peacefully. Years later, when he had already become a steadfast disciple of Reb Shneur Zalman, this scholar recalled: "When those four problems resolved themselves in my mind, I felt like a small child."

❦ ❦ ❦

In 1804 an elder chassid of Reb Shneur Zalman by the name of Reb Avraham Sheines of Shklov told this story to the rebbe's grandson, Reb Menachem Mendel of Lubavitch. It was on the basis of this story that Reb Menachem Mendel later wrote his long chassidic discourse beginning with the words לְהָבִין עִנְיַן טְעָמִים which explains, among other things, the kabbalistic connotations of the musical cantillation symbols that adorn the printed Hebrew text of the Torah.

◆§ *No More Questions (ii)*

In his youth the tzaddik of Pshischah once heard a dissertation delivered by Reb Moshe Leib of Sasov, in which he resolved an apparent textual difficulty by pointing out that one of the authorities involved presented his arguments in the reverse of the expected order.

After the lecture was over he said to his young guest: "I did not approach this subject with the express intention of solving that textual difficulty. The solution I proposed is no major matter, and in fact I did not even notice the need for it — until while I was studying, the rationale underlying my solution occurred to me, as a matter of academic interest. Once I had thought of it, I cast about for some problem to use it on, and this was the best I could find.

"To take this one step further, my son," he continued, "I would like you to know that Maimonides in his *Guide for the Perplexed* did not start out by posing philosophical problems and thereafter seek ways and means of solving them. For if this were the case, then whenever he was waiting for an answer — even if only for a moment — then *for that moment* he experienced separation from the Creator, God forbid. We are therefore forced to the conclusion that he had all the answers to start with, and not even for a single moment was his faith bothered by any philosophical objections. For the edification of his contemporaries, however, he was obliged to demonstrate that the learning that he had mastered could serve to answer certain philosophical problems. Today, however, if someone were to study the

Guide according to the sequence in which its arguments appear — first each question and then its answer — then for the moment that elapses between question and answer he is (God forbid) separated from his Maker!"

From that time on, whenever the tzaddik of Pshischah studied Maimonides' *Guide for the Perplexed*, he did so in this fashion: first the answer, then the question.

◈ *Exemplary Virtue*

אֶת ה׳ אֱלֹקֶיךָ תִּירָא
You shall fear the Lord your God (10:20)

Reb Yaakov Yitzchak, the Yid HaKadosh of Pshischah, studied under Reb David of Lelov, under whose influence he was to become the disciple of the Chozeh of Lublin. He used to make the journey to Lelov with the clear intention of learning from Reb David how to fulfill a particular mitzvah richly — *ahavas Yisrael*, the obligation to love one's fellow Jew as oneself. To this end he made a point of accompanying his rebbe on his visits to the neighboring towns and villages, watching his every word and move.

Finding himself in this way in a certain village, he took an outdoor seat where he could rest after the journey, while Reb David visited one of the villagers to ask how he was keeping. The rebbe took so long over doing this that the Yid HaKadosh asked him what had delayed him.

"I found a man at home doing his work," said the tzaddik, "while his son abused him for being lazy. These were his words: 'You are so lazy that if I didn't fear God I would kill you!' Now when I heard words such as these, I stayed on: I simply couldn't leave the presence of a man so God-fearing!"

◈ *Service of the Heart (i)*

וּלְעָבְדוֹ בְּכָל לְבַבְכֶם
And to serve Him with all your heart (11:13)

And to serve him with all your heart: That is, with a service which is in the heart, namely, prayer *(Rashi).*

When he was at prayer the Baal Shem Tov used to tremble exceedingly. Once, in preparation for *Tefillas Geshem*, the prayer for rain which is chanted once a year on the festival of Shemini Atzeres, he robed himself in his white *kittel.* His disciple, Reb Dov Ber of

 Mezritch, stretched out his hand to straighten a wrinkle which he had noticed on the shoulder, but at the mere touch of the *kittel* he began to tremble so much that he took hold of the table that stood in front of him, and it too shook. On another occasion the Baal Shem Tov became engrossed in prayer while standing next to the eastern wall of a dwelling, and the grain in the barrels which were ranged against the opposite wall was seen to tremor.

The tzaddik once said: "Whoever wants his prayer to ascend to heaven, let him say his prayers with me, word by word."

A certain disciple undertook to do this, and for a long period he would echo the prayers of his rebbe, one word at a time, from the first to the last. One *Shabbos*, while they were making their way through the morning prayers in this way, the Baal Shem Tov came to the verse: שֶׁקֶר הַסּוּס לִתְשׁוּעָה — "A horse is a vain thing for salvation" — which he repeated over and over again. The disciple repeated it once only, according to his custom, and then was left to wonder: On what mysteries could his rebbe now be concentrating? He consulted the relevant books but could find no possible explanation, so he decided to stop praying with the Baal Shem Tov.

He did visit his house some time later, though, and when the tzaddik asked him why he had decided to stop, he told him the truth. Whereupon the tzaddik explained the circumstances of that *Shabbos* morning: "On his way home from a journey some distance from here a certain Jew found that he would be unable to reach the nearest settlement before the eve of that *Shabbos*, and had no alternative but to spend the holy day out in the fields. A highwayman nearby came to hear of this, and leaped on to his horse in order to kill him and rob him of his possessions. But when I said that verse he lost his way, and the lone traveler was left in peace."

Service of the Heart (ii)

Reb Dov Ber, the Maggid of Mezritch, was accustomed to praying alone, but every morning, when toward the end of the service he came to the rhymed paean of praise which begins with the words אֵין כֵּאלֹקֵינוּ – "There is none like our God" – he would ask someone to call together the quorum of ten men required for congregational prayer, and conclude his devotions with this *minyan.* One day, one of the ten happened to be a young man called Reb Yaakov Yitzchak Horovitz, who was many years later to become renowned as the Chozeh, or Seer, of Lublin. The Maggid asked to have someone else brought in his place, for this young man, he said, was a *batlan*, an impractical good-for-nothing. No one else happened to be available at the time, however, so it was decided to proceed with those present.

The Maggid barely managed to proclaim: "There is none like our God!" – when the young man fainted, and only with difficulty did his friends manage to bring him to.

"Didn't I tell you that you should not let this young man be here because he is a *batlan?*" said the Maggid when he had concluded his prayers. "All I said was: 'There is none like our God,' and as soon as he saw all the hosts of heaven, he straight away fainted from fright. If someone else had been here instead of him, he would have seen nothing, and would therefore have had nothing to be afraid of."

◆§ *Service of the Heart (iii)*

The disciples were spending the Days of Awe with their rebbe, Reb Dov Ber of Mezritch. When they had concluded the prayers of Rosh HaShanah, the New Year, the rebbe stood looking out of the window for a long time, instead of going home to recite *Kiddush* over a goblet of wine. So long did he tarry that finally Reb Menachem Mendel of Vitebsk approached him and asked him why he did not go home.

"What can I do about it," replied the Maggid, "if Reb Pinchas of Korets is still at his prayers, setting up a clamor in all the heavens!"

◈ Service of the Heart (iv)

A few chassidim once asked Reb Pinchas of Korets why when he prayed his voice could not be heard, nor could one see any hint of ecstasy.

"The essence of prayer," he explained, "is *dveikus*, cleaving to the Creator, and the essence of *dveikus* is *hispashtus hagashmius*, divesting oneself of one's corporeality. This is something like the departure of the soul from the body. Now the departure of the soul from the body at the end of a man's lifetime — in the words of our Sages — sometimes resembles the dragging of a rough cable though a narrow hole, while at other times, resembling a kiss, it is like drawing a wisp of hair out of the milk. During prayer, likewise, in some people the temporary elevation of soul from body is as tortuous as the hauling of a ship's cable; in others, it is more like a kiss."

◈ Service of the Heart (v)

"A thought once beset me," said Reb Mendel of Bar, a chassid of the Baal Shem Tov, "right in the midst of the ecstasy of prayer: 'How dare you pray to the Almighty, when you are so full of sin?'

"I felt duly contrite, and for a long time was unable to rid myself of that thought, which I believed was motivated by a holy source. But then I considered: If this is indeed a holy thought, why does it not come to disturb me while I am *eating*?

"And I banished it!"

◈ Service of the Heart (vi)

A certain freethinker who lived in Berditchev was always scoffing at Reb Levi Yitzchak and his chassidim.

"If you were in the synagogue when our rebbe is at his prayers," they assured him, "then you too would be prompted to repent."

The *apikores* laughed and said: "I'll go along, just to show you that it will make no impression on me whatever!"

True to his word, he visited the *shul* and waited from the beginning of the morning prayers until the end of *Shemoneh Esreh,* and then snickered as if to say: "What did I tell you?"

But within minutes the tzaddik came to the words: וּבָא לְצִיּוֹן גּוֹאֵל וּלְשָׁבֵי פֶשַׁע בְּיַעֲקֹב — "And a Redeemer will come unto Zion, *and to those among Yaakov who return from sin.*" The very depths of his soul cried out, as over and over again he spoke these last words. This the visitor could not withstand. Touched to the heart, he resolved there and then to tackle life afresh, to become one of those who return from sin.

◆§ *Service of the Heart (vii)*

Reb Levi Yitzchak of Berditchev once came to Reb Yisrael, the Maggid of Koznitz, and told him that he intended to make the journey to Vilna in order to argue in defense of Chassidism with the *misnagdim,* its opponents.

"Then let me anticipate their first question to you about your own conduct," said Reb Yisrael. "If you do not read out of a *Siddur,* then why, in seeming neglect of the Code of Jewish Law, do you recite the *Shemoneh Esreh* prayer with your eyes open?"

The Berditchever addressed him with his favorite Russian term of endearment. "*Serdtse* ('my beloved heart')," he said, "do you think I *see* anything at the time?"

"*I* know that you don't see," said Reb Yisrael, "but what will you answer *them?*"

◆§ *Service of the Heart (viii)*

In the course of their prayer, certain chassidim of the *Chabad* school pause at appropriate intervals to meditate on those tracts of chassidic philosophy that illuminate the particular passage which they have reached.

It was with this mode of worship in mind that Reb Shneur Zalman of Liadi, the author of *Tanya,* once asked his son, Reb Dov Ber of Lubavitch: "With what are you currently praying?"

Reb Dov Ber replied: "With the discourse that begins

 with the words: וְכָל קוֹמָה לְפָנֶיךָ תִשְׁתַּחֲוֶה — 'And all those who stand shall prostrate themselves before You.'"

He then went on to ask his father in turn: "And with what do *you* pray?"

"With the floor and the bench," he said.

❦ ❦ ❦

This exchange has also been handed down in another version.

The father asks: "With what did you pray last Rosh HaShanah?"

The son answers as above. Then, in response to his question, Reb Shneur Zalman answers: "With the *stender* ('lectern') — for all of the material creation comes into being through the Creator's infinite essence (הִתְהַווּת הַגַּשְׁמִיּוּת הִיא מֵעַצְמוּתוֹ)."

◆§ *Service of the Heart (ix)*

Chassidim, as everyone knows, are sometimes to be heard singing quietly to themselves while they are at prayer. In an analysis of this custom as it is practised among chassidim of the *Chabad* school of thought, Reb Shalom Ber of Lubavitch once distinguished between a number of modes of *niggun* — including melodies of joy, melodies of contriteness, melodies of spiritual yearning, and melodies that sing of the worshiper's rapturous love of God. Common to them all, he explained, is a characteristically *Chabad* kind of intensity, that is, an ecstasy anchored in measured meditation, and finding expression in *dveikus* — a cleaving to the Creator that encompasses the whole being.

Reb Shalom Ber went on to recount: "Reb Moshe Vilenker and Reb Pinchas Reizes were among the first disciples of Reb Shneur Zalman of Liadi, the *Alter Rebbe*. When they first came to him, and had been examined in their studies, he directed them to Reb Moshe Zalman Feldman, who was to teach them *niggunim*. This chassid was a middle-aged scholar who spoke little, but was a gifted singer; on the festivals and during the Days of Awe it was he would led the congregation in prayer in the *minyan* with which his rebbe prayed. During the languid summer days he liked to stroll out to the fields beyond the outskirts of the town, with a large volume under his arm, and spend tranquil hours in lone study and pensive song. In fact it was this custom of his that gave him his surname — Feldman, which is Yiddish for 'man of the fields.'

"One day," continued Shalom Ber, "Reb Shneur Zalman entered the small *beis midrash*, where he found his two new disciples, Reb Moshe and Reb Pinchas, deep in their studies together with several of their friends. He took a seat at their table, and after some moments during which his soul seemed to have soared elsewhere, he roused himself and said: בַּמֶּה בְּהֵמָה יוֹצְאָה בְּשַׁבָּת — 'The Mishnah discusses the question, *With what* [appurtenances] *may an animal go out* [from a private domain to the public domain] *on Shabbos?'* Reb Shneur Zalman saw in this a mystical hint toward the service of the Creator, and interpreted these words as follows: 'The prayer-time of each weekday is its own *Shabbos.* And during this prayer-time, בַּמֶּה בְּהֵמָה יוֹצְאָה — *With what does the animal go out?* That is: through what kind of service in his prayer can a man drive out his animal soul? And the Mishnah goes on to speak of various kinds of animals — the camel, the she-camel, the donkey and the horse. So, too, each level of the animal soul necessitates its own distinctive manner of divine service' — and here Reb Shneur Zalman went on to explain them all. Then he continued: 'But what is common to all these kinds of service is hinted at in the statement of the Mishnah: כָּל בַּעֲלֵי הַשֵּׁיר יוֹצְאִים בְּשֵׁיר וְנִמְשָׁכִים בְּשֵׁיר. [Literally: All animals bearing a chain or ring (שֵׁיר) may go out wearing their ring and may be led along by it.] *Going out* and *being drawn along* hint respectively at רָצוֹא וָשׁוֹב, two of the primal forces in the dynamics of the human soul — in turn seeking to *wrest itself free* from the body and to cleave to its Source, and then *resigning itself* to the discipline of inhabiting a physical body and illuminating it from within, for this is its divinely-appointed mission. And singing [שִׁיר] during his prayers can help a worshiper separate and distill the elements of holiness hidden within his animal soul, and arouse him to pray with devout intent.'

"With this teaching," Reb Shalom Ber concluded, "Reb Shneur Zalman of Liadi implanted in his chassidim a devotedness to the service of the heart, and endowed them with the ability to be aroused to worship singlemindedly through the power of a melody."

◈§ *Service of the Heart (x)*

Reb Yitzchak, the Chozeh of Lublin, once asked his disciple, the Yid HaKadosh: "My dear Yid, why do you snatch the words of your prayers so hastily?"

The disciple from Pshischah answered: "I find them so delicious that I want to swallow them quickly!"

"And don't *I* relish the words?" asked the Chozeh.

"Rebbe," the Yid replied, "the words of *your* prayer are like fiery flames, so it's hard to gulp them down ..."

◈§ *Service of the Heart (xi)*

Reb Yaakov Yitzchak, the Yid HaKadosh of Pshischah, was once asked from heaven whether he desired to undergo suffering; he replied that he was willing to do so for one hour. He was at once visited by such grievous pain that he was unable to bear it.

"A time like this is a good time to say my prayers," he thought, "for prayer involves הִתְפַּשְׁטוּת הַגַּשְׁמִיּוּת – divesting oneself of one's corporeality, and in that way I will not feel the pain."

And with that he began to recite the afternoon *Minchah* prayer.

◈§ *Service of the Heart (xii)*

Reb Uri of Strelisk once visited a town, and while in its synagogue prayed at length with the ecstatic abandon that earned him the reverent nickname "the Saraph," or fiery angel.

After the service the local *rav* asked him: "Do you not consider the possible inconvenience to the waiting congregation? For the Talmud tells us that when Rabbi Akiva prayed alone, his prayer was so ecstatic that a person might leave him in one corner of the room and find him later in another. When he prayed with the congregation, however, he used to pray briefly, in order to spare them inconvenience."

"But Rabbi Akiva," replied the tzaddik, "had twenty-four thousand disciples, and amongst them there must have been at least ten men — enough for a *minyan* — who did not find their rebbe's prayer burdensome. Why, then, did he not pray with them, and then he would not have to cut his prayers short? We are therefore forced to understand his practice as follows. When he used to pray *with* the congregation — that is, when the congregation prayed with devotion, as he did — then his prayer was accepted at once, and there was no need for him to pray at length. But if within that vast congregation he prayed *alone* — he alone prayed as one should — then because of the necessity of raising aloft and refining all the prayers of the whole congregation, Rabbi Akiva was forced to pray at length ..."

◆§ *Service of the Heart (xiii)*

Reb Yisrael of Ruzhin used to take a long time over his prayers; Reb Shalom of Belz would recite his prayers hastily. On this one of their contemporaries commented that both of them cherished every word of the prayers: the former loved them so much that he could not bring himself to part with them, while the latter — for the same reason — could not restrain his eagerness to make them his.

◆§ *Service of the Heart (xiv)*

The mode of worship traditionally favored by chassidim of the *Chabad* school of thought which flourished in Belorussia is characterized by the unhurried and systematic contemplation of themes in chassidic philosophy which underlie the prayer at hand; Polish chassidim, by contrast, are accustomed to reading their prayers ecstatically, but quickly.

Two chassidim once met — one a devotee of this school of thought, one of the other — and discussed the worshiper's task of warding off any extraneous thoughts which may interfere with his concentration during prayer.

Said the Polish chassid: "Suppose a farmer decides to put up a fence in order to keep his swine out of his vegetable patch. If he binds the canes close to each other, without leaving spaces between them, then he will achieve his aim; if he leaves spaces between them, then the pigs will certainly find their way in ..."

"You are right," said the *Chabad* chassid. "But this is only true if they are not yet in the garden. If, however, they are already inside, and one needs to drive them out, then if the canes of the fence are placed *too* closely together, there will never be any chance of driving them out at all!"

◆§ *Service of the Heart (xv)*

Another *Chabad* chassid once brought his plaint to Reb Hillel of Paritsh, the celebrated elder chassid of Reb Menachem Mendel of Lubavitch. When he studied chassidic writings in preparation for prayer, his soul was afire; when he then proceeded to read the daily prayers, this spiritual zest left him, and he was unable to pray as he should.

"We have a rebbe," said Reb Hillel. "Ask him."

"But is it possible to make the journey to the rebbe for every question that comes up?" objected the chassid.

"So if the festival of *Sukkos* came and you haven't got a *lulav* and an *esrog* with which to carry out the mitzvah of taking the Four Species in your hand," said Reb Hillel, "do you make do with a stick and shake it instead?"

The chassid was persistent nevertheless and entreated Reb Hillel to advise him what to do, until he finally obliged and said: "So what does it matter to you if you pray *before* you say your prayers?"

◆§ *Service of the Heart (xvi)*

Weary and famished after a long journey, Reb Zelig of Shrintzk once arrived at the home of his grandson, Reb Yechiel Meir of Gostynin. Not wanting to keep him waiting until after he had said his morning prayers so that they could eat together, Reb Yechiel Meir asked his grandfather to eat his breakfast at once, alone. At first the older man insisted that he would wait, but finally he agreed to eat alone — for does the Talmud not teach that a guest is obliged to accede to the requests of his host?

When Reb Yechiel Meir joined him at the table after having finished his prayers in another room, Reb Zelig said: "Here, let us say there is something I want to tell you which I learned through the inspiration of *ruach hakodesh* ... Today you did not pray with a settled mind. In fact you did not even take note of the words you were saying!"

Amazed, his grandson asked him how he knew.

Reb Zelig answered: "Rabbeinu Bachya writes in *Chovos HaLevavos* that he who prays without *kavanah*, without devout intent, is like a man who gives another a meal but does not eat with him. Since you gave me breakfast but did not eat with me, it is certain that you prayed without *kavanah*."

☙ *Service of the Heart (xvii)*

Reb Zalman Zlotopolski was a chassid who enjoyed the rare distinction of being held in such esteem by his rebbe, Reb Shmuel of Lubavitch, that he had entire chassidic discourses delivered exclusively to himself, in private. In 1878, in the midst of such a discourse, the rebbe quoted the well-known Talmudic dictum: "Rabbi Eliezer used to give a coin to a pauper, and then he would pray." Prayer, explained the rebbe, should be characterized by liveliness. When one gives alms to a poor man and thereby enlivens him, one's own prayer thereafter gains greatly in vitality — and to emphasize his point, Reb Shmuel threw his arms upward, as he was wont to do on such occasions.

As soon as Reb Zalman returned home to Kremenchug he repeated his discourse to Reb Chaim Dov, a chassid who was renowned for the depth of his grasp in the more profound reaches of chassidic philosophy. Starting the very next morning, Reb Chaim Dov made it his custom to provide vodka and cake on the table at the back of the *beis midrash* in order to enliven the spirits of all the poor folk who passed through the town.

When word of this came back to Reb Shmuel in Lubavitch, he commented: "Do you think that Reb Chaim Dov's erudition comes from his study of *Shaarei Orah* or *Ateres Rosh* [abstruse philosophical tracts of the speaker's grandfather, Reb Dov Ber of Lubavitch]? Not at all! It owes its success to the cake that he gives the underfed before he prays."

◆§ *Telling Half a Story*

פֶּן יִפְתֶּה לְבַבְכֶם... וְעָצַר אֶת הַשָּׁמַיִם
Lest your heart be beguiled... then will He close up the skies (11:16-17)

A man complained to Reb Yitzchak of Vorki that he was not earning enough to make a living. After the tzaddik had answered whatever he answered, he commented to one of his chassidim, Reb Feivl of Gritza: "This man was ashamed to repeat the first half of the quotation to me, so he only quoted the second half."

The other chassidim who were present did not understand this comment, but Reb Feivl later explained them Reb Yitzchak's meaning. "The rebbe," he said, "was alluding to a statement in the Mishnah: 'I have conducted myself wrongly, and I have ruined my livelihood ...' "

◆§ *The Land of the Living*

לְמַעַן יִרְבּוּ יְמֵיכֶם
That your days... may increase (11:21)

In order that your days ... may increase on the Land which God swore to your forefathers: Thus is it written — but not outside the Land *(Talmud, Tractate Berachos).*

Reb Eliyahu Yosef of Drivin was one of the elder disciples of Reb Dov Ber of Lubavitch and, after his passing, of Reb Menachem Mendel of Lubavitch, both of whom used to direct students to learn chassidic philosophy from his mouth. After he had moved from Drivin he became the *rav* of Polotzk, where he became dangerously ill, and his doctors despaired of saving his life. Now the disease from which he suffered is the subject of a conflict of opinion in the *Shulchan Aruch,* the Code of Jewish Law. If an animal were to contract this disease, Rabbi Yosef Caro holds it to be still kosher, while Rabbi Moshe Isserles holds the animal to become *trefah,* in which case it must be discarded.

Said Reb Eliyahu Yosef: "I known what I will do. I will go and settle in *Eretz Yisrael,* where Rabbi Yosef Caro — from his time onward — is the *mara de'asra,* the ruling legal authority for that region. In *Eretz Yisrael,* the law will be settled in accordance with *his* view!"

He set out at once for the Holy Land, where he lived on for over twenty years more. At length he passed away on the twelfth of Tammuz 1865 in Jerusalem, among whose hills he was brought to rest.

סדר ראה
Sidra Re'eh

◆§ *Life-Giving Waters*

כִּי תְאַוֶּה נַפְשְׁךָ לֶאֱכֹל
For you will desire to eat (12:20)

Towards the end of a fast which was to extend from one *Shabbos* to the next, Reb David of Lelov was out on the road when he experienced the most fearful thirst. The sudden sight of a spring bubbling with cool, clear water intensified his suffering so acutely that he was on the point of breaking his fast and drinking. He stood still for a moment to consider the matter briefly, and found the strength in himself to master his burning thirst.

Continuing on his way, he soon found himself overcome by a surge of unutterable joy: he had succeeded in vanquishing his Evil Inclination! A further moment's thought, however, taught him otherwise.

"This joy could not derive from the Good Inclination," he told himself. "It no doubt came from the Other Side. The Evil Inclination is contriving to trap me into becoming conceited!"

And in order to avoid becoming thus ensnared, Reb David returned to the spring, and drank his fill of its waters.

◆§ *A Healthy Appetite*

Reb Yitzchak Meir of Ger, accompanied by Rabbi Dov Meisels of Warsaw, once visited a wealthy individual in the capital city in order to ask him to utilize his connections with the authorities for some matter involving the public good.

When they were shown into his house they found him enjoying his lunch of non-kosher food. The tzaddik of Ger promptly gave him the customary greeting: "Good appetite!"

"Rebbe," said their host, "if you knew that I was now eating forbidden food, you would not have wished me such a good appetite!"

"Quite the contrary," said the rebbe, "I intentionally wished you just that, in the hope that in the eyes of heaven you would be classed only as a *mumar leteiavon* — an apostate who acts out of uncontrolled desire, rather than as a *mumar lehach'is* — an apostate who is motivated by wilful rebelliousness ..."

◆§ *A Matter of Taste*

A wealthy Jew from Pest, who did not observe the Sabbath and the festivals and who ate non-kosher food, happened to be present at a chassidic gathering presided over by Reb Chaim of Zanz. According to the custom at the *tish* in certain chassidic circles, the rebbe partook of the food which was served to him, and then offered the remaining portion *(shirayim)* to his disciples, each of whom tasted a morsel. Reb Chaim offered a little of the food to this individual too — but as soon as he reached home he complained of a stomach ailment, and from then on lost his appetite so completely that he balked at the sight of food. Since he steadily lost weight and the doctors were baffled, his family seized upon the suggestion that some passerby offered them — that they should seek the advice of a certain tzaddik who happened to be nearby at the time. His name: Reb Chaim of Zanz.

The tzaddik heard their story,and advised them to break all the *trefah* kitchen utensils in the house or to sell them to gentiles, and replace them with new ones, and to begin to conduct a kosher kitchen. The head of the house would soon be well.

As soon as these instructions were carried out the

waning patient began indeed to recover his appetite, and as he regained his former strength, the reason for his ailment became clear to them all: once he had tasted the *shirayim* which the tzaddik had offered him, he developed an instinctive aversion to any *trefah* food.

☙ *Feed the Body, Feed the Soul*

Rebbitzin Rivkah, the wife of Reb Shmuel of Lubavitch, developed such a serious lung condition that her doctors declared her case to be beyond hope.

Her father-in-law, Reb Menachem Mendel of Lubavitch, heard this and said: "On the verse וְרַפֹּא יְרַפֵּא — 'and he shall surely heal,' the Sages of the Talmud comment that 'from this we learn that the Torah permits a doctor to heal.' *This* is what the Torah permits — but when it comes to pronouncing the opposite verdict, God forbid, that is no affair of his at all."

He then instructed her to make a breakfast of bread and butter every morning immediately after washing her hands when she woke up — without observing the usual order of first saying her morning prayers — and gave her his blessing for long life. After some time she decided to allow this instruction to lapse, and told her father-in-law that she now hurried through the morning prayers, and immediately after that sat down to breakfast.

"It is better to eat in order to be able to pray," he said, "than to pray in order to be able to eat."

☙ *One Man's Meat*

While Reb Shmuel of Lubavitch was on a visit to St. Petersburg for some communal matter, one of his chassidim came to him with a complaint: "Rebbe, in this city it is hard to come by meat that is really strictly kosher."

"And who says that one has to eat meat altogether?" asked the rebbe. "Have not the Sages of the Talmud taught us that 'an ignoramus is forbidden (אָסוּר) to eat meat'? Now this word אָסוּר at root means *bound*. That is to say, an ignoramus feels *bound* to eat meat ... One can survive *without* such meat that one lusts to eat."

◆§ In the Eyes of God and Man

וְזָבַחְתָּ... כַּאֲשֶׁר צִוִּיתִךָ
And you shall slaughter...as I have commanded you (12:21)

Reb Nachum of Chernobyl was making one of his accustomed rounds of the Jewish towns and villages collecting money for the ransom of captives. Arriving one morning at the outskirts of a certain village he asked one of the local citizens: "Where does your *shochet* live?"

Now the man he met was in fact the local *shochet* himself, but because he was dressed in tattered clothes he did not want to introduce himself as such to the visitor, who was obviously a man of stature. He therefore gave him instructions as to how to reach the house of the *shochet* — by a roundabout route, while he himself took a short cut home, and changed his clothes before the prominent guest arrived.

Some time after Reb Nachum found the house he explained to his host — gently and apologetically — that it was his custom, wherever he traveled, to ask to be shown the knife of the ritual slaughterer, in order to satisfy himself as to its unblemished sharpness and validity. After his prayers, could he therefore be shown his host's knife?

While the tzaddik was praying, the *shochet* took out his own knife, examined it, and found it to be in excellent condition. "Nevertheless,' he thought, "since I am about to show it to someone, perhaps I might as well sharpen it just a little bit more?"

But this thought was immediately replaced by another: "Now let us see. If someone were to ask me right now to slaughter for him, would I not use this knife right away, exactly as it is? Is it not then unthinkable that in the sight of the Almighty the knife is valid, but if it is to be submitted to the scrutiny of flesh and blood it needs to be sharpened *just a little bit more?"*

He therefore decided to do nothing more to it, and simply to show it to the tzaddik as it was.

After Reb Nachum had finished praying, and his host presented him with his knife for examination, the tzaddik said: "If in the eyes of the Almighty your knife is valid, then it is most certainly so in my eyes too. Take it and use it: there is no need for me to examine it."

◆§ Not Gone, but Returned

בָּנִים אַתֶּם
You are sons
(14:1)

In most congregations it is customary to add to the number of seven statutory worshipers who are honored by being called to the Torah during the *Shabbos* morning service in the synagogue. Reb Henich of Alisk, the son-in-law of Reb Shalom of Belz, used to make a point of never making any such additions until the first six worshipers had each been called to their allotted passages. He himself was customarily called up in the sixth place and only thereafter, if at all, were additional passages allocated.

In the year 1884, however, on the *Shabbos* on which the weekly Portion of *Re'eh* is read, he gave instructions in his synagogue that the first part of the weekly reading should be divided into sections shorter than usual, so that the sixth man — himself — should be called to the reading of the passage which opens with the words בָּנִים אַתֶּם — "You are sons to the Lord your God."

None of those present understood this change of policy — until on the following Friday the tzaddik passed away. The chassidim then lighted upon a telling interpretation of that very verse in *Or HaChaim*, the Biblical commentary of Rabbi Chaim ben Attar. This Oriental scholar writes as follows: "One needs to understand why these words appear immediately before the words לֹא תִתְגֹּדְדוּ — the prohibition against gashing oneself in token of mourning. It would seem that the Torah is hinting here that a man's death does not imply a loss to the deceased. He is, rather, like a son whose father sent him off to do business in a distant city, and then in the course of time sent for him. True enough, the son is now no longer present at the place of his sojourn — but he is still alive. Moreover, the son is pleased to be able to return to his father, who is the source of life. For this reason, the Torah reminds us first בָּנִים אַתֶּם — that we are sons to the Almighty, and then teaches us a corollary of this: לֹא תִתְגֹּדְדוּ — that we are not to gash ourselves and to cut bald patches in our hair, nor to give vent to any of the other once-common manifestations of violent grief."

◆§ Discernment

לֹא תְאַמֵּץ אֶת לְבָבְךָ
You shall not harden your heart (15:7)

It sometimes happens that a man is in two minds as to whether or not to give alms. For this reason is it written: "You shall not harden your heart" *(Rashi).*

A chassid once brought a gift of three hundred rubles to Reb Nachum of Chernobyl, who was a poor man all his days. The family was overjoyed — but most of all the chief *gabbai,* who was relieved that now the household would at last be able to pay off some of the debts which were owed to the baker and the butcher and so on.

Soon after that chassid had left, the rebbe received a few dozen visitors at *yechidus,* and made a break for the evening prayer. He then closed himself in his study for a time, and later resumed the series of private interviews, which continued until late into the night.

When the last visitor had left, the chief *gabbai* — who was responsible for the household expenses — called on the rebbe in order to receive the long-awaited money needed to settle the accounts. In fact as soon as he had heard of the three hundred rubles he had prepared a list of all the creditors, and had calculated how much he would now be able to give each of them in part payment. The tzaddik opened the drawer of his table and asked the *gabbai* to take whatever was there. Seeing only sundry silver and copper coins, but no sign of the bills that made up the gift of three hundred rubles, the *gabbai* stood still in unquestioning silence.

Seeing how his face had dropped, the tzaddik asked: "Why do you look so sad? Has He Who provides bread for all creatures not shown us — in His lovingkindness — undeserved generosity?"

The *gabbai* could no longer restrain himself. The debts and the privation that hung over the rebbe's household caused him anguish, and he spoke out in words that came straight from the heart: "But were are the three hundred rubles which that chassid brought? That sum could have helped us pay off some of our debts!"

"It is true," conceded the tzaddik, "that he brought

me three hundred rubles. My first reaction was to wonder why I deserved such a large sum, and then I was happy that I had found favor in the eyes of the Almighty and that He had chosen to sustain my family and myself with a generous hand. But when I thought into the subject a little more deeply I became distressed, lest He had given me material benefits instead of spiritual riches. Now among the chassidim who visited me soon after that gift arrived was one who poured out his troubles to me: for a whole year he had not paid the village *melamed* for his children's tuition; the local squire had threatened to drive him out of his house because of his arrears on the rental of the millstones; and to make the situation even more acute he now had to arrange a wedding for his eldest daughter.

"So then I thought that perhaps the Almighty had given me the special privilege of being the agent for the disbursement of charity in a way that would earn me three mitzvos at once — the support of his children in their Torah study, the saving of a family from homelessness, and dowering a poor bride. I asked him how much he needed, and he said that three hundred rubles would solve all his problems. I decided therefore to present him with the whole amount I had received.

"But then another thought came to mind: an amount such as this could bring relief to a considerable number of poor families. This view too seemed to be right — and I could not decide between them. And that is when I closed myself in my room so that I could weigh both arguments. After a little while I arrived at the conclusion that these two views came from the Good and the Evil Inclinations, and that the view which proposed dividing up the amount for several families did *not* come from the Good Inclination. How did I know that?

"Because if this had been the view of the Good Inclination, then as soon as the money reached me he should have expressed his opinion, as follows: 'Nachum! Here, take the three hundred rubles and divide it up into six parts. Give away five to the needy, andd keep one for yourself.' But he did *not* say that. Only *after* the Almighty had made it my privilege to heed the Good Inclination, and I had decided to give the whole amount to that poor chassid, only *then* did this voice come along and try to speak to me craftily.

"I therefore took the advice of the Good Inclination — I called in that poor fellow and gave him the whole amount."

❀ ❀ ❀

When Reb Yosef Yitzchak of Lubavitch told this story, he commented: "From this we learn that *discernment* is more essential to the practical aspects of divine service than is comprehension or emotional involvement. Even an accomplished tzaddik, even God-fearing Jews, even Torah scholars — all need to apply intellectual discernment to their practical service of the Creator."

◆§ *Someone Agrees With You*

Reb Menachem Mendel of Kosov had a simple and honest brother by the name of Reb Yitzchak — a poor man, who was supported by the tzaddik as part of his household.

Now the rebbe was visited one day by an individual who had won notoriety as an antagonist of his. This man brought his sorry situation to the rebbe's attention — his daughter had reached marriageable age — and since he was penniless he sought advice as to how he could earn some money. In response to the rebbe's question he said how much he needed, whereupon Reb Menachem Mendel emptied out his drawer and handed him its contents — a few hundred gold rubles.

When Reb Yitzchak heard of this he was incensed. Whenever his brother was asked for money to cover his own household expenses he said he had none, and now — for his antagonist, mind you! — he suddenly had plenty.

He went straight off to ask his brother: "How could you do such a thing?"

"My dear brother," answered the tzaddik, "only a few minutes ago someone was here, and he said *exactly* what you are saying now. But I took no notice of him — for reasons best known to myself — nor do I intend to take notice of you."

"Who was this who agreed with me?" asked Reb Yitzchak.

Replied his brother: "Satan — the Evil Inclination!"

☙ To Humor a Fool

דֵּי מַחְסוֹרוֹ
Sufficient for his need (15:8)

Reb Menachem Mendel of Kotsk once received a rabbinic guest with all the traditional trappings of respect, including a festive meal in his honor. His chassidim were surprised, for they knew that their rebbe did not at all hold this pretentious guest in esteem.

When they asked him for an explanation of his conduct he said: "In defining the financial support which the Torah obligates us to give or lend a poor man — דֵּי מַחְסוֹרוֹ: 'sufficient for his need' — the Talmud says that these words imply 'even a horse on which to ride, and a servant to run before him.' Now the first half is understandable: perhaps our poor man is too weak or sick to walk, so he needs a horse. But 'a servant to run before him'?! Why, if he desires such a thing, it is sheer foolishness. Why should we be obliged to give it to him?

"But from this we may learn that even to humor the whim of a fool counts as the mitzvah of charity..."

☙ Self-Serving Charity

וְלֹא יֵרַע לְבָבְךָ בְּתִתְּךָ לוֹ
Let your heart not grieve when you give to him (15:10)

On his way home from a business trip to Danzig before he became a rebbe, Reb Simchah Bunem of Pshischah passed through a town called Sheps. As soon as he arrived at his lodgings he sent for one of the local chassidim, a poor man by the name of Reb Zalman, and asked him to arrange a festive meal in his home in honor of the guest from Pshischah, as chassidim are accustomed to do. In order to make this possible he gave him ample money to buy fish and chickens and all kinds of delicacies besides.

When Reb Zalman had gone off to begin his purchases, Reb Simchah Bunem sent his attendant to summon a furrier to his lodgings. To the fur hat and coat that he bought from him he added shoes, and generous lengths of white material which could be made up according to need. He wrapped it all up into one outsize bundle, and sent it off with his sturdy attendant to the cottage of the destitute family. When the messenger brought back word of how ragged the whole family looked, Reb Simchah Bunem promptly dispatched him with enough money to buy them all the clothes they could conceivably need. And that was not all — for after the festive meal Reb Simchah Bunem asked his host to treat all his guests to vodka, and for this too he gave him more money than was needed. In a word, Reb Zalman was left with money to spare.

When the guest of honor was about to leave, he offered his host a substantial sum as a parting gift.

"But from all the money that you have given me until now," protested Reb Zalman, "I have quite an amount left over, apart from the clothes and other goods that you bought me." And he refused to accept it.

"In giving us the commandment to give *tzedakah* to the poor," answered Reb Simchach Bunem, "the Torah tells us the following: 'You shall surely give him, and let your heart not grieve when you give to him.' That is to say...' — and here the tzaddik lent an interpretation of his own to the plain meaning of the above verse — "...that whoever gives alms to a pauper out of compassion, because his tender heart cannot bear to look upon the sufferings of the poor man, has not given *tzedakah* at all. For such a man is in fact serving his own interests, alleviating his own distress. *Tzedakah* should be given in such large amounts that one reaches the point where 'your heart will not grieve when you give to him' — when one no longer feels compassion for his situation. Only then does one fulfill the commandment of giving *tzedakah.*

"Now in my case, too: once I had given you whatever you lacked my heart was no longer pained by your condition. Now, therefore, I can finally fulfill the mitzvah of giving *tzedakah* as one should. For all the trouble I went to in giving my previous gifts was only a preparation that would enable me to do this mitzvah now. If at *this* stage you refuse to accept this gift from me, then (God forbid!) all my efforts until now will have been in vain..."

In response to this explanation Reb Zalman accepted

the gift with good grace, and they parted company amidst warm expressions of friendship.

◆§ *The Joy of Giving*

Reb Chaim of Zanz is widely remembered for the way in which he distributed charity with an open hand. Once his son, Reb Baruch of Gorlitz, asked him to help bear the financial burden of marrying off his daughter.

"I have no money now," said Reb Chaim.

A few days later a number of wealthy chassidim visited Zanz and made him a gift of a large sum of money. His son was pleased to hear of this: surely he would now be given what he had requested. Instead, however, the tzaddik sent for a certain poor townsman who had a whole line of daughters to marry off, and gave him the entire amount.

When the son came to speak to his father and was told what had happened, he wept and said: "Why should I be less eligible to receive help than some other poor man? Don't I also need money to marry off a daughter?"

The tzaddik explained his reasoning: "You, my son, will be able to go traveling about in places where you are known, and our brethren will no doubt help you out generously. But as for this obscure pauper — if *I* don't give him money, who will look after him?"

❀ ❀ ❀

Reb Chaim once asked: "Among the tzaddikim whom I visited in order to learn from their various ways was Reb Zvi Hirsch ('the Beadle') of Rimanov, to whom I went in order to learn how *tzedakah* is to be given — but in this I did not succeed. For when he had money he gave it all to the poor, leaving himself nothing; if he did not have money he was still just as happy as if he had it and as if he was giving it to the poor. But as for me, if I haven't any money to give the needy I pine away from distress."

◆§ *The Wheel of Fortune (i)*

כִּי בִגְלַל הַדָּבָר הַזֶּה יְבָרֶכְךָ

*Because for the sake of (*בִּגְלַל*) this thing (i.e., charity), He will bless you:* Fortune is a wheel

(גִּלְגַּל) that turns in the world *(Talmud, Tractate Shabbos).*

Because for the sake of this thing He will bless you (15:10)

Hearing that Reb Feivish of Zabriza was going to spend *Shabbos* in Skole, his young disciple Reb Menachem Mendel of Kosov set out to greet him — on foot, because he could afford no other way. As evening fell on Thursday a village inn came in sight. He had not tasted a morsel of food all day long, and he was weary from trudging across the Ukraine, so he asked the innkeeper if he could spend the night in his hostelry.

"You may certainly sleep here," was the answer, "but I have nothing to give you for supper. I have not even got a slice of bread left to give my little ones. There is no income from this inn, and if I do not pay the owner of this village what I owe him for the lease within a few days, he will throw me and all my family into his dungeon. And I have not a solitary coin to start paying with."

Reb Menachem Mendel was so distressed to hear this story that he could not sleep all that night. In the morning he said farewell, gave the poor man his blessing that the Almighty should help him, and resumed his slow tramp along the highway.

A carriage soon overtook him, and as it slowed down the Jew sitting within called out to him: "Young man! Where are you heading?"

"To the rebbe of Zabriza," answered the walker.

"In that case," said the owner of the carriage, "come and join me up here, because I am headed in that very direction."

"But I will not travel with you," stipulated Reb Menachem Mendel, "unless you give me twenty silver coins."

"It is not enough that I offer to take you in my carriage without charging any fee!" fumed the other. "On top of that you demand payment?!" Then he added: "I shall give you a respectable contribution — but not such a large sum as that!"

"Believe me," said Reb Menachem Mendel, "that I do not need the money for myself. My request is made for the benefit of others — and for your benefit, too."

The rich man in the carriage now wanted to know what benefit he could expect to derive from his contribution, apart from having earned a mitzvah.

"Who knows what ups and downs each new day can bring?" said Reb Menachem Mendel in reply. "For life is a wheel that turns in the world ..."

These words had their effect. The rich man took out twenty silver coins and handed them to his prospective passenger, who said: "Now I shall not move from here until you return with me to the nearest inn, so that you will be able to see with your own eyes what a great mitzvah you have fulfilled."

The rich man agreed, and they rode back together along the highway until they reached the village they sought. Reb Menachem Mendel handed the innkeeper the money he had just been given, sent him off to town to buy up a stock of vodka for his inn, and assured him that from that day on he would prosper in all his affairs.

He now turned to the owner of the carriage and said: "As you know from the words of our Sages, 'One mitzvah brings another in its train.' Let us stay here for the morning prayers, and in the meantime, if you give your coachman some money, he will be able to go and buy bread so that our host's children will have what to eat, and we will be able to eat some of it for breakfast."

This was done, and there was enough bread left over for *Shabbos* meals for the whole family, as well as for provisions to last the travelers for the remainder of their journey.

As they were about to leave, Reb Menachem Mendel whispered in the ear of the innkeeper: "From now on you will prosper more and more, and in the course of time my rich companion will utterly lose his fortune. When the time comes, remember to repay one kindness by another!"

When they arrived at Zabriza they were unable to make their way through the bustling throngs of chassidim, until Reb Feivish himself called out: "Make way for the people who have just performed a mitzvah!"

In response to Reb Menachem Mendel's account of how his traveling companion had saved an entire family from starvation, the tzaddik — borrowing the words of the patriarch Yaakov — said: "I know, my son, I know. But did you tell the innkeeper how he is to act when the time comes?"

"I told him," said Reb Menachem Mendel, "and he undertook to discharge his obligation."

After *Shabbos* the rich man drove off in his carriage, a contented man. In due course, however, he was tossed by the tempests of time and fortune. Every transaction was a disappointment, every investment was a failure. He was left literally penniless. Dire necessity drove him to wander from town to town, knocking on the doors of the well-to-do in quest of alms. During this same period Reb Menachem Mendel became renowned as the rebbe of Kosov — and the innkeeper became a prosperous man, just as his young guest had promised him long ago.

In the course of his years on the road, the destitute wanderer arrived at Kosov. He did not know that the tzaddik who had made the name of the town famous was the same young man to whom — in such different circumstances! — he had once given twenty silver coins. The itinerant paupers who knew Kosov from previous visits now told the newcomer: "Let us come along and visit the local rebbe. *There* is a man who knows how to provide for the likes of us!"

Recognizing him at once, the rebbe called him aside and said: "Take my advice, my friend, and may God prosper your path. I will give you a letter to a certain wealthy individual, and through him you will be helped."

The pauper wondered at these words, but was too weary to ask for an explanation. With the letter in hand he set out in the direction he was told to take, and eventually found himself treading the length of the long-forgotten dirt track that meandered its way to a certain remote village inn. The innkeeper did not recognize him after his fifteen long years of privation, but before he opened the envelope he said: "I know this letter is from the rebbe of Kosov, for this very night he appeared to me in my dream and told me that the time had come for me to repay one kindness by another."

He then reminded the wanderer of their first encounter, and told him what it was that their mutual friend had whispered in his ear at the time. For the first time in years, a smile now warmed the strained features of the dusty traveler.

The innkeeper went on: "Be my guest until I make an honest reckoning of all the prosperity with which the Almighty has blessed me. Then we will travel together to Kosov, and we will do whatever the rebbe tells us."

It is not known what instructions were given by the tzaddik for the settling of their accounts, but one thing is certain — the innkeeper made the wanderer an exceedingly generous gift, the tzaddik blessed him with success, and when he re-established himself in business he prospered in every venture.

☙ *The Wheel of Fortune (ii)*

One of the chassidim of Reb Avraham Yehoshua Heschel journeyed to Apta to tell his rebbe to what wretched straits he was reduced.

"I will give you a letter to one of my people," said the tzaddik, "instructing him to give you two hundred rubles on my account. He is a very wealthy man."

When the poor man arrived at the home of the addressee, he merely told him that he had been sent by the rebbe, and was received warmly. Only after he had enjoyed his host's hospitality for several days did he hand him the letter. At the sight of it the rich man went purple with rage.

"I don't know what business affairs the rebbe has with me that he should take it upon himself to instruct me to give you such a large sum on his account!" he protested. "I can give you a certain amount — but definitely not two hundred rubles!"

The guest argued that it would not be proper for him to disobey the rebbe's orders by receiving less. In the end he left empty-handed, and returned to Apta to repeat his sad story.

"Very well," said the tzaddik, "I will now give you a letter to another one of my chassidim. This man is not so rich, so I will tell him to give you only one hundred rubles."

This letter received a different welcome altogether.

"My brother," said this chassid to the stranger at his door, "please stay in my house for a few days until I manage to put together the amount that the rebbe named."

After he had handed it over with a happy heart, the poor man took his leave and brought this story, too, back to the tzaddik.

Now the recipient of the first letter noticed after a short time that his fortunes were steadily waning. He even came to a stage at which he was compelled to beg for bread from the houses of the rich. In the course of his wanderings he came to Apta, and the mere sight of the town reminded him of the letter he had received from the tzaddik who lived there. As the misfortunes that had overtaken him since then came to mind one by one, he could not forgive himself for not having obeyed the rebbe's instruction unquestioningly — for he saw his own willful disobedience at the time as the root of all his sufferings since then.

He begged and pleaded to be admitted to the rebbe's presence for an audience, but the rebbe had left orders that this was not to be. Seeing him weep day and night, one chassid advised him to stand outside the rebbe's window, where the tzaddik would be able to hear his anguish for himself. The rebbe in fact asked his attendants whose voice this was, and when they told him, they added that he was full of regrets for his earlier conduct.

Said the tzaddik: "If he has any claims against me, I am willing to appear with him at a hearing before a rabbinical court."

A *beis din* of three rabbinical judges was duly constituted — one of their number was Reb Moshe Zvi of Savran — and the tzaddik stated his case: "This is the background to the story. When I was due to come down to This World, the Almighty entrusted me with the amount of gold and silver that I would need for the discharge of my divine service in the course of my lifetime down here. I divided it up, and distributed it amongst the disciples with whom I came in touch. Now all the property that this man ever owned — was mine. When he refused to give that pauper two hundred rubles on my account, I claimed my own, and gave it over to the other chassid, the one who followed my instructions."

After due deliberation the court ruled that the man could not reclaim his property, for it was not his. Nevertheless, compassion dictated that he be awarded sufficient for his upkeep, provided that he regretted his earlier action and made amends with the rebbe.

The verdict became fact. Throughout his days he earned sufficient for his support, but left no estate behind him; the other chassid prospered in all his affairs and became a wealthy man.

◈ *Open Your Hand (i)*

פָּתֹחַ תִּפְתַּח אֶת יָדְךָ *You shall surely open your hand (15:11)*

Therefore do I command you, saying, You shall surely open your hand: As if to say, "I would like to give you some sound advice" *(Rashi).*

Reb Shneur Zalman of Liadi, the author of *Tanya*, used to make a point of conducting his household frugally, and would explain his attitude by saying: "Our Sages observe that the Torah is wary of spending the money of Israel — and since the upkeep of my household depends on the support of the public, it follows that I should be sparing in my expenses."

Indeed, when one of his children or grandchildren wore a costly garment, they did not do so in his presence, lest he object.

One day his young grandson — Reb Menachem Mendel of Lubavitch, who later became renowned as the author of *Tzemach Tzedek* — wore an expensive belt, and forgot to take it off when his grandfather called for him unexpectedly.

"Tell me," opened Reb Shneur Zalman, "how much did that belt cost?"

"Fifteen rubles," answered his grandson.

"And are you such a rich man," protested the tzaddik, "that you should be wearing such an expensive item?"

The grandson was silent, and the tzaddik continued: "How much was the dowry you received from your bride's father?"

"Two thousand silver rubles," was the answer.

"And what do you intend to do with this sum?"

"I will hand it over to a trustworthy merchant, and earn something on it."

"But perhaps he will return you neither the capital nor the interest?"

"This man is very wealthy, and utterly reliable"

"So what if he is very wealthy now," persisted the tzaddik. "In time he can become very poor."

"What, then, should I do with the money?" asked the grandson.

"My firm advice," said the tzaddik, "is that you should put the entire sum into this box, and that way it will certainly be preserved in its entirety."

The box, it should be mentioned, was a charity box... The grandson's first thought was that Reb Shneur Zalman was joking — until he heard him speak on: "I really meant that I would like you to give the money away to *tzedakah*, and then both the capital and the interest will remain intact — whereas if you give it to some wealthy merchant, I fear that you will lose even the capital."

The grandson heard what was being said, but soon left the rebbe's study nevertheless, and decided to entrust the money into the hands of a scholarly and utterly trustworthy merchant of means. Some months later all the possessions of this man were destroyed in a fire, and he was literally reduced to poverty.

In due course Reb Shneur Zalman asked Reb Menachem Mendel: "Well, did you earn anything through your investment?"

And when he was told of the total loss that had befallen him, he continued: "But why did you not heed my advice? Had you put all your money in this box, then both the capital and the interest would have remained intact. Why does each man here not trust the advice of his rebbe like the people of Volhynia, who are great believers? Let me tell you what I mean.

"I was once on my way home from Mezritch during a bitterly cold winter, and by the time we reached our wayside inn, I was so stricken by frostbite that the coachman carried me indoors from the wagon. The innkeeper, an elderly and God-fearing Jew, rubbed my feet with snow and vodka until I recovered.

"I then asked him: 'How long have you been living here?'

" 'More than fifty years,' he said.

" 'And do you have a *minyan* of ten men with whom you can pray according to the Law as part of a congregation?' I asked.

" 'No,' he answered. 'Only on the Days of Awe do I go to a nearby township to worship with the people there.'

" 'Now tell me,' I said, 'do you think it is right that an elderly man should pray all his life without a congregation, and hardly ever be able to say *Kedushah,* and *Barechu,* and all the other responses which a solitary worshiper cannot make? Why should you not go to live in the town?'

" 'And from what will I earn my livelihood over there?' he asked.

"So I asked in return: 'How many householders live in that township?'

" 'I should say around a hundred,' he replied.

" 'In that case,' I concluded, "we see that the Almighty can find a livelihood for a hundred families. Tell me — don't you think He can manage the same for one man more?'

"Then I added: 'By the way, I am a disciple of Reb Dov Ber, the Maggid of Mezritch.'

"He left me at once. Half an hour later I saw a number of wagons drawn up in front of the inn, loaded high with household goods and chattels of every description.

" 'What is this?' I asked him.

" 'Why,' he said, 'I am on my way to settle in that township, just as you told me to do.'

"You see, then," — Reb Shneur Zalman wound up his talk with his grandson — "how strong was the faith of that old man. I was still a young man at the time, but as soon as he heard that I was a disciple of the Maggid of Mezritch he dropped everything at once, including the dwelling and the livelihood which had supported him respectably for over fifty years. And you heard from me twice that there was a risk that you would lose both the capital and the interest — yet you did not believe!"

◆§ Open Your Hand (ii)

A number of chassidic leaders once convened in Berditchev to discuss some grave threat which hung over the Jews of Russia. The meeting was presided over by Reb Shneur Zalman of Liadi, who proposed that the funds needed to save the situation should be raised by the imposition of a tax of a quarter of a ruble on every Jew — or, according to another version, by the payment of a quarter of their dowries by every bridegroom.

A knock was heard at the door which was behind the speaker's back. He said: "The grandfather has arrived." (Reb Aryeh Leib of Shpola was known since his infancy by this Yiddish nickname — *der Shpoler Zeide.)*

Reb Aryeh Leib came in, and was invited by Reb Shneur Zalman to wash his hands for bread and to join the company at the table for a meal. The new arrival walked up and down the room, but gave no answer.

When he ignored the invitation a second time, Reb Levi Yitzchak of Berditchev said to Reb Shneur Zalman, who was his relative by marriage: "*Mechutan*, do you not know that the Zeide fasts from one *Shabbos* to the next?"

Reb Shneur Zalman nevertheless turned to the Zeide a third time, inviting him to eat — and this time the invitation was accepted.

There was another knock at the door.

"The emissaries of Reb Baruch of Mezhibuzh are here," said Reb Shneur Zalman.

And when they entered they turned to him and said: "Our rebbe sent us here to tell you that in the days of Mordechai and Esther people were not told to contribute quarters: other measures were taken!"

"Do you hear that?" Reb Shneur Zalman said to those at his table. "Reb Baruch [who was known as an outspoken critic of his] holds that I am the Mordechai of this generation!"

He then turned to the emissaries and said: "I would ask you to tell Reb Baruch that there are three modes of repentance — fasting, prayer, and charity. The first was the means appropriate to the city of Nineveh; the second was practiced by Mordechai and Esther; the outstanding means which is the especial task of our generation is *tzedakah*, charity."

◆§ Open Your Hand (iii)

Two of the disciples of Reb Shneur Zalman of Liadi who were known for their grasp of the revealed and hidden aspects of the Torah, and for the manner in which they served their Maker, were particularly outstanding in the mitzvah of *tzedakah*. These two philanthropists were called Reb Zalman of Dubrovna and Reb Pinchas of Shklov. A note in the will of Reb Zalman says that on the Day of Judgment he sees no merits on which he will be able to rely — apart from the mitzvah of *tzedakah*, and the power of his rebbe.

He was a wealthy man, and kept his copper, silver and gold coins in separate boxes. When a poor man visited him with a request for alms he would estimate what sum would be appropriate, and then dip his hand into the box required; whatever came up in the first handful he would give away.

Reb Pinchas was also wealthy, and he made the journey to Dubrovna for the express purpose of learning from Reb Zalman how to go about performing the mitzvah of *tzedakah*. Some time after he had learned to give alms in the same way he visited their rebbe, Reb Shneur Zalman of Liadi, and told him: "I have learned a new way to give *tzedakah* from Reb Zalman."

Then, when he had described it, he added: "But there is one difference between us. Reb Zalman does not open his hand to see how much is in it, whereas I — even though I too give the pauper whatever comes up in my hand — still open it first just to catch a glimpse."

◆§ Open Your Hand (iv)

Like many Jews of his time, the father of Reb Menachem Mendel of Rimanov earned his livelihood as an *arendar* — by leasing the rights to an inn from the squire who owned the village.

One day the squire came to him with a proposition:

 "Moshke, I want to move to a distant province, so I have to sell all my property here. I know you to be an honest and trustworthy man, and have grown to like you. If, therefore, you will pay such-and-such an amount — which is only a tenth of the real value of all my estates around these parts — then I am willing to sell you my entire property, on condition that you pay me this amount in cash within a few days."

The leaseholder's first reaction was to rejoice at the rare opportunity that had been brought his way to become so wealthy without exertion — but he soon realized that even the price the squire had quoted was well beyond his means.

His wife offered the following suggestion: "We do have a house, with some silver utensils and gold ornaments. If we sell all of these we will have ready money, and whatever is still lacking we will be able to borrow from our friends and relatives. Then we will not have to forgo the good fortune which the Almighty has sent our way."

Having followed this advice, he set out cheerfully for the squire's mansion with his purse of money, ready to finalize the details of the transaction.

His spirits were suddenly chilled by an agonizing shriek. He looked around and ran towards a dilapidated cottage that stood alone not far from the road. Opening the door, he saw the corpse of a man lying on the floor. It was surrounded by a distraught woman and her seven ragged children, all wailing in despair. They had obviously been left without food or clothing, so the leaseholder turned to the poor woman and said: "Here, take this purse. It's for you and all your little ones."

She could not believe her ears. Could he be joking at her expense? At first she refused to accept it, and only after some time did he succeed in convincing her that this was a gift offered in earnest.

This little encounter fired all the heavens with excitement. Here was a Jew who had given away everything he owned for the sake of a mitzvah! Not only had he forgone the vast wealth which was within moments of his reach, but he had left himself utterly destitute, for in order to raise the money which he had just given this widow he had sold his home and everything in it!

No sooner had the Heavenly Court decided to reward him handsomely than word of the verdict reached the grudging ears of Satan. He hastened to appear before the Court and argued as follows: "Before any of your tzaddikim are given a gift from heaven they are always put to a test. I will therefore plummet down to That World and test this mortal too. Only then shall he be granted whatever reward you have decided upon!"

At that moment there appeared from the opposite direction the Prophet Eliyahu, of blessed memory.

"If there must be a test," he said, "then it is I that shall go down to administer it. For if the Adversary is entrusted with the task, who knows if in his zeal he will not impose more than even this saintly man can bear?"

And the Heavenly Court accepted his view.

The leaseholder, in the meantime, realizing that he now owned nothing but the shirt on his back, thought to himself: "What point is there in going home the way things are at the moment? I had better take up the staff of the wanderer and visit one town after another. Who knows? Perhaps the Almighty in His mercy will bring a bit of good fortune my way... "

By evening he had already reached a certain town, and made his way to the local *shul*. He resolved that he would ask no mortal for bread to eat nor for a nook in which to sleep. If one of the worshipers invited him home to eat, he would follow him; if not — he would do without. The prayers came to an end, but not one solitary person approached him to ask the stranger in their midst whether he had a place where he could satisfy his hunger and lay his head to rest. He was weighted down by fatigue, and hunger, and thirst — but his spirit was strong, and he allowed no second thoughts to tarnish the noble decision of that morning. On the contrary, he said: "Whatever happens, I thank God, Who gave me the opportunity of carrying out such a great mitzvah!" And with that the famished wanderer took down a tall volume from the synagogue shelves, and nourished his soul with the study of the Torah.

A dignified presence appeared now before him, and addressed him in these words: "May peace light upon you, man blessed by God! From where do you come, and what brings you here?"

And as the wanderer unfolded his story to the patient listener, he came to the episode of that morning.

"Listen to what I have to tell you, my friend," said the venerable stranger. "Since the Almighty has blessed me with great wealth, please accept from my hand a certain sum — enough to support your family throughout your entire lifetime. In exchange for this, sell me the merit of the mitzvah which you performed today. And if God makes your affairs prosper, you will be able to perform many more mitzvos like this one."

This tantalizing offer roused a tremor of eager anticipation in the heart of the wanderer — but only for a moment. His strength of purpose did not fail him, and he replied emphatically: "No! Since the Almighty gave me the rare privilege of doing a mitzvah at such cost — with *mesirus nefesh,* one might even say — I will not sell my mitzvah for all the money in the world!"

"Very well," said the aged stranger, "then sell me only half of the mitzvah, and for that half I will give you the full amount I promised."

"I will not part with even half a mitzvah," the wanderer insisted.

So eager was the old man to buy himself a share of that spiritual treasure that he went as far as to offer the whole payment for even one hundredth part of the other man's mitzvah. Even this offer was rejected outright.

Seeing before him a man of spirit, the venerable stranger said: "Know my son, that I am Eliyahu the Prophet, sent from heaven to put you to the test. Blessed indeed is your lot, for you not only earned a rich mitzvah, but withstood the temptation of selling even the tiniest fragment of it! One of three rewards is now yours: make your choice between them. Either you and your wife will be blessed with long life, or else you will be granted exceptional wealth, or you will be blessed with a son who will grow up to be a tzaddik."

"My sole wish is to be blessed with such a son," said the man without hesitation. "For what profit is there in riches and in long life if all those years we have not been blessed with a child?"

"The son whom you will beget," said the Prophet Eliyahu, "will be a man of such sanctity that his learning and his saintliness will illuminate the world. Be forewarned, though, that if this is to be so, then you and your wife will have to accept the lot of perpetual wanderers throughout your lives."

The man hastened home to consult his wife, and together they undertook to pay the price of their reward with loving patience. In the fullness of time a son was born to them, and they called him Menachem, which means "the consoler." This infant grew up to be Reb Menachem Mendel of Rimanov, who proved indeed to be a shining light of learning and saintliness, and comfort to his People.

May the merit of his beautiful life protect us and all of Israel!

◌§ *Open Your Hand (v)*

It was not a new problem, but it was nonetheless urgent: a chassid by the name of Reb Ben-Zion of Ostrov, with not a penny of his own, had to marry off his daughter. He hired a wagon and set off to Ger in order to consult his rebbe, Reb Yehudah Aryeh Leib, the author of *Sfas Emes.*

"Since you will be passing through Warsaw," said the tzaddik, "call on Reb Bunem Eybeschuetz, and ask him to endeavor to put together the amount you need."

Reb Bunem, who was a chassid of means, gave him a royal welcome in true chassidic style — a long table in his honor laden with refreshments, around which a melodious company of scores of chassidim sat together into the wee hours of the night, exchanging stories of tzaddikim and choice tidbits of Torah lore. When Reb Ben-Zion told him of his request at breakfast the next morning, his host reassured him: "Do not worry. With God's help everything will work out smoothly."

The next day the guest said: "Since today is Thursday, I must set out already in order to reach my hometown in time for *Shabbos.*"

Reb Bunem thereupon opened his safe and took out a thousand rubles, which he presented to his guest in the friendliest manner imaginable.

After taking his leave, Reb Ben-Zion decided to return to Ger in order to spend *Shabbos* in the company of his rebbe. When the tzaddik heard how things had worked out, he said: "I certainly did not intend that he should give the whole amount himself, but rather that he should persuade wealthy philanthropists to contribute the money."

"Rebbe," said Reb Ben-Zion, "that chassid in fact fulfilled your request — except that since he himself is a wealthy philanthropist, it was himself whom he persuaded to give the money."

◆§ *Forewarned is Forearmed (i)*

וּפָנִיתָ בַבֹּקֶר וְהָלַכְתָּ לְאֹהָלֶיךָ
And you shall turn in the morning, and go to your tents (16:7)

No harm befalls men who journey forth for a mitzvah, neither on their way out nor on their way home, as it is written, "And you shall turn in the morning, and go to your tents" *(Talmud, Tractate Pesachim).*

Reb Shneur Zalman of Liadi, the author of *Tanya,* used to dispatch his most prominent disciples to towns and villages in all directions, for the purpose of instructing their brethren in the teachings and life-style of Chassidism, and to arouse them to a service of God made alive by the experience of awe and the love of Him. At the same time, it was the task of these emissaries to collect contributions for the poor scholars who had settled in the Holy Land.

One of those upon whom such a mission was imposed was a celebrated chassid by the name of Reb Zalman Zezmer. He undertook to fulfill the rebbe's request, of course, and when he came to receive his farewell blessings, the tzaddik said: "Take extreme care not to spend the night in a house whose door faces east."

The chassid hired a wagon and set out. The Almighty made his mission prosper, so that he succeeded in stimulating hundreds of people to strive to new heights of piety. He likewise succeeded in raising substantial sums for the relief of the distressed scholars in far-off *Eretz Yisrael,* who looked for succor to the *maamad* funds which were thus replenished from time to time by their fellow chassidim in Russia.

On his way home, while he was enjoying the quiet satisfaction of having fulfilled the rebbe's command, he suddenly realized that the wagon had veered from the road and had lost its way in unfamiliar side-tracks. The wagon-driver too was alarmed, for in the pitch blackness of midnight they had no idea where they should turn. After continuing aimlessly for a short distance they suddenly spied a light in a distant house. They knocked on the door, and it was opened by an old man who greeted them with the traditional *Shalom Aleichem,* and invited them to rest in his house from their tiring journey.

Having washed his hands, Reb Zalman's first thought was to ask his host which wall was the eastern one, for this was the direction traditionally faced in prayer, and he had not yet had time for his evening devotions. But when the master of the house pointed at the eastern wall, Reb Zalman was seized with a fearful trembling, for that was the wall in which the door was to be found. His rebbe's warning was still fresh in his ears. He immediately ordered the coachman to load their chattels back on the wagon, to harness the horses, and to prepare for departure. The poor fellow could not begin to understand what had suddenly overcome his passenger, but Reb Zalman's voice was decisive, so he began to collect their bundles.

Their preparations were interrupted by a voice thundering from the doorway. It was their host, and his words struck terror in their hearts: "I take guests *into* my house; I do not let them *out.* You two are staying here!"

With that he strode out, and bolted and locked the door behind him. In the moment of shocked silence that followed, the two prisoners were startled by the raucous shouts and curses of a fearsome gang of ruffians who clattered their way into an adjoining room.

"Tell me, whose carriage is that out in front?" asked one of the voices. "Did you manage to trap us a fancy bird today?"

"Such a rare catch we haven't made for a long, long time," returned the voice of their host. "They've got a whole stack of bundles, and you can even hear the shiny coins clattering in their boxes."

"Let's go in and see them for ourselves!" shouted another voice.

The door burst open, and the chassid and his wagon-driver found themselves facing six bloodthirsty savages, who leered at them and said to each other: "First things first! Let's fill up our bellies before we get down to business. These birdies won't escape from the cage!"

Reb Zalman looked the robbers squarely in the eye and said: "I was sent out to do a mitzvah by a holy man who knows hidden secrets. He foresaw that I would fall into danger and ordered me not to spend the night in a house whose entrance faces east. The owner of this house is my witness that as soon as I became aware that this door faces that direction I tried to flee — but I did not succeed. Listen now to a warning: you had better let us out of here, for my holy master will avenge our blood!"

Uproarious laughter burst forth from all sides — except from the mouth of the householder, who fell silent and thoughtful.

Throughout the night Reb Zalman and his coachman poured out their hearts over verses from the Book of *Psalms*. Before dawn they heard hushed footsteps approaching their room. It was their host, who whispered to them: "Quick! Follow me! I will help you escape from here."

This was hard to believe, but there was no time to pause, and without a word they followed him to their wagon. As they clambered up to their seats he whispered: "I saved you because of your rebbe!" — and with that he gave Reb Zalman a bill of fifty rubles for the tzaddik.

When they reached Liadi the rebbe said to his chassid: "I did not sleep all that night because of you."

And he took the fifty-ruble bill and stuck it into a crack in the wall.

Years later a pauper came to Liadi and asked to be admitted to speak with the rebbe. When the *gabbai* brought this message to the tzaddik, he declined to receive him. Instead, he took out the fifty-ruble bill from the crack in the wall and asked the *gabbai* to hand it to the man outside.

And no one there knew who that pauper was, except for two — the rebbe and the pauper.

סדר שפטים
sidra shoftim

◆§ Forewarned is Forearmed (ii)

צֶדֶק צֶדֶק תִּרְדֹּף
Pursue justice, only justice (16:20)

He who is neither lame nor blind nor crippled but feigns to be one of these will not die of old age without first becoming one of these, as it is written: "Pursue justice, only justice" *(Mishnah, Tractate Pe'ah).*

A chassid by the name of Reb Yosef Moshe, the son of Reb Avraham Yehoshua Heschel of Apta, once needed to travel to Jassy. He decided first to seek the opinion of Reb Yisrael, the Maggid of Koznitz, who gave his blessing to the journey.

One day before he left for Rumania he visited Koznitz again to take his leave of the Maggid, who in the course of their conversation said the following: "Now you are a man who spends a good deal of his time traveling. Tell me, what do you do when your carriage overtakes a poor man who is going in your direction on foot and asks to be given a ride?"

"Why, that is something that happens quite often," said Reb Yosef Moshe, "and my men of course have instructions to stop and take in the poor man, and to take him to his destination."

"And suppose you overtake a lame pauper leaning on a walking-stick — what happens then?" asked the rebbe.

"I would say that it is even more important to take such a man," said the chassid. "It must be hard to make a journey on foot when one needs the help of a cane."

"And I would say exactly the opposite," said the Maggid. "A healthy man depends on his legs. If a carriage comes by, so much the better; if not, he can always continue on foot. But if a man is lame, and needs a cane, how can he undertake a long journey and rely on the miracle of a carriage at the right moment that will be able to take him exactly where he wants? I would say that in such a case one should be wary in case he is only feigning lameness — and who knows what evil designs he has!"

The chassid was of course surprised to hear these words. Whatever could the rebbe be talking about?

He set out the next day according to plan, and being an old man, lay down in the carriage and fell asleep. On the way his companions saw a lame man who was somehow making his way along the highway with the help of two crutches. He begged them to stop and take him with them, so they called out to the coachman to draw rein and to wait until he caught up with them. Reb Yosef Moshe, awakened by the sound of their shouting, asked them why they had stopped. As soon as he heard the reason he recalled his visit to Koznitz and cried out to the surprised coachman at the top of his voice: "Quick! Gallop ahead as fast as you can!"

The coachman cracked his whip, and at the same moment the lame man called out to them: "Have pity! Wait for me!"

This made the chassid urge his coachman to drive off even faster. At this point the passengers who were facing the lame man saw him hold both crutches aloft in one hand and bolt furiously after them. Soon realizing that he would not be able to overtake them, he expressed his frustration by hurling one of his crutches at the carriage — but apart from a hole in the hood, he caused them no harm.

◆§ *Controversy*

דִּבְרֵי רִיבֹת בִּשְׁעָרֶיךָ
Matters of controversy within your gates (17:8)

A delegation of the chassidim who lived in a certain town once called on Reb Avraham of Sochatchov, the author of *Avnei Neizer*, with a complaint. They claimed that the *rav* of their town had ruled with undue leniency in a certain question involving the dietary laws, and since they were therefore reluctant to accept his ruling in any other ritual question that should arise in the future, they requested that their rebbe send them some other *rav* who would be able to serve as a reliable and competent authority on the *halachah*.

Replied the tzaddik: "Even according to your claim, what this *rav* did was to pronounce as permissible something that the Sages of the Talmud have ruled to be prohibited — an *issur derabbanan.* But what you yourselves are about to do is to transgress an *issur de'oraysa,* for according to all opinions to sustain a controversy is explicitly forbidden in the Torah itself. Not only that, but through engaging in controversy people come to err, and to transgress other prohibitions which appear in the Law."

Now there is a verse in the Torah which is addressed to the judges of the rabbinical courts: "If there should be a matter too obscure for you in judgment, between blood and blood, between plea and plea,... matters of controversy within your gates ..." In concluding his audience with the dissident delegation, Reb Avraham gave this verse a novel interpretation by inserting a few explanatory words of his own: "If there should be a matter too obscure for you in judgment, between blood and blood, between plea and plea,... *it is because there are* matters of controversy within your gates ..."

⸎ *In Lonely Majesty*

שׂוֹם תָּשִׂים עָלֶיךָ מֶלֶךְ *You may appoint a king over you (17:15)*

A certain individual who lived in Lublin used to buy up a stock of combs every Friday and then hand them out in the communal bathhouse that afternoon to whoever wanted them. When word of this original custom reached Reb Yaakov Yitzchak (the Chozeh) of Lublin he spoke very warmly of the practice, citing it as an instance of the *mitzvah* of *gemilus chassadim,* doing a favor to one's fellow. Report of the tzaddik's reaction was brought to the attention of Rabbi Azriel, the official *rav* of the city, whose admirers nicknamed him "the iron-headed" on account of the solid logic which he applied to the study of the Talmud. This scholar was known to be an opponent of Chassidism in general and of the Chozeh in particular.

"The chassidic rebbe," he commented, "has forgotten an explicit statement in the Talmud, where it is said: 'When King David entered the bathhouse he realized that he was naked and said, *Woe is me that I should be left bare of any mitzvah!'* Now if what the rebbe praises so highly were in fact a mitzvah, then King David too could have bought up stocks of combs and distributed them to all comers in the bathhouse ..."

This comment in turn was brought back to the ears of the rebbe.

"My learned colleague," he said, "has overlooked an explicit statement in the Mishnah, where it is said: 'Nor may one see the king when is having his hair cut, nor when he is naked, nor when he is in the bathhouse, as it is written, *You may appoint a king over you;* stand in awe of him.' It follows, then, that it was impossible for King David to have performed this mitzvah ..."

◆§ *The Succession*

נָבִיא אָקִים לָהֶם...כָּמוֹךָ
I shall raise them up a prophet... like you (18:18)

In 1826, when one of the emissaries of Reb Uri of Strelisk returned from his travels, he told the rebbe that a certain chassid had begged to be excused for not having visited Strelisk for the festival of Shavuos as he always did, and planned instead to come for Rosh HaShanah.

"Fool that he is!" said Reb Uri. "If he comes here for Rosh HaShanah, who will answer him?"

Soon after came the *Shabbos* on which the weekly Portion of *Shoftim* is read. The tzaddik read aloud from the Torah Scroll in the synagogue, according to his custom, with Reb Yehudah Zvi of Stretyn at his right and his own son, Reb Shlomo, at his left. In the course of his reading he came to a verse which gives the words of the Almighty to Moshe Rabbeinu: "I will raise them up a prophet from among their brothers, like you, and I will put My words in his mouth, and he shall speak to them all that I command him." But instead of reading "from among their brothers, *like* you" (מִקֶּרֶב אֲחֵיכֶם כָּמוֹךָ), he read "from among their brothers, *from* you." (מִקֶּרֶב אֲחֵיכֶם מִמְּךָ). Reb Yehudah Zvi read out the word to him as it appears in the Torah, but though Reb Uri repeated the whole verse, he again read as before. This was repeated once more, and again a third time. But now, still seeking to correct him, Reb Yehudah Zvi showed the rebbe the printed text so that he could see it for himself.

שפטים

This time Reb Uri began the verse afresh, and read as follows: "I will raise them up a prophet from among their brothers, *like you, like you, like you!*" And, having said כָּמוֹךָ three times, he placed his hands on the head of Reb Yehudah Zvi and said the word once more, with a burning intensity — *"like you!"*

It was clear to all the chassidim present that this elder disciple of the tzaddik had just been ordained his successor.

Less than three weeks later, on the twenty-third day of the month of Elul, Reb Uri returned his fiery soul to heaven — one week before the Rosh HaShanah to which he had once made reference...

His son, Reb Shlomo, expressed himself soon after: "I do not know how it is possible to live after a father like that" — and within four months he had joined him.

◆§ *No Academic Question*

הוא יָנוּס אֶל אַחַת הֶעָרִים הָאֵלֶּה וָחָי
He shall flee to one of these cities, and live (19:5)

If a disciple is exiled, his rebbe is sent into exile with him, for it is written, 'and live' — to teach us that he is to be afforded a source of vitality *(Talmud, Tractate Makkos).*

Reb Simchah Bunem of Pshischah once asked his disciple, Reb Menachem Mendel of Kotsk: "If in the World Above they order me to go to *gehinnom,* what shall I do?"

Reb Menachem Mendel answered not a word. After a pause of a few moments, his rebbe said: "If that happens, I will ask them to bring me my teachers, Reb Yaakov Yitzchak (the Chozeh) of Lublin,and Reb Yaakov Yitzchak (the Yid HaKadosh) of Pshischah. For does the Talmud not say: 'If a disciple is exiled, his rebbe is sent into exile with him'?"

"Rebbe," said Reb Menachem Mendel, "to you this rule is not really a matter of interest. But I stand to gain by it ..."

◆§ *Natural Justice*

לֹא תַסִּיג גְּבוּל רֵעֲךָ

A poor widow earned her livelihood from the lease which she held on an inn — known among East

You shall not move your neighbor's landmark (19:14)

European Jews as an *arenda* or *michyah* — until along came some other villager, offered the local squire a higher fee, and displaced her. The widow had him summoned to a lawsuit which was to be heard before the local rabbinical court on a charge of *hasagas gvul* — "moving one's neighbor's landmark," the Biblical metaphor which means not only depriving one's neighbor of his land rights by moving a fence or landmark, but also the prohibition of encroaching unfairly on another's source of sustenance. The newcomer refused to appear.

Hearing that he was a frequent visitor to the court of Reb Shalom of Belz, the widow persuaded her local *rav* — whose summons this man had ignored — to write to the tzaddik, asking him to order his follower to appear before the court. She arrived at Belz with the letter in hand and delivered it to the tzaddik, but was shocked to see that he ignored both her request and the letter from her *rav*. Returning home, she told the *rav* of her disappointment. He was so incensed that in his indignation he made some very critical remarks about the tzaddik's motives: he no doubt sought to flatter his moneyed follower rather than ruffle his relations with him. In a more sober moment some time later, he came to regret having spoken this way about the holy man, and resolved to make the journey to Belz to request forgiveness of the tzaddik.

"I bear no grudge against you," Reb Shalom reassured him. "You should know, however, that flattery plays no role with me. I did not accede to your request because justice is on the side of the new innkeeper. You see, the grandfather of this *arendar* held this same lease many years ago, until the father of this widow's late husband offered the local squire a higher fee, and displaced him. Left penniless, that old man eventually had to find some other place to live, and since he and his family left your region so long ago, the whole connection of his family with that inn has been completely forgotten. But, as the Psalmist says, 'the steps of man are ordered by God' — and through the unseen workings of Divine Providence things so worked out that this very man, the grandson of the original lessee, succeeded in hiring the same inn which had been held by his own forebears. This livelihood is his by right: would it be proper to wrest it from him?

"The facts of the case, by the way, may be checked to your own satisfaction."

The *rav* took up this offer, and found that this was indeed the history of the inn.

סדר כי תצא
Sidra Ki Seitzei

☙ *Lost and Found*

הָשֵׁב תְּשִׁיבֵם לְאָחִיךָ
You shall surely return them to your brother (22:1)

A stranger once walked into the *shtibl* frequented by the chassidim of Chernobyl who lived in Berditchev, and asked them if they were chassidim of the tzaddik of Chernobyl. Hearing that they were, he gave them money for *tikkun*, and asked them to prepare a festive meal at his expense.

When they were all seated together around the table he said: "Do you people know who your tzaddik is, Reb Aharon of Chernobyl? I have just come from him now. Let me tell you what happened to me, and then you will know what manner of man he is.

"When I happened to be here in Berditchev a few years ago, a certain businessman who worked on a commission basis came here to buy up various goods for the shopkeepers of his town. Even after he had paid for them he had quite a sum left. Anyway, his wallet fell from his pocket unnoticed, and I picked it up. I wavered for a moment whether to return it or not, but the stranger was already on his way. I followed him at once, but lost him in the crowd and could not find him. I went about my affairs, and in the course of time the Almighty prospered my way and I became a rich man. But when that agent came home to his town his creditors gave him no peace, for the money he lost was theirs. In addition he lost his livelihood, for the shopkeepers were no longer willing to trust him. He died in misery soon after, leaving his wife in wretched poverty, and his sons illiterate — for there was no one to pay their tuition fees.

"After some time he appeared to me in a dream. 'Why did you kill me?' he said. 'And worse still, look at the state my widow and children are left in — all because of you! I now demand that you appear with me in a lawsuit to be heard here in the World of Truth!'

"I woke up in alarm. But then I told myself: 'Does the Prophet Zechariah not teach that *Dreams speak falsehood?* And does the Talmud not tell us that *A man is shown in his dreams only that upon which his heart ponders by day?* It is only because I have thought of this incident so often that it figured now in my dream!'

"But when the same dream repeated itself the next night, and the next night again, and so on I saw that this was no joking matter. So one night I answered him in my dream: 'Very well, I agree to the lawsuit — but not in the World of Truth. For what will you gain from it if my wife and children will be widowed and orphaned too?'

" 'In that case,' he replied, 'tell me where the hearing should take place.'

" 'Give me time to think it over,' I said, and he agreed.

"First thing in the morning I set out to consult Reb Aharon of Karlin, but he said that he couldn't get involved in a matter of this sort, and recommended that I go off to see Reb Aharon of Chernobyl. Your rebbe, Reb Aharon, told me that when this man came to me again in a dream I should tell him that the hearing would be held before him. I returned home, and when I passed on this suggestion at the next opportunity the plaintiff agreed, and I set out at once for Chernobyl.

"I appeared at the date and time set by the tzaddik, and he opened the hearing by inviting the deceased to state his claim. Not a word of what was said reached my ears, but after a few moments the tzaddik turned to me and said: 'The deceased has various well-founded claims against you — that you brought about his death, and so on. What do you have to say in your defense?'

"I explained that I had in fact wanted to return the wallet, but had lost him in the crowd; and since I had no idea who he was, what was I to have done?

" 'Will you agree to accept whatever verdict I hand down?' the tzaddik asked me.

"I said I would, and the tzaddik said the plaintiff was also agreeable.

" 'This, then, is my verdict,' he said after a pause. 'You are to return home and to make an honest stocktaking of whatever you own in money and property, down to the last thread and shoelace. Half of the total you may keep for yourself. As to the other half, you are to make the journey to the township where this man's widow lives, and hand it over personally to her. While you are there, hire competent tutors to teach her children. In addition, you are to set aside a certain proportion of your half and distribute it as *tzedakah* to the needy.'

"Stage by stage I did exactly as I was told — first at home, then in the widow's hometown — and then I made another journey to Chernobyl to express my gratitude to the tzaddik for having looked after the whole affair for me. I am now on my way home from there, so I thought that since I was passing through Berditchev, I would like to drop in here and hold a thanksgiving meal in the company of you folk.'

◆§ *Whispers from Another World (i)*

לְמַעַן יִיטַב לָךְ
That it may be well with you (22:7)

That it may be well with you — in the World in which all is good; *and prolong your days* — in the World which is endless *(Talmud, Tractate Kiddushin).*

When he had reached a ripe old age, one of the respected citizens of the community of Uman sold all his belongings and set off to live out his remaining years in *Eretz Yisrael.* He wanted to be buried in the soil of the Holy Land when his time came — "after a hundred and twenty years," as people say.

After only a few days there he decided to leave *Eretz Yisrael,* and a few months after having farewelled him, his old friends were surprised to see him back in his hometown. He was showered with questions from all sides: What made him go? What made him return? But he gave no answer whatever, and the whole episode remained a puzzle in the eyes of his townsmen.

A short while later he took ill, and called for the officials of the *Chevrah Kaddisha,* the voluntary burial society of the town, for he had something of importance to tell them. They hastened dutifully to his bedside, but when they arrived he merely made conversation on all manner of trifling subjects. The officials were surprised, and left his room. The next day he summoned them again, and though their first impulse was to ignore him, they finally decided to accede to his request. Once again he took up their time on inconsequential small talk, as if he were out of his mind, and they eventually left him in annoyance. When he called for them again on the third day they refused outright to be bothered in vain, but when he received this message he sent word that this time he would explain his invitations; he earnestly requested that they not take offense, but come to see him.

They took up seats around his bed, and the pale little man said: "The time has come to reveal a certain episode from the story of my life.

"When I was a young man I used to travel to various fairs and markets, earning my living from merchandising. Most of my business was in the region of Berditchev, and every time I passed by the town I would spend a day or two there in order to be able to see the tzaddik who lived there, Reb Levi Yitzchak.

"On my way from a certain fair one morning, I passed through Berditchev and went straight to the house of the tzaddik. He was walking up and down his study, robed in his *tallis,* and whispering the preliminary passages of the daily prayers in an ecstasy that was beautiful to see. I did not dare to disturb him at a moment like this, of course; so I waited in the adjoining room, and listened to his voice. Suddenly an angry little knot of noisy men and women brushed past me and stormed their way straight into the rebbe's study, where they kept up their raucous arguments. It was clear that they had come to the *rav* with a lawsuit, and as I heard their bitter claims and counter-claims, I pieced the story together.

"It transpired that a poor Jew had made a bare living by working as a money-changer. Having no capital of his own, he conducted his entire business with money which he borrowed from acquaintances. Every so often he would pay his debts from his meager earnings, and so continue. Now during the previous night this man had lost three hundred rubles — all of it borrowed money. He was in great consternation: he would lose his entire means of support, and be spurned as a bad debtor as well. He suspected the maid of his household, but despite her protestations of innocence he abused and cursed her, and even beat her in order to persuade her to return the money. She reported this treatment to her parents. They of course descended upon his house in a fury, and now, at the height of their violent dispute, they had all decided to bring it to the rebbe for adjudication.

"After listening to all parties the rebbe said: 'I can see that the maid is utterly innocent. This was an unfounded suspicion. At the same time it is clear that the money was in fact lost, and that this man did not simply invent this story in order to cast aspersions on her. As to where the money is — that, I am afraid, I do not see.'

"And Reb Levi Yitzchak walked up and down his room in distress, not knowing how to find a way out of this confused situation.

"Suddenly he stood still and said: 'If some person were to be found who would give me three hundred rubles so that we could make good this man's loss, I would promise him a share in the World to Come!'

"Hearing this from the adjoining room, I walked straight into his study and said: 'Rebbe, are you prepared to give this promise in writing?'

'I am,' he said.

"I took three hundred rubles out of my pocket and gave them to the tzaddik, who handed them directly to the money-changer.

"Then he said to the maid: 'Because you were suspected in vain, I give you my blessing that you will make a good match.'

"And to the man he said: 'And as for you — you have my blessing that you will never again suffer a loss.'

"The little group left the rebbe's presence in good spirits, and I retired to the waiting-room, allowing him to proceed with his morning prayers.

"When he was ready I entered his study again and reminded him about the written promise. He immediately asked his *gabbai* to bring paper, pen and ink, and sat down to write a note. As he folded it up he said: 'Here is your note, but take care never to open it or read it all the days of your life. When your time comes, and you sense that your last day in This World has arrived, hand over the note to the officials of the *Chevrah Kaddisha,* and ask them to place it inside your grave.'

"I took it joyfully from his hands, and of course took good heed of his instructions. Moreover, in order that it should be preserved safely, I decided to hide it in a special place: I had it bound by a bookbinder into the cover of my *Siddur.*

"When I left for *Eretz Yisrael* I forgot that prayer book in all the excitement of my preparations, and only when I arrived there did I realize that I had left it behind me, here in Uman. I lost no time in deciding what to do, and left the Holy Land at once. So you now understand that I did not leave there because of confused thinking. Now two days ago, when I fell ill, and thought my time had come, I called for you. By the time you arrived I felt somewhat better. I saw that this was not yet my last day, so I had to start talking on some other subject. The same thing happened yesterday. Today, however, I feel that my end is in fact drawing near. Gentlemen, here is the note. I beg of you to fulfill the instruction of the tzaddik. Place it in my grave."

He stretched out a wrinkled hand, and in exchange for their solemn promise, entrusted them with the folded note. A few hours later the man was no more.

After his passing the officials said to one another: "It was only this man alone whom the tzaddik forbade to read the note. There is clearly no prohibition on our reading it, now, after his death."

Accordingly, before carrying out their promise to the deceased, in a funeral that showed all honor to his memory, they unfolded the tiny note and read these words: *Open for him the gates of the Garden of Eden. – Levi Yitzchak the son of Sarah.*

☙ Whispers from Another World (ii)

A once-prosperous merchant who had lost his entire fortune came to Reb Avraham Yehoshua Heschel of

Apta with the request that he intercede in heaven on his behalf, and advise him as well what to do: he had a daughter of marriageable age, and hardly a penny left to his name. The tzaddik asked him how much he needed and how much he had, and he answered that he needed a thousand rubles for the wedding and the dowry, and in his pocket he had exactly one ruble.

"Go in peace," said the tzaddik, "and take up the first offer of a transaction that comes your way. May God make your way prosper!"

A strange instruction, indeed: business without capital? ... But after this first thought the man relied on his faith in the words of his rebbe and set out on his way.

He arrived at an inn which he found was frequented by dealers in gems. He approached the table around which a group of them were crowded, and examined the diamonds that were set out on it.

"What are you looking at here?" asked a Jewish dealer. "Are you perhaps interested in buying one of these diamonds?"

"I am," replied the man.

"And how much money do you have, if I may ask?" said the dealer.

"One ruble," was the reply.

The whole group burst out in uproarious laughter.

The dealer continued boldly: "Listen here! I've got a deal for you that needs only one ruble. Buy my share in the World to Come!"

"I am agreeable," said the new arrival, "on condition that you confirm the sale in writing, and sign it according to law."

The gem dealer agreed, and egged on by the derisive laughter of his friends, he wrote out and signed a contract of sale, which he duly handed over to the purchaser in exchange for his last ruble. Having nothing more to do in the company of these people, the traveler found himself a quiet corner, took out of his pack the volume of the Talmud that he always carried with him, and was soon deep in thought.

While they were still chuckling with scorn at the hapless *batlan* who had just paid out his last ruble for a commodity that did not yet exist, in walked the wife of that gem-dealer. As it happened most of his gems in fact belonged to her; in fact, his whole wealth had come to him through an estate which she had inherited. She asked what they were snickering about, and they told her.

Incensed, she turned upon her husband: "So just in case you *did* have a share in the Next World coming to you, did you have to go and sell it, and remain naked like some heathen? I'm not going to live with a pagan like you! Come along with me to the *rav* and give me a bill of divorce!"

He stammered out an attempt at an excuse: he had only meant the whole thing to be a joke, and so on. His wife remained unconvinced. *She* was not going to be the wife of a pagan who had no share in the World to Come!

Her husband begged one of the employees of the inn to search around urgently for the new arrival.

When he joined the distraught couple, the dealer addressed him as follows: "Listen here, Reb Yid. I'm sure you realize, don't you, that everything that passed between us was one big joke? Here take your ruble back, and return me the contract. Okay?"

"Not at all," said the traveler. "Business is business. *I* certainly had no joke in mind!"

"If so," said the gem-dealer, "I'll let you make a profit of a few rubles on the deal, and you can sell me back again what you bought from me."

"The profit I demand," said the traveler, "is one thousand rubles."

"Are you out of your mind?" shouted the dealer, red with rage. "For some miserable little bit of paper that I gave you, you're demanding such a fortune?"

At this point his wife chimed in decisively: "Even if he demands five thousand rubles you must ransom your share in the World to Come."

The dealer quietly offered the stranger a hundred rubles, but he refused.

"I would like you to know," he said, "that I am not the impractical *batlan* that you and your friends take me for. I too was once a businessman, except that I lost my fortune, and it was the *rav* of Apta who advised me to accept the first offer of a transaction that presented itself

— because I need a thousand rubles with which to marry off my daughter. And I am not going to forgo one solitary kopek out of that one thousand rubles!"

Two hundred, three hundred — each successive offer received the same answer: not a kopek less than one thousand rubles. Words were never going to make any impression on a man as stubborn as this, and in the end the gem-dealer had no option but to give him that whole sum in exchange for his bill of sale.

His wife now turned to the stranger: she would very much like to see the tzaddik of Apta.

"My pleasure," he said. "Allow me to direct you to him."

When they arrived there, the woman said to the tzaddik: "I am of course pleased that through my agency such good fortune should come the way of that poor fellow. But I have one queston of you, rebbe. Is my husband's share in the World to Come in fact worth one thousand rubles?"

"At the time of the first sale," replied the tzaddik, "when he sold his share in the World to Come for the price of one ruble, his share in it was not worth even that one ruble. But at the time of the second sale, when he bought back his share in the World to Come for a thousand rubles and helped to marry off the daughter of a poor fellow Jew, his share in That World was worth far, far more than a thousand rubles. No money can measure its worth."

◆§ *Whispers from Another World (iii)*

When Reb Menachem Mendel of Rimanov was a young man, before he became known as a tzaddik, he married the daughter of a prominent householder from Fristik who supported the young couple at his table for some time after their marriage, according to the custom. During this period, the young man devoted himself to the service of his Maker through study and prayer by day and by night. He indulged as well in ascetic practices, such as fasting for long periods, and rolling in the snow in the bitter winter mornings. When his father-in-law saw that nothing else interested him, and that he neglected to provide for his young wife, he ordered his daughter to demand that her husband give her a bill of divorce. She refused this demand outright. Her father reacted by driving them out of his house, and cutting them off utterly from any share in his inheritance.

The young couple found themselves a humble dwelling of their own, where they lived in unrelenting privation. The young woman suffered all in silence, and with whatever work she could get in sewing and embroidery supported herself and her husband on the barest of rations.

It once happened that for three days on end she earned nothing, and they were left without even a loaf of bread to eat. So she said to herself: "If we sit here in silence, we will both die of hunger. I'll go along to the baker. Perhaps he will give me a cake on account, something that I can take along to my husband. The poor tzaddik has been fasting in the *beis midrash* for three days now!"

The baker refused her request, and she left him in tears. He called her back immediately and said: "If you give me your share in the World to Come, I will give you the bread."

She was in a dilemma, and pondered her situation earnestly. Finally she said to herself: "Whatever happens to me, I'm not going to let my husband die of hunger."

Turning to the baker, she said: "Give me the bread, and some cheese as well — and I am now giving you my share in the World to Come."

He gave her what she requested, and she made her quiet way to the *beis midrash*. She spread out a little tablecloth for him, laid out the bread and cheese, and remained standing there — not according to her usual custom of retiring modestly from the House of Study once she had brought him his meal.

He washed his hands in preparation for the breaking of bread, pronounced the benediction, and ate what she had brought him. Then he said: "Tell me, what makes you stand here still?"

"My dear husband!" she wept. "You know what toil and suffering I have undergone in order to make my soul worthy of enjoying the bliss of the World to Come — and now I have lost my share in it!"

When he had heard the whole story from her innocent lips he consoled her: "Do not regret what has happened, for a moment before you came I was seized by a fainting fit. If you had not brought me the bread I would have died. That means that with this loaf of bread you have earned yourself a *new* share in the World to Come, for the Sages teach us — do they not? — that 'Whoever saves the life of one fellow Jew, it is as if he saved an entire world!' Why, then, do you need your *old* share in the World to Come?"

☙ *Whispers From Another World (iv)*

The old man languishing on his sickbed was clearly about to breathe his last: it was time to call the members of the *Chevrah Kaddisha* brotherhood, according to custom, so that they could help him utter the words of *Vidui*, the confession which is recited by one who is about to return his soul to his Maker. The sick man suddenly turned in bed to face the wall. A moment later he turned to face the men of the fraternity, and said: "You may go your separate ways. My time has not yet come."

The next evening, after the twilight Third Meal, when *Shabbos* was drawing to a tranquil close, he called for them once more. When they arrived he told them quietly: "The time has now come for me to take my leave from This World."

"How do you know that?" they asked — and they leaned over the wan face to hear the urgent whisper of an old man straining to tell his last story.

"In my youth," said the old man, "I was a servant in the household of a villager who was the father-in-law of the tzaddik Reb David of Lelov. Before daybreak one bitterly cold morning my master sent me to have a ram slaughtered by the local *shochet*. On my way I was shocked to see a man lying on the frosty ground with arms and legs outstretched. I came closer, and saw who it was — the tzaddik Reb David, almost killed by the cold. He had broken the ice to immerse himself in the nearby river, and on coming out of the water had fainted from sheer cold. I quickly took off my fur coat and put it on him, hoisted him on my shoulders, and carried him to his home. There I boiled a kettle and gave him tea, and laid him in his bed. After he had regained his strength he made me swear that I would not reveal what had happened until my time came. Then he added these words: 'In return for the great favor that you have done for me, I owe you some reward. You may choose between wealth — and a share in the World to Come.'

"When I told him that I chose the latter reward he said: 'Before you pass away from This World you will see me while you are awake. But so long as you do not see me, even if you appear to be breathing your last, you may be certain that your time has not yet come.'

"And that, my friends, explains why yesterday evening I turned my face to the wall. I thought my minutes on earth were counted, and was therefore certain that I would see the tzaddik, as he had promised. I did not see him, however, and there is a reason for that. For when in the World Above they called for Reb David and told him that the time had come for him to fulfill his promise and visit a certain old man on his deathbed, he said: 'I am now enjoying the bliss of the Sabbath day. Now is no time to be sent down to the coarse materiality of the World Below! Let me go after *Shabbos* has passed.'

"Just now, a moment before I summoned you, the tzaddik appeared to me. I saw him clearly, so I am certain that within a very short time I will depart this life. My friends, help me say my last *Vidui* on earth!"

Word for word they pronounced the solemn confession; word for word he mouthed it after them. His time on earth had come to a close, and he was now in a World which is beyond the bounds of time.

◆§ *Whispers From Another World (v)*

In Helochov in the 1870's there lived a chassid called Reb Chaim Yehoshua, who was eighty-seven years old. For a week he had felt his strength waning, though his mind remained clear and unwavering. Sensing that his days on earth were coming to an end, he requested that the inner circle of elder chassidim in the town should assemble at his bedside, and when they arrived, he asked that they invite as well a distinguished chassid who was then in their town — Reb Dov Ze'ev of Yekaterinoslav, an emissary of Reb Shmuel of Lubavitch.

"One request I have of you all," he told the venerable gathering, "but first I must tell you of a singular incident that once befell me.

"In 1833 or 1834 I spent all of the eight days of the festival of Channukah in the court of Reb Menachem Mendel of Lubavitch. In the course of that time I heard three chassidic discourses from his mouth, all of them based on the idea that the struggle of the Maccabees against the Seleucids was a spiritual battle. It was a revolt against the desire of the invaders to impose Hellenism on the People of Israel, as expressed in their proud demand: 'Inscribe it for yourselves on the honor of an ox that you have no share in the God of Israel!' And it was only through the self-sacrifice of our ancestors for their faith they ousted the invaders. The rebbe then spoke at length in praise of this *mesirus nefesh* shown by our forefathers for the sake of sanctifying the Divine Name.

"I was forty-odd years old at the time, and lived with my four brothers and two brothers-in-law in a village near Kalisk in the Vitebsk region. Our father, Reb Avraham Yisrael — a chassid of Reb Shneur Zalman of Liadi and then of his son Reb Dov Ber of Lubavitch — had settled there, and brought us up as farmers with a particular zest for fulfilling the mitzvah of hospitality.

"Late one night during the winter of 1835 or 1836 I heard a knock on the door. I got out of bed and opened the door, and saw before me two Jews wearing heavy fur coats and covered in snow. I extended my hand in the traditional greeting of *Shalom Aleichem*, and invited them to come inside and warm themselves by the stove. When I had prepared them hot tea, and a meal of bread and butter and milk, I left them to eat alone, and went out to the cowshed. On the way there I thought I heard the wailing of a child. At first I dismissed it as the meow of a cat, but as I came nearer, it was unmistakable.

" 'Who is that crying over there?' I asked.

"'It's me, Binyamin,' answered a trembling little voice.

"I soon traced the sound to the covered wagon which my two guests had stood at the far end of the farmyard. I climbed up to see, and my blood froze — for inside lay two small children trussed up in ropes, one asleep, and the other crying.

"Those were the days of the *chapers*, brigands who used to kidnap Jewish children. They would sell them to farflung communities who were forced by the authorities under fearful threats to hand over a certain number of children to the terrors of conscription in the Czarist army. So these were the guests who were supping so placidly in my kitchen! My first thought was fear lest they kidnap our own children likewise. I quicky unbound the ropes from these two shivering little waifs, and took them in my arms to the house of my brother Michael, which stood among the trees in our orchard. My brother was already awake, so I quickly told him what was happening and hastened home.

"Entering my kitchen I saw that one of the guests was making conversation with one of our children. I excused myself, woke up the rest of the family, and whispered to them what we should be wary of. When I came back to the kitchen the same man said to me: 'What a nice, good boy this is! But I have been punished by heaven with two crazy children who talk nonsense. In fact, I had to tie them up with ropes, and I am now on my way to take them to a very important doctor in Vitebsk.'

"My brother Michael had managed meanwhile to give the two little prisoners a solid breakfast, and to hide them away in a safe place in his house. He now stormed into my kitchen in a rage, and addressed my guests: 'A very good morning to you, kidnappers that you are! Either you leave this very minute, or you will suffer a bitter end!'

"The child-snatchers did not yet realize that they had been caught redhanded, so one of them said to the other, in tones of righteous indignation: 'Let us pick up and leave this place. You can see that we have fallen among heartless people who do not even have pity for an unfortunate fellow like yourself who is taking his mentally-disturbed children to see a doctor. You see' — he continued, turning now to my brother and myself — 'I too live in a village, just as you do. But when I saw that my dear friend who lives in the nearby forest has this most unfortunate problem with his dear children, and there was no doctor in our district who could deal with such an illness, I felt sorry for him. I quickly harnessed my horses, and I am now taking him to consult a very important doctor in Vitebsk.'

"The kidnappers left the house with long faces that expressed offended sensitivity. A moment later, though, when they saw that their passengers were no longer in their wagon, they ran back to us, shouting and cursing. It did not take them long now to realize that this would not be at all to their advantage, so they turned around soon enough, and galloped out of our village as fast as they could.

"A month later, when my brother Michael paid one of his periodic visits to Reb Menachem Mendel of Lubavitch and told him of this episode, the face of the tzaddik beamed with joy. He blessed us all and told us to watch over the children for a year, and only then to return them to their homes. We of course followed his instructions. For a whole year they studied together with our own little ones, and did very well indeed.

"From that time on, I was overcome by a burning desire to do what I could for the ransom of captives. In fact I even made the journey to Lubavitch especially to tell the rebbe of my wish, and he told me how I should go about doing this mitzvah. Three or four months of every year — partly in summer, partly in winter — I would travel to various places and ransom children such as these, who are known in these parts as 'Cantonists.'

"This went on for seven years — until one day I was trapped by a vicious ambush. I was a hairsbreadth from death. When I was eventually freed I again traveled to see the tzaddik, who chose Helochov as the place I should live in, and gave me his blessing for long life. In addition to that, he gave me his promise that when my time came to go up to the Other World, I would be — and these were his very words, which he took from the Talmud — עִמִּי בִּמְחִיצָתִי, 'with me, in my abode.'

The old man drew a deep breath, and let it out slowly. "My masters," he said, speaking now more deliberately, "either today or tomorrow my soul will return to its Creator. My parting request to you is that after the soil will have filled my grave, a *minyan* of ten men should stand next to it, and say these words: 'Reb Menachem Mendel, son-in-law of Reb Dov Ber, and grandson of Reb Shneur Zalman! Your servant Chaim Yehoshua the son of Esther is dead. Before his passing he appointed us his agents for the mitzvah of informing you of this, and of reminding you of your promise to Chaim Yehoshua the son of Esther that by virtue of the mitzvah of the ransoming of captives, he would be *with you, in your abode.*' "

They all promised together to fulfill his request, and the next morning — after he had completed all of his usual morning devotions — Reb Chaim Yehoshua returned his soul to his Maker with a clear mind, his last words being *Shema Yisrael.*

❦ ❦ ❦

The whole of the above episode was recorded by the emissary from Yekaterinoslav, Reb Dov Ze'ev, who concluded his account as follows: "On the same day Reb Chaim Yehoshua was brought to rest. When his grave had been filled by soil, we stood around it together, all ten of us, and — in the very words that we had been given — faithfully reminded the departed rebbe of his promise to his chassid."

◈§ *Responsibility*

וְלֹא תָשִׂים דָּמִים בְּבֵיתֶךָ
You shall not bring blood upon your house (22:8)

Reb Menachem Mendel of Rimanov was once presented with a costly table as a gift. His little boy and one of his playmates from the neighborhood immediately began a game of chasing each other noisily around it. In the midst of all the excitement the neighbor's child knocked his head against one of the corners of the table and began to cry. A moment later he was laughing again, but nevertheless, since someone had come to harm by it, the tzaddik decided at once to remove the stumbling-block from his house by having the corners of the expensive table cut off.

◆§ For the Sake of Peace (i)

כי יקח איש אשה
If a man take a wife (22:13)

The bridal party was ready, the *chuppah* was standing in place, but the distinguished guests were kept waiting — for the bride's father, Reb Yaakov Yitzchak of Lublin, was spending far longer than usual over his afternoon prayers. No one thought it proper to ask for an explanation, but at the wedding breakfast the Chozeh himself raised the subject.

"You are no doubt surprised," he said, "that I took so long this afternoon over the *Minchah* prayer. Well, here is the reason. As you all know, the Talmud teaches that 'Forty days before the formation of an infant a heavenly voice proclaims: *The daughter of so-and-so is destined to marry so-and-so* — and at the same time they announce in what year the marriage will take place, as well as the week, the day, the hour, and the moment. Now if the parents of a young couple in their eagerness to perform a mitzvah arrange to hold the ceremony *before* the time announced years earlier, then some kind of dispute is bound to come up in order that the *chuppah* take place at the required time. As our Sages say: 'There is no marriage contract — *kesubbah* — that does not involve some controversy.'

"Now since I knew that the moment fixed in heaven had not yet arrived, I deliberately took my time over the *Shemoneh Esreh* prayer, in order to spare us from that other method of filling in the last few minutes ... "

◆§ For the Sake of Peace (ii)

In his fourteenth year Reb Avraham of Sochatchov married the daughter of Reb Menachem Mendel of Kotsk. When they were already in the carriage on the way to the *chuppah*, his father — Reb Ze'ev Nachum of Biala — suddenly realized that in all the bustle of the wedding preparations he had completely forgotten to remind his son to prepare a learned dissertation. This would have to be delivered, according to custom, at the reception held in honor of the bridegroom immediately before the ceremony.

"Do you have something prepared?" he asked his son. But he too had overlooked the matter.

"What will you do now?" his father asked in distress. "You can be sure that all the most prominent scholars will have assembled at Kotsk for the occasion, and without a doubt they will be expecting to hear some profound *pilpul* from you!"

"Don't worry, father," said the little fellow. "I still have time to prepare while we are traveling."

With that he opened up the volume of the Talmud that he had with him, and after a quarter of an hour of intense concentration he cried out happily: "No worries — I now have a good *pilpul!*"

What with all the clatter and lurching of the carriage his father had no opportunity to hear the discourse before its delivery; he had no option but to rely on his son.

On their arrival in Kotsk the young bridegroom amazed the learned multitude by the breadth of his erudition and the brilliance of his analytical acumen. His discourse lasted several hours, and was appropriately based on a Mishnah in Tractate *Nedarim* that deals with the marriage of the daughters of scholars.

While the marriage contract was being drawn up, the bride's father, Reb Menachem Mendel, said to the father of the bridegroom, Reb Ze'ev Nachum: "*Mechutan,* I am told that you have provided your son with expensive clothes. Now tell me: is it right to spend so much money on clothes that will soon be outgrown by a bridegroom who can still draw himself up to his full height — and even spring up on tiptoe for *Kadosh! Kadosh!* — while standing under the table?

"Since, as you recall, the Talmud assures us that 'There is no marriage contract that does not involve some controversy,' *this* is the subject on which I have chosen to have a difference of opinion with you!"

◈§ *The Honor of Your Presence*

In honor of the marriage of his daughter to the present Lubavitcher rebbe in 1929, Reb Yosef Yitzchak Schneersohn of Lubavitch delivered a *maamar* — a discourse on the teachings of the *Chabad* school of chassidic philosophy — based on the words *Lechah Dodi:* "Come, my beloved, to greet the bride."

In introducing his discourse, the rebbe addressed the distinguished assemblage in the *Tomchei Temimim* yeshivah in Warsaw as follows: "As is widely known, the forefathers of a bridal couple come as guests from the World of Truth to grace the ceremony with their presence. In the House of Israel at large, as many as three generations come to a wedding. There are those who are honored by even earlier generations, each according to his spiritual level. Now, by way of invitation to the tzaddikim who were our forefathers to join us at the *chuppah* and to bestow their blessings on the bride and groom, let us now open with a chassidic discourse; its content is partly from Reb Shneur Zalman of Liadi, partly from his son and successor Reb Dov Ber of Lubavitch, partly from his nephew and successor Reb Menachem Mendel of Lubavitch, partly from his son, my grandfather Reb Shmuel, and partly from my father, Reb Shalom Ber. And, as our Sages remind us, 'He who quotes a teaching in the name of a sage, let him see that sage in his mind's eye standing before him!' "

◆§ *Man, Wife, and Tzaddik (i)*

וְכָתַב לָהּ סֵפֶר כְּרִיתֻת
And he shall write her a bill of divorce (24:1)

In 1740 the greatest scholars of Slutsk and all that district went out to greet the Baal Shem Tov, who had come to the city on a visit. Among them was the aged scholar Reb Uri Nasan Nata, who as a youth was known as the Ilui ("prodigy") of Karinik, a township near Brisk. One of the wealthy householders of Brisk had taken him as a son-in-law, and after he was left a widower he had moved to Slutsk.

His son Reb Shlomo had been educated by him at home, and then at the age of fourteen he had left home to seek a scholarly environment — first in Vilna, then in Horodna, and then in Cracow. There he had encountered a prominent scholar by the name of Reb Menachem Aryeh, who was a hidden tzaddik, and grew to be his close disciple in the study of the teachings of Chassidism — though on condition that their connection be kept secret. At the age of about twenty-two he returned to Slutsk. His father was overjoyed with his progress in learning, and arranged a match for him with the daughter of a leaseholder who lived in a villager nearby. Half a year after their marriage, however, the young wife lost her sanity, and since she was in no state to accept a bill of divorce, he was of course unable to remarry. When the Baal Shem Tov now visited Slutsk, the young man's father brought their sad plight before him, and the unfortunate woman's father likewise asked the tzaddik for advice and a blessing for her recovery.

The Baal Shem Tov then invited both fathers to meet him together and asked them if either of them bore a grudge against the other. The bridegroom's father, Reb Uri Nasan Nata, spoke first. He was full of praise for his *mechutan,* the bride's father. Here was a man who despite the pressure of business fixed times for the study of Torah, maintained a hospitable house which was open to all comers, supported Talmudic scholars generously, and maintained his son-in-law in the most respectable manner. Since the young man had been mentioned, Reb Eliyahu Moshe now spoke most highly of his noble character. He was clearly proud of his assiduous son-in-law, who throughout his stay in the village always found time on weekdays to conduct study circles for the simple farming folk who lived round about, teaching them *Chumash* with Rashi's commentary, and the moral lessons of *Ein Yaakov;* and on *Shabbos* he would read for them from the Midrash and the Ethics of the Fathers. While teaching he imbued them with a comradely love for each other, explaining to them that no man's profit ever came at the expense of that which Divine Providence had destined for another. In a word, he was well loved by the villagers from all around. They were saddened by his present plight, and prayed that his young wife would be restored to complete health, and that he would return to teach them as in happier times.

The Baal Shem Tov listened attentively to them both, and then said: "With God's help, I will be able to heal the young woman completely, and restore her mind to its original clarity — but only on condition that when this happens the young couple do not live together, and when several days have passed, and she is in a fit state according to the Law to accept a bill of divorce, she accepts such a document from her husband with a willing heart."

The *mechutanim* were stupefied at these words. The aged father of Reb Shlomo proposed various legal objections to such a divorce, and Reb Eliyahu Moshe argued that his daughter would be grieved by such a procedure, since she respected her husband highly. He was certain that his son-in-law would likewise be distressed. He himself was prepared to contribute an enormous sum to charity — in the merit of which he begged the tzaddik to pray for her recovery, but to allow the young couple to rejoin each other in the love and harmony to which they were accustomed. The Baal Shem Tov answered unequivocally — that if they did not agree to the condition that he had stipulated, he would not be able to help them.

A few days later they called on the tzaddik together with the young Reb Shlomo, and told him that they accepted his condition — though of course they could not guarantee that the young woman would agree. The Baal Shem Tov heard their reply, and told Reb Eliyahu Moshe to go home and tell his ailing daughter that the Baal Shem Tov had come to Slutsk and asked her to come to speak with him about a matter of importance.

The *mechutanim* looked at each other in amazement.

"But for the last six years," Reb Eliyahu Moshe protested, "she has not uttered a syllable! She has found herself a nook between the stove and the wall, and can barely be fed. In a word, the poor young woman is utterly out of her mind. How can I possibly speak to her?'

The Baal Shem Tov gave no answer.

Making his way homeward with a heavy heart, Reb Eliyahu Moshe remarked to his *mechutan* that if the tzaddik had seen the state in which his daughter was to be found, he would not have spoken as he had. And from the very depths of his heart, Reb Uri Nasan Nata sighed in sympathy with the sufferers from all sides. Not so his son, Reb Shlomo. For when before his marriage he had been a disciple of Reb Menachem Aryeh, he had felt an intellectual affinity with the teachings of the Baal Shem Tov. Now that he had met him, and had heard his teachings from his mouth, he became attached to him with all his heart. He therefore told his father-in-law that he held that they should follow the instructions of the Baal Shem Tov implicitly. His father added that since they had already accepted a far more difficult condition, they should certainly fulfill an instruction which required merely that they attempt to speak to the young woman.

Opening the door Reb Eliyahu Moshe found his daughter sitting in her accustomed corner behind the stove. He began at once to tell his wife what the Baal Shem Tov had said, adding that he was widely reputed as a wonder-worker. To their amazement, their daughter rose from her place as soon as she heard her father's words. She approached them quietly, and in a voice they had not heard for six years, asked who this was who worked wonders. They told her that the man about whom they were speaking was a renowned tzaddik, and she answered that before hearing any more she first wanted to immerse herself in a *mikveh* for purification.

Fearful lest the Evil Eye reverse this unbelievable transformation, her parents bolted their door fast. The young woman ate and spoke and slept as if completely normal, though she felt very weak. On the third day they saw that she had contracted malaria, and in her delirium spoke partly about the Baal Shem Tov. When her father heard her crying and asking to be taken to the wonder-worker, he was suddenly reminded of what this cataclysm in his life had made him forget — that the tzaddik had asked to see her. She was visibly happy to receive the message, and on the very next day, accompanied her parents, she made the journey to Slutsk.

Reb Shomo had heard by now of his wife's recovery, for his father-in-law had sent a special messenger with the news. He now began to speak with his father about the principles of Chassidism taught by the Baal Shem Tov, for he considered this to be a teachable moment. He explained the emphasis which the tzaddik gave to the mystical teachings of the Kabbalah; the workings of Divine Providence not only on humanity but even on the mineral and vegetable kingdoms; the intrinsic worth of even the simplest fellow Jew; the central role of the obligation of *ahavas Yisrael;* and so on. The aged scholar pondered these matters all that day and throughout the following night. On the next day he set out to tell the Baal Shem Tov what his son had told him of these principles, and added that he would dearly love to become a disciple of his. At the same meeting he told the Baal Shem Tov of the good news which had just reached his son. To this the tzaddik replied that on that same day the young woman was again unwell, but that when her father would carry out his mission she would recover and come to see him.

When the young woman and her parents arrived at Slutsk, she and her husband entered the room of the tzaddik, who told them that they would have to divorce. With bitter tears the unfortunate young woman told the Baal Shem Tov how highly she respected her husband for his refined character. If the tzaddik decreed that they should divorce, he must surely know that she was unworthy of so righteous a husband, and she felt it her duty to obey. Reb Shlomo, likewise moved, told the tzaddik that his wife exemplified all the noble attributes by which the Sages define a good wife. If, however, the tzaddik ordered that they divorce, he too would be agreeable.

The Baal Shem Tov arranged to see them four days later; he would then arrange the legalities required.

The next three days the young couple and their parents spent in fasting and prayer. When on the fourth day they made their cheerless way to the tzaddik, they found a *rav,* a scribe and two witnesses already waiting. The Baal Shem Tov asked them if they agreed wholeheartedly to the divorce. They answered that they believed that whatever the tzaddik told them would be for their good, and since they loved each other, each of them was willing to proceed with the divorce — for the good of the other.

The Baal Shem Tov retired for some time to another room.

When he returned he said: "Six years ago a threat of fearful suffering hung over your lives because of the accusations of the Prosecuting Angel. The verdict was then issued that you should each undergo what you have gone through these last six years. Now that your faith in the instructions of your rebbe has been so strong that you were even willing to proceed with a divorce on account of it, this very faith has at this moment freed you from the continuing sentence of the Heavenly Court. The charge against you has been annulled. Live on happily together, and you have my blessing that your house be filled with sons and daughters, and that you both live to a ripe old age."

The young couple remained in Slutsk for three years, after which they moved to Minsk, where Reb Shlomo became one of the pillars of the chassidic community. They then settled with their family in Bayev, until Reb Shneur Zalman of Liadi moved to Liozna, where Reb Shlomo and his family joined his circle of chassidim. Finally, in 1796, they settled in *Eretz Yisrael* where they lived on for another fifteen years — until Reb Shlomo was some ninety-nine years of age.

◆§ *Man, Wife, and Tzaddik (ii)*

When a man divorces his first wife, the very altar sheds tears for him *(Talmud, Tractate Gittin).*

A wealthy chassid once came to Lubavitch to ask Reb Menachem Mendel to recommend a fine young man as a match for his daughter. The rebbe sent at once for one of the students then at the yeshivah, and in introducing him said: "Here is a good match for her."

Without hesitation the chassid invited the young man to his home, and within a short time the young couple were betrothed and married.

Not long after, the young woman began to complain that this husband of hers was not to her liking. After a period of unrest and various attempts at restoring harmony, she insisted on a divorce.

Her father set out at once to consult the rebbe on this step, and he answered: "God forbid! This is her match."

Returning home the father exerted himself to bring peace into the lives of the young couple, but it did not last. His daughter was soon demanding a divorce as before, so he made the journey to Lubavitch once again.

The rebbe answered him sharply: "Did I not tell you that they should not divorce?"

After the father had again attempted to restore domestic harmony his daughter repeated her demand more insistently than ever. She would not even allow her father to visit the rebbe, for, as she said: "Is the rebbe some kind of governor-general that he should order me to spend my life with someone whom I do not want?"

She had her way, and she and her husband divorced.

Some time later she married a God-fearing widower, and for a long period they lived in peace. Their marriage, however, was not blessed with children. The husband did not feel the lack so acutely, for he had children from his previous marriage — but his wife suffered intensely. Consequently, when one day he had occasion to make the journey to Lubavitch, she asked him to mention her name to the rebbe with the request that she be granted a child.

When he duly raised this question at the conclusion of his *yechidus*, the rebbe said: "Am I some kind of governor-general, that I can give the order for children to be born?"

The husband found this answer unintelligible. When repeated he it at home, however, his wife understood it all too well.

☙ *Not Quite a Mitzvah*

וְהָיָה אִם בִּן הַכּוֹת *And if he be worthy of stripes (25:2)*

At the time that Reb Yitzchak of Vorki succeeded Reb Avraham Moshe of Pshischah as rebbe, he lived in a village near Warsaw that belonged to a lady by the name of Tamar'l, who was renowned for her philanthropy, and whose estates he managed.

On one occasion a large group of chassidim who came to consult him there made their way to his house by way of the surrounding fields, and on their way caused damage to the grain crops through which they passed.

One of the owner's employees responsible for these farms was a chassid by the name of Reb Moshe Plotzker. Seeing the damage caused by the visitors, he stormed into the rebbe's room and exclaimed: "It would be a mitzvah to beat them!" — for this was the custom among the gentile landowners of the time.

Reb Yitzchak gave no answer. Assuming that the rebbe concurred with his view, the angry man strode out to give the offenders their deserts.

But the tzaddik called him back and said: "When a man is about to perform a mitzvah, he usually articulates his lofty intention by first contemplating and pronouncing the evocation that opens with the words *LeSheim Yichud*. If he is a chassid, then even before that he usually purifies himself in preparation for the holy act by immersing himself in the waters of a *mikveh*. In that case, you should first go to the *mikveh*, then say *LeSheim Yichud* devoutly, and only then go ahead to perform your mitzvah ..."

◆§ *To Preserve a Name*

וְלֹא יִמָּחֶה שְׁמוֹ
That his name not be wiped out (25:6)

While speaking to Reb Avraham of Sochatchov, a well-meaning chassid commented about a certain freethinker: יִמַּח שְׁמוֹ – "May his name be wiped out!"

The tzaddik reacted abruptly: "Do you know what the Law prescribes in the case of an apostate who dies without leaving children, God forbid?"

The chassid was silent.

The tzaddik went on: "The Jerusalem Talmud explains that the widow of such a man is obliged to undergo *chalitzah*. This ceremony, as you know, takes the place of *yibbum*, the obligation which the Torah places upon a deceased man's brother to marry the widow *for an express purpose* — in order 'that his name be not wiped out from Israel.'

"So you see that the Torah is concerned that even the name of an apostate should not be erased — and you take the liberty of saying what you said about this freethinker?!"

◆§ *Weight-Watchers (i)*

אֶבֶן שְׁלֵמָה וָצֶדֶק יִהְיֶה לָּךְ
A perfect and just weight shall you have (25:15)

Once a month, on the eve of Rosh Chodesh, it was the custom of Reb Menachem Mendel of Rimanov to send out two supervisors to all the shops in town to see whether the weights and measures being used were sound. One of those sent on a certain occasion was Reb Zvi Hirsch, who was later to succeed his rebbe. Arriving with his partner at the shop of a certain wealthy businessman who had once dabbled in scholarship, he found an undersized liquid measure. When Reb Zvi Hirsch rebuked him for his carelessness, the shopkeeper answered that it was not used for measuring.

"But there is an explicit law on the subject," said Reb Zvi Hirsch. "Our Sages teach us that a man is forbidden to have an oversized or undersized measure in his house, even if it is used as a pail for garbage."

The shopkeeper's retort was brazen. Borrowing a phrase remembered from the Book of *Samuel,* he asked: " 'Is Shaul also one of the prophets?!' Does our Reb Zvi Hirsch too go about laying down the Law?"

In reaction to this, Reb Zvi took the measure in hand, and trampled on it.

When he returned from his day's rounds and was asked by the rebbe if everything was in order, Reb Zvi Hirsch concealed that incident, being afraid that the wrath of the rebbe would be kindled against the arrogant offender. But Reb Menachem Mendel got to hear of the story from the man who accompanied him.

He immediately instructed his *shammes* to announce that the townsmen should all assemble in the synagogue to hear a sermon, but though he was to knock with his cane on all the shutters according to custom, he was to ignore the house of that offender. The shopkeeper heard that the rebbe was speaking on the subject of weights and measures, and realized that this whole tempest was brought about on his account. He went to the synagogue of his own accord, and as a sign of contriteness removed his shoes in preparation for begging forgiveness of the tzaddik. Reb Menachem Mendel promised to forgive him on condition that by way of a fine he undertake to donate fifty gold ducats to charity.

Before the shopkeeper arrived at the synagogue to humbly make amends, someone noticed that the lips of Reb Zvi Hirsch were muttering something. Asked what he was saying, he replied: "Only a little prayer that the man should not be punished before he comes to make peace with the rebbe."

❧ Weight-Watchers (ii)

"I was once in the house of Reb David of Lelov at dawn," recounted Reb Yitzchak of Vorki. "He was garbed in *tallis* and *tefillin*, ready to begin his morning prayers. Suddenly a gentile walked in and asked the tzaddik to sell him half a gallon of beer. No other member of the family was in the house at the moment, so Reb David went ahead with amazing alacrity and measured out the beer himself. At this point, though, the gentile wanted to buy it more cheaply, so he asked the tzaddik to measure him out an additional quantity for the same price. Reb David cut the conversation short, poured what was in the container back into its barrel, returned to his study and began his prayers.

"I was baffled by the entire little episode. What made him start? What made him stop? And if he had already decided to get himself involved in selling beer to the gentile, why did he not come to an agreement with him on the price, and settle the matter?

"So Reb David explained it all to me. 'Listen, my friend,' he said. 'My guiding principle is בְּכָל דְּרָכֶיךָ דָעֵהוּ — *Know Him in all your ways.* Before a man begins any action he first needs to know what pleasure the Almighty will have from it. When I first went to measure out the beer, I intended thereby to fulfill the mitzvah of keeping just weights and measures, and so I did it energetically. But from the moment I saw that our encounter had become no more than plain commerce, I withdrew from it. For what do I have to do with him? And what pleasure would the Almighty now derive from our encounter?"

❧ The Wife of One's Youth

וְאֵשֶׁת נְעוּרִים כִּי תִמָּאֵס
Can the wife of one's youth be reviled? (Haftarah)

In the household of a certain chassid there lived a maid whose husband had been conscripted into the Czarist army at the outbreak of the Russo-Turkish war of 1877, and had never been heard of since. She therefore asked her mistress to ask her husband to raise the subject when he next visited his rebbe, Reb Shmuel of Lubavitch.

The rebbe was riding in his carriage just outside Lubavitch, as he often did, and when he saw this chassid approaching, he invited him to join him. The chassid utilized the opportunity well.

"Rebbe, I have been given a message for you," he said, and went on to tell him all about the unfortunate *agunah*, who neither knew whether she had a husband alive nor was able to remarry.

"My father," said the rebbe, referring to Reb Menachem Mendel of Lubavitch, "was good at these things — but I know nothing. Let me tell you a somewhat similar story that involved my father.

"My father had a relative whose husband had deserted her, claiming that she was ugly and an evil woman. She came to our household, and my mother took her in as a house-help. She asked my mother several times to raise the subject with my father, but every time my father would get out of it. Once, before the Days of Awe, my mother insisted, and said: 'Is it not written וּמִבְּשָׂרְךָ לֹא תִתְעַלָּם — *And hide yourself not from your own flesh?'*

" 'You too?' my father replied. 'Haven't I got enough heartache from all the people who come here with their bundles of woes, that you have to add some more?'

" 'Then make up your mind,' countered my mother. 'If you are unable to help, then tell that to all your chassidim so that they will stop coming to see you; if after all you *are* able to help everyone, then why don't you give an answer to our relative?'

" 'But the Dnieper is not on fire,' said my father.

" 'Very well,' said my mother, 'then fix a time.'

"And my father told her that after the coming festivals — within a few weeks — he would see what could be done.

"During the Ten Days of Penitence between Rosh HaShanah and Yom Kippur my father called his *gabbai* and told him that if a certain leaseholder from the region of Orsha should arrive during the Intermediate Days of the festival of Sukkos — since every year this man came to Lubavitch especially for the last days of this festival — he should send him to see him at once.

"He was duly called to see my father, who said: 'I have a mission for you involving a mitzvah — to pass on a letter to a man called Chaikl who lives about twenty miles from your home.'

" 'It will be my pleasure to obey, God willing,' said the leaseholder, 'immediately after the festival.'

" 'No,' said the rebbe, my father. 'What I meant was that you should set out immediately, and spend the last days of the festival at home.'

"The man was not exactly overjoyed at the prospect, after all the trouble he had gone to in order to be able to spend those very days in the company of the rebbe and all the chassidim – but for him this was an order, and he felt obliged to obey. But no sooner had he left the study with the letter in hand, than my father called him back and said: 'Remember, do not fail your mission!'

" 'God forbid!' replied the man. 'Of course I will fulfill it faithfully.'

"Back at his lodgings, he told his fellow chassidim of his hard luck – he had come all the way here for *Yom-Tov*, and the rebbe was sending him back home. His comrades cheered him up. This was, after all, a mission to be undertaken for the sake of a mitzvah, and surely there must be some profound reason behind it. If anything, they told him, he should rejoice that he was the one fortunate enough to be chosen to undertake this urgent task. In brief, they set the table with whatever refreshments they could afford, were happy themselves and made him happy as well, and he set out cheerfully in an open carriage drawn by two horses, accompanied by his gentile wagon-driver. It was the eve of Hoshana Rabbah, a little over twenty-four hours before the final days of the festival. As soon as they set out they were drenched by a continuous downpour of rain, and the first thing the chassid did on his arrival home was to change his clothes and warm himself over the enormous built-in stove. A short time later his driver came in to tell him that one of their horses had died.

" 'So let it be an atonement for my sins,' said the leaseholder, dismissing the incident as insignificant.

"A little later the gentile came in to say that the second horse had died too.

" 'What can be done?' the leaseholder consoled himself. 'The Almighty will make good my losses.'

"But then the gentile came in a third time — the mill-house was on fire. Something jogged the man's memory.

" 'What on earth has happened to me?' he cried. 'What have I done with the rebbe's letter?'

" 'What letter?' his family wanted to know — and when he went through the pockets of his drenched clothes he found it. Without losing a moment he instructed his coachman to set out on horseback to deliver the letter to Chaikl. He refused at first, being wet and tired from their journey, but the leaseholder offered him payment for his pains, and poured him a glass of vodka to warm him up. Before he set out he was given a covering letter as well, in which the leaseholder solemnly warned Chaikl that he should fulfill the rebbe's request without delay; he himself had already received his just deserts for not having acted promptly enough.

"Chaikl opened the rebbe's letter. Without any delay, he was to send off the miller who worked for him, in time to spend the last days of *Yom-Tov* in Lubavitch. The miller was promptly summoned, but being a simple coarse fellow, he merely answered: 'What is there for me to do over there? What business has the rebbe got with me?'

"Seeing that pleading did not help, Chaikl threatened to dismiss him if he did not oblige — and on Hoshana Rabbah the miller arrived in Lubavitch.

"When he walked in for *yechidus,* my father took hold of him and said: 'Young man! Why have you deserted your wife for these last three years?'

" 'Rebbe,' said the miller in alarm, 'I can't support her.'

" 'Then I will write to your employer and tell him to increase your wages so that there will be enough for the two of you,' said my father.

" 'But rebbe, he protested. 'She is an evil woman!'

" 'No doubt her only *evil* is that she doesn't cook meals that are good enough for you,' said my father. 'But now that you will be able to afford to give her more money for household expenses, you can be sure she will cook better.'

" 'But she is ugly,' complained the miller.

" 'So what *would* suit you — a countess?!' said my

father. 'Come with me to the kitchen, please.'

"Then, when they arrived there, he continued: 'Here is your wife. Go along happily, the two of you, and live in peace together according to the Law of Moses and Israel.'

"And that, for the rest of their lives, is exactly what they did."

Reb Shmuel had concluded his story. "That kind of thing," he said to the chassid who accompanied him in his carriage, "my father was able to do — but not me."

"If I may ask," ventured the chassid, "what answer can I take home to that unfortunate maid who does not know her husband's whereabouts?"

Replied Reb Shmuel: "Write to the army headquarters in St. Petersburg, and ask them to investigate."

An answer eventually arrived from the capital to notify the young woman that her husband was dead. A rabbinical court was set up, and after due deliberation it pronounced her free to remarry.

סדר כי תבוא
SIDRA KI SAVO

☙ *The Art of Giving (i)*

וְעַתָּה הִנֵּה הֵבֵאתִי
And now, behold I have brought (26:10)

If one brings a gift to a sage, it is as if one made an offering of the First Fruits in the Temple *(Talmud Tractate Kesubos).*

Reb Mordechai of Nadvorna once felt a deep desire to perform the mitzvah of offering the First Fruits of *bikkurim* in the only way possible since the Destruction of the Temple — that is, in the spirit of the above teaching of the Sages. He therefore bought a lamb and had it slaughtered. Its meat he distributed to needy families in honor of *Shabbos*, and gave part of the wool to an upright chassid who was little steeped in the vanities of This World, with the request that he spin it into yarn from which *tzitzis* could be made. He then wrapped up the bundle of long woolen threads, hired a special messenger, and personally sewed the precious little package into a safe pocket in the man's overcoat. The messenger was then dispatched to deliver the gift to Reb Chaim of Zanz.

On his arrival in Zanz, he explained to the tzaddik that Reb Mordechai had sent this gift in fulfillment of the mitzvah of bringing the First Fruits to the Temple.

Reb Chaim was radiant with joy. He not only untied the gift from its hiding place with his own hands, but — as the messenger was later to relate — he even preserved the paper in which the tzaddik of Nadvorna had wrapped it.

◆§ *The Art of Giving (ii)*

It was a principle with Reb Tzadok HaKohen of Lublin not to accept gifts from anyone, not even a *pidyon* from his chassidim. The only payment he would ever agree to accept was the money paid by the father of an infant in the ceremony of the Redemption of the Firstborn, *pidyon haben*, for the Torah explicitly made him entitled to it as a *kohen*, a descendant of the priestly clan. And even this money he used only for the purchase of sacred literature, never for any other purpose.

His daily living expenses were paid out of the income which his *rebbitzin* made in her secondhand clothes shop. When she passed away his chassidim wanted to support him generously, but he flatly refused to accept any help. However, when one of his chassidim asked to be allowed to reopen the shop, he agreed — but only on condition that he would be given no more than his daily needs. These were modest enough, to be sure — one meal every evening, which consisted of tea and a bun, or a little porridge.

Despite all this, one chassid got it into his head that he would like to present the tzaddik with a bottle of pure olive oil and a costly package of fish. Realizing that nothing would ever be accepted as an outright gift, he tried to outwit the tzaddik, and said: "I am bringing First Fruits" — and he quoted the teaching of the Sages, that "If one brings a gift to a sage, it is as if one made an offering of the First Fruits in the Temple." Reb Tzadok was overawed, as always, by the mere quotation of words from the Talmud, so he accepted.

On the following *Shabbos*, however, he opened his discourse to the chassidim at his table by quoting the same statement: "If one brings a gift to a *talmid chacham*" and so on. Then he continued: "But *am* I a sage? One cannot say that one has not studied, because one has. But what if one *has* studied? For in *Proverbs* it is written: 'Why is the price of wisdom in the hand of a fool, seeing he has no sense?' And the Sages teach us that this verse refers to those who study the Torah but do not observe it..."

When the *tish* was over and the chassidim had dispersed disconsolately, one of his elder disciples approached the tzaddik and said: "Rebbe, we were all shocked to hear such words from your mouth!"

"And is that a good enough reason for me to be a liar?" returned Reb Tzadok. "If I received the gift from that man, that implies that I am a Torah scholar worthy of being called a *talmid chacham*. Now I do not hold that to be the case, so I was obliged to state the truth in the hearing of you all."

◆§ *The Art of Giving (iii)*

On his way to *Eretz Yisrael* in 1929, Reb Yosef Yitzchak of Lubavitch passed through Alexandria. The moment his train drew up at the railway station, the door of the carriage burst wide open and a man leaped inside. His arms were loaded with a basket full of exotic fruit, and his eyes were streaming with tears of joy.

"Rebbe!" he exclaimed as soon as he was able to catch his breath. "When I was a little boy in Russia my grandfather took me along with him to visit your grandfather, Reb Shmuel of Lubavitch, so that he should give me his blessing. My grandfather brought the rebbe a basketful of fruit as a kind of *bikkurim*, a gift of First Fruits.

"You, rebbe, were also a little boy at the time, and you were playing in your grandfather's study. So when he received the gift, Reb Shmuel said to my grandfather: 'May it be God's will that your grandson will one day bring First Fruits to my grandson.'

"Many long years have passed since that meeting, and in the meantime my business affairs brought me here to settle in Egypt. But when the other day I heard that you, rebbe, would be passing through the city, that blessing of Reb Shmuel's came to life in my memory, and I thought: 'The time has come!' I bought this fruit and I hurried here to see you.

"I thank God for granting me the privilege of seeing Reb Shmuel's blessing come true!"

◆§ *It's the Thought That Counts*

הַקְּלָלוֹת הָאֵלֶּה
These curses
(28:15)

People who came to see Reb Shlomo of Radomsk in request of a blessing were sometimes shocked to discover that instead of kindly sympathy or advice he showered them with curses. Those whose *kvitl* was received in this manner were always pleased to discover later, however, that their affairs prospered exceedingly — whether by natural means, or by means beyond the predictable.

A learned and wealthy chassid once came from Pietrikov to consult with the rebbe about an important forthcoming transaction. Using plain logic and business sense, the rebbe gave him a piece of advice which produced such a vast profit that the businessman sent one of his friends to inform him of it. This messenger was himself a man of learning, and when he saw how pleased the rebbe was with the news he had brought he ventured to begin: "I hope you will not mind, rebbe, if I take the liberty of asking you one question. It is clear that in this case you gave my friend a piece of advice which can be comprehended by pure reason. Why, then, do you often help people through curses, if you can achieve the same result by blessing them?"

Replied the tzaddik: "My rebbe, Reb Meir of Apta, used to act this way, and would explain himself as follows. 'It is very probable that in the World Above they will punish me for cursing my fellow Jews — but I have no option in this matter, and the Torah absolves those who act under duress.'

"In fact we have a hint of this situation in the words of Moshe Rabbeinu: 'Not a single donkey have I taken from them, nor have I done evil to a single one of them' — for one cannot be helped by a tzaddik except by either of two means: either the tzaddik has to accept the gift of a *pidyon*, or he has to curse the supplicant. And this is what Moshe Rabbeinu is arguing here to the Almighty — since he has neither accepted as much as a donkey from the Children of Israel, nor has he said as much as a harsh word to them, it is impossible for him to help them."

The messenger had not expected to hear such a rationale for the tzaddik's bizarre behavior, and he hastened to pass it on to his fellow chassidim.

In his book *Tiferes Shlomo*, the tzaddik gave a further explanation of the use of harsh words. He opens by asking why the rebukes and curses of *Parshas Ki Savo* are read in the synagogue on the *Shabbos* preceding the last week of the outgoing year, the week during which the penitential prayers of *Selichos* are said. His answer is based on an analogy with the promise in the Book of *Hosea:* וּנְשַׁלְּמָה פָרִים שְׂפָתֵינוּ — "With our lips we will compensate for oxen" — a reference to the replacement of the sacrificial service by prayers. Reb Shlomo cites the assurance of the Sages that "He who studies the passage in the Torah concerning the burnt offerings is considered to have actually sacrificed a burnt offering." Applying it to the above-mentioned rebukes and curses of the *Tochachah* passage, he argues that even if Israel were found punishable by the sufferings described there, the reading of the words alone is no doubt accounted by the Heavenly Court as if they had already undergone them — and with that the tribulations which had been prescribed for the passing year, but which never materialized, are struck off the list.

◆§ *Classified Information*

יַכְּכָה ה׳ בְּשִׁגָּעוֹן
God will smite you with insanity (28:28)

One weird delusion obsessed the deranged mind of a certain unfortunate fellow. He was somehow convinced that the commander of the local gendarmerie was Eliyahu the Prophet, and that the governor of the city was the Messiah himself. His family were sorely vexed by this, because he never tired of telling all and sundry of his singular discovery. They decided therefore to take him along to Reb Simchah Bunem of Pshischah.

The poor man had barely opened the door of the rebbe's study when he excitedly gave him the news: "The Prophet Eliyahu and the Messiah live in my city!"

"Who are they?" asked the rebbe.

"One is the military commander, and the other is the governor," explained the other.

"And who am I?" asked the rebbe.

"Why, you are the rebbe!" answered the visitor.

"Is it possible, then," asked Reb Simchah Bunem "that I — who am a rebbe — do not know that Eliyahu and the *Mashiach* are in your city?"

"Of course you know it," said the man, "and you know it well — except that you don't want to reveal it to anyone."

"Very well," said the tzaddik. "You too can know it, and nevertheless reveal it to no one — just like I do. Don't breathe a word of it to anyone!"

The man returned to his hometown and never raised the subject again — then at length he recovered his sanity completely.

☙ *Hardly a Blessing*

הוא יַלְוְךָ
He shall lend to you (28:44)

A certain chassid asked Reb Menachem Mendel of Rimanov to pray that the Almighty should cause him to find favor in the eyes of a certain noble, from whom he wanted to borrow money.

"I cannot pray for that," said the tzaddik, "for it is with reference to the stranger in our midst that the Torah warns us of one of the punishments for our disobedience: 'He shall lend to you.' "

סדר נצבים
SIDRA NITZAVIM

☙ *Melodies for the Ears of Heaven (i)*

מֵחֹטֵב עֵצֶיךָ עַד שֹׁאֵב מֵימֶיךָ
From the hewers of your wood to the drawers of your water (29:10)

It was the way of the Baal Shem Tov to show a particular fondness for simple, God-fearing folk, and many such people became his warm admirers. For the more intellectually sophisticated among his disciples this affinity was a bitter pill to swallow — nor did it become more palatable even after their rebbe had sent them to associate with such folk in order to learn from their example such desirable traits as unquestioning trust in the Creator, simple faith, and the love of a fellow Jew.

Among those who flocked to be near the tzaddik one *Shabbos* in summer were many such people — innkeepers, farmers, craftsmen, poultrymen, market stall-keepers, and the like. And it was these visitors to whom the Baal Shem Tov showed especial tokens of affection at his Friday night table. With one he shared the wine over which he sanctified the Sabbath; to another he lent his own *Kiddush* goblet; some were offered slices of the sweet *Challah* over which he had pronounced a blessing; and others tasted a morsel of fish from his plate. The inner circle of scholarly disciples who made up the holy brotherhood — the חֶבְרַיָּא קַדִּישָׁא — wondered at the conduct of their rebbe.

The custom in the household of the Baal Shem Tov was that the guests who came to Mezhibuzh for *Shabbos* joined him at the Friday night *tish* and again at the twilight Third Meal on the following day, while the midday meal of *Shabbos* was reserved for the inner circle alone. This gathering strangers were not even allowed to watch from a distance. The unlettered folk who had come for that *Shabbos* therefore ate their midday meal at their lodgings, and then found their way back to the *shul* of the Baal Shem Tov, where they engaged in the only kind of divine worship that their meager schooling had given them — pouring out their hearts in singing the praises and entreaties of the Book of *Psalms*.

As the Baal Shem Tov took his place at the head of the long table, he first seated each of his disciples in a particular place, according to his custom, and then revealed to them such secrets from the world of the Torah that their hearts were aglow with spiritual delight. Their rebbe too was living through a moment of rare joy, and they thanked their Maker for having brought them into his radiant orbit.

But the hearts of a few were clouded by a critical thought. Why did their rebbe show such marks of favor to men so simple that they did not understand his teachings?

At once the face of the tzaddik took on a serious appearance. In a tone of restrained ecstasy and with eyes closed, he said: "In a place where penitents stand, the most righteous of men have no place. So our Sages teach us. There are two paths in the service of the Creator — the righteous service of tzaddikim, and the contrite service of *baalei teshuvah.* The service of simple folk belongs to the second level, the loftier level of the penitent — for they are lowly of spirit, regretting the imperfect past, and striving nobly to improve the future."

A haunting melody began imperceptibly from around the table, and those disciples who had harbored doubts as to their rebbe's conduct realized that he had sensed what they had been thinking. The music faded away. The Baal Shem Tov opened his eyes, gazed long and deeply into the faces of his disciples, one by one, and then told them each to rest their right hand on the shoulder of their neighbor. When they had sung quietly together for a further space, he asked them to close their eyes, and not to open them until they were told to do so. He then rested his right hand on the disciple who was seated at his right, and his left hand on the shoulder of the disciple seated at his left — and the circle was closed.

From that moment the sweetest of tender melodies stole into their ears, melodies that bore with them the heartfelt entreaties of honest souls.

"Ribbono shel Olam!" said one manly voice, appealing to the Maker of the Universe in gentle terms of his own, before going on to address Him in words first used by King David: "בְּחָנֵנִי ה׳ — Examine me, O God, and test me; refine ... my heart."

"Zisser fotter, father dear!" another voice prefixed his verse from *Psalms.* "חָנֵּנִי אֱלֹקִים חָנֵּנִי — Be gracious to me, O God, be gracious, for my soul trusts in You; and in the shadow of Your wings will I take refuge until woes are past."

"Father!" came the piteous cry of a storm-tossed life, desperately seeking anchorage in a haven of its own. "גַּם צִפּוֹר מָצְאָה בַיִת — Even the sparrow has found a home, and the swallow a nest for herself ..."

The holy brotherhood of learned chassidim trembled in the face of such innocent supplication. Their eyes were closed, but they shed tears of contriteness, and humbly envied the worship that was the daily portion of these simple singers of *Psalms*.

The Baal Shem Tov lifted his hands from the shoulders of the disciples, and the music vanished from their ears. He told them all to open their eyes, and again the brotherhood sang softly together.

One of that circle who was present on that *Shabbos* was Reb Dov Ber, the Maggid of Mezritch. Years later he told his disciple, Reb Shneur Zalman of Liadi, that at that moment he experienced a rapturous love of the Creator with an intensity that he had never before known. Indeed his whole being was seized by such a paroxysm of desire for *teshuvah* that his very slippers were soaked with perspiration and tears.

The singing had come to an end, and the brotherhood sat in pensive silence. For some time the Baal Shem Tov sat with his eyes closed in a trance of *dveikus*, then he looked again at his chassidim and said: "The music that you heard was the innocent singsong of the simple folk in the synagogue, intoning their verses from the *Psalms* from the bottom of their trusting hearts. Consider now. We mortals are made up of a body, which is not a thing of truth, and a soul, which is truth — and even the soul is only part of the Whole. Being thus creatures of imperfect truth, we are called *sfas emes*, 'the lip of truth,' a mere hint of truth. Nevertheless, even we are able to recognize and sense the truth, and be overwhelmed by it. How much more so must the Almighty — the ultimate Truth — recognize the truth in the psalm-singing of these simple men."

For a long time thereafter — so the Maggid of Mezritch told Reb Shneur Zalman of Liadi — he had been distressed by the fact that he had previously entertained doubts as to his rebbe's closeness with simple people. Though he had undertaken various penances to clear himself of this past guilt, he could find no rest — until one night he saw a vision which brought peace to his soul. In one of the palaces of the Garden of Eden, a group of little children were clustered around a long table, learning *Chumash.* At the head of the table sat their schoolmaster — Moshe Rabbeinu. They were studying the passage which speaks of the seeming disbelief of the Patriarch Avraham when he was given the divine promise that in their old age he and his wife would beget a child. One of the little students read aloud the verse: "And Avraham fell on his face, and laughed and said in his heart, 'Shall a child be born to him that is a hundred years old?" Moshe Rabbeinu thereupon explained them that all the Midrashic commentaries woven around this sentence were of course true — but at the same time, no verse in the Torah utterly leaves its plain meaning. As to the question of how it was possible to conceive of doubt in the mind of the Patriarch Avraham, the answer was that this doubt stemmed from the fact that he had a body — and even a holy body is flesh.

When the Maggid heard that by the mere fact of having a body a person can experience doubts that arise of themselves, he was no longer troubled by the recollection of his misgivings about his rebbe's conduct. At long last, his soul found response.

◆§ *Melodies for the Ears of Heaven (ii)*

Reb Moshe Zvi of Savran was once on visit to Berditchev where he stayed at the house of his *mechutan,* a chassid by the name of Reb Moshe Yosef Chodorov. The craftsmen of the town at the time were busy deciding on the regulations which would govern their newly-found *Chevrah Tehillim,* a comradely fraternity whose chief aim was to bring together groups of artisans to chant the *Psalms* in unison. Once agreed upon, their regulations were entered for posterity in the *pinkas,* the community register. Most of the members of the fraternity were unlearned, though honest and God-fearing. And in case in any future communal situation they should require the services of someone more learned than themselves, they asked two of the respected young married scholars of the town to add their names to the list of members — and these two *talmidei chachamim* obliged.

When the founders of the *Chevrah* heard that Reb Moshe Zvi of Savran was in town they decided to send him the *pinkas,* with the request that he append his signature to their newly-inscribed regulations. And if he wanted to add or change anything they had written, they indicated that their agreement was assured in advance.

One of their two young scholarly members was chosen to be honored with this mission. When he arrived at the lodgings of the visiting rebbe he found that there was already an erudite caller sitting importantly there — a local heavyweight pedant, a veritable *lamdan.*

When this pillar of learning heard that the new arrival had joined the commoners as a member of their *Chevrah,* he turned to him in amazement and exclaimed: "What on earth are *you* doing in a *Chevrah Tehillim?* Leave *Psalms* for the artisans and the simple folk, who can do no better. You should be reserving your talents for the Talmud and the legal codes, not spending your time on *Tehillim!"*

"And since when should a Torah scholar not read the *Psalms?"* challenged the young man. "You recall what the Midrash says on the verse from *Psalms:* יִהְיוּ לְרָצוֹן אִמְרֵי פִי — 'May the words of my mouth find acceptance.' On this verse the Midrash elaborates that King David prayed that whoever read the *Psalms* should be accounted in the sight of heaven as of equal worth with him who engaged in the study of the laws of purity and impurity."

Replied the *lamdan:* "And I once heard from the mouth of a prominent scholar — *he* was no chassid, for sure! — that this Midrash says that King David made a request; it does not say that his request was *accepted.* In support of this view allow me to cite another case in which we see that King David made a request that was not granted. For we find in Tractate *Bava Basra* that 'There were seven people whose bodies were not overcome in the grave by worms.' And the Talmud goes on to say: 'There are those who say that the same applies to King David, as it is written, אַף בְּשָׂרִי יִשְׁכֹּן לָבֶטַח — *My flesh too dwells secure.* Another view holds that David prayed for this.' From this we see that this was only a *request* of his — but that it was not granted."

Reb Moshe Zvi of Savran had been listening quietly to this dialogue, but these last words of the *lamdan* were more than he could bear in silence.

"Who is it you say whose prayer was not granted?" he exclaimed excitedly. "Are you talking about David, King of Israel?! Woe is me, that I should hear such words! And besides, your learned colleague has misunderstood the meaning of that passage from the Talmud. The Sages had listed the seven people who were granted this privilege *without having requested it,* while 'David — prayed for this.' Because it came to him as the result of his request, his name does not appear among the seven. This passage, therefore, proves the very opposite of your thesis. The prayer of David *was* accepted."

With that he took the *pinkas* in hand, opened up at the page on which the artless worshipers had entered the statutes of their *Chevrah Tehillim,* and signed there with gusto.

◆§ *What Angels are Made Of*

Rebbitzin Mirl -- the wife of Reb Yitzchak Meir of Mezhibuzh, and the daughter-in-law of Reb Avraham Yehoshua Heschel of Apta — was a saintly soul. Once she was in synagogue, and hearing an unaccustomed bustle, she opened the door that led from the women's section to where the men were assembled, to ask what had happened. She was told that Reb Yaakov the wagon-driver had died.

"What?!" she cried aghast. "Is Reb Yaakov dead? Do you know who Reb Yaakov was?"

And when she had calmed down from her sudden anguish, she said: "It once happened that on a freezing winter's day I was left without a single splinter of firewood in the house. I went off to Reb Yaakov. He immediately harnessed his horse, drove off to the forest, and came back with a wagon stacked high with firewood. I stoked up the stove in the *beis midrash,* and dozens of people were then able to sit there and study Torah.

"On another occasion I ran out of water — not a single drop left. Again I went off to Reb Yaakov, and he brought me a huge barrel full of water, so that I was able to cook in honor of *Shabbos*.

"Master of the Universe!" she pleaded in conclusion. "May it be Your will that from every piece of wood that he brought, an angel be born — to speak up now on his behalf. And may all those drops of water be transformed into so many merits — to turn out and greet him as he arrives in the World Above!"

When the tzaddik came to *shul* a little later, the chassidim told him what his *rebbitzin* had said.

"I marvel at it!" he said. "Where did the woman get that divinely-inspired gift of *ruach hakodesh*? For what she said down here is exactly what they said in the World Above."

◂§ *Unsung Heroes (i)*

When at the circumcision of his son Reb Menachem Mendel of Lubavitch gave him the name Shmuel, no one present knew after whom the infant had been named.

At the festive meal which followed the ceremony the infant's grown brother, Reb Yehudah Leib — later rebbe in Kopust — asked his father: "After whom is the baby named? I don't know of anyone of that name in our family. Perhaps," he ventured in a whisper, "he is named after the Prophet Samuel?"

Replied his father, the Tzemach Tzedek: "The baby is named after a certain water-carrier in Polotzk who was called Shmuel."

◂§ *Unsung Heroes (ii)*

A chassid by the name of Reb Monye Monissohn, who was a wealthy dealer in gems, was once sitting in the presence of Reb Shalom Ber of Lubavitch. In the course of their conversation the rebbe spoke highly of certain unlettered folk.

"Rebbe," asked Reb Monye, "why do you make such a fuss of them?"

"Why, they have many noble qualities," said the rebbe.

"Well, I can't see them," said the chassid.

The tzaddik was silent. Later on, he asked Reb Monye whether he had brought his package of diamonds with him. The dealer said that he had, but he would prefer to show them to the rebbe a little later, not in the sunlight, so that they could be seen to their best advantage.

He later opened the package in a nearby room, arranged the gems carefully on a table, and pointed out a particular stone to the rebbe, saying: "This one is something really special!"

"I can't see anything in it," said the rebbe.

"Ah, but you have to be a connoisseur to know how to look at diamonds!" said the chassid.

"Every Jew too is something really special," said the rebbe, "but you have to be a connoisseur to know how to look at him."

☙ The Torah is For Mortals (i)

לא בַשָּׁמַיִם הִיא
It is not in heaven (30:12)

Reb Yaakov Yitzchak of Lublin — known as the Chozeh, or Seer, on account of his clairvoyancy — was visited one day by a butcher. He wanted the tzaddik to advise him as to whether he should slaughter his cattle before the forthcoming festival, or sell them; he was afraid that after they were slaughtered and their vital organs examined they might be found to be *trefah*, in which case their carcasses would have to be discarded.

The tzaddik asked the butcher to write down a description of each of his animals, and then went through the list with him, telling him that this one was kosher, the next one *trefah*, and so on. About one of them he said: "I do not know — for when it is opened it will be found to involve a legal query. Whether the *rav* who is consulted will determine that this *she'elah* makes the animal kosher or *trefah*, I do not know. For it is on decisions on *halachah* that it is written that the Torah is 'not in heaven.' "

☙ The Torah is For Mortals (ii)

In the summer of 1804, while Reb Nachman of Breslov was on a journey, his infant daughter Feige passed away. When he came home his family hid the news, which was possible because she had been staying in the home of a wetnurse in the nearby town of Ladizin.

Coming straight from his carriage into his house, the tzaddik found a large number of people there waiting for him, and began at once to deliver a mystical discourse which touched on the subject of mourning. His hearers sensed that he was aware through *ruach hakodesh* of what had happened, and those who had accompanied him in his carriage on the way home had received the same impression. After the discourse he asked after his daughter from his family, but they still kept the news from him. And the tzaddik observed none of the rites of mourning.

In that year, Rosh HaShanah fell on Thursday and Friday. At sunset on the following day, the chassidim were seated at the *Seudah Shlishis* meal in a room near his study, uncertain whether he would join them and deliver a discourse, for only on rare occasions would he sit with them at the Third Meal of *Shabbos*.

Suddenly Reb Nachman opened the door as if in alarm, to the surprise of all the assembled chassidim. He called for his elder daughter, and when she had joined him in his study he raised the subject of the passing of the little girl. When she began to speak evasively, he assured her: 'But I already know the truth myself.'

And then she was obliged to state the unfortunate fact explicitly. Reb Nachman did not join his chassidim for the Third Meal. Instead, after the Day of Rest had passed, he observed the rites of mourning for one hour, as the Law prescribes in the case of evil tidings which reach a person after thirty days have elapsed from the decease of a near relative.

No matter what a person may perceive through supernatural means, explained Reb Nachman, he may not observe the rites laid down by the Law until he is informed of the facts in the conventional way.

◆§ *Pastures that are Even Greener*

כִּי קָרוֹב אֵלֶיךָ הַדָּבָר מְאֹד
For this thing is very near to you (30:14)

Reb Chanoch Henich of Alexander used to repeat in the name of his rebbe, Reb Simchah Bunem of Pshischah, that anyone planning his first visit to a tzaddik should first know the story of an honest man from

Cracow by the name of Reb Aizik Reb Yekeles. This Reb Aizik lived in the days before surnames were invented; the appendage to his name tells us that he was the son of a certain Reb Yekele, in order to distinguish him from other people called Aizik who no doubt lived in the same courtyard. Until recent years there stood in Cracow the very synagogue that he built, and it was called — the *shul* of Reb Aizik Reb Yekeles.

This Reb Aizik dreamed several times that he should make the long journey to Prague, and there, near the royal palace, under the bridge, he should dig in the ground, where an unbelievable treasure was waiting for him. He set out for Prague, and headed straight for the bridge which stands near the palace. But he discovered to his consternation that the area was heavily guarded night and day by half a mounted regiment of burly hussars. How could a little Jew from Cracow sneak in under the gaping muzzles of their fearful muskets and blunderbusses, and start digging under the bridge for hidden treasure? It was a disappointing climax to such a fatiguing journey, and he would now have to make that whole exhausting journey home again — emptyhanded. All day long he walked up and down near that bridge feeling very sorry for himself, and when night fell he returned to his lodgings, where he tossed and turned until daybreak. His odd behavior day after day attracted the attention of the brass-helmeted officer of the guards, who called him across and demanded that he explain himself.

Reb Aizik told him the whole story of the dreams, and the bridge, and the treasure — and the brass hat exploded in laughter.

"Do you mean to tell me that on the strength of a dream you came all this long way? Who on earth believes the kind of nonsense they see in dreams? Why, I myself dreamed the other day that I should travel all the way to Cracow, where I would find some Jew called Reb Aizik Reb Yekeles; I was to dig under the fireplace of his house, and find an unbelievable treasure. Now I ask you: do you think it would occur to me to take notice of the kind of stuff you hear in dreams and to set out and make the long journey to Cracow?!"

At long last Reb Aizik understood why he had to come all the way to Prague. He went straight back to his own hometown, headed straight for his own house, dug away furiously under his own fireplace — and found an unbelievable treasure of hundreds of shiny gold coins. It was from this very fortune that he built the *shul* in Cracow that bore his name.

"And so it is," Reb Chanoch Henich would say in the name of Reb Simchah Bunem, "with anyone setting out to visit a rebbe. It should be clear in his mind that the purpose of his visit is to find out from the tzaddik that the treasure is to be sought not with the tzaddik but in his own house. And when he comes home, his task is to dig and seek the treasure in his own soul — '*for this thing is very near to you*, in your mouth, and in your heart, that you may do it.' "

☙ *The Best Attorney*

Reb Shalom Ber of Lubavitch once entered the study of his father, Reb Shmuel of Lubavitch, to ask his advice on how to achieve a certain goal which he had set himself in the course of the divine service of self-refinement.

"Through meditating with profound concentration," was the answer.

"But the concept to be grasped is an exceedingly difficult one," said the son.

"If a subject really matters to a person," replied the rebbe, "then he comprehends it well. You will have observed the intellectual giants of each generation at work throughout the Talmudic and Rabbinic literature. In the course of solving questions of jurisprudence, they often construct hypotheses as to the kinds of involved arguments that could theoretically be put forward in court by the untutored women or ignoramuses who might be involved in the various kinds of legal disputes. Now the Torah is a Torah of truth. How, then, can one imagine such ingenious arguments coming from the mouths of simple folk who are unschooled and unlettered?

"The answer is simple. When a cause really matters to

people, then even the weakest intellects produce forceful lines of argument."

◆§ How To Love Your Competitor

בְּפִיךָ וּבִלְבָבְךָ לַעֲשֹׂתוֹ
In your mouth, and in your heart, that you may do it (30:14)

A shopkeeper once complained to Reb Moshe of Kobrin that his neighbor, who sold exactly the same goods as he did, always did a lively trade, while he himself could not eke the merest livelihood out of his shop.

"I can promise a generous income to you, too," said the tzaddik, "but only on condition that when you see your neighbor making a handsome profit, you thank the Almighty for his success. Something like this: Thanked be the Lord, Who gives such a rich livelihood to a fellow Jew.' It may be difficult to say this wholeheartedly at the beginning, but as you train your mouth to say the words, then with time they will find their way into your heart as well — until you will in fact be saying them with all your heart. For, in the verse בְּפִיךָ וּבִלְבָבְךָ לַעֲשֹׂתוֹ — 'in your mouth, and in your heart, that you may do it' — we first find the words 'in your mouth,' and only later is it written 'in your heart.' "

◆§ Ornament of God

הַעִדֹתִי... אֶת הַשָּׁמַיִם וְאֶת הָאָרֶץ
I call heaven and earth to witness (30:19)

The Russo-Japanese War broke out in 1905, the last year in the lifetime of Reb Yehudah Aryeh Leib of Ger, the author of *Sfas Emes*. Thousands of his young chassidim were conscripted and dispatched to the battlefields of the Far East.

In giving them his blessing and advice before they set out, he would begin by quoting a verse in the Torah which in ancient times was part of the announcement made to armies about to march forth: מִי הָאִישׁ הַיָּרֵא וְרַךְ הַלֵּבָב יֵלֵךְ וְיָשֹׁב לְבֵיתוֹ — "Who is the man who is afraid and faint of heart? Let him go and return to his house." He gave the verse a non-literal interpretation, however, as follows: "Who is the man who fears heaven? Let him return in repentance; and then," the rebbe would continue, "he will certainly return home from the battlefield."

So anxious was he for the welfare of these young soldiers that throughout the time they were at the Eastern front he did not once go to sleep in bed. He chose instead to sleep on the floor, lying on a single garment, which by morning was drenched with the tears he had shed over the anguish of his brethren.

And they in turn warmly reflected his faithful attachment to them. From out of the trenches they would write to him — hasty dissertations on fondly-remembered Talmudic themes, and touching descriptions of their daily lot.

One gifted scholar who hailed from Ostrov utilized every hour of respite in his bunker and wrote a long paper that discussed some learned comment of the medieval luminary Rabbeinu Yonah. After it had reached Ger, his rebbe wrote him a loving reply which opened with the words of a verse in the Torah: הַעִדֹתִי בָכֶם הַיּוֹם אֶת הַשָּׁמַיִם וְאֶת הָאָרֶץ. In the plain meaning of its context, this verse is spoken by Moshe Rabbeinu, and may be translated as follows: "I call heaven and earth to witness this day against you." In his letter, however, the tzaddik gave this verse too a non-literal interpretation. The verb הַעִדֹתִי is in fact related to the word עֵד, meaning "witness," but for the moment the tzaddik regarded it as if stemming from the noun עֲדִי, meaning "ornament."

Putting the words into the mouth of the Almighty, so to speak, he wrote the following: הַעִדֹתִי בָכֶם הַיּוֹם אֶת הַשָּׁמַיִם וְאֶת הָאָרֶץ — "With young Jews like yourself have I ornamented heaven and earth."

סדר וילך
Sidra Vayeilech

◆§ A Mere Child

וּבְנֵיהֶם... יִשְׁמְעוּ וְלָמְדוּ
And their children...shall hear and learn (31:13)

And their children, who have not known, shall hear and learn: This refers to small children — not infants, but children of tender years *(Ramban).*

When Reb Menachem Mendel of Lubavitch was a child of four or five, he was often to be found in the study of his grandfather, Reb Shneur Zalman of Liadi. In fact it was known among the chassidim that when the tzaddik was praying, the toddler would take the toy *tefillin* which he had carved out for himself from two potatoes, tie them with string to his head and arm, sway his little body as if in prayer, and sing happily away. When his grandfather removed his *tefillin* at the conclusion of his morning prayers, he would mimic that action too. That done, he would run up and down and around the room as little boys do. Once, when the rebbe's door was left ajar, some chassidim peeked through the chink and saw that as the child was running around and dragging his potatoes along the floor, one of the strings was caught around the leg of the table. The rebbe bent down and disentangled it, and the boy played on as before.

On a certain occasion Reb Shneur Zalman delivered a chassidic discourse on the statement in the Ethics of the Fathers that "the world stands on three things." It was so abstruse that the chassidim did not fully grasp it, and asked the rebbe to repeat it. He promised to do so three days later after morning prayers, on condition that no more than thirty people would be present.

One of the fortunate ones was the distinguished chassid Reb Yitzchak Aizik of Homil, who later recounted: "When the rebbe began to repeat the *maamar*, I saw that his little grandson had made a path for himself right in the thick of the chassidim who were assembled there. I imagined that at any moment the strings that were attached to his toy *tefillin* would be caught up somewhere, and I was afraid that he might distract us during the repetition of the discourse. I was about to say something to him, and to ask him not to disturb me, but before I managed to open my mouth I was amazed to hear the rebbe saying to me: 'Let him be. He wants to listen; he is listening; you will know that he is listening.' "

These words spread quickly among all the chassidim, though no one could understand their import, and in the course of time were forgotten.

Decades elapsed. In 1813 the tzaddik passed away, and Reb Dov Ber, the son who succeeded him, passed away in 1827. After a great deal of persuasion by their chassidim, the leadership of the movement was assumed by the son-in-law of Reb Dov Ber, Reb Menachem Mendel, who was this same grandson of Reb Shneur Zalman of Liadi. And the very first discourse which he delivered as rebbe was a repetition of the discourse which had been delivered over thirty years earlier by his grandfather, and which was based on the words: "On three things the world stands." One of those present on this occasion was Reb Yitzchak Aizik of Homil, and as soon as the newly-inducted rebbe began to speak, the elder chassid recalled that occasion on which Reb Shneur Zalman had repeated this very discourse. He recalled too a little boy racing his way through the assembled chassidim ... But most clearly of all he recalled the words which in retrospect rang out clearly like a prophecy: "Let him be ... You will know that he is listening."

Reb Yitzchak Aizik's soul lit up.

"Now that's the kind of trick that only a rebbe can do!" he thought to himself.

This thought was cut short. The rebbe interrupted his lecture, turned for a moment to Reb Yitzchak Aizik, and said: "Do not suspect me of having what I have not. How can I help it if my grandfather orders me to repeat this discourse?"

When he had completed his presentation, the chassidim present were so overjoyed at the fact that they now had this personage as their rebbe that a happy song burst spontaneously from their lips, and they accompanied him joyfully to his home.

Only one riddle remained — the two cryptic sentences which the newly-appointed rebbe had directed in the middle of his *maamar* to Reb Yitzchak Aizik. So when the chassidim returned to their *beis midrash* they crowded around him inquisitively, and pressed him to let them into his secret. And it was then that the old man shared with them his treasured memory of the little boy — a mere child — who was listening to an abstruse philosophical dissertation while playing with his potatoes and his strings.

◆§ Thy Day Draws Nigh (i)

הֵן קָרְבוּ יָמֶיךָ
Your days are approaching (31:14)

In Berditchev there lived a man who was reputed to be a tzaddik, and who was known by his birthplace as "the *rav* of Merchov. His differences with Reb Levi Yitzchak of Berditchev were superficial; beneath them lay a warm friendship. When Reb Levi Yitzchak passed away the *rav* of Merchov was one of the many who came to his funeral, and as the bier was carried out of his home he followed it, then approached it and leaned over to whisper, as if to be heard by the deceased: שִׁבְעָה שָׁבֻעֹת תִּסְפָּר לָךְ — "Seven weeks shall you count."

And seven weeks from that day, the *rav* of Merchov passed away.

◆§ Thy Day Draws Nigh (ii)

Reb Menachem Mendel of Lubavitch used to give his grandchildren five kopeks every day as pocket money.

One Sunday in 1866 they came along on their usual visit, and he said: "Today I am going to give you thirty kopeks, for the whole week in advance. But if anyone of you wants to, he can come along every day instead."

All the grandchildren took their week's allocation in advance, except for Zalman Aharon and Shalom Ber, the sons of Reb Shmuel of Lubavitch. They decided to continue calling every day. On one of the days of that week the older brother came later than usual, and when he met his brother, Shalom Ber told him that he had already been to see their grandfather.

"Let us go again," said Zalman Aharon.

They arrived at their grandfather's house only to find it crowded with somber chassidim. The rebbe had just passed away.

❀ ❀ ❀

When later that day Zalman Aharon told his father, Reb Shmuel, that he had come too late to his grandfather's house, the father said with emotion: "What have you done, my son? Why, he gave your brother everything!"

Some sixteen years later, when after their father's passing in 1882 Reb Zalman Aharon absolutely refused to accept the leadership, and Reb Shalom Ber became rebbe in Lubavitch, the older brother once told a small group of elder chassidim that one of the reasons for his refusal was what he had then heard from his father — that his grandfather Reb Menachem Mendel "had given his brother everything."

◆§ *Thy Day Draws Nigh (iii)*

Reb Meir of Premishlan was clearly overjoyed that Reb Chaim of Zanz was visiting him, and showed him every mark of respect.

After a lively and learned debate Reb Meir said to his guest: "You, rabbi, are a member of a rabbinical court of repute. Tell me. Should Meir live in modest lodgings such as these? Would it not be proper that he dwell in a grander residence?"

"Of course it would be fitting for you to live in more beautiful and spacious lodgings," said the guest.

"If that is your opinion," said Reb Meir, "Then I will take your advice."

Reb Chaim suddenly realized that there had been some unsuspected intention lurking behind these simple words of his host. He now sought to correct what had been said: "What I meant was — more beautiful lodgings in This World!"

"It is too late," said Reb Meir. "I only wanted your agreement; and if you have already given it, then that is no doubt what will be."

And within a few weeks the tzaddik of Premishlan had departed to another abode.

◆§ *Thy Day Draws Nigh (iv)*

During the night of Yom Kippur, the Day of Atonement, Reb Yitzchak Meir of Ger would always study the Mishnah of Tractate *Yoma* in the hearing of an inner circle of elder chassidm. In the last year of his life tears appeared in his eyes in the midst of his study, and the expression on his face was completely transformed.

The chassidim were alarmed, and one of them, who was very close to the tzaddik, waited till all the others left, and then asked him why he was so morose.

"I suspect that I will not live out this year, God forbid," answered the tzaddik.

"Rebbe," asked the chassid, "why should you say such a thing?"

"Every year," explained the tzaddik, "on the eve of the Day of Atonement, immediately after the *Shemoneh Esreh* prayer, two guests call on me — the Prophet Eliyahu and another old man wearing a cloak. And they always speak to me with smiling faces. But when I welcomed them on their arrival tonight, they returned my greeting with faces clouded by sorrow. May God have mercy on us all!"

❀ ❀ ❀

On the fifteenth day of Shvat in the same year the tzaddik was in Warsaw, where he called on his old friend, Reb Yeshayahu of Prague. Their meeting was a happy one, and after a time Reb Yitzchak Meir told his host that he wanted to speak to him in private. For a long time they remained alone. After the distinguished guest later took his leave affectionately, it was clear to all who saw Reb Yeshayahu that his mind had been thrown into turmoil. He did not even explain his sudden metamorphosis to his immediate family; he said only that the tzaddik of Ger had insisted that he divulge his words to no man.

When a few weeks later word reached him of the passing of the tzaddik, he wept bitterly and said: "Now I can reveal the secret which the rebbe of Ger told me. He said that he had come to me in order to be farewelled from This World, for he would be leaving it within a few weeks. When I asked him what made him think so, he said that the Prophet Eliyahu had visited him that day, and had told him the exact *day* of his passing — the *day*, the month, and the hour."

❀ ❀ ❀

When during the same week these tidings reached Reb Shlomo of Radomsk, he broke out in tears, took hold of his beard, and said: "Look, my beard is already white."

Then he added: "I have it on the authority of my holy teachers that when the tzaddik of my generation passes away, I too will be called to heaven, and I will be given the honor of leading the congregation there in Friday evening's prayers of welcome to the *Shabbos* Queen" — for during his life in This World, Reb Shlomo had often led his own congregation in prayer with his mellow and melodious voice.

And so it was. That same week, on Thursday night, while he was sitting at his table engrossed in the sacred mysteries of the *Zohar*, his soul flew aloft and found its rightful place in the congregation of the righteous — in time for Friday evening's prayers of loving welcome to the *Shabbos* Queen.

◆§ *Thy Day Draws Nigh (v)*

One of the chassidim of Reb Yitzchak Aizik of Zhidachov dearly wanted to make the journey to *Eretz Yisrael*, and went to consult his rebbe.

"Wait," said the tzaddik, "and make the journey with me."

Assuming that his rebbe intended to set out shortly for the Holy Land, the faithful chassid waited patiently. But not for long — for soon after, the tzaddik of Zhidachov passed away.

When the news reached the chassid, he said to his townsmen: "It seems that the hour has come for me to make my preparations for the great journey, for my rebbe told me that I would set out together with him."

He immersed himself tranquilly in the purifying waters of the *mikveh*, called for the wardens of the *Chevrah Kaddisha* burial society, pronounced the solemn confession of *Vidui*, and wrote out a will for his children.

And within a few days the whole community of Zhidachov learned that the faithful chassid had indeed set out on his last journey — together with his rebbe.

◆§ *Thy Day Draws Nigh (vi)*

Reb Mordechai Dov of Hornisteipl was the grandson of Reb Yaakov Yisrael of Chercass, and the great-grandson of Reb Mordechai, the Maggid of Chernobyl. The young man once set out to visit Chercass at the invitation of his grandfather, who had earlier asked him to begin leading a community of chassidim as their rebbe during his own lifetime.

When a day or two had passed since his warm welcome, Reb Mordechai Dov decided it was time to ask his grandfather for the purpose of his invitation.

"Come along with me to Bobbe's room," said the tzaddik.

And when the young man had greeted his grandmother, the tzaddik said: "I have a disagreement with your Bobbe, and so we agreed to abide by whatever you decide on the matter. Now here is the subject of the argument. Bobbe says that she should leave This World before me, because if she is left a widow and the chassidim will no longer come to our house, she will not be able to accustom herself to the loneliness. I claim that I should pass away first, because being left half a man, I will not find life pleasant.

"Now, young man," he concluded, "give us your ruling. We rely on your judgment."

Said Reb Mordechai Dov: "In fact Bobbe is right. Life for her as a widow would be harder to bear. But you, Zeide, hold otherwise, and I would certainly not want to contradict you. I would therefore say that when the time comes, the passing of you both should be in the same year."

And so it was. The *rebbitzin* — who was the daughter of Reb Menachem Mendel of Lubavitch — passed away in the month of Sivan 1876, while her husband, the tzaddik of Chercass, followed her in Elul, three months later.

◆§ *Brevity is the Soul of Wit*

עַד תֻּמָּם
Until their completion (31:30)

Reb Simchah Bunem of Pshischah once entered the study of his rebbe, Reb Yaakov Yitzchak, who is better known as the Yid HaKadosh of Pshischah.

"Quote me some verse from the Torah," said the rebbe, "and I will give you an interpretation of it."

The *pasuk* that happened to come to mind was the last verse of the weekly Portion of *VaYeilech:* וַיְדַבֵּר מֹשֶׁה

בְּאָזְנֵי כָּל קְהַל יִשְׂרָאֵל אֶת דִּבְרֵי הַשִּׁירָה הַזֹּאת עַד תֻּמָּם – "And Moshe spoke in the ears of all the congregation of Israel the words of this poem, until their completion."

The chassid having quoted his verse, the rebbe now gave his interpretation — which he did by simply echoing its last two words: עַד תֻּמָּם ("until their completion").

Reb Simchah Bunem was overjoyed at this "interpretation."

But also present was another disciple, Reb Chanoch Henich of Alexander, who turned to his colleague and asked him: "What is the meaning of this joy? And what did the rebbe explain here?"

"Here, you're a clever fellow," replied Reb Simchah Bunem. "You work out the rebbe's meaning yourself!"

"It would seem," suggested Reb Chanoch Henich, "that this was the rebbe's meaning. If the word תֻּמָּם ('their completion') was intended to refer to the poem, then it should have appeared in the singular form — תֻּמָּהּ ('*its* completion'). Why, then, does the plural form appear? And we must answer that Moshe Rabbeinu no doubt went about among the Children of Israel, repeating over and over again the words of this poem, which sings of the historic covenant — past and future — of the Creator with His People. He repeated its words to his brethren until it entered their very hearts: indeed, עַד תֻּמָּם — 'until *their* completion,' until *they* were perfected."

"That's it!" exclaimed Reb Simchah Bunem.

סדר האזינו
sidra ha'azinu

⁂ *Fair Play*

אַסְתִּירָה פָנַי מֵהֶם
I will hide My face them them (32:20)

Reb Yechiel of Alexander and the son who was to succeed hm, Reb Yisrael Yitzchak, were once in an isolated village where they had gone for a rest cure. In the middle of the night the father suddenly took ill and was in danger of his life. There was no doctor for many miles around. The tzaddik thought his end was near, and wept, whereupon his son embraced him and *swore* that no harm would befall him.

Then he left his father for a few moments, walked out into the thick of the forest, and cried out: "Master of the Universe! Is this what you do to the rebbe of Alexander? In the forest, with no one at hand?! Do our Sages not teach us that 'The Almighty cares for the honor of tzaddikim'?"

He quickly returned to his father and found him feeling better.

"How were you able to swear?" asked Reb Yechiel.

"I relied on the words of Reb Yisrael of Ruzhin," answered his son. "In the Book of *Psalms,* King David pleads: עַד אָנָה תַּסְתִּיר אֶת פָּנֶיךָ מִמֶּנִּי, עַד אָנָה אָשִׁית עֵצוֹת בְּנַפְשִׁי— 'How long will You hide Your face from me? How long shall I take counsel in my soul?' These words the tzaddik of Ruzhin reads as a question and an answer, as follows: 'How long will You hide Your face from me?' And the supplicant answers his own question: 'So long as I can take counsel in my soul.' That is to say, when the supplicant can do nothing whatever to remedy his situation, and help can come from God alone, — in such a time the Almighty *cannot* hid His face.

"And here, out in the middle of the forest, when there was no way in which we could possibly take counsel and help ourselves, and no one could help us but God alone, I was perfectly certain that no harm would befall us. So that is why I swore as I did."

סדר וזאת הברכה
Sidra V'zos Habracha

☙ *Attuned*

וְזֹאת לִיהוּדָה
And this was for Yehudah (33:7)

Reb Avraham of Sochatchov was once out on a journey on the first day of the month of Nissan with his nephew, Reb Yitzchak Menachem of Shidlitz. Strangely, his learned conversation throughout the entire day was related exclusively to one subject — the many Talmudic references to Yehudah, the son of the Patriarch Yaakov. His traveling companion found this something of a riddle.

Towards the end of the day the rebbe suddenly realized that the first of Nissan was a date mentioned in the Torah in connection with the dedication of the *Mishkan* in the days of Moshe Rabbeinu. This was the day on which the representative of the tribe of Yehudah had brought his offering as part of the dedication of the Sanctuary in the wilderness.

The riddle was solved — for both of them.

"So *that* is why I have been speaking about Yehudah all day!" exclaimed the rebbe.

◈ *Mortal Remains (i)*

לֹא כָהֲתָה עֵינוֹ
His eye was not dim (34:7)

His eye was not dim: Even when he died. The body of Moshe Rabbeinu did not crumble, nor did his countenance alter *(Rashi).*

In 1943 word reached the Jewish community of Chechanov that the Nazis were about to desecrate the burial place of Reb Avraham of Chechanov, who had passed away in 1875, by plowing over the site and erasing it from mortal memory.

The wardens of the *Chevrah Kaddisha* burial society immediately met in secret with the elders of the community. They decided together that they would foil this plot, even if it cost them their lives. Late one night they went out in stealth to the old cemetery on the outskirts of the town, and opened the grave of the tzaddik in order to remove his last remains to another resting place. But as they moved aside the tablet that lay above the body they were dumbstruck. For though some sixty-eight years had passed since the burial, the holy body of the tzaddik lay intact and whole, as though he had been buried a moment before. Even the shrouds had not decomposed.

With brave hands trembling in awe they lifted the body from its resting place, enveloped it in a *tallis,* and bore it reverently to the grave which they had prepared in the new cemetery, between the two tall trees which were to serve as a sign.

The Nazi invaders soon heard of this exploit. They hunted and tracked down the townsmen, and dragged them out of the cave in which they had hidden for almost two weeks. Finally, after dreadful torture, their racked bodies *(May God avenge their blood!)* were hanged.

◆§ *Mortal Remains (ii)*

While troops of Nazis were on their frenzied rampage through the towns and villages of Poland and Galicia, they arrived at Lyzhansk. They first razed the town to the ground, and then turned to the old Jewish cemetery, where they found a number of aged Jews praying softly at the graveside of Reb Elimelech. This was the same tzaddik who until his passing in 1787 had been a source of inspiration to such luminaries as the Chozeh of Lublin, the Ohev Yisrael of Apta, the Maggid of Koznitz, and Reb Menachem Mendel of Rimanov.

The troops demolished the modest edifice which had been built over the gravesite, tore open the grave itself, but were shocked by what they saw — a countenance, as in life, which bespoke quiet joy and dignity.

Leaving the grave open they fled in sheer fright, and the aged Jews were left to resume their whispered prayers at the graveside of Reb Elimelech.

Glossary

Glossary

All terms are in Hebrew unless otherwise indicated

agunah — woman unable to remarry because she has neither a divorce nor evidence of her missing husband's death

ahavas yisroel — the love of a fellow Jew

amora [pl. amoraim; Aramaic] — authority quoted in the *Gemara*

apikores [pl. apikorsim] — freethinker

arenda [Polish/Yiddish] — lease on an inn or other source of livelihood commonly held by East European Jews; the leaseholder was called the *arendar*

atzilus — one of the supernal levels of Creation described in the Kabbalah

av beis din — chairman of a rabbinical court

avodah — the service of God, whether in sacrifice, prayer, or self-refinement

Baal Shem — (as a common noun) lit. "master of the Name"; a wonder-working *tzaddik*

baal teshuvah [pl. baalei teshuvah] — a penitent

bankess [Yiddish] cupping glasses formerly heated and used as a universal remedy

bar mitzvah — religious coming of age on a boy's thirteenth birthday

batlan — impractical fellow

beis din — rabbinical court of law

Beis HaMikdash — the Temple (First or Second) in Jerusalem

beis midrash — communal House of Study

berachah — blessing, benediction

bikkurim — First Fruits of the seven species which were brought to the Temple and given to the *Kohanim.*

chacham — sage

chalitzah — ceremony exempting a man from marrying the widow of his deceased childless brother

challah [pl. challohs] — braided loaf baked in honor of the Sabbath

chametz — leavened products forbidden for Passover use

Chanukah — eight-day festival commemorating the Maccabees' re-dedication of the Temple

Chaunkah gelt [Hebrew/Yiddish]. Pocket money traditionally distributed to children on Chanukah.

chapers [Yiddish] — kidnappers of children for conscription in the Czarist army

Chassidism — Movement within Orthodox Judaism founded in 18th century Eastern Europe by Reb Yisrael, known as the Baal Shem Tov. Stresses emotional involvement in prayer; service of God through the material universe, the primacy of wholehearted earnestness in divine service; the mystical in addition to the legalistic side of Judaism; the power of joy, and of music; and the collective physical and moral responsibility of the members of the informal brotherhood, each chassid having cultivated a spiritual attachment to their saintly and charismatic leader — the rebbe or *tzaddik.*

chazzan — cantor

cheder — elementary school for religious studies

Chevrah Kaddishah — voluntary burial society

Chevrah Tehillim — brotherhood for the communal reading of *Psalms*

Chillul Hashem — desecration of the Divine Name

cholent [Yiddish] — stew cooked on Friday afternoon and kept simmering until the Sabbath lunch meal

Chumash — the Pentateuch

chuppah — canopy under which the marriage ceremony is solemnized. Also, by extension, the ceremony itself

darshan — preacher

daven [Yiddish] — to pray

Days of Awe — the New Year period of judgment, from Rosh Hashanah to Yom Kippur

dayan — judge

deitsch [or Deitsch'l; Yiddish] — nickname for the assimilationist Jews of the "Enlightenment" movement

derush — exegetical or homiletical interpretation

divrei Torah — discourse or conversation on Torah subjects

drashah — a sermon or discourse

dveikus — the ecstatic state of cleaving to the Creator

Eretz Yisrael — the Land of Israel

esrog [pl. esrogim] — the citron fruit used in the festivities of Succos

farbrengen [Yiddish] — gathering of *chassidim* for mutual edification and comradely criticism

fertziger [Yiddish] — coin

gabbai — (a) attendant of a *tzaddik;* (b) master of ceremonies in a synagogue

galus — exile, the Diaspora

gartl [Yiddish] — belt worn in prayer

gefilte fish [Yiddish] — traditional Sabbath delicacy

Gehinnom — purgatory

Gemara [Aramaic] — that portion of the Talmud which discusses the *Mishnah;* also, loosely, a synonym for the Talmud as a whole

gemilus chassadim — the *mitzvah* of doing good deeds

get — a bill of divorce

glatt kosher — ritually fit for consumption, without any query

golem — a man of clay; a dummy

goy [pl. goyim] — gentile

graf [Polish] — noble

guter yid [Yiddish] — lit: "a good Jew"; the popular Yiddish term for a chassidic rebbe

gut Shabbos [Hebrew/Yiddish] — greeting; "A good Sabbath to you!"

haftarah — the passage from the Prophets read in the synagogue after the Pentateuchal reading

hakadosh — "the holy" — traditionally suffixed to certain names

Halachic [English adjectival form] — referring to the *halachah,* the corpus of Torah law

Hamavdil — hymn sung at the close of the Sabbath

Hamotzi — blessing pronounced over bread

Haskalah — the 18th century "Enlightenment" movement which sought to introduce Western culture into traditional Jewish circles

Havdalah — the Saturday evening ceremony by which the sanctity of the outgoing Sabbath is separated from the workaday week

hekdesh — (a) something sanctified for Temple use; (b) a communal hostelry for vagrants

Hoshanah Rabbah — the seventh day of the festival of Succos, when seven circuits are made around the *bimah* in *shul.*

hrubnikess [Russian/Yiddish] — fireplace-kindlers; specifically, those in the circle of the disciples of the *Maggid* of Mezritch

Kabbalah — the body of Jewish mystical teachings

kapote [Yiddish] — black frockcoat, worn usually in honor of the Sabbath

kavanah — devout intent

kesubah — marriage contract

kevitsas haderech — miraculous abbreviation of a *tzaddik's* journey

ketz [pl: kitzim] — different dates calculated to be auspicious for the Messainic Redemption.

Kiddush — blessing over wine, expressing the sanctity of the Sabbath or a festival

kiddush Hashem — sanctifying the Divine Name, especially through self-sacrifice

kittel [Yiddish] — white gown worn on certain solemn occasions

Kohen [pl. Kohanim] — priest, *Kohen Gadol*: High Priest

kopek [Russian] — small copper coin

kosher — ritually fit for use

K'suvim — the Writings; the third division of the Biblical Books

kugel [Yiddish] — a delicacy of baked noodles or potatoes traditionally prepared in honor of the Sabbath

kvater [Yiddish] — person honored by bringing the infant to circumcision

kvitl [pl. kvitlach; Yiddish] — note handed to a *tzaddik* bearing the name of a supplicant and his mother's name, and the nature of the request

L'ag Ba'omer — minor festival celebrated on the thirty-third day of the *Omer*.

lamdan — scholar of repute

lashon harah — lit: "the evil tongue"; slanderous talk

l'chaim — lit: *"to life;"* greeting of congratulation

lulav — palm branch. One of the four species used on the festival of Succos.

maamad — regular contribution made by a chassid for maintenance of his rebbe's household

maamar — chassidic discourse

maggid — preacher

malach — angel

manna — the food from heaven which sustained the Children of Israel in the wilderness

mara de'asra [Aramaic] — the recognized halachic authority for a particular region

Mashiach — Messiah

maskil [pl. maskilim] — adherent of the *Haskalah* movement

matzah [pl. matzos] — unleavened bread eaten on Passover

mazel tov — lit., "Good Luck!" — greeting of congratulation

mechutan — the parent-in-law of one's son or daughter

mekubal [pl. mekubalim] — experts in the *Kabbalah*

melamed — schoolmaster or tutor

melaveh malkah — Saturday evening meal eaten after *Havdalah* in honor of the departing Sabbath Queen

meshorerim — choirboys accompanying a *chazzan*

mesirus nefesh — self-sacrifice

mezuzah [pl. mezuzos] — tiny parchment scroll affixed to doorpost

michyah [Hebrew/Yiddish]: lit: sustenance; in Yiddish usage, a synonym for *arenda*

Midrash — (a) classsical anthology of the Sages' homiletical teachings on the Torah; (b) a particular passage therefrom

mikveh — pool for ritual immersion

Minchah — the afternoon prayer service

minyan — quorum of ten required for communal prayer

Mishnah [pl. Mishnayos] — (a) the germinal statements of law elucidated by the *Gemara*, together with which they constitute the Talmud; (b) any paragraph from this body of law

misnaged [pl. misnagdim; adj. misnagdish,-er] — opponent of the teachings of *Chassidim*

mitzvah [pl. mitzvos] — a religious obligation; loosely, a good deed

mohel — circumcisor

Motzaei Shabbos — the time of the departure of the Sabbath, i.e. Saturday night

Mussaf — prayer added to the service in honor of the Sabbath and festivals

nasi — civil and religious head of the community

nebbich [Yiddish] — "poor wretch"

nefesh — soul; specifically, name for one of its levels

Ne'ilah — concluding service of the Day of Atonement

neshamah — soul; specifically, name for one of its levels

netilas yadayim — ritual washing of the hands

Neviim — the Prophetic Books of the Bible

niggun — melody, usually wordless

nu, nu — untranslatable Yiddish expression meaning (among its scores of uses) something like "Well, well!"

paritz — local squire in Eastern Europe

parnas haChodesh — communal functionary, in office by rotation for a month

pasuk [pl. pesukim] — Biblical verse

Pesach — the festival of Passover

Peyos — earlocks

pidyon [or pidyon nefesh; pl. pidyonos] — the contribution for charity which accompanies a chassid's request to his rebbe

Pidyon HaBen — ceremony of Redemption of the Firstborn

pilpul — involved legalistic dissertation

pinkas — communal register

posek [pl. poskim] — decisors; rabbis whose legal decisions are authoritative

Priestly Blessing — the three Biblical verses pronounced by the *Kohanim* in the course of the synagogue service

rav — rabbi

rebbe [Hebrew/Yiddish] — (a) a *tzaddik* who is spiritual guide to a following of chassidim; (b) a Torah teacher

rebbetzin — wife of a rav or a rebbe

Reb Yid [Yiddish] — informal term of address to an individual whose name is not known

Ribbono Shel Olam — Master of the Universe

Rosh Chodesh — New Moon; i.e. one or two semi-festive days at beginning of the month; the first of the month

Rosh Hashanah — the New Year festival

ruach — soul; specifically, name for one of its levels

Sabbath Queen — the Sabbath personified

Sefer Torah — Scroll of the Law

segulah — spiritual remedy; talisman

Selichos — penitential prayers

seudah — meal, especially a festive one

seudah shlishis — the Third Meal held at sunset on the Sabbath

seudas mitzvah — meal held in celebration of a religious obligation

Shabbos — the Sabbath

Shabbos HaGadol — the Sabbath preceding the festival of Pesach

Shacharis — the morning prayer service

Shalom — greeting — "Peace!"

Shalom Aleichem — (a) greeting — "Peace be upon you!" (b) Friday evening hymn of welcome to ministering angels

shammes — sexton in a synagogue or beadle in attendance on a rabbi

Shavuos — Pentecost; the festival commemorating the Revelation at Sinai

she'elah — legal query

sheiner yid [Yiddish] — a fine, dignified Jew

Shema Yisrael — opening words of the Jew's declaration of faith — "Hear O Israel"

Shemini Atzeres — the eighth day of Succos. In many respects, it is a festival in its own right

Shemoneh Esrei — the silent standing prayer which is the main feature of each of the three daily prayer services

shidduch — a matrimonial match

shiur [pl. shiurim] — lesson or lecture

shochet — ritual slaughterer

shofar — ram's horn blown on Rosh Hashanah

shomrim — pious congregants who meet in synagogue before dawn for non-mandatory devotions

shtendar — movable lectern

shtibl [pl. shtibluch] — a place for informal prayer meetings

shtreimel [Yiddish] — fur-rimmed hat worn on Sabbath and festivals

Shul — synagogue

Shulchan Aruch — the Code of Jewish Law

siddur — prayerbook

succah — booth lived in during the festival of Succos

Succos — one of three pilgrimage festivals celebrated for seven days, marked by living in a *succah*

Tachanun — prayer requesting forgiveness, omitted on festive occasions

tallis — shawl worn in prayer

Talmid Chochom — Torah scholar of standing

Talmud — the basic compendium of Jewish law, thought, and Biblical commentary; comprises *Mishnah* and *Gemara; Talmud Bavli*: the edition developed in Babylonia; *Talmud Yerushalmi:* the edition of the Land of Israel

Tanna [pl. Tannaim] — authority quoted in the *Mishnah*

Tashlich — riverside ritual of atonement on Rosh Hashanah

Tefillas Geshem — prayer for rain

tefillin — phylacteries; small black leather cubes containing parchment scrolls inscribed with *Shema Yisrael* and other Biblical passages, bound to the arm and forehead at weekday morning prayers

Tehillim — the Biblical Book of Psalms

tenaim — betrothal agreement

terumah — the first portion of the crop which must be separated and given to a *Kohen*

teshuvah — repentance

third meal — see **Seudah Sh'lishis**

tikkun — [pl. **tikkunim**] — **lit.** "improvement"; (a) refreshments for a *yahrzeit.* The blessings made upon eating the food are a source of merit for the departed soul. (b) refreshments for a *farbrengen;* (c) the task of uplifting the universe by revealing its hidden sparks of spirituality

Tikkun Chatzos — midnight lament over the exile of the Divine Presence

tish [Yiddish] — lit: "table;" ceremonial Sabbath meal conducted publicly by a chassidic rebbe, characterized by spontaneous Torah discourses; and singing by all present

Tishah B'Av — the ninth day of the month of Av; fast day commemorating the Destruction of both the First and Second Temples in Jerusalem

Tosafos — commentaries on the Talmud

treifah — ritually unfit for use; opposite of kosher

tzaddik — (a) saintly individual; (b) specifically, a chassidic rebbe

tzedakah — charity

tzitzis — the fringes worn at the corners of the **tallis.**

Vayikra — the Book of Leviticus

Vidui — the confession recited on the Day of Atonement, and during the final stocktaking of a lifetime

vort [Yiddish] — lit: "word"; a quotable and insightful morsel of moral teaching or Biblical interpretation.

yahrzeit [Yiddish] — anniversary of the passing of a near relative

yechidus — private interview at which a chassid seeks guidance and enlightenment from his rebbe

yeitzer hara — the Evil Inclination

yeshivah — Talmudic academy

yibum — marriage with the widow of one's deceased childless brother

yichud — a union in the spiritual spheres, effected by devout divine service in This World

yichus — distinguished lineage

Yom Kippur — the Day of Atonement

Yom Tov — festival

zal — [suffix] "of blessed memory" [acronym]

zechuss — the merit of a good deed, especially as deserving a spiritual reward

zemiros — Sabbath and festival table hymns

Zohar — the basic work of the *Kabbalah*

This volume is part of
THE ARTSCROLL SERIES®
an ongoing project of
translations, commentaries and expositions
on Scripture, Mishnah, Talmud, Halachah,
liturgy, histroy, the classic Rabbinic writings,
biographies, and thought.

For a brochure of current publications
visit your local Hebrew bookseller
or contact the publisher:

Mesorah Publications, ltd

4401 Second Avenue
Brooklyn, New York 11232
(718) 921-9000

Notes

Notes

Notes

Notes

Notes

Notes